Treat this book with care and respect.

*It should become part of your personal
and professional library. It will
serve you well at any number
of points during your
professional career.*

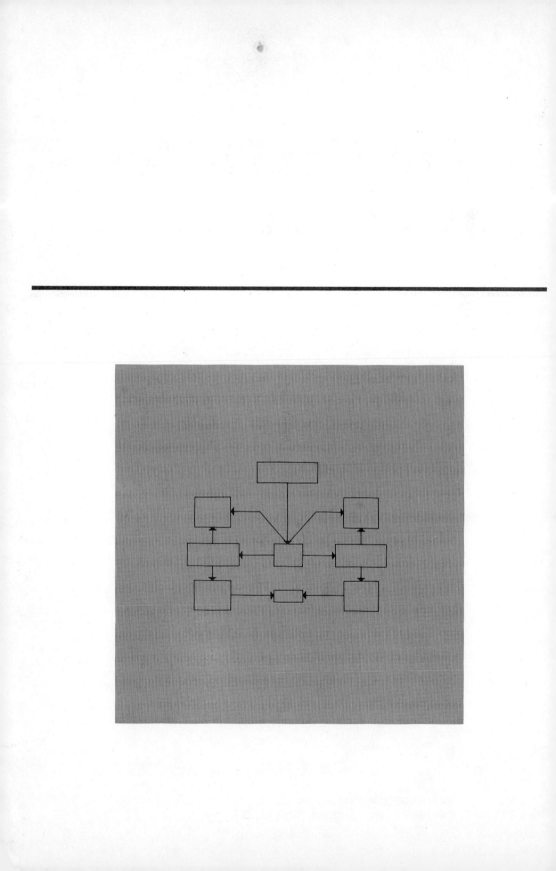

OPERATIONS MANAGEMENT

ARTHUR C. LAUFER

PROFESSOR OF MANAGEMENT
CALIFORNIA STATE UNIVERSITY
LONG BEACH

Published by

G07 **SOUTH-WESTERN PUBLISHING CO.**

CINCINNATI   WEST CHICAGO, ILL.   DALLAS   PELHAM MANOR, N.Y.
PALO ALTO, CALIF.   BRIGHTON, ENGLAND

PREFACE

A preface is an accepted convention. It is also somewhat anomalous. In the first place, most readers ignore it. In the second place, while it precedes everything else, it is the last thing written. However, tradition will out, and to satisfy those who would be disappointed by a lack of a preface (including the author), the following remarks are presented.

Many management writers have noted the semantic difficulties encountered in this discipline. There are even some ambiguities surrounding the term management itself. It can be used to describe a process, or it can be used in reference to the people who engage in the process. A similar difficulty exists in regard to the term operations management. Many books addressed to the same problems have different titles. Initially, Industrial Management was the favored terminology. Then Production Management became the standard. More recently a movement to Production and Operations Management has been noted, and some have used Operations Management alone.

Operations Management has been selected as the title of this book because it is felt that this more adequately expresses the viewpoint of universality of the activities covered than does any other title. Operations is viewed as a more inclusive term; production is treated as only one element of operations.

In line with the premise of universality, a generic approach has been followed to the greatest extent possible. The discussions and examples are drawn from diverse kinds of enterprises to accomplish this end.

The material is presented from a managerial viewpoint. No attempt is made to provide an exhaustive treatment of any one topic. Therefore, only enough detail is given to supply understanding for decision-making purposes. Since this book is expected to be used mainly in a course typically offered at the junior level, it must be somewhat generalized in covering the various topics. Each chapter contains material that could be expanded into a whole book.

The chapters have been grouped into four parts to provide some direction and continuity of subject matter. In a survey course, each chapter is somewhat self-contained. Often there is not a direct flow of thought from one chapter topic to the next. The chapter grouping used proceeds from the generalized to the specific. A foundation for analysis of the decision problems is first developed, followed by some of the applicable models for decision making. The broad problem areas are then considered. Finally, techniques for synthesizing the individual approaches are presented. A preview is included before each section.

The book emphasizes the behavioral element in operations management. Wherever applicable, this element is woven into the material. A special treatment is included in the discussion of manpower planning. The chapter on ergonomics is an example of this emphasis. The ergonomics approach to work design and the material on physiological work measurement receive a more expanded treatment than is usual. Other noteworthy features are the strong presentation of the sociotechnical relationship in the operations system, and the development of the logistical elements of the system.

Quantitative models are discussed generally, and in regard to specific problem areas. These models are presented in a way understandable to nonmathematicians. While some preparation in mathematics and statistics is helpful, it is not necessary for comprehension.

In addition to discussion questions at the end of each chapter, many chapters have problems designed to illustrate techniques discussed. A number of chapters include incidents. The incidents are general in form, designed to present concepts rather than specifics. They are purposely open-ended, and no definite answers or conclusions are expected. Comments and suggested answers to the questions, problems, and incidents are provided in the teacher's manual.

Clearly, a book is never the exclusive product of a single individual. In the first place, many people influence an author while he is developing the ideas that he gathers together in book form. In the second place, direct contributions are made by numerous individuals. It would be impossible to acknowledge the contributions of everyone in either of these two categories. However, to ignore certain contributions would be ignoble. The acknowledgements made are, therefore, only a partial listing. Anyone overlooked must pardon the poor recollections of a grateful author.

Many organizations contributed material used in the preparation of the text. Some must be mentioned because of the special efforts undertaken to make this material available. I particularly want to express my appreciation to: The American Telephone and Telegraph

Co.; Cincinnati Milicron; General Electric Corp.; General Motors Corp.; Holiday Inns, Inc.; IBM; and Douglas Aircraft Division of McDonnell Douglas Corp. A special expression of thanks for an unaccountable amount of help must be made to my friend and associate of many years, the late Don Wheeler of Grayson Controls Division, Robertshaw Controls Co.

Many associates at C.S.U.L.B. contributed in a variety of ways. Two former deans, A. E. Prell and John Martinelli, gave much support. The Director of Research of the School of Business, Dale Yoder, offered considerable encouragement and many suggestions. In my department, my most heartfelt thanks go to all my colleagues. My chairman, V. A. Metzger, not only provided what resources he could, but he reviewed certain parts of the manuscript. Without mentioning specifics, I also gratefully acknowledge the invaluable contributions of Robert DeVoe, William Lyle, Thomas Penderghast, Gordon Robinson, Ronald Rudkin, Roger Stanton, Herbert Stone, and Michael Quinn.

Finally, I want to acknowledge the enormous contribution of Ms. Ann Merta who read, criticized, typed (at least twice), and proofread every page of this book.

Long Beach, California   A.C.L.

Contents

PART **1** **INTRODUCTION AND FUNDAMENTAL CONSIDERATIONS**

Chapter 1 / Historical Overview   1
Evolution of Management   2

Chapter 2 / The Operations System   14
Enterprise Strategy and Operations Policies   14
The Operations Function   16
Systems Approach   19

Chapter 3 / Decision Making   35
The Decision Process   35
Certainty, Risk, and Uncertainty   39
Probability   42
Utility   49

Chapter 4 / Computers and Decision Making   61
The Nature of Computers   61
Computer Programming   67
The Role of the Computer in Decision Making   69
Computer Applications   71
Computers and Thought   80
Limitations of Computers   82

PART **2** **MODELS FOR OPERATIONS MANAGEMENT DECISIONS**

Chapter 5 / Conventional Decision Models   87
"General" Decision Models   87
Accounting Models   90
Economic Analysis Models   93
Schematic Models   99

Chapter 6 / Quantitative Models   115
Mathematical Programming   116
Graphical Solution Method of Linear Programming Problem   117
Simplex Method   123
Distribution Models   128

Chapter 7 / Quantitative Models (Continued)   146
Simulation   146
Waiting-Line Theory   157

PART **3** **PLANNING THE OPERATIONS SYSTEM**
Chapter 8 / Product and Plant Planning   173
Operations Management Planning   173
Design of Product or Service   173
Equipment Investment Analysis   177
Plant Location   189

Chapter 9 / Forecasting   200
Premises   200
Types of Forecasts   204
Forecasting Techniques   209
Reliability of Forecasts   223

Chapter 10 / Process Planning   233
Nautre of Processes   233
Numerical Control of Machine Tools   245
Layout of Facilities   249
Maintenance   260

Chapter 11 / Manpower Planning   269
Elements of Manpower Planning   269
The Learning Curve and Manpower Planning   273
Manpower Loading   281
Motivation   283

Chapter 12 / Design of the Work System   297
Nature of Work   297
Work and Job Design   298
Man-Machine Systems   298
Job Design   300

Chapter 13 / Ergonomics   322
Nature of Ergonomics   322
Factors in Ergonomics   323
Sociotechnical Systems   342

Chapter 14 / Work Measurement   350
Nature and Purpose of Work Measurement   350
Time Study   351
Elemental Standard Data Systems   362
Motion-Time Data Systems   363
Work Sampling   368
Physiological Work Measurement   373

PART **4** **FUNCTIONING AND CONTROL OF THE OPERATIONS SYSTEM**

Chapter 15 / Logistics Systems   385
Components of the Logistics System   385
Operation and Control of the Logistics System   393
Logistics and Operations Management   405

Chapter 16 / Inventory Systems   409
Nature of the Inventory Problem   409
Types of Inventory Systems   413
Economic Lot Size   416
Inventory System Variations   424
Practical Inventory Management   433

Chapter 17 / Integrated Control Systems   441
Types of Control Systems   441
Output Scheduling   446
Large-Scale Project Control   460

Chapter 18 / Output Quality Control Systems   474
Basic Quality Control Systems   474
Process Control by Inspection for Variables   480
Acceptance Sampling for Attributes   486
Statistical Tests of Significance in Quality Control   492
Human Performance and Quality Control   496

Chapter 19 / Cost Control Systems   502
Cost Concepts   502
Standard Cost Control Systems   505
Control of Labor Costs   508
Cost Reduction   519
Cost Effectiveness Analysis   521

Chapter 20 / Perspective   527
Present Status of Operations Management   527
Future Status of Operations Management   531
L'Envoi   533

Index / 535

PART 1

Introduction and Fundamental Considerations

In this section, background material is presented to establish a foundation for the later decision-problem analysis. On the assumption that we can learn from history, the past, as it has influenced the present, is reviewed. The evolution of operations management is viewed as a series of logical steps that have set the stage for current techniques. The operations function has a specific relationship to the management of the total enterprise. The systems approach as a means of achieving better decisions follows. The operations function can be placed in the context of a system. The decision-making process is described, followed by a discussion of some of the generalized approaches to decision making. Finally, the computer, and its particular influence on decision making are surveyed. Computer applications, potential, and limitations are given special attention.

CHAPTER 1 | Historical Overview

The process of managing the present-day industrial enterprise has become extremely complex. Most of these enterprises are enormous, with large amounts of capital invested in physical facilities, and with many people performing diverse activities that have to be directed and coordinated. Consequently, those people responsible for the successful performance of the enterprise are repeatedly required to make difficult decisions which will have far-reaching effects. These decisions invariably involve the determination of the most efficient ways to use available resources in the proper mixture to result in the desired product or service.

Every enterprise or organization faces similar decisions. The necessary activities must be directed toward the achievement of the enterprise goal. Even in the very common two-person organization, the family, the participants must strive to use their resources properly to achieve their established goal.

Management is the directing and guiding of the required activities. The activities needed to produce the desired result, product or service, are the essence of the operations function of any enterprise.

The dictionary definition and the synonyms for operation(s) denote action. Operations involves the performance of an undertaking which is of a practical nature. The word has achieved diverse meanings in specific areas. In the field of medicine, it is used in reference to surgical procedures. It is used to describe military actions or missions. In business, it has come to have several meanings, all of which involve some sort of transaction, change, or conversion.

The specifics of operations are different in every enterprise. For manufacturing firms, operations encompasses the production activities. However, the problems faced in this area by I.B.M. are different from those faced by U.S. Steel. Even more diverse are the operations problems of enterprises engaged in nonmanufacturing endeavors. The scope of operations differs in aviation, in financial institutions, in educational institutions, in health-care activities, and in nonprofit enterprises. Operations at Los Angeles International Airport is essentially concerned with getting the flights into and out of the airport. For Merrill, Lynch, operations consists of processing the security transactions initiated on behalf of customers. The operations function of all enterprises is concerned with the accomplishment of the end output created for the customers or users of that output. Therefore, the approaches to the problems of operations management are essentially identical for all enterprises. The same decision-making techniques can be utilized.

Not everyone who enters management will be directly engaged in operations. Probably a majority will find themselves in one of the other functional areas.

1

However, no matter what phase of management an individual finds himself in, he must have some understanding and knowledge of the other functions. Since operations is a pervasive function that is found in all enterprises, all potential managers need to know about the problems found in operations.

Marketing's objective is placing the output of the enterprise into the users' hands. This requires knowledge of the output — its method of creation, and the abilities and requirements of the operations function in order to provide the output needed. There is little value in having sold a product or service which cannot be produced at the quality, price, or time required.

Finance must know the capital requirements of all the other functions. The influence of various decisions on cost are an important consideration in achieving success. The establishment of a budget for the operations activities must take account of the feasibility of achieving the desired output under the budgeted allocations. Financial management needs to have some background in operations problems to do this.

People are an essential resource in any enterprise. It is through people that all management is accomplished. The operations function requires a given number of people with appropriate skills to create the output. Without awareness of the needs of the operations function, the personnel department will find it difficult to fulfill these needs.

These illustrations indicate the importance of understanding the operations function by management of the other functional areas. All managers must make decisions that contribute to the achievement of the overall goals of the enterprise. Without a fundamental knowledge of all functions, this achievement is unlikely. The basic decision-making approaches utilized in operations management are frequently useful in all areas of management decision making.

EVOLUTION OF MANAGEMENT

The modern enterprise has evolved over a period of time into its present form. Concurrent with this has been the development of the management concepts now prevalent. A review of the evolution of management is a prerequisite to an understanding of the application of present-day techniques. The value of a historical approach was summarized by one writer as follows:

> Today is not like yesterday, nor will tomorrow be like today; yet today is a synergism of all our yesterdays, and tomorrow will be the same. There are many lessons in history for management scholars; the important one is the study of the past as prologue.[1]

The usual beginning point for a discussion of modern industry practices, and the subsequent evolution of modern management techniques, is the Industrial Revolution. The Industrial Revolution began about 1770. It originated largely in the textile industry of England as an outgrowth of the introduction of

---

[1]Daniel A. Wren, *The Evolution of Management Thought* (New York: The Ronald Press Company, 1972), p. 5.

200 yrs

various types of power-driven machinery. The year 1790 is considered as the beginning of this movement in the United States.

The term revolution, as applied to this movement, is perhaps somewhat misleading. The usual picture that comes to mind from the word revolution is one of a violent upheaval with rapid changes. While some violence occurred and some significant changes took place rather quickly, the overall process took a long period of time. In fact, some observers feel that certain aspects of the "so-called" Industrial Revolution are still being experienced. The term "so-called" is used here because it seems plausible that what really is involved is more of an evolutionary process, as opposed to a revolutionary one.

Carrabino refers to three industrial revolutions starting with the 1770 date, and carrying on to the present.[2] These three revolutions are named Mechanization, Scientific Management Movement, and Automation.

The overall movement which has led to the present state of management is more conveniently viewed as merely separate phases of the same process. These phases are:

Phase 1. Industrial Revolution
Phase 2. Scientific Management Movement
Phase 3. Quantitative Techniques
Phase 4. Automation

Industrial Revolution

While it is usual to think of the beginnings of modern industry as an outgrowth of the Industrial Revolution, this period was really only an acceleration and synthesizing of a process going on for centuries. The dramatic change occurred primarily as a result of the mechanization of the English textile industry.

There is considerable evidence that management practices have existed since the beginning of recorded history.[3] If we were able to move back to the days of prehistoric man, a very crude form of management would be found. Perhaps the first time management occurred was when two of the cave dwellers decided they needed to cooperate to move a large boulder from in front of a cave. Someone had to decide where and how they were to move this boulder, and someone had to count the equivalent of "One, two, three; heave." This man would have been the first "manager."

It is sufficient to begin the examination of the development of operations management with the period referred to as the Industrial Revolution. At this time, the development of modern management techniques began in a systematic fashion, and the first evidences of many changes in the total production process were seen. Present-day production methods developed out of this period.

---

[2]Joseph D. Carrabino, "The Metamorphosis of Industrial Engineering into Management Engineering — Plea for Change in Name," *The Journal of Industrial Engineering*, Vol. XII, No. 1 (January–February, 1961), pp. 51–56.

[3]Claude S. George, Jr., *The History of Management Thought* (Englewood Cliffs: Prentice-Hall, Inc., 1968), pp. 1 ff.

75 yrs old

WILL WE GO BACK

As a result of mechanization, and the consequent substitution of the machine for a great deal of handwork, the factory system replaced the domestic system of manufacturing. Accompanying this change was the evolving concept of specialization or division of labor. Ultimately, this mechanization and specialization made feasible the development of mass production techniques. Interchangeable parts and the assembly line were important results.

Credit for the development of the concept of interchangeable parts manufacture is usually given to Eli Whitney.[4] The original assembly line was probably used by Oliver Evans in 1783 in a flour mill. However, what might have been the first modern assembly line in the United States was described and illustrated in vivid terms in *Harper's Weekly* of September 6, 1873.[5] In the packing houses of Cincinnati, the hogs were hoisted onto an overhead rail at a 24-inch interval. They were moved past the men, each of whom performed his specialized operation. The first was the executioner. After this the carcass went through the scalding vat, the scrapers and the shavers took over. After disemboweling, the carcass moved to the final man who washed it out with a hose.

The keynote of this phase was the substitution of mechanical power for the muscle power of the worker.

FORD

Scientific Management Movement

The second phase in the development of operations management is usually thought of as having its inception in the United States, approximately at the beginning of the 20th century. Frederick W. Taylor, who is referred to as the "father of scientific management," gave leadership to this movement. Many of the principles expounded by Taylor had been developed and practiced by others throughout the years prior to Taylor's writings.[6] Taylor served largely as a synthesizer of ideas, and put them into a formal framework that became widely disseminated.

Contributions of Charles Babbage. The best-known predecessor of Taylor was Charles Babbage (1792–1871). Babbage is remembered today mostly for the development of the "Difference Engine," the forerunner of the modern-day digital computer. Of more significance, however, are his unique contributions to the development of management thought as exhibited by his unswerving belief in the potential use of scientific processes in the operation of business firms.

An illustration of Babbage's scientific attitude is found in the preface to *On the Economy of Machinery and Manufactures:*

> Having been induced during the last ten years to visit a considerable
> number of workshops and factories, both in England and on the Continent,
> for the purpose of endeavoring to make myself acquainted with the various

---

[4]*Ibid.*, p. 62.

[5]*Harper's Weekly*, Vol. XVIL, No. 871 (September 6, 1873), pp. 776–778.

[6]L. Urwick and E. F. L. Brech, *The Making of Scientific Management*, Vol. I, *Thirteen Pioneers* (London: Management Publications Trust, 1949), p. 17.

resources of mechanical art, I was insensibly led to apply to them those principles of generalization to which my other pursuits had naturally given rise.[7]

Babbage anticipated Taylor in the area of work measurement when he used a crude form of time study to analyze the processes and manufacturing of pin making. His presentation of the processes, time, labor cost, worker earnings, and per unit cost certainly presages latter-day approaches.[8]

He also showed an understanding of the problems of time study when he pointed out:

> If the observer stands with his watch in his hand before a person heading a pin, the workman will also almost certainly increase his speed, and the estimate will be too large. A much better average will result from inquiring what quantity is considered a fair day's work.[9]

While there might be some disagreement with parts of this statement today, it is an indication of Babbage's keen awareness of the need for the application of a scientific approach to the problems of the industrial organization.

Contributions of Taylor. There were other writers in the interim between Babbage and Taylor who appeared to sense a change in the management of industrial organizations. Not, however, until Taylor appeared upon the scene did anything approaching a systematic concept of management emerge in practice. Taylor's major contribution was that he showed *how* to substitute a fact-finding approach to management problems for the old rule-of-thumb method prevalent in industry at that time. Taylor suggested that in order to develop a science of management there were four duties of management:

1. The development of a science of management for each element of a man's work, thereby replacing the old rule-of-thumb method.
2. The selection of the best worker for each particular task and then training, teaching and developing the workman in place of the former practice of allowing the worker to select his own task and train himself as best he could.
3. The development of a hearty cooperation between the management and the men in the carrying on of the activities in accordance with the principles of the developed science.
4. The division of work in almost equal shares between the management and the workers, each department taking over the work for which it is better fitted instead of the former condition in which most of the work and the greater part of the responsibility were thrown on the men.[10]

In addition to developing a philosophy of management, he also was instrumental in the introduction of specific management tools that were important

---

[7]Charles Babbage, *On the Economy of Machinery and Manufactures* (4th ed.; London: Charles Knight, 1835), p. III.

[8]*Ibid.,* p. 184.

[9]*Ibid.,* p. 117.

[10]Frederick W. Taylor, *The Principles of Scientific Management*, reprinted in *Scientific Management* (New York: Harper & Bros., 1947), p. 36.

in the implementation of such a philosophy. Among those of particular interest to students of operations management are:

Modern techniques of stopwatch time study. ✓
Planning of the job. ✓
The exception system of management at the shop level. ✓
Modern cost systems and other tools of measurement and control. ✓

COST ACCT & CONTR

Other Contributors. Any discussion of the early years of scientific management must include at least a mention of the contributions of some of the other pioneers of this movement. Foremost among these contributors were the Gilbreths, Frank and Lillian. While their contributions are wide and varied, it is their original work in the area of motion study for which they are best known. One significant outgrowth of this work was the development of a classification of motions into seventeen fundamental motions called therbligs (Gilbreth spelled backwards with the *th* reversed).

 Report

Another important pioneer was Henry L. Gantt. Gantt, who worked for Taylor at an early age in his career, is, as is Taylor, often remembered more for the tools he devised than for his far greater contributions to the advancement of the philosophy of scientific management. Perhaps, most significant of these contributions was his emphasis on the human element in management. Gantt's contributions were summarized when he was posthumously awarded the first Henry Lawrence Gantt Medal in 1929, by the Institute of Management and the American Society of Mechanical Engineers, "For his humanizing influence upon industrial management and for the invention of the Gantt Chart."[11]

Harrington Emerson and the term efficiency almost seem to be synonymous. Emerson maintained that the principles of efficiency were essential to the successful operation of any organization. He listed twelve principles of efficiency in a book of that title.[12] The majority of this book was devoted to an elaboration of these twelve principles. He thought of efficiency primarily as the elimination of waste.

Report

Emerson is also well remembered for his testimony before the Interstate Commerce Commission, in 1910, in the Eastern Rate Case. He was called as an expert witness by Louis Brandeis who represented the shippers. Emerson did much to further the cause of scientific management when he stated that the railroads could save a million dollars a day if they adopted the proper efficiency system, or scientific management.[13]

RR

The contributions of Morris L. Cooke to the advancement of the scientific management movement are unique. He showed potential applications to a diversity of fields. In two books, *Our Cities Awake*[14] and *Academic and Industrial*

---

[11]Urwick and Brech, *op. cit.*, p. 80.
[12]Harrington Emerson, *The Twelve Principles of Efficiency* (New York: The Engineering Magazine Co., 1913).
[13]Louis D. Brandeis, *Scientific Management and the Railroads* (New York: The Engineering Magazine Co., 1911), p. 83.
[14]Morris L. Cooke, *Our Cities Awake* (Garden City: Doubleday, Page & Co., 1918).

Efficiency,[15] Cooke presented the case for the systematic application of the techniques and principles of scientific management to municipal government and to university administration. These applications served the purpose of underlining the claim of the universality of this movement.

The contributions of others to the early development of scientific management could be mentioned. However, those included here are a representative sample of this group.

The philosophy of scientific management was not readily accepted by everyone. As with any new idea, strong resistance came from many quarters: labor, scholars, government, and segments of management itself.

One of the most widely-read of the early criticisms of the movement was a book by Robert F. Hoxie, entitled, *Scientific Management and Labor*.[16] Hoxie, at points, was highly critical of scientific management, particularly with reference to what he saw as its detrimental effects on the labor movement. Such critics as Hoxie, and there were many others, served to force the proponents of the movement to reexamine their beliefs. After such an evaluation, their faith in the new philosophy of management was strengthened when it was found to meet the tests of the critics.

The scientific management movement gave impetus to many new tools and concepts widely accepted today. The emphasis on human relations in industry is one example. The research carried on at the Hawthorne Works of the Western Electric Company, under the direction of Elton Mayo, is considered as the classic work in the area that created a foundation for the development of the human relations techniques now in use. The details of this experiment were published in *Management and the Worker*, by Roethlisberger and Dickson.[17] The later work of men such as Max Weber, Douglas McGregor, and Rensis Likert, and the application of group sociology, psychology, social psychology, and related tools to the management of human resources was largely encouraged by the Hawthorne experiments.

Quantitative Techniques   *w w I*

Before the beginning of World War II, new approaches, based primarily on the quantitative techniques of mathematics and statistics, were applied to the management of the industrial enterprise. These techniques have been generally grouped under the titles of operations research, management science, or some other all-inclusive term. Many of these techniques have specific applications to the operations function of the enterprise.

During the war, these techniques were widely used to assist in the management of the war effort in both the military and the industrial segment.

---

[15]Morris L. Cooke, *Academic and Industrial Efficiency* (New York: Carnegie Foundation for the Advancement of Teaching, 1910).

[16]Robert F. Hoxie, *Scientific Management and Labor* (New York: D. Appleton and Co., 1915).

[17]F. J. Roethlisberger and W. J. Dickson, *Management and the Worker* (Cambridge: Harvard University Press, 1939).

Essentially, the use of quantitative techniques appears to be an extension of the scientific approach to decision making. The quantitative approach to decision making of today has many antecedents in history which made the achievement of the present state of the art possible.

A great deal of the work of the early contributors to the scientific management movement is akin to the present-day quantitative approach. One example is the work of Carl Barth, an associate of Taylor, who developed a slide rule to determine the operating speeds and feeds for a machine to perform a specific metal-cutting task in the fastest time. This device permitted solving a problem with twelve independent variables by a worker who had no mathematical understanding. This application certainly falls into the realm of operations research.

Other early contributors in this area include T. C. Fry and Walter Shewhart of the Bell Laboratories. Fry introduced the concept of applying probability theory to engineering, and Shewhart laid the groundwork for modern methods of statistical quality control. Later, H. F. Dodge and H. G. Romig, also of Bell Laboratories, developed statistical sampling tables, for use in the control of quality, which are widely used today.

Ronald A. Fisher showed how to use numerous statistical methods and how to apply them to management, as in the design of experiments for predictive purposes. The development of the basic economic lot size formula for use in inventory control is generally credited to F. W. Harris. The first applications of the concepts of queuing or waiting line theory were made by A. K. Erlang in his work with the telephone company in Copenhagen.

Operations Research. All of these contributions were made prior to World War II. It was in England that the first applications of what came to be called operations research were found. Initially, these applications were aimed at the military, but as time passed, the applications were industrial in nature as well. Today *operations research* is generally taken to define the application of the scientific method, with emphasis on the use of mathematical and statistical techniques, to industrial problems, to arrive at the "best" or optimal solution.

Some students of management see operations research as nothing more than a direct line descendant of the techniques and approaches advocated by Taylor and his disciples. Operations research and scientific management have the same general goal of aiding management in determining the best course of a future action. Operations research has been called more "scientific," however, because it makes greater use of the basic sciences and of mathematics.

Operations research has shown that similar and relatively standardized techniques can be used to solve a variety of management problems. Many operations problems have analogous structures for which specific decision rules can be developed. The use of quantitative techniques and of operations research methods is an attempt to develop a uniform way to accomplish optimality. More recently, this objective of uniformity has been sought through the application of the systems approach.

Systems Approach. Studying the parts and relating the findings to the whole to achieve a solution to a problem is currently finding considerable acceptance in management decision making. Through this approach, management has moved to the use of systems analysis as a problem-solving approach. Systems analysis uses the techniques of systems engineering and applies them to management decision making. Basically, systems analysis sees the enterprise as an integrated whole, and makes use of this viewpoint when a problem is studied for the purpose of determining the best solution.

From the systems standpoint, the enterprise is an assemblage of interrelated parts. Because of the interrelationships, a decision made in one part of the enterprise system will have an effect on all other parts of the system. These effects must be considered in all decisions. Viewing the enterprise in this way facilitates an understanding of the relationships of a problem to the total enterprise. Better decisions will result because of an awareness of all the influences found in a decision problem.

Perhaps no activity in recent times better exemplifies the systems approach than the effort involved in the Apollo program in its attempt to place man on the moon. There is little question that this program required the highly integrated functioning of every segment involved in achieving this goal. All decisions, whether they involved the ground controllers, the flight engineers, those at the tracking stations throughout the world, or the astronauts themselves took the total objective into consideration. Without this systems viewpoint it is, at the very least, questionable that the program would have succeeded.

Since World War II, there has been widespread application of quantitative methods to the operations of business firms. Quantitative techniques, along with a variety of others, have had great influence on the field of operations management, and have made it possible to handle many classes of decision problems previously subject only to intuitive or empirical methods.

The virtually concurrent arrival on the scene of the electronic computer has made the use of quantitative techniques practical. The vast complexity of calculations required to solve the mathematical formulation of most business problems would make such solutions impossible without high-speed computers.

Automation

Many people see automation as merely the extension of the process of mechanization of industrial activity. It is considerably more than that. *Mechanization* is the substitution of some form of mechanical energy for the muscle power and brawn of the worker. *Automation*, on the other hand, is the substitution of machines for the sensory mechanisms of the worker. The process of automation taking place today will not further reduce the total percentage of physical labor performed by man by any appreciable amount. What automation will do is to reduce the amount of repetitive and routine sensory and mental tasks that man has heretofore had to perform. The machine will not obsolete man and his thinking processes. On the contrary, the computer, the real heart of any automated system, will force man to be more precise in thinking about what he is doing.

Not everyone views automation in this light. Norbert Wiener, who was the leader of a group of scientists at M.I.T. whose basic research during World War II led to the modern electronic computer, was extremely pessimistic about the effects of these machines when he wrote:

> Let us remember that the automatic machine, whatever we think of any feelings it may have or may not have, is the economic equivalent of slave labor. Any labor which competes with slave labor must accept the economic conditions of slave labor. It is perfectly clear that this will produce an unemployment situation, in comparison with which the present recession and even the depression of the thirties will seem a pleasant joke. This depression will ruin many industries — possibly even the industries which have taken advantage of the new potentialities.[18]

Of course, these dire predictions have not materialized to this time. On the contrary, most knowledgeable people today would probably view automation and the computer as a beneficial development.

Automation has resulted in considerable changes in the operational methods used by a large number of firms. There are many examples of the automation of individual production processes, the automation of office and clerical procedures, as well as the completely automated plant or office.

The use of numerically controlled machine tools in industry has gained considerable acceptance in today's factories. Briefly, numerical control is the use of automatic equipment to control the actual movement of a machine tool. This control is achieved through a series of programmed instructions fed into the input device of the system, through a computer, and then to a controller which guides the movements of the cutting tool.

The automation of office and clerical procedures is exemplified by the data processing systems so widely adopted. Applications to various accounting procedures, payroll records, billing procedures, and the registration procedures at large colleges and universities are well known. The computer has many uses in these areas because it is particularly adaptable to highly routinized work.

Most outstanding examples of complete automation of factories are found in the process industries. The process industries use bulk materials such as liquids or powders, and change their form. These industries are characterized by petroleum refining, sugar refining, chemical companies, and soap manufacturing. In these industries, there is a flow of material to be processed in a highly standardized manner from batch to batch. This characteristic makes them extremely well suited to a great degree of automation.

The automating of information systems and of management decision making is perhaps the most significant area of application of the computer. Present-day technology permits the manager to receive information quickly, as soon as it is generated, or "on line," and in "real time." He can make decisions that enable him to control the problem while it is developing, and continuously thereafter. An improvement in the speed and the quality of decision making has

---

[18]Norbert Wiener, *The Human Use of Human Beings* (Garden City: Doubleday and Co., Inc., 1954), p. 162.

resulted. The influence of the computer on the management of the operations of the organization has only started. In the future, the computer will have an increasing impact on all aspects of operations management.

This historical overview is designed to show the logic of the development of the management of the operations function. It will serve to put the individual tools into some perspective as they relate to the entire kit of tools available to the operations manager. The plan of this book is to examine these tools in detail and to determine their applicability to the management of the operations function. Virtually all of the tools and techniques mentioned in this overview will be described in detail, with particular reference to applications. The operations manager of today has available to him a large variety of methods to assist him in carrying out his function effectively and efficiently. He must be able to select the proper method for the problem at hand if he is to make a good decision. The objective of the remainder of this book is to develop the appropriate tools and techniques of operations management to assist the manager in selecting and applying the appropriate one for the decision problem at hand.

SUMMARY

Operations management is concerned with the guiding and directing of the activities required to produce the product or service of an enterprise. While operations differ between enterprises, the problems in all are basically the same. Operations is a functional area, comparable to the other functions of the enterprise. For this reason, an understanding and knowledge of operations is essential for managers. All managers need knowledge of the other functions if the objectives of the enterprise are to be achieved. The techniques of operations management can be utilized in all management decision making.

The historical development of management thought and techniques has been a long and gradual movement which has brought us to our present-day state. The Industrial Revolution is the usual starting point in considering the development of modern day industry, but it was actually only a synthesizing of a long-term movement which was accelerated by the introduction of power-driven machinery.

The scientific management movement was the outgrowth of attempts to substitute a fact-finding approach for the old rule-of-thumb method of managing. Primarily under the impetus of the pronouncements of Frederick W. Taylor, this movement saw the beginnings of many of the management tools which have been prevalent in industry since the beginning of the 20th century. Among those which have particular application to the operating function of the organization are motion and time study. During this period the foundations of the present-day emphasis on the human element were also established.

Quantitative techniques which have become so significant in the decision-making process of the operating manager received their greatest impetus from wartime applications. The variety of these techniques is quite extensive, and, as a result, such tools have been applied to a broad spectrum of management problems. The application of quantitative techniques to industrial problems is often grouped under the title of operations research.

The systems approach views the enterprise as an integrated whole. It recognizes the necessity of considering all parts of the enterprise when a decision is made. An understanding of the interrelationships of the different parts of the enterprise will lead to decisions that are better for the enterprise as a whole.

The computer has extended the practical application of quantitative techniques to many areas where they would have been inapplicable. The computer has also been a major force in the process of automation which has been, and will surely continue to be, so evident in the operation of the firm. The full impact of the computer and the resultant automation is as yet not fully ascertainable. However, there is little doubt that it is having a significant effect on operations management.

QUESTIONS FOR DISCUSSION AND ANALYSIS

1. What are the four phases in the development of management which have brought it to its present state?

2. What is the keynote of the first phase?

3. Do you consider it unusual that we should find a similarity of ideas expressed by Babbage and Taylor? Why?

4. What were the major contributions of Frederick W. Taylor to the evolution of management?

5. Give the principal contributions of the following pioneers of the scientific management movement:
   The Gilbreths
   Henry L. Gantt
   Harrington Emerson

6. What is the significance of the application of quantitative techniques to management problems?

7. How would you define operations research?

8. How does automation differ from the process of mechanization?

9. Do you see any logical pattern in the development of management to its present state? Do you feel that automation is the final phase of such development, or do you foresee some future development? If so, in what direction?

SELECTED ADDITIONAL READINGS

Beer, Stafford. *Cybernetics and Management*. New York: John Wiley & Sons, Inc., 1964.

Churchman, C. W., R. L. Ackoff, and E. L. Arnoff. *Introduction to Operations Research*. New York: John Wiley & Sons, Inc., 1957.

Filipetti, George. *Industrial Management in Transition*. Homewood, Illinois: Richard D. Irwin, Inc., 1953.

George, Claude S., Jr. *The History of Management Thought.* Englewood Cliffs: Prentice-Hall, Inc., 1968.

Morris, William T. *Management Science in Action.* Homewood, Illinois: Richard D. Irwin, Inc., 1963.

Simon, Herbert A. *The Shape of Automation for Men and Management.* New York: Harper and Row, Publishers, Inc., 1965.

Taylor, Frederick W. *The Principles of Scientific Management.* Reprinted in *Scientific Management.* New York: Harper & Bros., 1947.

Tillett, Anthony, Thomas Kempner, and Gordon Wills (eds.). *Management Thinkers.* Harmondsworth, England: Penguin Books, Ltd., 1970.

Urwick, L., and E. F. L. Brech. *The Making of Scientific Management,* Vol. I, *The Thirteen Pioneers.* London: Management Publications Trust, 1949.

Wiener, Norbert. *The Human Use of Human Beings.* Garden City: Doubleday and Co., Inc., 1954.

Wren, Daniel A. *The Evolution of Management Thought.* New York: The Ronald Press Co., 1972.

CHAPTER 2

The Operations System

Before undertaking an examination of operations management and its tools, it is necessary to recognize its constituent parts. To do this requires a knowledge of what is meant by the operations function. It then becomes incumbent to understand the concept of a system and the relationship which the operations function as a system has to the other systems within the total enterprise. This means that in considering the operations system there must be a realization that it is one of a number of functional systems within the enterprise, such as the marketing system, the finance system, and others that will vary with the type of enterprise. Viewing the operations function as a system makes its relationship to the other functional systems clearer.

ENTERPRISE STRATEGY AND OPERATIONS POLICIES

Operations management, while differentiated from the overall management of the enterprise, should not be considered as separated from it. Part of the problem in describing the position of operations management is that in many enterprises the role of this function is not fully understood by top management, and very often it is not completely under its control.[1] A delineation of the nature of the operations function will be deferred to a later point. What is of primary concern now is to establish the relationship of operations management to the strategy and policy making activities of the enterprise.

Enterprise Strategy

A variety of meanings have been given to the term strategy. The one adopted here is that *strategy* is the means by which an enterprise makes use of its primary skills and resources, and selects the most logical route required to achieve its stated end in response to the forces of the environment in which it exists.

No specific prescription can be set forth for the development of the strategy of an enterprise. However, there is a certain set of factors that should be considered. The external environment must be taken into account in the development of enterprise strategy; this would include the economic, social, technological, and political conditions currently in existence. These conditions must be related to the enterprise's skills, resources, strengths, and weaknesses which constitute the internal environment.

---

[1]Wickham Skinner, "Manufacturing — Missing Link in Corporate Strategy," *Harvard Business Review*, Vol. 47, No. 3 (May–June, 1969), pp. 136–145.

The development of a strategy for the enterprise leads to the creation of plans for each of the significant areas such as marketing, product or service, and finance. What results, as far as the operations function is concerned, is that the specific demands which will be placed on the operations facilities will be determined by the strategy adopted. Different strategies will place differing demands on the operations facilities and on the operations managers.

This would be true even in enterprises which are engaged in the same basic activity. For example, consider two firms that manufacture kitchen cabinets. If one produces standard cabinets, and the other produces custom-made ones, it is only natural that the strategies of the two firms would be different. It also follows that the demand on the operations facilities would differ as well.

The key to the success of the management of the operations function is the ability of these managers to meet the demands placed upon their function by the strategy of the enterprise. Specific operations policies must be developed if the operations function is to be performed effectively.

Operations Policies

If strategy is important to the success of the enterprise, and if strategy determines the task of the operations function, it follows that it is necessary to develop a framework for the implementation, performance, and control of the task. The *operations policies* of the enterprise flow from the strategy adopted and create this framework. It is a framework which sets the limits within which important decisions must be made.

In formulating these policies, it is necessary to select a criterion which will be useful in measuring the effectiveness of the decisions which are made. In making these decisions, the operations manager will find that because there are restrictions and limitations in the enterprise's skills and resources, he will have to compromise. For instance, in many operations systems there has been a tendency for managers to place undue emphasis on lowest cost as the ultimate criterion of success. While this is a desirable goal, it usually cannot be achieved without an adverse effect on some other significant aspect of the performance of the enterprise. The achievement of the lowest cost position may lead to neglecting the needs of the customers. This condition may result in a failure to satisfy the customer's needs for proper service when and where it is needed. Such a situation is not likely to lead to a successful operation. Management will have to compromise on its desire for lowest cost and provide a proper level of service. Each enterprise must evaluate the restrictions which are imposed on it and which limit the use of the skills and resources available. From such an evaluation will evolve the enterprise's operations policies.

In setting the operations policies, a large number of decision alternatives must be weighed one against the other. Some of the broad operations policy areas include product design, product planning, manpower planning and utilization, process planning, and production-inventory planning and control. Within each of these areas the operations manager faces a variety of decisions, and there will be numerous alternatives that he must evaluate relative to each decision from among which he must choose the most appropriate to the strategy and operations policies of the enterprise.

THE OPERATIONS FUNCTION

No function is more pervasive than the operations function. It is found in all enterprises in some form. The form may vary with the type of enterprise. The function will differ between those enterprises that are profit oriented as compared with nonprofit enterprises. There will also be a difference in the operations function when the output is a product and when the output is a service.

There is a wide diversity of terminology in use regarding activities which are performed in enterprises. The examination of what is identified as operations in a large sample of organizations would reveal this to be true. The result would be an extensive list of activities. There would naturally be some overlap, but even after a distillation of the unique elements of the activities the list would be formidable.

A close examination of the activities identified as operations would find, however, that production or something similar to it appeared frequently. This would be true because virtually all enterprises which have a physical output are engaged in production. Therefore, production is an important element of the operations function. It may well be the single most common form of operations.

Production as a Part of the Operations Function

Inasmuch as a great proportion of the operations function is concerned with what we have called production, a closer look at production itself will assist in achieving an acceptable and workable definition of the operations function. The economist is usually concerned with the so-called "factors of production," and these "factors of production" serve as inputs, which when combined in some way result finally in the creation of some goods or services, or, in other words, an output of some sort. The economic approach to the most efficient utilization of the factors of production is to find the best or optimum combination or allocation of these factors of production.

Viewing the operations function strictly as production is inadequate. The term production is naturally associated almost exclusively with the concept of manufacturing. If the operations function is considered as consisting solely of production or manufacturing activities, the scope and application of the tools of operations management are limited. These tools are applicable to the management of the operations function irrespective of the nature of the enterprise: whether it provides a product or a service; whether it is a profit or nonprofit organization; whether it is purely a marketing-type organization, a financial-type organization, or some other type. In any kind of enterprise, similar operations problems are found. Managers may have to decide on the location of buildings, the layout of facilities within the buildings, or the control of inventories of various types. The problems differ in degree and in specifics, but all fall within the domain of operations management.

Definition of the Operations Function

It is necessary to recognize that the operations function encompasses a variety of activities that are all too frequently viewed in a restricted context. A broad conception is required to satisfy the need to include all aspects of operations. The *operations function* is concerned with the interaction of any of the various resources (people, money, machinery, facilities, information, or materials) which are used in some combination to provide the product or service for which the enterprise was established. The operations manager is primarily concerned with finding the best combination or allocation of the resources, and seeing that they result in the desired product or service, in the proper amount, and at the desired quality level.

Operations in Relation to Other Functions

Operations problems are subdivisions of the large and complex problems of the total enterprise, and are related to the problems of the other functional areas such as marketing, finance, and others. In many cases solutions to the total problem are the result of solutions that have been made in various subdivisions of the enterprise and brought together as a whole. To solve the enterprise problem, it is helpful to segregate and consider individually the problems of the various functional areas of marketing, finance, operations, and others. In considering the problems of operations management separately, the interrelationships that exist among the various parts of the enterprise must be included. In examining the individual tools and techniques available, concern for the specific methods for solving problems of operations management cannot be ignored. These methods should not be considered as abstractions of the total process of managing the enterprise, but rather should be considered as part of the total management process.

A Logical Approach to Operations Problems

The attempt to arrive at solutions to operations problems requires a systematic and logical approach. In the problem-solving process, the manager will find that the problems vary in their degree of difficulty. If the problem is a familiar one, a direct approach will be possible. New problems will create a more difficult situation. A methodology for approaching all problems will be helpful in reducing the difficulty. A logical approach to the resolution of operations problems can be found in the scientific method. The method, used in the physical and biological sciences, progresses to a solution as follows:

1. Formulation and statement of the specific problem.
2. Development of a hypothesis.

3. Development of an experimental design.
4. Experimentation.
5. Observation and measurement.
6. Collection and analysis of data.
7. Interpretation of results.
8. Statement of conclusions and possible new hypotheses.
9. Recommendations.
10. Implementation of the solution.

To illustrate, examine an operations problem with a factual background: jet engine overheating occurred shortly after a new passenger aircraft started in airline service. The following is an application of the scientific method to that problem:

1. The engines on the aircraft are overheating to a danger point which is causing delayed or cancelled flights as well as costly maintenance.
2. It is hypothesized that this is the result of improper design of the fan blades of the engines.
3. The engine manufacturer has redesigned the fan, and laboratory and field tests of engines with the new design will be carried out. Records of actual performance data will be maintained. These data will be subjected to a series of statistical tests of difference to determine the relative merit of the new design.
4. Engines of both designs will be operated for various periods of time and under a variety of operating conditions normally encountered while in actual flight.
5. The operations of the engines will be observed and all pertinent measurements will be made.
6. The data will be collected and recorded. These data will be analyzed by subjecting them to the statistical tests that were designated in the experimental design.
7. The results of these statistical tests will be examined to determine what inferences can be drawn, and what interpretations can be placed on the data analysis.
8. A statement regarding the operations of the jet engines with the newly designed part as compared with previous operations results can now be made. Depending on the outcome of the above steps, this statement might indicate that the new design is satisfactory; that it is unsatisfactory; or it might include a new hypothesis that suggests some other change in the engine design is required.
9. A recommendation could be made to rebuild or replace all engines with the new fan, if the results indicated this. Other recommendations might be for further research, or for further tests of the new design.
10. If the recommendation was to rebuild or replace the engines, it would be necessary to issue instructions to put into effect the actions required to initiate and carry out the program.

This method is essentially a way of thinking about all problems. All aspects of the problem are considered. A logical approach such as this one insures that the total picture will be taken into account. Thus, while useful for solving operations problems, this method does not ignore the interrelationships between all parts. The problem is viewed in the framework of the systems approach. The design of any system will be facilitated by the application of this logical approach.

SYSTEMS APPROACH

The systems approach has been increasingly applied to the solution of business problems. Systems analysis in business requires the decision maker to visualize the internal and external environment as a whole. This is in opposition to the approach of solving the individual problems of the various functional areas as subdivisions of the total problem. By using systems analysis, it is expected that solutions to problems will take into consideration the total organization. Operations managers will not make decisions primarily to optimize their own function within the organization, but will select alternatives beneficial to the entire enterprise.

An extreme situation will serve to illustrate the circumstance where a decision optimizes the function at the expense of enterprise efficiency. Production might make a processing decision which in some way alters output. This decision would show improved efficiency when measured against criteria established by production management. The improvement could be higher productivity, lower cost, or better quality. Any of these might be considered as optimum from the viewpoint of production. If, on the other hand, this decision resulted in a condition where sales found the change a disadvantage, it would not be a good decision for the total firm. A market might not exist for the increased output, or the change in quality could alter the firm's relative competitive position. Thus, it would be better to make some other decision regarding production which in the aggregate is better for the firm, even if it is not optimum for production. *over time*

Color of Plastic

What Is a System?

Most of us intuitively have a cursory understanding of what is meant by the term system. Certain aspects of systems, however, can be useful in developing an understanding of what is actually meant by the term.

The concept of a system carries many connotations. Almost anything that is made up of parts, which in some way are related or connected together, may be called a system. Any group of things which are interrelated and combined so as to form an integrated whole can be called a system. It is not the individual parts that are important, but it is the connecting together or the interrelationship of these parts which is important to the making of a system. For example, the transistor or a group of transistors taken individually are not a system, but when they are in some way connected together and begin to interact somehow, they then become a system, an electronic system such as a radio. As may have been surmised at this point, almost anything can be called a system. This may appear to be an exaggeration, but it is literally a true statement. If you look around you, you will note that almost everything within your area of vision is made up of constituent parts. In most instances the parts are in some way interrelated or combined to make a whole. For instance, if there is a table in the room, it has four legs (presumably) and a top. None of these parts is very useful on its own, but, by assembling them, the parts interact and become a whole. Thus, the table may be considered as a system. A more formal definition which has found wide acceptance is the one set forth by Hall and Fagen. They state: "*A system* is a set of objects together with relationships between the objects and between their attributes."[2] For this definition to be useful, some of the terms will require definitions themselves.

Objects or Entities. *Objects, or entities,* as they are sometimes called, are the parameters of the system; inputs, processes, outputs, feedback control, and restrictions. Specific examples of objects might be machinery, materials, operators, or some form of measure of effectiveness.

Attributes. The term *attributes* refers to the characteristics or properties of a particular object; that is, they describe the object. For example, a particular object such as a piece of material may be described by its price, its size, its color, its chemical composition or hardness as in the case of a piece of metal, and so on. The attributes of an object will usually be changed as a result of the operation of the system when this piece of material enters into the system and is processed

Relationships. The *relationships* which exist between the objects and their attributes are what actually hold the system together. The relationships which can exist are virtually unlimited. Examples of relationships that can be found in an operations system would be those such as between volume of output and cost, quality and cost, cost and selling price, volume and selling price, and many other possible relationships.

Environment. Each system, of course, must operate in some environment. *Environment* may be viewed as the set of all the objects, which if changed, either internally or externally, will affect the way in which the system operates.

The objective of the systems approach in the management of the operations function of an enterprise is to establish a framework for making decisions that take into consideration all of the objects, attributes, and relationships, as well as the environment of the system, so that these decisions make the attainment of the goals of the enterprise easier.

Types of Systems

Systems can be classified or grouped in a variety of ways. The more important of these classifications follow.

---

[2]A. D. Hall and R. E. Fagen, "Definition of System," *General Systems Yearbook of the Society for the Advancement of General Systems Theory*, I, edited by L. von Bertalanffy and A. Rapoport (New York: The Society for General Systems Research, 1956), p. 18.

Natural vs. Man-made Systems. The first such classification is that of a natural system. *Natural systems* are those which come about as a result of natural phenomena such as the actions of nature. The most common and obvious example of a natural system is man himself viewed as a biological system, made up of a series of smaller systems referred to as subsystems, such as the nervous system, the circulatory system, the muscle system, and other such subsystems. Another example is the universe with the galaxies subdivided into units such as the solar system, and then the various planetary subsystems such as the earth-moon set. Opposed to natural systems are *man-made systems;* systems which man creates and operates. Examples of man-made systems are the social system or an economic system. HiWAy SYSTEM ,

Physical vs. Abstract Systems. Systems may also be classified as physical or abstract. A *physical system* consists of real-life objects such as machinery, tools, or equipment. In an *abstract system* we find the system objects are much more nebulous, such as strategies, objectives, or plans. LAWS . ⁻

Open vs. Closed Systems. Systems may also be viewed as either open or closed. The business firm is an example of an *open system* because there is an interchange in some form or another between the system and its environment. This interchange can take many forms such as products, advertising, and various types of information. On the other hand, the system is *closed* if no such exchange takes place between the system and its environment. Closed systems are, of course, very difficult to find because they tend to be stagnant, and unless in some way they were self-perpetuating, would ultimately cease to function. An example of a system which was at least approaching a closed state would be the human body in syncope or a state of coma. In this condition, the body system has virtually ceased to have any interchange with its environment. Another case that might typify a closed system would be a radio with one component not functioning properly. This electronic system would no longer be interacting with its environment as desired, and could be viewed as a closed system. Of course, this might only be a temporary situation if the necessary repairs were made. The system then would again be open. It is unlikely that any form of business enterprise could be identified as a closed system. Such a system, if found, would be short-lived.

Adaptive vs. Nonadaptive Systems. A very similar classification to the open and closed systems just discussed has been suggested by Cyert and March.[3] They have held that the business firm may also be viewed as an adaptive system as contrasted with a nonadaptive system. The business firm is held to be an *adaptive system* because it reacts to environmental pressures. The response engendered changes the state of the system. This change is one that is desirable in view of the current objectives of the system. This kind of system is essentially the same as an open system. A *nonadaptive system* would be one which did not

---

[3]Richard M. Cyert and James G. March, *A Behavioral Theory of the Firm* (Englewood Cliffs: Prentice-Hall, Inc., 1963), p. 99.

SHAKERS

respond to the needs imposed upon it by its environment. Such a system, if not already so, would soon be identical to a closed system.

The Total System

Reference to the systems approach in the context of the business enterprise frequently carries a connotation variously referred to as the total system, the unified management approach, integrated management, or the synthesis approach, among others. The *total system* is concerned with the achievement of the objective for which all of the components of the enterprise system have been brought together in an organized fashion. Implied is a further interest in the way in which the enterprise carries on the necessary activities in its attempt to reach the stated goal through the effective utilization of the resources required and available. The medium through which all of this is accomplished is, of course, good management.

Phys!
History

The notion of the enterprise as a total system includes the problem of the transmission of information. Information can be said to be the lifeblood of any organization. Without the development and transmission of information it would be impossible for the organization to operate effectively. Only with the receipt of meaningful information is a manager able to make a good decision. Since management and information are integral parts of the total systems approach, the term management information system is often used.

At this point it should be evident that the task of designing and implementing the total system approach in a business enterprise is very complex. This problem would apply to any size of enterprise, large or small. In attempting to complete this task, one of the first steps is to identify and define the system with which we are concerned. Additionally, it would be helpful to include an identification of the problem, the recognition of the objectives and requirements of the system, and an understanding of the nature and purpose of all of the related subsystems.

The application of the total systems approach to management problems is of relatively recent origin, but it has wide potential. It makes possible the establishment of a framework which serves as the limits of the particular problem area. Once the structure of the system under study is established, it then becomes possible to concentrate on the specific problem. The relationships and the behavior of the constituent parts of the system in all of its possible states can be observed.

Mq!
DID?

→ BALANCE ←
The System Structure

The structure of a system may be determined by examining the parameters of that system. This examination can best be accomplished by means of a series of schematic models of the system parameter relationships. The elements of a system along with their relationship to each other can be shown by the models.

A system can be assumed to consist of a series of inputs which yield an output, and are collectively a function of some action or process. Thus, a model of a system could be expressed in the following terms:

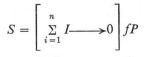

$$S = \left[\sum_{i=1}^{n} I \longrightarrow 0 \right] fP$$

Where:

S = the system

$\sum\limits_{i=1}^{n} I$ = total inputs = $I_1 + I_2 + I_3 + \text{-------} I_n$

O = output

P = process

This relationship can also be illustrated by a schematic model as in Figure 2-1.

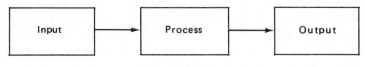

FIGURE 2-1

Schematic Model of a System

The three principal elements of a system are input, process, and output (Figure 2-1). Output and process need only to be defined here, but a detailed investigation of input is required. *Output* is the final result of the system operation. The output of a system is the reason for which the system exists: output is the goal or the objective of the system. *Process* is the ongoing action of the system which must be carried on to effect the transformation of the input into the desired output.

Input. *Input* is the generating function of any system and supplies it with the specific necessity to make the system operative in a variety of different forms. Optner states that input may take one of three different forms:

1. The result of a previous process, in line, serially.
2. The result of a previous process, randomly generated.
3. The result of a process that is being reintroduced.[4]

The first form of input can be shown by an expansion of the basic structure of a system into a series of subsystems as shown in Figure 2-2. Here the output of subsystem 1 becomes the input of subsystem 2, and the output of subsystem 2 serves as the input of subsystem 3. This relationship could continue in the same type of a series for a large number of subsystems. The total of all of the

[4]Stanford L. Optner, *Systems Analysis for Business and Industrial Problem Solving* (Englewood Cliffs: Prentice-Hall, Inc., 1965), p. 36.

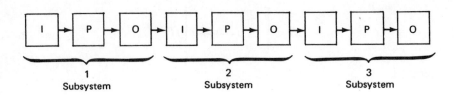

FIGURE 2-2

Schematic Model of Input Introduced Serially

subsystems in this line would equal the total system itself. It is also possible to identify each of these subsystems as systems within themselves. This is true when each of the subsystems is actually producing a final output of its own.

This first form of input may also be found in a total system wherein each of the individual subsystems is producing an output which is not a final output in itself, but is really only a part of the final output of the system. This can be exemplified by the special case of an assembly process where subsystem A produces a subassembly which becomes a part of another subassembly resulting from subsystem B, which when combined with components of subsystem C results in the final output. Such a total system is identified in Figure 2-3 where subassembly A, which is the output of subsystem A, becomes one of the inputs of subsystem B. These inputs when combined produce subassembly B, which becomes a part of the various inputs of subsystem C which then produces a final assembly as its output.

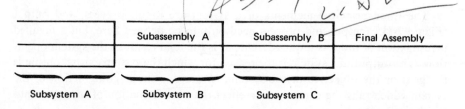

FIGURE 2-3

Schematic Model of Input Introduced Serially — Assembly Line Case

When the input is generated randomly rather than serially, we have the second form of input mentioned. The essential difference here is that the inputs of the subsystems may be introduced at any point in the total system process. The timing of their introduction is purely random.

If we consider the manufacturing system of a firm, we recognize that not all of the inputs, in the form of raw materials, need to be introduced initially, nor must they be introduced in series. There are many cases where new inputs may be introduced at a number of different points in the processing. These inputs may be new parts or raw materials directly out of stock. The essential feature here is that the inputs are introduced at purely random times, not in sequence as

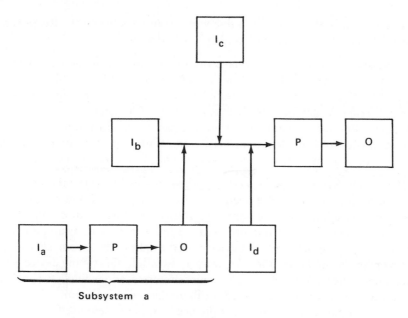

FIGURE 2-4

Schematic Model of Randomly Introduced Input

in the first type of input. Figure 2-4 can be used to illustrate this condition. Inputs c and d are examples of random introduction. Subsystem a is an example of input serially introduced.

Input which is the result of the reintroduction of the output of a process is the third form of input. In order to examine this type of input, it is necessary to consider another of the parameters of a system, that of feedback control. Reintroduced input as a result of feedback control is illustrated in Figure 2-5.

In a case where the system is strictly an information system, the inputs could be sales forecast data. As the system operates, the actual sales figures become the output of the system. These actual data are fed back for purposes of comparing the results with the forecast. If the data deviate from the initial forecast, it will be necessary to change some of the inputs going into the system to bring

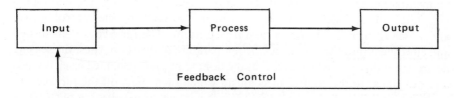

FIGURE 2-5

Schematic Diagram of Reintroduced Input Resulting from Feedback Control the system state and the output in line with the initial objectives. Reference to Figure 2-5 shows us this type of system in schematic form.

Feedback. In Figure 2-5 we have the reintroduction of the output of the system as input. This is shown by means of the feedback loop which has as its object the control of the system, returning the ouput as input into the same system. *Feedback* may be described as that part of a system that is concerned with controlling the system by means of comparing the operation or output of the system with some predetermined criterion. With respect to control there are two types of systems: the open-loop system and the closed-loop system.

OPEN-LOOP SYSTEM. An *open-loop system* is one in which the control is completely independent of the operation of the system itself, but rather results from some outside element or some prearranged element. An example of an open-loop system would be the turning on of lights in a room by an individual. Even if you were to put a timing device onto the light in that room, such as that used by many people when they are away on vacation, this timing device would depend upon the tripping of a switch at a pre-set time, and would have no direct relationship, necessarily, to the need for illumination in the room. This type of control is completely independent of the needs of the system itself.

CLOSED-LOOP SYSTEM. If, on the other hand, a device was attached to the wiring of this room which sensed the intensity of light in the room and turned on the lights when the intensity lowered to a specific level, this controlling device would be in direct connection with the needs of the system. When the control of a system is exerted by means of some feedback device, which is directly related to the operation of the system itself, we have a *closed-loop system*.

An early application of feedback is the Watt governor, which was used in connection with the Watt steam engine. As the speed of the engine increased, the weighted arms, which were mounted on pivots, began to rise as the speed of the shaft to which they were attached increased. The rise was a result of the application of centrifugal force. As the speed increased and the arms rose, they served as a valve which was closed as they rose, consequently admitting less power to the engine. This represents a closed-loop feedback system which permitted more power to be admitted when the engine was running slowly, and the reverse occurred when it was going at high speed.

Another very common example of the closed-loop system is the thermostatic control which is found in most homes or offices today to maintain or control the temperature of the room. As the temperature in the room falls, the sensing device notes this and sends out a signal which is received by the control device, and which in turn is relayed to the furnace itself. The furnace is then started and emits heat into the room. As the temperature in the room rises, the sensing device notes this, and when it reaches the desired or predetermined level, it sends a return signal to the control mechanism which then shuts off the furnace. In these examples it is easy to see that there is a constant monitoring of the state of the system, and a continuing comparison of the actual output is made against the desired output. If the output is deviating from the desired level, the input is modified by means of the feedback channel so that the processing element of the system can operate in such a fashion as to produce the desired output.

Control. The general function of control consists of the establishment of some measure of effectiveness of the system operation. Specifically, *control* involves the evaluation and interpretation of information regarding the actual operation of the system, the comparison of this information with the measure of effectiveness, and the institution of any corrective action needed to maintain the system output at the desired state.

State of System

USUAL CONCEPT OF CONTROL. Despite the wide and varied use of the concept of control in many disciplines, the most commonly held understanding of what is meant by control is incorrect from the systems viewpoint. Most people tend to think of control as a form of containment, or of some form of action which is taken after the fact. For example, at large gatherings we hear reference made to "crowd control," when talking about the techniques used by security officials. This is not control in the proper sense, but is merely containment. Corrective action taken after examination of the completed operating results which are found not to be up to the predetermined criterion is also mistakenly referred to as control. Changing a dull cutting tool which has produced oversized parts after completion of the run is not control.

HOMEOSTATIC CONTROL. Real control exists when the system operates in a consistent and optimal state. When a system operates in this fashion, so as to counteract any changes in its internal state which are the result of either changes in the external environment or the result of the action of the system itself, it is referred to in the biological sciences as a condition of *homeostasis*. One of the best examples of a homeostat is the way the body temperature is regulated. It is controlled by means of mechanisms in such a way that when the temperature of the body changes in any direction, these mechanisms react so as to offset this change in temperature and return the body to its normal level of heat. A homeostat is actually an example of *negative feedback* control. This simply means that it performs in a fashion to minimize the difference between the output of the system and the predetermined criterion. *Positive feedback* would occur when the action of the control system was to increase the response difference. Servomotors, used to amplify automatic pilot control signals in aircraft operation, are an example of this.

A homeostatic control system consists of several components:

1. A sensing device.
2. A comparator which measures the actual output against that of the predetermined criterion or measure of effectiveness.
3. An error signal which is the difference between the measure of effectiveness and the actual system output.
4. An effector which takes the error signal and acts to minimize the difference between the actual and the desired level of performance.
5. A response.

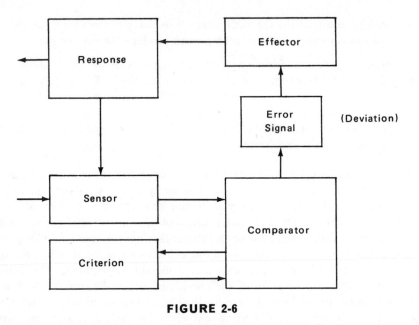

FIGURE 2-6

Schematic Diagram of a Homeostatic Control System

Figure 2-6 illustrates the elements of a homeostatic control system.

CONTROL AND FEEDBACK. A very high degree of feedback control is required for accurate system control. In this way the effects of any changes in the input, the environment (internal or external), or any other parts of the system will be moved in the direction of zero. If the feedback system is slow in its response time, the system will tend to be unstable. A homeostatic control system may only operate within a certain range with respect to its parameters, especially its inputs. If there is a reduction in the input, or a marked change in one of the other parameters, the effector may not be able to function properly and return the system to the desired operating level. While it may be true that systems in industry may not be of a homeostatic nature in a large number of cases, the ideal system will have this type of control. The ideal system, while difficult to achieve, should always be the goal in the design of any industrial system.

The Operations Management System

The operations function and the systems approach have been examined. The next logical step is to examine the operations function in the context of a system and as one of the many subsystems of the total enterprise. Figure 2-7 schematically shows the operations subsystem in relation to the enterprise as a whole within the framework of a total management system.

This diagram is drawn from the viewpoint that the management system encompasses all characteristics involved in the planning, organizing, directing,

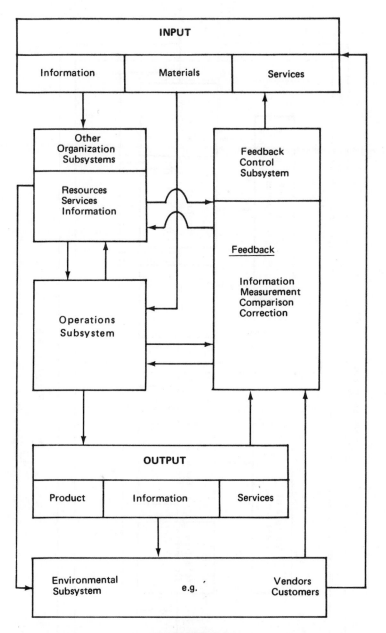

FIGURE 2-7

Schematic Diagram Showing Operations Subsystem
as a Part of the Total Management System

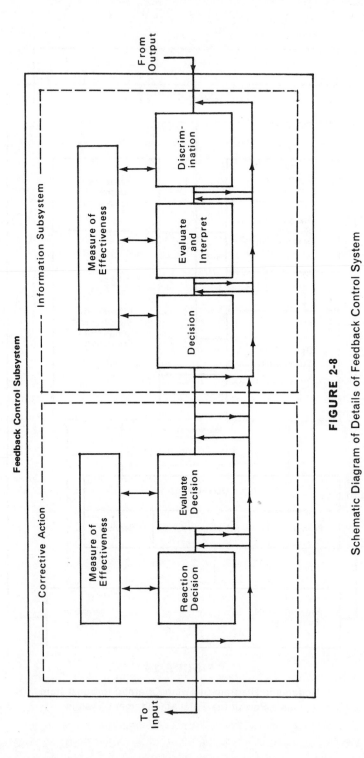

FIGURE 2-8

Schematic Diagram of Details of Feedback Control System

staffing, and controlling of the enterprise. This system is not conceived of as being involved only with the processing of material things or solely with information processing, but with any possible combination of these elements. Examination of the diagram makes it readily apparent that the inputs can be in the form of information, materials, or services. The inputs of the system may flow to the operations system and to the other organizational subsystems in various combinations.

The outputs of the system may be in a variety of forms such as products, information, or services. These outputs may flow to the environment as indicated in any or all of the forms.

The inclusion of the environmental subsystem allows the relationship of the environment to the total management system to also be pictured. The environment has interchanges of many sorts with the components of the management system, such as receiving output, providing inputs, and receiving or providing information to various subsystems of the enterprise.

The total management system as depicted is, of course, a closed-loop system. As such, it has as an integral part a feedback subsystem. This feedback control system is displayed in more detail in Figure 2-8.

In this figure we find the feedback control system viewed as consisting of two subsystems. These two further subdivisions are labeled as the information subsystem and the corrective action subsystem. The information subsystem is that subsystem wherein the feedback is evaluated and a decision as to its meaning and significance is made. The corrective action subsystem takes this decision and makes a further decision as to what action is necessary to bring the feedback up to criteria.

Of course, the operations subsystem could be further broken down into its integral parts, or into what might be called sub-subsystems. These would be concerned with the various functions performed by the operations subsystem such as product and plant planning; process planning; work design and measurement; and inventory, quality, or cost controls.

SUMMARY

Operations is only one of a number of functional areas which comprise the total enterprise. To be able to study the techniques of the management of the operations function, it is necessary to have a grasp of its relationship to the total enterprise. Top management of any enterprise deals primarily with the problems of the determination of the strategy to be followed and with the development of policies to successfully pursue this strategy. The nature of the strategy adopted will play an important role in the effectiveness of the operations function.

The formulation of the operations policies will lead to the selection of a measure of effectiveness for the operations system. The operations manager should recognize that the formulation of policies for his function is not as obvious as it might at first appear. The most meaningful operations policies will require a series of trade-offs between the numerous alternatives available.

The operations function is viewed as being a function found in any type of enterprise. This view is in contrast to the older idea of considering operations only as consisting of production activities. The significance of production activities is not denied, but recognition is given to the fact that production is only one form of the operations function. While operations is recognized as only one of the functional areas found in an enterprise, its relationship to the other functions must not be ignored. Operations managers should always be aware of these interrelationships with all the other functions. To achieve this awareness, a logical approach similar to the scientific method can be employed in the solution of management problems.

The recent trend toward the application of the principles of the systems approach to management is recognized. The value of visualizing the enterprise as an integrated whole is that it assists in achieving better decisions for the total enterprise. Systems can be divided into a number of categories. Such classifications make it easier to identify a particular system, and to understand its functioning. The enterprise system can fit into a number of these groups. The enterprise system is frequently referred to as the total system or as the management system. This emphasizes the necessity of applying the systems approach to the total enterprise. It also emphasizes the importance of management in the operation of an enterprise system.

To better understand the systems approach, an examination of the elements of a system is helpful. The basic elements of any system are input, process, and output. Another element which is important to the proper functioning of systems such as the operations system is feedback. Feedback is essential to the achievement of control of a system.

Thus, the operations management system is a subsystem of the total management system. As such, it contains all of the elements of any system. From this standpoint it is possible to examine the various relationships which exist between the operations subsystem and all other pertinent subsystems. In investigating the operations function as a system, it is possible to get a better idea of its constituents and of its performance. Such an investigation leads to a detailed analysis of the feedback control subsystem. The importance of the decision-making process to the effectiveness of the operations system can be seen. Therefore, clearly, it is important to examine the decision-making process.

INCIDENT

THE JOINT CHIEFS OF STAFF

In September, 1970, the Secretary of Defense announced that he was changing the responsibilities of the Joint Chiefs of Staff. The announcement indicated that the joint chiefs would no longer be responsible as a group for the control of the operations of the military services. They would, from that time, be concerned only with planning and policy making.

The day-to-day operations would be under a new and separate command. No change was anticipated in the various commands of the individual armed services which have field control. A recommendation had been made that the field command structure be replaced with three major command groups called strategic, tactical, and logistic. However, this recommendation was not accepted by the Secretary at this time.

Questions

1. From a management standpoint do you see any reason for the change?
2. Do you approve or disapprove? Why?
3. Do you agree or disagree with the recommendation which was not accepted?

QUESTIONS FOR DISCUSSION AND ANALYSIS

1. What is your understanding of the meaning of enterprise strategy? Why is the determination of strategy an important function of the top management of any enterprise?

2. Discuss the reason why the development of the proper strategy is important to the success of the operations manager.

3. Why is it important to view the operations function more broadly than as though it were essentially the same as the production function?

4. Consider a variety of nonmanufacturing firms, and identify those activities which you would place under the area of operations. For example:
   (a) A department store
   (b) A stock broker
   (c) An airline
   (d) A bank

5. Select a specific problem of operations management, and develop the framework of a logical approach to the solution of this problem.

6. Define a system. Of what specific value is the concept of a system to an operations manager?

7. Complete the following chart by placing a check mark in the appropriate column for each named system or subsystem to indicate under which classifications it belongs.

System	Classification							
	Natural	Man-Made	Physical	Abstract	Open	Closed	Adaptive	Non-Adaptive
Human Body	X		X		X		|	
Factory		X	X			|		
Airplane	X		X			|		
Urban Development Plans	X			X		|		
City Council	X	X			|			
University	X	X			√			X

8. Give specific examples of operations systems which exemplify the three different forms of input mentioned in the chapter.

9. What is feedback? Distinguish between an open-loop and a closed-loop system.

10. What are the components of a homeostatic control system? Is such a control system possible in operations systems?

11. Describe the relationship that exists between the total management system and the environment.

SELECTED ADDITIONAL READINGS

Cleland, David I., and William R. King. *Systems Analysis and Project Management.* New York: McGraw-Hill Book Co., 1968.

Kast, Fremont E., and James E. Rosenzweig. *Organization and Management: A Systems Approach.* New York: McGraw-Hill Book Co., 1970. Chapter 5.

Koontz, Harold, and Cyril O'Donnell. *Principles of Management,* 6th ed. New York: McGraw-Hill Book Co., 1972. Chapter 10.

McMillan, Claude, and Richard F. Gonzalez. *Systems Analysis: A Computer Approach to Decision Models.* Homewood, Illinois: Richard D. Irwin, Inc., 1965. Chapter 1.

Optner, Stanford L. *Systems Analysis for Business and Industrial Problem Solving.* Englewood Cliffs: Prentice-Hall, Inc., 1965.

Prince, Thomas R. *Information Systems for Management Planning and Control.* Homewood, Illinois: Richard D. Irwin, Inc., 1966.

Sisk, Henry L. *Principles of Management,* 2d ed. Cincinnati: South-Western Publishing Co., 1973. Chapters 6 and 7.

Starr, Martin Kenneth. *Production Management: System and Synthesis.* Englewood Cliffs: Prentice-Hall, Inc., 1964. Chapters 1, 2, and 3.

Steiner, George A. *Top Management Planning.* New York: The Macmillan Co., 1969. Chapters 9, 10, 14, and 16.

SELECTIONS FROM READINGS BOOKS

Greenwood, William T. *Decision Theory and Information Systems.* Cincinnati: South-Western Publishing Co., 1969.
  Johnson, Kast, and Rosenzweig, "Systems Theory and Management," p. 220.
  Young, "Designing the Management System," p. 242.
  Reilley, "Planning the Strategy of the Business," p. 547.
  Greenwood, "Business Policies — Controls for Strategic Decisions," p. 569.

Richards, Max D., and William A. Nielander. *Readings in Management,* 3d ed. Cincinnati: South-Western Publishing Co., 1969.
  Ansoff, "A Quasi-Analytic Approach to the Business Strategy Problem," p. 350.
  Peirce, "The Planning and Control Concept," p. 375.

3 | # Decision Making

The process of decision making is an inherent part of the efficient functioning of the enterprise system. This is emphasized by the fact that many people view the process as the primary function of management. The decision problem evolves from the fact that the manager frequently finds himself in the position of having to select what direction he must take relative to a specific problem. Unfortunately, when he makes his decision, the manager is not able to use the techniques of the fortune-teller nor does he have the ability to gaze into a crystal ball and receive sage advice relative to the problem.

This selection is the essence of the decision-making problem. The effect of the choice made will largely be to determine the form of the ultimate solution. It is also necessary to emphasize that a good solution to the wrong problem will often be worse than no solution at all. Therefore, a large part of the decision-making process involves the identification of the problem as well as the achievement of a solution.

THE DECISION PROCESS

Decision making has been divided into three steps by Kimball.

First: Discovering the possible avenues among which the choice can be made.

Second: Analysis of the consequences of taking each of the possible avenues.

Third: Choosing the best avenue of action.[1]

In this third step it is very simple to make a decision when the possible choices are clear and the consequences of each choice are not in doubt. Kimball labels these as the decisions of the first kind.[2] Most of the time, however, the consequences are unknown. This condition results in a second kind of decision where there is always a possibility that the decision might be wrong. The use of probability techniques will be found useful in making such decisions. There are also decisions of the third kind, which involve unknown elements, and where the consequences are unpredictable. Situations where these types of decisions are required are quite common in operations management. A schematic representation of the decision-making process can be found in Figure 3-1. This diagram can be related to the steps in the decision process listed above. The first step is represented by the box labeled, Evaluation of Alternatives. The next two boxes,

---

[1]George E. Kimball, "Decision Theory: Operations Research in Management," *Advanced Management*, Vol. XX, No. 12 (December, 1954), pp. 5–7.

[2]*Ibid.*

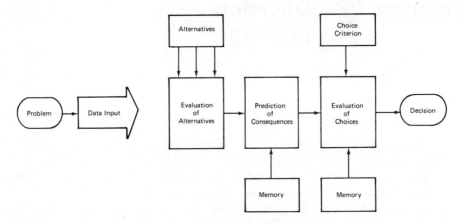

FIGURE 3-1

Schematic Diagram of the Decision-Making Process

Prediction of Consequences and Evaluation of Choices, would parallel the second step. The actual decision is the same as the third step.

In Figure 3-1 two forms of memory are illustrated and are labeled Memory 1 and Memory 2. Each of these memories flows to separate activities represented by other boxes. Memory is an important element in the decision-making process. It plays a significant role in the recognition of past happenings, and then in the prediction of results based on these past events. One uses this type of memory when considering past performance of the teams in predicting the outcome of a sporting event. This is identified as Memory 1 in Figure 3-1.

Memory is also an essential element in the next step, the choice evaluation process, which must precede the decision. Such memory is designated as Memory 2. Any such evaluation is affected, in the first place, by an analysis of similar previous situations which depends on this type of memory. The established criteria which relate to the current decision also have a bearing. These criteria include the level of risk which is permissible and the required amount of assurance as to the correctness of the decision.

How Managers Make Decisions

The way a manager will make a particular decision depends largely on the nature of the problem facing him. If the problem is similar to others that the manager must decide on a day-to-day basis, his approach to a solution will be quite different than if the problem is new and unique. Simon differentiates between decisions on these two bases and calls them either programmed decisions or nonprogrammed decisions.[3]

---

[3]Herbert A. Simon, *The New Science of Management Decision* (New York: Harper & Row, Publishers, Inc., 1960), pp. 5–6.

SOFT SELL SAM

"While the boss is sick, where's that coin he flips on major decisions?"

Reprinted by permission of The Register and Tribune Syndicate, © 1970.

FIGURE 3-2

Programmed decisions are those types of decisions that are made frequently and that are related to the normal day-to-day performance. These decisions result from the application of established standard procedures. Consequently, the making of such decisions can often be delegated to middle and lower levels of management. A specific decision rule can be stated for this type. A typical example is the reordering of an item in stock when the inventory of that item reaches some predetermined level.

Nonprogrammed decisions are required when the problem or the conditions are not uniform or recurrent. These are the exceptional, unexpected decisions which must be handled on an individual basis. No specific procedure can be stated for making such decisions.

Simon further compares the traditional and modern decision-making techniques applied to these two types of decisions.[4] While it is only natural that modern decision-making techniques are of greatest interest, the fact that the traditional methods still can play a large role in the manager's decision-making processes should not be overlooked. In some situations, it is not possible to ignore such time-honored managerial methods as habit, judgment, hunch, or intuition. Certainly, the intention here is not to suggest that such personalized and subjective approaches to decision making should be the rule. The experienced manager will find that resorting to such techniques can still be useful.

----

[4]*Ibid.*, p. 8.

Algorithms. The modern decision-making techniques applied to programmed type decisions depend on deductive and systematic methods. These methods are usually referred to as algorithmic methods. An *algorithm* is essentially any calculating method such as a mathematical formula or model. Algorithms will always lead to a solution where a solution is possible, and such a solution is usually optimal.

Heuristics. In contrast, nonprogrammed decisions depend largely upon heuristic methods. A *heuristic* is an intuitive approach based on rules-of-thumb for finding solutions to problems. A heuristic will not always result in the best decision; for that matter, it may not result in any solution to the problem at all. However, when it does, the solution is a good one. The decisions achieved are usually reached in a much shorter period of time than would be possible using an algorithm. In fact, there are some problems that are not possible to frame as an algorithm, and must be subjected to heuristic methods. Heuristic problem solving is not limited to problems composed of quantifiable variables.

Research in heuristic problem solving has been aimed at simulating the human problem solving process. Simon and Newell conducted studies in this direction by setting up a problem and requesting a subject to vocalize his thinking in the process of arriving at a solution. Both his oral thinking and his problem solving commands were recorded on tape. These recordings or protocols were studied, and a computer program was written to simulate the human thought processes followed in arriving at a decision.[5] While the applications have been limited to date, the potential of combining heuristic techniques with the computer appears to be very promising. Studies of heuristic problem solving have added to our knowledge of human thought processes.

Models

After the problem has been identified, constructing a model to represent the system in which the problem exists is useful. In order to make a satisfactory decision, some knowledge of how the system will behave as a result of some new input is necessary. Experimenting directly with the system to determine the results of a decision empirically is not always possible. Nor is it always possible to break down a complex system into smaller parts to evaluate the total system's operation by observing the behavior of the components. A model makes such experiments of the performance of the system feasible. A *model* can be defined as something which can be manipulated economically, and which represents the actual system under study. Four types of models are:

1. Iconic — a schematic representation of the real thing; a picture, a photograph. This type of model is static. Iconic models may also take physical forms such as scale models. While these models may represent many properties of the real thing, they may also possess characteristics which are not necessary for the purpose at hand.

---

[5]*Ibid.*, p. 23.

2. Abstract — various forms of physical models used to explain or demon-
   strate certain phenomena, such as a globe of the earth. Another form
   of an abstract model is a verbal model.
3. Analog — a representation of one set of properties by another set of
   properties. For example, representation of the flow of gasoline through
   pipelines by some mechanical analogy such as electricity.
4. Symbolic — an equation or group of equations that describe mathematically a real situation. It relates factors involved in such a way that
   they can be operated mathematically.

The use of symbolic or mathematical models in recent years has been
responsible for the development of many of the modern techniques of decision
making available to operations managers. Coupled with the development of
high speed computers, many types of problems heretofore unsolvable can now be
solved through combination of the mathematical model and the computer.

CERTAINTY, RISK, AND UNCERTAINTY

When a decision is made, the conditions that exist at that time will have a
significant influence on the actual decision process. The nature of the problem
will, in a large part, dictate what these conditions are. In addition, the available
alternatives will structure the process, as will the possible consequences and the
choice criterion. Thus, it is possible for the decision maker to find himself faced
with different decision-making conditions. The basic conditions under which
decisions are made are usually identified as certainty, risk, and uncertainty.
These conditions closely parallel the previously discussed decisions of the first,
second, and third kind respectively.

Certainty

Earlier in this chapter the various types of decisions were discussed. Mention
was made of decisions of the first kind where the possible choices were clear and
the consequences of each of the choices were not in doubt. When decisions are
made under these circumstances, they are described as decisions made under
conditions of *certainty*. For example, if by some chance the demand for the
product during a coming period of time was known, the decision of the number
of units to produce for sale in that period of time would be quite simplified.
The number of units which were going to be sold would be produced.

It is very unusual for the operations manager to find a decision situation
fitting the category of decision making under certainty. Certainty implies a
decision problem where each alternative or strategy, if chosen, results in a known
consequence or state of nature. Under this unusual or possibly nonexistent
approach to decision making, decisions would be highly simplified since all that
is necessary is to choose from among the known possible outcomes. Not all
decisions under conditions of certainty are as simple as they might first appear.
The sheer magnitude of the problem can add to the difficulties, even under

certainty conditions. These types of decision situations are possible because the aim of many of the techniques applied to any decision problem is to reduce the problem at hand to circumstances that approximate certainty. This condition is accomplished by ignoring some of the complexities, by assuming certain parameters have no significant effect on the results of the decision, or by making assumptions as to the value of some of the problem parameters.· If the decision maker has some knowledge of decision making under conditions of certainty, he possesses an understanding of the decision process that makes him better able to solve decision problems.

Risk

A large number of decisions are identified as being made under conditions of risk. Conditions of *risk* occur when the decision maker has information or firm knowledge of the probability or expected occurrence of the outcome. By way of example, assume for a given decision situation that the evaluation of past history reveals: a certain outcome, or state, occurs approximately 30% of the time; a second outcome, or state, occurs about 70% of the time; and these conditions are expected to continue to apply in the future.

Assume the first state (S_1) is that GNP will increase, and state two (S_2) is that GNP will decline in the next year. The operations manager is faced with two alternatives: making one of two products. These alternatives or actions are designated as A_1 and A_2. Past experience indicates that the sales of these products are related to the movement of GNP. The following table shows the expected sales revenue of each of these two actions under the two possible states.

Products (Actions)	S_1 GNP+ $p = .30$	S_2 GNP− $p = .70$
A_1	$50,100	$15,950
A_2	$20,250	$40,300

The expected value of each of these two actions can now be computed. *Expected value* is the long run weighted average result anticipated. In this case it is the average sales of the two products which would be obtained over an extended period of time. The sales for the two different states are weighted by the probabilities of their occurrence, and the results are summed. The expected values in this instance are as follows:

$$E_{(A_1)} = \$50,100(.30) + \$15,950(.70) = \$26,195$$

$$E_{(A_2)} = \$20,250(.30) + \$40,300(.70) = \$34,285$$

Therefore, the best decision indicated under these conditions is to take action A_2 (make product two). To illustrate the importance of the probability: if the probabilities had been 50% for each state, the expected revenue would have been greatest for A_1 ($33,025 vs. $30,275) and the decision would have been reversed.

Uncertainty

Probably the most frequent types of decision situations found in the "real world" are referred to as decision making under *uncertainty*. In this decision-making condition, the decision maker does not have any information regarding the possible outcomes, such as the probability of occurrence of any of the possible states. Uncertainty conditions are sometimes subdivided into two categories: total ignorance and partial ignorance.[6]

Total Ignorance. *Total ignorance* is found when the decision maker possesses absolutely no information about the several possible states that may exist. He is unable to even apply any probability distribution to the possible outcomes. Thus, the decision maker must select some decision criteria for making his specific choice from among the alternatives available. While there are a variety of criteria to which one might resort, and each of these criteria can be justified rationally, there is no single criterion for decisions under uncertainty that can be termed best. The criterion finally selected will be based on what, in the decision maker's judgment, is the most satisfying, based on his own attitudes, or on the policies of the enterprise. From among the numerous criteria, two will be examined for purposes of illustration.

MAXIMIN CRITERION. The first criterion is the *maximin criterion*, or the criterion of pessimism. This rule assumes, as is obvious from its name, that the decision maker takes a pessimistic viewpoint of nature. The decision maker is most concerned with minimizing his risk, and therefore, he calculates the minimum result for each alternative or strategy that he faces. He then selects from among the minimum payoffs the one which gives him the maximum result. Assume the same conditions as in the example of risk above. The sales revenues are the minimums to be expected.

	Maximin		
	S_1	S_2	
Products (Actions)	GNP+	GNP−	Minimum
A_1	$50,100	$15,950	$15,950
A_2	$20,250	$40,300	$20,250

Therefore, the decision in this case would be to make product two.

MINIMAX CRITERION. The *minimax, or regret criterion*, is based on the idea that the decision maker will attempt to minimize the regret which he suffers

[6]William Emory and Powell Niland, *Making Management Decisions* (Boston: Houghton Mifflin, Co., 1968), p. 104.

when the actual outcome is one that results in a lesser payoff than he might have received had he selected a different course of action.

When the actual state of nature is known, and the decision maker is cognizant of the results of his decision, he will have this regret when he realizes that he may not have selected the best alternative. His regret can be gauged by the difference between the maximum payoff which he might have received, if he had known the state that would occur, and the lesser amount he actually received. In the case where he received the maximum payoff, he has no regret and it is represented as zero.

Under the same assumptions as outlined in the above examples of the maximin criterion, the following table can be constructed for the regret criterion.

Minimax

Products (Actions)	S_1 GNP+	S_2 GNP−	Regret
A_1	0	$24,350	$24,350 (minimum)
A_2	$29,850	0	$29,850

Therefore, if GNP increased and he had selected A_1, given the sales as estimated, he would receive the largest payoff under S_1 and have zero regret. On the other hand, if he had selected A_2, his regret under this state would be $50,100 − $20,250 = $29,850. This is the amount he would have lost as a result of selecting this alternative compared with what he might have received. If GNP had decreased and he had selected A_1, his regret would be $24,350 ($40,300 − $15,950). If he had selected A_2, his regret would be zero since this would have given the largest payoff under this state. Thus, the minimum regret in this illustration, derived from the estimated sales, amounts to $24,350, which would lead to a decision to produce product A_1, using this criterion. Therefore, by producing A_1, the decision maker is assuring himself that no matter which state occurs his maximum regret will be the lowest possible one.

Partial Ignorance. Another circumstance under conditions of uncertainty is partial ignorance. Under this circumstance, the manager has just enough information to permit him to assign some likelihood to the occurrence of the various outcomes or states of nature. This likelihood takes the form of subjective or personal probability. Because of their importance in the decision-making process, under all conditions other than certainty, it will be useful to briefly examine probabilities.

PROBABILITY

Everyone has an intuitive idea of probability since it is related to a variety of familiar games of chance. The use of probability is found in the daily weather forecasts when the weatherman states that there is a certain probability of the occurrence of rain in the next period of time. In essence, what he is saying is that there is a certain likelihood of rain in the period for which his forecast is made. When he assigns a certain numerical evaluation to this likelihood, he is actually expressing a probability, e.g., "There is a 70% chance of rain tomorrow." Probabilities are then a means by which the uncertainties about events can be expressed. Attaching a numerical value to these uncertainties permits quantitative judgment in addition to qualitative judgment regarding the uncertainty.

Basic Concepts of Probability

The determination of the probability of a specific outcome is usually thought of in terms of the long-run relative frequency of the occurrence of that event, assuming that the event is repeated many times. The probability of any given event is expressed by the percentage of the time a specific occurrence results in relation to the total number of observations. For example, in the usual coin flipping experiment, a "fair" coin is flipped a given number of times and the occurrences of heads and of tails are recorded. Then, it is possible to determine the probability of the occurrence of heads by the ratio of the number of heads to the total number of times the coin was flipped. Conversely, it is also possible to determine the probability of the occurrence of tails in the same way. If the coin was flipped 2,000,000 times, heads would be expected to appear approximately ½ of the time and tails approximately ½ of the time. Therefore, the probability of heads is .50, and the probability of tails is also .50. Note that this is the long-run probability or relative frequency of the occurrence of either heads or tails, and does not in any way indicate the probability of a given flip of that particular coin.

Probability Formulas. If events are such that they are equally likely to occur, the basic probability formula is expressed as follows:

$$P(\text{success}) \, = \, \frac{\text{number of equally likely successful events}}{\text{total number of equally likely events}}$$

A particular coin may not be "fair," but may be unbalanced in some way to favor heads. This condition would result in a head appearing more often than ½ the time. In such a circumstance the probabilities of the two events (heads and tails) occurring would not be equal. The probability of heads appearing with a flip of that particular coin is the ratio of the number of heads to the total number of flips. The basic formula for this is as follows:

$$P(\text{success}) \, = \, \text{relative frequency of success}$$

$$= \, \frac{\text{number of "successful" occurrences}}{\text{total number of occurrences}}$$

"*Successful*" *occurrences* are defined as any occurrences that fall into any category arbitrarily designated as "success." In this case, heads is the designated successful occurrence.

Objective and Subjective Probabilities. Whenever a large amount of information regarding the occurrence of a given event exists, and it is possible to state the probability of the occurrence of that event, this is referred to as an *objective probability*. This probability is in contrast to subjective probability to which it is often necessary to resort when no really definitive or reliable information about the event is available. *Subjective probabilities* are the result of the personal judgment or belief that one places in the occurrence of a particular event.

Frequency Tables. A useful tool for displaying the frequencies with which the events occur is a frequency table. Table 3-1 is such a table representing 100 flips of a coin.

TABLE 3-1

Frequency Table for 100 Flips of a Coin

Result	Frequency	Relative Frequency (Probability)
Heads	52	.52
Tails	48	.48
Total	100	1.00

Often the frequency data are more detailed than in a simple coin flipping experiment. For example, consider a specially constructed deck of 100 playing cards of which 60 are black and 40 are red. The following distributions of the two colors are contained in the deck.

Black Cards	Red Cards
20 are Jacks	15 are Jacks
15 are Queens	20 are Queens
25 are Kings	5 are Kings

These data can be depicted in a two-way frequency table as in Table 3-2.

If each of the cards in the deck has an equal chance of being chosen on a random draw, the probability of choosing one particular card is 1/100, or .01. Thus, since there are 20 red Queens in the deck, the probability of drawing a red Queen can be computed using the basic equally likely events formula set forth above.

$$P(\text{Red Queen}) = \frac{\text{number of equally likely successful occurrences}}{\text{total number of equally likely occurrences}}$$
$$= 20/100 = .20$$

Note that the total of the probabilities expressed for the occurrence of heads or tails in the flipping of a coin equaled one (1.00). This is always the case:

TABLE 3-2

Two-Way Frequency Table

Color of Cards	Value of Cards			Total for Each Color
	J	Q	K	
Black	20	15	25	60
Red	15	20	5	40
Total for Each Value	35	35	30	100

that the total of all probabilities of all possible events is assumed to equal one. At the same time, probabilities may never be less than zero. When the probability of an event is stated as zero it is impossible for that event to occur; if the probability of an event is expressed as equal to one, then that event is absolutely certain to occur. This range of probabilities is expressed by the following statement of inequality:

$$0 \leq P(E) \leq 1$$

Probability Rules

There are circumstances where probability problems become quite complex. A series of probability rules are applicable to these complex problems. A very brief look at some of these rules will yield a better understanding of the applications of probabilities to decision making in operations management.

Mutually Exclusive Events. The first of these rules deals with mutually exclusive events. If two or more events are *mutually exclusive*, it is impossible for any two events to occur at the same time. The probability of either of these events is the sum of their individual probabilities. For example, if one card is drawn randomly from a standard deck of cards, the probability of drawing a heart is .25, the probability of a diamond .25, the probability of a club .25, and the probability of a spade .25. The probability of drawing either a heart or a diamond is the sum of the probabilities of each of these events, or .25 plus .25 = .50. Of course, the probability of drawing a heart or a diamond or a club, or any combination of three suits would be .75, and, therefore, the probability of a heart or a diamond or a spade or a club would be equal to 1.00. This rule is also referred to as the additive rule, which can be illustrated as follows:

$$P(H) = .25 \text{ or } (1/4)$$
$$P(D) = .25 \text{ or } (1/4)$$
$$P(C) = .25 \text{ or } (1/4)$$
$$P(S) = .25 \text{ or } (1/4)$$

Thus:

$$P(H \text{ or } D) = P(H) + P(D)$$
$$= .25 + .25$$
$$= .50 \text{ or } (1/2)$$

Where:

$H = $ Heart
$D = $ Diamond
$C = $ Club
$S = $ Spade
$P(H) = $ the probability of drawing a heart.

The logic of mutually exclusive events is illustrated by Figure 3-3.

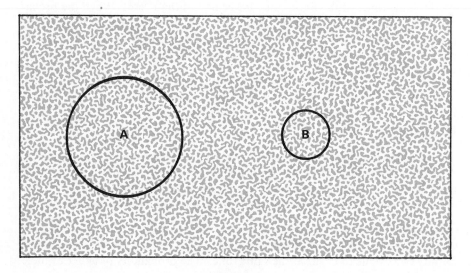

FIGURE 3-3

Mutually Exclusive Events

This figure illustrates that mutually exclusive events cannot occur at the same time. Any point within the sample space represented by the rectangle must be either in A or in B or in neither. Since the circles do not intersect, no point can be within A and B at the same time.

Not Mutually Exclusive Events. The second rule deals with events that are not mutually exclusive, and is another addition rule. Again, use a regular deck of 52 cards and ask, "What is the probability that a randomly chosen card will be either a heart or a face card (Jack, Queen, or King)?" Here is an example of events that are not mutually exclusive. This is true because a face card may also be a heart. Therefore, the selection of either a heart or a face card can mean the selection of either one of the two, or both of them.

If the basic addition rule as stated above is used, those cases where the card will be both a heart and a face card will be counted twice. The probability then, of a heart or a face card is the sum of the individual probabilities of these two events minus the probability of the occurrence of both of the events. In this case the probability of a heart and a face card is $3/52$. This is true because there are 3 cards in the deck which are both hearts and face cards, i.e., the Jack, Queen, and King of hearts. Thus, the probability of drawing a heart or a face card, or both, equals $22/52$ as expressed below:

$$P(H) = 13/52$$
$$P(J, Q, K) = 12/52$$

Thus:
$$P(H \text{ or } J, Q, K) = P(H) + P(J, Q, K) - [P(H) \text{ and } P(J, Q, K)]$$
$$= 13/52 + 12/52 - 3/52$$
$$= 22/52$$

This rule can also be illustrated by a diagram. Figure 3-4 represents the case of events which are not mutually exclusive.

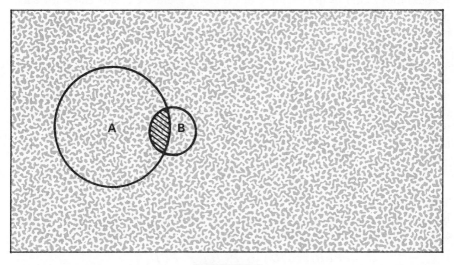

FIGURE 3-4

Events Not Mutually Exclusive

This figure illustrates that some points in the sample space are within both A and B. This fact is represented by the shaded area where the two circles overlap. Points falling within this area are not mutually exclusive.

Independent Events. The third rule evolves because there are also *independent events*. Independence is found when the occurrence of one event does not in any way depend on whether another event has occurred or not. If, from a deck of cards, two cards are drawn at random, and the first card is replaced before the second one is drawn, the probability attached to drawing a heart on the first draw is .25, and the probability of drawing a diamond on the second draw is also .25. Because the first card was replaced, the second draw does not depend on whether the first card was any particular suit or not. Thus, the two events are said to be independent events. The probability of drawing a heart and a diamond on the two consecutive draws is the same as the joint probability of the two events, and thus is the product of the probabilities of the independent events, or .0625. This multiplication rule applies for any number of independent events, and is expressed by the following statement:

$$P(H \text{ and } D) = P(H) \times P(D)$$
$$= .25 \times .25$$
$$= .0625 \text{ or } (1/16)$$

Dependent Events. The fourth rule, which is also a multiplication rule, relates to *dependent events*. Here, the occurrence of one event depends on the occurrence of another and will consequently affect the probability of the occurrence of the second event. If, from a deck of cards, only the four aces are used, the same probabilities found in the example of mutually exclusive events exists for each of the suits, that is, .25. If one card (ace) is drawn, and then a second card (ace) is drawn, this time not replacing the first card (ace), these draws are dependent events. In this case, the probability of the second ace being a particular suit is affected by the first ace drawn. What is the probability of drawing a heart and a diamond? The probability of a heart on the first draw is still .25. After drawing the heart only three cards remain, and the probability of drawing a diamond on the second draw is reduced to .333. This probability is referred to as the conditional probability of drawing a diamond, given the fact that a heart has already been drawn. The symbol for this is:

$$P(D|H)$$

The probability of a heart and a diamond is equal to the product of the probability of drawing a heart and the probability of drawing a diamond, given that a heart was drawn the first time. The expression for this rule is:

$$P(H \text{ and } D) = P(H) \times P(D|H)$$
$$= .25 \times .333$$
$$= .0833 \text{ or } (1/12)$$

An understanding of these rules will provide a good foundation of the circumstances surrounding probability events. This foundation will permit the application of the concept of probability to almost any set of circumstances relative to a decision problem in operations management. To be assured of complete clarity of these rules, another set of examples will be useful.

Additional Examples. To illustrate the above four rules further, a series of examples will be taken from data in the two-way frequency table presented above in Table 3-2.

Assume that it is desired to know the probability of drawing a Jack or a Queen from the special deck of 100 cards. These are mutually exclusive events as defined. Hence, from the table we can determine:

$$P(\text{Jack or Queen}) = P(\text{Jack}) + P(\text{Queen})$$
$$= 35/100 + 35/100$$
$$= 70/100$$

If the interest is in events that are not mutually exclusive, such as the probability of drawing a King or a black card, reference to the table shows:

$$P(\text{King or Black}) = P(\text{King}) + P(\text{Black}) - [P(\text{King}) \text{ and } P(\text{Black})]$$
$$= 30/100 + 60/100 - 25/100$$
$$= 65/100$$

Independent events can be exemplified by determining the probability of drawing two red cards on successive draws, replacing the first card after it is drawn. From the data on Table 3-2:

$$P(\text{Red and Red}) = P(\text{Red}) \times P(\text{Red})$$
$$= 40/100 \times 40/100$$
$$= 16/100 \quad .16$$

Dependent events can be illustrated with the data on Table 3-2 as well. An example is the determination of the probability of drawing a red card given that a red card has already been drawn. That is, determining the probability of drawing two successive red cards without replacing the first card. Thus:

$$P(\text{Red and Red}) = P(\text{Red}) \times P(\text{Red}|\text{Red})$$
$$= 40/100 \times 39/99$$
$$= 26/165 = .1570$$

UTILITY

In the decision process the decision maker is concerned with the selection of the best alternative from among those available. The decision maker may be viewed as a single individual or as a group of individuals such as an enterprise. No matter what conditions appertain, or whether the decision maker is an individual or a group, the primary function is to appraise the possible results of each alternative. One means of appraising the outcomes is to attach a value to each one. That one which has the greatest value is then chosen. The value given to the alternative outcomes can be identified as a measure of the utility of that outcome.

The Nature of Utility

The concept of utility is in itself not new; economists have been concerned with utility for many years. Their use of utility has been in relation to the measuring of satisfaction that results from some action taken or from some item that an individual acquires. *Utility*, then, is the measure of the ability of an action or item to satisfy a human need. The concept of utility can be applied to the decision-making process. It can be used to measure the satisfaction which is achieved as a result of the selection from among the alternatives available. The preferred outcome is that one which has the greatest utility. The application of utility and its measurement to the decision-making process is a somewhat "new" utility when compared with the economist's approach.

Individual Aspect of Utility Measurement. Utility is, in the first place, completely an individual or personal thing. So long as the concern is only with the utility that the manager (or decision maker) establishes, relative to the possible states, little problem exists. On the other hand, if comparing the utilities that different individuals possess is involved, utility measurement would be useless. In addition, note that utility is a subjective measurement. Utility is the specific value that any person, group, or organization may set. As such, it is not subject to question, since it reflects only the relative judgment of the satisfaction achieved by the person or persons stating the utility. From this follows the fact that in order to establish a utility measurement for the decision maker, relative to the various alternatives available, it is necessary to have a better understanding of the logic of the decision process.

Ordinal and Cardinal Utility. In relating the utilities of the various alternate choices available, it is necessary to develop some sort of ranking of the items. This ranking can be done in two different ways: ordinal ranking and cardinal ranking.

Ordinal utility is the ranking of the utilities of the alternatives in order of their value, e.g., first, second, third. This ranking does not establish the relative value of the utilities, merely that one is of greater worth than the other.

To establish a relative ranking of the utilities, it is necessary to resort to a cardinal ranking. *Cardinal utility* is the ranking of the worth of the choices on the basis of some specific utility value attached to it. The values attached are measured in the same units; and, thus, the ranking gives the relative relationship of the utilities. For example, if one utility is 5 and another is 10, the second is valued at twice that of the first. The idea of cardinal and ordinal utility will subsequently be examined further.

Utility and Specific Values. It is often assumed that a specific value or measurement such as lowest cost or highest return is coincidental with the utility attached to a specific alternative. This relationship is not always the case. Rather the utility given is frequently not directly related to the specific measurement or value involved. The following is offered as an illustration of this point. Assume you are offered the opportunity to participate in a game and to gamble on this game. The game consists merely of cutting a deck of cards. If the card turned up is red, you will win \$20, but you must pay \$10 if the card is black. Given this possibility, most people would certainly accept the opportunity to participate in such a game. You have an equal opportunity to win on every play of the game, and the payoff is two times the cost of playing. Surely, this is a situation that would tempt even a typical non-gambler. Now, assume that the chance to play this same game is offered to you, but instead the money values involved are \$2,000 for winning, and \$1,000 for losing. The response might be different. Even though the probabilities of winning are not changed and the payoff odds still are two-to-one, many people would not accept the offer. In the first instance, the utility of winning would obviously be greater than the utility of losing. In the second instance, however, because of the larger amounts of money involved, the relative utility of winning could be much reduced as compared to the utility of losing. If you have a relatively small amount of money, the possibility of losing \$1,000 would affect your utility judgment. It can readily be seen that the amount of money to be won or lost in these two instances did not have a one-to-one relationship with our utility valuation. If utility was directly related to the amount of money involved, a person would always put a higher utility on playing the game than not playing it, irrespective of the amount that could be lost, whether it be \$10, \$1,000, or \$1,000,000. It is true that different individuals would have different utility values with respect to these games. Certainly there are some people who would, under any circumstance, play the second game, and still others who would gamble regardless of the amounts of money involved. If a person can afford to lose the amount of money involved, whether it be \$1,000, or \$1,000,000, or any other amount, then he would undoubtedly place a high utility on the playing of the game because the probabilities are so good. This illustrates the point made above that utility is a strictly personal matter and utilities of different individuals are impossible to compare for this reason.

Utility Assumptions[7]

There are certain assumptions that underlie utility. If the decision maker has certain tastes which satisfy the assumptions, it is possible to measure the utility which he attaches to the various possible outcomes. It may be said that there is a utility function, u; and for each outcome, 0, there is a value, $u(0)$, designated as the utility of the outcome, 0, which is the numerical utility for that specific outcome. In any given situation, utility becomes greater when the outcome is considered better.

[7] A complete discussion of utility assumptions may be found in various sources: e.g., Herman Chernoff and Lincoln E. Moses, *Elementary Decision Theory* (New York: John Wiley & Sons, Inc., 1959), pp. 81–86, and R. Duncan Luce and Howard Raiffa, *Games and Decisions* (New York: John Wiley & Sons, Inc., 1958), pp. 23–31.

Therefore:

$$u(0) > u(0')$$

When:

The individual prefers 0 to $0'$

It is also true that the utility of several outcomes can be computed and found to be equal to the expected value or weighted average of the individual utilities. So, in the case of outcome, 0, where the decision maker finds $0'$ with probability p and $0''$ with probability $(1 - p)$ then:[8]

$$u(0) = p[u(0')] + (1 - p)u(0'')$$

The assumptions regarding utility measurement may be stated as follows:

First Assumption. There is a complete ordering of the alternatives available relative to the satisfactions the decision maker derives. That is, when faced with two alternatives, A and B, he will be able to decide which of these alternatives he prefers if he has a preference of one over the other. If he finds A is preferable or equal to B, this can be stated as $A \geq B$ or conversely, if he finds B is preferable or equal to A, as $B \geq A$.

Second Assumption. This complete ordering or transitivity of the alternatives makes it possible to state that if $A \geq B$, and $B \geq C$, then $A \geq C$.

Third Assumption. If the same preferences for the potential outcomes, A, B, and C, as stated in the second assumption still hold, and there is a probability value p attributable to A and a probability $(1 - p)$ attributable to C, it is consistent that $[pA, (1 - p)C] > B$. This would be the case where the probability of A is high (close to 1). If on the other hand, the probability of A is low (close to 0) the preference would be reversed. That is to say, the combination of A and C is now of such low value that B will be preferred to the mixture of A and C.

Fourth Assumption. If outcome A is preferred to B, and C is another outcome, then a mixture of A and C will be preferred to a mixture of B and C if the same probability p applies to both mixtures.

Inconsistencies of Assumptions. Since utility measurement is such an individual matter, these assumptions may not apply universally. There are, in other words, certain inconsistencies that may be applicable to some of the above assumptions. Assume A is two hamburgers, and B is one hamburger, while C is getting ptomaine poisoning, and you had a choice between an uncertain combination of A and C or the certain outcome B. Is there then any probability p, no matter how small or close to zero it might be, which would make you indifferent between the two possible choices? If not, then you are rejecting the third assumption.

---

[8]Herman Chernoff and Lincoln E. Moses, *op. cit.*, p. 81.

Examples of Utility Rankings

Even though this and other inconsistencies may exist relative to the assumptions about utility, such a condition does not negate the existence of utility functions as far as individuals are concerned. While such utilities are difficult to ascertain, empirical evidence points to the existence of utility functions for individuals. Not only is the utility function plausible, but it is possible to establish specific scales of preference for varying outcomes. If A is preferred to B which is preferred to C, then an ordinal ranking can be given to these three possible outcomes. Thus, if these outcomes are ranked 1 for the most preferred, 2 and 3 in that order, it is a preference ranking, but this does not tell how much greater was the preference or the utility of A relative to B, and B relative to C. Emory and Niland[9] show how this difficulty is complicated when the decision maker must rank the preferences of alternatives or outcomes in several different dimensions.

Take as an example a situation where an enterprise is attempting to choose from among four alternative sites for the location of a new facility. Management may use as evaluating factors such characteristics as cost, climate, labor supply, utility services, and community services. The rankings with respect to the four sites may result as follows:

Characteristic	Ranking of Alternative Sites			
	A	B	C	D
Cost	3	1	4	2
Climate	4	1	2	3
Labor Supply	1	4	3	2
Utility Services	4	2	3	1
Community Services	2	3	1	4

This example very explicitly points out the lack of a comparison of the degree of preference which results from an ordinal utility ranking. In order to show relative utility, it is necessary to resort to a cardinal ranking. The utilities assigned are weighted. To compare costs: if site B had twice the utility of site D, three times the utility of site A, and six times the utility of site C, the numbers attached would show this relative weighting. In this situation the utility value of 30 can be assigned to site B, 15 to site D, 10 to site A, and 5 to site C. To do this, however, assumes that the individual is actually aware of and able to attach these relative utility values to the outcomes under consideration. In most cases this would be very difficult, if not impossible, for a decision maker. However, if specific numerical values can be assigned to each of the possible outcomes under consideration, there are at least two ways in which this information might be presented for a specific decision problem.

Payoff Table. The first of these is the payoff table which is essentially the same sort of arrangement presented earlier in illustrating the maximin and

[9]Emory and Niland, *op. cit.*, p. 99.

minimax decision criteria. The payoff table shows for each state of nature and for each act a utility value corresponding to the outcome attributable to each of the states and actions. Table 3-3 shows such a payoff table.

TABLE 3-3

Payoff Table

Actions	S_1	States $S_2 \ldots \ldots \ldots S_n$	
A_1	$u(0_{11})$	$u(0_{12}) \ldots \ldots u(0_{1n})$	
A_2	$u(0_{21})$	$u(0_{22}) \ldots \ldots u(0_{2n})$	
.	.	.	.
.	.	.	.
.	.	.	.
.	.	.	.
.	.	.	.
A_m	$u(0_{m1})$	$u(0_{m2}) \ldots \ldots u(0_{mn})$	

In this table the actions or the alternatives are identified as A_1 through A_m. These actions could be alternative sales promotion programs such as the various percentages of expenditure in the different media. The states, identified as S_1 to S_n, could be the ensuing consumer demand for the firm's products. The resultant utility of the outcomes of the combinations of the actions and the states are represented by the series of utility functions $u(0_{mn})$. Thus, the utility of the combination of Action A_1 and State S_1 would be represented by the value assigned to the Utility Function $u(0_{11})$ located in the first column and the first row. All other utility functions would appear on the table in the appropriate locations.

Decision Trees. A second device for depicting utility functions is the decision tree. The decision tree is a visual representation of the decision problem and its alternative outcomes. It has been found useful for clarifying purposes for decision makers. Assume a situation of three actions and three states along with the corresponding utilities. Figure 3-5 is a decision tree for such a case.

The same notations for the actions, states, and utility functions are used in Figure 3-5 as were set forth above for Table 3-3. The decision point represents the selection from among three alternative capital investments. The selection of each of these alternatives leads to a particular event. Each of these events occurs under three different states, say increased demand, decreased demand, or no change in demand. Therefore, a utility value can be attached to each of the nine outcomes represented by the individual $u(0_{mn})$ notations.

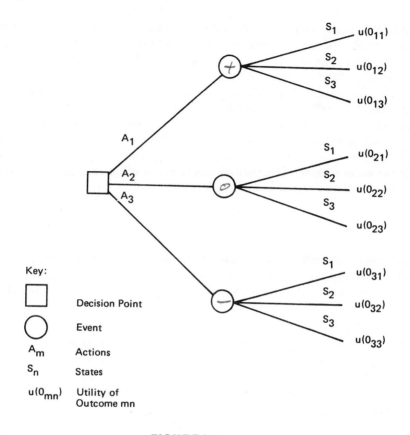

FIGURE 3-5

Decision Tree

Practical Application of Utility

The examples of a payoff table and of a decision tree as representations of a decision problem are obviously oversimplifications of a typical decision facing a manager. The way that the utility values were achieved is not indicated by these two devices. These utility values are essentially nothing more than the decision maker's estimates of outcomes. These estimates are based largely on subjective evaluations. Still, the manager must make a decision despite the fact that an element of uncertainty remains. Even though the utility value is not always related to the money value involved, there are many cases where the manager would make his decision based on these money values. Under these circumstances, utility is assumed to be related to a money value in a linear relationship. Obviously, in this condition, the decision is much easier because the money values supply a scale for the decision. However, there are conditions, as in the illustrations above, where utility and money are not linearly related.

OBTAINING
UTILITY FACTOR

Therefore, it can be concluded that all decisions are made on the basis of the assigned utility value even though this may or may not be the same as the monetary value involved.

Thus, while the decision can be made strictly on the basis of monetary value, there are circumstances that necessitate the establishment of a separate utility value in order to apply modern decision techniques. Typical are those involving very large sums of money or those where non-monetary considerations are the determining factor. The decision maker must then determine for each of the actions the expected utility by summing the utility value of each of the outcomes under the various states. This result is multiplied by the probability attached to each state. This is denoted as follows:

$$E(u_{ij}) = \sum_j \{u_{ij}p(S_j)\}$$

The example applied to the decision tree above can be used to illustrate. In this case, there were three alternative investments under consideration. Assume that the decision maker places a utility value on each of the outcomes as follows:

$$u(O_{11}) = 12 \qquad u(O_{21}) = 30 \qquad u(O_{31}) = 22$$
$$u(O_{12}) = 20 \qquad u(O_{22}) = 5 \qquad u(O_{32}) = 25$$
$$u(O_{13}) = 8 \qquad u(O_{23}) = 15 \qquad u(O_{33}) = 10$$

In addition, the decision maker has assigned the following probabilities to the three possible states which were indicated:

$$S_1 = .5$$
$$S_2 = .2$$
$$S_3 = .3$$

Thus, the expected utility for each of the three alternatives is calculated in the following manner:

Action 1: $12(.5) + 20(.2) + 8(.3) = 12.4$
Action 2: $30(.5) + 5(.2) + 15(.3) = 20.5$
Action 3: $22(.5) + 25(.2) + 10(.3) = 19.0$

The decision maker would consequently select Action 2 because it yields the greatest expected utility.

Clearly, the determination of a utility measure in a real decision situation is not easy. Since the determination of a utility value is such an individual matter, it can be closely related to the whole problem of human behavior. When the process of decision making is considered from the context of the application of utility measures to the potential outcome, a more rational approach to the decision process is achieved. But man is not a rational being at all times. Therefore, the manager, or decision maker, cannot determine a utility measure for a given set of alternatives on a consistent basis, particularly if he is required to do this repetitively. More likely, he can assign some percentage or probability value to his preference statement, and thus indicate that one outcome is preferred to another outcome a certain percentage of the time, that is, with a certain probability.

Therefore, decision theory tools, such as probability and utility measures, and other quantitative tools which will be discussed subsequently, are merely that; they are tools which it is hoped will give a certain level of consistency or rationality to the decisions that are forthcoming. By the use of these tools then, a more logical and "better" decision will be the result. However, there is no guarantee that the resultant decisions are the "best" or, for that matter, that they are even good decisions. The whole idea here is to reach the point where the decision maker uses a logical, analytical method. The decision that he makes appears to him to be a good decision insofar as the information he possesses, and what he believes to be the facts in the problem. The "goodness" of the decision will be determined by the correctness of the information and of the facts which the decision maker applies.

Because of the extreme complexity of most business problems facing the operations manager today, there are many who would doubt the advisability or even, for that matter, the possibility of using the decision techniques under discussion. The contention here is that the use of these techniques will materially assist any manager in making his decision. The very fact that these techniques require a specific and structured approach to the decision problem, in itself, is important. This structured approach requires a decision maker to have a much greater understanding of the problem before he attempts to make a final decision. Because he does this, he brings to bear a much larger amount of information and a much greater understanding of the decision problem than would normally be available under other decision-making approaches. The resultant decisions are more likely to be "better" decisions than any less rigorous or less analytical process would provide.

SUMMARY

The decision-making process is basic to the management of the enterprise system and of the operations subsystem. An examination of the decision process and of the way in which managers make decisions is necessary for an understanding of the way in which efficient functioning of the operations system can be achieved. A fundamental tool in the manager's decision making is the model. A model enables him to evaluate a potential decision economically without disruption of the actual system operation. While there are a variety of types of models, the symbolic model is of greatest significance for managerial decision making.

Decisions can be made under varying conditions. Three conditions typically identified are: certainty, risk, and uncertainty. While conditions of certainty do not appertain to most decisions, it is useful to examine decision making under these conditions. The primary usefulness of such an examination is that by comparison, decision making under other conditions becomes more readily understood. Operations managers are more frequently faced with the more difficult conditions of risk or uncertainty. An examination of the different criteria which may be used for decision making under these two conditions leads to the conclusion that there is no single best criterion.

Such an examination, however, does result in a recognition of the importance of the role of probabilities in the decision-making process. Thus, the basic concepts of probability must be examined, and the difference between objective and subjective probability determined. Also, certain rules bear upon the use of probabilities. The two addition rules deal with mutually exclusive events and not mutually exclusive events, and the two multiplication rules deal with independent and dependent events.

Another approach to the decision-making process, in addition to probability, is utility. Utility must be viewed as a purely personal measure which enables the individual to establish either an ordinal or a cardinal ranking of his preferences. Since the determination of a utility value is an individual matter, it is impossible to compare the utility functions of different individuals. Thus, utility is not necessarily related to any specific value such as money amounts. A number of assumptions underlie the utility concept, and a full comprehension of utility demands a knowledge of these assumptions.

While there are some inconsistencies connected with these assumptions, they are not such that they deny the value of the utility concept. There are a variety of methods available for determining utility rankings. Still, in some instances, the determination of a meaningful ranking is difficult. However, there are some practical applications of utility for decision-making purposes. A combination of the utility concept with probabilities seems to offer the most realistic approach.

The use of decision tools such as those reviewed are useful in establishing an approach to a problem, and are of value in establishing a logical decision-making process. Through their use the decision maker will be able to arrive at better decisions.

QUESTIONS FOR DISCUSSION AND ANALYSIS

1. What are the steps in the decision process?
2. Differentiate between programmed and nonprogrammed decisions. What would be some typical examples of programmed decisions in operations management?
3. What are algorithms? What are heuristics? To what types of decisions does each apply? Give examples of specific problems to which the operations manager might apply these two techniques.
4. What is a model? What is the function of the model in the decision-making process?
5. Identify and describe the four types of models discussed in the chapter.
6. "It is very unusual for the operations manager to find a decision situation which fits into the category of decision making under certainty." If this is true why

is it useful to understand the concept of decision making under conditions of certainty?

7. Illustrate the difference between a decision problem under conditions of uncertainty and one under conditions of risk. Is it possible that a problem which initially was classified as uncertainty could be changed to one of risk? If so, how?

8. Assuming the case of total ignorance, and the conditions which were used on page 41 to illustrate the maximin and the minimax criteria, which of these criteria would you use to make your decision? Why?

9. What is the difference between objective and subjective probabilities? Why is it frequently necessary for the operations manager to use subjective probabilities in making his decisions?

10. Describe the four probability rules given in the chapter and give an illustration of each.

11. What is your understanding of the nature of utility as it applies to the decision-making process of the manager?

12. Explain the difference between ordinal utility and cardinal utility. What is the major drawback of ordinal utility from a decision-making standpoint? Why is the establishment of cardinal utility more difficult to determine?

PROBLEMS

1. If A represents the fact that a retail store sells an item in inventory and B represents the fact that an item may be defective, write each of the following probabilities in symbolic form:

(a) The probability that an item which is sold is defective.
(b) The probability that a defective item is sold.
(c) The probability of an item being sold and defective.
(d) The probability of an item being sold or defective.

2. The Knockdown Demolition Co. has the opportunity to submit a bid on one of two contracts with Megalopolis City. They are restricted by city code from bidding on more than one contract. The company estimates that their chance of getting the central city job if they submit a bid is 25%. For the harbor job their chance is estimated at 75% since it is expected that the number of firms bidding will be fewer. Knockdown believes that the profit from a successful bid would be $200,000 and $56,000 respectively for the two jobs.

(a) What is the expected return on each of the two jobs?
(b) For which contract should they submit a bid?

3. Assume the following payoff table:

	S_1	S_2	S_3
A_1	12	6	24
A_2	8	26	10
A_3	18	8	2

(a) Using the maximin criterion, what would your decision be?

(b) What would your decision be if you resorted to the minimax criterion?

4. Assume that you are the manager of a mine which has experienced an explosion and fire trapping 300 men. Fifty of these men are in a part of the mine which is more readily accessible to rescue efforts. However, if you proceed to rescue these men, you will doom the other 250. You have two alternatives:

(a) Attempt to rescue the 50 men, in the process of which poisonous gas will spread to the other part of the mine assuring the death of 250 men.

(b) Seal off the section of the mine in which the 50 men are trapped. If the seal is effective the 250 men will be rescued, but the 50 will be sacrificed. How-ever, the seal may not be effective, in which case the gases will seep through the location of the 250 men and result in their deaths as well.

Construct a payoff table and make the decision. (This is based on an actual occurrence.)

SELECTED ADDITIONAL READINGS

Bierman, Harold, Jr., Lawrence E. Fouraker, and Robert K. Jaedicke. *Quantitative Analysis for Business Decisions.* Homewood, Illinois: Richard D. Irwin, Inc., 1961: Chapters 1, 2, 3, and 7.

Bross, Irwin D. J. *Design for Decision.* New York: The Macmillan Co., 1953.

Chao, Lincoln L. *Statistics: Methods and Analyses.* New York: McGraw-Hill Book Co., 1969. Chapter 3.

Chernoff, Herman, and Lincoln E. Moses. *Elementary Decision Theory.* New York: John Wiley & Sons, Inc., 1959.

Emory, William, and Powell Niland. *Making Management Decisions.* Boston: Houghton Mifflin, Co., 1968. Chapters 1, 5, 6, and 7.

King, William R. *Probability for Management Decisions.* New York: John Wiley & Sons, Inc., 1968.

Luce, R. Duncan, and Howard Raiffa. *Games and Decisions.* New York: John Wiley & Sons, Inc., 1958. Chapters 2 and 13.

Simon, Herbert A. *The New Science of Management Decision.* New York: Harper & Row, Publishers, Inc., 1960.

SELECTIONS FROM READINGS BOOK

Greenwood, William T. *Decision Theory and Information Systems.* Cincinnati South-Western Publishing Co., 1969.

Wilson and Alexis, "Basic Frameworks for Decisions," p. 63.

Magee, "Decision Trees for Decision Making," p. 83.

Gordon, "Heuristic Problem Solving," p. 154.

| # Computers and Decision Making

The impact of the computer is impossible to ignore today. Tremendous amounts of material have been written regarding present and future wonders of these machines. Numerous miraculous accomplishments have been attributed to these "giant brains," and predictions about computers in management, and, for that matter society as a whole, have occasionally given rise to the feeling that a replacement of the human race by computers is imminent. This statement is not meant to impugn in any way the potential benefits of the computer, for they may well prove to be, as some have suggested, one of the most beneficial developments in the history of mankind. It merely serves to place the computer in its proper perspective. The output of a computer is completely dependent upon the human input which has been developed in the form of a program which considers the limitations of the machine. The output of a computer will only be as good as the accuracy of the input and the correctness of its operation as prescribed by the program.

Since the major concern is with the role of the computer as a decision-making tool, it is appropriate to examine briefly certain details of the computer.

THE NATURE OF COMPUTERS

Essentially the electronic computer is a device which is used for rapidly processing data and information. Any factual matter presented as symbols which can be identified or manipulated in some predetermined fashion is called *data*. *Information*, on the other hand, is derived from data as a result of the analysis or manipulation of the data. As one of the forms of input into the enterprise system, information may be considered as relevant data that is necessary for the proper functioning of that system.

There are many ways in which data processing can be performed. Data can be processed by manual methods. In addition, there are a variety of mechanical devices for processing data. The conventional tabulating equipment using the familiar punched card is one such device. Man and "tab" equipment can also perform certain amounts of information processing. However, the efficiency of these methods is low, and only since the arrival on the scene of the electronic computer has meaningful information processing been feasible. By making information available rapidly and efficiently, the computer has become a useful tool for decision-making purposes in all types of enterprises.

Types of Computers

The primary type of computer used by managers today is a digital computer, although there are some analog computers in use as well. In the previous chapter when the types of models were discussed, analog models were described as representations of one set of properties by another set of properties.

Analog Computers. An analog computer uses physical measurements to represent numerical quantities. The variables to be analyzed are represented by other variables which are parallel or have similar properties. For instance, the flow of fluids or gases can be represented by electrical current or voltages. Mechanical measurements can also be made by means of lengths, angles, or shaft rotations. The simplest example of the analog computer, often cited, is a slide rule. This device provides answers to arithmetic problems by means of physical measurements; i.e., the lengths or distances, which are changed by sliding the rule back and forth to reach a solution. Another familiar analog is the automobile speedometer. The physical rotation of the cable resulting from the movement of the wheels is translated into a numerical representation of the speed of the car. These two examples can be utilized to illustrate another property of the analog computer. The physical variables are usually continuous. This means that the measurements are virtually infinite. For instance, the speed represented on the dial of the speedometer is not either 60 mph or 61 mph. In moving to the next highest speed indicated by the dial markings, the car passes through many intermediate speeds. Theoretically, this continuous data could be represented by having a more discriminating dial with more markings.

Most analog computers are used for engineering or scientific applications rather than for business problems. These types of computers are usually special purpose in that the program is built into the machine. In most cases, these machines are designed for solving a specific problem or a single class of problems. If reprogramming is possible, it requires substantial time and money. Even in the case of the slide rule this is true. For example, slide rules can be used to compute navigational data or for setting speeds and feeds of machine tools. However, converting a standard slide rule to one of these specialized uses would require a complete revision of the scales used.

Digital Computers. *Digital computers*, the type most frequently used, are essentially very rapid counting machines. A digital computer will take information which has been coded, will digest this information, and will remember, without fail, what it has received. It can choose between alternatives, and it can communicate by giving answers or by controlling some activity. Digital computers are more flexible than the analog type, and can be programmed to perform virtually any desired sequence of computation within the range of their capacities. Of course, the programs are not built into the machine, and consequently, it is necessary for the user to develop his own program.

Components of Digital Computers

Inasmuch as the digital computer is of great significance to operations managers, it will be useful to have an understanding of the nature of these machines. A digital computer can be broken down into six major functional components. These components are input devices, the storage or memory unit, the auxiliary memory, the arithmetic unit, the control unit, and output devices.

Input Devices. These are the various mechanisms which are used to feed data into the computer. Among the more commonly used methods for input are punched cards, punched paper tape, magnetic tape, and printed material which is optically or magnetically read.

Storage or Memory Unit. The memory is the component which holds all of the data which is being processed. All data must enter the memory of the computer before it can be manipulated in any way. The memory also contains the instructions which are fed to the computer telling it what operations are to be performed on the data being inserted. These instructions are, of course, the program. Because of its obvious functional importance, the capacity of the memory unit is extremely critical in the performance ability of a given computer.

The size of the digital computer memory capacity can vary greatly from one computer system to another. In most of the present-day computers the basic storage unit is referred to as a byte. A *byte* is made up of a certain number of digits or bits which are used to represent a character such as a number or numbers, a letter, or some special character such as $ or (. The number of digits or bits in a byte will also vary according to the machine. The IBM 370 system uses an eight bit byte, as one example. In some computers, the unit which is *addressable*, that is, which can be called out of storage individually, is called a word. A *computer word* is a grouping of a certain number of bytes. The size of a computer word also differs from computer to computer. A word in the IBM 370 series consists of four bytes or 32 bits. The 370 series has a maximum memory capacity range of from about 64,000 bytes to over 8,000,000 bytes depending on the system model.

Another important characteristic of a digital computer memory is the speed with which the system can retrieve a piece of information. This is known as the *access time*, and on larger and faster computers is measured in nanoseconds (.000000001 seconds). The type of memory device used will largely determine access time since different types of memory devices have different speeds.

Auxiliary Memory. The auxiliary storage of a computer usually has a much smaller total capacity than the main memory. This memory supplements the main memory unit to add to the total storage capacity of the machine. The information stored in this unit is that which is not currently needed. While the auxiliary memory is usually slower with respect to its access time, it can only be reached through the main storage unit and cannot communicate directly with the other components of the computer.

Arithmetic Unit. The arithmetic unit performs the necessary operations to solve the problem presented. It is here that the adding, subtracting, multiplying, and dividing take place. In addition, the arithmetic unit performs a logic function which makes it possible for the computer to make comparisons of alternatives and then make decisions. It is this logic ability of the computer that makes it a valuable decision-making tool.

The speed with which the computer performs its calculations is also important. For the faster computers, operations such as addition are also measured in nanoseconds. Again, systems differ, and as newer developments are brought forth, operating times will speed up.

Control Unit. The control section of the computer is not readily identifiable to an observer. The reason is that the control is mostly automatic. There is a physical portion of the system concerned with a limited amount of control. This is the console. The console is, however, essentially a means of communication between the operator and the computer. The internal control mechanism of the computer coordinates the activities of all other components of the system. This unit monitors the feeding of the data in and out of the system. When data is moved to, or extracted from, the storage unit, the message is checked. If, for example, the decimal digit is required to be expressed as an even number of bits, this fact will be checked by the internal automatic control. If the number of bits is odd instead, the machine will stop, and a signal will appear on the console. The performance of the necessary operation by the arithmetic unit is initiated by the internal control. The general function of the control segment of the computer is to oversee and to synchronize the operation of the entire system. This element of the system can be likened to the homeostatic controls found in the human body.

Output Devices. The output unit has the function of presenting the information from the computer. The forms that the output takes are similar to the input as listed above: punched cards, punched paper tape, magnetic tape, or printed material. Other output forms are also available, but the specific output form is usually determined by the desired function of the computer system. Figure 4-1 is a schematic diagram of a digital computer which shows the relationship of the major components.

Input-Outout Forms

In discussing the input and the output of computers, reference was made to the fact that they often appear in the same forms. Two of the forms specifically mentioned deserve closer attention because they are so widely used. The first of these is the punched card, and the second is magnetic tape.

Punched Cards. The punched card is familiar because it is used in so many ways. It is seen in the form of a bill, a check, and other information-bearing documents. The punched card uses codes to convey information to processing equipment. These codes appear in the form of punched holes in the card.

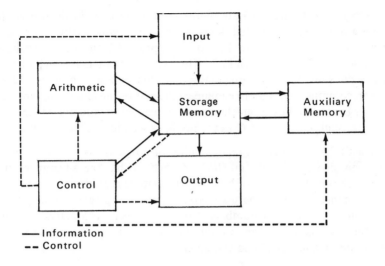

FIGURE 4-1

Schematic Diagram of a Digital Computer

The IBM 80-column card has, as its name indicates, 80 columns across its face. In addition, it has ten printed digits (0-9) in each of these columns. In the space above the printed portion, there is space for two more horizontal rows, thus, allowing for 12 possible punched rows for each column.

The way in which letters and numbers are represented on the punched card is illustrated in Figure 4-2. By reference to columns 42 to 51, note that the decimal digits are represented simply by punches in the corresponding printed

Reproduced by permission of IBM.

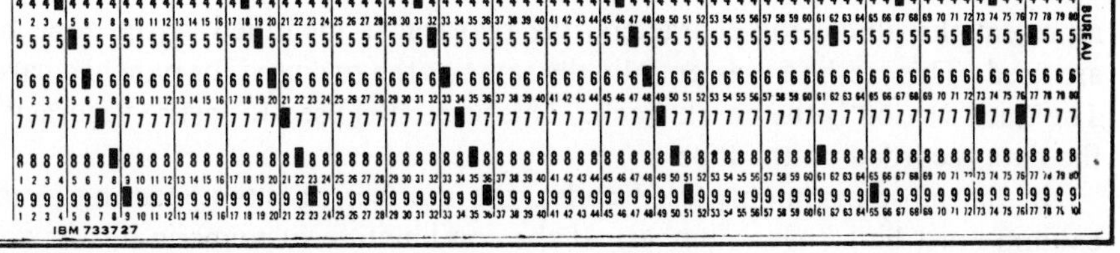

FIGURE 4-2

IBM 80-Column Punched Card, Punched for Letters and Numbers

digit. The letters A through I are represented by a punch in the top or twelfth row and a punch in the printed digits 1 through 9 sequentially. For example, the letter A has a punch in row 12 and in the printed 1, the letter B is shown by a punch in row 12 and a punch in 2. The remaining letters through I are represented in the same fashion sequentially preceded by a punch in row 12 as can be seen in columns 1–9. In a like manner, the rest of the letters are represented; J through R preceded by a punch in row 11, as seen in columns 15–23, and the letters S through Z using row O as the prefix as seen in columns 29–36.

Magnetic Tape. Magnetic tape, in addition to its use as a form of input and output, can also be used for auxiliary storage. It has the advantage, in comparison with punched cards, of high speed. Data is recorded on the tape in the form of magnetic spots. The magnetized spots in a single column across the tape are used to represent numbers, letters, or special characters. Figure 4-3 shows the way a magnetic tape would appear if the magnetic spots were visible for the numeric and alphabetic characters.

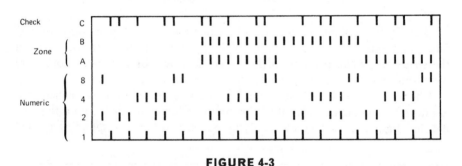

FIGURE 4-3

Section of Magnetic Tape

The tape has seven horizontal tracks, as can be seen in Figure 4-3. Each magnetized spot is equivalent to a bit as described earlier. Numbers are formed by various combinations of bits recorded in the numeric section. In order to represent the alphabetic characters, the two tracks identified as the zone bits are used. This method is essentially the same as the one used for punched cards. The third section is the check track. This section is used to insure accuracy of the data recorded on the tape.

In the most commonly used codes, the number of bits appearing in any column must be an even number. If the combination of numeric bits or zone and numeric bits is an odd number, a check bit is automatically added. For example, in the case of the digit 1, the number of bits is one. Therefore, a check bit is added to make the total number of bits in the column even. The same situation can be seen for other numbers. For the alphabetic characters, the letters A, L, and Z, as examples, have a check bit added to bring the total number of bits to an even number. Thus, an automatic check is provided, whereby the machine can signal an error whenever a column has an odd number of bits because a numeric or zone bit is dropped or not recorded.

COMPUTER PROGRAMMING

Programming consists of presenting the necessary instructions and data so that the computer may respond by carrying out the required operations as prescribed. Programming, then, is the way in which the user "speaks" to the computer. A digital computer speaks only one language, and that language, machine language, is comprised wholly of numerical symbols. In this way the machine can accept the data presented in machine language without translation. The process of learning to speak machine language is a long and difficult one, and the writing of a program in machine language is very time-consuming and very costly.

While some may feel that learning machine language programming is useful for a full understanding of the operation of the computer, it is not absolutely necessary for an operations manager to learn machine language to be able to program a computer.

Problem-Oriented Languages

Fortunately, a number of other languages have been developed which are much less complex and much less tedious to use. These other more simplified languages, however, must be translated by the computer into machine language. These other languages, referred to as problem-oriented languages, are translated from their original form into machine language by means of an intermediate program called a *compiler*. Languages that make use of compilers typically require more computer time than do programs written in machine language. This is more than offset, however, by the saving in time which is effected through the use of these other languages when compared with the time required to write a program in pure machine language.

FORTRAN, derived from FORmula TRANslation; ALGOL, from ALGOrithmic Language; and COBOL, which is an abbreviation of Common Business Oriented Language, are examples of languages for which compilers have been written in order to translate them into machine language. Each of these program languages is designed to handle different types of problems. FORTRAN is basically arithmetic in nature and is used primarily for mathematical, engineering, and scientific problems. ALGOL is designed for problems of a logic nature and has been limited primarily to scientific research applications. COBOL is, as its name suggests, concerned mostly with processing business data.

FORTRAN is probably the most widely used of these languages. This is true, even though there are a number of versions of FORTRAN, because FORTRAN is more generally useful. The other languages, in other words, are more usable for specialized problems. The most recent of the FORTRAN systems is FORTRAN IV.

Example of FORTRAN IV Program

To illustrate problem-oriented programs, a very simple and routine problem encountered regularly by all enterprises will be written in FORTRAN IV. It is a problem of calculating the weekly pay of an employee. Figure 4-4 is the program for this problem.

```
C    SAMPLE PAY PROGRAM
C    INPUT CARD INFORMATION : EMPNO, HOURS, RATE
     READ (1,10) EMPNO, HOURS, RATE
  10 FORMAT (I5, F6.2, F5.2)
C    COMPUTE WEEKLY PAY
     PAY = RATE*HOURS
     WRITE (3,20) EMPNO, PAY
  20 FORMAT (//, I5, F9.2)
     STOP
     END
```

FIGURE 4-4

Sample Fortran IV Program

The problem illustrated by this program is simply to calculate an employee's weekly pay from his hours worked and his hourly rate. By reference to the sample program the individual statements in the program will be explained.

The input data is derived from punched cards. This is indicated in the input statement. The input card contains the employee number, EMPNO, the hours worked, and his hourly rate. It will be noted that this statement, along with others, is preceded by a C to the left. This C indicates that this is a comment card. The computer does not utilize the data on these cards in its computations. These cards are only included to show the logic of the program, and are not executed.

The third statement is READ (1, 10) EMPNO, HOURS, RATE. This is an instruction to read the data on the input card. The number 1 in the brackets is the data set reference number assigned to the input device used. In this case, it would be a card reader. The 10 is the identification of the applicable FORMAT statement. The items following the parentheses are called the list which enumerates the variables to be given a specific value.

The FORMAT statement specifies the specific form which the data will read into the computer. The I5 indicates an integer value for which 5 columns are available on the data card. This value is the employee number. It is not necessary to use all of the available columns. Many programmers indicate more columns than are necessary to have spacing between the different variables when they are written. The F6.2 indicates that the number of hours will have 6 columns available, with a decimal point which will have two decimal places to the right of the decimal point. The F5.2 can be interpreted in the same fashion for the hourly rate.

The arithmetic statement PAY = RATE∗HOURS calls for the multiplication operation of the rate of pay times the hours worked to determine the weekly pay. The multiplication operation is indicated by the ∗ symbol.

The WRITE statement is similar to the READ statement. In this case, the 3 would indicate a printer. The FORMAT statement calls for two blank spaces by means of the two / marks. The remainder of the statement is the same form as explained for the 10 FORMAT statement above.

The STOP means to stop computation and the END signifies the finish of the program. It is possible to have more than one STOP in a program, but only one END can be used.

THE ROLE OF THE COMPUTER IN DECISION MAKING

The primary area in which the computer can play a role in the management decision-making process is as a part of the integrated information system of the organization. Computer oriented information systems are designed to provide managers with information useful for making a variety of decisions. For example, information can be provided for use in decisions concerning market analysis, material and inventory problems, output control, capital equipment purchases, manpower requirements, plant location, and facilities. In addition, computers have potential for use in policy formulation and in various aspects of planning, but have not yet been utilized to their full potential in these areas. The use of the computer in conjunction with a variety of quantitative models has provided a means of significantly increasing the information available to the manager for decisions. The operations manager who can evaluate the importance of information, who understands the potential of the computer in decision making, and who uses the computer to acquire the desired information, will be in a position to reduce the uncertainty inherent in any decision he faces. A computerized information system for management only supplies the desired information. It is the manager who still must make the decision.

An examination of management's information needs and the means of generating the information can best be accomplished in the context of the management information system. Out of this examination will come a foundation for the evaluation of the computer's role in this type of system.

Management Information Systems

Many people view an organization as being made up of a group of information subsystems. The total of these connected information subsystems results in one complex information system, which is the total enterprise. In this way then, each of the separate functional areas can be viewed as an information network. To view the organization as an information system is not entirely new. However, it is possible to take this view seriously today because of recent developments in high-speed data processing equipment. A *management information system* (MIS) is concerned with the receiving and perception of the information transmitted, the translation of the information into the language in which the system operates, the discrimination of the information so that it can then be processed and analyzed on the basis of information already contained within the system, the making of a decision, and the eliciting of a response that results in the system output.

Types of Management Information Systems

There are two useful forms of models for classifying management information systems. The first of these models is called the traditional information system, and the other model is the on-line type of information system.

Traditional Management Information System. The *traditional management information system* is the type that has been most usually found and still is to some extent. This type of information system is highly defined and fixed with respect to the flow of information and the responsibilities attached to the system. It is formalized to an extent that it is closely related to the organization structure of the enterprise. This type of system depends almost entirely on fixed, scheduled reports, supplemented in part by word-of-mouth communication. Intended as one of the principal control mechanisms for management, the very nature of such a system makes it sluggish and behind time relative to the need for the information supplied. In most cases, the information is received by those responsible for action too late for them to make many of the necessary decisions.

Because the traditional information system is, to a great extent, ineffective, or at least limited, in its ability to react quickly, an informal information system usually exists virtually parallel to the official information system. This informal system develops simply because it is necessary to have an information system that is more sensitive to the functioning of the total system itself. In this informal system, communication and information take place quite regularly outside of the formal channels of authority-responsibility relationships as officially established. The informal system may be found to operate almost daily when the formal lines of the organization are crossed in order to get around the slow-moving formal system. This informal action is undertaken to achieve results that will be more in line with the objectives of the system. If the informal system did not exist, without doubt the typical formal information system could not satisfy the information needs of the enterprise.

On-Line Management Information System. The *on-line management information system* is designed to furnish information as soon as it is generated. It thus reacts to the information immediately. In this way the current status of the system is available whenever it is needed.

The instrument that makes the on-line information system possible is the electronic computer. The computer is able to assimilate information as soon as it is received, to remember it, and to make comparisons with previously received information. The computer is also able to produce information at command or automatically when the information received indicates any deviation from a previously determined condition.

A brief example may serve to make the operation of such an information system clearer. Many manufacturing firms have developed systems to keep track of the current status of production orders. Remote input devices connected directly to the central computer are placed in the production area. When a worker starts on an order he is able to communicate this information to the computer through this input device. In the same fashion, he also "notifies" the computer when he completes the order. Management is able to call for information regarding any order when it wishes. The actual status can be compared with the schedule, and necessary corrective action instituted immediately if the order is behind schedule. There is no need to wait until the daily or weekly reports arrive, or until the scheduled completion date, to learn that the order will be delivered late.

In this type of information system, it is irrelevant whether the information received is the result of a planned or unplanned happening. Such an information system does not eliminate the need for various types of reports, including the periodic report, but only serves to make these reports more meaningful to managers. Information systems of this type have also been referred to as transaction-oriented information systems.[1]

COMPUTER APPLICATIONS

Most initial applications have tended to use the computer almost entirely as a very rapid calculating machine. These installations have often resulted in a situation of very expensive equipment simply replacing either human operators or much less complex machinery such as tabulating equipment. Perhaps the classic example of this would be the use of the computer by an insurance company to perform the clerical activities connected with the billing of policy premiums. The machine will regularly examine all policies; determine the amount of the premium; ascertain whether the premium is paid monthly, semi-annually, annually, or however; and, when the due date arrives (with appropriate lead time), will reproduce a premium notice to be mailed to the policy holder. When the premium payment is received, this information will be recorded in the machine. This, of course, is just an electro-mechanical method of performing a purely clerical operation originally done by a human being. This does not imply that such applications of computers are not desirable. On the contrary,

---

[1]D. B. Thompson, "Transaction-Oriented Information-Handling Systems," I, *Control Engineering*, Vol. XI, No. 1 (January, 1964), pp. 87–94.

many such applications have resulted in very large savings and have justified the computer installation. It can be pointed out, however, that the computer has a potential in the decision-making process which has not been realized in a large number of instances.

Developments in Computer Technology

Before examining specific examples of applications of computers to decision making in operations management, it will be useful to look at some developments in computer technology which have a bearing on computer utilization in this area. Since most practical applications make use of one or more of these developments, an understanding of them will facilitate the comprehension and appreciation of the specific examples. Among the developments which are of interest from the standpoint cf operations management are real-time systems, time-sharing, data communications, and computer graphics.

Real-Time Systems.   The first of these developments in computer technology is the creation of what are known as real-time systems. A *real-time system* is one in which the centralized processor is capable of digesting input data immediately and returning output so that the information may be used for decision-making purposes as soon as a problem arises. This type of system is opposed to batch processing. In the latter instance, a group of similar transactions are gathered together before processing. In batch processing, the manager has to make a decision based on historical data or after the fact, not in "real-time." An inventory control system which is constantly updated with information regarding receipts and withdrawals, and which can immediately supply information regarding the current status of any item in that inventory is an example of a real-time system.

Real-time systems are often referred to as being *on-line.* On-line means that the peripheral equipment, usually in the form of distant input-output terminals, is connected directly to the central computer. In this way information can be fed into the computer either automatically or at the discretion of an individual manager as soon as the relevant data are generated. The real-time nature of the system will make it possible for the manager to make the necessary decision to control the problem virtually as the problem develops. Of course, with numerous terminals continuously feeding data into the central computer, the computer cannot process all of this information as it is received. Consequently, a queue or waiting line will form, and some sort of priority system for handling the information input must be programmed. Initially this was usually a first-come, first-served priority rule. More recent developments in the form of time-sharing have changed this processing sequence of programs.

Time-Sharing.   *Time-sharing* is a development which enables a large number of users at remote locations with input-output terminals to use the services of a single computer with results which would be essentially the same as if each user had his own individual computer. As greater use of computers occurred, the total time required to get a program through the computer system increased considerably. The reason for this was not in the computing time itself, because this time was small even in early computers, and became shorter as new generations of computers came into use. The major delay was in the waiting time involved in getting the program to the computer.

The development of a time-sharing system eliminated these long waiting periods, and enabled a computer to operate as if it were working on a number of programs at the same time. Each program is allocated a certain period of time which might vary for each user from a few seconds to less than a second for some. The program or problem is processed in sequence for the allotted unit of time. The computer then proceeds to the next program for its allotted time, and ultimately returns to the first program for another period of processing. This cycle continues for as long as necessary. The high speed of the processing unit gives the effect of the computer dealing instantaneously with each user at the same time. The advantage of time-sharing is that, for all practical purposes, each user appears to have immediate access to his own computer with no perceptible delay in the processing of his program. In addition, there is an economy to the firm since it is only necessary to have a single processing unit of its own. For companies with limited requirements, time-sharing allows them to buy time on a computer only to the extent of their needs.[2] Such a circumstance means that the organization does not incur the investment in equipment or related facilities.

Data Communication. Another rapidly growing and important technology is data communication or data transmission. *Data communication* is the transmission of data or information, usually in some coded form, by means of an electronic communication system. A variety of general examples of presently used applications can be given. Among these are:

1. Governmental agencies maintain data banks of information relating to their function which can be transmitted to the point of need. Examples of this are the weather information prepared by the National Weather Service, and the data files maintained by the Federal Aviation Agency and the Social Security Administration among others.
2. Doctors or hospitals transmit patient data to distant points for diagnostic purposes.
3. Law enforcement agencies transmit data regarding suspects.
4. Production shop control systems designed to handle such elements as order and stock control, scheduling, status reports, planning data, and procedures for developing required corrective actions.
5. Design changes accomplished by the transmission of the revised drawing of the part to a graphic display receiving terminal.
6. Information retrieval systems in which a variety of different classes of information can be called from central storage when needed.
7. Financial transactions of which banking transactions, credit card account processing, and stock transactions are typical examples.

[2]R. M. Fano and F. J. Corbató, "Time-Sharing on Computers," *Scientific American*, Vol. CCXV, No. 3 (September, 1966), pp. 129–140.

Most of these examples are real-time systems, and they use time-sharing. Naturally, it is possible to have data communication that is not on-line, such as batch processing, and that does not operate on a time-sharing basis. Any

Reproduced by permission of The American Telephone and Telegraph Company.

Teller in bank uses Touch-Tone^R telephone to check an account balance. She also can "input" debit holds or retrieve other information necessary for her position. This is being used in certain banks throughout U.S. This is a Savings Bank, thus you can't mention *checks*. But you can of course for Commercial Banks. Incidentally, his pass-book in this picture may in the future be eliminated when we reach a "Passbook-Less" or "checkless" society. Not here yet, but certainly a future possibility.

FIGURE 4-5

Touch-Tone^R Telephone Used in Data Communications

real-time system and any case of time-sharing can, of course, be classified as data communication.

Types of Terminals. Because of the real-time and on-line nature of so many systems, there have developed a variety of devices by which the operator "talks" to the machine, and by which the computer can "talk" back. The very rapid nature of the communication in such systems is very much akin to a conversation between man and machine.

KEYBOARD TERMINALS. Probably the most common type of device in use for "talking" with the computer is the keyboard type of terminal. In many of these systems, the operator sends his message by using a keyboard similar to a typewriter. His message is visible to him, and the response of the computer is printed out for him as well. There are a variety of keyboard configurations which are specialized for the input required. An example of this might be found in banking uses where the teller has a keyboard terminal which is used to insert the account number, the type of transaction (withdrawal or addition), the amount involved, and other such information. A typewriter keyboard would not be required here.

TELEPHONE TERMINALS. Another form of terminal that is finding considerable application is the telephone. Special data-set telephones are used to transmit data from computers over distances. This is done by converting the

Reproduced by permission of The American Telephone and Telegraph Company.

FIGURE 4-6

Data Set Used with Touch-Tone^R Telephone
for Transmission over Communication Lines

signals from the machines into tones for transmission over communication lines.[3] Telephones may be used with a variety of transmission instruments which input the data by means of such devices as punched tape or punched cards. They may also be used with keyboard terminals such as described above. In addition, the Touch-Tone dialing keyboard can be used as an input mechanism. The Touch-Tone keyboard uses pushbuttons instead of the usual rotary dial on the telephone. After the call to the computer has been completed, data can be transmitted by means of the pushbuttons. Many systems using the telephone as an input device are designed to give a voice answer. For example, if someone wishes to check on the location of a quantity of stock of some item in a number of possible locations, the request for the information may be made as input to the computer through the Touch-Tone telephone. The request may be for the location of 3,200 units of part number 75638. This can be fed to the computer from the telephone instrument by some code. The data will be transmitted over the communication lines, and the tones converted into signals at the receiving end for processing by the computer. The response will be transmitted back to the sending telephone set verbally. The response may be, "5,000 units of part number 75638 are in stock at the Kansas City warehouse." In some systems the computer may even end its message with "Thank you."

COMPUTER GRAPHICS.   One of the most interesting developments in computer technology is the use of terminals which display pictures. Basically, computer graphics refers to the use of a cathode ray tube (C.R.T.), similar to a television picture tube, on which can be displayed a variety of input and output material. Some of these terminals can display only alphanumeric input and output on the tube. Typical of this are the various units used for displaying the latest information regarding the various stocks listed on the New York Stock Exchange. Using a keyboard, a broker or a customer can input the exchange code for the company and request various information such as the latest bid and ask prices, high and lows for the day, and number of shares traded.

In addition to the alphanumeric terminals, there are those which display diagrams or pictures. Such things as engineering drawings or graphs can be exhibited on these terminals. Still other terminals, which go a step beyond the type just described, are those which have the ability to permit an interaction between the computer and the operator. One of the most widely used interactive devices is the light pen. The light pen is a tool which enables the operator to mark positions on the screen to indicate interest in a display item to the computer, or it can be used to draw on the screen. This is only one of a variety of interactive devices available. Graphic displays and interactive devices can also be used for the design of parts or products, as part of management information systems, and in process planning and control.

Companies such as General Motors and Lockheed have been using computer assisted design systems for a number of years. General Motors has utilized its DAC system (Design Augmented by Computers) since 1962.

---

[3]Edgar C. Gentle, Jr., (ed.), *Data Communications in Business* (New York: American Telephone and Telegraph Co., 1965), pp. 118–132.

Applications of computer graphics in the area of management information systems are numerous. Companies such as Westinghouse and Boeing, among others, use such systems. In these systems, the desired information is displayed to the manager on the C.R.T. By means of an interactive device, the manager can highlight certain information and ask "what if" questions. The manager can ask the computer to determine the effect of the changes which would occur as a result of the "what if" inquiry. It is possible for the manager to ask as many of these types of questions as he wishes before making a decision.

With this brief survey of some of the recent developments in computer technology, we should have some appreciation of the potential of the electronic computer in assisting the manager in his decision-making process.

Reproduced by permission of General Motors Corporation.

FIGURE 4-7

Operator Using Light Pen with
DAC (Design Augmented by Computers) Console

Examples of Computer Applications

Virtually all large enterprises have devised ways in which the computer can be used to assist managers. It would be impossible to cite examples of all of the innumerable types of applications which might be found. A representative number of different types will be discussed briefly as typical of certain categories of managerial use.

SAGE System. One of the first large-scale applications of computers to decision making is SAGE (Semi-Automatic Ground Environment) developed for the Air Defense Command of the Air Force to monitor the air space surrounding the United States. Plans have been made to phase out SAGE, but at present the details of the new system for protection against surprise air attack have not been declassified. Despite its ultimate replacement, SAGE is still an excellent example of a computerized decision-making system. The system constantly watches for any object entering this air space, tracks it, and analyzes the situation based on the information which it contains. The human operator can also question the computer about any object on the display by the use of an interactive device. The system memory contains information in the form of airline schedules and flight plans to account for the entrance of an object into this air space. It is the human monitor who checks out any unscheduled entrances with the proper authorities, and, if necessary, notifies a designated individual. This individual then decides what action, if any, is to be taken, such as authorizing interceptors or missiles to be launched. While it is possible to program the system to make this decision, it is a human who actually makes the final decision after seeking alternatives from the machine. The SAGE system also guides the interceptor airplane or missile to its target. In the case of a manned airplane, however, the pilot can override the system control.[4]

Holidex System. One of the largest computer systems of its type is the Holidex computerized reservation system used by Holiday Inns, Inc., of Memphis, Tennessee. This system handles an average of more than 100,000 messages a day. All of the reservation offices of the company and of over 1,200 Inns in the United States and Canada, as well as some of the locations outside these two countries, are connected with the company's computer center in Memphis. The system consists of cathode ray display terminals and typewriter-like keyboards at each of the reservation centers. The reservation clerk can obtain information about any Inn in a particular section of a city, or a specified area of the country by pressing the code-letter buttons for the area. A printed confirmation in the form of a ready-to-mail post card can be obtained from the terminal if one is desired.

This part of the system is in addition to the terminals located at the individual Holiday Inns. Reservations can also be made through the central computer from these locations as well. The information is fed into a terminal, and

---

[4]Gilbert Burck and the Editors of FORTUNE, " 'On Line' in 'Real Time,' " *The Computer Age and Its Potential for Management* (New York: Harper & Row, Publishers, Inc., 1965), pp. 29–30.

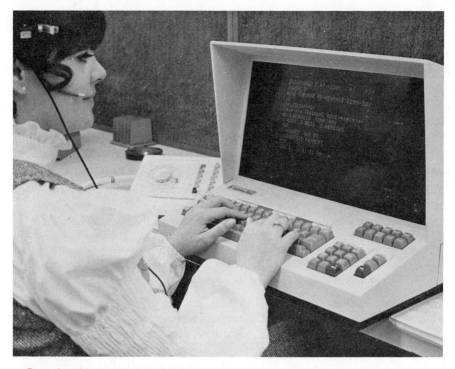

Reproduced by permission of Holiday Inns, Inc.

The Holidex Reservation System is the first of its type in the hotel industry and is the world's largest commercial computerized communications system.

FIGURE 4-8

Holiday Inns, Inc. Reservation Terminal

the reservation is automatically made if the desired accommodations are available. A printed confirmation is prepared for the guests; the Inn at which the reservation was made is simultaneously notified by a computer written notice.

If the requested accommodations are not available, the computer indicates the types of accommodations available at three alternate Holiday Inns in the vicinity. Each location must keep the computer notified of its current room status so that the system can keep an up-to-date record.

The terminals at the individual Inns are also used for the simultaneous transmission of messages from the parent company to all locations in the system. Holiday Inns, Inc., also uses the computer for administrative communications and total data processing and management information services.

Most of the major airlines have similar systems for handling reservations. The first of these large-scale airline reservation systems was SABRE which was developed for American Airlines by IBM.[5]

---

[5]*Ibid.*, pp. 31–34.

Hospital Applications.   Recently attempts have been made to apply computers to decision-making activities in previously ignored areas.   One such area has been in the management of hospitals.   In addition to the obvious applications dealing with business office activities, record keeping, and admission procedures, computers have been found to be useful in certain nonclerical areas.   Among these areas of application is a patient's medication program including ordering, scheduling, and discontinuing specified medications.   Also the same sort of procedure can be applied to the laboratory in much the same fashion as with medications.   Further projected uses will permit the hospital to have complete information regarding each patient.   For example, these uses have been projected to the point where,

> Each doctor on the staff will have a terminal in his office, tied into the hospital computer and set to receive all information about his hospital patients.   He could know from moment to moment exactly what was happening with his patients.   He could even change orders or add orders, to be printed out at the nurses' station in the ward, *and without the need to make an interrupting telephone call to a very busy nurse.*[6]

Educational Institution Uses.   Another area of recent application of the computer is in the management of educational institutions.   A very large number of universities, colleges, and school districts have been using computers for some time for the normal data processing activities such as payroll.   Also, there have been a large number of instances where the registration procedure at universities has been computerized.   It is in the area of long-range planning, policy determination, and resource utilization, however, where recent applications have begun.   Sisson tells of such a system developed for the Philadelphia, Pennsylvania, school district which was designed for use by top administrative levels in evaluating policies, planning, and resource allocations.[7]

Computerization of decision-making activities in institutions such as hospitals and schools is relatively new.   It will undoubtedly expand as more experience is gained and more is realized about the potential in these areas. Because they are so recent, such applications are difficult to evaluate fully.

COMPUTERS AND THOUGHT[8]

Can computers think?   Many questions have been raised regarding the abilities of computers to display intelligence in the same fashion as humans, but they still have not been answered completely.   The idea of a computer being called "intelligent" seems to fit into the fiction of "Buck Rogers and the 25th Century."   There are those who hold that the computer is simply a machine

---

[6]Blaine M. Lair, "Computerizing Total Hospital Activities — A Pioneer Effort," *Computers and Automation*, Vol. XI, No. 7 (July, 1969), p. 30.

[7]Roger L. Sisson, "Computer Simulation of a School System," *Computers and Automation*, Vol. XI, No. 3 (March, 1969), pp. 20–23.

[8]For a full exploration of this topic, the reader is referred to an anthology of papers on this theme in: Edward A. Feigenbaum and Julian Feldman (eds.), *Computers and Thought* (New York: McGraw-Hill Book Co., 1963).

that is only capable of serving as a tool to man. On the other hand, there are those who contend that the computer is capable of performing the process of the human brain. To this point, research has not provided a conclusive answer to this disagreement. However, the answer appears to lie somewhere between the two extremes.

The development of computers that are capable of displaying artificial intelligence seems to be only a matter of time (and money). These machines will not be capable of duplicating the human brain. They will be able to simulate some functions of the brain, and, thus, behave in an "intelligent" manner in the performance of specific tasks. The need is to develop programs for computers that can achieve solutions to difficult problems by means of apparent "intelligence." To achieve this requires a program that permits the machine to write new program instructions. These new elements of the program will result from a continuous analysis by the computer of its own performance. In effect, the computer will "learn" from its experience. There are some interesting results in the area of artificial intelligence that seem to have potential implications for operations management.

Reference was made in Chapter 3 to heuristic problem solving. Heuristic problem solving techniques were likened to the process by which the human brain solves a problem or arrives at a decision. There have been some heuristic programs developed for computer use. Perhaps the best known such program is the General Problem Solving program (GPS) which attempts to use the computer for solving problems by the same method as that used by the human brain.[9] The GPS is designed to achieve a goal by means of establishing a number of subgoals whose achievement will satisfy the primary goal.

Some specific examples of intelligent behavior can be found in programs that have been written for computers to play games such as checkers and chess. These programs are written to provide for a selective evaluation of the alternatives (possible moves). A set of rules are included in the programs to ascertain when it is fruitful to continue the search and when to stop assessment of the alternatives. While such programs do not produce champions, these game-playing computers can perform at an above average level.

Computers are being tested as a means of medical diagnosis. These programs are in their infancy. Limited medical diagnosis programs have been developed using pattern recognition.[10] Essentially, this approach utilizes discriminating factors identified with a disease to make diagnosis. Other approaches utilize a search of categories of information organized on a hierarchal basis.[11]

There are numerous researchers working on "intelligent robots." These projects are in an early stage of experimentation. Attempts are being undertaken to have these robots perform such tasks as material handling; advanced

---

[9]Allen Newell and Herbert A. Simon, "GPS, A Program That Simulates Human Thought," *Ibid.*, pp. 279–293.

[10]D. James Croft, "Is Computerized Diagnosis Possible?" *Computers and Biomedical Research*, Vol. V, No. 1 (August, 1972), pp. 351–367.

[11]Paul M. Wortman, "Medical Diagnosis: An Information-Processing Approach," *Computers and Biomedical Research*, Vol. V, No. 1 (August, 1972), pp. 315–328.

automation, including the manufacture of a part or product directly from reading the engineering drawing; broken object repair; and quality inspection.

There is, by no means, complete agreement as to the potential of the computer in the area of problem solving using the same approaches as the human mind. There have been a number of attempts at writing programs to accomplish this, but generally speaking such programs are for rather specific problems. Even the GPS, despite its name which implies general application, is limited to rather specific types of problems. The problems facing the operations manager are very complex, as previously indicated, and the ultimate usefulness of the computer in solving management problems is still undetermined.

LIMITATIONS OF COMPUTERS

Much has been written and said about the power and potential of computers in our society. When electronic computers first came into use, a great deal was said about their capabilities, and the application of terms such as "giant brain" to computers led many to expect the computer to virtually eliminate the necessity for human effort in almost any type of activity. The very wide introduction of computers into the business firms of this country, and throughout the world for that matter, eventually led to speculations as to the role of the computer in management. There were those who predicted that the time was not far distant when the general manager of a business firm would be a computer. The enthusiasm of computer manufacturers, computer experts, and others was so great that it was not surprising that this enthusiasm was transferred to the managements of many enterprises. They saw the computer as the panacea for all management problems of the past.

Of course the computer was not without detractors. There were those who saw it exclusively as a threat to themselves or to their areas of interest. Many feared its effects on the employment picture of the future. Some saw it as a potential for invasions of personal privacy and still others cited the dehumanizing effect of computers. Examples of problems which individuals have encountered in their dealings with business firms through the computer are familiar to anyone who reads the newspaper. Situations like the following are not unusual:

COMPUTER CONFUSION[12]

The following notice was sent by the publisher of a group of magazines to the subscribers:

> Last December, in an effort to improve service to our subscribers, we installed a computer. Unfortunately (but, we are told, not unprecedentedly), this technological wonder has since repeatedly broken down or malfunctioned. As a result, issues have been mailed late, payments have not been processed promptly, and complaints have not always been acknowledged.

---

[12]"Computer Confusion," *Michigan Business Review*, Vol. XXI, No. 5 (November, 1969), p. 31. © 1969 by The University of Michigan. Reproduced by permission.

The benighted instrument is now showing signs of life and we devoutly hope that by the end of June we will have caught up on the work that has been accumulating.

Meanwhile, we can only beg your continued indulgence and we apologize for the inconvenience you have been caused.

Faithfully yours,
THE PUBLISHER

There is little doubt that the computer has not always lived up to the expectations of its ardent supporters. In many cases, this has been the result of exaggerated claims for the equipment, the improper designing of the system itself, the overselling of equipment for the particular task at hand, or simply improper application and operation on the part of the users. Consequently, many reports are now forthcoming which indicate disenchantment with and disappointment in the computer on the part of management of user firms. Most users report that they are not achieving what they had originally expected when the system was introduced. The principal area of disappointment seems to be in the lack of application to the more complex areas of potential utilization such as decision making. What is now being realized in the words of a title of a *Fortune* article is, "Computers Can't Solve Everything."[13]

There is no doubting the tremendous impact that the computer has had upon management. There is no reason to doubt that it will have still more impact in the future as additional technological developments come about. There is, however, little evidence to lead to the conclusion that the computer will displace management completely (although there are those who would hold to this viewpoint). At this point in time, it is clear that the computer is strictly a tool, although a valuable tool, of management. Most present applications find the computer playing a very small role in the decision-making process of the firm. It will undoubtedly play an increasing role in this area in the future, but the full extent of computer decision making is unclear. Present evidence would probably lead to the conclusion that it will be limited in its application to certain types of problems only, and will never supplant management; but it would be foolish to say that anything is impossible.

SUMMARY

Computers are viewed primarily as tools in the management decision-making process. The two broad categories of computers are the analog and the digital computer. The digital computer is the most significant for managers.

The digital computer consists of six basic functional components. These components are input devices, the storage or memory unit, the auxiliary memory, the arithmetic unit, the control unit, and output devices.

To communicate with the computer, it is necessary to feed instructions and data to the computer in a fashion understandable to the machine. The process by which this is done is referred to as programming. While the digital computer

---

[13]Tom Alexander, "Computers Can't Solve Everything," *Fortune*, Vol. LXXX, No. 5 (October, 1969), pp. 126ff.

speaks only machine language, it is not necessary for the operations manager to learn machine language to program a computer.

There are a number of problem-oriented programming languages available. Through their use, the programming process is much easier than if one had to resort exclusively to machine language. These languages use an intermediate program known as a compiler which converts the problem-oriented language into machine language for internal use. Among the best-known languages for which compilers have been written are FORTRAN, ALGOL, and COBOL. FORTRAN is the most widely used of these languages, largely because it is applicable to a greater variety of problems.

The primary role of the computer is as a part of the integrated management information system. An organization can be viewed as an information system. In turn, each of the parts of the organization can be considered information networks connected to form the larger information network of the total enterprise. Management information systems are considered of two types: the traditional management information system and the on-line management information system. The former type is highly formalized and conforms closely to the structure of the organization. However, the traditional system is inflexible and ineffective in providing for management's information needs.

The on-line management information system is designed to furnish the needed information on a current basis. The computer makes this type of information system possible, and, thus, management is able to achieve a better level of control and better system performance.

Most of the original applications of computers were made as substitutes for routine clerical operations, but the computer is finding an expanding role in the decision-making process. More recent applications have been made in providing managers with needed information for a wide variety of problems. Specific applications such as the SAGE and Holidex systems, as well as applications to hospitals and educational institutions, are typical examples.

Recent technological developments have made possible the expansion of the potential contributions of the computer for management use. Among some of the most important developments are real-time systems, time-sharing, data communication systems, and special types of input-output terminals such as telephone terminals and computer graphics.

Many unanswered questions exist regarding the potential of the computer as a substitute for man's thought processes. The computer has great potential for benefiting mankind, although there are limitations to its use. However, the full capability of the computer has not as yet been realized, particularly in the area of management decision making.

QUESTIONS FOR DISCUSSION AND ANALYSIS

1. How would you differentiate between data and information?
2. Compare analog and digital computers. Why do you think that the digital computer is most frequently used for management purposes?

3. List and describe briefly the functional components of the digital computer.

4. What is a problem-oriented programming language? What is the purpose of a compiler in such a language?

5. Discuss the importance of management information systems.

6. Describe the two types of management information systems discussed in the chapter. What is the role of the computer in MIS?

7. What is meant by a real-time system? Is a real-time system possible if the computer operates on a first-come, first-serve basis?

8. Describe your understanding of time-sharing. What is the advantage of such a system?

9. Describe in detail a data communications system with which you have had some experience.

10. Discuss some of the recent technological developments in the computer field as they apply to management decision making.

11. What is your opinion of the potential of the computer in substituting for human thought?

12. What are the possible impacts of the computer for operations management? What are some of its limitations?

SELECTED ADDITIONAL READINGS

Alexander, Tom. "Computers Can't Solve Everything." *Fortune*, Vol. LXXX, No. 5 (October, 1969), pp. 126ff.

Brightman, Richard W., Bernard J. Luskin, and Theodore Tilton. *Data Processing For Decision-Making.* New York: The Macmillan Co., 1968.

Burck, Gilbert and the Editors of FORTUNE. *The Computer Age and Its Potential for Management.* New York: Harper & Row, Publishers, Inc., 1965.

Feigenbaum, Edward A., and Julian Feldman (eds.). *Computers and Thought.* New York: McGraw-Hill Book Co., 1963.

Gentle, Edgar C., Jr. (ed.). *Data Communications in Business.* New York: American Telephone and Telegraph Co., 1965.

Lair, Blaine M. "Computerizing Total Hospital Activities — A Pioneer Effort." *Computers and Automation*, Vol. XI, No. 7 (July, 1969), pp. 30–32.

Laurie, Edward J. *Modern Computer Concepts.* Cincinnati: South-Western Publishing Co., 1970.

Martin, James. *Telecommunications and the Computer.* Englewood Cliffs: Prentice-Hall, Inc., 1969.

Parslow, R. D., R. W. Prowse, and R. Elliot Green (eds.). *Computer Graphics.* London: Plenum Press, 1969.

Popell, Steven D. *Computer Time-Sharing.* Englewood Cliffs: Prentice-Hall, Inc., 1966.

Sanders, Donald H. (ed.). *Computers and Management.* New York: McGraw-Hill Co., 1970.

Sisson, Roger L. "Computer Simulation of a School System." *Computers and Automation*, Vol. XI, No. 3 (March, 1969), pp. 20–23.

PART **2**

Models
for Operations
Management
Decisions

Analytical methods applicable to a wide variety of operations management decisions are summarized in this section. The first group of models are essentially non-quantitative. Many of these models have been used in management for a long time. The second group has found more recent application to operations management problems. These models are quantitative. The models discussed have been found to be useful in a wide variety of problem areas. Linear programming models are valuable in determining the best allocation of resources. Simulation models provide a manager with a means of evaluating the effects of decisions before they are made. A wide variety of problems possess characteristics which make solution by waiting-line models feasible.

| # Conventional Decision Models

The operations manager has available to him a substantial number of models to assist him in making and improving the quality of his decisions. Decision models are arbitrarily classified into two broad categories in this book: conventional decision models and quantitative models. In this chapter the first category will be discussed, and in Chapters 6 and 7 some of the newer quantitative models will be examined. Attaching the adjective conventional to some of these models is not intended to give them any special significance. This distinction is made to indicate that most of these models have been widely used by operations managers both in the past and at present.

The conventional models, while perhaps less sophisticated and less powerful than the quantitative models, still can have broad application for decision-making purposes by the operations manager. In many cases these conventional models can serve the manager's purpose better than the quantitative techniques now available. In fact, many believe that it is to the manager's advantage to use these less complex models whenever a decision can be reached through their utilization.

The models examined in this chapter are not intended to be an all inclusive list of those available. Only a sampling has been selected for presentation here, largely on the basis of the extent of their common utilization. Among the decision models included here are "general" decision techniques such as logical decision methods, "open" decision models, and non-quantitative simulation. Other categories of decision-making models to be considered are accounting models, certain types of economic analysis models, and schematic models for decision making. Most of these models will be given only a limited examination. For one reason, it would be impossible to look at each of them in complete detail, since many of them could conceivably consume an entire book themselves. For another, many of the models introduced here will be found to have specific application to the various problem areas of operations management and can better be examined in the context of the specific problems to which they are applied.

"GENERAL" DECISION MODELS

Many decision models classified as "general" do not require detailed exposition because they are quite simple and virtually self-explanatory. For example, a verbal model can be used to describe and evaluate a problem for the purpose of making a decision. Reports made under a variety of situations are primarily a verbal description of a problem, a verbal analysis of the alternatives involved in the problem, and a suggested solution, again, strictly in verbal terms.

Rule-of-Thumb Models

One of the most generalized decision-making tools is a rule of thumb. The rule-of-thumb approach is based largely on a subjective evaluation by the individual. However, many rules of thumb have been found to be quite valuable and very accurate as a result of the large backlog of experience which underlies the rule. In the early days of aviation when flight instruments were nonexistent, pilots often "flew by the seat of their pants." This was essentially rule-of-thumb decision making based on the experience and judgment of these early-day pilots. Of course, pilots of large jet aircraft do not fly their planes this way. However, in an emergency, a modern airline pilot might resort to rule-of-thumb decision making based on his backlog of experience and judgment. The same can be said of the complex industrial organization of today. In certain areas of operations management, managers do use rule-of-thumb techniques. For example, in the areas of procurement and inventory control it is common to find rules of thumb which state, "Order every thirty days," or, "Hold thirty-days' supply of this item," being utilized.

The use of rules of thumb in decision making can also play an important role in more complex decision models. For example, it may be recalled, when referring to heuristic problem solving techniques, it was pointed out that this method may resort to the use of such devices as rules of thumb in attempting to arrive at a decision. Heuristic models may involve very complex processes in decision making. They are perhaps best understood by means of examples. Consequently, we will defer detailed discussion of these types of models to Chapter 17 where specific applications will be viewed.

Logical Models

Logic in decision making is essentially the process of reasoning to draw conclusions which serve as a basis for a decision. The two primary forms of logical reasoning or inference are induction and deduction. *Induction* is the process of drawing generalizations from specifics, while *deduction* is the process of proceeding from the general to the specific. These two forms of reasoning are not mutually exclusive, but may be used jointly. The process of deduction may begin with a generalization which has been established previously by the process of induction. Conversely, it is possible that the inductive process may start with a specific which was arrived at by means of deductive reasoning. Morell differentiates the deductive reasoning approach from inductive reasoning as follows:

> In deduction, unlike induction, "validating forms and rules" have been developed to assist the decision-maker in drawing a valid decision from logically related premises. The validating forms and rules governing

deduction are those of the syllogism, the syllogism being the typical form of deductive reasoning.[1]

A *syllogism* is the process of reaching a conclusion or a decision which necessarily results from two premises, the major and minor premises. An example of a simple syllogism might be as follows:

Major premise: Increased productivity lowers operating costs.
Minor premise: Improved methods increase productivity.
Conclusion: Improved methods result in lower costs.

The validity of the conclusion reached by means of a syllogism is dependent upon the truth of the premises which is not generally determined by the deductive process. However, the premises are assumed to be valid and to have been arrived at through proper induction methods. One specialized form of logic — symbolic logic — has found some limited application in the solution of operations problems. Symbolic logic states the premises in symbolic form and uses the techniques of Boolean algebra to manipulate the symbols. The explanation of symbolic logic is beyond the scope of this book, but reference will be made to its potential use in particular problem areas.

"Open" Decision Models

It has been suggested that greater emphasis on *"open" decision models* is needed in preference to the "closed" models so widely utilized.[2] These open models permit the inclusion of environmental factors in the decision model and take into account the influence of human behavior on the particular decision being considered.

"Closed" models, such as quantitative models, do not include many of the aspects of the environment in which the decision is to be made. As pointed out in discussing utility theory, and in discussing logical decision models, the decision maker is presumed to be rational in his decision-making techniques. Human behavior makes this assumption suspect if not false. Therefore, any model which does not take into account the human behavioral aspect of the decision-making process would be of limited value.

Non-Quantitative Simulation Models

In Chapter 7, the use of simulation models for decision-making purposes will be discussed. These simulation techniques are based on quantitative methods. However, simulation as a decision-making tool, in the strictest sense of the term, is not new in business decision making. In its broadest interpretation,

---

[1]Robert W. Morell, *Managerial Decision-Making* (Milwaukee: The Bruce Publishing Co., 1960), p. 58.

[2]A discussion of the "open" decision model is found in: Charles Z. Wilson and Marcus Alexis, "Basic Frameworks for Decisions," *Journal of the Academy of Management*, Vol. V, No. 2 (August, 1962), pp. 151–164.

simulation means representing reality by some abstraction appearing to be the same as the original. Verbal models and logical models are non-quantitative simulation models. Essentially, all schematic models are a representation of a particular situation or problem in schematic or graphical form. Most of the schematic models discussed below are also non-quantitative simulation models.

Frequently, before many of the newer quantitative decision-making models can be used, it may be necessary to resort to one of the non-quantitative simulation techniques; for example, before resorting to digital simulation, it may be desirable to schematically represent the system under study. Then the actual quantitative aspects of the simulation can begin. This schematic representation of the system is, of course, a non-quantitative simulation model.

ACCOUNTING MODELS

The accounting system of an organization is a model of the total organization, designed to assist management in the proper operation of that organization. The traditional purpose of the accounting system has been to serve as a historical record of the operations of the organization. However, the role of the accounting system in decision making has been greatly expanded through the approach of managerial accounting techniques. Managerial accounting techniques are primarily aimed at supplying the necessary information to managers at all levels on a timely basis according to the individual manager's needs.

Balance Sheet and Income Statement

The basic form of the accounting model of the firm is the accounting equation which states: assets = liabilities + net worth or assets = equities. This equation states the financial position of the organization at any given time. Individual terms in the equation are subdivided and broken down into many different categories or accounts. The number of accounts in a large organization may be quite numerous. The balance sheet of a firm is a representation of this accounting equation. Figure 5-1 is an example of a typical balance sheet.

THE CAREFREE MANUFACTURING CO., INC.
and Subsidiaries

Consolidated Balance Sheet
December 31, 19—

Assets

Current Assets:		
Cash and short-term investments		$ 52,650,000
Notes and accounts receivable	$278,572,000	
Less: Allowance for doubtful accounts		
and notes	2,879,000	
		275,693,000

Inventories:		
Finished goods	$189,916,000	
Work in process	122,793,000	
Raw materials	107,746,000	420,455,000
Prepaid expenses and other current assets		14,844,000
Total current assets		$ 763,642,000

Property — at cost:		
Land	$ 49,578,000	
Buildings	214,680,000	
Machinery and equipment	569,927,000	
Total	$834,185,000	
Less: Accumulated depreciation and amortization	357,977,000	
Net property		476,208,000

Other Assets		87,417,000
Total Assets		$1,327,267,000

Equities

Current Liabilities:		
Notes payable	$137,810,000	
Accounts payable	168,583,000	
Estimated income taxes payable	57,321,000	
Dividends payable	2,807,000	
Total current liabilities		$ 366,521,000

Long-term Debt		204,420,000

Other Liabilities:		
Deferred revenues	$ 10,921,000	
Minority interests	22,415,000	
Total other liabilities		33,336,000

Shareowners' Equity:		
Capital stock, $1 par value	$ 32,856,000	
Additional capital	178,849,000	
Retained earnings	511,285,000	
Total shareowners' equity		$ 722,990,000
Total Equities		$1,327,267,000

FIGURE 5-1

Illustration of a Balance Sheet

In addition to the balance sheet, an important accounting report is the income or profit and loss statement. To many managers, this is the most important accounting document because it gives them information about the operations of the firm over the period of time represented by the statement. Figure 5-2 is an example of a typical profit and loss statement.

THE CAREFREE MANUFACTURING CO., INC.
and Subsidiaries
Consolidated Income Statement
Year Ended December 31, 19—

Sales and Other Income:		
Sales	$2,346,728,000	
Other income	17,169,000	
Total		$2,363,897,000
Cost of Sales		1,285,570,000
Gross profit		$1,078,327,000
Operating Expenses:		
Selling expenses	$ 471,376,000	
General and administrative expenses	385,671,000	
Total operating expenses		857,047,000
Net Operating Income		$ 221,280,000
Other Expenses:		
Interest expense	$ 32,316,000	
Miscellaneous other expenses	2,528,000	
Total other expenses		34,844,000
Net Income Before Taxes		$ 186,436,000
Taxes on Income		108,200,000
Net Income		$ 78,236,000

FIGURE 5-2

Illustration of an Income Statement

These two statements, the balance sheet and the profit and loss statement, represent better than any other models yet devised the past operation of the firm and the current financial status of the firm.

Other Accounting Reports

In addition to the two basic accounting reports discussed above, there are other accounting reports which can be considered as sub-models of the main accounting model. Reports that show the flow into and out of certain types of accounts are used. Such reports can explain the increases or decreases that take place in any account category. The basic flow reports, beside the income statement, are the source and application of funds statement and the cash flow statement. These statements measure the flows of net working capital and of cash. All changes in these two categories are included, whether the changes result from operations or from some other activities of the firm.

In a manufacturing firm, the statement of manufactured costs of goods sold would be of particular interest. Revenue and expense forecasts are often used to project anticipated operating results. These forecasts can be prepared for individual products or services, projects, and individual departments. At the end of operating periods, expense summaries of products, projects, or departments may also be prepared and used to compare the actual results with the anticipated results as set forth in the revenue and expense forecast. Analysis of these actual data will often result in identification of problem areas and assist in effectuating corrective action to improve the operation of inefficient segments of the organization. Such analysis will also reveal the strengths within the organization.

Accounting Ratios

The operations manager will find the analysis and interpretation of certain accounting ratios useful. These ratios, derived from the accounting model, are essentially rules of thumb or standards of measurement which have been established by management for comparison purposes. The analysis of any particular accounting ratio gives the operations manager some indication of how well any specific segment is performing as compared with the objectives or standards previously established. The number of accounting ratios available is legion. Some which may serve to be valuable in particular situations to the operations manager are: cost per unit of output, direct labor costs vs. indirect labor costs, direct labor costs vs. direct material costs, productivity per unit of output.

Value of the Accounting Model

The accounting model has been criticized as not being a dynamic model, and, therefore, of limited value to the manager for decision-making purposes. It is true that the accountant has been primarily interested in recording past transactions. Managers, however, need information that is more detailed and up-to-date. The development of managerial accounting techniques has tended to focus the use of accounting data toward the needs of managers. With the use of the computer and its application to the information systems of the firm, the accounting model has taken on greater significance. It is now possible for the accounting model to contain a much larger amount of information which is useful in the manager's decision-making process. The speed of the computer and the on-line characteristics of modern management information systems have made it possible for managers to receive up-to-date information from the accounting model. Thus, the accounting model has become more dynamic. Even in its older format, the accounting model was unique because there was no other model which demonstrated better the financial position of the firm. With modern techniques and modifications now taking place, the accounting model will continue to be of great importance to the manager in his decision-making role.

ECONOMIC ANALYSIS MODELS

Closely akin to the accounting model are certain types of models identified as economic analysis models. Much of the data used in these economic analysis models are derived from the accounting model. However, an analysis of costs and of the cost-revenue relationship, separately, can be a valuable adjunct to accounting reports.

Costs

It is possible to classify costs into a number of categories. Among the cost classifications which may be useful to the operations manager are: long-run as compared with short-run costs, avoidable vs. unavoidable costs, traceable vs. non-traceable costs, and current vs. historical costs. Certain other classifications of costs are not as readily identifiable, but they can be more significant to the operations manager; consequently they require some elaboration.

Opportunity Costs. *Opportunity costs* are actually alternative profits or earnings which can be achieved from some alternative use of the organization's funds. A comparison of the returns anticipated from the alternative utilizations is made. If it is found that an investment could be yielding a higher return than the current use, the difference is considered as a cost. This cost, or lost return, is an opportunity cost.

Fixed and Variable Costs. Another important and widely used differentiation of costs is variable costs vs. fixed costs. This differentiation is generally well understood, primarily because it is so widely used. These two cost categories have unique relationships to output. *Variable costs* are those costs which will change as the level of output or operation changes. These costs may change or vary from perfectly variable costs, where there is a one-to-one relationship between cost and operation level changes, to semi-variable costs, where the relationship between cost changes and operation changes are other than on a one-to-one relationship. In the latter case, costs may vary only by a very small percentage with a large percentage change in the operational level, or conversely, a very large change in costs may result from a small change in the level of operations. Typical of variable costs would be direct labor and direct material costs. *Fixed costs* are those costs which do not change, irrespective of any change in the level of operation. Examples of these costs might be investment in certain types of equipment or insurance on fixed investment.

Incremental Costs. Perhaps the most important and useful cost concept for the operations manager in his decision making is that of incremental or marginal costs. *Incremental costs* may be defined as the added costs which would be incurred as the result of a decision. Any decision where the added out-of-pocket (incremental) costs are below the additional revenues gained by the decision is advantageous. Thus, if we are faced with a simple decision to manufacture one more item of a product, incremental analysis would show us what additional costs would be incurred by manufacturing this item as well as what additional returns we could expect from selling this item. If the return exceeded the cost, the decision would be to manufacture the item. Almost any decision which involves additional outlay can be subjected to incremental cost analysis. Every new program, every new product or service, every additional employee, and so forth, will result in changing the cost structure of the firm. Such a change must then be subjected to an analysis which will reveal the comparisons between the additional costs and additional revenues which can be expected. Incremental analysis can be used in a very large number of decision situations. It can be used in making a decision regarding a marketing program which would involve wider distribution of a product or service. It can be used to evaluate the effects of a sales promotion program wherein the costs can be weighed against the anticipated increased sales. It can be used by an airline to evaluate the advisability of adding a flight to its existing schedule. In the consideration of adding an employee to some phase of the company's operation, incremental analysis will provide a comparison of the additional cost of this employee with his anticipated worth or contribution to the organization.

Incremental analysis offers a means of answering the question: What will be the effect upon profits of an anticipated decision? It is opposed to the often misleading concept of average costs which have been so widely depended on by many managers. Incremental cost analysis takes into account the many parameters of a decision.

Thus, incremental cost analysis has very broad potential in the decision-making process. Wherever data are available regarding incremental cost and incremental revenue, it may be advantageous to use incremental analysis as a basis for many operations management decisions. The concept of incremental analysis will be emphasized in many places throughout this book. There will be a number of decisions where the basis for the selection of alternatives will be incremental cost. It is important that the reader of this book have a basic understanding of incremental cost analysis before proceeding into the specific problem area.

Break-Even Analysis

Break-even analysis is a relatively simple and very widely used method for determining the relationship between total costs and total revenues at various potential levels of operation. The relationship expressed by the break-even analysis is a static one existing at a particular point in time. This means that both the cost and revenue functions are fixed as of the time in which the analysis is being made. The typical presentation of the break-even analysis is by means of a break-even chart. A break-even chart may be considered as a still photograph of the cost-revenue-output relationship, and thus is fixed as of that particular time. Figure 5-3 illustrates a typical break-even chart as related to a decision regarding adding a new product to an existing line. The point at which the total cost line and the total revenue line intersect is identified as the break-even point. As can be seen, output (or sales) beyond or to the right of the break-even point represents a profit, and any level below this point represents a loss. Note that break-even analysis makes use of the already described concepts of fixed costs and variable costs. If these two classifications of costs are known,

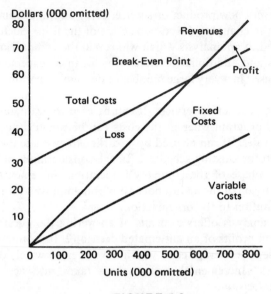

FIGURE 5-3

Break-Even Chart

and the volume of sales is known, it is a relatively simple matter to draw a break-even chart.

Break-Even Formula. It is also possible to find the break-even point by a mathematical formula. One formula is:

$$X = \frac{FC}{SP/U - VC/U} \text{ or } \frac{FC}{SP/U} - VC/U$$

Where:

$$SP/U = \text{selling price per unit}$$
$$VC/U = \text{variable cost per unit}$$
$$FC = \text{fixed cost}$$
$$X = \text{break-even point}$$

Thus, assume the same data used to draw the chart in Figure 5-3: a selling price of 10¢ per unit, a variable cost of 5¢ per unit, and a fixed cost of $30,000. By substituting into the formula:

$$X = \frac{\$30,000}{.10 - .05}$$

$$= \frac{\$30,000}{.05}$$

$$= 600,000 \text{ units}$$

Under the conditions assumed, and for the period of time in which these cost and revenue figures are applicable, a sales volume of 600,000 units would be required for the company to break even. Anything above that would be a profit and anything below would result in a loss. Thus, if the sales forecast for this new product was above this point, a decision to add it to the line would be favored. A negative decision would likely result if the forecast was less than 600,000 units.

Limitations of Break-Even Analysis. Although break-even analysis appears to be simple, it does have drawbacks. In the first place, the data used for both the cost function and the revenue function are based upon estimates; thus, it follows that break-even analysis will only be as valid as the accuracy of the estimates of costs and revenues.

In the second place, break-even analysis is a static situation, and assumes there will be no changes in other variables. The dynamic nature of the business enterprise makes for a weakness in this assumption.

Perhaps the most critical point about break-even analysis has to do with the determination of the organization's total cost curve. Reference to Figure 5-3 indicates that break-even analysis assumes a straight line total cost curve. There is no particular logic to this assumption, and it is very possible that the cost curve of the organization under consideration will take some other form, i.e., curvilinear or some more complex form.

Usefulness of Break-Even Analysis. Discussion of the limitations of break-even analysis is not meant to indicate that the usefulness of this form of analysis is lacking. In actual practice, the use of break-even charts has been found to be very valuable. In addition to the situation illustrated above, the adding of a new product, break-even analysis can be applicable to a number of fairly common operations problems. It can be used for making a decision about the dropping of an existing product from the line as well. Break-even analysis is also useful in plant capacity decisions, in equipment replacement problems, and in decisions regarding making a part as opposed to buying it.

The manager who uses this form of analysis for decision-making purposes must understand its limitations. The linear cost functions used in break-even analysis are usually sufficiently close to the true cost function in the typical range of activity to give reasonably good results. One final comment with respect to break-even analysis seems appropriate at this point: because of the degree of uncertainty resulting from the estimates used, the operations manager should be aware that the break-even point is not to be taken as an absolute. Surrounding this point is a range of reliability. If the projected level of operations falls within this range, the break-even point would probably be considered as questionable. Above the upper limits of this range the achievement of profit would be highly likely. Below the lower limits, a loss would probably be experienced. If the level of operations is within this range of reliability, the operations manager would be well advised to resort to some form of further analysis before making a decision.

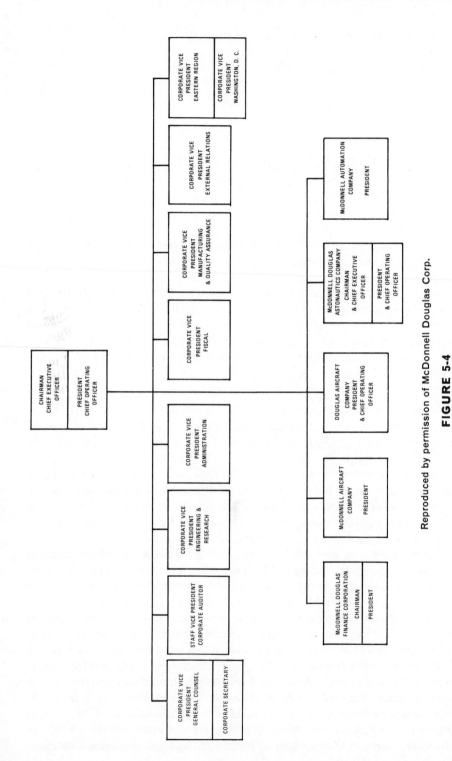

Reproduced by permission of McDonnell Douglas Corp.

FIGURE 5-4

Representative Organization Chart

SCHEMATIC MODELS

There are innumerable ways in which various segments of the problems of the enterprise can be represented. These have been designated as *schematic models*. Included in this designation are all those techniques available for analyzing various problems facing management which can be represented by some graphical or diagrammatic means. Perhaps the best known schematic model so widely utilized in manufacturing is the blueprint. All schematic models are essentially abstract representations of the system or problem under consideration, developed by a drawing instrument such as a pen or pencil.

Organization Charts

One of the types of schematic models widely used in almost any type of organization is the organization chart. The organization chart is an attempt to depict the relationships between various departments, functions, or individuals. Certainly any organization needs to have such a schematic representation. It is undoubtedly the easiest way of showing the existing relationships. As with many of the conventional models already discussed, the organization chart is static since it is representative of a particular point in time. Also, it does not show the many informal relationships that always exist, and it must be revised periodically to keep pace with the dynamics of the typical organization. As with any schematic model it must, of necessity, leave out some aspects of the "real" thing. Figure 5-4 shows a typical organization chart.

Flow Charts and Diagrams

Flow charts are designed to represent symbolically the sequence required to complete a wide variety of activities. For example, they are used to represent the operations required to complete a specific product. Figure 5-5 is an example of such a flow chart.

There are a number of specialized forms of the flow chart and the flow diagram. In the area of design of jobs and work methods, specific applications are found. Among these are flow process charts, activity charts, and operation charts. These applications will be discussed in detail in Chapter 12.

The flow diagram shows the same information as found on flow charts, but with a spatial relationship. This schematic model has application in several problem areas of operations management. It is used in conjunction with the flow process chart in work design, and in the area of process planning; specifically, in connection with relative location of facilities. This latter application will be discussed in greater detail in Chapter 10. Figure 5-6 illustrates a form of a flow diagram which relates to the flow chart shown in Figure 5-5.

Another specialized example of the flow chart is the illustration of a computer program. A flow chart is useful to the programmer in assisting him to grasp the logic of the total program. In a computer program, proper sequencing of the

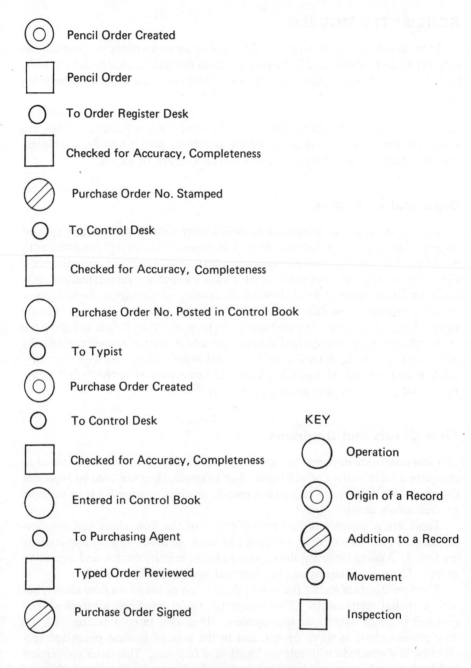

Pencil Order Created

Pencil Order

To Order Register Desk

Checked for Accuracy, Completeness

Purchase Order No. Stamped

To Control Desk

Checked for Accuracy, Completeness

Purchase Order No. Posted in Control Book

To Typist

Purchase Order Created

To Control Desk

Checked for Accuracy, Completeness

Entered in Control Book

To Purchasing Agent

Typed Order Reviewed

Purchase Order Signed

KEY

Operation

Origin of a Record

Addition to a Record

Movement

Inspection

Source: Clarence B. Randall and Sally Weimer Burgly, *Systems & Procedures for Business Data Processing* (2d ed.; Cincinnati: South-Western Publishing Co., 1968), p. 175.

FIGURE 5-5

Flow Chart for Purchase Order Preparation

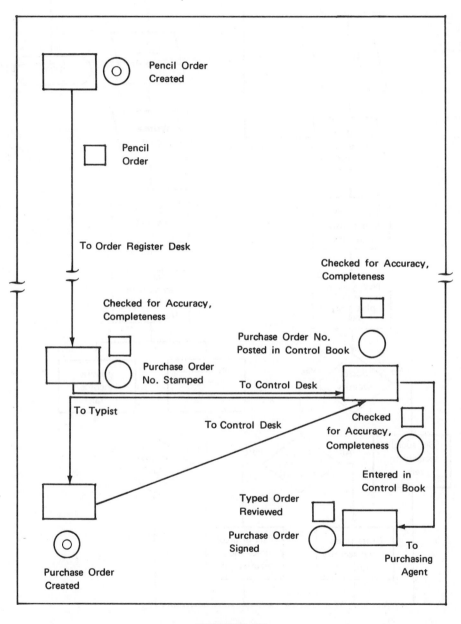

FIGURE 5-6

Flow Diagram for Purchase Order Preparation

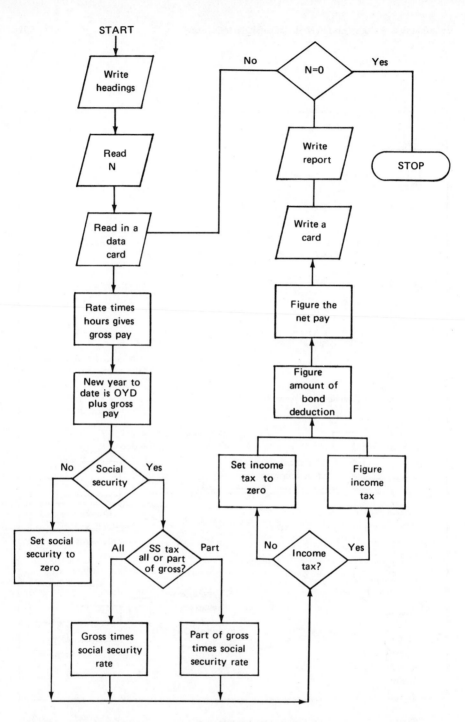

Source: Edward J. Laurie, *Modern Computer Concepts* (Cincinnati: South-Western Publishing Co., 1970), p. 526.

FIGURE 5-7

Computer Program Flow Chart of Payroll Procedure

various steps is essential. The use of the flow chart in this case can result in the avoidance of errors in the program. An example of a flow chart for a computer program is found in Figure 5-7.

Information Distribution Charts

These schematic models are variously called routine sequence diagrams, information flow charts, and forms distribution charts. They are used to illustrate how various types of information flow through pertinent segments of the organization. These charts also show the action taken by those receiving the information. Such devices have found wide use in analyzing paper work procedures. An example of an information distribution chart is found in Figure 5-8. This chart is for a simple paper work flow procedure used in processing a purchase order and the receiving documents. The departments or groups involved in this procedure are listed across the top of the chart. The distribution of information and the actions taken are shown in the columns under these headings. Often in a complex system where more details are needed, a separate list is made to show the actions taken. This may be particularly true when the organization develops a detailed procedures manual.

Assembly Diagrams

An *assembly diagram* is a graphic representation of the sequence followed in the assembly of a part or product. Figure 5-9 is an assembly chart for a ball-point pen. The pen consists of a barrel, a top cap subassembly, a spring, and a ball-point unit. A sketch of the main subassemblies with the component parts of each identified is shown in the figure. The chart is for a production lot of 5,000 units.

As can be seen in Figure 5-9, a time scale is shown horizontally, and the component parts are shown by means of a vertical list on the left side or by labels on the lines that represent the time required to make the individual parts. The length of each of these lines indicates all of the time needed to complete the part, including setup time, move time, expected delay time, as well as the standard processing time. These charts are useful in estimating completion times, and for overall scheduling. Examination of assembly diagrams will often reveal ways in which the total time can be compressed, thus resulting in an earlier completion date.

Block Diagrams

The designation of block diagrams as a separate form of schematic models is subject to question since some of the models already discussed are often categorized as special forms of block diagrams. For example, the organization chart as illustrated in Figure 5-4 can be considered as a form of block diagram. In addition, flow charts for computer programs have sometimes been designated

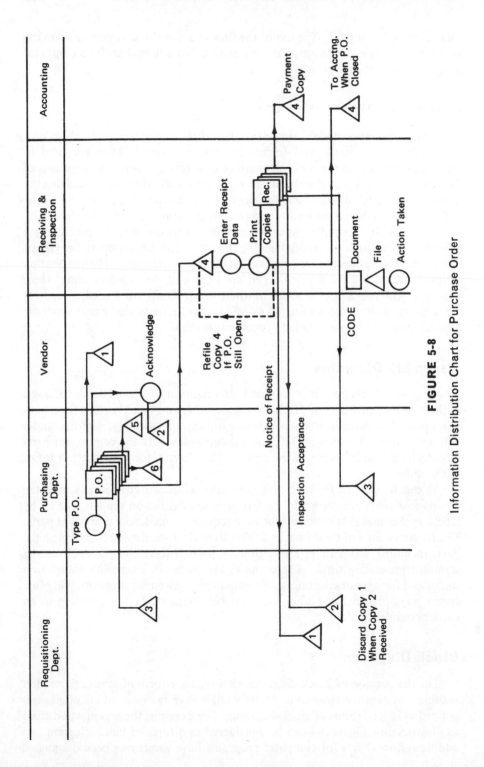

FIGURE 5-8

Information Distribution Chart for Purchase Order

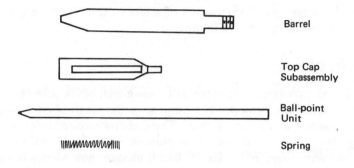

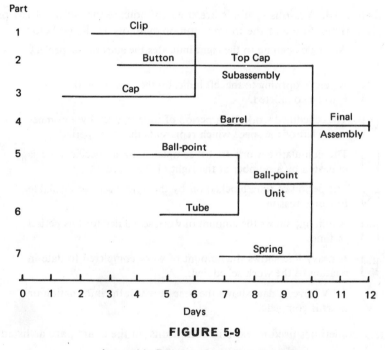

FIGURE 5-9

Assembly Diagram for a Ball-Point Pen

as block diagrams. However, there are circumstances where a more generalized form of the block diagram is useful. In the discussion of systems in Chapter 2, use was made of block diagrams. The reader is referred to Figure 2-5 as another example of a block diagram. Block diagrams are frequently valuable as a graphic presentation of systems relationships. This type of model often presents these relationships more clearly than any other technique. Figure 2-5 represents a very simple system, but block diagrams can also be used to represent complex operations systems. Examination of a block diagram of a given system often is useful in finding ways to improve it.

Gantt Charts

The Gantt chart is one of the best known methods of schematic presentation of the status of a project. The purpose of the Gantt chart is to present load and progress in relation to time. These charts receive their name from their originator, H. L. Gantt, one of the pioneers in the field of management.

The vertical axis of the Gantt chart is used to show what is being planned or measured. For example: machines to be loaded; facilities to be allocated; and departments, operations, or orders to be scheduled are found on this axis. The horizontal axis becomes the time scale against which available time is apportioned for the item to be controlled.

Symbols Used. Various symbols are used to indicate the status of the plan at any given time. Some of the more common symbols are listed below:

An angle opening to the right indicates the start of the project.

An angle opening to the left indicates the time when the project is to be completed.

The scheduled work for a period of time is given by a number at the left of the space which represents that time period.

The cumulative work to be completed by a specific time is indicated by a number at the right of the space.

The period of time blocked off by this symbol is not available for some reason.

A thin line shows the amount of work scheduled for this period of time.

A heavy line shows the amount of work completed to date in relation to the work scheduled.

A "V" over a date shows the time at which the information or chart is complete.

Letters, sometimes used to explain conditions on the charts, are as listed:

E = Waiting for setup
M = Lack of material
O = Lack of orders
R = Down for repairs
A = Operator absent
I = Idle capacity

Chart Types. Three widely used forms of the Gantt chart are the layout chart, the load chart, and the progress chart. An example of each is shown in the following illustrations.

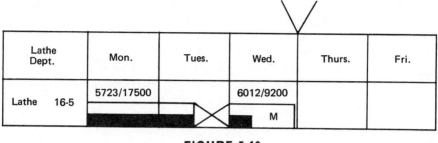

FIGURE 5-10

Gantt Layout Chart

LAYOUT CHART. Figure 5-10 shows a portion of a layout chart. This example shows that order number 5,723 for 17,500 pieces was scheduled for completion by approximately noon of Tuesday. This order amount is completed now. Tuesday afternoon was unavailable for an undetermined reason. Order 6,012 for 9,200 pieces is behind schedule at this time (Wednesday night) because of the lack of material.

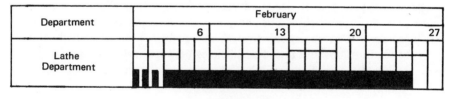

FIGURE 5-11

Gantt Load Chart

LOAD CHART. An example of a part of a load chart is found in Figure 5-11. In this figure the light lines show work scheduled by weeks while the heavy lines show the cumulative work schedules. The broken lines represent work not finished and carried over to a later period.

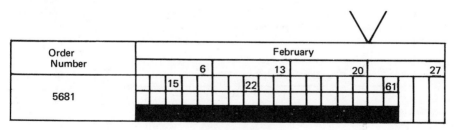

FIGURE 5-12

Gantt Progress Chart

PROGRESS CHART. In Figure 5-12, which depicts a sample of a section of a progress chart, the heavy lines show work that is finished. They are used to determine what plans should be made. The numbers in the body of the chart indicate the number of pieces completed on the days where the figures appear.

These devices enable the planning group to schedule and record progress. When special or rush orders have to be scheduled, these charts make it possible to arrive at an answer quickly. The charts also permit the expeditious handling of other problems such as delays.

To summarize, the Gantt charts graphically represent what is planned. The progress of men, machines, materials, orders, departments or entire plants is recorded. This permits a ready comparison between planned and actual.

Network Techniques

The Gantt chart has limitations that impair its effectiveness as a decision model. In the first place, the Gantt chart, like other schematic models, is static. Secondly, it does not make clear certain restrictions which may exist in the schedule. This is of particular importance in large complex projects such as construction projects, shipbuilding, or similar large-scale projects.

Networking has been utilized to overcome some of the difficulties mentioned above. The basic idea behind this approach is to determine the necessary events which represent the completion of work. A network is established which indicates the relationships and interdependencies between tasks. A simplified network is illustrated in Figure 5-13. The arrows connecting tasks represent

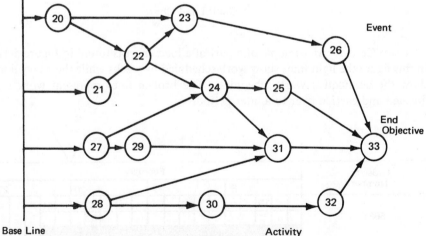

FIGURE 5-13

Example of Network Diagram

activities or the performance of a task. The length of the arrows has no time significance.

When the time requirement for each activity is known, the total time for completion of the project through each of the possible paths can be determined. The path which results in the longest time is designated as the critical path.

Network techniques have come into some degree of popularity in recent years. The use of these techniques in large project planning and control will be examined fully in Chapter 17.

Line of Balance

Another graphical technique which is, in essence, similar to the Gantt chart concept is line of balance (LOB). This technique is designed to set apart certain significant related factors in a project, and to assist management in comparing the factors with the objective. LOB may show possible areas of difficulty or delay in completion of the task before the problem becomes serious.

Project Plan. To illustrate, assume a manufacturer of heavy equipment where the required materials, components, and assembly operations are grouped homogeneously. A lead time exists for each of these groups. If we begin at the right of Figure 5-14 with the delivery of the completed product, each group is "set back" depending on its lead time. Each group is designated as a "control group" and is numbered consecutively from left to right. For example, forgings and castings which make up control group No. 1 are required five months before the delivery date of the completed item.

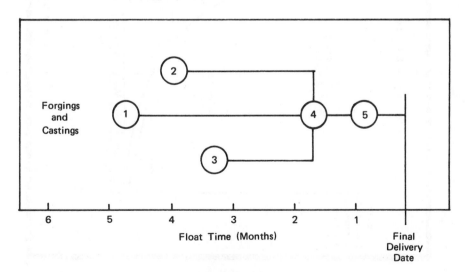

FIGURE 5-14

Scheduled Flow of Material and Components

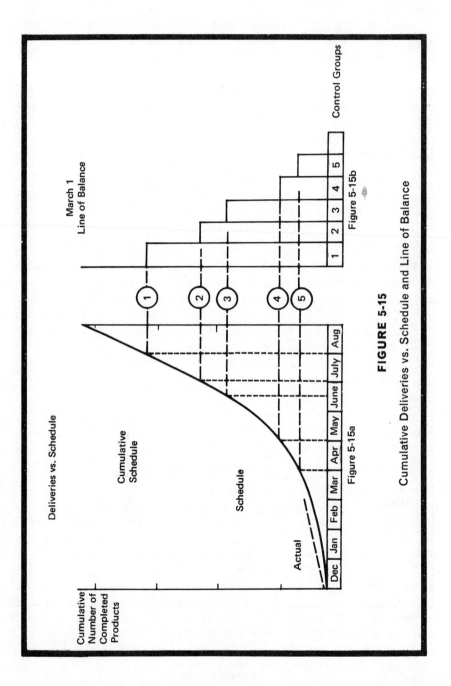

FIGURE 5-15

Cumulative Deliveries vs. Schedule and Line of Balance

Cumulative Deliveries vs. Schedule. Next a line chart is developed, as in Figure 5-15a, showing the cumulative schedule against a time scale. Cumulative deliveries are also indicated against the same time scale. Actual deliveries can then be compared with the schedule. Now, a determination can be made that, as of March 1, deliveries are ahead of schedule.

Determination of Balance. A bar chart is now developed on the same vertical scale as was used for the Deliveries vs. Schedule. There are the same number of bars on this chart as there are control groups. The bars are numbered consecutively to correspond to the control groups. A bar chart representing the line of balance for this project, as of March 1, is shown in Figure 5-15b.

Starting with control group No. 1, remember that it must be completed five months before completion of the final item. On the Deliveries vs. Schedule chart, count forward five months from the current date, March 1; this is August 1. A line is drawn vertically, from August 1, to intersect the schedule line. This point is projected horizontally to the bar chart to become the top of the bar representing control group No. 1. In a similar fashion, the other bars are projected until all control groups are represented. The resulting step pattern is the line of balance for March 1. The line of balance for any date can be developed in an identical fashion.

Status vs. Line of Balance. A final step in the overall line of balance technique is to compare the present status with that which should exist. In Figure 5-16 the shaded areas in the bars represent the current status of each of the control groups as of the March 1 date.

This total graphical technique offers relatively quick, economical, and easy presentation of data which may be of great value to the operations manager in making a decision about the project under consideration.

Summary of the Uses of Schematic Models

As can be readily ascertained from this overview of schematic models, they have wide potential application in management decision making. While the models have certain drawbacks, because they are of necessity not complete representations of the total problem, this does not preclude their wide utilization. Perhaps the most serious drawback of schematic models is that they are usually static. However, a static model can still be useful in evaluating a specific problem. As already indicated, schematic models are often a prerequisite to the use of the more complex quantitative models.

In many cases where the problem is not unduly complex, the use of the schematic model will be preferable to a mathematically oriented model. In such a case the schematic model is more economical since the examination of all possible alternatives can be carried out without resorting to a mathematical formulation. There may even be some situations where the problem can only be represented by a schematic model. This is frequently the case in the area of the design of work methods.

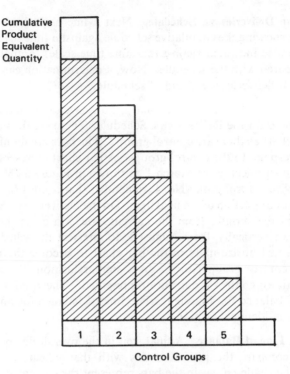

FIGURE 5-16

Status vs. Line of Balance

The schematic models reviewed here tend to have wide application. This is not intended to be an exhaustive treatment of these models as they are found in operations management. From time to time, other schematic methods will be noted as having value in the decision-making process, usually in a limited area. In addition, reference will be made, at appropriate points, to those models already discussed.

SUMMARY

A variety of decision tools available to the operations manager which are classified as conventional or traditional decision models are discussed. Such tools are those which have had wide usage for decision purposes in the past. They are also those which generally have wide applicability as to the decision problems. The discussion of most of the models is limited in nature as detailed examination is reserved for the point where the models have application to a specific problem area.

The first category of models examined is identified as "General" Decision Techniques. Under this classification are found rule-of-thumb models which are often of considerable value because they rely largely on accumulated experience. The use of logic in decision making falls into this category as well. A logical approach usually involves either inductive or deductive reasoning in arriving at the decision. Included under this classification of decision models are "open" decision models and non-quantitative simulation models.

The accounting system of the enterprise is viewed as another class of decision models. The various accounting statements, particularly the balance sheet and the income statement, are the basic accounting decision models. Also included are the numerous accounting ratios.

Economic analysis models are a third type of decision models examined. Of primary importance in this group of models are those which involve some sort of cost analysis. A wide variety of cost classification exists which may be of value to the operations manager. Of major interest are opportunity costs, fixed and variable costs, and incremental costs. Incremental cost analysis is singularly significant because it has wide potential application to the decision making of the operations manager. Break-even analysis is another form of economic analysis which has wide usage. While break-even analysis has its limitations, it can be used as a preliminary form of analysis in a large number of situations.

Schematic models are another category of conventional decision models. A number of the more widely utilized schematic models are surveyed. One of these is the organization chart. Flow charts and diagrams are another group which can be applied widely. Flow charts can take on many different forms depending on the specific application. Closely related to flow charts are information distribution charts, assembly diagrams, and block diagrams.

Perhaps the best known of the schematic models examined are the Gantt charts. These charts have found wide acceptance in a number of areas of operations management. Three of the major types are discussed: layout charts, load charts, and progress charts. Closely related to the Gantt charts are the various network techniques which have come into vogue in recent times for use in planning and controlling large-scale projects. PERT and CPM are typical of these techniques. Also in a similar relationship is the graphical technique known as the line of balance.

QUESTIONS FOR DISCUSSION AND ANALYSIS

1. Define conventional, or traditional, decision models. What is the relative value and application of such models by the operations manager as compared to the more modern and more sophisticated quantitative models?

2. Describe the various types of decision models which are classified as "general" decision techniques.

3. Discuss the role of induction and deduction in the decision-making process. How do these two types of reasoning relate to the logical method?

4. What is the relationship between "closed" decision models and "open" decision models?

5. What is the value of the use of accounting models to the operations manager for decision making?

6. Differentiate between fixed and variable costs. Give examples of each which might fall under the control of the operations manager.

7. What are incremental costs and what is their significance in operations management? Cite some types of decisions where incremental cost analysis might be useful in making an operating decision.

8. What is break-even analysis? Discuss its limitations. Give some of the possible areas of application.

9. Describe the general nature of the Gantt chart. Name and discuss the application of three types of Gantt charts.

SELECTED ADDITIONAL READINGS

Barnes, Ralph M. *Motion and Time Study — Design and Measurement of Work*, 6th ed. New York: John Wiley & Sons, Inc., 1968.

Bowman, Edward H., and Robert B. Fetter. *Analysis for Production and Operations Management*, 3d ed. Homewood, Illinois: Richard D. Irwin, Inc., 1967.

Clark, Wallace. *The Gantt Chart*. London: Sir Isaac Pitman & Sons, 1938.

Laurie, Edward J. *Modern Computer Concepts*. Cincinnati: South-Western Publishing Co., 1970. Chapter 5.

McGarrah, Robert E. *Production and Logistics Management*. New York: John Wiley & Sons, Inc., 1963.

Moore, Carl L., and Robert K. Jaedicke. *Managerial Accounting*, 2d ed. Cincinnati: South-Western Publishing Co., 1967.

Moore, Franklin G., and Ronald Jablonski. *Production Control*, 3d ed. New York: McGraw-Hill Book Co., 1969.

Nadler, Gerald. *Work Design*. Homewood, Illinois: Richard D. Irwin, Inc., 1963.

Randall, Clarence B., and Sally Weimer Burgly. *Systems & Procedures for Business Data Processing*. Cincinnati: South-Western Publishing Co., 1968.

SELECTIONS FROM READINGS BOOK

Greenwood, William T. *Decision Theory and Information Systems.* Cincinnati: South-Western Publishing Co., 1969.

Wilson and Alexis, "Basic Frameworks for Decisions," p. 63.

Morell, "Logic for Decision Making: The Stages of Decision Making," p. 179.

Morell, "Logical Analysis in Decision Making — A Demonstration," p. 189.

Boulanger, "Program Evaluation and Review Techniques . . . A Case Study Application with Analysis," p. 778.

CHAPTER 6 | Quantitative Models

The use of quantitative models in operations management has become quite widespread. Such techniques are more widely used in operations management than in any other area of management. The reason for this is that the problems facing the operations manager lend themselves more readily to quantitative analysis. In addition, the operations function in many firms is such that the people who fill operations management positions are more likely to have had quantitative training than those who are found in other functional areas. Naturally, quantitative models are not limited to use in operations management. While many of the initial applications have been in manufacturing activities, recent experience shows that these models are being applied in many diverse types of firms or enterprises. The rate of utilization in the functional areas other than operations and in nonmanufacturing activities has been relatively slow. However, the future will undoubtedly see a much faster rate of application to all areas.

All quantitative models are viewed as mathematical statements of the system under study. In their broadest form, all such models can be stated as:[1]

$$E = f(x_i, y_j)$$

Where:

E = the effectiveness of the system

x_i = controllable variables

y_j = noncontrollable variables

The type and form of model used depends on the problem at hand. Different quantitative models are used in the various problem areas of operations management. Thus, it is necessary to examine applications of these models which have been developed to solve specific problems. However, before doing this it is advisable to look at some of the specifics with respect to certain quantitative models which are widely used. The intention here is not to develop the high skill level necessary to build models for solving decision problems, but merely to gain some insight into the workings of a few of the more generally applicable quantitative models.

---

[1] Russell L. Ackoff, "The Development of Operations Research as a Science," *Operations Research*, Vol. IV, No. 3 (June, 1956), pp. 265–287.

MATHEMATICAL PROGRAMMING

Mathematical programming is the name given to a variety of techniques used to solve problems of allocation of resources or mixture problems. The most widely used of these techniques fall under the category of linear programming, therefore, attention will be concentrated here. The economist has long been concerned with the problem of the efficient allocation of scarce resources. Many operations management problems fall under this classification.

Allocation Problems

Examples of allocation problems are: financial budgeting; the assignment of production capacity to numerous product lines; and the assignment of workers to machine categories, when labor availability is a factor. Whenever resources (money, machinery, men) are not available in adequate quantities, and, when it is possible to use one resource in an alternate way, the operations manager is faced with an allocation problem.

Mixture Problems

Another large group of operations problems susceptible to solution by programming models are mixture problems. The make-or-buy decision is a mixture problem. Determining the quantities of various physical constituents to be used in a mixture to produce a given end product is another form of mixture problem. For example, what quantities of different chemicals are mixed together to produce a fertilizer? In oil refining, the proper mixture of different grades of crude oil used as input into the refining process to achieve a desired output is another such problem.

General Statement of Linear Programming Models

The general statement for linear programming models is as follows:

$$\sum_j a_{ij} x_j \leq b_i$$

$$\text{all } x_j \geq 0$$

$$f(X) = \sum_j c_j x_j = \text{maximum or minimum}$$

Where:

$$j = \text{output} = 1, 2, \ldots, n$$
$$i = \text{resources} = 1, 2, \ldots, m$$
$$b_i = \text{available quantity of resource } i$$
$$f(X) = \text{objective function}$$

$$c_j = \text{cost or profit attributable to output } j$$
$$a_{ij} = \text{units of resource } i \text{ per unit of output } j$$
$$x_j = \text{the unknown output rate for output } j$$

The above formulation states: for unknown variables, such as the output of a particular product, which is dependent upon the limited availability of some resources, values must be found which satisfy these restrictions and which also satisfy the objective function. The objective function may be established to achieve the highest profit, or to yield the lowest possible cost.

This formulation applies to a variety of operations problems. These problems are complex because of the interactions of the restrictions. The uniqueness of these interactions makes it impossible to arrive at solutions by intuitive decision processes. Note the descriptive word "linear" as used in connection with these models. Simply stated, *linear* means that a direct one-to-one relationship exists between all of the variables. Thus, the variables and their restrictions must have this type of relationship. In addition, the objective function must be stated as a linear equation. The meaning of this concept should become obvious as we proceed with the examples. Linearity is essential to the use of the models described. Not all problems are "linear," and, consequently, these models cannot be universally used. Techniques available for solving nonlinear problems will be discussed later.

GRAPHICAL SOLUTION METHOD OF LINEAR PROGRAMMING PROBLEM

The linear programming approach can be illustrated by a highly simplified example which can be solved by the graphical method. The graphical approach can be used for problems with two unknowns. A graphical solution can also be achieved for three unknowns, but this becomes difficult because it requires visualization of a three dimensional graph on a two dimensional plane.

A Maximizing Problem

Assume a company currently has a demand for two products, Abysmals and Brackishes. These two products can be made with various combinations of metal working machines: lathes, drill presses, and grinders. Table 6-1 shows the time requirements for each of the two products on the three different classes of machines and indicates the capacities available for each of the machine types. All times shown are in minutes. The capacities are in minutes available per week, and the time requirements for each product on the various machine categories are in minutes per unit of product. What is desired is to determine the most profitable product mix between the two products by assuming product A makes a $3.00 per unit contribution to profit and overhead, and product B makes a $2.00 per unit contribution.

TABLE 6-1

Summary of Production Data for Abysmals and Brackishes

| | Production Time Required | | |
	Product A per Unit	Product B per Unit	Weekly Capacity Available
Lathes (m_1)	40	20	20,000
Drills (m_2)	70	60	42,000
Grinders (m_3)	25	45	22,500
		Times in minutes	

Contribution: Product A $3/unit
                Product B $2/unit

Solution Method. To build the model for this problem, let the following symbols represent weekly output:

x = the weekly output of Abysmals and,
y = the weekly output of Brackishes.

Reference to Table 6-1 reveals that the total time required on lathes is represented by $40x + 20y$. Considering the available capacity, the restriction on lathes is shown in the first of the following statements of inequality. The other restrictions, on drill presses and grinders, are represented by the remaining statements:

$$40x + 20y \leq 20,000$$
$$70x + 60y \leq 42,000$$
$$25x + 45y \leq 22,500$$
$$x \geq 0$$
$$y \geq 0$$

The objective is to achieve the most profitable product mix. The objective function is expressed mathematically as maximizing the following:

$$p_{max} = 3x + 2y$$

Values for x and y which are subject to the above stated inequalities must be found to make p as large as possible.

The graphical solution to this problem is shown in Figure 6-1. The quantity of product B is shown on the vertical, or y-axis, and the quantity of product A is shown on the horizontal, or x-axis. The capacity limitation for lathes is shown by a straight line drawn from 500 on the x-axis to 1,000 on the y-axis. This line represents the fact that if the entire lathe capacity of 20,000 minutes was used to produce the weekly output (x) of product A, the resulting 500 units

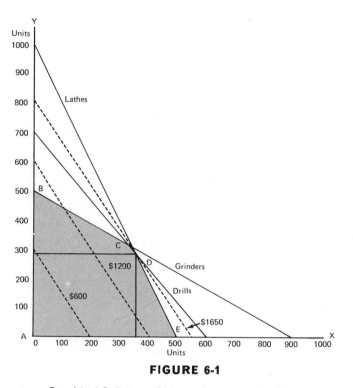

FIGURE 6-1

Graphical Solution of Linear Programming Problem

as represented comes from 20,000 ÷ 40; similarly, 20,000 ÷ 20 gives the number of units (y) of product B if lathe capacity was devoted exclusively to the production of this product.

Any point along this line represents the total of 20,000 minutes available for lathe operation. For example, if 5,000 minutes were devoted to product A, and 15,000 minutes to product B, x would be equal to 5,000 ÷ 40, or 125 units, and y would be equal to 15,000 ÷ 20, or 750 units. All other possibilities of using the 20,000-minute capacity for lathes lie along this line. This illustrates the "linear" nature of the problem, and consequently, the reason for referring to this technique as linear programming. The linear programming technique is applicable only when the restrictions in such a problem can be represented reasonably by a straight line. It is not necessary for the lathes to be operated at full capacity as this line represents. Consequently, there are many other points which may be feasible points relative to the stated restriction of $\leq$. Such points would be represented by any point inside this line and closer to the origin point (the point of no production where $x = 0$, $y = 0$). Any point outside the line that represents lathe capacity is, of course, not feasible.

Similarly, the lines that represent the restrictions on drill presses and grinders can be determined. For drill presses, the two points on the axes are found as follows: $42,000 \div 70 = 600x$, and $42,000 \div 60 = 700y$. For grinders, $22,500 \div 25 = 900x$, and $22,500 \div 45 = 500y$.

Solution Polygon. The polygon ABCDE, shown by the shaded area in Figure 6-1, is referred to as the *polygon of technical feasibility.*. Any point inside this shaded area will satisfy the stated restrictions. Then it is necessary to find the point (or points) that represents the best mix between these two products to satisfy the objective function. This can be done by drawing a series of straight lines to show a constant contribution. These lines are referred to as *isocontribution lines*, or equal contribution lines.

The slope of these lines is determined by the relationship of contributions of the two variables x and y. The axis intersections are determined by a method similar to that used for the restriction lines. However, for isocontribution lines, the objective function equation determines the end points. Arbitrarily, assuming a total contribution of $600, entirely from product A, a contribution of $600 ÷ $3 = 200x results. Conversely, if the entire $600 contribution comes from product B, it results in $600 ÷ $2 = 300y. These points are joined with a dotted line from 200 on the x-axis to 300 on the y-axis to yield an equal contribution line representing a $600 contribution. Any point along this line would result in a $600 contribution. A second line can be drawn, using the same method, where the total contribution equals $1,200; $1,200 ÷ $3 = 400x; $1,200 ÷ $2 = 600y. This line also appears on the graph as a dotted line. The two lines are parallel. This is true of all of the equal contribution lines in a given problem. This process can continue, moving away from the origin as far as possible, until an equal contribution line is found that is tangent to some point (or series of points) within the polygon of technical feasibility. This point graphically represents the optimum solution to the problem. The equal contribution line tangent to point D represents a $1,650 contribution. This is the optimum contribution. The product mix can be determined by reading the x and y coordinates of point D. Read from the graph, $x = 360$, $y = 283$.

Algebraic Check. It is desirable to check this answer, since graphical representations obviously can only be approximations as a result of the errors which generally occur when plotting graphs. Since point D is the intersection of two lines which have known equations, an algebraic solution can be found to check the graphical solution. Point D is the intersection of the lathe capacity line and the drill press capacity line. Solving the equations of these lines simultaneously:

$$40x + 20y = 20,000$$
$$70x + 60y = 42,000$$

Multiply the first equation by 3 to get:

$$120x + 60y = 60,000$$
$$70x + 60y = 42,000.$$

Then, subtract the second equation from the first; y is canceled out leaving:

$$50x = 18,000$$
$$x = 360.$$

Now substitute this value of x into the first of these equations to get:

$$40(360) + 20y = 20,000$$
$$20y = 20,000 - 14,400$$
$$20y = 5,600$$
$$y = 280.$$

This answer of $x = 360$ and $y = 280$ is slightly different, but more accurate, than the graphical solution. It means that the best product mix which satisfies all the restrictions set forth at the outset results in a weekly output of 360 units of Abysmals and 280 units of Brackishes. The resultant weekly contribution to profit and overhead is:

$$p_{max} = 3(360) + 2(280)$$
$$p_{max} = \$1,080 + \$560$$
$$p_{max} = \$1,640.$$

Summary. An additional comment or two, regarding the linear-programming-graphical-solution technique as related to this problem, is in order. First, since the optimum solution was at the intersection point of the restriction lines for lathes and drill presses, these two resources were used to their fullest capacity. Secondly, since the solution point was inside (closer to the origin) the restriction line for grinders, not all of the grinder capacity was utilized, and *slack time* on the grinders results.

The explanation for finding the optimum solution stated that this solution could be a point or series of points within the polygon of technical feasibility. In the example used, the solution was a single point. However, the solution can also be represented by more than one point. This indicates a number of alternate and equal optimum solutions. In the graphical method, this type of solution occurs when the slope of the isocontribution lines (or isocost lines in minimization problems) is identical to the slope of one of the restriction lines used in the solution, and when the tangency of these two lines (the isocontribution line and the restriction line) occurs within the feasible polygon. Any point of tangency along these lines yields the same optimum solution to the objective function. The actual solution chosen from among the many possible ones then becomes strictly a matter of subjective judgment on the part of management.

A Minimizing Problem

The problem just solved resulted in a maximizing of contribution. However, the general statement of the linear programming model (pp. 116, 117) indicated that the model could also be used to minimize an objective function. Therefore, the model could result in a solution which minimized total cost. To achieve such a solution by the graphical method, isocost lines are drawn in the technically feasible polygon. The object is to find a point of tangency as close to the origin as possible.

The concept of the *isocost lines* is identical to that described for the isocontribution lines. They are equal cost lines since any point along them represents the same cost, regardless of the values of x and y at that point. The slope of these lines is determined by the relationship between the costs of the variables in the problem.

To illustrate a minimization problem, assume a fertilizer manufacturer is concerned with the determination of the optimal mixture for a particular fertilizer product. This product can be made up of two different chemicals, A and B. The constituents of these two chemicals and the restrictions which appertain to the mixture, stated in standard nutrient units, are summarized on Table 6-2.

TABLE 6-2

Summary of Chemical Constituents and Fertilizer Mixture Restrictions
(In Standard Nutrient Units)

| | Per Pound | | Restrictions on Mixture |
	Chemical A	Chemical B	
Total Nutrient Units	600	1200	At least 1800 At most 2400
Nitrogen	500	250	At least 750
Phosphorus	40	35	At most 140

The totals of the nutrient units of the individual constituents do not equal the totals for the two chemicals. While they contain additional elements, the only restrictions involved are for nitrogen and phosphorus.

Let x equal the number of pounds of Chemical A to be used in the mixture, and y equal the number of pounds of Chemical B. Follow the same procedure outlined for the previous problem to develop these statements of inequality for this problem:

$$600x + 1200y \geq 1800$$
$$600x + 1200y \leq 2400$$
$$500x + 250y \geq 750$$
$$40x + 35y \leq 140$$

If the cost of Chemical A is \$1.20 per pound, and the cost for Chemical B is \$1.00 per pound, the objective function of minimizing the total cost is stated as follows:

$$c_{min} = 120x + 100y$$

Use the method already outlined to find the solution to this problem by graphical means. The graphical solution is shown in Figure 6-2. Since this is a problem of minimizing costs, isocost lines are used to move to a point tangent to the area of feasibility as close to the origin as possible. In Figure 6-2 this is point B, which yields a solution of 1 pound of Chemical A and 1 pound of Chemical B at a total cost of $2.20.

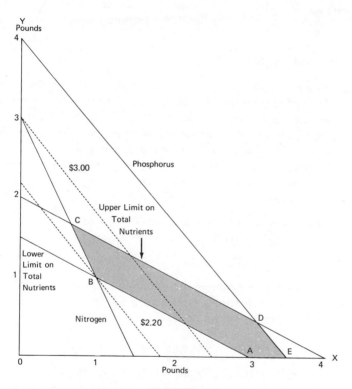

FIGURE 6-2

Graphical Solution of Linear Programming Problem
Minimizing Objective Function

SIMPLEX METHOD[2]

The simplex method of linear programming is an algebraic approach with a greater general application than the graphical method. For all practical purposes, the graphical method is limited to problems with only two unknowns. The simplex method is an iterative process. Therefore, changes are made in the

---

[2]The solution technique used here follows that suggested in: Robert W. Metzger, *Elementary Mathematical Programming* (New York: John Wiley & Sons, Inc., 1958).

existing solution, one at a time, until a point is reached where further change will not improve the objective function. This indicates an optimum solution. The word simplex is not related to the word simple, but is derived from the techniques of simplex algebra. While the simplex method is not really difficult, it is somewhat tedious because it requires numerous computations when solved by pencil and paper methods. Fortunately, simplex linear programming models can be solved with a computer. If this were not true, most business problems susceptible to solution by simplex linear programming models would require time-consuming efforts. To illustrate the simplex method, the problem previously solved by graphical methods will be used.

Solution Technique

The first step normally undertaken in the simplex method is the formulation of the statements of restrictions. The restrictions for this problem have already been developed as inequalities. However, when using the simplex model, it is necessary to state the original inequalities as equations. To accomplish this, the appropriate slack capacity for each of the machine types is added to each statement of inequality. The slack variables are represented in the equations by the symbols m_1, m_2, and m_3; therefore, the resulting equations for lathes, drills, and grinders are:

$$40x + 20y + m_1 = 20,000 \text{ (lathes)}$$
$$70x + 60y + m_2 = 42,000 \text{ (drills)}$$
$$25x + 45y + m_3 = 22,500 \text{ (grinders)}$$

Now it is necessary to establish the initial solution in a matrix form. In matrix form the three equations, considering all of the variables, slack or otherwise, would appear as shown on Table 6-3.

TABLE 6-3

Linear Programming Problem Variables in Matrix Form

	x	y	m_1	m_2	m_3
20,000	40	20	1	0	0
42,000	70	60	0	1	0
22,500	25	45	0	0	1

Initial Solution. For an initial solution, the worst possible solution, or the origin solution in the graphical method, is selected. This solution represents zero production, which is undesirable; however, it is feasible. The origin solution is used because it is a feasible solution which can be stated rather readily. It is also necessary to consider the objective function in developing the full initial solution matrix. The previously developed objective function was:

$$3x + 2y = p_{max}$$

The full initial solution matrix, with identifying labels for the constituent parts, is shown in Table 6-4. The size of the matrix will depend, of course, on the number of variables and the number of equations involved.

TABLE 6-4

Initial Solution Matrix with Identifying Labels

Objective Column	Variable Column	Constant Column	3 x	2 y	0 m_1	0 m_2	0 m_3	Objective Row Variable Row
0	m_1	20,000	40	20	1	0	0	
0	m_2	42,000	70	60	0	1	0	Equations
0	m_3	22,500	25	45	0	0	1	
	Solution Stub			Body		Identity		

The initial solution is uneconomical because it has no production; consequently, it makes no contribution. Therefore, it must be evaluated for improvement.

Index Number Calculation. One method for improving a solution is to develop index numbers. *Index numbers* are determined for the constant column, and for each column in the body and in the identity of the matrix. The index numbers developed for the body and identity columns represent the evaluation of the improvement which can be achieved by adding that particular variable into the existing solution. The index number for the constant column always represents the value of the objective function. The index number is computed as follows: multiply each entry in the body, identity, and constant columns by the corresponding entry in the objective column; total the products for each column; then subtract the number located above the respective columns in the objective row. Implicitly, the number in the objective row for the constant column is zero at all times. The calculations for the index numbers for the present solution are as follows:

$$\text{Constant column} = (20{,}000 \times 0 + 42{,}000 \times 0 + 22{,}500 \times 0) - 0 = 0$$
$$x \text{ column} = (40 \times 0 + 70 \times 0 + 25 \times 0) - 3 = -3$$
$$y \text{ column} = (20 \times 0 + 60 \times 0 + 45 \times 0) - 2 = -2$$
$$m_1 \text{ column} = (1 \times 0 + 0 \times 0 + 0 \times 0) - 0 = 0$$
$$m_2 \text{ column} = (0 \times 0 + 1 \times 0 + 0 \times 0) - 0 = 0$$
$$m_3 \text{ column} = (0 \times 0 + 0 \times 0 + 1 \times 0) - 0 = 0$$

Note that the index numbers are nearly the same as the objective row, except that all positive numbers are now negative. This occurs only in the initial solution. The index row can now be developed. This is shown in Table 6-5. The index row values indicate the possible improvement in the objective function.

The column which has the greatest potential for improvement is the key column. This column is the one with the largest negative number in the index row. Therefore, the x column is the key column. It indicates the variable which must now be added into the existing solution. When a variable is added to the solution, another variable must be taken out of it. The key row determines the variable to be removed. The key row is the variable which has the greatest limitation on the variable to be added to the solution. The key row is determined by dividing the numbers in the constant column by the corresponding numbers in the key column. The key row yields the smallest non-negative number after this computation. Computations to determine the key row are as follows:

$$m_1 \text{ Row } \quad 20,000/40 \; = \; 500$$
$$m_2 \text{ Row } \quad 42,000/70 \; = \; 600$$
$$m_3 \text{ Row } \quad 22,500/25 \; = \; 900$$

The m_1 row has the smallest non-negative number, therefore, it is designated as the key row. The number in the matrix at the intersection of the key row and the key column is the *key number*. The initial solution matrix with the key column, key row, and the key number identified, is shown in Table 6-5.

TABLE 6-5

Initial Solution with Key Column,
Key Row and Key Number Identified

			3	2	0	0	0	
			x	y	m_1	m_2	m_3	
0	m_1	20,000	40	20	1	0	0	Key Row
0	m_2	42,000	70	60	0	1	0	
0	m_3	22,500	25	45	0	0	1	
		0	−3	−2	0	0	0	Index Row
			Key Column		Key Number			

These computations indicate that units of product x are going to be added in by utilizing the capacity of m_1, which will be removed from the solution. The amount to be added is determined by the most limiting restriction. The graphical solution indicated the following: in moving from point A (the origin) along the x-axis, the three restriction lines intercepted the x-axis at 500, 600, and 900. The 500 is most restricting; the other two points are outside the poly-gon of technical feasibility. The decision to add 500 units of product x is iden-tical to moving from point A to point E in the polygon of technical feasibility.

Second Solution Matrix. It is now necessary to calculate the main row for Matrix II. The new values or coefficients must be computed to replace the coefficient values for the variable being removed. Compute this by dividing the key row numbers by the key number. The main row for Matrix II is shown in Table 6-6.

TABLE 6-6

Matrix with Main Row of Matrix II
Replacing Variable Removed from Solution

				3	2	0	0	0	
				x	y	m_1	m_2	m_3	
Matrix I	0	m_2	42,000	70	60	0	1	0	
	0	m_3	22,500	25	45	0	0	1	
			0	−3	−2	0	0	0	
Matrix II	3	x	500	1	1/2	1/40	0	0	Main Row

Continue by computing the remaining new coefficients for Matrix II. These are computed by the formula:

$$\text{New Number} = \text{Old Number} - \frac{\begin{array}{c}\text{Corresponding} \\ \text{Number} \\ \text{of Key Row}\end{array} \times \begin{array}{c}\text{Corresponding} \\ \text{Number} \\ \text{of Key Column}\end{array}}{\text{Key Number}}$$

Examples of the calculations required for completing Matrix II follow:

$$\text{Second Row, constant column} = 42,000 - \frac{20,000 \times 70}{40} = 7,000$$

$$\text{Second Row, } x \text{ column} = 70 - \frac{40 \times 70}{40} = 0$$

$$\text{Index Row, constant column} = 0 - \frac{20,000 \times -3}{40} = 1,500$$

$$\text{Second Row, } m_1 \text{ column} = 0 - \frac{1 \times 70}{40} = -1\,3/4$$

All of the remaining coefficients are similarly calculated. The second matrix with the key column and the key row identified is shown in Table 6-7.

TABLE 6-7

Matrix II with Key Column and Key Row Identified

			3	2	0	0	0
			x	y	m_1	m_2	m_3
3	x	500	1	1/2	1/40	0	0
0	m_2	7,000	0	25	−1 3/4	1	0
0	m_3	10,000	0	32 1/2	−5/8	0	1
		1,500	0	−1/2	3/40	0	0

Optimum Solution

By repetition of the above procedure, Matrix II is evaluated and the appropriate substitutions made. Matrix III then results. This is depicted in Table 6-8. All the numbers in the index row for Matrix III are non-negative. This indicates an optimum solution has been achieved, and that any new change would not improve the total contribution. Also note that the solution proposed by Matrix III is to produce 360 units of product A, and 280 units of product B with a total contribution of $1,640. The graphical solution and algebraic proof of that solution were identical to the optimum solution achieved at this point.

TABLE 6-8

Matrix III — Optimum Solution

			3	2	0	0	0
			x	y	m_1	m_2	m_3
3	x	360	1	0	3/50	−1/50	0
2	y	280	0	1	−7/200	1/25	0
0	m_3	900	0	0	1 13/20	−1 1/2	1
		1,640	0	0	8/200	1/50	0

DISTRIBUTION MODELS

Certain problems are more easily handled by different linear programming models than the simplex model. The most useful models are the distribution, or transportation models. They are widely used to solve problems involving the shipping of goods from various sources to various destinations. Actually these models are valuable in many different types of problems in which limited resources must be utilized to satisfy a known requirement or demand at minimum cost. If such models are to be usable, the available resources and the requirements for the use of these resources must be capable of expression in the same units of measurement. Generally, any problem that can be solved by the distribution method can also be solved by the simplex method. However, the distribution models are more easily handled, and any problem framed in the simplex model format which can also fit the distribution model should be formulated as a distribution problem.

Examples of other types of problems fitting the distribution model format are machine assignment problems, production-routing problems, scheduling problems, and certain types of personnel assignment problems.

Illustrative Problem

To illustrate this model, consider an example of four sources which must supply materials to three users, a, b, and c. Each source has a maximum capacity of goods available, and each destination has an established requirement. Each of the twelve possible shipping routes has its own distinctive cost. These data are shown in Table 6-9. The problem is now expressed in a matrix format. Next, an initial solution to the problem must be developed. An initial solution of a distribution model may be established in various ways.

TABLE 6-9

Distribution Matrix
Shipping Costs, Capacities and Requirements Shown

To / From	a	b	c	Capacity
1	6	6	2	110
2	4	14	6	80
3	18	16	8	120
4	4	12	10	40
Required	150	100	100	350

Northwest Corner Solution

For illustration purposes, the systematic approach known as the "northwest corner rule" can be used. This rule receives its name because the matrix is viewed the same way a map is viewed. Consequently, cell 1-a would be the extreme northwest corner of the matrix. This rule states that the maximum allocation possible is made into the most northwestern corner of the matrix that is available. Then continue downward and to the right (or southeast) through the matrix until all allocations are complete.

Following this rule, allocate into cell 1-a the maximum quantity possible, as determined by the restrictions of row 1 and column a. In this case, it is 110, the smaller of the two restrictions, derived from the 110-unit capacity of source 1. The restrictions for row 1 are now entirely satisfied. Next, moving to row 2, column a, which is now the most northwestern cell available; allocate the maximum possible, which is 40. This results because column a now has a remaining unallocated capacity of 40 units, and row 2 has an available capacity of 80 units. The 40 units is the most restrictive, and, consequently, the maximum amount which can be allocated without violating the stated restrictions of requirements and capacities. This satisfies the limitations for column a. Next move to cell 2-b, and follow this procedure to achieve an initial solution shown in Table 6-10. The objective function of $3,220 represents the total cost of this solution. This is achieved by summing the products of the allocated amounts and the costs of each assigned cell. That is, for this solution matrix; $110 \times \$6 + 40 \times \$4 + 40 \times \$14 + 60 \times \$16 + 60 \times \$8 + 60 \times \$10 = \$3,220$.

TABLE 6-10

Distribution Matrix
Northwest Corner Initial Solution

From \ To	a	b	c	Capacity
1	6 110	6	2	110
2	4 40	14 40	6	80
3	18	16 60	8 60	120
4	4	12	10 40	40
Required	150	100	100	350

Objective Function: $3,220

Stepping-Stone Method

This initial solution must be evaluated to try to improve the solution by a reduction in the total distribution cost. There are numerous methods available to solve distribution models. Of the solution techniques available, only the "stepping-stone method" will be examined. References at the end of the chapter contain information about other methods used to achieve optimal solutions to distribution models. In the stepping-stone method, each unoccupied cell must be evaluated one by one. To accomplish this, a closed path is developed by moving either clockwise or counterclockwise from the unoccupied cell being evaluated, using only occupied cells, and making a right angle turn at the appropriate occupied cell to reach another occupied cell. It is possible to skip over both occupied and unoccupied cells to achieve this path, and it should be emphasized that for each unoccupied cell there is one, and only one, possible closed path. The path is developed by placing alternating plus and minus signs in the cells to indicate the addition, or removal, of an allocation in the cell concerned; starting with a plus in the cell to be evaluated. When establishing the path, it is important to remember that when a unit is added to, or subtracted from, a given cell, the row and column totals (the rim requirements) must be kept in balance. In the evaluation of a cell in row 1, when a unit is added to that cell (plus sign), a unit must be removed from another cell in that row (minus sign) to balance the rim requirements for row 1.

To illustrate this procedure, four contiguous cells, 1-a, 1-b, 2-a, and 2-b, have been removed from the matrix for examination. Closer scrutiny reveals that of the four cells 1-b is unoccupied. This cell must be evaluated to determine whether it presents a possible improvement in the attempt to minimize total costs.

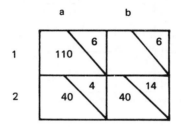

Following this procedure, place a plus sign in 1-b, a minus sign in 2-b, a plus sign in 2-a, and a minus sign in 1-a. The rows and columns are kept in balance. Determine the effect of placing a unit in cell 1-b, from the algebraic sum of the costs, using the plus and minus signs in the four cells involved. The result of this evaluation is shown below:

$$
\begin{array}{cc}
+ & - \\
6 & 14 \\
4 & 6 \\
\hline
10 & 20 \\
\end{array}
$$
$$-10$$

Thus, the net result of an allocation into 1-b would be a $10 cost reduction per unit.

Some closed paths are more complex than the one illustrated. For example, evaluation of cell 4-a requires a more complex path. Starting from cell 4-a (plus) move clockwise to cell 2-a (minus), to cell 2-b (plus), to cell 3-b (minus), to cell 3-c (plus), to cell 4-c (minus), and thus back to 4-a. This path is indicated by the arrows on Table 6-11.

Repeat this procedure for all other unoccupied cells in the matrix. The results are shown in Table 6-12. The anticipated changes in cost per unit are entered in the unoccupied cells, and circled.

When all of the unoccupied cells have been evaluated, it is necessary to decide what change to make, if any. Any evaluated cell with a minus quantity represents an advantageous possibility of total cost reduction. The most common decision rule used is: select the cell which indicates the largest improvement

TABLE 6-11

Closed Path for Evaluating Changes Required
for Possible Improvement of Square 4-a

To From	a	b	c	Capacity
1	6 110	6	2	110
2	− 4 40	+ 14 40	6	80
3	18	− 16 60	+ 8 60	120
4	+ 4	12	− 10 40	40
Required	150	100	100	350

TABLE 6-12

Anticipated Per Unit Shipping Cost Changes
Shown Circled in Unoccupied Cells

To From	a	b	c	Capacity
1	6 110	6 (−10)	2 (−6)	110
2	4 40	14 40	6 (0)	80
3	18 (+12)	16 60	8 60	120
4	4 (−4)	12 (−8)	10 40	40
Required	150	100	100	350

possibility; move the maximum amount possible into that cell. Therefore, the desired move is cell 1-b with a − 10 cost improvement. Reference to the above illustration shows the evaluation path for this unoccupied cell was: 1-b (plus); 2-b (minus); 2-a (plus); and 1-a (minus). The amount which can be moved into an improvement cell is limited to the smallest amount in the minus cells of the evaluation path; specifically, the quantity of 40 found in cell 2-b. Thus, make the necessary adjustments as indicated by the minus and plus signs in the cells in the evaluation path. Move 40 units into 1-b, remove 40 units from 2-b, add 40 units to 2-a, and subtract 40 units from 1-a. The resulting solution is shown in the new matrix in Table 6-13.

The new objective function results from subtracting $40 \times \$10 = \$400$ from the previous objective function, \$3,220 (derived because moving 40 units resulted in saving \$10 per unit). Consequently, the new objective function shown below the table is \$2,820.

Again, follow the same evaluation procedure used for the initial solution. The circled symbols indicate the evaluation results for the new solution. The actual figures are shown only in cases resulting in a minus quantity. In the other cases, encircled plus signs indicate undesirable moves. The most advantageous move is to transfer as many units as possible into cell 4-a as determined by the stated decision rule. The evaluation path and the appropriate plus and minus signs for this route are indicated in the matrix in Table 6-14. It was necessary

TABLE 6-13

First Improved Solution Matrix with Unoccupied Cells Evaluation
Results Shown Circled

From \ To	a	b	c	Capacity
1	6 / 70	6 / 40	2 / ⊕	110
2	4 / 80	14 / ⊕	6 / ⊕	80
3	18 / ⊕	16 / 60	8 / 60	120
4	4 / −14	12 / −6	10 / 40	40
Required	150	100	100	350

Objective Function: $2,820

TABLE 6-14

Closed Path for Evaluating Changes Required
for Possible Improvement of Square 4-a, Matrix II

To / From	a	b	c	Capacity
1	− \ 6 70	+ \ 6 40	\ 2	110
2	\ 4 80	\ 14	\ 6	80
3	\ 18	− \ 16 60	+ \ 8 60	120
4	+ \ 4	\ 12	− \ 10 40	40
Required	150	100	100	350

TABLE 6-15

Optimum Solution

To / From	a	b	c	Capacity
1	\ 6 30	\ 6 80	\ 2	110
2	\ 4 80	\ 14	\ 6	80
3	\ 18	\ 16 20	\ 8 100	120
4	\ 4 40	\ 12	\ 10	40
Required	150	100	100	350

Objective Function: $2,260

to skip occupied cell 2-a in order to complete the closed evaluation path. Again, the limitation is determined by the smallest amount in the minus cells (40).

Follow this procedure to make the move, developing the third solution matrix as displayed in Table 6-15. The new objective function is $2,260.

Evaluation of the third solution matrix indicates the unoccupied cells will not yield an improvement in the objective function. Since the objective function cannot be reduced, an optimum solution has been achieved. The desired objective has been satisfied when no move yields an improvement. In some circumstances, it is possible an unoccupied cell will show zero change, rather than either a positive or a negative change; this indicates another solution which is also optimum. For example, a move into the zero change cell could be made without causing any change in the objective function. The decision is then a subjective one by the manager, rather than an objective one based on minimizing cost.

Vogel Approximation Method

The Vogel Approximation Method is another method used to achieve an initial solution to a distribution model. VAM is a method which can be used in place of the northwest corner rule. The advantage it has over the northwest corner rule and other initial solution methods is that the VAM allocation very frequently is also an optimum solution. VAM does not always result in an optimum solution, but it reduces the number of iterations required to achieve an optimum solution.

The same problem solved by the stepping-stone method can illustrate the VAM. First, determine the differences between the two lowest cost cells in each row and each column. These figures are shown on the right of the rows and below the columns in Table 6-16.

Select the row or column indicating the greatest cost difference; in this case, row 3. Then allocate to the nearest cost cell in the selected row or column the maximum quantity possible (determined by the rim requirements). Thus, allocate 100 units to cell 3-c. Put X's into the remaining cells in column c, which is now fully allocated, as illustrated in Table 6-17.

Repeat this procedure for the remaining rows and columns in the matrix. The new differences are shown. This time row 2 has the greatest cost difference. A quantity of 80 is allocated to cell 2-a. Row 2 is eliminated and the remaining unoccupied cells in that row are crossed out (Table 6-18).

Calculate the cost differences again to find the greatest cost difference is 8 for row 4. Thus, 40 units are allocated to cell 4-a, and the requirements for row 4 are now satisfied. Table 6-19 illustrates these results.

Repeat the same procedure to find the greatest difference in column a. Allocate the maximum amount possible to the lowest cost cell 1-a to satisfy the requirements of column a. This fourth assignment is shown in Table 6-20.

Column b is now the only remaining column available. Thus, make an allocation into this column starting with the lowest cost cell. Continue making allocations until all rim requirements are satisfied. The resulting allocations are

TABLE 6-16

VAM Differences Shown

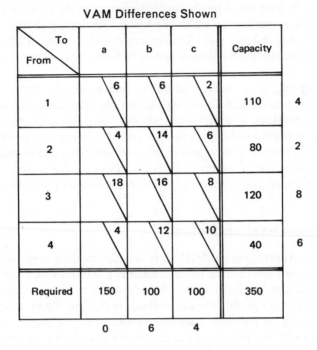

From \ To	a	b	c	Capacity	
1	6	6	2	110	4
2	4	14	6	80	2
3	18	16	8	120	8
4	4	12	10	40	6
Required	150	100	100	350	
	0	6	4		

TABLE 6-17

First VAM Assignment Made

From \ To	a	b	c	Capacity	
1	6	6	2 X	110	4
2	4	14	6 X	80	2
3	18	16	8 100	120	<u>8</u>
4	4	12	10 X	40	6
Required	150	100	100	350	
	0	6	4		

TABLE 6-18

New VAM Differences Shown and Second VAM Assignment Made

To \ From	a	b	c	Capacity		
1	6	6	2 / X	110	~~4~~	0
2	4 / 80	14 / X	6 / X	80	~~2~~	<u>10</u>
3	18	16	8 / 100	120	~~8~~	2
4	4	12	10 / X	40	~~6~~	8
Required	150	100	100	350		

0   6   ~~4~~

TABLE 6-19

Recalculated Differences and Third VAM Assignment Made

To \ From	a	b	c	Capacity		
1	6	6	2 / X	110	~~4~~ 0	
2	4 / 80	14 / X	6 / X	80	~~2 10~~	
3	18	16	8 / 100	120	~~8~~ 2	
4	4 / 40	12 / X	10 / X	40	~~8~~ <u>8</u>	
Required	150	100	100	350		

~~0~~
2   6   ~~4~~

TABLE 6-20

Fourth VAM Assignment Made

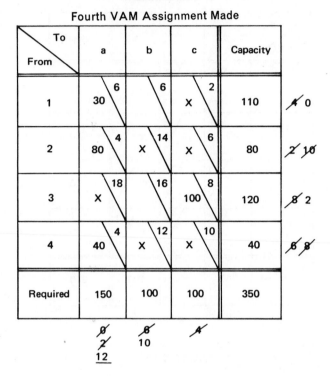

80 units to cell 1-b, and 20 units to cell 3-b. The completed VAM solution is found in Table 6-21. This allocation is an optimum solution identical to the solution achieved by the stepping-stone method. (Compare Tables 6-21 and 6-15). While this VAM allocation resulted in an optimum solution, it does not always produce this result. Therefore, it is necessary to evaluate the VAM allocation by one of the solution techniques, such as the stepping-stone method. If the VAM allocation is found not to be optimum, the indicated improvement is made in the allocation. The evaluation procedure continues for as many iterations as necessary to reach an optimum solution.

Distribution Model Variations

While most distribution models are as illustrated, some deviate from this general form of the model. Some of the variations are as follows:

Excluded Cells. In some problems, allocations to certain cells must be zero, that is, these cells must be excluded from the solution. An example is an assignment problem in which certain machines or machine categories cannot be used to make some of the products being considered. In this circumstance, the costs for the excluded cells are set at infinity (∞). Proceed with the solution as under normal circumstances.

TABLE 6-21

Fifth VAM Assignment Made
VAM Optimal Solution

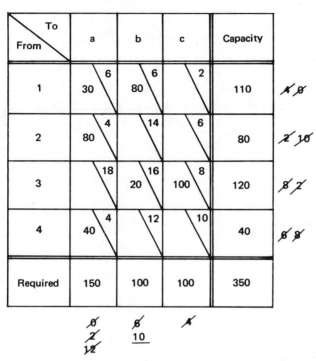

For computational purposes, "infinity" is viewed as a *very* large number and is not really infinite. Thus, in the evaluation process, $\infty + 10$ is considered greater than $\infty + 4$.

Unequal Supply and Demand.   Occasionally, the total amount available (supply) exceeds the demand requirement. To handle this situation, an artificial destination, or *slack column*, is established. The amount at the bottom of the column is the excess of supply over demand. If it makes no difference where the unrequired quantity is located, the costs for each cell in the slack column will be zero. On the other hand, if it is preferred that the unneeded supply be located at a particular point of origin, a cost entry in the appropriate cell or cells would indicate this preference or set of preferences. An optimum solution of a distribution model matrix, where the total available supply exceeds the demand requirements, is illustrated in Table 6-22. In this illustration zero costs are indicated in all cells in the slack column. To evaluate unoccupied cells, follow the identical procedure used when the available amount equals the requirements. All unoccupied zero cost cells are evaluated the same way as any other unoccupied cell. In this case, source 3 would have 65 units of unused capacity.

TABLE 6-22

Optimal Solution Matrix —
Capacity Greater Than Requirements

To / From	a	b	c	Slack	Capacity
1	6 / 10	6 / 100	2 / 40	0 /	150
2	4 / 90	14 /	6 /	0 /	90
3	18 /	16 /	8 / 60	0 / 65	125
4	4 / 50	12 /	10 /	0 /	50
Required	150	100	100	65	415

An excess of demand at the destinations over the available supply is also possible. To account for this excess demand, establish an artificial source or a slack row in the same way. This row signifies that some of the demand cannot be satisfied by the existing sources. This row can also be used to represent the subcontracting of some of the requirements to an outside source.

In certain situations, determination of the costs used to minimize the objective function of the total cost may require consideration of costs other than shipping costs, such as the manufacturing costs, for each origin. Thus, the costs in each cell will be the manufacturing costs of the origins plus the appropriate costs applicable to each shipping route.

Frequently, operations beyond a particular level can be especially expensive. Under these circumstances, regular operations and extraordinary operations (e.g., overtime costs) are shown as separate sources which have identical shipping costs, but different operations costs resulting from the level of operations.

Maximizing Models. Certain problems may require maximizing the objective function instead of minimizing it. Recall the development of such an objective function in the graphical and simplex linear programming model illustrations. This same type objective function can also be developed for distribution models. This type function does not alter the computational procedure in any way.

In the stepping-stone method, the objective is to make moves into cells which result in the greatest increase for an unoccupied cell instead of the greatest decrease. When the VAM technique is utilized to achieve a solution to maximize the objective function, calculate the differences between the two highest contribution cells in each row and column, then make the allocation into the highest contribution cell in the selected row or column.

Other Programming Models

Linear programming models are the most frequently utilized mathematical programming models; however, other types of programming models are available to fit specialized situations. Nonlinear models are one type of model needed to represent those relationships which are not linear; i.e., cannot be expressed as a linear equation. However, in many situations where linear programming is used, the relationships involved are not truly linear; but the assumption of linearity is sufficiently accurate to make linear programming feasible. The theory relating to nonlinear models, in which at least one restriction is nonlinear or the payoff function is nonlinear, is extremely complicated and will not be considered. It is merely sufficient to recognize the availability of such models.

Certain types of problems require the operations manager to make sequences of related decisions. Such problems can often be solved by dynamic programming, a form of mathematical programming. In the dynamic programming model, an optimum solution is reached by means of a series of interim optimum solutions. The result of a single decision within the sequence frequently can be related to the present outcome; at the same time, it can be related to the conditions surrounding the following decisions in the sequence. Dynamic programming is an integrated process. Optimum decisions unite with existing states at the decision point to arrive at an optimum solution for subsequent conditions. The optimum solution at each individual decision point (not all the prior states) is focused to achieve a new optimum solution. The decision maker using the dynamic programming model is able to achieve an initial solution without considering the entire chain of future decisions. Once the initial decision has been made, it then becomes possible to arrive at a subsequent solution in the chain.

The computational procedure in the dynamic programming model can become rather complex. Dynamic programming models require utilization of computing equipment for most realistic problems. There are various forms of dynamic programming models; they may involve many combinations of characteristics such as nonlinear relationships and uncertain conditions which may require the application of probabilities.

Examples of problems requiring sequential decision making, of the nature described, and which fit into the dynamic programming model format follow.[3]

1. A production scheduling problem.
2. An equipment purchase problem.

[3]Richard Bellman, "Some Applications of the Theory of Dynamic Programming — A Review," *Journal of the Operations Research Society of America* (August, 1954), pp. 275–288.

3. An employment stabilization problem.
4. An optimal inventory problem.
5. An engineering control problem.
6. A reinvestment of earnings problem.
7. Production bottleneck problems.
8. Learning and testing theory.

The various types of mathematical programming models discussed in this chapter have broad application potential. The operations management problems to which they apply are quite diverse, and as progress is made in the use of mathematical programming it is probable that the number of problem areas will probably expand. The illustrations of certain mathematical programming techniques were highly oversimplified; most of the actual problems facing the operations manager would be more complex. Therefore, computers are necessary to accomplish solutions to most practical programming models.

SUMMARY

The role of quantitative models in operations management, and the general nature of the quantitative approach is recognized. While there is a wide variety of useful quantitative techniques, there are certain models which appear to have broad applicability. They may be valuable to decision making in several problem areas.

A number of these models are classified under the mathematical programming category. These models are useful primarily to solve allocation and mixture problems. The operations manager is responsible for many decisions of this variety; therefore, an examination of some types of programming models is necessary. Of primary concern are those models classified as linear in character.

A number of linear programming solution techniques are examined. The graphical method is first. This approach is feasible in very simple problems having only two variables. Its primary value is its clear illustration of the general form of the linear programming model and the solution technique. The graphical technique can be applied either to problems which maximize the objective function or to those which minimize the objective function.

The simplex method offers wider application because it can be used for any number of variables. It is an algebraic technique which enables the achievement of an optimum solution by an iterative process.

Distribution models are a better method for solving some types of linear programming problems. The simplex method is more generally applicable; however, the distribution model is less cumbersome for those problems which can be solved by either method. The northwest corner method and the Vogel Approximation Method of achieving initial solutions are examined. The stepping-stone method of evaluating a distribution model is illustrated as an example of solution techniques available. Some distribution model variations encountered are also viewed.

Not all mathematical programming models are of the linear programming type. Certain other types are acknowledged; namely, nonlinear models and dynamic programming models. Their potential applications are briefly described. The next chapter illustrates other quantitative models which also apply to problem areas of operations management.

QUESTIONS FOR DISCUSSION AND ANALYSIS

1. What is the general form of all quantitative models?
2. To what types of problems do the various kinds of mathematical programming techniques apply?
3. Show and explain the general statement of linear programming models.
4. Discuss the value of the graphical solution technique of linear programming problems. What are its limitations?
5. Define isocontribution and isocost lines as used in the graphical linear programming technique. What determines the slope of these lines?
6. What is the polygon of technical feasibility?
7. What is the nature of the simplex method of linear programming?
8. Describe the types of problems for which the distribution models are most useful.

PROBLEMS

1. The Bonbon Candy Co. makes two types of candy weekly, Fudgies and Dewdrops. Each candy uses three ingredients: sugar, chocolate, and nuts; however, the quantities available are limited. The other ingredients used do not limit the output. The amounts of these three ingredients available per week are:

Sugar	20,000 lbs.
Chocolate	28,000 lbs.
Nuts	24,000 lbs.

Both candies require the following ingredients per dozen:

	Sugar	Chocolate	Nuts
Fudgies	5 lbs.	4 lbs.	2 lbs.
Dewdrops	4 lbs.	7 lbs.	8 lbs.

Fudgies contribute $4 per dozen to profit and overhead, and Dewdrops contribute $5 per dozen.

Use the graphical technique of linear programming to determine the amounts (in dozens) of each candy the company should produce weekly to maximize the contribution.

2. The Nordic Shops, Inc., manufacture three types of high quality furniture: harvest tables, captain's chests, and deacon's benches. The tables can be

made by two different processes. The company can sell all the furniture of these types it can produce. Three classes of woodworking equipment are used to manufacture these items. The following table shows: the amount of time, in minutes per piece, required on each of the three classes of machines; and the total number of minutes available on these machines per week. The profit per unit realized from each item is also shown.

	Tables Method 1	Tables Method 2	Chests	Benches	Total Available
Drills	0	3	6	6	4,800 minutes
Lathes	6	18	0	12	5,400 minutes
Routers	15	0	30	3	19,200 minutes
Profit	$115	$70	$244	$67	

Determine the product mix which will maximize profits for the Nordic Shops.

3. The Rocket Delivery Service has contracted to deliver a total of 109,000 gallons of fuel to four lunar exploration sites weekly. These four sites, designated as Alpha, Beta, Gamma, and Delta, have the following weekly requirements:

Alpha	17,000 gallons
Beta	30,000 gallons
Gamma	38,000 gallons
Delta	24,000 gallons

These shipments can be made from three launching pads, Sigma, Tau, and Upsilon, with the following launching capacities:

Sigma	48,000 gallons
Tau	40,000 gallons
Upsilon	21,000 gallons

Determine the optimum shipping schedule for this company which will minimize the total delivery cost. The individual delivery costs are indicated in dollars per gallon:

From	To			
	Alpha	Beta	Gamma	Delta
Sigma	28	64	43	34
Tau	50	37	75	48
Upsilon	41	90	68	56

All costs, dollars per gallon

4. The Etude Manufacturing Co. supplies its single product to three warehouses from four plants. The weekly unit capacities of the plants, the requirements of the warehouses, and the appropriate transportation costs, are displayed in the following table, in cents per unit:

Plant	Warehouse			
	Accordion, New York	Bassoon, Illinois	Clarinet, Missouri	Capacity
Viola, Ark.	1	6	4	400
Woodwind, N.D.	4	10	6	600
Xylophone, Fla.	5	3	8	200
Yodel, Maine	7	2	5	800
Zither, Texas	3	5	7	500
Requirements	600	700	900	

(a) Determine the minimum cost weekly production schedule for these factories.

(b) What is the cost per week under this schedule?

SELECTED ADDITIONAL READINGS

Bellman, Richard, and Stuart Dreyfus. *Applied Dynamic Programming.* Princeton: Princeton University Press, 1962.

Bowman, Edward H., and Robert B. Fetter. *Analysis for Production and Operations Management,* 3d ed. Homewood, Illinois: Richard D. Irwin, Inc., 1967. Chapters 3 and 4.

Charnes, A., and W. W. Cooper. *Management Models and Industrial Applications of Linear Programming.* 2 vols. New York: John Wiley & Sons, Inc., 1961.

Chung, An-min. *Linear Programming.* Columbus: Charles E. Merrill Books, Inc., 1963.

Dorfman, Robert. "Mathematical, or 'Linear' Programming: A Non-mathematical Exposition." *The American Economic Review,* Vol. XLIII, No. 5 (December, 1953), pp. 797–825.

Eisemann, Kurt, and William M. Young. "Study of a Textile Mill with the Aid of Linear Programming." *Management Technology* (January, 1960), pp. 52–63.

Metzger, Robert W. *Elementary Mathematical Programming.* New York: John Wiley & Sons, Inc., 1958.

7 | # Quantitative Models (Continued)

Many specific operations problems cannot be fitted into the various types of programming models, nor into any algorithmic model. One reason is the complexity of many operations management problems arising from the large number of variables. In addition, the restrictions involved in the interrelationships which exist also limit the usable models. Under these circumstances, the computational procedures required could be so enormous that it would not be practical, either from a time or cost standpoint, to attempt an optimum solution. Additionally, the variables differ extensively with respect to their linearity or nonlinearity. Sometimes, no known algorithmic technique is available for solving such a model.

In certain circumstances, a decision may require investigation of a variety of different courses of action. The best procedure under these circumstances is to experiment with the alternative courses of action, to attempt to determine the consequences of each action, before arriving at a final decision. However, experimenting with operations systems cannot be fitted into the pattern of the controlled experiment, as used in laboratory procedures of the physical sciences. Such experiments necessitate long interruptions in the existing system which are not feasible. System changes of an experimental nature can be highly expensive, with the resultant outcome by no means certain. Consequently, many possible improvements which could result in substantial savings are never made.

SIMULATION

Fortunately, operations managers now have available to them a technique which has been useful in overcoming some of the aforementioned problems. This technique, called simulation, enables the manager to avoid a trial and error approach, but at the same time to investigate the effects of alternate courses before having to make a final decision.

Simulation Defined

Simulation,

> . . . has the most useful property of permitting the researcher and management to experiment with and test policy, procedure and organization changes in much the same way the aeronautical engineer tests his design in the laboratory or in the wind tunnel. Thus we might think of System Simulation as a sort of 'Management Wind Tunnel' which is used

to pretest many suggested changes and eliminate much needless 'experimentation' with the 'real' people, machines, and facilities.[1]

It is possible to conclude that simulation is a new technique because of its recent popularity in management circles. Actually, the basic mechanics used in simulation have been in use for a considerable period of time. Simulation is, in a general way, an evolutionary attempt to put systems and procedures, and in fact, operations management, on a sounder analytical foundation. It might be paraphrased as an attempt to put some scientific method into the "looking" part of the old adage, "Look before you leap."

When a company contemplates a change in an operating system, there will be a cost associated with eliminating the existing system, as well as with installing and operating the new one. Management will want some assurance that the change will result in a savings of operating cost which will justify the installation of the new plan. If some way could be found to operate the proposed plan on a small, economical scale, it might be possible to work out the bugs and to assess its value without exposure to the risk of a major investment. This is essentially what has been done for some time by the use of pilot plants or pilot runs. A retail store may try a new sales check procedure in a branch store; a college may test a new registration procedure using a single class of students, e.g., graduate students only; or a manufacturing concern may build a small scale plant to produce a newly developed product. These experiments are virtually identical to full operation except in scale. The investment is limited until management is sure the action is desirable.

Monte Carlo Simulation

A different form of simulation, referred to as Monte Carlo Simulation, is currently being used to solve certain management problems. *Monte Carlo Simulation* may be defined as, ". . .the technique of setting up a stochastic model of a real situation and then performing sampling experiments upon the model."[2] This type of simulation is used to study the output of systems which have many interacting variables of a *stochastic* nature (are not constant, but are affected by conditions such as time, resulting in a probability distribution).

Thus, the proposed system is approximated by something quite different in nature, which at the same time observes identical rules of behavior as the system under study. In Monte Carlo Simulation, systems can be a computer program; set up on a differential analyzer; or expressed as a set of mathematical equations, as a probability analysis, or as a set of flow charts. It becomes possible then to test the major system by maneuvering the values, volumes, or other factors going into the experimental system (which acts like the real system), and observe the results.

[1]D. G. Malcolm, "Forward," *Report of System Simulation Symposium*, 8th National Convention of the A.I.I.E. (New York: American Institute of Industrial Engineers, Inc., 1957), p. v.

[2]John Harling, "Simulation Techniques in Operations Research — A Review," *Operations Research*, Vol. VI, No. 3 (May–June, 1958), pp. 307–319.

A flow chart, described in Chapter 5, is actually a simulation of a system. It is a symbolic representation of a system of actions performed to achieve some given purpose. In planning a system change, a manager need not juggle people, or any other system element in the attempt to improve the system; he simply juggles the flow chart symbols.

Introduction of mathematical analysis, statistics, and computers to simulation does not change its basic nature; it merely adds some useful new tools.

Product Development Simulation Example

To acquire a fuller understanding of the simulation technique, consider the following examples where simulation may be applied as a decision-making tool. In the first illustration, the Harlow Company has $300,000 available to invest in a research and development program. They wish to find some new products to introduce into the already existing product line. Before proceeding with this investment, the company feels it must first examine the probabilities of the success of such a program. Investigation of pertinent conditions yields the following information:

a. It will cost about $100,000 to get a product through the development stage and onto the market.
b. A successful product will provide an average net profit, after taxes, of $1,000,000.
c. A failure of the product on the market will result in a loss of the total $100,000 investment.
d. About one out of every four products developed will be successful.

The Harlow management decide to simulate the histories of a number of research projects, making use of the above information. A flow chart is designed for a simulation which will enable them to evaluate, by flipping a coin, the probability of achieving their goal. When a net profit of $2,000,000 is achieved through this program, the Harlow Company will sell out to one of the groups which has currently made offers. On the other hand, if the entire $300,000 is lost, they will continue the present operations. The flow chart appears in Figure 7-1.

The flow chart as shown indicates the procedure for simulating the desired histories by using a coin. This is a highly simplified and idealized example of a problem which could be subjected to simulation. Management would seldom want to make an important decision involving the expenditure of $300,000 merely by the flipping of a coin. However, this example illustrates a typical class of problems to which the simulation technique might be applied. It is conceivable that a simulation procedure as described could be used, if, in fact, all of the conditions listed were exactly as set forth. Naturally, a considerable number of simulated histories would be required before reaching a point where this information was useful as a basis for making a decision. These simulated histories are only samples, and in no way can they be used to represent exactly

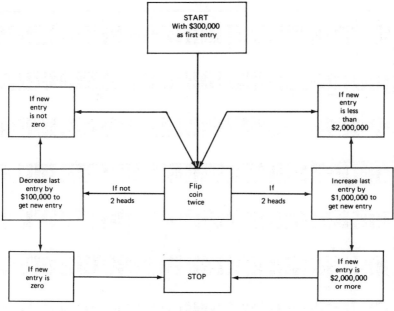

FIGURE 7-1

Flow Chart of Harlow Company Simulation

what would happen in the future. However, if the model is properly developed, and the simulation carried out correctly, using a sufficient sample size, a predictable accuracy could be attributed to the results.

Schedule Simulation Example

Another class of problems to which simulation techniques are applicable is illustrated by the following example: Doctor Molar, a dentist, has a series of appointments scheduled for a particular morning. That afternoon he has arranged to speak at a professional conference. In order to arrive at the meeting on time, it is necessary for him to leave the office no later than noon. He wishes to know what his chances are of being out of the office by this time. The use of simulation is a device which will enable him to predict with a predetermined degree of accuracy what his chances are. His appointment schedule for the morning in question is:

9:00 Mr. Gardener
9:15 Mr. Carpenter
9:30 Miss Universe
10:00 Mr. Shoemaker
10:20 Mr. Farmer
10:45 Mr. Teacher
11:10 Mr. Baker
11:35 Mr. Butcher

TABLE 7-1

Table of Random Numbers

Line	(1)	(2)	(3)	(4)	(5)	(6)	(7)	(8)	(9)	(10)	(11)	(12)	(13)	(14)
1	10480	15011	01536	02011	81647	91646	69179	14194	62590	36207	20969	99570	91291	90700
2	22368	46573	25595	85393	30995	89198	27982	53402	93965	34095	52666	19174	39615	99505
3	24130	48360	22527	97265	76393	64809	15179	24830	49340	32081	30680	19655	63348	58629
4	42167	93093	06243	61680	07856	16376	39440	53537	71341	57004	00849	74917	97758	16379
5	37570	39975	81837	16656	06121	91782	60468	81305	49684	60672	14110	06927	01263	54613
6	77921	06907	11008	42751	27756	53498	18602	70659	90655	15053	21916	81825	44394	42880
7	99562	72905	56420	69994	98872	31016	71194	18738	44013	48840	63213	21069	10634	12952
8	96301	91977	05463	07972	18876	20922	94595	56869	69014	60045	18425	84903	42508	32307
9	89579	14342	63661	10281	17453	18103	57740	84378	25331	12566	58678	44947	05585	56941
10	85475	36857	53342	53988	53060	59533	38867	62300	08158	17983	16439	11458	18593	64952
11	28918	69578	88231	33276	70997	79936	56865	05859	90106	31595	01547	85590	91610	78188
12	63553	40961	48235	03427	49626	69445	18663	72695	52180	20847	12234	90511	33703	90322
13	09429	93969	52636	92737	88974	33488	36320	17617	30015	08272	84115	27156	30613	74952
14	10365	61129	87529	85689	48237	52267	67689	93394	01511	26358	85104	20285	29975	89868
15	07119	97336	71048	08178	77233	13916	47564	81056	97735	85977	29372	74461	28551	90707
16	51085	12765	51821	51259	77452	16308	60756	92144	49442	53900	70960	63990	75601	40719
17	02368	21382	52404	60268	89368	19885	55322	44819	01188	65255	64835	44919	05944	55157
18	01011	54092	33362	94904	31273	04146	18594	29852	71585	85030	51132	01915	92747	64951
19	52162	53916	46369	58586	23216	14513	83149	98736	23495	64350	94738	17752	35156	35749
20	07056	97628	33787	09998	42698	06691	76988	13602	51851	46104	88916	19509	25625	58104
21	48663	91245	85828	14346	09172	30168	90229	04734	59193	22178	30421	61666	99904	32812
22	54164	58492	22421	74103	47070	25306	76468	26384	58151	06646	21524	15227	96909	44592
23	32639	32363	05597	24200	13363	38005	94342	28728	35806	06912	17012	64161	18296	22851
24	29334	27001	87637	87308	58731	00256	45834	15398	46557	41135	10367	07684	36188	18510
25	02488	33062	28834	07351	19731	92420	60952	61280	50001	67658	32586	86679	50720	94953
26	81525	72295	04839	96423	24878	82651	66566	14778	76797	14780	13300	87074	79666	95725
27	29676	20591	68086	26432	46901	20849	89768	81536	86645	12659	92259	57102	80428	25280
28	00742	57392	39064	66432	84673	40027	32832	61362	98947	96067	64760	64584	96096	98253
29	05366	04213	25669	26422	44407	44048	37937	63904	45766	66134	75470	66520	34693	90449
30	91921	26418	64117	94305	26766	25940	39972	22209	71500	64568	91402	42416	07844	69618
31	00582	04711	87917	77341	42206	35126	74087	99547	81817	42607	43808	76655	62028	76630
32	00725	69884	62797	56170	86324	88072	76222	36086	84637	93161	76038	65855	77919	88006
33	69011	65795	95876	55293	18988	27354	26575	08625	40801	59920	29841	80150	12777	48501
34	25976	57948	29888	88604	67917	48708	18912	82271	65424	69774	33611	54262	85963	03547
35	09763	83473	73577	12908	30883	18317	28290	35797	05998	41688	34952	37888	38917	88050
36	91567	42595	27958	30134	04024	86385	29880	99730	55536	84855	29080	09250	79656	73211
37	17955	56349	90999	49127	20044	59931	06115	20542	18059	02008	73708	83517	36103	42791
38	46503	18584	18845	49618	02304	51038	20655	58727	28168	15475	56942	53389	20562	87338
39	92157	89634	94824	78171	84610	82834	09922	25417	44137	48413	25555	21246	35509	20468
40	14577	62765	35605	81263	39667	47358	56873	56307	61607	49518	89606	20103	77490	18062
41	98427	07523	33362	64270	01638	92477	66969	98420	04880	45585	46565	04102	46880	45709
42	34914	63976	88720	82765	34476	17032	87589	40836	32427	70002	70663	88863	77775	69348
43	70060	28277	39475	46473	23219	53416	94970	25832	69975	94884	19661	72828	00102	66794
44	53976	54914	06990	67245	68350	82948	11398	42878	80287	88267	47363	46634	06541	97809
45	76072	29515	40980	07391	58745	25774	22987	80059	39911	96189	41151	14222	60697	59583
46	90725	52210	83974	29992	65831	38857	50490	83765	55657	14361	31720	57375	56228	41546
47	64364	67412	33339	31926	14883	24413	59744	92351	97473	89286	35931	04110	23726	51900
48	08962	00358	31662	25388	61642	34072	81249	35648	56891	69352	48373	45578	78547	81788
49	95012	68379	93526	70765	10592	04542	76463	54328	02349	17247	28865	14777	62730	92277
50	15664	10493	20492	38391	91132	21999	59516	81652	27195	48223	46751	22923	32261	85653

Source: Interstate Commerce Commission, Bureau of Transport Economics and Statistics, *Table of 105,000 Random Digits*, Statement No. 4914, File No. 261-A-1 (Washington, D.C., May, 1949), p. 1.

Since he knows what must be done with each of these scheduled patients, Dr. Molar estimates the time necessary for each of these appointments will be:

Mr. Gardener	15 minutes
Mr. Carpenter	15 minutes
Miss Universe	30 minutes
Mr. Shoemaker	15 minutes
Mr. Farmer	20 minutes
Mr. Teacher	25 minutes
Mr. Baker	20 minutes
Mr. Butcher	20 minutes

Examination of his past records enables the doctor to estimate that, for any given appointment, a patient will arrive for his appointment with the following probabilities:

10% of the time a patient will arrive 20 minutes early.
20% of the time a patient will arrive 10 minutes early.
50% of the time a patient will arrive exactly on time.
10% of the time a patient will arrive 10 minutes late.
10% of the time a patient will not show up at all.

Further examination of the records indicates that it can be anticipated the following distribution will apply with respect to the actual time taken for any of the appointments:

10% of the time, 80% of the allotted time will be utilized.
20% of the time, 90% of the allotted time will be utilized.
20% of the time, 100% of the allotted time will be utilized.
20% of the time, 110% of the allotted time will be utilized.
20% of the time, 120% of the allotted time will be utilized.
10% of the time, 130% of the allotted time will be utilized.

In the first example, a coin was used to generate the necessary random data for the problem at hand. This problem will use a different form of random generating device, known as random numbers. For pencil and paper simulation, random numbers are available on tables. These tables are developed by a deterministic process (a computer program); therefore, they may not be truly random. However, they are sufficiently close to purely random numbers to serve the purpose at hand. The digits appearing on a random number table are sequences chosen independently from the ten decimal digits, 0 through 9, wherein each digit is equally probable. Thus, assuming any series of these digits to be decimals, and placing the decimal point to the left of the first digit, round off to the number of decimal places required. Sequences can be developed from the random digits to represent any proportion desired. Part of a random number table is reproduced in Table 7-1.

There is no specific rule for using a random number table. Any point on the table can be used as a starting point to select the digits to be used. One commonly used procedure is to simply pick a point at random, select the required number of digits for the initial occurrence being simulated, and then proceed down the table to the next set of digits, and again select the required number. This process can be followed until all of the random numbers needed have been acquired.

The digits on a random number table may be used in pencil and paper computations, and also as input into computers for running simulations. Also available are so-called random number generator sub-routines for use in computers. These sub-routines can be incorporated into the simulation program. They appear to be much more efficient than using previously generated digits.

In this example consider the arrival data, and relate this to the ten decimal digits which will appear on the random number table with equal probability. Then assign the digit 1 to represent the patients who appear 20 minutes early; the digits 2 and 3 for 10 minutes early; 4, 5, 6, 7, and 8 for on time; 9 for 10 minutes late; and 0 for those who do not show at all. In a similar fashion, assign random number digits to the estimated appointment duration data. This latter distribution is shown in Table 7-2, along with the arrival time data just developed.

TABLE 7-2

Arrival Time and Appointment Duration
Random Number Distribution

Arrival Time Distribution

Time	20 mins. Early	10 mins. Early	On-Time	10 mins. Late	Not Show
Percentage of Occurrence	10	20	50	10	10
Random Numbers	1	2-3	4-8	9	0

Appointment Duration Distribution

Duration	80%	90%	100%	110%	120%	130%
Percentage of Occurrence	10	20	20	20	20	10
Random Number	1	2-3	4-5	6-7	8-9	0

With this scheme established, it is now possible, by reference to the random number table, Table 7-1, to simulate potential histories of Dr. Molar's appointment schedule. Table 7-3 shows one such simulated history, indicating waiting time for each patient, as well as idle time experienced by Dr. Molar.

On the basis of this single simulation, Dr. Molar could leave his office by noon; in fact, at 11:57. However, this would not necesarily be the actual circumstance in which Dr. Molar would find himself. Again, this is only one sample, and is not sufficient to predict the actual results. A larger sample of simulated histories is necessary to determine the probability that Dr. Molar could leave his office by the desired time.

TABLE 7-3

Simulation of Appointment Schedule

Scheduled Time	R.N.	Arrival Time	Service Begun	R.N.	Service Length min.	Service Ended	Waiting Time	Idle Time min.
9:00	7	9:00	9:00	0	19.5	9:19.5	0	
9:15	5	9:15	9:19.5	8	18	9:37.5	4.5	
9:30	3	9:20	9:37.5	1	24	10:01.5	17.5	
10:00	3	9:50	10:01.5	5	15	10:16.5	11.5	
10:20	1	10:00	10:16.5	6	22	10:38.5	16.5	
10:45	1	10:25	10:38.5	1	20	10:58.5	13.5	
11:10	2	11:00	11:00	7	22	11:22	0	1.5
11:35	5	11:35	11:35	6	22	11:57	0	13.0

Total Waiting Time:	63.5 min.
Total Idle Time:	14.5 min.
Average Waiting Time/Patient:	7.94 min.

Random Arrival and Servicing Simulation Example

For a final example of the simulation technique, consider an outpatient clinic which has patients arriving at random from 8:00 a.m. up to 4:00 p.m. Examination of past records indicates that the arrivals may vary from four to eight patients during any given hour the clinic is open. Available information also indicates that processing of the patients arriving takes from 7 to 13 minutes per patient, also on a random basis. Table 7-4 summarizes the arrival and service probability data, and indicates the appropriate random number scheme which

TABLE 7-4

Arrival and Servicing Time Random Number Distribution

Arrival Time Distribution					
Number of Arrivals	4	5	6	7	8
Probability	.10	.25	.30	.25	.10
Cumulative Probability	.10	.35	.65	.90	1.00
R.N.	01–10	11–35	36–65	66–90	91–00

Servicing Time Distribution							
Length of Service	7	8	9	10	11	12	13
Probability	.05	.10	.20	.30	.20	.10	.05
Cumulative Probability	.05	.15	.35	.65	.85	.95	1.00
R.N.	01–05	06–15	16–35	36–65	66–85	86–95	96–00

can be used to simulate this particular system. What is desired is to determine whether all the patients arriving can be processed during the hours the reception desk is open, or whether it is necessary to have additional service facilities available. The reception desk will remain open beyond the normal 4:00 p.m. closing time, to complete the processing of all patients who arrive during the 8:00 a.m. to 4:00 p.m. period each day.

The same data found in Table 7-4 can also be shown in a graphic form. Figure 7-2 is a cumulative frequency distribution of the servicing time data found in this table. The relationship of the probability, and hence the random number, to the value of the service time is made quite clear by this device.

The procedure for carrying out this simulation is to first select a random number which represents the number of patients arriving during the first hour of operation from 8:00 to 9:00 a.m. If the random number selected is 23, this would represent the arrival of five patients during that hour. Now five random numbers must be selected to represent the servicing time. These are related to the data in Table 7-4. These five random numbers represent the total servicing time required for this hour. The resulting random numbers and service times are summarized in Table 7-5. Thus, 47 minutes would be required to service the patients arriving between 8:00 and 9:00 a.m.

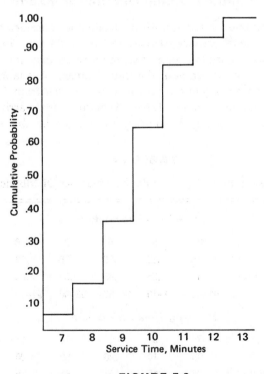

FIGURE 7-2

Service Time Cumulative Frequency Distribution

TABLE 7-5

Simulation of Service Time for First Hour

R.N. Selected	21	13	71	33	45
Service Time (min.)	9	8	11	9	10

Total Service Time: 47 minutes

If the same procedure represents that in the second hour eight patients arrive, the resulting computations of the service time are shown in Table 7-6. In this instance, the service time would be 73 minutes and, consequently, the receptionist would be handling these patients beyond 10:00 a.m. The patients who arrived between 10:00 and 11:00 a.m. would have to wait until the completion of the service for all previously arrived patients.

TABLE 7-6

Simulation of Service Time for Second Hour

R.N. Selected	15	45	04	65	21	37	24	60
Service Time (min.)	8	10	7	10	9	10	9	10

Total Service Time: 73 minutes

Table 7-7 summarizes the simulated arrivals and total servicing time for one day's operation of this system. Further reference to Table 7-7 indicates that the total waiting time of patients is 35 minutes, and that the receptionist's idle time is a total of 44 minutes. In this particular simulated day, the processing

TABLE 7-7

Summary of Results of Outpatient Clinic Simulation

Hour	Patients Arriving	Total Service Time Min.	Waiting Time Min.	Idle Time Min.
8– 9	5	47	0	13
9–10	8	73	13	
10–11	6	55	8	
11–12	7	63	11	
12– 1	5	48	0	1
1– 2	5	53	0	7
2– 3	4	37	0	23
3– 4	7	64	4	

Total Waiting Time: 36 minutes
Total Idle Time: 44 minutes

continues for 4 minutes beyond the normal 4:00 p.m. closing time. This is the result of the total simulated service time of 64 minutes required during the last hour of operations.

As can be seen from the examples, simulation is a technique which is applicable to a variety of types of problems in the area of operations management. The process of simulation enables the manager to observe the operations of a particular system in response to varying conditions, in an attempt to determine what sort of activity might be expected.

The value of the simulated results is determined very extensively by the accuracy of the past data used for the simulation procedure. To achieve reliable simulation results, future conditions must be essentially the same as the past conditions from which the data were generated.

Most actual problems which will be subjected to simulation are extremely complex. Thus, for effective and economic results, the simulation problem must be handled by means of a computer. Without the use of a computer program, most simulation problems would be impossible to solve because of the tremendous amount of computation required. This volume of computation implies that the cost of a simulation decision may be high. However, proper use of simulation techniques presents operations managers with an opportunity to investigate many problems. Simulation will lead to good decisions to these problems, which otherwise might be extremely difficult, if not impossible, to solve.

Determination of Sample Size

In referring to the examples, it has been stated that simulation is a sampling process, and consequently, subject to the limitations of sampling. Among the problems encountered is the determination of the proper sample size. Sample size is important because the confidence which can be achieved in the results of a given simulation is determined by the use of a proper sample size. Primarily, this is a matter of applying the statistical rules which relate to the establishment of confidence intervals.[3]

A general rule which has been stated for establishing the confidence in a simulation study is that its accuracy increases directly with the increase in the square root of the number of simulated histories. In addition, it is considered to be good practice to not discontinue a simulation study as long as the mean of the simulated data is significantly different from that which is empirically determined.[4]

To illustrate this latter point: if the results in the Harlow Company example, after 100 trials, specified the products developed were successful 50% of the time, more sample trials would be indicated. The coin flipping would not be expected to deviate so far from the expected results of one success in four.

---

[3]The reader is referred to any general statistics book such as those listed in the bibliography for a full discussion of confidence intervals.

[4]Edward H. Bowman and Robert B. Fetter, *Analysis for Production and Operations Management* (3d ed.; Homewood, Illinois: Richard D. Irwin, Inc., 1967), p. 425.

Areas of Simulation Application

Reference will be made to simulation as it applies to the specific problem areas of operations management. In the area of process planning, some use of simulation has been made in the actual design and control of a proposed new processing method. Simulation is also used in the determination of the relative location of processing facilities and, on occasion, for the physical design of the total processing facility.

The evaluation of the effects of different forecasts on the operations system is another area in which simulation can be used. For example, management could evaluate what might happen to sales as a result of different levels of expenditures for sales promotion. Along with this would come an evaluation of the effects of the resultant forecasts on the operations system of the enterprise.

Simulation has had a great deal of value in analyzing certain inventory related problems. An entire inventory system can be simulated to determine the optimum level of inventory to carry in order to satisfy some measure of effectiveness such as lowest cost or improved customer service.

Simulation has been valuable in production-distribution-inventory systems, particularly those of large scale. One technique, industrial dynamics, has been successfully used for evaluating these systems. Simulation has also been applied to numerous types of scheduling problems of varying magnitude. Of interest here are applications which have simulated large job shop operations, and those which have been used to determine overall schedule decision rules, such as priority dispatching rules.

This list represents only a sample of the practical applications of simulation to operations management problems. While the applications are only briefly mentioned, they are evidence of the large number of potential areas of use.

WAITING-LINE THEORY

A variety of situations encountered almost daily can be classified as waiting-line situations. There are also many operations management problems which fit into this classification. Generally, a *waiting-line* or queuing problem is one where units of some sort arrive at an entrance point into the system, are processed in some way within the system, and then depart from the system. If the entrances, or processing, are not specifically scheduled, but are random in nature, a waiting line or queue can develop. The system will then become congested. If either the entrances (arrivals) or the processing (servicing) can be expressed as a probability distribution, the system can be represented by means of a waiting-line model.

Specific examples of waiting-line problems are: selling tickets in a booth; collecting tolls on a bridge; servicing bank customers by a teller; the check-out procedure in a supermarket; a maintenance system where machines require the services of repairmen; and even certain inventory problems concerned with the stocking of adequate, but not excessive, numbers of items. Examples of waiting-line situations and the conditions attendant to them are listed in Table 7-8.

TABLE 7-8

Examples of Typical Waiting-Line Situations

Description	Units to be Serviced	Service Performed	Servicing Facility	Waiting-Line Discipline
Toll Booth	Cars	Collect Tolls	Booth and Collector	First-come, First-serve
Market Check-out Stand	Customers with Purchases	Ring up, Collect, and Wrap	Clerk, Cash Register, and Wrappings	First-come, First-serve
Medical Clinic	Patients	Medical Treatment	Receptionist, Nurse, Doctor, Equipment	Appointment or First-come, First-serve
Beauty Shop	Women	Hair Dressing	Beauty Operator and Equipment	Priority by Appointment
Forms and Typist	Form	Type Form	Typist and Typewriter	First-come, First-serve or Some priority
Telephone Switchboard	Calls	Make Connection	Operator and Switchboard	Random
Bus Terminal	Buses	Arriving and Departing	Loading Area, Dispatcher, Driver	Schedule

It is possible to classify waiting lines in various ways. The nature of a specific waiting-line situation is determined by four essential factors. To characterize a waiting line and to establish a model, these factors must be known. They are the distribution of the time intervals between arrivals; the distribution of the servicing time; the number of servers or channels in the system; and the waiting-line discipline, or priority system, which determines the sequence in which the arrivals are processed. A further factor of classification of waiting lines is concerned with whether the queue forms from a finite or an infinite source. A *finite source* indicates the units requiring service are limited to a specific number. An *infinite source* implies that, theoretically at least, the waiting-line source is unlimited. Often in practice when the source is a very large finite number, it is assumed to be infinite. The number of possible variations of waiting lines can be very large, and many of them become quite complex.

Phases

One widely used method of classifying waiting lines is according to the number of phases or sequential servicing stations in the system. A *single-phase case* is where the arrivals pass through only one station in order to complete the required service. From the examples already cited, the toll booth, the theater ticket window, and the market check-out stand exemplify such a condition.

A *multiple-phase or multiple-station case* involves the situation where the units to be served pass through a series of stations in sequence. One example of this case is an assembly line, where units being produced are required to pass through a series of assembly operations, each one a service station. A second example illustrating the multiple-station waiting line is found in the typical registration procedure experienced by college students each semester. They must go through a number of stations: program approval, pick up of class cards, fee payment, parking permit, and so forth.

Channels

Waiting lines can also be classified according to the number of channels, or servers, available to the units in the queue. The channels or servers may be classified either as single or multiple, the latter meaning any number greater than one. If the system is a *single-channel* waiting line, the units arriving and forming the queue have only one server available to them. A small market where there is only one check-out stand, or a physician treating patients in his office, is a typical example.

A large market with more than one checker available to the customers, or a medical clinic with more than a single doctor to treat the patients, is an example of the *multiple-channel* waiting-line case. The large market situation is a multiple waiting-line condition with multiple channels; the clinic case is a single waiting line with multiple servers, if the waiting-line priority was first-come, first-serve. Under the former condition of multiple line, multiple channel, it is possible to have a restriction against line switching. Typically, in these cases, however, the units are free to switch from one line to another. Who hasn't stood in a line at the teller's window at the bank only to find that the person in front of you has a very complicated transaction, but the line next to you is moving along rapidly? You may then move into the fast-moving line in hopes of being served faster (not always successfully, unfortunately). From a mathematical treatment viewpoint, the case of the multiple-line, multiple-channel case without switching is really a number of one-line, single-channel cases.

When possible, it is advantageous to resort to a single line in the multiple-channel case. Some banks have recently adopted the practice of having their customers form a single waiting line, from which the first person in the line moves to the teller who becomes available. This assures an absolute-first-come, first-serve discipline, and eliminates the line-switching situation.

Since waiting-line problems can result in many variations, and can develop into a high degree of complexity, the models developed require a high degree of mathematical sophistication. In fact, there are quite a few problems which become so complex that it is impossible to arrive at any solution by means of a mathematical model. In these cases, simulation techniques have often been found to be useful for achieving solutions to these problems. The outpatient clinic example used earlier in this chapter to illustrate simulation is an example of the application of this technique to a waiting-line problem. It will be sufficient to examine only the single-phase case of waiting-line problems in detail.

Single Channel. Perhaps the simplest form of the waiting-line problem, which can be solved through the use of relatively uncomplicated equations, is the *single-channel, single-phase case*. In this case, units arrive at the single-service facility, and require only one service activity before moving out of the system. The theatre ticket window example is typical. The schematic diagram in Figure 7-3 illustrates this case.

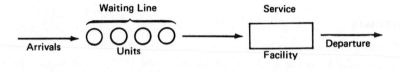

FIGURE 7-3

Single-Channel, Single-Phase Waiting-Line Case

CONDITIONS ASSUMED. To illustrate this case, certain conditions are assumed; in the absence of these conditions, a different model must be used. The first condition is that an infinite waiting-line source exists. Thus, it is assumed that the arrival rate follows the Poisson distribution. The *Poisson distribution* is a statistical distribution used to describe situations where the actual occurrence

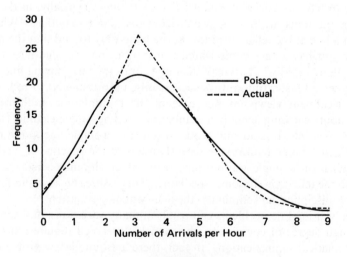

FIGURE 7-4

Poisson Distribution Compared with Actual Distribution

of an event is usually small, but the possibility of its occurrence is large. It is possible to show that there is also a distribution of the time intervals between arriving units which corresponds to the Poisson arrival rate distribution. This distribution of the time intervals is a *negative exponential distribution* where the arrival times are the reciprocal of the arrival rates, and indicates that the intervals of time are also random.[5] An example of a Poisson distribution is shown in Figure 7-4, and a negative exponential distribution is indicated in Figure 7-5.

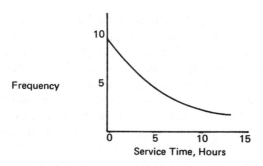

FIGURE 7-5

Example of Typical Negative Exponential Distribution

Many examples of the Poisson distribution in arrivals are found in actual day-to-day occurrences. This is true because the population, from which potential units to be served in a waiting-line situation arrive, is frequently large in number and individual units will act in an manner independent from other units. A typical example of a Poisson distribution is the toll booth case cited

---

[5]The reader is referred to any of the statistics references listed at the end of the chapter for a full explanation of the Poisson and the negative exponential distributions. The formula for the Poisson distribution is:

$$P(n) = e^{-\lambda}\ \frac{\lambda^n}{n!}$$

Where:

  n = any number which the random variable involved can assume; e.g., the number of units which can arrive per unit of time.
  ! = the factorial of the number; i.e., $n! = n(n-1)(n-2)\cdots(1)$.
  e = a constant, equal to 2.71828.
  λ = the mean number of occurrences, or arrivals.
  $P(n)$ = probability of n occurrences.
  Tables are available to determine the Poisson distribution for different values of n and λ.
  The negative exponential distribution corresponds very closely to the Poisson. It is the distribution of the time intervals between arrivals. The formula for the exponential distribution is:

$$f(t) = e^{-\lambda t}$$

Where:

  t = the time between arrivals.

in Table 7-8. The number of cars which arrive at toll booths on the Golden Gate Bridge on any given day is large, and the pattern of their arrival is certainly determined by various factors which affect the drivers of the cars. The same type of arrival distribution would apply to a large bank or a large market.

A second condition required is that the service time must conform to the negative exponential distribution. Consequently, the service rate has a corresponding Poisson distribution. Real-life situations, where service rates follow the Poisson distribution, are much less likely to occur than for arrival rates. This assumption, however, is necessary for the mathematical techniques to be described.

A third condition required for the solution technique to be described is that the waiting-line discipline must be on a first-come, first-serve basis. It is possible to have some other waiting-line situation where other priority rules apply. For example: the service discipline may be random; it may be on some scheduled basis; or it may be by some other specific discipline such as last-in, first-out.

A fourth and final condition is: the average service rate must be greater than the average arrival rate. When the arrival rate and the service rate are equal, the average waiting time and the average length of the waiting line become infinitely large. In most real-life circumstances, however, it would be virtually impossible for this infinite waiting line to occur for several reasons. In some cases, an arrival may leave the system rather than wait, or some action may be taken to reduce the size of the waiting line and the waiting period. Such action may consist of slowing down the arrival rate in some way, or speeding up the service rate. Thus, if the average arrival rate exceeds the average service rate, the system cannot achieve a steady state, because the waiting line will continuously grow larger.

EQUATIONS FOR SINGLE-CHANNEL CASE. Under these conditions the following equations apply to the waiting-line problem. General terminology uses the small Greek letter lambda (λ) to represent the average number of arrivals per unit of time, and the small Greek letter mu (μ) to represent the average number of services per unit of time. To express the intervals between arrivals and between services, the reciprocals of these two symbols are used: $\dfrac{1}{\lambda}$ = the average time between arrivals, and $\dfrac{1}{\mu}$ = the average time between services.

The probability that there are n units in the system:

$$P(n) = \left(1 - \frac{\lambda}{\mu}\right)\left(\frac{\lambda}{\mu}\right)^n \tag{1}$$

Since;

$$\left(\frac{\lambda}{\mu}\right)^0 = 1,$$

Then:

The probability that there are zero units in the system:

$$P(0) = 1 - \left(\frac{\lambda}{\mu}\right) \tag{2}$$

The probability that an arriving unit will have to wait:

$$P(w) = 1 - P(0) \tag{3}$$

The average number in the waiting line:

$$E(m) = \frac{\lambda^2}{\mu(\mu - \lambda)} \tag{4}$$

The average number of units in the system (the number in the waiting line plus the number being served):

$$E(n) = \frac{\lambda}{\mu - \lambda} = E(m) + \frac{\lambda}{\mu} \tag{5}$$

The average time spent waiting:

$$E(w) = \frac{\lambda}{\mu(\mu - \lambda)} \tag{6}$$

The average time in the system including servicing:

$$E(s) = \frac{1}{\mu - \lambda} \tag{7}$$

ILLUSTRATION OF SINGLE-CHANNEL CASE. The use of some of these equations can be illustrated by a simple example. Assume students in the process of registering for classes at a university, and they must go to a cashier's window to pay the necessary fees. The students arrive at the rate of 15 per hour, and are serviced at the rate of 20 per hour, on the average. The times between arrivals and times required for servicing the students are randomly distributed. First, what is the average length of the waiting line?

$$\lambda = 15 \text{ students per hour arriving}$$

$$\mu = 20 \text{ students per hour serviced}$$

$$E(m) = \frac{\lambda^2}{\mu(\mu - \lambda)} \qquad \textbf{Equation (4)}$$

$$= \frac{225}{20(20 - 15)}$$

$$= \frac{225}{100} = 2.25 \text{ students in the average waiting line}$$

The probability that a student will have to wait before being served can also be determined. Since $P(0)$ = the probability of zero units in the system, this represents the probability that the arriving student will not have to wait. Therefore, $1 - P(0)$ = the probability that the student will have to wait.

$$P(0) = 1 - \left(\frac{\lambda}{\mu}\right) \qquad \text{Equation (2)}$$

$$= 1 - \frac{15}{20} = \frac{5}{20}$$

Substituting:

$$P(w) = 1 - P(0) \qquad \text{Equation (3)}$$

$$= 1 - \frac{5}{20} = \frac{3}{4} = .75 \text{ probability of waiting}$$

To determine the average time that a student would have to wait in the line:

$$E(w) = \frac{\lambda}{\mu(\mu - \lambda)} \qquad \text{Equation (6)}$$

$$= \frac{15}{20(20 - 15)}$$

$$= \frac{15}{100} = .15 \text{ hours} = 9 \text{ minutes average waiting time}$$

Finally, the total time which a student will have to spend in the system is:

$$E(s) = \frac{1}{\mu - \lambda} \qquad \text{Equation (7)}$$

$$= \frac{1}{20 - 15} = \frac{1}{5} = 12 \text{ minutes average time in the system}$$

The administrator in charge of this registration system, upon examination of these results, could draw certain conclusions. A probability of .75 of having to wait in line, an average wait of 9 minutes, an average of 12 minutes in the system, and an average waiting line of 2.25 would require some action. It would probably be desirable to add another cashier window in order to cut down on the length of the waiting line and the average waiting time. This additional window, however, would create a multiple-channel, single-phase case of a waiting-line model, which would alter the analysis required.

Multiple Channels. To analyze a single-phase system using multiple channels, it is necessary to resort to another series of equations. The multiple-channel, single-phase case is illustrated by the diagram in Figure 7-6.

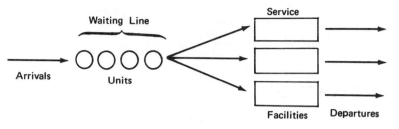

FIGURE 7-6

Multiple-Channel, Single-Phase Waiting-line Case

EQUATIONS FOR MULTIPLE-CHANNEL CASE. If the same conditions listed above for the single-channel case exist, the following set of equations apply for analyzing the multiple-channel situation:

$$P(0) = \frac{1}{\left[\sum_{n=0}^{N-1} \frac{(\lambda/\mu)^n}{n!}\right] + \left[\frac{(\lambda/\mu)^N}{N!(1 - \lambda/\mu N)}\right]} \tag{8}$$

$$E(m) = \frac{(\lambda/\mu)^{N+1}}{(N-1)!(N - \lambda/\mu)^2} \times P(0) \tag{9}$$

$$E(n) = E(m) + \frac{\lambda}{\mu} \tag{10}$$

$$E(w) = \frac{(\lambda/\mu)^{N+1}}{\lambda(N-1)!(N - \lambda/\mu)^2} \times P(0) = \frac{E(m)}{\lambda} \tag{11}$$

$$E(s) = E(w) + \frac{1}{\mu} = \frac{E(n)}{\lambda} \tag{12}$$

ILLUSTRATION OF MULTIPLE-CHANNEL CASE. To illustrate the use of these equations, the data from the single-channel example will be used. This system will now operate with two cashiers' windows available. First, the probability of $P(0)$ (the probability of zero units in the system) is calculated.

$$P(0) = \frac{1}{\left[\frac{(3/4)^0}{0!} + \frac{(3/4)^1}{1!}\right] + \left[\frac{(3/4)^2}{2!\left(1 - \frac{3}{(4)(2)}\right)}\right]} \qquad \textbf{Equation (8)}$$

$$= \frac{1}{\left[\dfrac{1}{1} + \dfrac{.75}{1}\right] + \dfrac{.5625}{2(1 - .375)}}$$

$$= \frac{1}{1.75 + .45}$$

$$= .455$$

The average number of students in the waiting line can now be calculated. Note that $P(0)$ must be calculated first, before proceeding with further analysis of the multiple-channel waiting-line case.

$$E(m) = \frac{(3/4)^{2+1}}{(2 - 1)!(2 - 3/4)^2} \times .455 \qquad \text{Equation (9)}$$

$$= \frac{(3/4)^3}{1(1.25)^2} \times .455$$

$$= .1229 \text{ students}$$

The average number of students in the system, including those being served, can now be determined.

$$E(n) = .1229 + .75 \qquad \text{Equation (10)}$$

$$= .8729 \text{ students}$$

Next, the average waiting time is found.

$$E(w) = \frac{.1229}{3} = .0410 \text{ minutes} \qquad \text{Equation (11)}$$

Finally, the average time a student will spend in the system, including servicing, is computed.

$$E(s) = \frac{.8729}{3} = .2910 \text{ minutes} \qquad \text{Equation (12)}$$

The results of adding an additional service channel can be determined by referring to the single-channel analysis. Clearly, the critical factors of average waiting time, average time in the system, and average number in the waiting line are substantially reduced. It would be necessary to calculate the costs of adding additional service channels to a system in order to have a full evaluation of the decision. Also, it is necessary to evaluate the utility of waiting in such a system. If the system is one where waiting is a problem, low values for the critical factors measured above may be desirable, irrespective of cost considerations.

Situations may also exist where each unit must go through a series of service stations, as in an assembly line. Frequently the arrival and service patterns will be other than random. For instance, some examples can be found where the service time is constant. When the service time is constant, the values sought equal one-half those found with random service time. Thus, in the single channel, single phase with constant service time, we find the following:

$$E(n)_1 = \frac{1}{2}E(n)$$

$$E(m)_1 = \frac{1}{2}E(m)$$

$$E(w)_1 = \frac{1}{2}E(w)$$

Where:

$E(n)_1$ represents the average number of units in the system when the service time is constant.

$E(m)_1$ represents the average number in the waiting line when the service time is constant.

$E(w)_1$ represents the average time spent waiting when the service time is constant.

Frequently, there are waiting-line situations in which the arriving population is finite. A good example of a finite waiting-line problem is a factory with a specific number of machines which require maintenance. The problem which must be solved is to determine how many repairmen are needed to keep the machines operating at the desired rate at minimum cost. Again, a more complex mathematical computational technique is required. There are tables which are useful for solving many of these more involved waiting-line problems. For the finite model, Peck and Hazelwood have compiled a series of tables.[6]

The waiting-line problem may take myriad forms. There are many cases where the waiting-line problem becomes so detailed that the mathematical techniques are either unworkable or uneconomical. Under such circumstances, the use of simulation may not only be practical, but necessary, if a solution is to be achieved.

SUMMARY

Programming models cannot be used to solve all types of problems. Many conditions make it impossible to frame a problem in any algorithmic form. Often before making a decision, the results of a variety of alternatives must be evaluated. Simulation is a technique which has found a high degree of

[6]L. G. Peck and R. N. Hazelwood, *Finite Queuing Tables* (New York: John Wiley & Sons, Inc., 1958).

acceptance in these types of situations. A particular form, Monte Carlo Simulation, is especially applicable to management problems. By means of this form it is possible to approximate a system and to study its potential behavior.

To illustrate Monte Carlo Simulation, different types of problems are subjected to simulation. One example deals with a problem of investment in a program of product development. A second is a scheduling problem, and a third is a random arrival and servicing situation. These are only representative of the potential areas of simulation usage. Simulation will be found to apply to the solution of problems in process planning, inventory systems, manpower planning, and large-scale production-inventory systems, among other areas. The examples used are necessarily oversimplified to illustrate the concepts involved.

Another type problem which characterizes many operating situations is identified as a waiting-line problem. Any time a unit arrives for processing within a system, is processed, and then departs, a waiting-line problem exists. Numerous examples are found to represent the waiting line in daily activities.

Certain characteristics pertaining to waiting lines determine their exact nature. The distribution of the arrival time, the distribution of the service time, the number of channels, and the waiting-line discipline must be known. Whether the source of the units arriving is finite or infinite must be determined, in order to develop the solution model.

The classification of waiting lines, according to the number of phases or sequential servicing stations, is necessary for the development of the proper model. It is also necessary to determine the number of channels or servers available to a unit coming for service. Only the single-phase case waiting line is examined.

For the single-phase case, certain conditions are assumed. First, the source of units is infinite. This implies that the arrival rates follow the Poisson distribution. Second, the service times conform to the negative exponential distribution. The third condition is that the waiting-line discipline is first-come, first-serve. Finally, the average service rate must be greater than the average arrival rate.

Equations for a single-channel case are illustrated, as are the more complex set of equations which apply to the multiple-channel case. Many variations of waiting lines exist, such as constant arrival and service times. When the source is finite, the problem increases in its complexity. Tables are available to assist in solving finite source problems.

Some of the quantitative techniques which have general application to the problems of operations management have been examined. An exhaustive treatment of the use of quantitative models in operations management is not intended. The models reviewed are applicable to a variety of problem areas. Some instances of their use, with respect to specific problem areas, will arise later.

It was not deemed necessary to look into the derivations of these models. This chapter is merely an introduction to these techniques, with an emphasis on their potential use as decision-making tools for the operations manager. There are many other quantitative models which may also be useful to the operations manager. Many of these, however, have specialized application because they are designed for use in a single problem area. For example, certain specific quantitative techniques will be useful for solving problems of investment decisions and forecasting.

The use of quantitative models as an aid to decision making has become an integral part of the function of the operations manager. If he is to be successful in performing his job, this understanding of the concepts underlying the various models and the potential areas of their application is vital.

QUESTIONS FOR DISCUSSION AND ANALYSIS

1. Define simulation. What is its value as a decision-making tool for operations management?

2. Cite some examples of typical operations management problems where simulation might be useful for decision-making purposes.

3. Discuss the significance of the computer in the use of simulation. What are the implications with respect to the effectiveness of the results and the cost of the simulation?

4. Comment on the relationship between the confidence a manager may place in the results of a simulation, and the size of the sample used. Are there any other factors which may have an effect on the accuracy or the confidence which can be achieved?

5. What is the nature of a waiting-line problem?

6. Describe what is meant by:
   (a) Arrivals
   (b) Servicing
   (c) Service facility
   (d) Waiting-line discipline

7. Develop a table in the same form as Table 7-9, using other examples of waiting-line situations you have encountered.

8. Differentiate between a finite and an infinite source of a waiting line.

9. What are the required conditions for using the equations for the single-phase waiting-line case?

10. Describe and illustrate by example the single-channel, single-phase, and the multiple-channel, single-phase waiting-line cases.

11. What is the nature of the multiple-phase waiting-line situation? Describe the single-channel, multiple-phase, and the multiple-channel, multiple-phase waiting-line cases.

12. What are some of the decisions the operations manager might approach, using the waiting-line equations in the chapter?

PROBLEMS

1. The Miles Manufacturing Co. is a small job shop which has ten machines which run continuously for three shifts, 24 hours a day. Even though the

management has in operation a preventive maintenance program, the machines break down and require repairs from time to time. The machines are such that only one serviceman can work on the repairs at any time. Past data reveal the following random distribution with respect to the number of machines which break down in any given hour of the day:

Number of Machines	Percentage
0	5%
1	15%
2	25%
3	25%
4	15%
5	10%
6	5%

The length of time needed to repair the down machines is also randomly distributed. This is as follows:

Length of Repair	Percentage
15 min.	35%
30 min.	30%
45 min.	20%
1 hr.	15%

Simulate eight hours of operation for two servicemen, and for three servicemen; compare the idle time of machines as a result of waiting for service. Assume that all machine breakdowns occur at the beginning of the hour, and that service times are in the order simulated.

2. In a two station subassembly line, the two operators take approximately the same time to perform their respective operations. However, the actual time taken by each operator varies randomly. The distribution of the times taken by the two operators is listed below:

Time in Hrs.	Percentage Station 1	Occurrence Station 2
.22	8%	4%
.23	31%	16%
.24	47%	42%
.25	11%	21%
.26	2%	14%
.27	1%	3%

(a) Simulate the movement of 15 parts through the two stations.
(b) Determine the average length of the waiting line between Station 1 and Station 2.
(c) What is the average waiting time of a part between Station 1 and Station 2?
(d) Show the idle time (if any) of operator 2.
(e) What is the output per hour?

3. An airport has a mean of 10 airplanes per hour taking off, and an average of 3 minutes per takeoff to clear the runway, or 20 services per hour. Assume that both the arrivals and the service times for takeoff are random and are

Poisson and exponential distributions respectively. For this single-runway airport, determine the following:

(a) The probability of a plane having to wait before taking off.

(b) The average number of planes waiting to take off.

(c) The average time a plane will have to wait before takeoff.

4. A nursery has an arrangement where all customers are required to take a number upon entering the shop, to insure a first-come, first-serve priority. Past data indicated that the average number of customers arriving in an hour is 15, and that these arrivals follow the Poisson distribution. In addition, a single clerk can wait on an average of eight customers in an hour. The service times are exponentially distributed. The customers are served by one of 5 clerks, available according to the number the customer holds. Determine from the data:

(a) The average number of customers in the waiting line.

(b) The average number of customers waiting and being served.

(c) The average time a customer waits.

(d) The average time the customer spends at the nursery.

SELECTED ADDITIONAL READINGS

Bierman, Harold, Jr., Charles F. Bonini, Lawrence E. Fouraker, and Robert K. Jaedicke. *Quantitative Analysis for Business Decisions.* Homewood, Illinois: Richard D. Irwin, Inc., 1965.

Bowman, Edward H., and Robert B. Fetter. *Analysis for Production and Operations Management*, 3d ed. Homewood, Illinois: Richard D. Irwin, Inc., 1967.

Chao, Lincoln L. *Statistics: Methods and Analyses.* New York: McGraw-Hill Book Co., 1969.

Clark, Charles T., and L. L. Schkade. *Statistical Methods for Business Decisions.* Cincinnati: South-Western Publishing Co., 1969.

diRoccaferrera, Giuseppe M. Ferrero. *Operations Research Models for Business and Industry.* Cincinnati: South-Western Publishing Co., 1964.

Freund, J. E., and F. J. Williams. *Modern Business Statistics.* Englewood Cliffs: Prentice-Hall, Inc., 1958.

McMillan, Claude, and Richard F. Gonzalez. *Systems Analysis.* Homewood, Illinois: Richard D. Irwin, Inc., 1965.

Miller, David W., and Martin K. Starr. *Executive Decisions and Operations Research.* Englewood Cliffs: Prentice-Hall, Inc., 1964.

Panico, Joseph A. *Queuing Theory.* Englewood Cliffs: Prentice-Hall, Inc., 1969.

Ruiz-Pala, Ernesto, Carlos Avila-Beloso, and William W. Hines. *Waiting-Line Models.* New York: Reinhold Publishing Corp., 1967.

SELECTIONS FROM READINGS BOOK

Greenwood, William T. *Decision Theory and Information Systems.* Cincinnati: South-Western Publishing Co., 1969.

Davis, Ambill, and Whitecraft, "Simulation of Finance Company Operations for Decision Making," p. 390.

Bhatia and Garg, "Basic Structure of Queuing Problems," p. 452.

Goetz, "Monte Carlo Solution of Waiting-Line Problems," p. 465.

PART **3**

Planning
the Operations
System

The problems encountered in planning the operations system, and methods available for solving these problems are surveyed in this third section. An initial step in the planning process is to determine the character of the output of the enterprise. Once this decision is made, the way the output is created must be set. To complete the planning of the system, techniques for acquiring and using the necessary resources have to be chosen. The resources considered in making the planning decisions may be financial, may be physical (machinery or equipment), or may be human. The role of the human element is considered from a motivational standpoint, and in regard to its importance in job design and job performance.

8 | # Product and Plant Planning

The task of planning any system must be undertaken with considerable care. Planning is a function of management at all levels. Of course, planning activities vary at different management levels. Planning begins with a statement of goals or objectives, and proceeds with the development of policies and procedures. The determination of the activities necessary to achieve the stated objectives then follows. Planning is a dynamic activity which continuously considers the environment in which the enterprise exists. Planning cannot be an intermittent activity, but must be conducted in a thorough and regular pattern.

In essence, planning encompasses evaluation of all alternative courses of action, and selection of a particular course of action from those alternatives. In other words, planning is essential to the process of making the decisions necessary to reach the stated objectives. The decisions made are related to the enterprise strategy and operations policies. The strategy and the policies of the enterprise will greatly influence the planning function of the operations manager.

OPERATIONS MANAGEMENT PLANNING

The planning activities of the operations manager differ from planning by other functional area managers. *Planning* the operations system involves: product design, the determination of processes required; the decision establishing the capacity of the system; the forecasting decision; the development of manpower plans, with respect to both numbers and kinds of people; and the design and measurement of the work system. The planning function of the operations manager will be examined in this and succeeding chapters in this section. Establishing a sequence for planning is difficult, as a great deal of the planning function is correlative and executed simultaneously. Therefore, the order in which operations planning activities are discussed does not necessarily represent the actual sequence in which it will occur. Many of the planning steps take place concurrently.

DESIGN OF PRODUCT OR SERVICE

An early step in the planning process for the operations of an organization is to design the product or service which will be offered. Perhaps the foremost consideration, at this stage, is the market the organization plans to service. The term *market* is used in a very broad sense to include both a competitive market, and any user of the product or service. This differentiation is made to point out that all types of organizations, nonprofit as well as profit-oriented ones, must consider their market. For example, an educational institution must consider the student population it will be serving in designing its service (or curriculum). While most of the discussion will be oriented to product design, many of the same types of decisions must be made for nonmanufacturing firms.

A product must go through numerous steps from the inception of the planning until it reaches the market. Many of these steps are accomplished over a long period of time, and will overlap. An example of the sequence and timing needed in planning a product, from the initial research stage until it is marketed, is shown in Figure 8-1.

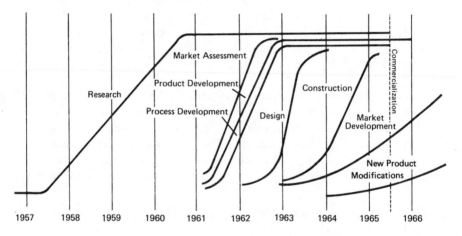

Source: "The D of Research and Development," *This is Du Pont 30* (Wilmington, Delaware: E. I. Du Pont de Nemours & Co., 1966), pp. 14–15. Reproduced by permission of E. I. Du Pont de Nemours & Co.

FIGURE 8-1

Steps in the Planning of a Product
The Case of Du Pont's "Kapton" Polyimide Film

Nature of the Design Problem

When company policy indicates the need to consider a new product, many forces within the organization are set into motion. The industry must be surveyed to evaluate the possible success of the program. The effect of the new product or service on all aspects of current operation must be reviewed. Among the factors which must be considered in the design process are the current resources of the organization, and possible modifications in the operations. The designer must also take account of the various characteristics of the product, the production design, and the economic factors involved.

Characteristics of the Product. In designing a new product, all characteristics of the product must be considered. The functional use of the product cannot be viewed exclusive of all other aspects. The designer considers both the use to which the product will be put, and the operational characteristics of the product as well. The way the product is to be used will affect its design. The product must also be designed so the user can operate it easily and efficiently. There are other characteristics of the product which are also important. Among these is its appearance. In the case of services, similar considerations regarding the characteristics of the service to be offered would be necessary.

Production Design. To the operations manager, the most important aspect of the design phase is designated as production design. When a product or service is designed, the functional, operational, and appearance characteristics are probably foremost in the mind of the designer. However, these are of little significance if the product cannot be produced for some reason or other. When, what appears to be a well designed product is subjected to analysis for the purposes of planning production, the company may find it is not able to manufacture it. This situation arises because the designer did not consider the manufacturing facilities of the company. The product may require a manufacturing process which the company does not possess, or it may require the use of equipment which is beyond the know-how of the organization.

Tolerances. Sometimes a part is designed with a very tight tolerance. A *tolerance* is a permissible deviation from an established standard. For example, a dimension may be stated as $1.00 \pm .001$. The $\pm .001$ is the tolerance, or the range of acceptability, for that dimension. Any part produced outside that range would be unacceptable. In designing a product and establishing tolerances, a designer must consider the functional necessity of a tolerance, and the ability of the production department to maintain it. The type of manufacturing equipment will determine, in part, the ability to attain the specified deviations. Equipment is itself built to tolerances. Consequently, a machine which was built to loose tolerances will not be able to hold tight tolerances on the parts it produces. Tighter tolerances lead to greater costs. A tighter tolerance may require better equipment, material with higher specifications, and more highly skilled workers. Usually, there will be a greater percentage of rejects and hence scrap. Undoubtedly, the result will be to increase the cost of the item.

Economic Considerations. In addition to the cost increase resulting from tighter tolerances, there are other economic considerations in the design process. These considerations are just a part of the total production costs of the product. In evaluating the design of a product, all cost factors attendant to its production must be calculated, including direct costs of production, and overhead costs allocated to production.

The quantity of the product to be produced and sold will have a major bearing on the total cost. Production of a larger quantity of a product usually results in a lower unit cost. This is true because even if the variable costs per unit remain constant, fixed costs can be spread over a larger number of units. An important element in this analysis is the forecast.

Another economic consideration related to the design function is the determination of the need for an expansion of capacity resulting from adding a new product. In most cases, adding a new product or service to an existing line will require additional capital investment. The capital investment decision is an integral part of product and plant planning by the operations manager. It is perhaps one of his most difficult decisions, and requires separate treatment.

It is difficult to isolate the variables involved in the design function. The characteristics of the product cannot be considered without also being aware of the production design requirements. Any evaluation of the production design is closely intertwined with the many economic considerations. None of these parts of the design problem can be solved independently and in isolation from the others.

Standardization

In product design, it is desirable to standardize as much of the product as feasible. *Standardization* means that certain criteria are established which will be applied to all items of a product produced. Standardization has broad application: it may apply to dimensions, shape, color, or some other characteristic. Standardization makes it possible to take an automobile in for service, have a defective part removed, and have a new part taken from a stockroom shelf to replace the old one. Standardization also applies to soft goods. If you wish to purchase a pair of stockings, it is merely necessary for you to go to a store and ask for a particular size, and you can be assured that they will fit. There are an extensive number of examples of standardization encountered daily.

Standardization in operations management is found in areas other than product design. A variety of standards relating to the quality of a product or a service have been established. Standards are set for worker performance, for the types of personnel needed, and for costs.

Methods of Establishing Standards. Standards may be established as an outgrowth of company policy. Standards may result from past usage, or from a systematic approach to the problem. Some standards are established by industry-wide action. An example is the plumbing industry, where certain pipe thread standards have been established. Some standards result from the actions of an outside body or organization. Many quality requirements have been established by governmental buying agencies and imposed upon industry supplying these agencies. Those standards established for firms doing business with the Department of Defense are perhaps the best illustration. Examples of government imposed standards are those which result from a concern for the health and safety of the public. Health standards are established for drug manufacture by the Food and Drug Administration. Safety standards are exemplified by recently established norms for the automobile industry.

Advantages and Disadvantages of Standards. Standards have the distinct advantage of reducing numbers, kinds, and sizes of parts and materials which must be stocked by a company. They are also beneficial because they reduce the number of necessary production runs. Controls are usually more effective because of the existence of standard practices and procedures.

Standardization also has disadvantages. Perhaps the most critical point about standardization is that it may lead to inflexiblities. Once a design is standardized, or a standard practice or procedure set, there is a tendency for it to become frozen. The real danger is that once a standard is established, there will be no attempt to improve what exists. New developments which could be applied to improve the standardized item are ignored, and the organization does not progress as it should. Establishing standards too soon, and then failing to recognize the need for revision, can be disastrous. Sometimes standardization of a product eliminates a competitive advantage. Most sales promotion programs attempt to prove that the product being promoted is different. However, if the alleged difference is real, and the product is a distinct improvement, such nonstandardization can create a truly competitive advantage in a standardized industry.

EQUIPMENT INVESTMENT ANALYSIS

All types of organizations, profit or nonprofit, at certain times must make a decision about their operation capacity. The decision setting the capacity of the system is crucial in determining the nature of the outputs of the system. The operation capacity of the organization is a primary determinant of the kind, amount, and quality of its output; and of the cost structure of the enterprise.

In the planning of the operations system, the capital investment decision is of great significance. In making this decision, management commits the organization to a specific operational capability, by making an investment, usually of long-range significance. In the capital investment decision, equipment is acquired to be used to produce the system output for a period of time into the future. Management's major concern should be the return which an investment can be expected to produce, whether this investment is for replacement purposes, to acquire a more efficient system; for expansion purposes, to satisfy increased demand; or to produce a new product.

When faced with the decision of whether or not to make an investment, or with choosing from among possible alternative investments, the operations manager must have some means available to help him evaluate the potential investment. In most cases, the primary consideration will be economic, but there are times when certain subjective factors will weigh heavily in the final decision.

Many investment decision models are available for use by the operations manager. Some models are of a general nature; they can be utilized in almost any situation. Others are highly specialized, having been developed for use in specific situations. Irrespective of the case involved, all equipment investment models should have certain characteristics: they must represent the particular problem at hand so it can be adequately analyzed; they must be reasonably simple and economical to operate; and the necessary data should be readily available in a usable form. Computers have increased the utility of some models because more data are available, and because of the increased computational capacity of these machines.

Return on Investment

Management is primarily concerned with the return it will receive from any new investment. In many organizations, one of the primary control devices used to evaluate overall performance is return on investment. Probably the foremost example of this technique, used by top management, is the DuPont approach. However, concern at this point is the application of the return on investment concept to operational equipment investment.

Simple Rate of Return. Each organization uses its own method to determine the return on investment. Perhaps the most frequently used method is the simple rate of return on the annual return on investment. Assume that a potential investment in a turret lathe requires an initial investment of $2,500,000. This lathe will yield a return of $600,000 a year. The expected salvage value of the lathe at the end of its useful life is $500,000. Calculation of the simple rate of return follows:

$$\text{Annual Rate of Return} = \frac{\text{Annual Income}}{\text{Original Investment} - \text{Salvage Value}}$$

$$= \frac{\$600,000}{\$2,500,000 - \$500,000}$$

$$= 0.30 \text{ or } 30\%$$

This method has some limitations. It does not always give a true measure of the value of an investment. For instance, it assumes that the return from the investment will be constant throughout the life of the equipment. Detailed study of the revenue functions of investment opportunities reveals that this is not the case in a great majority of instances. The revenue function may take many different forms. It may be a decreasing function; that is, its earnings will decline in some pattern from year to year. It may be an increasing function, where the earnings become greater each year. The revenue function may sometimes take a more complex form, such as a fluctuating yearly pattern.

Unadjusted Rate of Return on Average Investment. In this method, the depreciation of the investment is considered. The annual income is reduced by the amount of the annual straight-line depreciation. This is then related to the average investment instead of the total investment. This method and the simple rate of return calculation are "unadjusted" because they do not take into account the decreasing value of the invested capital over time. The formula for calculating this form of rate of return is:

$$\text{Return on Average Investment} = \frac{\text{Annual Income} - (\text{Net Investment}/\text{Estimated Life})}{1/2\ \text{Net Investment}}$$

Consider the same potential investment used in the example for simple rate of return, with the added factor of an estimated life of 10 years. The calculations are as follows:

$$\text{Return on Average Investment} = \frac{\$600,000 - (\$2,000,000/10)}{1/2(\$2,000,000)}$$

$$= \frac{\$600,000 - \$200,000}{\$1,000,000}$$

$$= 0.40 \text{ or } 40\%$$

This approach to return on investment takes into account certain additional factors left out of the simple rate of return calculation. Most criticisms of the simple rate of return approach would also apply to this latter method.

There are other approaches available for calculating the rate of return, but in the area of equipment investment analysis, the two illustrated are probably most frequently used. Despite possible inaccuracies which might occur, these methods are widely used, because they offer a quick, easy evaluation of investment alternatives. Most organizations develop an acceptable rate of return as part of their capital budgeting policies. This established rate may either be general for the entire organization, or there may be different rates established for various classes of investment. Whenever the calculated rate of return is greater than the rate established by policy, management will approve the proposed investment.

Payback Method

The payback method is undoubtedly the easiest and probably the most widely used criterion for investment decisions. It is nothing more than the determination of the period of time in which a potential investment will pay for itself. The payback method is closely related to the simple rate of return method. The formula for calculating the payback period is the reciprocal of that used for computing the simple rate of return.

$$\text{Payback Period} = \frac{\text{Original Investment} - \text{Salvage Value}}{\text{Annual Income}}$$

Using the same conditions stated in our simple rate of return example we get:

$$\text{Payback Period} = \frac{\$2,500,000 - \$500,000}{\$600,000}$$

$$= 3.33 \text{ years}$$

This investment will pay for itself out of its annual income in 3.33 years. Most organizations set an acceptable payback period as a matter of policy. If the calculated payback period is less than the management-established criterion, the investment will be made.

Inasmuch as the payback method is the reciprocal of the simple rate of return method, the same criticisms apply. Critical evaluation of the payback method and the return on investment method for capital investment decision making leads to the conclusion that for short-term investments, these methods would have to be considered only as initial evaluations. Before making a final decision, a more thorough and more accurate method should be utilized.

Present Value

The present value technique overcomes some of the criticisms of the methods already discussed. This technique presents a more reliable means of evaluating possible alternative investment opportunities having cost and revenue functions that are distinct from each other. It takes into account the possible earnings of an investment alternative beyond the first year. By using present value, a manager can determine what the potential investment is worth today, based on what it may earn over its expected life. Present value calculations reflect the pattern of earnings and the absolute earnings. Present value computations reveal that if one of two otherwise equal alternatives returns more than 50% of its earnings during the first half of its anticipated usefulness, it will be preferred to another alternative with an increasing earnings pattern (more than 50% of its earnings in the latter half of its useful life span).

The present value technique determines the value of future income at a current point in time. The future income is discounted at the expected rate of interest. This means that $100 you possess today, which can be invested at 8% interest per annum, will give you $108 one year from now. By the same logic, $100 income a year from now is worth a lesser amount because it is discounted by the appropriate rate of interest. After discounting $100 at 8% is $92.60.

Specifically, the present value of an invested principal, P, which earns an interest rate, i, in n years in the future will return an amount, S, if the earnings are accumulated at a compound rate for the entire period. Therefore:

$$S = P(1 + i)^n$$

Solving for P:

$$P = \frac{S}{(1 - i)^n} = S(1 + i)^{-n}$$

Using the above example of $100 invested at 8%, substitute into the formula above to get:

$$P = \$100(1.08)^{-1}$$

It is not necessary to calculate the quantity within the parentheses as available tables give the values for $(1 + i)^{-n}$. Such tables are referred to as Present Value of $1. Table 8-1 reproduces a portion of such a table. This table shows that the value of $1.00, invested at 8% for 1 year, is equal to 0.926. Inserting this value into the above example and carrying out the multiplication, the present value of $100 at 8% for 1 year is $92.60. In a similar fashion the value of this same $100 invested at 8% for any number of years can be determined. For example, Table 8-1 shows that if this investment was for 10 years, the present value of the $100 would be $46.30 (0.463 × $100).

The process of determining the present value of an investment alternative is not complex. This task is easily accomplished using a table for present value of $1. By applying the appropriate discount rate to the annual expected income for the expected useful life, the present value of the investment can be determined.

Assume that management is considering an investment alternative of $21,000, which is expected to return $6,000 a year for its anticipated life of 10 years. Management has a policy that it will approve any investment of this class which will yield 18%, assuming the necessary funds are available. Calculation of the present value of this investment proposal is as follows, using data from Table 8-1:

Year	Annual Return	P.V. of $1 at 18%	P.V. of Return
1	$6,000	0.847	$ 5,082
2	6,000	0.718	4,308
3	6,000	0.609	3,654
4	6,000	0.516	3,096
5	6,000	0.437	2,622
6	6,000	0.370	2,220
7	6,000	0.314	1,884
8	6,000	0.266	1,596
9	6,000	0.225	1,350
10	6,000	0.191	1,146
		Total 4.494	$26,964

This analysis indicates the investment exceeds the 18% return demanded by management policy. If the proposed investment had yielded exactly 18%, the total present value of the return would have been exactly $21,000. The analysis shows a return of $26,964, assuming the estimates of the annual return of $6,000 and the 10-year life span are accurate.

Close examination of the analysis shows that the total present value of the return is approximately equal to the product of the annual return, and the total of the present value of $1 at 18% ($6,000 × 4.494 = $26,958). Table 8-2, which is the Present Value for an Annuity, shows the cumulative sums of the present values of $1, given in Table 8-1. Thus, reference to the annuity table in the 10-year row at 18% shows the present value figure of 4.494, which is the

TABLE 8-1

Present Value of $1

Years Hence	1%	2%	4%	6%	8%	10%	12%	14%	15%	16%	18%	20%	22%	24%	25%	26%	28%	30%	35%	40%	45%	50%
1	0.990	0.980	0.962	0.943	0.926	0.909	0.893	0.877	0.870	0.862	0.847	0.833	0.820	0.806	0.800	0.794	0.781	0.769	0.741	0.714	0.690	0.667
2	0.980	0.961	0.925	0.890	0.857	0.826	0.797	0.769	0.756	0.743	0.718	0.694	0.672	0.650	0.640	0.630	0.610	0.592	0.549	0.510	0.476	0.444
3	0.971	0.942	0.889	0.840	0.794	0.751	0.712	0.675	0.658	0.641	0.609	0.579	0.551	0.524	0.512	0.500	0.477	0.455	0.406	0.364	0.328	0.296
4	0.961	0.924	0.855	0.792	0.735	0.683	0.636	0.592	0.572	0.552	0.516	0.482	0.451	0.423	0.410	0.397	0.373	0.350	0.301	0.260	0.226	0.198
5	0.951	0.906	0.822	0.747	0.681	0.621	0.567	0.519	0.497	0.476	0.437	0.402	0.370	0.341	0.328	0.315	0.291	0.269	0.223	0.186	0.156	0.132
6	0.942	0.888	0.790	0.705	0.630	0.564	0.507	0.456	0.432	0.410	0.370	0.335	0.303	0.275	0.262	0.250	0.227	0.207	0.165	0.133	0.108	0.088
7	0.933	0.871	0.760	0.665	0.583	0.513	0.452	0.400	0.376	0.354	0.314	0.279	0.249	0.222	0.210	0.198	0.178	0.159	0.122	0.095	0.074	0.059
8	0.923	0.853	0.731	0.627	0.540	0.467	0.404	0.351	0.327	0.305	0.266	0.233	0.204	0.179	0.168	0.157	0.139	0.123	0.091	0.068	0.051	0.039
9	0.914	0.837	0.703	0.592	0.500	0.424	0.361	0.308	0.284	0.263	0.225	0.194	0.167	0.144	0.134	0.125	0.108	0.094	0.067	0.048	0.035	0.026
10	0.905	0.820	0.676	0.558	0.463	0.386	0.322	0.270	0.247	0.227	0.191	0.162	0.137	0.116	0.107	0.099	0.085	0.073	0.050	0.035	0.024	0.017
11	0.896	0.804	0.650	0.527	0.429	0.350	0.287	0.237	0.215	0.195	0.162	0.135	0.112	0.094	0.086	0.079	0.066	0.056	0.037	0.025	0.017	0.012
12	0.887	0.788	0.625	0.497	0.397	0.319	0.257	0.208	0.187	0.168	0.137	0.112	0.092	0.076	0.069	0.062	0.052	0.043	0.027	0.018	0.012	0.008
13	0.879	0.773	0.601	0.469	0.368	0.290	0.229	0.182	0.163	0.145	0.116	0.093	0.075	0.061	0.055	0.050	0.040	0.033	0.020	0.013	0.008	0.005
14	0.870	0.758	0.577	0.442	0.340	0.263	0.205	0.160	0.141	0.125	0.099	0.078	0.062	0.049	0.044	0.039	0.032	0.025	0.015	0.009	0.006	0.003
15	0.861	0.743	0.555	0.417	0.315	0.239	0.183	0.140	0.123	0.108	0.084	0.065	0.051	0.040	0.035	0.031	0.025	0.020	0.011	0.006	0.004	0.002
16	0.853	0.728	0.534	0.394	0.292	0.218	0.163	0.123	0.107	0.093	0.071	0.054	0.042	0.032	0.028	0.025	0.019	0.015	0.008	0.005	0.003	0.002
17	0.844	0.714	0.513	0.371	0.270	0.198	0.146	0.108	0.093	0.080	0.060	0.045	0.034	0.026	0.023	0.020	0.015	0.012	0.006	0.003	0.002	0.001
18	0.836	0.700	0.494	0.350	0.250	0.180	0.130	0.095	0.081	0.069	0.051	0.038	0.028	0.021	0.018	0.016	0.012	0.009	0.005	0.002	0.001	
19	0.828	0.686	0.475	0.331	0.232	0.164	0.116	0.083	0.070	0.060	0.043	0.031	0.023	0.017	0.014	0.012	0.009	0.007	0.003	0.002	0.001	
20	0.820	0.673	0.456	0.312	0.215	0.149	0.104	0.073	0.061	0.051	0.037	0.026	0.019	0.014	0.012	0.010	0.007	0.005	0.002	0.001	0.001	
21	0.811	0.660	0.439	0.294	0.199	0.135	0.093	0.064	0.053	0.044	0.031	0.022	0.015	0.011	0.009	0.008	0.006	0.004	0.002	0.001		
22	0.803	0.647	0.422	0.278	0.184	0.123	0.083	0.056	0.046	0.038	0.026	0.018	0.013	0.009	0.007	0.006	0.004	0.003	0.001	0.001		
23	0.795	0.634	0.406	0.262	0.170	0.112	0.074	0.049	0.040	0.033	0.022	0.015	0.010	0.007	0.006	0.005	0.003	0.002	0.001			
24	0.788	0.622	0.390	0.247	0.158	0.102	0.066	0.043	0.035	0.028	0.019	0.013	0.008	0.006	0.005	0.004	0.003	0.002	0.001			
25	0.780	0.610	0.375	0.233	0.146	0.092	0.059	0.038	0.030	0.024	0.016	0.010	0.007	0.005	0.004	0.003	0.002	0.001	0.001			
26	0.772	0.598	0.361	0.220	0.135	0.084	0.053	0.033	0.026	0.021	0.014	0.009	0.006	0.004	0.003	0.002	0.002	0.001				
27	0.764	0.586	0.347	0.207	0.125	0.076	0.047	0.029	0.023	0.018	0.011	0.007	0.005	0.003	0.002	0.002	0.001	0.001				
28	0.757	0.574	0.333	0.196	0.116	0.069	0.042	0.026	0.020	0.016	0.010	0.006	0.004	0.002	0.002	0.002	0.001	0.001				
29	0.749	0.563	0.321	0.185	0.107	0.063	0.037	0.022	0.017	0.014	0.008	0.005	0.003	0.002	0.002	0.001	0.001	0.001				
30	0.742	0.552	0.308	0.174	0.099	0.057	0.033	0.020	0.015	0.012	0.007	0.004	0.003	0.002	0.001	0.001	0.001					
40	0.672	0.453	0.208	0.097	0.046	0.022	0.011	0.005	0.004	0.003	0.001											
50	0.608	0.372	0.141	0.054	0.021	0.009	0.003	0.001	0.001	0.001												

TABLE 8-2

Present Value for an Annuity

Years (N)	1%	2%	4%	6%	8%	10%	12%	14%	15%	16%	18%	20%	22%	24%	25%	26%	28%	30%	35%	40%	45%	50%
1	0.990	0.980	0.962	0.943	0.926	0.909	0.893	0.877	0.870	0.862	0.847	0.833	0.820	0.806	0.800	0.794	0.781	0.769	0.741	0.714	0.690	0.667
2	1.970	1.942	1.886	1.833	1.783	1.736	1.690	1.647	1.626	1.605	1.566	1.528	1.492	1.457	1.440	1.424	1.392	1.361	1.289	1.224	1.165	1.111
3	2.941	2.884	2.775	2.673	2.577	2.487	2.402	2.322	2.283	2.246	2.174	2.106	2.042	1.981	1.952	1.923	1.868	1.816	1.696	1.589	1.493	1.407
4	3.902	3.808	3.630	3.465	3.312	3.170	3.037	2.914	2.855	2.798	2.690	2.589	2.494	2.404	2.362	2.320	2.241	2.166	1.997	1.849	1.720	1.605
5	4.853	4.713	4.452	4.212	3.993	3.791	3.605	3.433	3.352	3.274	3.127	2.991	2.864	2.745	2.689	2.635	2.532	2.436	2.220	2.035	1.876	1.737
6	5.795	5.601	5.242	4.917	4.623	4.355	4.111	3.889	3.784	3.685	3.498	3.326	3.167	3.020	2.951	2.885	2.759	2.643	2.385	2.168	1.983	1.824
7	6.728	6.472	6.002	5.582	5.206	4.868	4.564	4.288	4.160	4.039	3.812	3.605	3.416	3.242	3.161	3.083	2.937	2.802	2.508	2.263	2.057	1.883
8	7.652	7.325	6.733	6.210	5.747	5.335	4.968	4.639	4.487	4.344	4.078	3.837	3.619	3.421	3.329	3.241	3.076	2.925	2.598	2.331	2.108	1.922
9	8.566	8.162	7.435	6.802	6.247	5.759	5.328	4.946	4.772	4.607	4.303	4.031	3.786	3.566	3.463	3.366	3.184	3.019	2.665	2.379	2.144	1.948
10	9.471	8.983	8.111	7.360	6.710	6.145	5.650	5.216	5.019	4.833	4.494	4.192	3.923	3.682	3.571	3.465	3.269	3.092	2.715	2.414	2.168	1.965
11	10.368	9.787	8.760	7.887	7.139	6.495	5.988	5.453	5.234	5.029	4.656	4.327	4.035	3.776	3.656	3.544	3.335	3.147	2.752	2.438	2.185	1.977
12	11.255	10.575	9.385	8.384	7.536	6.814	6.194	5.660	5.421	5.197	4.793	4.439	4.127	3.851	3.725	3.606	3.387	3.190	2.779	2.456	2.196	1.985
13	12.134	11.343	9.986	8.853	7.904	7.103	6.424	5.842	5.583	5.342	4.910	4.533	4.203	3.912	3.780	3.656	3.427	3.223	2.799	2.468	2.204	1.990
14	13.004	12.106	10.563	9.295	8.244	7.367	6.628	6.002	5.724	5.468	5.008	4.611	4.265	3.962	3.824	3.695	3.459	3.249	2.814	2.477	2.210	1.993
15	13.865	12.849	11.118	9.712	8.559	7.606	6.811	6.142	5.847	5.575	5.092	4.675	4.315	4.001	3.859	3.726	3.483	3.268	2.825	2.484	2.214	1.995
16	14.718	13.578	11.652	10.106	8.851	7.824	6.974	6.265	5.954	5.669	5.162	4.730	4.357	4.033	3.887	3.751	3.503	3.283	2.834	2.489	2.216	1.997
17	15.562	14.292	12.166	10.477	9.122	8.022	7.120	6.373	6.047	5.749	5.222	4.775	4.391	4.059	3.910	3.771	3.518	3.295	2.840	2.492	2.218	1.998
18	16.398	14.992	12.659	10.828	9.372	8.201	7.250	6.467	6.128	5.818	5.273	4.812	4.419	4.080	3.928	3.786	3.529	3.304	2.844	2.494	2.219	1.999
19	17.226	15.678	13.134	11.158	9.604	8.365	7.366	6.550	6.198	5.877	5.316	4.844	4.442	4.097	3.942	3.799	3.539	3.311	2.848	2.496	2.220	1.999
20	18.046	16.351	13.590	11.470	9.818	8.514	7.469	6.623	6.259	5.929	5.353	4.870	4.460	4.110	3.954	3.808	3.546	3.316	2.850	2.497	2.221	1.999
21	18.857	17.011	14.029	11.764	10.017	8.649	7.562	6.687	6.312	5.973	5.384	4.891	4.476	4.121	3.963	3.816	3.551	3.320	2.852	2.498	2.221	2.000
22	19.660	17.658	14.451	12.042	10.201	8.772	7.645	6.743	6.359	6.011	5.410	4.909	4.488	4.130	3.970	3.822	3.556	3.323	2.853	2.498	2.222	2.000
23	20.456	18.292	14.857	12.303	10.371	8.883	7.718	6.792	6.399	6.044	5.432	4.925	4.499	4.137	3.976	3.827	3.559	3.325	2.854	2.499	2.222	2.000
24	21.243	18.914	15.247	12.550	10.529	8.985	7.784	6.835	6.434	6.073	5.451	4.937	4.507	4.143	3.981	3.831	3.562	3.327	2.855	2.499	2.222	2.000
25	22.023	19.523	15.622	12.783	10.675	9.077	7.843	6.873	6.464	6.097	5.467	4.948	4.514	4.147	3.985	3.834	3.564	3.329	2.856	2.499	2.222	2.000
26	22.795	20.121	15.983	13.003	10.810	9.161	7.896	6.906	6.491	6.118	5.480	4.956	4.520	4.151	3.988	3.837	3.566	3.330	2.856	2.500	2.222	2.000
27	23.560	20.707	16.330	13.211	10.935	9.237	7.943	6.935	6.514	6.136	5.492	4.964	4.524	4.154	3.990	3.839	3.567	3.331	2.856	2.500	2.222	2.000
28	24.316	21.281	16.663	13.406	11.051	9.307	7.984	6.961	6.534	6.152	5.502	4.970	4.528	4.157	3.992	3.840	3.568	3.331	2.857	2.500	2.222	2.000
29	25.066	21.844	16.984	13.591	11.158	9.370	8.022	6.983	6.551	6.166	5.510	4.975	4.531	4.159	3.994	3.841	3.569	3.332	2.857	2.500	2.222	2.000
30	25.808	22.396	17.292	13.765	11.258	9.427	8.055	7.003	6.566	6.177	5.517	4.979	4.534	4.160	3.995	3.842	3.569	3.332	2.857	2.500	2.222	2.000
40	32.835	27.355	19.793	15.046	11.925	9.779	8.244	7.105	6.642	6.234	5.548	4.997	4.544	4.166	3.999	3.846	3.571	3.333	2.857	2.500	2.222	2.000
50	39.196	31.424	21.482	15.762	12.234	9.915	8.304	7.133	6.661	6.246	5.554	4.999	4.545	4.167	4.000	3.846	3.571	3.333	2.857	2.500	2.222	2.000

cumulative total. The slight difference in the total present value of the return figures ($26,958 vs. $26,964) is a result of rounding off. Thus, wherever the annual return is constant throughout the estimated life of the investment, use the present value factors in Table 8-2. When the annual savings vary, use the present value of $1 found in Table 8-1, and follow the procedure outlined in the example.

The flexibility of the present value approach can be illustrated by relating it to the payback period. The values appearing in the annuity table, Table 8-2, are actually payback periods. In other words, the value 4.494 is the amount of time, in years, it will take for an investment, with a life span of 10 years and a rate of return of 18%, to pay for itself. To find the true rate of return of an investment alternative, first determine its payback period; then find that figure on the annuity table opposite the anticipated life of the investment. Thus, the payback is $21,000/$6,000 = 3.50 years. In Table 8-2, on the 10-year line, this exceeds 25%. Therefore, if the annual return and the life span estimates are correct, the investment alternative under analysis exceeds the criteria set by management by approximately 7 percentage points.

The MAPI System[1]

An interesting approach to the investment decision is the one developed by the Machinery and Allied Products Institute. The MAPI formula is designed for relatively easy application by managers concerned with an equipment replacement problem. The actual formula is complex, but the manager does not need to apply the formula directly. He is able to get reasonably good output by means of a relatively simple process, using charts and graphs.

The MAPI system is usually considered as an adjusted after-tax rate of return method. It is concerned with determining next year's rate of return if the proposed investment is undertaken now, rather than delayed for one year.

Absolute and Relative Rates of Return. The MAPI system distinguishes between the absolute and relative rates of return anticipated from an investment. The absolute rate of return is the relationship between the investment and the revenue generated by it in excess of the operating costs it incurs. The relative rate of return, on the other hand, is derived from the difference in the return which occurs as a result of not having the equipment item, but continuing without it for a period of time. The MAPI system assumes the absolute rate of return is usually not available. Whenever an investment alternative exists, a relative rate of return can be calculated. For every alternative, there exists a relative return, but only one relative return can be determined for any given project. Even when the absolute rate of return can be determined, the relative rate of return is preferred, because it best shows the complete effect of an investment on the total organization.

---

[1]The material in this discussion of the MAPI system is based on: George Terborgh, *Business Investment Management* (Washington: Machinery and Allied Products Institute, 1967).

The Next-Year Deferment Concept. The MAPI system is concerned with determining the rate of return if the investment is delayed until next year. This period is chosen because it applies to a wider range of decisions than any other possible period. For most investment alternatives, the analysis of a short-term deferment of the investment is as meaningful as an analysis involving a longer period of time. In some cases, the one-year deferment period is the only logical one. In addition, annual analysis is standard for most managements; it requires less adjustment in planning than any other period of time. Annual data are usually readily available, and annual capital budgeting is becoming the prevalent trend. If an investment alternative is rejected, the usual period before it will be revived and reconsidered is one year. Thus, the next-year criterion is assumed to be the most acceptable.

While an anticipated return continues beyond the one-year period, and throughout the life of the investment; the one-year period is felt to be the best period for comparison purposes. Relative rates for longer periods are not considered as accurate or as meaningful in the decision process.

Calculation of the Next-Year Relative Rate of Return. Calculation of the next-year relative rate of return is done by a formula containing five basic factors:

a. Next-year operating advantage. The sum of the expected increase in revenue, and the estimated cost reduction accruing from the investment next year.

b. Next-year capital consumption avoided. This is really nothing more than the fall in the salvage value of the alternative at the end of the year.

c. Next-year capital consumption incurred. This is the decrease in the value of the investment during the year.

d. Next-year income tax adjustment. This is the net increase in income tax incurred, as a result of the investment.

x. Average net investment. This is the average of the installed cost of the investment, less the initial investment in the alternative; and the retention value of the investment at year-end, minus the salvage value of the alternative.

Using the above symbols, the following formula is used for calculating the after-tax return:

$$\text{After-tax return} = \frac{a + b - c - d}{x}$$

Comparisons for More Than One Year. A shortcut method for calculating the rate of return for periods of more than one year is also available. The formula for the one-year period as shown above is used. The only change is that the factors in the formula are annual averages for the longer period of time involved.

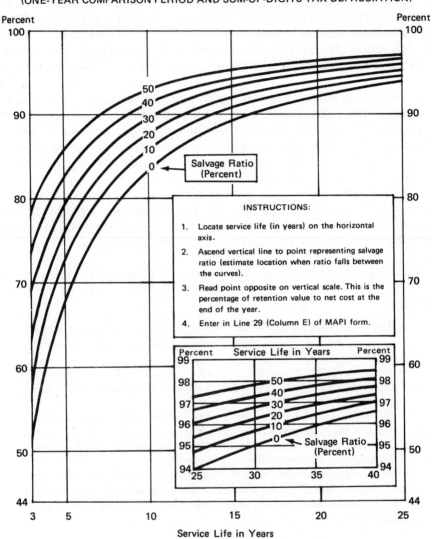

(ONE-YEAR COMPARISON PERIOD AND SUM-OF-DIGITS TAX DEPRECIATION)

INSTRUCTIONS:

1. Locate service life (in years) on the horizontal axis.

2. Ascend vertical line to point representing salvage ratio (estimate location when ratio falls between the curves).

3. Read point opposite on vertical scale. This is the percentage of retention value to net cost at the end of the year.

4. Enter in Line 29 (Column E) of MAPI form.

Service Life in Years

Reproduced by permission of Machinery and Allied Products Institute.

FIGURE 8-2

MAPI Chart No. 1A

Calculations of the Return. In calculating the rate of return, the MAPI system uses a set of forms and charts. The forms are worksheets on which certain known or estimated data are entered. Some of the estimated data must be obtained from the MAPI charts. The charts come in two series, A and B.

The A charts are for one-year periods, and the B charts for longer periods of time. Each series consists of four charts for various tax depreciation methods. These depreciation methods are:

1. Sum-of-digits tax depreciation
2. Double-declining tax depreciation
3. Straight-line tax depreciation
4. Expensing

Figure 8-2 is a reproduction of the MAPI Chart No. 1A. Figure 8-3 is a sample of the completed MAPI Summary Form, filled out to evaluate an investment in vibratory finishing equipment to replace a tumbling machine now in use.

The MAPI system is designed for easy use with the forms and the charts provided. For short-term investments, this system is reasonably satisfactory. There is some concern when it is used for long-term investment analysis. Also, there is a danger that use of the computational method of the MAPI system without some knowledge of the underlying theory and assumptions which make up this system will lead to highly unsatisfactory results.

Other Equipment Investment Models

There have been many attempts at developing more sophisticated and more generally applicable models for equipment investment decisions. Many of these models depend on very high-level mathematics, and are beyond the scope of this chapter. Readers interested in pursuing these models in detail are referred to original sources.[2]

There have also been attempts at developing what might be characterized as ideal models for investment analysis. Most of these ideal models consider equipment investment as a process of making a chain of decisions, involving not just a single choice of an alternative at the present time, but as a virtually infinite series of decisions over future time.[3] These models are based on the assumption that each successive decision involves consideration of unique factors. The sequential items in the chain are not identical to, or even similar to, the item which they are replacing.

These ideal models can be very helpful in setting forth a broad understanding of the equipment investment analysis problem. Their operational usefulness is questionable, however, because they require estimates for a series of investments with unknown characteristics, and unknown cost and revenue functions.

---

[2]Some of the original sources are listed at the end of this chapter. Models are summarized in: R. L. Ackoff (ed.), *Progress in Operations Research* (New York: John Wiley & Sons, 1961), I.

[3]cf. A. Reisman and E. S. Buffa, "A General Model for Investment Policy," *Management Science*, Vol. VIII, No. 3 (April, 1962), pp. 304–310; and Edward H. Bowman and Robert B. Fetter, *Analysis for Production and Operations Management* (3d ed.; Homewood, Illinois: Richard D. Irwin, Inc., 1967), pp. 386–388.

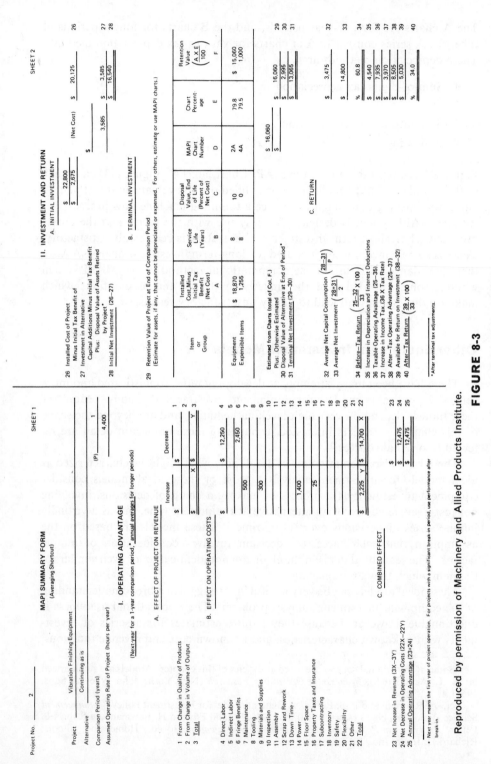

FIGURE 8-3

MAPI Summary Form for a Vibration Finishing Equipment Project

Reproduced by permission of Machinery and Allied Products Institute.

PLANT LOCATION

The decision regarding the location of a plant is relatively infrequent. Many managers may spend an entire career without ever being faced with this decision. It is also possible the operations manager will not have the final authority for making this decision, as it may well rest with top-level management, or possibly even with the owners or the board of directors. However, when a decision regarding location must be made, it is one which can have far-reaching effects on the future success of the organization. It is important to point out before proceeding further that the word "plant" is used in a very broad context here. The usual connotation given to the word plant is of a factory or some form of manufacturing facility. However, its current usage should be taken to mean any buildings or physical equipment available for carrying out the operations function. Thus, this can mean that plant location may refer to the location of a hospital, a restaurant, or facilities of an educational institution.

Conditions Which Create the Need for a Location Decision

Various conditions may require an organization to make a location decision. The most obvious of these is when the organization is first formed. At this stage, every organization must make a decision as to the location of its operating facilities. Unfortunately, many new organizations do not give proper attention to this problem. Frequently the organizers of a new undertaking are unaware of the potential importance of a good location. The other activities requiring their attention to form the new enterprise tend to overshadow the location problem. Even when location is considered, the personal wishes of the organizers to locate for their own convenience may prevail.

The location decision for an existing organization may arise as a result of several conditions. One may be a need for expansion of the present activities. This may arise when the demand for the product or service of the organization increases beyond the capacity of the present facilities.

Circumstances have, on occasion, led existing organizations to decentralize their operations in order to increase their efficiency. Often, as an organization expands and becomes more complex, the economic efficiency of a single plant is questionable. The advantages of a multi-plant operation may outweigh the continuation of a single plant; even an expanded one. Among these advantages are the possibilities of better service to the market, a more adequate labor supply, and improved operations at a lower cost, resulting from a more modern facility.

It is virtually impossible to separate completely the factors which may lead to the need for a new location. They are almost always interrelated. For example, economic factors may create a need for a new location. Economic factors which might be listed are changes in the market, increased costs at the present location, or a deficiency in the kinds and quantity of labor available. However, it is obvious that these economic factors may be critically involved in other circumstances creating a need for a new location. Also, closely related to the already mentioned conditions is the obsolescence of the existing facilities. Obsolescence may result either from technological advancements or from the age of the presently utilized plant.

Sequence of Location Decisions

In approaching the decision about a new location, two categories of factors must be considered sequentially. The first is a decision regarding the general area or region where the plant is to be located. The second is consideration of the actual site. Naturally some of the same factors will be considered in both cases, but there are some unique factors as well.

Area or Regional Factors. Historically there has been a trend toward regional specialization of industry in the United States. Many factors have been in influential in the development of this regional specialization. In some cases, it has simply been a matter of a particular industry starting in the area, such as the original concentration of the textile industry in New England. This industry subsequently moved to the South to take advantage of lower costs. Other examples are the steel industry, primarily found in Pennsylvania, Ohio, and the Great Lakes region to take advantage of transportation facilities for shipping the ore. The pottery industry is located in parts of California, Ohio, and New Jersey because of a ready supply of raw materials. The motion picture industry was originally located in California because of a climate which provided bright sunshine needed for illumination in the early days of filming. As can be seen, the factors which influence regional location are many. Among the more significant factors to be considered, which deserve mention, are:

1. Nearness to the market. Today this factor is not taken so much to mean geographical nearness, but nearness in the sense of the time required to reach the market served. With today's rapid transportation facilities, a national market may be served from a single location. For certain products, serving a market at the opposite end of the continent may not be detrimental if the products can be shipped quickly and economically.
2. Transportation facilities. This is closely related to the above factor. The primary considerations are the availability of transportation facilities and the cost of these facilities. Differential freight rate schedules in use are not necessarily related to the distance factor.
3. Nearness to sources of raw materials and supplies. Essentially, the same types of considerations given regarding the nearness to the market would prevail here. In both cases, the bulk of the items to be transported is an important factor.
4. Labor market. Here we should be concerned about the quantities, and the kinds (i.e., skilled or unskilled) of labor required, and the structure of the wages paid in the area.

This is by no means an exhaustive list of the factors which need to be evaluated in choosing a regional location. Each organization will have different needs; consequently, not only will the factors to be considered take on differing importance, but the actual factors themselves will vary. What may be significant in one case may not be in another.

Specific Site Factors. The selection of the region or area is probably the more difficult part of the location decision. This choice of region is usually more critical to the success of the organization than the selection of the site. However, the importance of the selection of a specific site should not be minimized. For certain types of organizations, this may be the only location decision to be made. In many cases, the region may not be a factor for consideration in this decision. For example, region would not be a factor in the location of a hospital or an educational institution. It is necessary that the site selected be suitable, and that it meets all the needs of the organization. It must, of course, meet all the criteria used in the regional selection decision as well. Enumeration of all of the possible factors to be considered for site location would require an unwarranted amount of space; they are extensive in number, and also vary in importance for each individual situation. Some of the factors to be considered in the site decision are:

1. Nature of the community. Included are the living facilities available for employees; the community services available for the plant and workers; and the economic characteristics of the community, such as average income, purchasing power of the residents, and the population trend.
2. Political stability of the community. The primary consideration is the attitude of the government toward a similar organization. Along with this would be the tax structure prevailing in the community, building code requirements, and any restrictive legislation which might have an effect. Of particular significance are the existing conditions, and a survey of past practices in the community. If the community has a history of an unstable attitude in these matters, it should serve as a warning. The fact that the community offers some sort of a tax advantage to a new firm may be a temporary condition that will disappear once the plant is located.
3. The actual site itself. The size of the piece of property; its accessibility to transportation facilities needed by employees and shipment of goods; the availability of services such as fire and police protection, and utility services; and the cost of the land are important factors.

Sources of Data and Assistance. When the manager is faced with a location decision, he can find a great deal of information and assistance available. Much of this aid will be offered with hope of enticing him to select a certain area or community. Most states have industrial development agencies to furnish help to industries considering location in the state. Such industries are a potential source of tax revenue and an addition to the state's economy. Local Chambers of Commerce also will gladly furnish assistance to organizations searching for a location. Public utilities, transportation companies, banks, and realtors cooperate willingly. Many of these firms have specialized departments which have as their prime purpose the job of attempting to persuade industry to locate within their area of business. Various federal government agencies are potential sources of useful information as well. Most management consulting firms will furnish service to find a new location. There are a few consultants who specialize in plant location advice.

Methods for Analyzing the Location Decision

In addition to merely making a personal evaluation of important factors for arriving at a location decision, managers may use techniques which are not influenced by personal bias. Since the location decision is largely an investment decision, proposed alternative locations may be subjected to techniques of investment analysis discussed earlier in this chapter.

In addition, the manager may resort to a variety of specialized economic analyses. For example, it may be valuable to prepare proforma profit and loss statements for the various locations under consideration. A comparison of these statements will provide some indication of the relative potential of the alternatives. An evaluation may also be made of the total costs involved (fixed and variable), and of the expected returns for each location, at the anticipated level of operation. This can be done by using break-even analysis. The break-even point for the alternatives can be calculated or charted by using the methodology outlined in Chapter 5.

Some companies have utilized a point-rating system for analyzing alternative locations. Using this technique, the manager must first make a list of the important factors to be considered in making the decision. He assigns a weight to individual factors by allocating each one a certain number of points which gives them a relative value with respect to all others being considered. For example, the following list of factors and their maximum possible points might be developed:

Factor	Points
Labor Supply	500
Wage Structure	400
Transportation Facilities	450
Utility Services	250
Climate	150
Community Services	100
Taxes	300
Economy of the Community	150
Building Costs	200
Total Points Possible	2,500

Each location alternative would be evaluated according to the factors listed, and a point value assigned. When this has been completed, a total point rating for each location is available, and a comparison can be made. The points assigned to each location result from a subjective judgment by the manager doing the rating. It is also possible that some negative factor might exist for one location and would not be indicated in the point rating. The selection of the location with the highest total point value would not necessarily be the most desirable decision, but the high points would undoubtedly carry a lot of weight in arriving at the final choice. It is advisable to resort to evaluative techniques other than the point-rating system before making a decision on a matter as important as location. The real value of the point-rating approach is that it forces the manager to attempt to consider all of the important factors when he compiles the list. In arriving at the point value for each location, he is also forced to evaluate that location with respect to the important considerations for each factor.

In the case of a company faced with a decision of locating an additional plant, the distribution model of linear programming is a useful analytical tool. Assume that a company which now has plants in Los Angeles and Seattle is considering the addition of a new plant. Locations under consideration for the new plant are Kansas City and Minneapolis. The warehouses to which this company now ships are located in San Francisco, Denver, Chicago, Pittsburgh, and Atlanta. Table 8-3 lists the pertinent data for this situation. This relatively simple problem can easily be formulated into a distribution linear programming model. Table 8-4 shows the final solution matrices for the two alternative locations. Based on this analysis, the new plant should be located in Kansas City.

Whatever method management uses to make the location decision, there is no guarantee that the outcome will be profitable. Both current and estimated data, based on the best predictions of the future, are used. After the choice is

TABLE 8-3

Summary of Shipping Costs, Demands, Capacities,
and Production Costs for Existing and Proposed Plants

From	Existing Plants		Proposed Plant		Monthly
To	Los Angeles	Seattle	Kansas City	Minneapolis	Demand
San Francisco	$.12	$.15	$.21	$.24	25,000
Denver	.20	.23	.17	.19	30,000
Chicago	.28	.34	.09	.06	20,000
Pittsburgh	.36	.43	.14	.18	27,000
Atlanta	.45	.52	.31	.28	15,000
Plant Capacity Monthly	47,000	38,000	32,000	32,000	
Production Cost per Unit	$1.70	$1.50	$1.80	$1.76	

The heading "Distribution Costs per Unit" spans the Existing Plants and Proposed Plant columns.

TABLE 8-4

Optimum Solution Distribution Matrices
for Two Alternative Plant Locations

From / To	L.A.	Seattle	K.C.	Demand
San Francisco	182	165 25	201	25,000
Denver	190 17	173 13	197	30,000
Chicago	198 15	184	189 5	20,000
Pittsburgh	206	193	194 27	27,000
Atlanta	215 15	202	211	15,000
Capacity	47,000	38,000	32,000	

Total cost: $20,982

made and the new plant built, conditions may change. The expected market acceptance may not materialize, new competition may develop to reduce the forecasted sales, cost of production may be higher than anticipated, other operating costs may increase, and many other unforeseen developments may arise. Management has no way of being certain about the future, and the location decision must be based on the best available information. The use of techniques, as suggested, will reduce the probability of error.

Foreign Location Problems

The impetus toward the development of the multinational firm in recent years has added a new facet to the location problem. Many of the same factors considered for a domestic location decision apply to a foreign location. However, some unique factors bear on the foreign location decision.

The selection of the area (in this case the country) would be influenced by additional factors such as any entry requirements the country may have. Among the considerations would be any restrictions placed on foreign firms

TABLE 8-4 (Cont.)

From / To	L.A.	Seattle	Minn.	Demand
San Francisco	182	165 / 25	200	25,000
Denver	190 / 17	173 / 13	195	30,000
Chicago	198	184	182 / 20	20,000
Pittsburgh	206 / 15	193	194 / 12	27,000
Atlanta	215 / 15	202	204	15,000
Capacity	47,000	38,000	32,000	

Total cost: $21,827

which may give the home firms a competitive advantage. Certain import barriers on materials, services, and capital may also exist. In addition, there are often stricter governmental controls imposed by the host countries on outside firms. Consideration should be given to the security of the investment. What guarantees of the safety of the investment, the protection of property, and protection of nationals of other countries working for the firm exist? Special consideration must be given to the social and cultural differences which will affect the marketing of the product or service, the workers' attitudes and performance, and the methods of management.

Regarding the foreign site selection, Robinson states that the major variation from a domestic decision is that differences in relative costs and product mobility between markets may be greater.[4] Thus, it would appear that in approaching a foreign location decision, essentially the same types of analysis used in the domestic location would apply. While specialized conditions appertain, the same may be said if one considers individual domestic location problems. Each case is unique unto itself, and must be evaluated as such, weighing those factors which are significant to the decision at hand.

[4]Richard D. Robinson, *International Management* (New York: Holt, Rinehart and Winston, Inc., 1967), p. 55.

SUMMARY

The planning of the operations system involves a number of specific activities; generally it can be said to be an important and dynamic endeavor. In this chapter, product and plant planning are examined.

In planning the operations system of any enterprise, one of the first activities must be concerned with the design of the product or service to be offered. In the design process, a variety of factors must be considered. The characteristics of the product or service to be offered are significant. It is necessary to be aware of the fact that, from the operations manager's viewpoint, perhaps the most important consideration is the production design. This aspect largely determines whether the enterprise is capable of creating the product or service. The permissible deviation, or tolerance, from an established standard must be realtistic. Economic considerations may have an effect on the design process.

It is also possible that standards or criteria of different sorts may be applied which will influence the results of the design process; hence, the functioning of the operations system. While standardization may be advantageous under certain circumstances, the establishment of inflexible standards, or ill-timed standards may have a negative effect on the efficiency of the operations system.

Another planning decision which bears heavily on the operations system is the capacity decision. Thus, planning and evaluation of capital investment is of great significance. There are numerous models which can be used to evaluate such problems. Whether they are general in nature or highly specialized, the primary consideration must always be the potential economic advantage of the proposed investment.

A selected group of models are discussed. The first types of models assist in finding the return on investment. The simple rate of return method and the unadjusted rate of return on average investment method are illustrated as typical of this type of evaluation. Closely related is calculation of the payback period, which is the reciprocal of the simple rate of return method. These techniques are not considered as highly accurate and reliable, but they are still widely used, at least for initial evaluations.

A more reliable means for equipment investment analysis is the present value technique. This method is used to determine the value of future income at the time of decision.

An operational approach to the equipment investment problem which has a degree of success is the MAPI system. Considered as an adjusted after-tax rate of return method, this system uses relatively simple graphs and charts to effectuate the complex theory.

The plant location decision is an infrequent one, but it may have a great effect on the successful operation of the enterprise. Such a decision must be made when the enterprise is first formed. An existing enterprise may face this decision when the demand for its output exceeds present capacity, or when the facilities have become obsolete. In addition, it may be desirable for the enterprise to decentralize for some reason.

In making the location decision, it is usually necessary to first consider certain regional factors to determine the general area. While factors differ in their significance for different enterprises, considerations of nearness to market, transportation facilities available, nearness to sources of raw materials and supplies, and the labor market are common.

It is next necessary to select the specific site, and again, while the importance varies with the situation, certain factors are generally applicable. The nature of the community, the political stability of the community, and the characteristics of the actual site itself are examples.

Some methods of analyzing the location decision are discussed. Different economic analysis methods are available, such as break-even analysis. In addition, point-rating systems have been useful, and in certain types of multi-plant decisions, the distribution model of linear programming can be valuable.

Because of the increasing importance of multi-national operations, it is necessary to examine the nature of the foreign location decision. While it is basically the same as the domestic decision, there are some unique aspects which differentiate the two.

INCIDENT I

WHAT'S THE PAYOUT?

George Service, Production Manager of the Dixter Company, read a request from his Supervisor of Inventory Control, Jim Roberts, for the purchase of some new storage bins for the parts stock room. He called Roberts on the telephone, and after referring to the request said, "Jim, before I can consider this request, I need to know what the payout is."

Roberts answered, "How can I calculate the payout on something like storage bins? If we were talking about a production machine it would be possible, but I just don't see how it is possible on this type of item. We just need more storage."

"Well, you had better figure out a way," replied Service, "because I'm not going to approve this request until I can evaluate it on the basis of its payout. In fact, from now on, all requests for equipment of any sort will have to have a three-year-payout, or they get turned down. And I expect proof, not just claims."

Questions

1. What is your opinion of this approach to equipment investment analysis?
2. Do you agree that the calculation of the payout period is impossible for equipment such as storage bins?

INCIDENT II

THE DELTA CONTAINER COMPANY

The Delta Container Company is a manufacturer of a newly designed polyethylene-coated paper milk products container on which it has an exclusive patent. Acceptance of its design has been so great that Delta must expand its production capacity considerably in order to meet the demand. Delta will be serving a national market, and it estimates output will exceed 2 billion containers annually. The company is evaluating the alternatives of a single-plant location and multi-plant locations.

Questions

1. Should the Delta Container Company choose a single-plant location, or a multi-plant arrangement?
2. What are the major factors to consider in this problem?
3. If a single plant is chosen, would a plant in the southeastern section of the United States be a good location? Do you have any suggestions for a better regional location? Why?

QUESTIONS FOR DISCUSSION AND ANALYSIS

1. What is the significance of the design of the product or service to the operations function of the enterprise?
2. Discuss the factors which must be taken into account in the design process.
3. What is standardization? Give examples of the application of standardization.
4. Give some methods by which standards are established.
5. In what ways is the establishment of standards desirable? What are some of the possible disadvantages?
6. What is the general nature of the equipment investment decision? To what types of enterprises is it important?
7. Compare the simple rate of return method and the payback method of investment analysis. What are the drawbacks of each?
8. Describe the general nature of the present value method.
9. What is the goal of the MAPI system? Briefly describe the approach of this method.
10. If the location decision is one which is made infrequently, why is it important for the operating manager to be concerned with the problem?
11. Describe some of the conditions which may arise to bring about the need for a location decision.
12. What are some of the more important factors which influence the choice of an area or region? Of the specific site?
13. Select a specific facility: factory, department store, hospital, university, etc., and discuss what you think would be the important factors in selecting its location.
14. What are some of the sources of information and assistance available to management in making a location decision? Evaluate the usefulness of these sources.

15. What, if any, are the differences in the factors and approach to a foreign location decision, as compared with a domestic one?

SELECTED ADDITIONAL READINGS

Ackoff, R. L. (ed.). *Progress in Operations Research*. Vol. I. New York: John Wiley & Sons, Inc., 1961.

Bowman, Edward H., and Robert B. Fetter. *Analysis for Production and Operations Management*, 3d ed. Homewood, Illinois: Richard D. Irwin, Inc., 1967. Chapter 10.

Dreyfus, S. E. "A Generalized Equipment Replacement Study." *Journal of the Society of Industrial and Applied Mathematics*, Vol. VIII, No. 3 (1960), pp. 425–435.

Goslin, Lewis N. *The Product Planning System*. Homewood, Illinois: Richard D. Irwin, Inc., 1967.

Hertz, David B. "Risk Analysis in Capital Investment." *Harvard Business Review*, Vol. XLII, No. 1 (January–February, 1964), pp. 95–106.

Moore, James M. *Plant Layout and Design*. New York: The Macmillan Co., 1962. Chapter 3.

Morris, William T. *The Capacity Decision System*. Homewood, Illinois: Richard D. Irwin, Inc., 1967.

Reisman, A., and E. S. Buffa. "A General Model for Investment Policy." *Management Science*, Vol. VIII, No. 3 (April, 1962), pp. 304–310.

Starr, Martin Kenneth. *Product Design and Decision Theory*. Englewood Cliffs: Prentice-Hall, Inc., 1963.

Steiner, George A. *Top Management Planning*. New York: The Macmillan Co., 1969. Chapter 19.

Terborgh, George. *Business Investment Management*. Washington: Machinery and Allied Products Institute, 1967.

9 | **Forecasting**

Many decisions which the operations manager must make are concerned with some point in the future; tomorrow, next week, next month, next year, or still further away. Before any plans can be made, a projection into the future is needed. In addition, a determination of the conditions under which the decisions will be put into operation must be made. It is not realistic to plan for a new product without having made some projection of the demand for that product over a period of time. A manager would not make a decision involving the investment of large amounts of capital without first attempting to find out the conditions which would exist over the period of time needed to recover the investment costs.

Naturally no one is able to predict the future exactly — not even the crystal-ball gazer at the carnival or the gypsy tea-leaf reader. The manager is neither a seer nor soothsayer possessed with mystical powers, nor is he able to hire someone to supply these powers. However, making some determination of the future is an essential part of the operations manager's function. It is the starting point in planning almost any aspect of the operations of the firm. The goals of any decision are established by considering the future.

Part of the operations manager's job is concerned with determining future conditions related to the operation of the enterprise. After a full examination and analysis of all available pertinent data, a forecast can be formulated.

This chapter will be concerned with examining various types of forecasts, available forecasting techniques, how forecasts may be controlled, and the measurement of accuracy of the forecast.

PREMISES

A primary prerequisite to the establishment of any forecast is to set forth the basis on which it is made. The assumptions made as antecedent to the actual forecast must be established. For example, certain economic and political conditions have to be assumed before forecasting the sales volume of the firm. These become the *premises* of the forecast, and the forecast is only valid as long as the premises under which it was made hold. If the premises change as time passes, a reevaluation must be made in light of the new ones. Certain forecasts become the premise for another forecast. The prediction of the political environment may well be the premise for the forecast of general economic conditions. This, in turn, may be an important factor in the prognosis of the sales volume of the firm, which may serve as basis for the specifics of the cost and revenue forecast for new capital investment.

Selection of the proper premises is an important process in the establishment of accurate forecasts. The decision involving the determination of specific premises is not easy. Premises must be developed, analyzed, and evaluated in the process, and this may involve commitment of considerable resources to guarantee success. What may be a significant premise for one firm may be irrelevant for another. In making a forecast, certain assumptions about environmental factors affecting the firm are usually considered. An example of this is the future level of economic activity, as expressed by the projected Gross National Product. However, the importance of even this rather basic premise may vary from firm to firm.

The same can be said with respect to the relative importance of certain premises in enterprises in different industries. For example, the consideration of the competitive environment for an automobile manufacturer is a significant factor in developing a sales forecast. On the other hand, such a premise is not really important to a public utility firm such as a local gas, electric, or water company.

Typical Forecasting Premises

Forecasting premises are categorized in several different ways. They are frequently considered on the basis of their relationship to the environment of the enterprise; i.e., internal or external. Another way of viewing forecasting premises is in accordance with the amount of control the enterprise has in relation to the premises. This category breaks down further to controllable, partially controllable, and uncontrollable. Generally, most of the external premises are beyond control of the firm, and most of the internal ones are controllable. Those partially controllable tend to be divided between internal and external.

Another way the premises of forecasting can be classified is to identify them as implied, high impact, analytical, or procedural.[1] Implied premises are those not clearly enumerated, but assumed to exist for a variety of reasons. High and low impact premises are determined by the force of the effect they will have on the particular enterprise. Analytical premises result from a detailed study of the area under consideration. Where policies, or some other established methods of operation, are related to the assumptions expected to prevail, the premises are identified as procedural.

Factors Underlying Premises

Usually the way a premise is classified differs from enterprise to enterprise. Thus, no attempt will be made to suggest a grouping. Instead, some of the more common factors underlying premises are discussed.

---

[1]George A. Steiner, *Top Management Planning* (New York: The Macmillan Co., 1969) pp. 200–202.

Economic Factors. The assumptions about the future economic conditions play a large role in forecast results. The overall picture is important, and the constituent parts of the total level of activity must be considered. For example, many elements interact to result in a particular level of GNP. While the total GNP is of interest and a significant factor to most enterprises, certain elements will be more important to a particular forecaster. Factors such as the amount of consumer disposable income, the level of the labor force and the percentage of employment or unemployment, the level of productivity, and price levels are general economic premises to be developed.

General economic factors are not the only important considerations. The firm must also assess the conditions that will exist for its particular industry, and for the enterprise itself. Thus, the premises about the total economy must be examined for their effect on the industry and the firm to develop the required additional premises.

Governmental Factors. Today it is virtually impossible to make assumptions regarding the level of economic activity without consideration of various governmental factors. Obviously the role of the government in influencing the level of economic activity is great. To develop premises about the economy, assumptions about government policy and the predominant political philosophy must be made.

The existence of a particular political philosophy, and the likelihood of its continuance, can be important. If an election is upcoming, the forecaster needs to make some prediction regarding the results, and about the stability of existing political thought. The presumption of stability, as opposed to a significant change, can have a strong influence on other assumptions.

These political considerations will have far-reaching effects in terms of the international picture and other important factors: war or peace. Also to be considered are the relationships to domestic politics at all governmental levels: national, state, or local.

Recently, the influence of government fiscal policy on the level of the economy has been evident. The enterprise, in developing its forecasting premises, must also take account of government policy in regulation and control.

These types of premises are not always easy to develop, and often the amount of reliable information available for analyzing the situation is not great. Still, because of the strong influence they can have on the forecast, these assumptions cannot be ignored. The forecaster must develop the appropriate premises with respect to government, despite the difficulties.

General Environmental Factors. Forecasting premises already discussed are clearly related to the external environment where the enterprise must operate. Other external environmental factors requiring assumptions should be mentioned. In almost any type of enterprise, note must be made of the expected trend in population over the forecast period. This trend will almost assuredly have an influence on the demand for the product or service of the enterprise.

Population data are readily available and this determination should not create a serious problem.

Additionally, premises will have to be developed regarding a variety of cultural and social forces. While these premises may be more difficult to establish, they must most certainly be considered. They can have a substantial effect upon a particular enterprise. For example, a manufacturer of clothing will undoubtedly find these forces to have an influence upon the styling of his product. The emphasis upon ecology has developed into a social force, and it touches literally every enterprise.

Closely related are the ethical factors which exist in respect to all types of enterprises. These are quite evident in medical, educational, and religious institutions, but they have become more of a force in respect to industrial concerns as well. In part, this has arisen out of the price-fixing cases and similar happenings in certain industries.

A final set of factors deserving mention are technological in nature. Technology has become an extremely pertinent area of concern because of the rapid growth experienced. Because of its importance, many firms are developing a specific technological forecast.

Market Factors. When developing premises for the factors already discussed, the primary concern is with the influence they will have on the market for the product or service of the enterprise. Analysis of the position of the industry where the enterprise operates is of first consideration. Thus, some determination of total industry sales will have to be made. Useful data are usually readily available from several sources. Past industry records, trade associations, financial institutions, and governmental agencies are typical of these sources.

Once the industry premises are set, the position of the particular enterprise within that industry must be developed. Therefore, an evaluation must be made of the competitive structure of the industry. This evaluation requires some knowledge of what the other enterprises are planning. In a competitive industry, this type information is not easily obtained. Some information is available from trade associations, government sources, and certain published data. However, to obtain all the information needed, the enterprise must resort to other techniques. Foremost among these is to engage in market research activities. For the small enterprise this may not be feasible because of cost. Smaller firms may have to play "follow the leader" and emulate the larger firms, taking it for granted they have the right information. Another approach found in practice is a form of industrial intelligence used in an attempt to learn something about the activities of a competitor.

Enterprise Factors. Assumptions must also be made about factors peculiar to the enterprise. Most of these premises concerning the enterprise would be controllable by management, at least to some degree. One factor of this type will undoubtedly play a large role in the premises of the forecast. This factor is the policies of the enterprise. Certainly, in developing a forecast relative to any aspect of the future activities of the enterprise, it is necessary to consider the existing policies, the continuing policies, and those policies newly put into operation.

Specific enterprise's policies, and those policies presumed for competitive firms, are a significant consideration. For example, in the automobile industry, any company, say Ford, must consider sales promotion and pricing policies. However, they cannot do this without some consideration of the sales promotion and pricing policies of General Motors, Chrysler, and American Motors. Thus, premises within the control of the firm will have to be based on premises regarding policies of competitors over which they have no control.

Another group of factors related to the individual enterprise encompasses the various resource factors. This group includes the capacity of the enterprise and assumptions about changes in capacity. The capacity level relates to availability of funds for capital investment. Among the resources to be considered are manpower and various supplies, including raw materials. These may or may not be controllable by the enterprise directly, but premises must be established for these factors.

Certain forecasts of the enterprise become premises upon which other forecasts are made. This is certainly true with regard to the basic forecast — the sales forecast. For example, forecasts for production, material requirements, and manpower needs must surely use the sales forecast as a premise.

TYPES OF FORECASTS

Literally, it is possible to make a forecast about anything in the future. We daily read or listen to the weather forecast. At the start of the season, the "experts" forecast the participants in the World Series some seven months away. Throughout the fall, weekly "peerless pigskin prognostications" are available. In addition, numerous analysts forecast the movement of the stock market and of individual stocks. Every four years there are forecasts of the results of the presidential election. These predictions are not necessarily derived by any formalized technique; after all, who hasn't made such forecasts himself?

The concern of the operations manager, however, is with specific types of forecasts fundamental to many decisions that he has to make. One of these forecasts, the economic forecast, becomes a premise of other more specific forecasts of the enterprise. The sales forecast can be another premise for enterprise planning in other areas. These two types have traditionally been the most widely developed forecasts of any enterprise. Any other forecasts have largely depended on these two. Recently, another rather unique type of forecast has come to be considered as important for many enterprises. Technological factors are fundamental in establishing the general environmental premises. With the rapidly accelerating pace of technology, this factor has become more intangible; it has created a greater need for enterprises to engage in technological forecasting as a separate activity. Because of their significance to most enterprises, an examination of economic forecasting, sales forecasting, and technological forecasting should prove beneficial.

Economic Forecasting

Probably no single factor is more important in managerial planning than the level of future business activity. It is certain that the first businessman, whoever he might have been, was concerned with predicting the level of economic activity in the future; even with crude techniques or probable inaccuracies. While the present-day approaches are more refined, and the methods used may be viewed as more scientific, the process of economic forecasting is still subject to error. Even so, the economic forecast is a necessary and important tool for any manager. Notwithstanding anticipated inaccuracy, these forecasts provide some idea of the consensus of projections regarding the future business climate. Inasmuch as opinions about the level of the economy play an important role in the decisions made for the period of the forecast, this consensus is valuable. Thus, the process of economic forecasting is essential to the manager's thinking in making decisions regarding coming periods.

Generally speaking, the time period for the forecast will affect the probable accuracy. Techniques available for forecasting the economy result in more reliable short-range forecasts than those for longer periods of time. Any forecast beyond a year would be of doubtful reliability. The accuracy of any attempt to go beyond three or four months is questionable.

The task of developing a forecast of an economy of the dynamic nature and complexity of the United States is formidable. Anyone who has studied the many annual forecasts published, and the components of these forecasts, is fully aware of this. The forecaster must attempt to determine the level of the major constituents of the economy: consumer disposable income, business expenditures for plant and equipment, government expenditure, and others. The determination of any one of the components of the Gross National Product requires the devising of difficult analytical techniques in itself. In addition, it must be recognized that any forecast of business conditions is almost entirely a result of the total of a large number of individual decisions made by many people. These decisions are not necessarily rational, but result from many unknowns influencing the behavior of the human being.

Economic forecasts are not usually the responsibility of the operations manager, but many general forecasting techniques apply to all types of forecasting. It is sufficient to recognize the nature of the economic forecast. It becomes a premise for the forecast of the enterprise, and despite its potential inaccuracy, the economic forecast itself may have an influence on the economy. With this understanding, the economic forecast can be a valuable input for the operations manager.

Sales Forecasting

While the operations manager is not primarily responsible for the sales forecast, he may be involved in its development. It is perhaps the primary planning document of the enterprise, and the one he will depend on most in formulating his own plans.

The level of demand for the product or service of any enterprise will determine many other aspects of the operations of that firm. The sales forecast will establish the level of output, and the output level will influence the capacity level of the facilities of the enterprise. Capacity will further affect the needs for other resources (financial and manpower requirements). There will also be a relationship between the sales and such aspects of the firm's operations as inventory levels, operating costs, and ultimately operating profits.

Obviously, development of the sales forecast is a springboard for making innumerable operating decisions. It is not merely a matter of stating that we anticipate a certain number of units will be sold, or that sales will reach a particular dollar level in the next year. More detailed data are needed. Sales must be subdivided according to product lines, geographically, by customer, and by organizational units or profit centers. From these details, the enterprise is able to translate the forecast results into the specifics of operational aspects. These specifics then become the plans of the operations manager in the form of schedules, capacity requirements, manpower needs, and inventory levels.

As with economic forecasting, the process of sales forecasting is not easy. It has been suggested that the sales forecast is wrong as soon as it is made. Despite this pessimism, even if true, it would be impossible to arrive at reasonable decisions about the operations of the enterprise without a sales forecast. This forecast is an integral part of the planning function of the operations manager of any enterprise.

Technological Forecasting

In discussing the premises common in the forecasting process, reference was made to technological factors as an important area. In recent years the increasing emphasis on this type of forecasting has elevated it to a high level of importance. These forecasts have particular significance to the operations manager because of the influence they have on his area of concern.

The reason technological forecasting has become so necessary is a result of the rapidly increasing pace of technological development. It does not require a very close examination of these types of changes in our society to recognize we are living in a period unprecedented throughout history in this regard. It is safe to say that in the last 50 years we have experienced greater technological change than the total changes prior to that time from the beginning of recorded history. It is also just as certain that by the end of this century a similar comparison using the then "last 50 years" will show an identical relationship. This implies that the rapid technological growth will continue at an increasing rate. After 26 years, Aldous Huxley reviewed the comments he had made in the *Brave New World*, and found that a majority of the technological changes foreseen for a 700-year period were already accomplished.[2] Because technology is such a dominant force and so dynamic, management must attempt to predict its develpoment.

2Aldous Huxley, *Brave New World Revisited* (New York: Bantam Books, Inc., 1958).

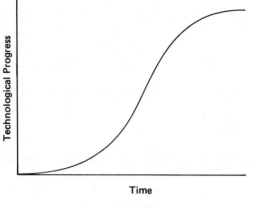

Time

FIGURE 9-1

Technology Progress-Time Curve

Undoubtedly, management's major interest in this type forecasting stems from the need to keep abreast of technological change in order to remain competitive. Nothing can be more damaging to an enterprise than to allow others in the industry to get the jump on new products or techniques. It becomes a matter of self-preservation to forecast technological developments. The planning of most areas affecting the operations of an enterprise will be predicated on some assumptions about future technology. Planning for capital investment in new machinery or equipment, planning of new facilities requirements, and the planning involved in the research and development activities of the enterprise are some examples.

Accuracy of Technological Forecasting. The need for technological forecasting is clear, but the ability to produce accurate forecasts is lacking. There are so many intangibles involved in the development of technological breakthroughs that the forecaster is severely limited. It is doubtful that anyone could have predicted the many technical spinoffs from the space program. Nor, for that matter, can we surmise the full results of the unforeseen development of some method of immunization against heart disease or cancer.

Once a breakthrough occurs, however, prediction of the growth of the development is more feasible. A historical analysis of the progress of the technology of any given development will most likely show an exponential improvement rate. The progress can be represented by a curve like that shown in Figure 9-1.

Reference to the curve in Figure 9-1 indicates certain assumptions. Early progress is very small for a period of time. At some point very rapid progress begins, probably as a result of a specific breakthrough. This may be the result of a discovery making a useful item possible; e.g., splitting the atom made atomic energy feasible. This discovery could result from a production technology making economic production possible. Following the period of rapid growth, a leveling off is seen. This could represent a period of saturation, where only by another breakthrough could any further significant progress take place. It is conceivable that another curve of the same shape could start where this curve left off. For example, television could be represented by two sequential curves: the first showing progress for black and white; the second, for color television.

Despite what has been said above about the problems of accurate technological forecasting, the enterprise should develop this kind of forecast. For short-term periods, acceptable forecasts should be possible by means of historical trends and statistical probability analysis. This does not mean that "history repeats itself," and, therefore, because a certain progress took place in the past that there will be a continued similar progress. It is possible to determine the pertinent elements of the environment and to take cognizance of them. Technological forecasting must recognize the strong influence of environmental factors. This type forecast is only a part of a total attempt to relate the enterprise to its environment. It is not possible to produce a techological forecast without this recognition. The relationship of technology to society appears to be of particular significance.

Technology and Society. Technology is dynamic; this characteristic makes it a strong force in our society. As a result of technology, man has reached the high level of life which he now enjoys. Continued technological growth should lead to even greater benefits. However, the beneficial effects will depend on how well society is able to accept and control the ever growing force of technology. Certainly, the ability to forecast technological change will assist in this social acceptance and control.

Recent concern with the ecological environment has brought attention to the mixed blessings of technology from a social viewpoint. Most pollution problems today are a direct result of technology. The technical improvements in products and processes contribute heavily to air, noise, and water pollution. Paradoxically, technology is the force that must, in a large part, solve these problems. In this attempt, society must be aware of the effects the new technical changes will have.

It is probable that technology alone will be unable to achieve a solution to these problems. Technology, while appearing to be the answer, may only result in the exchange of one problem for another. In considering technological change in the future, the needs and values of society are important. Arriving at solutions to problems will be more difficult because the consideration of human desires and needs is involved. This means that technological progress must be carried out in an atmosphere where the goals of society are considered.

One area of social concern involving technology, prevalent for some time, is the effect it has on jobs. Uneasiness about "technological unemployment" is long-standing. Increasing the pace of change will unquestionably cause this problem to be intensified. In addition, it will lead to a consideration of the way work will be performed, since machines are increasingly able to do more tasks, both of a physical, and of a sensory or mental nature. The character of the man-machine relationship is an integral part of the operations manager's area. It is related specifically to the design of jobs, and will be examined when this problem area is discussed.

Certainly it is clear that the technological future is not easily determined. Many factors cause difficulty in technological forecasting. Because of the potential effect on society, enterprises of all types must consider it as part of their total forecasting system. Technological forecasting is a most significant environmental factor for the enterprise. While precise forecasts are desirable, they can only be considered as having limited accuracy at this time. Continued improvement is to be expected, and will result in better planning for the enterprise, and improved technology for society.

FORECASTING TECHNIQUES

There is no way of being certain that the choice of a given technique is the best for the particular forecast. Certain methods are more commonly found in use, and, thus, these may be the more useful. Forecasting techniques can be broadly grouped as empirical and analytical. It is probable the latter type will be more reliable because of dependence on mathematical and statistical tools. However, good forecasting results can still be achieved by the use of the empirical techniques. In fact, there are many examples where excellent results have been consistently forthcoming by such methods. Very likely, a combination of empirical and analytical techniques will be used to arrive at the final forecast. It is doubtful that a serious forecast can be developed by using only a single technique. Comparison of the results of two or more methods serves as a check of potential accuracy. A wide disparity would tend to raise a question as to the reason for the divergent results.

Empirical Techniques

Empirical techniques for developing a forecast utilize a series of reports originating from a variety of sources supplying data considered to be reliable. The reports are usually in a form which makes them clear and easy to accumulate for a final forecast. However, such reports result from subjective judgments and biases, making any estimate of their reliability impossible. Forecasting is still at a stage where the use of hunch or intuition often yields good results. This will always be true in individual cases, and even with the use of analytical techniques, a certain amount of judgment will be called for. Three widely used empirical forecasting techniques are: the jury of executive opinion method; the sales force composite approach; and users' expectation reports.

Jury of Executive Opinion Technique. This technique uses the forecasts of executives from various parts of the enterprise. These forecasts can be collected either in a group meeting, or by means of reports sent in by each executive. Once the consensus is developed, it is usually reviewed by the president or by a group of top executives. The simplicity of this technique commends it to the attention of management. However, this technique is heavily weighted by opinion and judgment unsupported by any data. This technique can be used as an initial step in the forecasting procedure (if the cost of the use of executive resources is not too great); however, it would hardly seem logical to depend exclusively on a forecast developed by this means.

Sales Force Composite Technique. This is very much like the jury of executive opinion approach except that it uses the sales force to develop the forecast. This technique assumes that the salesmen are close to the action and should have the best information about the expectations for the next period. Each salesman is asked to give his forecast of sales in his territory. These are submitted to the territorial manager, then passed to the next level where further accumulation (and modification) takes place. Ultimately these accumulated and modified data arrive at the top level of sales management. The final result is reviewed by top management, and possibly revised in the light of its beliefs and knowledge of the total position of the company.

Certainly, salesmen should know the potential which exists for sales from their close contacts with the firm's customers. Salesmen are often highly optimistic individuals, and this characteristic may color their outlook when making the forecast. Also, it is possible the salesman may fear his forecast will become a quota or measurement of his future performance. With this attitude, he is unlikely to provide accurate data. Finally, the individual salesman is usually not in a position to see the total economic picture, nor can he fully gauge the strategy of the firm for the forecast period.

User's Expectation Technique. This empirical technique approaches the forecast with the premise that the users of the enterprise's product or service are the best source of information about future demand. This technique requires a carefully designed program for soliciting the users for this information. If a reliable picture of the users' intentions can be obtained, this information may be a useful base for developing the forecast.

This technique is most practical when the users are small in number, or when a few large firms dominate the demand for the product or service. Also recognize that the stated expectations are subject to change at some later time. The user may not really have a valid picture of his own needs. This technique is sometimes the only possible one available for making a forecast. This situation is especially true for a new product when no information regarding the past history of the product exists. The users' expectation technique may also be useful for a small enterprise where the necessary resources to use other forecasting techniques are not available.

Analytical Techniques

Analytical forecasting techniques can be described as those which depend on the use of mathematical or statistical methods. These techniques are most commonly used for forecasting purposes, because they yield the most accurate and reliable forecasts. The use of mathematics and statistics in forecasting reduces the element of subjectivity, and replaces it with a more objective, systematic approach. In addition, it is possible to determine the potential forecast error by developing confidence limits. The improvement in the methodology, along with the use of the computer to reduce the computational load, has played a large role in the growing utilization of analytical forecasting.

A large number of these techniques are available. Present examination will be limited to some of the more widely used ones. Included will be moving-average techniques; time-series analysis including secular, cyclical, seasonal, and irregular trends; correlation methods; and exponential smoothing.

Moving Averages. Eliminating the idea that things will remain as they are, the simplest analytical method is the moving average. The moving-average method accepts the assumption that what is being forecasted does not remain constant. Thus, there is some sort of trend, either upward or downward. This method attempts to smooth out the trend so the results are considered to be closer to the true value. It is assumed that the random error which exists is reduced. The larger the sample used, the smaller the deviation from the true mean.

Computation of the moving average consists of finding a series of sequential averages by excluding the first item in the series and adding the last item. For example, to obtain a three-item moving average, total the first three items in the series and divide by three for the first moving average. Next, drop the first item and add the fourth one; again divide by three for the second moving average. This process would be followed for all items in the series. To illustrate, Table 9-1 shows the results of a three-item moving average from a series of ten values.

A moving average can use any number of items or periods. For forecasting purposes, it uses the most recent observations; the last three months, six months,

TABLE 9-1

Example of Three-Item Moving Average

Series Value	Three-Item Moving Total	Three-Item Moving Average
46		
53		
44	143	47.67
50	147	49.00
53	147	49.00
64	167	55.67
70	187	62.33
67	201	67.00
72	209	69.67
65	204	68.00

or year. The number of items or periods of time utilized depends on the degree of variation. If the series values change little between periods, a larger number of items is preferred. Conversely, with wide fluctuations, fewer periods are more representative. If the number of periods is small, the most recent data have more significance.

Generally speaking, the moving average is considered less accurate than other analytical techniques. Moving averages, because of the influence of past periods, lag behind the trend; they are low on an upward trend, and high on a downward one. This is particularly true when more time periods are used. It is possible to use the moving average and give greater importance to the more recent data. Briefly stated, weighted moving-average techniques apply some factor to each value used to achieve the average. This weight assigned is assumed to be related to the importance of the factor. The total of the weights, or factors, must always equal one. Weighting may be equal for all values, may increase by a constant amount from the first item in the series to the last, or may increase at an increasing rate, or exponentially. The greatest problem in the weighted moving-average technique is how to determine proper weights on an objective basis. One special form of weighting, exponential smoothing, will be described below.

Time-Series Analysis. The classification of data according to the time intervals of occurrence is a very common method of presenting information regarding the operations of an enterprise. Usually the interest in such information is to analyze and measure the changes taking place over the time period involved. Data presented in this form are familiar to even the most casual observer. Typical of time series are the graphical representations of the level of business activity by months over a period of years, or the showing of the movement of stock prices over time.

The presentation of information by time series is, in itself, not of great value without analysis of the changes and movements which take place. These changes or movements are usually identified by four types: secular trend; seasonal variations; cyclical fluctuations; and irregular, or random variations. Each type of movement will be discussed with an examination of some of the applicable analytical techniques.

SECULAR TREND — THE LEAST SQUARES METHOD. Secular trend is the long-term change which occurs in a series. The trend may either reflect growth or decline. A secular trend can be represented by a straight line or a curved line on a graph. This type trend line, frequently referred to as a "line of best fit," can be drawn by "eyeballing" — drawing what appears to be the trend. However, the most frequently used method for establishing a secular trend line is the least squares method. Those trends represented by a nonlinear or curved line denote a varying rate of change. A constant, absolute change for each period throughout the series is represented by a straight line.

The least squares method for finding a linear trend line, or a first degree line, is based on the following equation for a straight line:

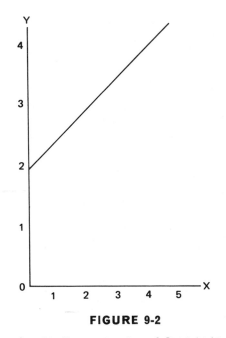

FIGURE 9-2

Graphic Representation of Straight Line

$$Y = a + bX \qquad \text{(1)}$$

Where:

$Y =$ that variable for which we want to determine the trend. (Dependent Variable)

$a =$ the Y intercept, or where $X = 0$

$b =$ the slope of the line, or the change in Y that occurs with a change of one unit in X

$X =$ the time against which the series is plotted. (Independent Variable)

Thus, if the values of X, given as 0 to 5, with $a = 2$ and $b = .5$, the equation for the straight line would be $y = 2 + .5X$. This results in the following values of Y for the given values of X:

X	Y
0	2.0
1	2.5
2	3.0
3	3.5
4	4.0
5	4.5

The graphic representation of this straight line is shown in Figure 9-2.

In utilizing the least squares method for straight-line trends, a set of "normal" equations are derived. These two equations are:

$$\text{(I)} \quad \Sigma X = Na + b\Sigma X \qquad\qquad (2)$$

$$\text{(II)} \ \Sigma XY = a\Sigma X + b\Sigma X^2 \qquad\qquad (3)$$

Where:

  X = the deviation of each year from the midpoint in the time series
  N = number of years
  Y = the value of the variable being measured, e.g., sales
  XY = the product of the deviation and the value of the sales for that year
  X^2 = the square of the deviations

Number each of the years sequentially, 1, 2, 3, . . . , N, and designate the deviations for each year before the midpoint as -1, -2, etc. Those years after the midpoint are designated as $+1$, $+2$, etc., with the middle year as 0, for an odd number of years. Therefore the $\Sigma X = 0$, and the normal equations reduce to:

$$\text{(I)} \quad \Sigma X = Na \qquad\qquad (4)$$

$$\text{(II)} \ \Sigma XY = b\Sigma X^2, \text{ or} \qquad\qquad (5)$$

$$\text{(I)} \quad a = \frac{\Sigma Y}{N} \qquad\qquad (6)$$

$$\text{(II)} \quad b = \frac{\Sigma XY}{\Sigma X^2} \qquad\qquad (7)$$

To illustrate this technique, assume the sales figures for a manufacturing company shown in column Y in Table 9-2. In addition, columns for values of

TABLE 9-2

Computation of Straight-Line Trend of Sales
Least Squares Method

Year	X	X^2	Y*	XY*
1	-4	16	11	-44
2	-3	9	15	-45
3	-2	4	16	-32
4	-1	1	17	-17
5	0	0	21	0
6	$+1$	1	20	20
7	$+2$	4	20	40
8	$+3$	9	23	69
9	$+4$	16	24	96
Total	0	60	167	87
N=9				

*Sales in dollars. 000,000 omitted.

X, X^2, and XY have been added, and the summations of these columns are included. With the information contained in this table, it is possible to calculate the regression line by using the least squares method, and to forecast next year's sales.

Thus, substituting into the two equations:

$$\text{(I)} \quad a = \frac{\Sigma Y}{N} = \frac{167}{9} = 18.56$$

$$\text{(II)} \quad b = \frac{\Sigma XY}{\Sigma X^2} = \frac{87.}{60} = 1.45$$

With the values of a and b computed, it is possible to determine the straight-line trend for the nine years. Also, the forecasted sales for year ten can be found using the equation of the straight line. In this case, the value of X would be 5. The calculations of this forecast, using Y_c to represent the trend values to differentiate it from the actual values of Y, are shown below:

$$
\begin{aligned}
Y_c &= a + bX \\
&= 18.56 + 1.45(5) \\
&= 18.56 + 7.25 \\
&= 25.81 \text{ or } \$25,810,000
\end{aligned}
$$

Sales data for the nine years, from Table 9-2, and the resultant straight-line trend are shown in Figure 9-3. From the already determined value of a above,

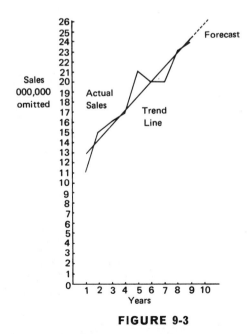

FIGURE 9-3

Actual Sales, Straight-Line Trend and Forecasted Sales

one point on the line is found, for year five, where X is equal to 0. Only one other point is needed to determine the line. Thus, using year one, $Y = 18.56 + 1.45(-4)$ or $18.56 - 5.80 = 12.76$. The forecast for year ten is indicated by a dotted line.

Secular trends may take a nonlinear form when changes do not occur at a constant rate or in a constant amount. The least squares method may also be applied to nonlinear trend lines. The simplest nonlinear trend line is the *second-degree parabola*, expressed by the following equation:

$$Y = a + bX + cX^2 \qquad \textbf{(8)}$$

From this equation are derived three "normal" equations:

$$\text{(I)} \quad \Sigma Y = Na + b\Sigma X + c\Sigma X^2 \qquad \textbf{(9)}$$

$$\text{(II)} \quad \Sigma XY = a\Sigma X + b\Sigma X^2 + c\Sigma X^3 \qquad \textbf{(10)}$$

$$\text{(III)} \quad \Sigma X^2 Y = a\Sigma X^2 + b\Sigma X^3 + c\Sigma X^4 \qquad \textbf{(11)}$$

As in the straight-line method, these equations simplify and reduce so they can be solved directly for the values of a, b, and c. Equation (7) for b, used in the straight-line method, still applies. For a and c:

$$a = \frac{\Sigma Y - c\Sigma X^2}{N} \qquad \textbf{(12)}$$

$$c = \frac{N\Sigma X^2 Y - \Sigma X^2 \Sigma Y}{N\Sigma X^4 - (\Sigma X^2)^2} \qquad \textbf{(13)}$$

Use the same sales data presented in Table 9-2 to compute the additional values required for Table 9-3. Since the trend line will now be a curve, all values of Y_c must be computed.

Computation of a and c is achieved by substitution into Equations (12) and (13). The value of b does not have to be computed; that was done above when it was found that $b = 1.45$. The computation of c must be done first, as follows:

$$c = \frac{(9)(1083) - (60)(167)}{(9)(708) - (60)^2}$$

$$c = \frac{-273}{2772} = -.098$$

$$a = \frac{(167) - (-.098)(60)}{9}$$

$$a = \frac{167 + 5.88}{9} = 19.21$$

TABLE 9-3

Computation of Nonlinear Trend of Sales
Least Squares Method

Year	X	X^2	X^4	Y*	XY*	X^2Y*	Y_c*
1	−4	16	256	11	−44	176	11.842
2	−3	9	81	15	−45	135	13.978
3	−2	4	16	16	−32	64	15.918
4	−1	1	1	17	−17	17	17.662
5	0	0	0	21	0	0	19.210
6	+1	1	1	20	20	20	20.562
7	+2	4	16	20	40	80	21.718
8	+3	9	81	23	69	207	22.678
9	+4	16	256	24	96	384	23.442
Total N=9	0	60	708	167	87	1083	

*Sales in dollars. 000,000 omitted.

The forecast for year ten is determined as follows:

$$Y_c = 19.21 + 1.45(5) + (−.098)(25)$$
$$= 19.21 − 7.25 − 2.45$$
$$= 19.21 + 4.80$$
$$= 24.01 \text{ or } \$24,010,000$$

This type curve represents only one form of nonlinear trend lines. It is possible to have higher degree parabola curves to represent the trend. It may be true that these advanced methods will tend to follow the data more accurately. However, if not applied judiciously, they may be more representative of seasonal or cyclical changes, rather than the secular trend.

In some circumstances, the pattern of the change cannot be represented by either a straight line or a parabola. This occurs when the growth or decline is a constant percentage. Exponential trends can be expressed by the equation:

$$Y = ab^x \tag{14}$$

There is no specific way to determine what approach best measures a secular trend. Often pure inspection will give a clue, but this is far from a surefire test. In most cases, several trend lines will fit well, and some choice must be made. Generally speaking, the use of the least squares method is as acceptable as any, if a good fit can be achieved. Any trend analysis is based on the assumption that past happenings are directly related to the future. The forecaster must be wary of this assumption, and most certainly must view other factors influencing the future. Other types of variations may also influence the movement of a time series.

SEASONAL VARIATION. A seasonal variation results in a time series with a recurring yearly pattern where certain months have high or low values. It is not unusual to find this type of change in a product or service. Many products have a definite pattern in their sales, related to the temperature norms for a particular time of the year. Not all seasonal variations are related to the climatic seasons, however. Virtually every product has some sort of seasonal variation. It is not always clear why seasonality occurs, but the fact it does is significant to the manager in developing a forecast.

There are various methods available for measuring seasonal variations. Most of them are essentially based on the idea of calculating some sort of index number for each month so that the average for the year is 100. A simple example of the calculation of an index number is as follows:

$$\text{Seasonal Index No.} = \left[\frac{\text{Monthly Sales}}{\text{Yearly Sales}} \times 100 \right] 12$$

Thus, if monthly sales were 8,897 units, and the annual sales amounted to 108,500 units, the computation of the index number would be:

$$\text{Seasonal Index No.} = \left[\frac{8,897}{108,500} \times 100 \right] 12$$

$$= (8.2)(12)$$

$$= 98.4$$

There are also more sophisticated means available for calculating seasonal index numbers which may be more accurate. No matter what method is used, the idea is to adjust the forecast data to take account of the seasonal variation. In forecasting, the seasonal index can be applied to the monthly trend forecast to make provision for the effect of the seasonal variation. This can be accomplished by multiplying the trend projection for a given month by the seasonal index for that month. Thus, if the trend indicated sales of 607 units, and the index of the seasonal variation for that month was .95, the seasonally adjusted forecast of sales for that particular month would be 607 × .95 = 577.

By taking into account the seasonal variation, it is possible to improve the quality of the forecast. The manager must constantly be aware of seasonal variations as they apply to his product. There is always a chance the seasonal pattern will change; the astute forecaster will consider this in his forecast.

CYCLICAL FLUCTUATIONS. While every enterprise will most certainly be affected by cyclical fluctuations, they are beyond the control of management. Consequently, it is important that management be aware of these movements. Cyclical fluctuations are variations in the level of business activity identified as periods of prosperity and depression. It is vital that management consider these fluctuations as they occur in their industry, to determine the cycle. Cyclical fluctuations are often the most significant movements occurring in a time series. Part of the logic behind this belief is that, to date, a reliable method for predicting

CHARTISTS

these variations has not been found. Since they cannot be predicted, they are potentially the most serious threats to the enterprise.

Even though no statistical techniques for forecasting cyclical fluctuations exist, some statistical methods can be used to measure the changes more accurately. Because of the significance of cyclical variations on the future of the enterprise, some form of forecasting must still be carried out. The forecaster must take into account all available information regarding cycles, making use of the best techniques possible (probably sprinkled generously with intuition and judgment) to develop the best forecast possible.

RANDOM OR IRREGULAR VARIATIONS. The level of business activity of an enterprise can be influenced by a wide variety of factors which cannot be foreseen. Among such factors are weather, strikes, or some onetime occurrence as a natural disaster. Most of these events are not of long-term duration which makes the prediction of their effect difficult. Generally speaking, the shorter the period of time covered by the forecast, the more influence these variations will have. While it is obvious the forecaster cannot predict individual events of this type, it is considered good practice to allow for random or irregular variations in the forecast.

Correlation. Occasionally it is useful to determine the relationship which exists between two or more series. It is possible the level of sales activity of an enterprise or industry is related to the movements of some other series. For instance, the sale of umbrellas may be related to the frequency of rain; the sale of gasoline might depend on the sale of automobiles; or the enrollment in a particular course upon the percentages of A's the students receive. This relationship between variables can be analyzed and measured by means of correlation. Correlation is particularly valuable in forecasting if there is a lead factor in the series related to sales. This means that the series changes at a predictable period of time, prior to a change in sales. It is essential to ascertain whether this leading change is a factor directly related to a change in sales, and is not a chance factor. If a relationship truly exists between the two variables, and this relationship can be accurately expressed, it becomes possible to forecast one when the other is known.

To calculate the relationship between two variables, it is possible to use a form of least squares to determine the values of the coefficients in the equation for the regression line. With these values known, it is possible to determine the value of Y_c for a known value of X in simple linear correlation.

The measure known as the coefficient of correlation determines reliability of the relationship. The coefficient of correlation (r) represents the degree of relationship, or association, existing between the two variables. A value of 1.00 indicates a perfect relationship, and a value of zero indicates no correlation exists. It is possible for r to have either a plus or minus value. A plus value means both variables increase together; a minus shows that the movements are in opposite directions, one increasing, the other decreasing. One equation commonly used for the computation of the coefficient of correlation is:

$$r = \frac{N(\Sigma\,XY) - (\Sigma\,X)(\Sigma\,Y)}{\sqrt{[N(\Sigma\,X^2) - (\Sigma\,X)^2][N(\Sigma\,Y^2) - (\Sigma\,Y)^2]}} \tag{15}$$

The relationship of the number of aerospace workers in California to the percentage of the total U.S. Defense and aerospace contract awards in California, for the period 1961-1970, is shown in Table 9-4.

Where:

X = the percentage of total aerospace contract awards in California

Y = aerospace workers in California in thousands of workers

TABLE 9-4

Computation of the Coefficient of Correlation

Year	X	Y	X^2	Y^2	XY
1961	23.5	390	552.25	152,100	9,165.0
1962	25.6	420	655.36	176,400	10,752.0
1963	27.7	415	767.29	172,225	11,495.5
1964	28.2	395	795.24	156,025	11,139.0
1965	28.1	400	789.61	160,000	11,240.0
1966	36.3	455	1,317.69	207,025	16,516.5
1967	41.3	485	1,705.69	235,225	20,030.5
1968	38.8	480	1,505.44	230,400	18,624.0
1969	37.9	455	1,436.41	207,025	17,244.5
1970	32.7	400	1,069.29	160,000	13,080.0
Total	320.1	4,295	10,594.27	1,856,425	139,287.0

The coefficient of correlation can be computed from the data in Table 9-4 by substitution into Equation (15).

$$r = \frac{1,392,870 - 1,374,829.5}{\sqrt{(3,478.69)(18,564,250 - 18,447,025)}}$$

$$= \frac{18,040.5}{\sqrt{(3,478.69)(117,225)}}$$

$$= \frac{18,040.5}{\sqrt{(407,789,435.25)}}$$

$$= \frac{18,040.5}{20,193.75}$$

$$= .893$$

Computation of correlation data can be quite complex and tedious. This is particularly true of nonlinear correlation, where the relationship between the two variables cannot be well expressed by a straight line. Computation methods are also complex for multiple correlation to measure the relationship between a dependent variable and two or more independent variables. It is fortunate that today there are available to the forecaster many standardized computer programs for computation of correlation data.

A final comment or caution seems appropriate with respect to correlation analysis. It is possible to find a high degree of correlation between two variables which was the result of purely unrelated factors. By way of illustration, it is possible to find a high correlation between the sale of bread and the number of students enrolled in colleges and universities. This correlation would undoubtedly be the result of another variable which has a relationship to the first two; possibly the population trend in this case. It is also possible a correlation may exist as a matter of pure chance, as the price of peanut butter and the attendance at the Rose Bowl game. In this case correlation would obviously have no validity for purposes of forecasting. Consequently, it is necessary for the forecaster to carefully develop the data used in correlation analysis.

Exponential Smoothing. Exponential smoothing is another technique used to level the variations encountered in a forecast. It does this by means of a weighting factor called an alpha factor (α). Alpha is a fraction used to discount the difference between the actual demand and the forecast previously made for the period. Exponential smoothing can be used for smoothing any time-series technique. The simplest form of smoothing is applied to average forecasts as the moving average. The alpha factor determined by management places greater emphasis on more recent data considered more valid.

The new forecast achieved by exponential smoothing results from adding the prior average forecast to the alpha factor fraction of the difference between actual demand and the old forecast. This is expressed by the following equation:

$$F_n = F_{n-1} + \alpha(D_n - F_{n-1}) \tag{16}$$

Where:

$$
\begin{aligned}
F_n &= \text{average forecast for next period} \\
F_{n-1} &= \text{average forecast for past period} \\
D_n &= \text{actual demand for period } n \\
\alpha &= \text{smoothing fraction alpha}
\end{aligned}
$$

Since the alpha factor is a fraction, it may have values only between zero and one. In actual use, the alpha factor usually is given a value between 0.1 and 0.3. It is more convenient to rearrange the terms of Equation (16) to express the new forecast as follows:

$$F_n = \alpha D_n + (1 - \alpha) F_{n-1} \tag{17}$$

The greater weight given to the most recent data can be illustrated by pointing out that the forecast for the present period (n) is based on the forecast for the immediate past period ($n - 1$) and the current demand (D_n). However, F_{n-1} is an average based on a previous period. Thus, F_{n-1} can be expressed:

$$F_{n-1} = \alpha D_{n-1} + (1 - \alpha) F_{n-2}$$

Substituting this for the value of F_{n-1} in Equation (17) we get:

$$F_n = \alpha D_n + (1 - \alpha)[\alpha D_{n-1} + (1 - \alpha)F_{n-2}]$$

$$= \alpha D_n + \alpha D_{n-1}[(1 - \alpha) + (1 - \alpha)^2 F_{n-2}] \qquad \textbf{(18)}$$

In a similar fashion, F_{n-2} was determined as a result of the previous period's average forecast (F_{n-3}), and the actual demand (D_{n-2}). This reasoning can be carried back to the original average forecast in the series so that the general equation for the nth forecast is as follows:

$$F_n = \alpha D_n + \alpha(1 - \alpha) D_{n-1} + \alpha(1 - \alpha)^2 D_{n-2} + \ldots + (1 - \alpha)^n F_{n-n} \qquad \textbf{(19)}$$

Where:

$$F_{n-n} = \text{initial forecast in series} = F_0$$

From this equation, it is clear that the most recent data get the greatest weighting. The latest actual demand receives a weight of α, the actual demand for one period removed is weighted by $\alpha(1 - \alpha)$, two periods removed by $\alpha(1 - \alpha)^2$, and so forth. To illustrate how the actual weights decrease, calculate the weights given to the actual demand for the case where $n = 5$, and $\alpha = 0.1, 0.2$, and 0.3. These values of α are used, since the normal range of alpha is from 0.1 to 0.3. The results of this computation are shown in Table 9-5.

Note from the weights in Table 9-5 that the higher the value of alpha, the faster the importance of the past data decreases. Thus, the significance of the determination of the correct value of α to be used can be seen.

Selection of Forecasting Technique

With such a variety of forecasting techniques available, management must select what approach to use. It is doubtful that any forecaster would wish to rely on any single technique. It would seem advisable to use a combination of available methods, empirical and analytical alike. Management will have to evaluate past experience with techniques used, consider the availability of the needed data, and compare the costs of various methods with the value of the results, to arrive at a decision regarding the techniques to be utilized. Should management decide on the users' expectations technique, trend line extrapolation, correlation, and exponential smoothing, the results of these forecasts will have to be reconciled. Generally the results of the different techniques used will be analyzed and compared by some predetermined procedure which consolidates the results into a single final forecast.

No one can say what technique or combination of techniques is best for a given enterprise. Almost any technique has some value, whether it is ease of computation or the past validity of its results; only experience can determine its total value in a specific case. Widespread use of statistical techniques has

TABLE 9-5

Weights Applied to Actual Demand

$n = 5$, $\alpha = 0.1$, $\alpha = 0.2$,   and $\alpha = 0.3$

Period	Equation	Exponential Weight		
n = 5		$\alpha = 0.1$	$\alpha = 0.2$	$\alpha = 0.3$
5	α	0.1	0.2	0.3
4	$\alpha(1 - \alpha)$	0.09	0.16	0.21
3	$\alpha(1 - \alpha)^2$	0.081	0.128	0.147
2	$\alpha(1 - \alpha)^3$	0.073	0.102	0.103
1	$\alpha(1 - \alpha)^4$	0.066	0.082	0.072
0	$\alpha(1 - \alpha)^5$	0.059	0.066	0.050

added greatly to the accuracy of forecasts in recent years. However, forecasting is far from being an exact science. Still, by attaching some degree of confidence to statistical forecasts, they are worth the effort.

RELIABILITY OF FORECASTS

In forecasting, it is desirable to have some measure of the reliability or confidence attached to a specific forecast. Any measure for the forecasts determined by empirical techniques would be strictly subjective. However, in the case of analytical techniques, statistical methods can be used to establish the reliability of the forecast. The standard deviation, the standard error of the estimate, the critical values of the coefficient of correlation, and the moving-range chart technique are examples of typical measures of reliability.

Standard Deviation

Perhaps the best measure of the error of a forecast, based on an average of past data, is the standard deviation. The *standard deviation* is computed by finding the square root of the sum of the squares of the deviations of the individual values from the mean, divided by the number of values. This can be stated as follows:

$$\sigma = \sqrt{\frac{\Sigma(X - \bar{X})^2}{N}} \tag{20}$$

Where:

σ = the standard deviation
X = the individual value
$\bar{X}$ = the mean
N = the number of items

The data on Table 9-4 are used to illustrate this computation. The mean for the number of aerospace workers is:

$$\bar{X} = \frac{390 + 420 + 415 + \ldots + 455 + 400}{10} = \frac{4295}{10}$$

$$= 429.5$$

The standard deviation for this data could be computed as follows:

$$\sigma = \sqrt{\frac{(390 - 429.5)^2 + (420 - 429.5)^2 + \ldots + (400 - 429.5)^2}{10}}$$

$$= \sqrt{1172.25} = 34.24$$

Once the computation of the standard deviation is completed, it is possible to make a statement of confidence about the forecast. The forecaster may wish to state that the forecast will fall within certain limits 95% of the time. This is done by establishing upper and lower limits equal to the mean plus and minus two standard deviations. In this case, $429.5 + 68.48 = 497.98$ is the upper limit, and $429.5 - 68.48 = 361.02$ is the lower limit. If it is desired to establish tighter limits which will be correct say 99.7% of the time, three standard deviations would have to be used.

Standard Error of the Estimate

In using the correlation technique, it is possible to use the regression equation to arrive at estimates. Thus, the values for Y_c can be computed for each period and equivalent value of X. The closer the relationship of X and Y, the more probable it is that the estimates are accurate. The values of Y_c represent points on the regression line. The differences between the actual values (Y) and the estimates (Y_c) are residuals. Measurement of the residuals, or the scatter of the values of Y about the regression line, is accomplished by a determination of the average of the residuals. The process is essentially the same as that used for finding the average deviations from the mean in computing the standard deviation. The computation of the standard error of the estimate can also be illustrated by using the data in Table 9-4.

The basic equation for the standard error of the estimate is:

$$S_y = \sqrt{\frac{\Sigma(Y - Y_c)^2}{N}} \tag{21}$$

However, it is possible to use a shorter method to compute the standard error of the estimate. This method utilizes much of the data available from the summations in Table 9-4. Only the computation of the values of the constants a and b in the regression equation for a straight line, Equation (1) is required.

This computation will not be illustrated. Only the equations and their final values will be given for substitution into Equation (24).

$$a = \frac{(\Sigma X^2)(\Sigma Y) - (\Sigma X)(\Sigma XY)}{N(\Sigma X^2) - (\Sigma X)^2} \tag{22}$$

$$= 263.49601$$

$$b = \frac{N(\Sigma XY) - (\Sigma X)(\Sigma Y)}{N(\Sigma X^2) - (\Sigma X)^2} \tag{23}$$

$$= 5.186$$

The shorter method equation for S_y is:

$$S_y = \sqrt{\frac{\Sigma Y^2 - a\Sigma Y - b\Sigma XY}{N}} \tag{24}$$

Substituting the known values, S_y is computed:

$$S_y = \sqrt{\frac{1{,}856{,}425 - (263.49601)(4{,}295) - (5.1860)(139{,}287)}{10}}$$

$$= \sqrt{\frac{2367.2551}{10}} = \sqrt{236.72551} = 15.39$$

15.39 indicates the average estimate error that can be expected in an individual forecast will be 15.39 thousand workers. If the distribution of errors is normal, 68% of the forecasts made by the regression equation will be within 15.39 thousand workers actually employed.

Coefficient of Correlation Critical Values

For the example, the coefficient of correlation (r) was computed to be .893. The question arises regarding the amount of confidence to be placed in this measure of the relationship between the two variables. It is possible, by means of statistical tests of the hypothesis, that the actual value of r = zero. This hypothesis will be rejected when the value of r exceeds certain critical values at a specific confidence level.[3] Where r = .893, and N = 10, the critical value for a 95% confidence level is 0.632; for a 99% confidence level it is 0.765. In this case, the value of r exceeds the critical value for both confidence levels. This means that we can be at least 99% confident that the correlation is not the result of chance.

[3] W. J. Dixon and F. J. Massey, *Introduction to Statistical Analysis* (2d ed.; New York: McGraw-Hill Book Co., 1957).

TABLE 9-6

Computations for a Moving-Range Chart

Period	Forecast	Demand	Forecast Less Demand	Moving Range
1	103	105	−2	
2	108	110	−2	0
3	99	112	−13	11
4	106	105	1	14
5	109	116	−7	8
6	121	110	11	18
7	125	111	14	3
8	126	125	1	13
9	124	135	−11	12
10	133	127	6	17
11	140	134	6	0
			Total	96

Moving-Range Chart Technique[4]

A comparison of the results with the forecast must constantly be maintained. It is important to recognize any significant change in the pattern of the actual demand, and to immediately determine why the changes have taken place. One device useful for this purpose is the moving-range chart. This device permits a comparison of the actual changes with the random variations that can normally be expected.

The moving range is the change in the deviation of the demand from the forecast between one period and the next. The mean of these values is then found. The control limits are determined by multiplying the average moving range by ±2.66, a constant. The difference between the forecasted demand and the actual demand can then be plotted on a control chart, and compared with the computed control limits. The control limits are designated as the upper control limit (UCL) and the lower control limit (LCL). To illustrate this technique, assume the demand and forecast data shown in Table 9-6, along with the computations required for the moving-range chart.

The average moving range equals 9.6 from these data. The computation of the control limits is shown below:

$$\text{UCL} = +2.66(9.6) = 25.54$$
$$\text{LCL} = -2.66(9.6) = -25.54$$

[4]John E. Biegel, *Production Control* (2d ed.; Englewood Cliffs: Prentice-Hall, Inc., 1971), Chap. 4.

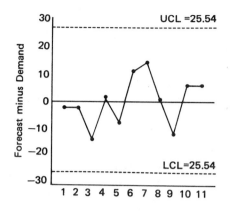

FIGURE 9-4

Moving-Range Chart

Results of these computations can be plotted on a moving-range chart (see Figure 9-4). The forecasts to date have been in control, since no points are outside the control limits.

This device is a useful method for maintaining a form of control of the accuracy of forecasts. The example used was a small sample, and the reliability of this device would be increased by a larger one.

This survey of methods for measuring reliability of forecasts should convey some idea of possible approaches for the achievement of this goal. An exhaustive treatment of the methods available was not attempted. Details of other statistical texts of significance are found in almost any standard statistics text.

SUMMARY

Many decisions are based on anticipations regarding the future. The process of forecasting is involved with predictions about future conditions which will be important to the enterprise.

Any forecast must be predicated upon certain assumptions or premises. Selection of the correct premises is vital to the ultimate accuracy of the forecast. Certain factors upon which premises are based are examined. Economic factors are of primary importance to most enterprises. In addition, governmental factors will influence assumptions made. A group identified as general environmental factors also bears on the premises adopted. Population trends, social and cultural forces, ethical forces, and technological factors apply here. The effect the premises have on the market for the product or service will have to be considered, as will any factors peculiar to the individual enterprise. This latter group would involve policy considerations, resource availability, and the fact that some forecasts become premises for other forecasts of the enterprise.

Three types of forecasts are examined, since they appear to have the most influence on the operations manager's decisions. These are economic forecasting, sales forecasting, and technological forecasting. Economic forecasting is necessary to any manager's planning for the future. The operations manager does not usually have a direct responsibility for developing this forecast. However, the economic forecast is important to the operations manager because it is a premise for the forecasts of more direct concern to him.

The sales forecast may be considered as the primary planning document of the enterprise. The operations manager must, of necessity, base many of his own plans on the sales forecast. Schedules, inventory levels, capacity requirements, and manpower needs are usually derived from the sales forecast.

Technological forecasting has gained in importance recently as a result of the rapid increase in technological developments. These forecasts are also related to many operating decisions of an enterprise. Changes in products, or in the techniques used, can have a great influence on the position of the enterprise. Since this type of forecasting is relatively new, the available techniques make accurate forecasts improbable. Technology is also a strong social force on the environment where the enterprise operates. This only adds to the need to develop some forecast of the future technology.

Forecasting techniques can be classified as either empirical or analytical in nature. Empirical techniques are, to a large extent, subjective, making any estimate of their reliability impossible. The three empirical techniques discussed are still widely used, however, and often lead to acceptable results. These techniques are the jury of executive opinion, the sales force composite, and the users' expectations approach.

Analytical techniques are considered to be more accurate and reliable. Because they rely on mathematical and statistical methods, they are considered more objective. In addition, some measure of confidence can be attached to forecasts developed by these methods. The simplest analytical technique is the moving average, which consists of finding a series of averages over some period of time by excluding the first item in the series and adding the last item. Time series analysis, concerned with the classification of data according to the time interval of occurrences, is another analytical technique. The analysis of the changes and the movements within a time series of the greatest value. Secular trends can be analyzed by means of the least squares technique to determine the long-term change in the series. Secular trend lines may be linear or nonlinear, and computational methods for both types are examined.

Seasonal variations, another form of change, can be analyzed for a time series. Most methods used for analyzing seasonal variations are based on some sort of index number. A simple index number calculating method is presented.

A third type of variation found in a time series is cyclical fluctuation. At present, no reliable methods for forecasting such fluctuations exist. However, some attempt must still be made to foresee these variations.

Random or irregular variations are the final category encountered in time series. As implied by their name, these variations are really unpredictable. It must be assumed that random variations will occur, and so some allowance is usually included in a forecast for unforeseen factors.

Correlation, or the determination of the relationship between two or more series, is another analytical technique. Computation of the coefficient of correlation, a measure of the degree of relationship, is illustrated.

A final analytical technique discussed is exponential smoothing. This may be viewed as a specialized form of weighted averaging. This method uses a weighting factor called an alpha factor. The alpha factor gives the greatest emphasis to the latest data since the weighted forecast is a result of the sum of the weightings of past periods.

Methods for evaluating the reliability of forecasts, developed by analytical techniques, are examined. These give a measure of the confidence which can be attached to a forecast. One widely used method for measuring the possible error in a forecast, based on an average, is the standard deviation. In correlation, the standard error of the estimate may be used to evaluate the forecast results. It is also possible to measure the reliability of the coefficient of correlation by means of critical values. A final means of measuring the accuracy of a forecast and controlling the forecasting process is the moving-range chart.

INCIDENT

POWER SHORTAGE

In 1964, the National Power Survey by the FPC indicated that electric utility companies of the northeastern section of the country had severe excess capacity. The forecasts of the industry were a declining rate of growth for peak capacity demand. The past 6% growth trend was moving below this level causing additional overcapacity.

Based in part on this study, the Kilowatt Electric Company adopted a plan which assumed a declining growth pattern. They increased their promotional efforts, and reduced some of their rates to encourage electric usage. In addition, they joined a program of pooling generating capacity with other utilities in the region. This would permit switching capacity when demands temporarily created a shortage for one of the member companies; thus, reducing the capital investment requirements.

The actual growth in demand in 1966 exceeded 7%; in 1967, it was about 1.5%; it soared to almost 14% in 1968; and was almost 6% in 1969. As a result, instead of overcapacity, Kilowatt, and other utilities in the region, found themselves with a severe shortage of generating capacity. This shortage resulted in requests to customers to reduce their use of electric power at certain times. It even led to occasional power blackouts like the famous incident in New York in 1965.

By 1966, Kilowatt found themselves in a position where their peak load capacity was more than 60,000 kilowatts less than the forecast peak load. Because of the slower increase in demand and an increase in capacity, in 1967, the forecast exceeded actual demand by more than 100,000 kilowatts. However, in 1968 and 1969, the forecast was more than 200,000 kilowatts below actual.

Questions

1. How could such a wide disparity between forecasted usage and actual usage occur, in view of the forecasting techniques available?
2. What are some factors which would affect peak load growth?
3. What factors might have contributed to a greater growth rate than was forecasted?
4. What can Kilowatt do to overcome its present difficulties, and what should they do to avoid such large forecasting errors in the future?

QUESTIONS FOR DISCUSSION AND ANALYSIS

1. What is the meaning of forecasting premises? Why are they significant?

2. Discuss briefly the different types of factors on which forecast premises are based.

3. Why is the economic forecast important? What are some problems encountered in developing an economic forecast?

4. Examine some past economic forecasts, and compare them with the actual results. What conclusions do you draw from this analysis?

5. What are the reasons the sales forecast is often referred to as the primary planning document? What is its significance to the operations manager?

6. Discuss the reasons why technological forecasting has received increasing emphasis in recent years. What is management's major interest in technological forecasting?

7. Comment on the relationship of technology and society. Cite some recent examples, from your own observations and experience, where technological advancement and society are in opposition. What are your recommendations for resolving these conflicts?

8. Describe and evaluate the empirical forecasting techniques presented in the chapter. Under what circumstances would you feel it useful to use any or all of these techniques?

9. What is the moving-average technique? What is its purpose? What conditions would influence the number of items used in computing a moving average?

10. Differentiate among the four major types of changes or movements identified with time series.

11. Identify the types of fluctuations found in the following cases, and suggest how each might be analyzed by management.

    (a) The yield of a particular crop may be identified as a "bumper crop," about every 10 to 12 years.
    (b) The sale of toys is highest in the period immediately preceding Christmas, and then declines sharply. It increases somewhat prior to Easter. It then slumps again until it starts upward again in the fall.
    (c) An earthquake in California increases the demand for building materials.
    (d) The value of shipments of synthetic rubber increased from $235 million in 1949, to $927 million in 1967.

12. What is correlation? How can it be most valuable in forecasting? What does the coefficient of correlation indicate?

13. Discuss the nature and purpose of exponential smoothing in forecasting.

14. In what ways is it possible to evaluate the reliability of a forecast? How can the level of confidence which can be held with respect to an individual forecast be determined?

PROBLEMS

1. Compute the three-year and the five-year moving averages for the following set of data. Compare the results. Comment.

[handwritten: 3 yr tot]   *[handwritten: 3 yr tot, 3 yr avg]*

Period	Value
1	69
2	84
3	90
4	94
5	93
6	112
7	120
8	129
9	147
10	162
11	178
12	196
13	220
14	236
15	260

[handwritten calculations, left column: 430 86, 473 95, 509 102, 548 110]

[handwritten calculations, right columns: 243 81, 268 89, 277 92, 299 100, 325 108, 361 120]

2. Using the least squares method, compute the equation for the straight-line trend of the data in Problem 1. Forecast the value for Period 16 from the result.

3. Forecast the sales for the next period, by means of the exponential smoothing technique, from the following:

Initial Forecast = 53

Actual Demand
Period 1   51
   2   56
   3   62
   4   63

Alpha Factor α = ~~0.3~~ *[handwritten: 0.2]*

SELECTED ADDITIONAL READINGS

Bean, Louis H. *The Art of Forecasting.* New York: Random House, 1969.

Biegel, John E. *Production Control,* 2d ed. Englewood Cliffs: Prentice-Hall, Inc., 1971. Chapter 4.

Buffa, Elwood S., and William H. Taubert. *Production-Inventory Systems*, Rev. ed. Homewood, Illinois: Richard D. Irwin, Inc., 1972. Chapter 2.

Dixon, W. J., and F. J. Massey. *Introduction to Statistical Analysis,* 2d ed. New York: McGraw-Hill Book Co., 1957.

Koontz, Harold, and Cyril O'Donnell. *Principles of Management*, 5th ed. New York: McGraw-Hill Book Co., 1972. Chapter 8.

Lewis, John P. *Business Conditions Analysis*. New York: McGraw-Hill Book Co., 1959.

Lovewell, P. J., and R. D. Bruce. "How We Predict Technological Change." *New Scientist*, Vol. XIII, (February 15, 1962), pp. 370–373.

McMillan, Claude, and Richard F. Gonzalez. *Systems Analysis*, 3d ed. Homewood, Illinois; Richard D. Irwin, Inc., 1973. Chapter 13.

Quinn, James B. "Technological Forecasting." *Harvard Business Review,* Vol. XLIV, No. 2 (March–April, 1967), pp. 89–106.

Redfield, J. W. "Elements of Forecasting." *Harvard Business Review,* Vol. XXIX, No. 6 (November, 1951), pp. 81–91.

Steiner, George A. *Top Management Planning.* New York: The Macmillan Co., 1969. Chapter 8.

Stockton, John R., and Charles T. Clark. *Introduction to Business and Economic Statistics*, 4th ed. Cincinnati: South-Western Publishing Co., 1969.

CHAPTER 10 | Process Planning

To further understand planning of the operations system, it is necessary to evaluate the specific nature of the actions or operations required to change inputs into the desired form of output. Discussion of the system's concept, in Chapter 2, referred to this as the process.

The manager must consider the types of processes which are applicable to his enterprise in planning the operations system. It may be necessary to design the process to be utilized, as opposed to selecting from existing alternatives. Once the process is determined, the most efficient flow of inputs through the system must be developed. This will involve consideration of the layout of facilities. Naturally, a great deal will depend on the operations carried out in the specific enterprise. In a manufacturing firm, it may also include the balancing of operations on the production line. Most processing will involve machinery or equipment to some degree; therefore, it is necessary to consider the program of maintenance required. The importance of automation cannot be overlooked in considering processes today, particularly in manufacturing. Of special relevance are numerically controlled machine tools.

NATURE OF PROCESSES

When the product or service of the enterprise is designed, certain specifications are established: physical dimensions, tolerances, standards, and quality are set forth. Then it becomes a matter of deciding the specific details of how to achieve the desired output. This decision is the essence of process planning. A *process* is defined as any group of actions instrumental to the achievement of the output of an operations system in accordance with a specified measure of effectiveness. Also involved is determination of the exact type of machinery or equipment needed, and the most desirable form of input into the system. The objective of these determinations is to achieve the best possible product or service. This concept of a process makes possible its application to the operations system of any type of enterprise.

Planning and designing the process are concerned with a broad view of the actions which are involved. Primarily this includes determination of the type of action required and the sequence in which each is to be done. The performance details for each of the actions is a function of the design of the job. The main concern is the way the input flows through the system, and the transformation of the input required to achieve the output. The prescribed curriculum a student must follow to acquire a degree is the process of an educational enterprise. One input of this system is the student, in one form. The output is the

233

same student, hopefully transformed as a result of his exposure to this process. In the case of a manufacturing enterprise, the processes required usually involve some sort of machining and assembly. The actions involved in writing a policy and collecting premiums by an insurance company are processes.

Types of Operations Systems

The nature of the process selected will largely depend on the type of operations engaged in by the enterprise. In manufacturing, it is typical to classify production into three categories. These categories, while generally limited to production, can be useful in considering all operations systems. They will also be useful in relation to other considerations, as facilities layout, and certain aspects of control of the operations system. Therefore, it will be helpful to take a brief look at these three forms of operations systems.

Intermittent Operations Systems. These types of systems are found when operations are unique and not standardized. This means that their output tends to depend entirely on the needs of the users of the product or service. This is *custom operations,* since the product or service is performed to specifications of the user. The quantity, dates, and all other aspects are set by him. Often this is a one-of-a-kind output the enterprise may never face again.

In other cases, it may be a repeat of something required only occasionally. In manufacturing, this situation is found in the job-shop type operation. Here, parts or products are produced to customer order, usually in small quantities. The cost per unit is high because of the large amount of planning involved. Unless it is indicated there will be repeat orders of this particular item, development of permanent specialized tooling and methods of production is not advisable.

Under these operating conditions, the problem of determining the type of equipment needed to perform the possible processes is a significant one. The problem of determining the capacity of the operations system is also difficult. The enterprise must have equipment available to perform any type of process required. It is possible to decide on a minimum capacity level, since the processes to be performed are diverse and are done intermittently. This reduces the investment, but it will mean a delay in processing an order when orders are numerous. Customer satisfaction is a factor in this decision. Will the customers be willing to wait for the product or service, or will a delay, because of low capacity, cause them to go elsewhere?

In the manufacturing situation, it is often possible to utilize a variety of processes to produce the same output. The problem resulting from small quantity output, and nonstandardized operations, forces the manufacturing enterprise to utilize flexible processing equipment to the greatest degree possible. This is accomplished by using general purpose machines.

General purpose machines can perform many different operations with relatively minor changes in the setup of the machine. The simplest example is the drill press in the metal or woodworking industries. By changing the size of the drill, these machines are able to perform a different operation; i.e., drill a different size hole. Most setup changes are not so simple, but numerous types of machines fit into this category. The standard engine lathe and the milling machine are typical.

In nonmanufacturing operations, the intermittent system faces much the same problem. In a hospital, for example, conditions will be quite different. Considering only the laboratory, the capacity decision will require another approach. It may be necessary to have a certain piece of equipment even though it will be rarely used. Here is a case where the customer will not be willing to wait. When it is a matter of the patient's life, such equipment must be available. This equipment may not be general purpose, since it may only be usable for one particular process or laboratory test. While the system in the hospital laboratory fits the intermittent format, it involves different considerations and ways of facing similar problems when compared with a manufacturing enterprise. Other examples are found in financial enterprises where the processes may be nonstandard; in marketing firms on occasion; or in many professional service enterprises like medicine, dentistry, and law. Thus, the term process may refer to a wide variety of actions.

Batch Operations Systems. The batch system usually involves a greater quantity of output, and tends to be more standardized when compared with the intermittent type. In essence, the *batch system* utilizes the processing facilities for a period of time to carry out the required work for accumulation of desired output. On completion of this processing, the facilities are then available for use on some other group of output items. Eventually, the system will return to the initial process for another group. In the interim, the processing facilities are utilized for other operations activities. These characteristics of the batch operations system lend themselves more readily to wider use of specialized equipment, tools, and other aids.

This system is easiest to exemplify in the manufacturing enterprise. In a foundry, several different shapes of products are made. Processing facilities may be used to produce one group of a single shape for two days, and then changed over to another group for an appropriate period of time. Eventually, possibly in a month or two, the facilities may return to processing the initial type of output.

Batch processing is also found in the nonmanufacturing enterprise. In certain types of clerical operations, such as processing of forms, the work may be accumulated, and all one type processed together. In the hospital laboratory, certain types of batch processing may be utilized if the information is not critical.

Major problems in these situations are determination of the proper size of the batch, and establishment of a workable schedule. The size of the batch will influence the amount of capacity needed. It will also relate to the schedule which can be a factor in customer satisfaction. More likely, the schedule will be of more concern internally, since this type processing is usually prerequisite to some other processing, or it is found in manufacturing, where production is for stock.

Continuous Operations Systems. In the continuous system, the output is usually highly standardized. While the quantity of output is high, it is limited in variety. In a manufacturing enterprise, this may be characterized by production of a single product without interruption throughout the entire period of time the facilities are operating. This is best illustrated by mass production of a part, or by the assembly-line type of operation, where parts are brought together in a specific sequence to form a finished item. This form of operations system is almost entirely characteristic of manufacturing, and it would be unusual to find it in any other type of enterprise. For instance, in a service enterprise the high degree of standardization typical of the continuous system is not found. Neither is the volume of services sufficiently great to require continuous operation.

Where the continuous operations system exists, it is possible to use equipment of a different type than that found in the other two systems. Since the processing is going to be virtually unchanged for a long period of time, the primary interest is to have as rapid a flow of the inputs as possible. It is unnecessary to have the flexibility which results from the general purpose machinery described above. Instead, it is possible to use equipment specifically designed for this process. Such equipment is called *special purpose machinery*. These machines perform only a single or limited series of operations needed to produce the output of this system. They are designed and built for this exclusive purpose, and cannot be modified to produce anything different without a very extensive alteration. Consequently, changes in the products of these types of systems can be very expensive. Cost of special purpose machines is typically high; this can be tolerated, since the initial investment can be amortized over a larger quantity of units. Since most of these machines are highly automatic and very fast, the per unit operating costs are low. Thus, over a high volume run, the unit production costs in the continuous system are lower than in the other two types of systems.

One specialized group of continuous operations systems may present certain unique problems. These are often referred to as the processing industries. Such industries are primarily concerned with the transformation of bulk materials such as liquids or powders. Processing industries require highly technical operations, and are subject to tight specifications. The processing is typically done within a very rigid scheme with a precise sequence of operations. It often is carried out in a self-contained system using pipes and vats. Perhaps the most typical processing industries are the chemical firms. The inputs flow through automatically, with necessary controls built in. Changes in these arrangements are extremely costly. All processing industries do not necessarily fall under the continuous operations classification. On occasion, they may fit into the batch operations category.

Rarely does a particular enterprise operate exclusively as one of these three systems. Most will be some combination. Assembly may be a continuous system while parts may be made on the intermittent basis or by batches. An example is the automobile industry. Some operations do not fit into any of these categories exactly. Special projects require a separate category, but for most purposes, these three categories will suffice.

Types of Processes in Operations Systems

Concern for processes for all types of enterprises requires consideration of a wide variety of classes of actions. A complete classification would result in a lengthy listing of almost every process performed to have discrete categories with no overlap. Consequently, it appears more logical to establish limited classes of those processes found in the operations system. Possibly certain types fit into more than one category; the lines between them are not always clear-cut. Processes are viewed as falling into four groups: facilitating, clerical, technical, and mechanical.

Facilitating Processes. Processes occur in all types of enterprises, including those providing services. *Facilitating processes* are those actions related to performance of a service. The processes in the activities of a nurse in a hospital would be one such example. The actions of a waitress in a restaurant, a teacher in an educational institution, a retail enterprise worker, and a social worker are also examples of facilitating processes. Most of these processes are performed directly for the users of the output; e.g., the customers, patients, students.

Clerical Processes. This category should be virtually self-explanatory. Any process which involves actions through the use of paper-work forms, usually referred to as office procedures, can be identified as a *clerical process*. It is also possible to consider some clerical activities as facilitating. One example of this type of overlap is a banking transaction. A deposit or a withdrawal would essentially be clerical, but it could also be considered as a facilitating process.

Technical Processes. Processes requiring a high degree of specialization, based on scientific principles, are identified as *technical processes*. The types of processes which are used in the hospital laboratory, or performed in many process industries like the chemical industry, can be included in this category.

Mechanical Processes. Differentiation between mechanical processes and technical processes is very fine, and is made arbitrarily here. Broadly speaking, *mechanical processes* involve manual operations or the use of tools or machines. Many mechanical processes also fit in the technical group. Some might also fit into other categories. Certain processes of the nurse may be classified as mechanical; some clerical activities involving office equipment could also be included.

Since the most frequently found form of operations is manufacturing, production processes are the most easily identified. However, since operations encompasses all forms of enterprises, the processes which can take place in the operations system must be viewed as broader than those in production. Therefore, this classification was developed to identify processes outside of production.

Production Processes

Inasmuch as production is so large a part of the total of operations systems found in the many types of enterprises, it is appropriate to take a closer look at some of these processes. Since the major types found in manufacturing are related to the metalworking industries, the emphasis will be on metalworking processes. Increasing automation of production processes is significant, particularly in the form of the numerically controlled machine tools. This aspect of production processes will be examined further.

Production processes can be conveniently divided into certain broad groups. In metalworking, the focus will be on forming, machining, joining or assembly, and finishing. In addition, certain other processes, involving plastics, woodworking, and the processing industries will be briefly described.

Forming Processes. *Forming processes* create the basic shape of the item. Most forming processes are the first of many steps required for the part to reach its finished form. Included in forming are casting processes, stamping and forming, forging and extrusion, and powder metallurgy.

Casting Processes. Any casting process involves infusion of molten metal into some type of mold formed to produce the properly shaped item. The mold is removed after the metal hardens. There are a variety of different casting techniques. Each technique is used to produce pieces with varying characteristics: dimensional accuracy, surface finish, and configurations. The principal variations in the different casting methods depend on the type of material used for the molds, and the way the molten metal is infused into the mold. The selection of the method to be used will depend on the characteristics of the part to be cast. In some cases, any method may be possible; in others, a single type is virtually dictated by the requirements of the finished part. Usually an evaluation will determine which method will be most feasible and economical. Among the most widely utilized methods are sand casting, plaster mold casting, permanent mold casting, die casting, and continuous casting.

Sand casting is one of the easiest and possibly the most economical of casting methods. Rather intricate parts can be made by this method. Any type of metal capable of being cast can be used for the parts. Because the parts produced by this casting method usually have a rough finish and cannot be held to very close tolerances, a considerable amount of machining may be required. This machining can lead to higher total costs than incurred for some more expensive casting method.

For small parts of nonferrous metals, it is possible to obtain smoother surfaces and much closer tolerances by plaster mold casting. These molds, made from a special plaster, are more costly than sand molds, and production costs are greater also. However, reduced machining requirements may more than offset these additional costs.

In certain cases, the molds may be made of metal; thus, are permanent. In permanent mold casting, the tolerances are usually still tighter, and a very good surface finish is possible. Costs of these molds are also higher than sand casting. In addition, the complexities of the parts cannot be as great as in sand casting. If the quantities are large enough, this method may result in lower total costs, because it can be mechanized to some degree.

A casting process similar to permanent mold casting is die casting. The principal difference is that molten metal is injected into the mold under pressure. The molds (dies), usually hardened steel, produce a very high degree of accuracy and surface finish. Because of the substantial costs of the dies and specialized machinery needed for the casting process, this method is only economical for relatively large runs. A certain degree of mechanization found in this process makes faster production possible.

The final type of casting is continuous casting. As the name indicates, this process is designed for high quantity runs, and would fit into a system as described under continuous operations systems. Essentially, this is very much like die casting, with the additional advantage that the machine is entirely automatic. Other casting methods would not fit well into the continuous system pattern. The shapes which can be produced by continuous casting are distinctly limited, and it cannot be used for intricate designs.

This is just a summary of some of the most widely used casting processes found in manufacturing. Other casting methods (shell mold casting, centrifugal casting, and investment casting, along with some specialized methods) are also utilized to form metal parts by this general process.

STAMPING AND FORMING PROCESSES. The primary nature of the processes in this group is that sheets or strips of metal are cut or shaped in some fashion. The parts formed by these processes are varied, primarily because they are some of the least costly types. This is particularly true where the size of runs are high.

Many stamping processes are performed on punch presses. The action of a punch press can probably best be described by comparing it with a cookie cutter on a rolled out sheet of dough. The difference is that the material is metal, and cutting requires some form of mechanical power. In addition to simply cutting, it is possible to form the part by passing the metal through a series of dies which will shape it by bending.

Another process which can be placed in this category is drawing, used to form a flat piece of metal into a shape such as a bowl or a cup. Drawing uses a series of steps which gradually "pulls" the metal into the final outline desired.

It is also possible to form metal by rolling the material between a series of rollers which gradually change its configuration.

FORGING AND EXTRUSION PROCESSES. Anyone who has watched the typical western on television is familiar with the basics of the forging process. The omnipresent blacksmith engages in forging when he heats the horseshoe and hammers the softened metal into the desired shape. All forging processes use this basic principle. The major difference is that most shaping is done by machines which exert the pressure or do the hammering. In some cases, since machines are capable of applying tremendous pressures, it is possible to perform these operations on cold metal. Other forging processes are open-die forging, drop forging, and press forging.

An extrusion process is most easily described by relating it to a tube of toothpaste. When you squeeze the tube, the soft paste is forced through the small opening and formed into a round shape. In the same way, heated metal is forced under very great pressure through a die with an opening of a desired configuration, forming a long ribbon-like piece. This strip is supported (on a conveyor) until it is cool. Later, the strips are cut into pieces and put through a straightening operation.

The extrusion process permits making rather complex shapes, particularly for the softer metals. The cost of the dies is relatively inexpensive; for small runs, it may be quite low.

POWDER METALLURGY. A final forming process with increasing application is powder metallurgy. In this process, powdered metals are mixed to achieve the desired combination. It is then poured into a cavity in the dies where it is subjected to extremely high pressure. The pieces formed are then heated to a temperature slightly below the melting point. This is called *sintering*. Many parts require no further processing, but some require a sizing operation where the parts are again placed into a die and subjected to higher pressure. This additional operation helps remove distortions, and makes the part conform to tighter tolerances.

The cost of the dies used in powder metallurgy is high, and this method requires quantity runs to make it economical. The quality of the parts is good, especially for small parts, often eliminating much of the need for machining.

There are other forming processes used in the metalworking industries. However, the ones described here constitute a representative sample of those in use. Those described should indicate the nature of the problem of selecting the proper process. Once the part is formed, it usually will require further processing before it becomes a finished part or product. Thus, other types of production processes must be considered.

Machining Processes. Possibly the most familiar metalworking processes are machining types. In fact, when one mentions the metalworking industries, the picture that comes to mind is some form of machining process. All machining involves removal of metal from the part made by some forming process. This removal involves a cutting tool to shape the part, to finish its surface, or to bring it closer to the desired dimensions. The basic machining processes are turning, drilling, milling, shaping and planing, and grinding.

TURNING. Turning, or the use of the lathe, is one of the most basic machining processes in manufacturing. A part being cut on a lathe is held firmly

FIGURE 10-1

The Five Basic Metalwork Machining Processes

and rotated on its axis. A cutting tool is moved along a path parallel to the rotating piece, and chips of metal are removed as the tool is forced against the work. The result is formation of a cylindrical piece as the diameter is decreased and the finish improved. By use of contoured or some other type of shaped cutting tool, specialized shapes can be produced. The lathe can also perform operations on the ends of the piece. The basic nature of the lathe operation is shown in Figure 10-1.

DRILLING. Drill presses are probably the most common type of machine tools found in the manufacturing facility. Drilling is accomplished by a rotating drill bit which is held firmly at one end while the tool is advanced against the fixed part so it removes metal and forms a hole. The drill press is a highly flexible tool in that it can drill many different size holes simply by changing the drill to one of a different diameter. The process of cutting screw threads in a hole, known as tapping, can be accomplished in much the same fashion, except the cutting tool is different. If many holes have to be drilled in fixed locations for a large number of parts, it is possible to use a multiple spindle drill. These machines can drill as many as 20 holes at the same time.

Drilling of large holes is referred to as boring. The boring tool may differ significantly from the standard drill press. In some cases the machine may be similar to a lathe where the part rotates and the tool is held stationary. Figure 10-1 also shows the basic nature of drilling processes.

MILLING. Milling machines remove metal with a rotating cutter which usually has multiple cutting teeth. The cutter rotates on a spindle which remains in a fixed position while the piece is moved against the cutter. The milling machine is very flexible and comes in many varieties. The cutting spindle may be vertical or horizontal. Cutters can vary widely with regard to size, shape, number of teeth, and size of teeth. It is also possible to use a series of cutters on milling machines. Reference to Figure 10-1 will show the nature of milling also.

SHAPING AND PLANING. These two processes are essentially identical. Both involve removal of metal from a flat or plane surface by a tool which makes a straight cut across the piece. In the shaper, the tool reciprocates while the piece is held on the table of the machine. The table moves after each stroke to position the piece for the next cut. The planer has a stationary tool, and the table with the workpiece moves back and forth. The tool on a planer moves to the next position after each stroke.

Shapers are usually used for smaller pieces, and planers for larger pieces. A standard planer may take a piece up to about 30 feet long, with larger capacities possible on special machines. Planers and shapers are not found in mass production operations, because they are slow and therefore costly.

For large quantities, other standard machining processes are more efficient and more economical. It is also possible to use special purpose machines described earlier. These processes are also illustrated in Figure 10-1.

GRINDING. The final basic metalworking machining process is grinding. In this process, metal is removed by some abrasive, usually in the form of wheels of numerous sizes, shapes, and degrees of abrasiveness. The metal is removed by rotating the wheel and feeding the part against it. The primary purpose of the grinding process is to improve the quality of the finish of the part. The amount of metal removed in grinding is very small. This process may also be seen in its basic form in Figure 10-1.

There are other types of metal machining processes. While some of them are fairly common and quite efficient, most are special variations of the above discussed machining processes. Included would be sawing, reaming, broaching, and threading. In addition, there are a few relatively new machining processes which are unique and deserve special comment. These are ultrasonic machining, chemical milling, electrical-discharge machining, and the use of lasers.

ULTRASONIC MACHINING. This process uses very high frequencies of electrical current to rapidly vibrate a cutting tool shaped for the desired cut. An abrasive mixture is fed to the point of contact, and the vibrations cause this abrasive to be forced into the cut.

CHEMICAL MILLING. This process involves removal of metal by immersing the part in an acid (some materials may require an alkaline solution). The part is first cleaned, then masked by applying an acid resistant coating (usually a plastic material). The coating over the portion to be etched is scribed or cut away. In some cases, the masking must be cured by heating. In some cases it can simply be cured by air.

The part is finally immersed into the acid to permit removal of the necessary amount of metal. Large parts, as well as small ones, can be processed by this means. Chemical milling is generally an economical process for removing up to one-half inch of metal when compared to machine milling. If the metal etched is thin, the tolerances are more easily held.

ELECTRICAL DISCHARGE MACHINING. This relatively new process has the ability of producing parts which are difficult to make by other methods. It can be used on very hard materials, and to produce pieces with high tolerances and good surface finishes. The metal must be an electrical conductor.

Metal cutting results from the electrical discharge which occurs between a formed tool and the piece. The discharge, in the form of sparks, is caused by a pulsing of direct current. The tool and the work are of opposite electrical polarity. In this way, the metal is removed from the piece. The process is relatively slow, and the electrical discharge causes the tools to erode rapidly. However, this method makes possible the production of intricate parts, like certain types of dies, which might be impossible otherwise.

LASERS. The use of this process is limited at this time, but it has potential application which could be significant. The laser (*l*ight *a*mplification by *s*timulated *e*mission of *r*adiation) can be used to remove metal using pulses to vaporize the metal. The primary application to date has been to perforate holes. It can do this on very hard metals and other materials, including diamonds. Other types of metal removal by lasers have been used, but the efficiency and the economy is low at this point. It is probable that as the technology of lasers improves, wider application to manufacturing processes will be found.

Joining or Assembly Processes. These processes include the various methods of fastening parts together (metal or otherwise). It is only necessary to mention a few of the many joining processes.

WELDING AND BRAZING. These processes involve joining of metals by applying heat so the parts are fused either by melting the metals themselves, or by melting a filler metal. *Welding* is accomplished when the pieces of metal to be joined are heated to their melting point so they fuse. This process forms a very strong joint; at least as strong as the material itself. There are various types of welding. The most important use the oxyacetylene torch or the electric arc.

Brazing is accomplished by heating a metal with a lower melting point than the metals to be joined, and flowing it between the original metals to bond them and thus join them. *Soldering* is, essentially, an identical process.

ADHESIVE JOINING. Adhesive joining uses a glue or other adhesive which serves as a bonding agent between two or more pieces of material. This type of joining is used for an almost unlimited variety of materials. Among these materials are wood, paper, plastics, and even metals to metals.

ASSEMBLY PROCESSES. Again, there are different kinds of processes included in this category. Some examples are: the use of fasteners, like bolts and nuts; screws; and special types of fasteners, like push fasteners, cotter pins, and retaining rings. In addition, riveting, stapling, and staking can be cited here. Assembly operations of various types can also be found in industries other than metalworking.

Finishing Processes. These processes give the piece its final appearance. In addition to imparting a changed appearance to the item, many finishing processes provide a protective covering. Possibly the most familiar kind of finishing is painting. Electroplating is another common type of finishing. In most electroplating processes, a thin covering of some conducting material is deposited on the part by electrolysis. Chromium plating and silver plating are familiar end results.

Galvanizing iron and steel parts is accomplished by hot-dip methods, to deposit a zinc coating to protect items like rain gutters and garbage pails from rusting.

Porcelain enameling, another commonly recognized finishing process, is used on sinks and household appliances. These examples represent only a few of the finishing processes used in the metalworking industries. Their significance is often greater than realized because of the impact the appearance which they impart will have on the potential user of the product.

Processes in Other Industries. There is a considerable amount of manufacturing not a part of the metalworking industry. Brief mention of some of the processes related to these industries is appropriate.

PLASTIC PROCESSES. Many plastic processes parallel certain ones used for metal. Particular similarity is found in forming, where many plastic parts are made by molding methods similar to casting of metals. Other similar processes are extrusion, drawing, and rolling. Some plastic parts require a limited amount of machining.

Many parts previously made from metal are now made from plastics. Despite shortages of petroleum, the basic material of plastics, plastic processes are significant.

WOODWORKING PROCESSES. A large number of parts and products are made from wood; we need only look around us to confirm this fact. A high degree of similarity is found between woodworking and metalworking. Many of the machining processes are virtually identical. The main differences are that the tolerances are looser for wood, and the use of automatic machines is less. This results from materials less standardized in their characteristics, like hardness, etc.

Woodworking assembly operations are also similar to those in metalworking but not as varied. Glueing, nailing, and use of screws or special fasteners are the most common methods. Wood finishing processes are primarily painting processes (stains, lacquers, varnishes, enamels, and paints). Other finishing processes are veneers, and certain synthetic finishes, including plastic. A set of unique woodworking processes are those found in the production of plywood.

Processing Industries. Processing industries use different types of manufacturing methods. Examples of these industries are chemical, rubber, petroleum refining, and food processing. A large part of the work in these industries is highly automatic; the primary problem is controlling the rate of flow of materials through the system. The equipment is unique, and often, in a given facility, the processes are small in number. Control of the processes in these industries is accomplished largely by electronic means. Probably no other group of industries is so highly automated. Most relatively large facilities are so completely automated that only a few people are needed, primarily for surveillance and maintenance purposes. Automation, however, is not found exclusively in these industries. An examination of this phenomenon as it relates to operations systems processes is in order. A particularly interesting development in automation is the use of numerically controlled machine tools.

NUMERICAL CONTROL OF MACHINE TOOLS

In the development of operations management to its present state, certain phenomena have had a significant impact. Automation is one of these phenomena. In this book, automation is differentiated from mechanization by the fact that automation consists of the substitution of machines for the sensory mechanisms of the workers, while mechanization only supplies mechanical energy.

Automation of Processes

Automation is certainly familiar to everyone today. Automation is frequently discussed in the daily news as well as in casual conversation. By no means is there universal agreement about the exact nature or meaning of automation. Some people see it only as an extension of further mechanization of manufacturing processes. For example, the use of transfer machines where the parts are moved automatically from one machine or operation to another is viewed as automation by some. Other people consider automation as more than additional mechanization. From this second viewpoint, automation does not occur until some form of control is exerted over the operation of the equipment by a type of energy other than human. The most frequent form of energy used for the newer automated processes is electronic.

An understanding of feedback control and of the computer is basic to an understanding of the automation of industrial processes. The underlying basis of automation of processes is feedback control. The closed-loop system is an essential element of automation. Information regarding the output of the processing system is used to keep the process in control. This control is most easily accomplished, with today's available technology, by electronic computer.

To illustrate automation of a process, consider a sheet of metal or plastic to be rolled to a certain thickness. The dimensions could be constantly monitored by some form of automatic gauge which recognized acceptable tolerance limits. If the part was too thick when it emerged from the rollers, the gauge would note this and relay a signal back to the machine. This signal would cause the rollers to adjust to the proper spacing to produce a sheet of desired thickness. The same sort of action would occur if the sheet was too thin as well.

This is an oversimplification of the actions of the control system, but it serves to illustrate the end result of this kind of automated system. As the discussion of numerical control proceeds, more of the specifics of the system will be made clear.

Nature of Numerical Control

The usual picture of the operation of a machine tool is as follows: An operator supplies all the inputs to operate the machine. He prepares the machine by setting it up, he sets the speeds and feeds, and performs the needed actions to cause the machine to operate as desired. In the case of a machine tool, he guides the cutting tool through the prescribed path to produce the proper part. As an outgrowth of the present trend toward the automation of production processes, a new concept is finding increasing importance in relation to operation of machine tools. This concept is called numerical control. Before proceeding, it should be made clear that it is possible to have automation without the use of numerical control. The numerically controlled machine tool is a specialized form of automation.

Numerical control is a means of operating a machine tool automatically by the use of coded numerical instructions. These are usually on tape and can cause the machine to move in a desired path when the numerical values are read and decoded. The numerical control process consists essentially of taking the engineering drawing of a part, and programming that part onto a tape for storage in a computer. The computer reads this program and provides digital direction or control of the tool as it passes over the metal, so that the finished part will conform to the engineering drawing specifications. A schematic diagram of this process is shown in Figure 10-2.

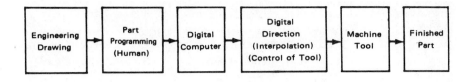

FIGURE 10-2

The Numerical Control Process

Figure 10-3 shows the basic nature of one system, General Electric's Mark Century Numerical Control System.

Two forms of numerical control are positioning (sometimes called point to point control) and contouring control. Positioning is by far the most frequently found (almost 90 percent of all installations). It involves the cutting of the piece on one axis. The simplest example of this type of control is drilling.

Contouring, or continuous path numerical control, moves the tool over a predetermined path. It is more difficult since it involves the cutting of complex shapes over more than one axis. Lathes are examples of contouring on two axes. Some skin milling machines used in airframe companies may require simultaneous control of up to five axes.

An illustration of a large numerically controlled machine tool is shown in Figure 10-4. This is a Cincinnati Milacron 5-Axis Aerospace Skin Milling Machine which can handle complex parts designs.

THE BASIC MARK CENTURY SYSTEM

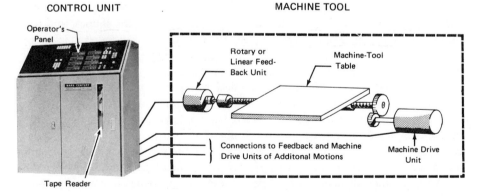

Reproduced by permission of General Electric Company.

FIGURE 10-3

The Basic Mark Century System

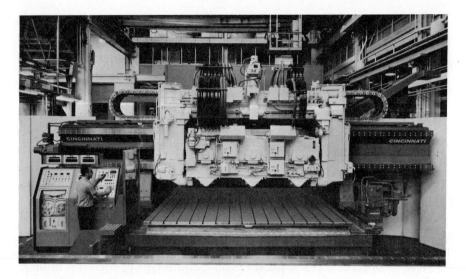

Reproduced by permission of Cincinnati Milacron Company.

FIGURE 10-4

A Large Numerically Controlled Machine

Economics of Numerical Control

The question of the feasibility of performing any process by numerical control hinges primarily on the economic justification for such a decision. A determination that the process can be performed by numerical control must be made before considering the economics of the problem. Where applicable, these machines are more accurate, can produce more complex shapes, and require fewer setups and operations in comparison with hand-operated machines.

The capital outlay for numerically controlled equipment is higher than for comparable hand-operated machines. The basic machine tool is more costly, as it requires certain modifications in its design to permit the greater speeds involved. In addition, there are the costs of the program and of the tapes used as input. Thus, the cost may range anywhere from $20,000 to $500,000 depending on the complexity of the equipment. Studies have shown that the numerically controlled machine will reach a break-even point and pay for itself sooner than a conventional machine because of greater performance efficiency.[1]

An important element of this operating efficiency is that numerically controlled machines are actually removing metal about 20 percent of the time the part is in the machine. This compares with about 5 percent for conventional machines. This is in addition to fewer operations, fewer setups, a reduction in the investment in fixtures, and less machining time. An example of the type of

[1]Herbert Wright, *Beginner's Course in Numerical Control* (Cincinnati: Cincinnati Milacron Co., Publication No. CTL-173), p. 1.

savings which can be achieved by the use of numerical control is summarized in Table 10-1. This is for a feed box, shown in Figure 10-5. This part was machined on a CIM-Xchanger machine which is manufactured by Cincinnati Milacron Company. This machine holds 24 tools; it has a five-second automatic tool change time.

Another example of the type of saving which can be achieved by the use of numerical control, as compared with conventional machines, is summarized in Table 10-2. The machine used for producing this part, which automatically drills, taps, mills, and bores in one setup, is shown in Figure 10-6. The machine panel of cast aluminum produced by this machine is shown in Figure 10-7. Thus, it would appear from these examples that numerical control is not only technically feasible, but also economical in the proper circumstance.

Potential of Numerical Control

Numerical control is still in an early stage of development, but its potential for the future is great. Certainly, the number of system installations now in operation is not great. Since the economic use of numerical control does not depend on large quantity runs (note that the lot size in Table 10-1 was only 30 parts), it has a potential for many manufacturing facilities, large and small. Consequently, its use will increase in those firms not using it, as well as in existing applications through expansion to new processes. Advances in numerical control will continue to improve the automation of production processes and to make more likely the possibility of the completely automated factory.

LAYOUT OF FACILITIES

In planning any operations system, no matter what type, intermittent, continuous, or batch, the major concern of the manager is to facilitate the flow of the inputs. The layout of the processing facilities is of practical importance in the achievement of this goal. This involves determination of the best location of the equipment within the physical facilities to make the flow as close to optimum as possible. The general perception of this problem is best developed with regard to manufacturing facilities. However, it is possible to use the same basic approach for any type of operations system. Certainly in an office, it is desirable to facilitate the flow of the paperwork by arranging the layout of the equipment in a fashion to achieve this end. It is always desirable to utilize available space as efficiently as possible. One way the flow may be optimized is to reduce the distances the inputs must travel within the processing system. In some cases, the need for flexibility in layout is of great importance. It should be clear that economic factors will have to be considered as well.

The achievement of the lowest cost is probably the most frequently used economic measure of effectiveness in connection with the layout decision. Usually the final layout is the result of a compromise among the many factors considered. It may be that providing needed flexibility will require a layout

TABLE 10-1

Summary of Savings for Feed Box
Produced by Numerical Control Machining

Method	Conv. Mach.	CIM-Xchanger
Lot Size	30 parts	30 parts
Fixturing Investment	$22,000	$1,300
Number of Setups	2*	1*
Setup Time	1.8 hours	1.0 hour
Machining Time	100.0 hours	20.0 hours
(Total 30 Parts)		
Total Time Savings	None	80.8 hours

*One prior operation same for conventional method and CIM-Xchanger.

Reproduced by permission of Cincinnati Milacron Company.

Reproduced by permission of Cincinnati Milacron Company.

FIGURE 10-5

Feed Box Produced by Numerical Control Machining

TABLE 10-2

Summary of Savings for Machine Panel of Cast Aluminum

	Machining Time	Load and Unload
Conventional methods	3 hrs. 20 min. (3 machines)	12 minutes (3 jigs)
Numerically controlled	46 minutes (1 machine)	5 minutes (no jigs)

Reproduced by permission of General Electric Company.

that does not minimize the travel required. Achievement of some other desired criterion may lead to an increase in costs. It is unlikely that the manager can arrive at a layout optimum in all respects. Certain tools may be helpful in the establishment of the best layout, but this problem is one where it is impossible to determine what the optimum solution is in most cases.

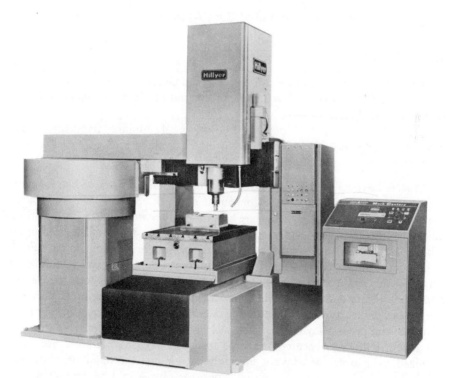

Reproduced by permission of General Electric Company.

FIGURE 10-6

A 3-Axis Positioning Control
Hillyermatic Numerically Controlled Machine

Reproduced by permission of General Electric Company.

FIGURE 10-7

Machine Panel of Cast Aluminum

Layout Types

Two basic types of layouts can be identified clearly in the operations function. Others have been set forth, but process and product layouts are the predominant ones in use.

A third type, the fixed-position layout, is of minimal importance, but deserves some mention. Each of these will be examined briefly, particularly as they relate to the kinds of operations systems.

Process Layout. The _process layout_ is found where all work of like function is gathered together in a single department or work center. This is probably the type most frequently found. Here all of the lathes would be in one location, all of the drill presses together, all of the typists in a stenographic pool in an office, or all the X-ray equipment grouped in a single location in a hospital. The process layout is related to the intermittent operations system discussed earlier in this chapter. Therefore, it is found where volume is low, the output nonstandardized, and a great deal of processing flexibility is required. General purpose machines are utilized to a large degree. A schematic illustration of the nature of the process layout is shown in Figure 10-8. A part moving through this layout will experience considerable travel. Since the parts are not standardized, each order will take a unique path. While the handling costs will generally be high in a process layout, any other type would be impractical because of the nature of the parts.

Product Layout. The _product layout_ is found in cases where the number of products is small, and these parts are highly standardized. They are also produced in large volume. Thus, this type layout is found largely in the continuous

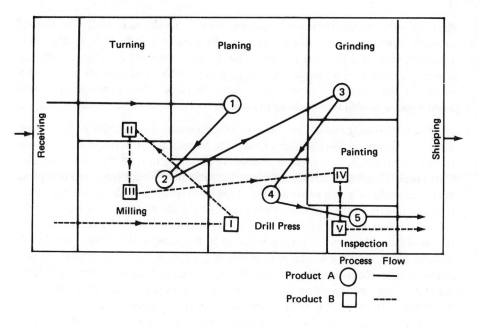

FIGURE 10-8

Schematic Representation of a Process Layout

operations system. Usually, the order of operations to be performed is the determining factor in the development of such a layout. The sequence of the operations virtually dictates the result. It is essentially a straight-line flow, in

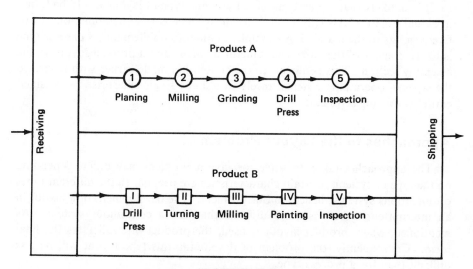

FIGURE 10-9

Schematic Representation of a Product Layout

that the parts move from one operation directly to the next with a minimum amount of movement required. This can be seen in Figure 10-9, a schematic representation of a product layout. This format is usually associated with the common concept of an assembly line in a mass production situation. As can be seen in the diagram, it is possible to have the same types of processing equipment located in different parts of the plant.

Fixed-Position Layout. In certain circumstances, the material or part does not move from one work center or machine to another as in the previous types of layout. Instead, the workers and the tools move to it. Of course, this circumstance is limited to situations where the machinery is not large and complex, and is capable of being moved. This type of layout, the *fixed-position layout*, is found mostly in the assembly operations where the movement of the product is inconvenient because of size, or because movement would be detrimental to the product. This type of layout is found in the computer industry, where the systems being built are too large to be moved, so the workers come to them; or, in some cases of custom production, where one worker builds the entire product. As stated, the fixed-position layout is not as significant as the other two types described. However, it is used in specialized circumstances.

Another case where this type layout may find utility is in the attempts to overcome some of the drawbacks of mass production techniques from the individual worker's standpoint. In some enterprises, the workers have been given responsibility for large segments of the production of the final output; this can be extended to the point where they make the entire part or product. The aim of this expansion of responsibility is the improvement of job satisfaction, through closer identity with the job. This concept, identified as job enlargement, is discussed more fully in Chapter 13.

It is unlikely that a pure example of any one type of layout would be found in actual practice. Usually what is found is some sort of combination at different points in the plant. For example, in an automobile plant, a process type is likely in most of the parts' manufacturing areas and a product layout in the assembly section. This conforms to the contention made earlier with regard to the types of operations systems; rarely would any single enterprise be classified entirely as a single system.

Approaches to the Layout Problem

The approaches taken to solve the layout problem may differ, depending on the type of system. Certain characteristics are peculiar to the different types of operations systems; hence, to this problem. The development of a layout in an intermittent system is more difficult than for a continuous system. As mentioned, where product layout is used, the product often dictates the final form. Consequently, the problem of developing this type layout will be less difficult than for a process type.

For the intermittent system, the product mix varies, and is hard to predict. Therefore, it is almost impossible to arrive at the ideal layout. There are, however, certain techniques which are useful in solving these kinds of problems. Some are of value for any type of situation, while others will have application only for one of the types of layouts.

Process Analysis. Reference to this method in one context was made while discussing schematic models for decision making in Chapter 5. At that time the use of the flow chart and the flow diagram was illustrated (Figures 5-5 and 5-6). This type analysis is a valuable aid for evaluating an existing layout, and for planning a new one. By using this approach, the manager is forced to look at the entire sequence of the process, or processes, being performed. Thus, he is able to get a full picture from which he can more readily see what the problems are, and where potential improvements may be found.

In a flow diagram, the plane view of the entire area is drawn to scale. In plant layout, the usual scale is 1/4 inch = 1 foot. There are also available templates which can be used for almost any item; machines, people, etc., in planning the layout. These templates may be either two dimensional, or three dimensional. It is possible to plan a layout by moving the templates around on a scaled representation of the area in order to visualize alternate layouts.

The process analysis approach can be utilized to evaluate any type of layout. Under any conditions, it is necessary to gather the facts, evaluate them, and attempt to make improvements. Use of the flow chart and the flow diagram is a means of accomplishing this end.

Quantitative Techniques. Some quantitative techniques have application to the layout problem. The use of mathematical programming is a particular example. Most especially, the distribution model can be used for determining the lowest cost path for moving material between departments. The details of the transportation model have already been discussed in Chapter 6.

It is also possible to use waiting-line theory in some aspects of layout. In most cases, the assembly line can be viewed as a system which is essentially a type of waiting line. In fact, Chapter 7 indicated that certain models of waiting lines could be best illustrated by a typical assembly line. The particular reference was in relation to the multiple-phase case of waiting lines.

Inasmuch as many waiting-line problems can best be solved by Monte Carlo simulation, it follows that this quantitative model has utility for solving the layout problem. It is also possible to utilize a different form of simulation for these problems. In this approach, a variety of alternate layouts could be simulated, and their appropriate operating results evaluated. One computerized technique which will be mentioned later uses simulation as a means of developing the best layout.

Reducing Travel Distances. In the process layout, the primary goal is to reduce the total travel distances to a minimum. Because the output will vary widely in the intermittent case, there is no guarantee that an optimum solution can be achieved. Usually, certain assumptions are made to which some measure of effectiveness is applied. A common measure of effectiveness used to develop a layout by analysis of travel distances is lot-feet-traveled. The *lot-feet-travel* is the product of the total number of lots, batches, or orders moved, and the sum of the travel distances (in feet) involved. It is assumed that, by reducing this figure, the handling costs will be lowered and the efficiency of the layout will be increased. Another measure of effectiveness used is the number of noncontiguous moves. Anytime a move must be made between two departments which do not adjoin each other, it is identified as *noncontiguous*. The assumption here is that if a move is made to an adjoining (or contiguous) department, the distance of travel is minimum. Therefore, the noncontiguous moves involve the greatest distance and hence the greatest cost. Reducing the number of these moves is assumed to lower the cost of movement.

A basic tool used to analyze travel distances is the travel chart. This chart is used to show the number of moves made between the departments in the facility. The travel chart in Table 10-3 is for a plant with six departments.

TABLE 10-3

Travel Chart

From	To						
	A	B	C	D	E	F	Total
A		20		15			35
B			27	9		22	58
C	30			21	18	12	81
D		45					45
E		18		32		10	60
F	28		36		7		71

From this chart, the manager can then develop a relative arrangement of these six departments. A good starting point is to locate, in the center, the department where the most moves originate and position the other departments around it. One possible arrangement, developed from this travel chart, is shown in Figure 10-10. The noncontiguous moves are shown by dotted lines in this schematic drawing, and total 60; i.e., E to D = 32 + F to A = 28.

This method depends entirely on inspection and subjective judgment to arrive at a solution. Consequently, it is limited in its use to cases where the number of departments is relatively small. Other constraints may be found in the use of this method, as far as the individual problem is concerned. In this example, no restrictions were placed on the physical size of the departments. Since the departments may have to be placed within an already existing area, their size and configuration could be limiting factors. In addition, diagonal

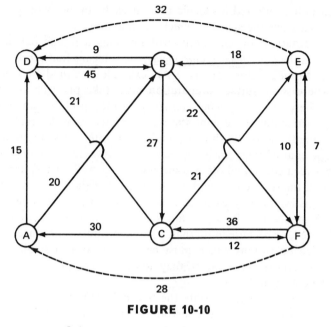

FIGURE 10-10

Schematic Layout for Six Departments

moves, as indicated in the schematic layout in Figure 10-10, may be impossible. Thus, some of the moves designated as contiguous in the diagram would become noncontiguous, and the solution would change.

This is a trial and error, iterative process, and there is no way to be certain the solution achieved is optimum. However, this kind of analysis should result in a reasonably good solution for the specific problem if the desired goal is to reduce the noncontiguous moves. This goal, in turn, assumes that the lot-feet-traveled will also be reduced as a result.

Improving Flow of Material. All plant layout analysis is aimed at improving the efficiency of movement of material or parts through the process. In process layout, this analysis tends to center primarily around the reduction of the travel distances. In product layout, the work passes through a series of operations in a line. A variety of problems are unique to the product type layout. A significant problem concerned with material flow is line balancing. Since many product layouts are of an assembly nature, this problem is also referred to as assembly line balancing. Primarily, these types of problems are concerned with determining how to divide the total work to be performed so each station in the line has an equal amount of work in terms of time. Perfect balance is an ideal circumstance. All operations do not require the same time, nor can they be divided equally by the same unit of time. Thus, line balancing arranges the work stations to minimize the idle time or the delay in the stations on the line. Certain factors determine the resultant line. The first is the output requirement for the line. Each unit is allotted a specific time at each station, which is called the *cycle time*. This sets the speed at which the line moves.

Certain limitations or constraints will also play a role in balancing a line. One of these is the *precedence requirements.* This means that certain operations must be performed before others. An example is found in woodworking finishing where some surface preparation must take place before staining or painting. There are also *zoning constraints* which prohibit some operations from being carried out at the same station. Zoning constraints can also be illustrated by using the wood finishing example. It is often necessary to apply more than a single coat of some finishing material. However, some drying period is required between coats, and often some rubbing as well. Thus, in an assembly line situation, the two coats could not be applied at the same station.

Other constraints may exist because the number of stations required is limited to a minimum. Possibly this is because a minimum number of machines is needed, or because more than a single product is produced on the line. There are also operations which must be performed at a single stage in the process. Whatever the constraints, they add to the complexity of the problem, and must be considered.

A simple example will illustrate the line balancing problem. Assume five operations without precedence constraints, and with the following time requirements:

Operation	Time in Minutes
A	10
B	5
C	8
D	2
E	5

If an output rate of six units per hour is required:

$$\text{Cycle time} = \frac{60 \text{ min./hr.}}{6 \text{ units/hr.}} = 10 \text{ min. per unit}$$

The resultant line with the minimum number of stations is shown in Figure 10-11.

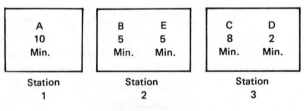

| A
10
Min. | B
5
Min. | E
5
Min. | C
8
Min. | D
2
Min. |

Station 1   Station 2   Station 3

FIGURE 10-11

Three Station Assembly Line

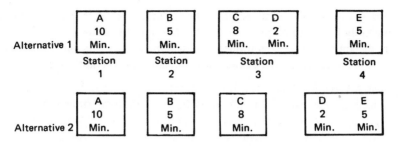

FIGURE 10-12

Alternative Four Station Assembly Lines

Thus, under the assumptions set forth, the line has three stations and a utilization factor of 100%.

If certain precedence requirements are added, the results will be different. Assume a simple requirement of a sequential precedence where A must precede B (indicated A → B), B → C, BC → D, and BCD → E. Given the same output requirement, with a cycle time of 10 minutes, the resultant minimum number of stations is shown in Figure 10-12. Note two solutions, each with four stations, are possible.

The utilization factor in this case can be computed as follows:

$$\text{Utilization Factor} = \frac{\text{Total Operation Time in min. /unit}}{\text{Total Man Minutes Available /cycle}} \times 100$$

$$= \frac{30 \text{ min. /unit}}{(4 \text{ stations})(10 \text{ min. cycle})} \times 100$$

$$= 75\%$$

This illustrates the possible effect of precedence requirements, and the problem of arriving at an exactly balanced line.

Many approaches have been developed to solve the line balancing problem. Most approaches have been extremely analytical in nature and have found little practical use. However, more recent attempts have made use of heuristics as a means of solving this very complex problem. The reader will recall that heuristic decision-making techniques were discussed in Chapter 3. No attempt will be made to detail these many approaches.[2]

Many of the difficulties surrounding the line balancing problem are concerned with human behavior. Some aspects of this factor are examined in the next chapter in regard to manpower planning. Some of the problems related to the individual and the assembly line have been recognized for a long time. Charlie Chaplin, in his film *Modern Times,* satirized this problem some years ago. Many of the same conditions on which this film was based, morale, boredom, and

---

[2]See, Edward J. Ignall, "A Review of Assembly Line Balancing," *Journal of Industrial Engineering*, Vol. XVI, No. 4 (July-August, 1965), pp. 244-254, plus other sources cited at end of chapter.

monotony, are still found in assembly line operations. Perhaps the epitome of the assembly line, and its problems, is the automobile industry. An interesting review of conditions in this industry was published in *Fortune*, which can be keynoted by a quote of one of the workers, "I don't like nothin' best."[3]

Computerized Methods. It is only natural to expect that the computer would be utilized in making plant layout decisions. Several heuristic techniques developed for line balancing use computer programs. One program, used where precedence requirements exist, is known as the *successive maximum elemental time technique*.[4] This method selects the combination of elements with the least amount of slack time for the initial station. With these elements eliminated from consideration, the program proceeds to consideration of the next station. This process is repeated until all of the elements have been assigned.

In situations where the process layout would be used, a computer approach, called CRAFT, has been suggested, paralleling the travel-chart technique.[5] An inspection method is really only applicable to cases where the number of departments is small. As the number of departments increases, the complexities of the problem become so great, because of the many possible combinations, that it is a virtual necessity to resort to a computer.

The CRAFT program uses a heuristic approach (in a similar fashion to judgment by the individual) to determine what changes can be made in a layout. In addition, it uses algorithmic methods to calculate distances and costs of movements between work centers. A form of physical simulation results in a printout of a block layout of any improvement. The program follows an iterative process to evaluate an existing layout for possible improvement; when one is indicated, one department is exchanged for another. After an evaluation of the newly developed layout, the next indicated one-for-one department exchange is made. This step-by-step process is repeated until improvement is no longer possible. While this program does not guarantee that the final printout will be an optimum layout, it has been found difficult to improve on the results by any other method. A serious drawback to this program is the restriction to a one-for-one exchange. Only departments with the same physical space requirements can be considered for exchange. This limits the practical application.

Not all approaches to the layout decision are applicable in any given situation. The manager must analyze his own particular problem to select the method or combination of methods which will assist him in arriving at the best solution.

MAINTENANCE

In planning the physical aspects of the operations system, it is necessary to consider the ability of the system to continue to function. This is especially

---

[3]Judson Gooding, "Blue-Collar Blues on the Assembly Line," *Fortune* Vol. LXXXII, No. 1 (July, 1970), p. 69 ff.

[4]Thomas R. Hoffmann, "Assembly Line Balancing with a Precedence Matrix," *Management Science*, Vol. IX, No. 4 (July, 1963), pp. 551–563.

[5]Elwood S. Buffa, Gordon C. Armour, and Thomas E. Vollman, "Allocating Facilities with CRAFT," *Harvard Business Review*, Vol. XLII, No. 2 (March–April, 1964), pp. 136–158.

true with regard to production processing equipment. Any equipment or physical system will on occasion fail to perform properly. This is true of machine tools, automobiles, office machines, computers, laboratory equipment, and the human body. Occasionally, the system will break down completely and cease to function. Whether the circumstance is improper performance or complete breakdown, the system must be repaired. This is one function of maintenance. The other is to devise a program designed to prevent these conditions from developing. This is the purpose of a preventive maintenance program, wherein the system is periodically inspected.

In many enterprises, this is the responsibility of the plant engineer instead of the operations manager. Regardless of the location of the maintenance function, the operations manager is concerned about development of policies and procedures regarding repairs and preventive maintenance. He wants a maintenance program which will uphold the efficiency of the system and will be economical.

Repair Policy

When a system or a piece of machinery ceases to function properly or breaks down completely, an attempt must be made to bring it back to an operable state. There are occasions where repair may not be possible or feasible. This means a decision must be made to replace the equipment. Considerations involved in equipment replacement were discussed in Chapter 8.

If repair is to be carried out, there are several available alternatives. These alternatives can be developed as a part of the policy of the maintenance program of the operations system. When a machine fails, it often requires the replacement of some part to repair it. This kind of repair usually requires disassembly of the equipment. The cost of this disassembly is incurred every time a repair must be made; therefore, it may be economically advantageous to repair or replace other parts at the same time. For example, if your television set fails and you take it for repair, there is usually a standard charge for diagnosing the difficulty. If the problem is a bad tube, it might be economically feasible to have more than just that single tube replaced. You could decide to replace all tubes while the set is disassembled. A third alternative is to replace all tubes that have been in service for longer than a specified period of time or those that tested below a certain level. This type of situation can have parallels to the repair policy of the operations system. In repairing a faulty bearing, the same alternatives may be applied. It is necessary, in developing a repair policy, to evaluate the possible alternatives in terms of total costs. The initial costs of a policy to replace more than the defective part will be higher. However, an evaluation of the total costs may show some other available alternative to be advantageous. The goal of these policies is fewer breakdowns, less idle machine time, and lower repair costs. The policy finally adopted will be the one judged to be most economical for the particular enterprise, after a complete evaluation has been made. Some techniques for this evaluation will be discussed below.

Preventive Maintenance Policy

The problem of a preventive maintenance program, facing the operations manager, is to establish a policy setting the frequency of inspection, and the extent of repairs to be made at the time of the inspection. Establishment of a period during which no breakdowns would occur is ideal. To achieve this state, if possible, would undoubtedly entail an excessive maintenance cost. Certainly, the greater the frequency of maintenance inspection, the fewer breakdowns expected. The problem to be resolved is the relative costs incurred.

When an automobile is lubricated and the oil and filter changed after so many miles, a preventive maintenance policy is in operation. The same type policy can apply to many kinds of equipment. Cleaning, oiling, and adjusting the office typewriter once a month is another example. Similar circumstances may be found with any type of machine or equipment utilized in the processing segment of the operations system.

Policies similar to those suggested for repair policy can be adopted for preventive maintenance. If, for example, an airline follows a policy of disassembling and inspecting the engines on its planes after a specified number of flying hours, what repairs or replacement of parts should be carried out? Should only those parts found defective or showing excessive wear be replaced? Should all parts of a particular class be replaced if one is found defective, or should only those parts exceeding the average service period be replaced?

Establishing a policy, in these cases, is often a result of evaluating past experience. The frequency of the inspection period can be established from past performance results. In many cases, the manufacturer suggests a schedule based on time or usage for automobiles. The inspection period may be imposed, as a result of a regulation of some governmental body, as in the case of airlines. Insurance requirements, as is the case for boiler insurance, may set the period.

Scheduling preventive maintenance creates certain problems for the operations manager which are particularly acute when the system is operating at a high level. If the enterprise is on a three-shift basis, all machines may be scheduled for continuous use. The shutting down of a machine means loss of a certain amount of capacity. Therefore, in scheduling a maintenance inspection, the operations manager must consider lost machine time. One possible way this can be avoided is to have standby or spare equipment. However, this requires additional capital investment, and, therefore, is in the area of equipment investment decisions.

Maintenance Decision Techniques

Much of the problem of planning the maintenance system can be identified as a specialized form of a waiting-line situation. The basic techniques available to the operations manager for making decisions in this area have been reviewed in Chapter 7. Other more complex methods have also been applied to the maintenance problem which are beyond the scope of this book. The reader is referred to specialized literature in this field for details of these approaches.[6]

Simulation of Maintenance Problems. Certain types of maintenance decisions are made with the assistance of simulation models as those discussed in Chapter 7. One problem to which this technique applies is determining the proper repair policy. The evaluation of the possible results of adopting alternative policies can be made by use of simulation.

Waiting-Line Theory and Maintenance. If we consider the machines requiring repair as arriving units, and repairs as processing of the arriving units, we have the structure of a waiting line. Thus, by applying the equations presented in the discussion of waiting lines, pertinent considerations as the most efficient size of the maintenance force can be determined. This can be related to many measures of effectiveness: minimum downtime, minimum idle time for the repairmen, or minimum total cost.

The maintenance problem can be extremely complex if all possible ramifications are considered. As must be realized, if the system is extremely large, with many machines, the difficulties of planning and operating the maintenance system are considerably magnified. The ultimate objective is to keep the system operative at the highest possible level, at lowest cost consistent with good service. This usually requires a combination of empirical judgments and analytical approaches. It is always possible to follow the policy of running the machines until they fail, and then replacing them. In other words, perform no maintenance. Such a policy would only be feasible where the replacement policy was more economical than a maintenance policy.

SUMMARY

Process planning is concerned with determining a substantial portion of the details of obtaining the output of the enterprise. Processes are viewed broadly, so that those needed to accomplish any form of output can be included. Process planning involves that part of the operations system where inputs are transformed to result in the desired product or service of the enterprise.

As a prerequisite to the examination of processes, three types of operations systems are described. The first is the intermittent one, found where the output is nonstandard. One of the significant characteristics of intermittent systems, from a process planning standpoint, is the fact that they tend to use flexible equipment identified as general purpose.

The second form of operations system identified is the batch type. A more standardized output is usual, as compared with the intermittent system. Processing takes place on a particular group of inputs for a period of time, then is changed to some other processing. In time, processing the original inputs occurs again for a similar period of time. Determination of the size of the batch

---

[6]Robert L. Bovaird, "Characteristics of Optimal Maintenance Policies," *Management Science*, Vol. VII, No. 3 (April, 1961), pp. 238–254.

to be processed and the development of a schedule are the major problems in this system.

Continuous operations systems are the final type considered. These systems produce a highly standardized output in large quantities. The major problems encountered center around maintaining a smooth and constant flow of the inputs through processing. In contrast to the intermittent systems, the type of machinery used is frequently special purpose.

A general classification of the kinds of processes found in operations systems is presented. These are not viewed as discrete categories, but as broad, generalized groups which can be used to identify the processes found in any type of enterprise. The processes are identified as facilitating, clerical, technical, and mechanical.

Since production constitutes such a large proportion of operations, a separate examination of the processes in this category is necessary. The primary emphasis is on the metalworking industry where the applicable processes are forming, machining, joining or assembly, and finishing. Processes in plastics, woodworking, and in the processing industries are used as illustrations outside of metalworking.

Automation of production processes is reviewed, particularly as it relates to the numerical control of machine tools. The nature of the numerical control process is discussed. Two types of numerical control are identified: positioning and contouring control. The economics of numerical control is examined by means of examples of pieces produced on numerically controlled equipment. Illustrations of savings achieved in specific cases are discussed. The potential of numerical control is also evaluated.

A problem area which is closely related to the processes employed is that of determining the layout of the facilities of the enterprise. The primary concern in this area is to facilitate the movement or flow of the inputs through the processing. Three types of layouts are identified. The process layout, usually found in intermittent operations systems, and the product layout, used in conjunction with continuous systems, are considered basic. A third type, the fixed-position layout, is found in some situations and is also examined.

A variety of approaches to the solution of the layout problem are available. One of these, process analysis, is essentially a schematic method. Certain quantitative methods are also applicable. Among these are the distribution linear programming models, waiting-line theory, and simulation. Another method which is particularly useful in process type layouts is designed to reduce the travel distances involved. In this, an inspection approach is used to try to reduce these distances by making the number of noncontiguous moves smaller.

The methods used in relation to the product type of layout are primarily aimed to improve the flow of materials. Of particular significance are the assembly line balancing techniques.

The application of computers to layout problems can be found in connection with both product and process layout. Some of the line balancing techniques depend on computer programs. There have also been developed programs for improving process layouts. One program parallels the inspection method used to reduce travel distances.

A final topic related to the process planning of the operations system is maintenance. While this is not always a responsibility of the operations manager, it certainly affects the efficiency of his system. Problems of repair policy and of preventive maintenance policy are relevant. Simulation techniques may be helpful in establishing repair policy. Many maintenance problems take the characteristics of a waiting line. Therefore, this technique has some applicability in solving certain maintenance problems.

INCIDENT I

BLAIR TELEVISION COMPANY

The Blair Television Company produced an average of 150 sets a day. Of these, about 80 percent were console models with high-quality wooden cabinets. These cabinets were manufactured by Blair at a separate facility, and trucked to the main plant where the chassis were assembled into the cabinets. Blair was planning a new facility to be built at the main plant so that the finished cabinets could be moved directly from the finishing line to the assembly area. A sketch of the overall layout is shown below.

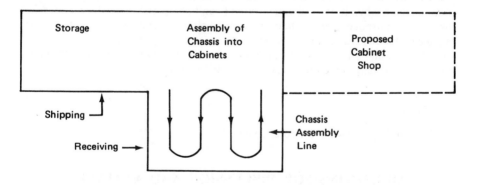

The management is considering the possibility of using a conveyor system in the finishing process for the cabinets. This conveyor would be an in-floor chain type. The cabinets would be placed on a wooden pallet which could be hooked to the continuously moving chain. In this way, the unfinished cabinets could be moved through the various finishing processes at a constant pace.

The cabinets were built in various popular furniture styles: Modern, Provincial, Colonial, etc. This meant that each required a different finish to conform to the style. Cabinets were also built in various sizes to accommodate different sized sets. Also some were large cabinets for TV, radio, stereo combinations. The finishes were equivalent to those found on high-quality furniture, and required numerous applications of stains, sealers, and varnishes, in addition to baking and hand rubbing.

Questions

1. What are the major considerations, other than costs, which must be evaluated in this situation?
2. Do you see any operational problems in using a conveyor in this type operation?
3. What advantages are there to this kind of system?

INCIDENT II

ZIPPY DELIVERY SERVICE

The Zippy Delivery Service provided package delivery to business firms in a large metropolitan area on a contract basis. Zippy used 175 trucks of various sizes for this service. The trucks averaged 150 to 200 miles a day. The president of the company, Ron Herman, was meeting with the general manager, John Foote, to review operations of the company for the past three months.

"John," he said, "I've been reviewing these figures on truck maintenance cost for the last quarter. I believe we are spending a lot of money for nothing. We have a crew of three men on duty during the day, and two at night when all the trucks are idle. That costs over $3,600 a month in wages. I've also been looking at the truck performance figures, and I find only three trucks broke down while on a delivery or pick-up run during this period. I realize we need a mechanic to get a truck running again when it has difficulty. What I can't comprehend is why we need five men for this purpose. I am particularly puzzled about what the two men at night do. We have standby trucks to take care of our needs when one is out of service. It seems to me that one, or, at most, two men during the day is all we need for maintenance, especially since our trucks seldom break down."

Question

How would you, as John Foote, answer this?

QUESTIONS FOR DISCUSSION AND ANALYSIS

1. What is a process, in the context of an operations system? Give some specific examples of processes in different types of enterprises.
2. Describe the characteristics of the three types of operations systems.
3. Differentiate between general purpose and special purpose machines. Under what types of conditions would each be most likely to be used?
4. Describe and give examples of the different types of processes found in operations systems.
5. Why are production processes in the metalworking industries of particular significance?
6. Describe the five basic metalwork machining processes discussed in the chapter.

7. Select a production process and write a detailed description of it. If possible, gather some of your information by actual observation of this process. Include a section on some of the recent developments in this process.

8. What is the nature of processes found in industries other than metalworking?

9. What is numerical control? How does numerical control operate a machine tool?

10. Explain the difference between positioning and contouring control.

11. When can numerical control be used? Is it only practical for large shops or for long runs?

12. Visit a plant where numerical control is in operation. Write a report on the economics of this process and its future potential, based on the information you were able to gather.

13. Describe and compare the two basic types of layout.

14. What is the nature of the line-balancing problem? What constraints may have a bearing on this problem?

15. Comment on the importance of maintenance from the viewpoint of the operations manager.

16. Consider the case of a four-engine jet airliner. Each engine has a fuel injection system. What are the possible repair policies which could be adopted by the airline?

17. Discuss the pros and cons of a preventive maintenance program. What are the major problems connected with preventive maintenance for the operations manager?

SELECTED ADDITIONAL READINGS

Ansley, Arthur C. *Manufacturing Methods and Processes*, Revised, Enlarged Edition. Philadelphia: Chilton Book Co., 1968.

Begeman, M. L. *Manufacturing Processes*, 5th ed. New York: John Wiley & Sons, Inc., 1963.

Bovaird, Robert L. "Characteristics of Optimal Maintenance Policies." *Management Science*, Vol. VII, No. 3 (April, 1961), pp. 238–254.

Bowman, E. H. "Assembly Line Balancing by Linear Programming." *Operations Research*, Vol. VIII, No. 3 (May–June, 1960), pp. 385–389.

Jackson, J. R. "A Computing Procedure for a Line Balancing Problem." *Management Science*, Vol. II, No. 3 (April, 1956), pp. 261–271.

Leone, William C. *Production Automation and Numerical Control*. New York: Ronald Press Co., 1967.

Mann, Lawrence, Jr. "Toward a Systematic Maintenance Program." *Journal of Industrial Engineering*, Vol. XVII, No. 9 (September, 1966), pp. 461–473.

Moore, James M. *Plant Layout and Design*. New York: The Macmillan Co., 1962.

Morse, Phillip M. *Queues, Inventories, and Maintenance.* New York: John Wiley & Sons, Inc., 1958.

Parsons, James A. "Preventive-Maintenance Policy Selection." *Journal of Industrial Engineering*, Vol. XVI, No. 5 (September–October, 1965), pp. 321–327.

Reed, Ruddell, Jr. *Plant Location, Layout, and Maintenance*. Homewood, Illinois: Richard D. Irwin, Inc., 1967.

Tonge, F. M. *A Heuristic Program for Assembly Line Balancing*. Englewood Cliffs: Prentice-Hall, Inc., 1961.

Vollmann, Thomas E., and Elwood S. Buffa. "The Facilities Layout Problem in Perspective." *Management Science*, Vol. XII, No. 10 (June, 1966), pp. 450–468.

Wester, L., and M. D. Kilbridge. "A Review of Analytical Systems of Line Balancing." *Operations Research*, Vol. X, No. 5 (September–October, 1962), pp. 626–638.

Wilson, F. W. (ed.). *Numerical Control in Manufacturing*. New York: McGraw-Hill Book Co., 1963.

CHAPTER 11 | Manpower Planning

To this point the planning problems have been related to the physical side of the operations system. Another important element of the operations system is manpower. Every enterprise system requires people as a significant part of its operation. It is imperative that the management of the enterprise conducts a concentrated and systematic program concerned with this element. The manager must develop a manpower plan.

ELEMENTS OF MANPOWER PLANNING

Manpower planning is concerned with determining the enterprise's future numerical requirement for people, establishing a program of recruiting and selecting these people, developing and training them to the level of skill required, and motivating them to achieve the desired performance. A mere determination that a certain number of people will be required in the future is not sufficient. The operations manager needs these people at specific times. Many of these requirements will be set by the forecasted level of operation for future periods of time. In other words, a specific quantity of lathe operators will be needed in the month of February. The economics of the manpower-planning process is also significant. Development, implementation, and control of an established manpower plan will involve expenditures of money. There is a cost attached to the manpower-planning process, and there are other costs associated with the various activities planned. Manpower must be paid, but management expects a return on this payment. A good manpower plan will insure that utilization of manpower will be efficiently carried out so manpower costs are within planned limits. Proper planning will contribute to the attainment of this goal.

The importance of manpower planning is greater today than at any time in the past. Some of the reasons for this can be readily recognized. Among the contributing factors are the rate of technological improvement, the demand for higher skills, the resultant lengthening of the training cycle, increasing shortage of certain specific skills, and greater mobility of manpower.[1] Thus, the manpower plan for an enterprise must consider many elements. In spite of its obvious importance, a recent survey found that only 72 percent of the firms in the study did any manpower forecasting, and a majority of these firms had

[1]Dale Yoder, *Personnel Management and Industrial Relations* (6th ed.; Englewood Cliffs: Prentice-Hall, Inc., 1970), pp. 170–173.

only begun these activities within the previous five years.[2] The approaches to manpower planning were quite diverse. None of the firms used all the available techniques, and most carried out only limited manpower planning, as opposed to planning for total manpower requirements.[3]

The variables used by the surveyed firms to develop their manpower forecasts tend to follow those factors indicated as important to create a need for manpower planning. However, the frequency of utilization of the important factors was quite low. The following list summarizes the factors considered and their percentage of utilization.[4]

Sales	62%
Quality of internal labor supplies	45%
Facilities expansion	36%
Workload	34%
External labor supplies	28%
Labor turnover	19%
New products	17%
Technological and administrative changes	17%
Budgets	11%

Even with the failure to use some important factors fully to develop the manpower forecasts, most resultant manpower plans will be derived from some type of forecast. This is true because forecasts serve as the primary source for determining the workload. This applies to the total enterprise, and to each department, including even the requirements for individual tasks. A firm understanding of the role ascribed to the manpower of an enterprise will be useful.

The Role of Manpower

Manpower, as an element of the operations system, plays a very specific role in the total scheme of the enterprise. From the economist's viewpoint, manpower is one of the factors of production. Thus, it is a resource that must be allocated and coordinated with the other factors to produce the output of the system. Today, many authorities would probably view manpower as the single most important element of an enterprise.

Popular definitions of management all tend to emphasize the "people" aspect. Management is concerned with accomplishment of enterprise goals through people. Most work of any enterprise is accomplished by people, and to a great extent, for people. Certainly if man was not so important an element, the function of management would be significantly changed. If everything was accomplished by machines, as in the totally automated plant, management

---

[2]U.S. Department of Labor, Manpower Administration, *Employer Manpower Planning and Forecasting*, Manpower Research Monograph No. 19 (Washington: U.S. Government Printing Office, 1970), p. 13.

[3]*Ibid.*, pp. 17–28.

[4]*Ibid.*, p. 15.

would essentially be a pushbutton process. However, manpower is still needed to push the button, to repair the machines, and to plan when to push the button. Therefore, manpower is a significant factor in the total operations system. Manpower can be the element which determines the ultimate outcome of the measure of effectiveness of the enterprise.

Visualize two identical enterprises, located side by side, having identical physical facilities. All other aspects of the enterprises are the same, except the manpower used to staff the two. It is virtually certain the success of one enterprise would be greater than the other. If this kind of controlled situation could be established, where the only changing element was manpower, the significance of manpower to the operation could be seen.

Manpower Policy

In Chapter 2, strategy was defined as the way an enterprise uses its primary skills and resources, responds to its environment, and selects the route required to achieve its stated end. Strategy determines the task; policies develop the framework for the implementation, performance, and control of the task. Manpower is one of the areas for which management must develop policies. Policy formulation is the initial step in the manpower-planning process. Manpower policy establishes the framework for management to develop specific programs and procedures to meet the manpower requirements. In view of the concepts of the total management system, manpower planning must be viewed as it pertains to the various subsystems of the firm. Because of the significant role of manpower, it is possibly the most pervasive element of the total system. Manpower policies determine the way this important resource is utilized. The objective of these policies should be to create an environment for the realization of the goal of optimum utilization and development of the manpower of the enterprise. Manpower policies must be developed for the determination of the quantity required, for a recruitment and selection program, and for a training and development plan of the manpower of the firm.

Quantity Determination. The first determination that must be made in developing a manpower plan is the quantity of people required. In addition to setting an absolute total number, the various classifications of manpower, according to the organization structure of the enterprise, must be set. It would be of little value to have a specific total provided for in the plan without reference to the types of manpower skills needed. Generally, the lower the skill requirement the easier it is to acquire that level of manpower. Thus, the necessity to plan for a future period is greater for more highly skilled classifications. The time period encompassed by a plan will largely be determined by the skill level required. The requirement for unskilled people can probably be handled by short-term plans.

As indicated in Chapter 9, the sales forecast is the primary planning document. Therefore, the manpower plan must use the sales forecast as a premise.

Additional forecasts related to manpower needs are also developed. Basically, the same types of forecasting techniques already discussed apply to the manpower area.

Ultimately, these forecasts for the total enterprise and for the individual organizational units are coordinated with the policies of the enterprise and with the appropriate budgets. From this will evolve the approved manpower plan. Specifics of the establishment of the unit manpower plan, as it applies to operations management, will be outlined in the discussion of manpower loading.

Recruitment and Selection. The recruitment phase of the manpower plan determines how the enterprise will obtain the manpower to meet its needs. The recruitment plan will revolve around the policies established for the staffing requirements. Included is a consideration of the sources the enterprise will solicit for these requirements. Broadly, these will either be internal or external. The selection of the sources to be used may be based on the existence of a policy to recruit from within the enterprise, as one example. Other areas of consideration will deal with establishment of policies regarding hiring of specific types of classes of people; e.g., college graduates, minority races, handicapped, etc.

In the selection process, the manager must review the candidates recruited, to determine who will fit the needs of the enterprise and who will not. Selection policy generally covers those activities required to acquire people who best fit the needs. From a planning viewpoint, the problem revolves around development of a program which specifies the techniques to be utilized to assure success. Should a series of interviews be used; what weight, if any, should be placed on work history and references; what role will testing play? The problem is essentially a matter of deciding what is required, then choosing the methods which serve as measures of the required specification. The ideal selection process has been described as a series of "go, no-go" gauges.[5]

Training and Development. The manpower plan must also provide for training the work force of the enterprise. In the first place, the people selected often need to go through a program of training to bring them up to the standards of the enterprise. This training may consist primarily of introducing the new worker to policies and methods. In a highly competitive labor market, a program of training may be required to satisfy the needs for a particular skill. Secondly, a program aimed at improving the level of productivity of all employees is usual.

Development can be distinguished from training, although the terms are often used synonymously. *Development*, as a separate activity, refers to the program of improving the abilities of an employee to prepare him for potential promotion or transfer. The importance of training and development in the total process of manpower planning is that they contribute to achievement of the goal of proper and efficient utilization of the manpower of the enterprise.

[5]Yoder, *op. cit.*, p. 298.

THE LEARNING CURVE AND MANPOWER PLANNING

The concept of the learning curve is not new; educators have recognized its existence for some time. It has been particularly conspicuous in learning of skills. Anyone who has learned to type is well aware of the learning phenomena. The same can be said for skills like swimming, skiing, driving, or operating a machine tool. The basic idea of the learning curve is that, as experience is gained, the ability to perform a particular skill will improve. This improvement would be faster at the beginning of the learning cycle. Acquiring a skill is not a smooth, continuously increasing process. Invariably, actual progress is uneven, with periods of rapid improvement followed by periods of regression before progress is made again. However, the individual learning curve is usually depicted as a smooth curve with the improvement measured against experience. A representation of a hypothetical learning curve for an individual is shown in Figure 11-1.

FIGURE 11-1

Hypothetical Learning Curve

Such a curve can be represented by the equation:

$$Y = aX^b \qquad \textbf{(1)}$$

Where:

Y = the improvement measure
a = a constant (e.g., the time to complete the first unit)
X = the number of repetitions
b = the exponent of the learning curve

Measurement of improvement is often difficult. Frequently, it can only be stated as a subjective judgment. The concept of the learning curve is useful to the managers of the operations function when considered from a slightly different viewpoint. In a production situation, it is more meaningful to consider the reduction in the cost per unit occurring with increased experience; or the change in actual or average time per unit taking place as the number of units produced increases.

Time-Reduction Curve

In manufacturing, improvement similar to and related to the learning curve occurs. This improvement is referred to as the production-progress function, the improvement phenomena, or time-reduction analysis. This improvement largely results from the learning phenomena. Factors other than the human effort contribute to this as well. Among these other factors are improved tooling, improved design, better equipment, and job design.

Initial applications of time-reduction analysis were made in wartime airframe firms for various production planning purposes. The time-reduction curve assumes the negative exponential distribution form. Thus, the equation for the curve can be expressed like Equation (1) except with a negative exponent. This equation becomes:

$$Y = aX^{-b} \tag{2}$$

Where:

Y = man-hours
a = the time to produce the first unit
X = the number of units produced
b = the exponent of the curve

An example of a time-reduction curve is shown in Figure 11-2. The designation of Y may either be in terms of man-hours per unit or cumulative man-hours per unit. Y most often represents cumulative average man-hours per unit, however, specific designation of Y can only be determined by the situation.

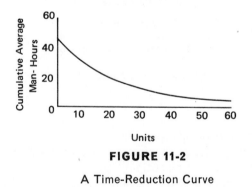

FIGURE 11-2

A Time-Reduction Curve

The underlying concept of the time-reduction approach is as follows: Every time the quantity of units produced doubles, the average cumulative hours decrease by a constant percentage. If the first unit required 50 hours, the average per unit time for two units would be 40 hours, and for four units it would be 32 hours. The average time requirement for each time the output doubles is 80 percent of the base. This is an 80 percent time-reduction curve. The 80 percent figure used here is for illustrative purposes only. Various factors determine the slope of the curve, and the learning percentage as well. The learning curve cannot be assumed to be any specific percentage curve. This percentage can only be determined after a full study of past experience yields a measure of the time-reduction relationship. Every industry may have a different percentage curve. Because a certain learning pattern has been the rule in a particular industry does not mean that the same pattern will be found in another industry. The same caution will apply to different firms in the same industry, and to different products in the same firm or plant. In fact, the same pattern found at an earlier time may no longer apply. In other words, management must investigate fully the time-reduction curve of the problem at hand before applying any percentage value to the learning curve.

Logarithmic Expression of Time-Reduction Curve. It is convenient to express the time-reduction curve in logarithmic form. One advantage is that the

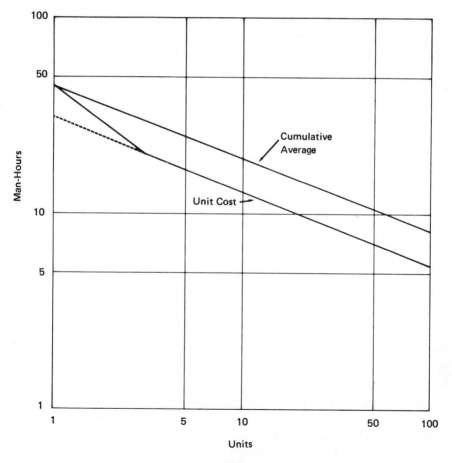

FIGURE 11-3

80% Time-Reduction Curve Plotted on Log-Log Paper

computation of Equation (2) using logarithms is easier. This is true because a number can be raised to any power by multiplying the log of the number by the exponent. Thus Equation (2) can be expressed as follows:

$$\log Y = \log a + b \log X \tag{3}$$

If the time-reduction curve is plotted on log-log paper where the two axes use a logarithmic scale, the curve is a straight line. Thus, it is possible to plot the time-reduction curve from only two points.

A second advantage of the logarithmic expression is that the straight-line representation more clearly depicts the decrease in the cumulative average time. It also makes possible estimation of time requirements for additional levels of production. This information is useful in preparing labor estimates for several different levels of output and in developing the manpower plan. An 80 percent time-reduction curve plotted on log-log paper is shown in Figure 11-3.

Computation of Exponent of Curve. Considering the condition of the 80 percent curve, the hypothetical times given can be used to compute the exponent of such a curve from Equation (2). The time for the first unit is Y_1 and the time for the second unit is Y_2:

$$Y_1 = aX_1^{-b} \text{ and}$$
$$Y_2 = aX_2^{-b}$$

Equation (2) can also be stated as:

$$Y = a/X^b$$

Thus, for $X = 1$ and $X = 2$ we can state the following relationship:

$$\frac{Y_1}{Y_2} = \frac{a/X_1^b}{a/X_2^b} = \frac{X_2^b}{X_1^b}$$

Substituting the known values gives:

$$\frac{50}{40} = \left(\frac{2}{1}\right)^b = 1.25 = 2^b$$

The following solution is achieved with logarithms:

$$b = \frac{\log 1.25}{\log 2} = \frac{0.0969}{0.3010} = 0.322$$

Computation of Cumulative Average Time. The cumulative average time for any value of X can be determined when the value of the exponent of the curve is known. The value of b (the exponent) determines the slope of the time-reduction curve. It can be computed in a similar fashion for any percentage curve. The values for the exponent (b) of different learning percentage curves are shown in Table 11-1.

TABLE 11-1

Values for Slope of Curve for Selected Learning Percentages

Learning Percentage	Slope Values (b)
95	0.074
90	0.152
85	0.234
84	0.252
83	0.269
82	0.286
81	0.304
80	0.322
79	0.340
75	0.415
70	0.515
65	0.622

Use Equation (3) with the exponent for an 80 percent curve and the first unit of production requiring 50 hours. The cumulative average hours for 100 units are:

$$\log Y = \log 50 + (-.322)\log 100$$
$$= 1.6990 - .322(2.000)$$
$$= 1.6990 - .6440 = 1.0550$$
$$Y = 11.35 \text{ hours}$$

Computation of Time for Individual Unit. Computation of the time for an individual unit can be determined by finding the difference between the total required for a given number of units (X) and the time required for one less unit $(X - 1)$ by applying Equation (3). To illustrate this, find the time required to produce the 100th unit from the data assumed above. The cumulative average time for 100 units was determined to be 11.35 hours; the total time, 1135 hours, is achieved by multiplying the average time by 100. Use Equation (3) to compute the cumulative time for 99 units. This is achieved as follows:

$$\log Y = \log 50 + (-.322)\log 99$$
$$= 1.6990 - .322(1.9956)$$
$$= 1.6990 - .6426 = 1.0564$$
$$Y = 11.39$$

The total time (11.39 multiplied by 99) is 1127.61 hours. The time for the 100th unit is 1135.00 − 1127.61 = 7.39 hours.

It is also possible to compute the unit time for an individual piece by the following equation:

$$Y_i = X_i^{(1-b)} - (X_{i-1})^{(1-b)} \tag{4}$$

Where:

i = the individual piece number

The total time for any number of units can also be computed directly using a slight modification of Equation (2). The equation for computing the total time is:

$$T = aX^{(1-b)} \tag{5}$$

Where:

T = the total time

To illustrate this equation, compute the total time for 100 units and compare it with the results above. Using logarithms, solve Equation (5) to achieve:

$$\log T = \log a + (1-b)(\log X)$$
$$= 1.6990 + .678(2.000) = 3.0550$$
$$T = 1135 \text{ hours}$$

Application of Learning Curves

By applying the concepts of the learning curve, an aircraft executive won a bet for a steak dinner from an executive of an appliance manufacturing firm by determining within 10 percent the cost of the 100,000th refrigerator. The aircraft executive arrived at a figure of $162.50, 50 cents too high.[6] This kind of occurrence can be misleading about the accuracy and usefulness of learning curves.

Table 11-2 shows how to utilize data from the production progress curve to develop a manpower forecast. These data are based on a 76 percent progress slope.

The primary interest in the learning curve is how it applies to manpower planning. However, it has other potential uses. It can be used as a basis for determining the capacity requirements. When the learning curve is used to determine the expected output using a specific sized work force, the amount of machinery needed can easily be derived. The rate of improvement expected will vary with the percentage of labor required, as compared with the percentage of machine time. The greater the machine time, the slower the rate of improvement management can expect. This emphasizes one important characteristic of learning curve analysis: It is primarily concerned with measurement of direct labor. However, savings can often result from factors other than labor improvement. Various actions by management may result in a reduction in the time required to produce a unit. These savings may incorrectly be attributed to labor improvement.

---

[6]Frank J. Andress, "The Learning Curve as a Production Tool," *Harvard Business Review*, Vol. XXXII, No. 1 (January–February, 1954), p. 87.

TABLE 11-2

Manpower Forecast

	A	B	C	D	E	F
Date	Monthly Quantity	Cumulative Position	Mid-Cum Position	Monthly Unit Cost	Total Monthly Manhours	Workers @ 38 Hr/Wk
December	1	1	1	5,830	5,830	35
January	2	3	2	3,600	7,200	44
February	6	9	6	1,850	11,100	67
March	15	24	16.5	1,170	17,550	107
April	25	49	36.5	850	21,250	129
May	35	84	66.5	665	23,275	141
June	46	130	107.0	550	25,300	154
July	50	180	155.0	480	24,000	146
August	50	230	205.0	425	21,250	129
September	50	280	255.0	390	19,500	118
October	50	330	305.0	365	18,250	111
November	50	380	355.0	342	17,100	104
December	50	430	405.0	325	16,250	99
January	30	460	445.0	313	9,390	57
February	15	475	467.5	308	4,620	28
Total	475					

Col. A = From Schedule   Col. D = From Production Progress Curve
Col. B = From Schedule   Col. E = A × D
Col. C = Monthly Mid-Point from B   Col. F = E ÷ 164.5 Hr/Worker (38 × 4.33)

Source: M. L. Bernsen, *Practical Application of the Production Progress Curve* (Long Beach, California: Douglas Aircraft Division, McDonnell Douglas Corp., August, 1967), p. 13. Reproduced by permission of McDonnell Douglas Corp. and the author.

A reduction in direct labor requirements may also occur when the total costs are actually increasing. This happens if more indirect labor is utilized, or if a different kind of labor is employed; i.e., higher skilled, at a higher cost. A reduction may also occur if management decides to subcontract a larger portion of the production, which will show a reduction in labor hour requirements. This is a false picture because there is no labor improvement, and no real savings will be realized.

It is also possible to show an improvement in the labor time requirement, as a result of changes in job design. Most operations managers constantly evaluate their present job methods with an eye to improve them and to achieve a saving. This type saving is obviously not a result of learning. Often when volume of output increases, it is possible to use techniques which are more efficient than would be possible at lower levels of activity. Improvements may be achieved as a result of improved management, increased motivation of workers, and improved organizational morale.

Other factors than learning can lead to the actual curve being different from the hypothesized one. Figure 11-4 illustrates how a production progress curve may vary as a result of factors other than learning.

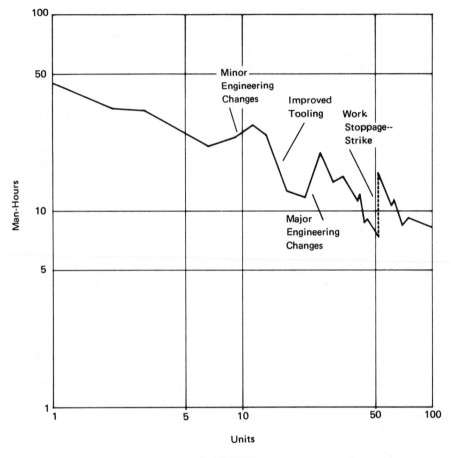

FIGURE 11-4

Variances in the Time-Reduction Curve

Additional areas of application of the learning curve concept are for estimating purposes, in assisting in make or buy decisions, and certain aspects of financial planning. In estimating, the learning curve has been widely utilized as a basis of establishing prices, when preparing bids for a customer. This has been particularly true in dealing with various contracting agencies of the Department of Defense. Aerospace firms have probably used the learning curve most for this purpose. The 80% curve has been found to parallel this industry's experience to a great extent.

The decision to buy a portion of a product outside, as opposed to making it internally, can lead to an unrealistic picture of the improvement experienced. This is a very common decision for the operations manager, especially in a manufacturing enterprise. The primary consideration is usually economic; that is, can we buy the part as cheaply (or cheaper) than we can make it? Since the learning curve is a valuable tool in determining price for an item, it can be useful in this decision. It is important to realize that factors other than economic may enter into this decision. On occasion a company may find itself in the position of operating at less than capacity. Thus, certain conditions may exist where the workers in some departments may have to go on short hours or be laid off. If this is viewed as a temporary situation, it may be desirable to make parts, even though they can be produced externally at a lower price, in order to retain the full work force and to utilize the available facilities. Also important in the decision to make a part internally is the assurance that the company has the know-how required. The experience of a medium-sized electronics firm illustrates this point.

The A & D Electronics Co. had produced an airborne radar unit for the U.S. Navy for over two years, and received a new contract for a quantity which would run for another 18 months. The competition had been great, and A & D lowered its price per unit by more than 10 percent from the previous contract. Consequently, management was looking for ways to reduce the costs of producing the new units. The learning curve had been considered in the bidding, but because of the competition, final negotiations had forced them to submit a price which cut their margin per unit considerably.

A major component of this unit was a highly complex, and delicate tuner which had been subcontracted on the original order. The assembly of this tuner required very specialized skills A & D's labor force did not possess. Despite this, management decided to make the tuner for the new contract, because it was the most costly part of the total unit. They felt that they could achieve a substantial saving in total costs.

The labor market was tight, and A & D was unable to hire workers having the necessary skills. They decided to train some of their more experienced workers. The learning curve analysis seemed to substantiate management's decision. However, no one in management had had experience with the type of production skill required, so the training immediately ran into difficulty. It took six months of training and experimentation before an acceptable tuner was produced. Thus, the decision to make the tuner resulted in a substantial loss and long delays in deliveries of the units on the new contract.

To summarize, learning curve analysis offers great potential to management for manpower planning when properly applied. The important things to recognize are the conditions required and the implicit limitations in using this tool.

MANPOWER LOADING

From the standpoint of the operations manager, one aspect in the total process of manpower planning, manpower loading, is of particular significance. This is especially relevant in manufacturing, but applies to any type enterprise. *Manpower loading* is the specific activity of assigning individuals to particular tasks for specified periods of time within a given department or enterprise unit. It might be viewed as the end process of total manpower planning.

In a manufacturing firm, the sequence of steps leading to the development of the manpower load is usually from the sales forecast to the master schedule to the loading of the manufacturing facilities. Development of the manpower load makes it possible to proceed to detailed production scheduling. Only after the loading has been accomplished is it possible to determine the starting and completion dates for work in the factory. This, in essence, is the concern of the schedule. Manpower loading assigns workers to production centers. Specific assignments of individuals to perform given operations, and the timing of this performance are part of the scheduling activity.

There is no set of rules which can be laid down concerning how a given enterprise should accomplish its manpower loading. One company may require a rather detailed procedure to develop loading information; another may find a highly informal, simplified approach satisfactory. At one extreme the supervisors or foremen are merely given indications of expected changes in order requirements, then left to do their own loading.

An example of a detailed manpower loading procedure might serve to illustrate the other extreme. The Westminister Manufacturing Co. produces a master schedule for a six-month period showing the beginning inventory figures of each item produced, the number of units in process, the amount to be produced, and the anticipated sales for each month. The manpower load for a given department is determined by first finding the hours required to produce the parts scheduled for each month. This figure is arrived at by making detailed calculations by part and by operation of the scheduled production. In this way, the percentage of the total load represented by each part and operation is established. The total monthly manpower load is finally computed by dividing the total actual hours required in the department (direct and indirect) for the month in question by the hours available.

The manpower load must be kept current. The master schedule is the controlling document; however, the schedule will not always be maintained. This can result from the fact that required manpower was not available. Thus, the schedule will require revision, and the manpower load will have to be recomputed.

The control of the manpower load can be achieved by a variety of techniques. All are primarily concerned with relating the manpower capacity with the level required. A widely used device is a form of the Gantt load chart as discussed in Chapter 5. The example dealt with machine loading, but the basic concepts can be applied to manpower also.

Certain quantitative approaches to the problem of manpower planning and loading are also available. However, most of these approaches deal with the problems of overall scheduling, and the manpower application is only a part of the total model used. One widely known quantitative method is the development of linear decision rules used to determine production and employment scheduling.[7] This approach uses a series of quadratic equations for making

---

[7]Charles C. Holt *et al., Planning Production, Inventories, and Work Force* (Englewood Cliffs: Prentice-Hall, Inc., 1960).

the aggregate scheduling decisions of the firm. A full description of these rules will be deferred until Chapter 17, where the problem of integrated systems will be viewed.

MOTIVATION

A discussion of the planning for the efficient utilization of the manpower of an enterprise would not be complete without some reference to the need for motivating the workers. The manpower plan is based on the premise that the workers will put forth a certain level of effort in order for the enterprise to achieve its desired output. However, men will not freely offer this required energy expenditure. Management must develop ways to encourage the work force to work at the desired level. If the manpower plan is to be considered complete, it must contain recognition of this need for encouragement. This is usually referred to as motivation. *Motivation* may be defined as the process of creating a reason, need, or desire, on the part of the workers, to perform at a level which will enable the enterprise to achieve its planned level of output. There have been many theories advanced with regard to motivation, but none can claim complete scientific validity. Oftentimes what appears to be sound procedure, in one case, will not be successful in another. This is undoubtedly a result of the fact that man is a complex being whose behavior is influenced by a variety of forces. The behavior of the individual and the group reflects the integration of many individual and interactive processes which take place. In an attempt to acquire a better understanding of motivation and human behavior, it will be valuable to examine some of the theories advanced.

Early Theories

Probably the earliest ideas about motivation tended to revolve around the belief that man was primarily an economic man. This grew largely out of the theories of the classical economists, and to some extent was perpetuated in the Scientific Management Movement. The basis of most of this theory was pecuniary. It assumed that money was the thing man desired the most, and it would provide him with the greatest satisfaction. The primary motivating devices assumed a direct relationship between the performance on the job and the amount of money received. Wage incentive plans, which offered a financial reward for increased productivity, were considered the best way to improve job performance.

This concept of motivation is still widely held today. Many managers still subscribe to it, and wage incentive plans are still utilized. The establishment of work standards by methods such as stopwatch time study, against which the worker's performance is measured, is quite common. A discussion of work measurement techniques will be undertaken in Chapter 14. A diversity of wage payment plans are used which reward the worker who exceeds the established standards through increased earnings. The most easily recognized of these wage payment plans is the piece rate, which enables the worker to increase his income by producing additional pieces of output. An examination of some types of wage payment plans utilized will be made in Chapter 19.

It is doubtful that enlightened management today would accept the idea that money is the primary motivator, and that it should be used for this purpose to the exclusion of other factors. This viewpoint does not mean that money as a motivator should be dismissed from consideration. There have been numerous studies which have substantiated the motivating characteristics of monetary rewards.[8] However, most managers would agree that money alone is not sufficient to sustain the desired level of productivity, but that something else is involved in motivation.

The Hawthorne Experiments

Perhaps the first documented recognition that factors other than money were involved in the level of productivity achieved resulted from the experiments starting in the 1920's conducted at the Western Electric Co. Hawthorne plant in Chicago. This twenty-year study is considered to be the foundation of many concepts which today are referred to as human relations, or behavioral science.

The original purpose of these experiments was to determine the effect of lighting on the productivity of workers. As the experiments progressed, it became apparent that something other than lighting influenced the workers' output. No matter what the experimenters did with respect to the lighting — improve it, appear to change it but actually not, or decrease the amount of illumination — productivity improved. When this was recognized, a series of additional experiments were undertaken to determine the real influence. Many theories regarding individual and group relations were developed as a result of these studies. The details of the full results are well documented.[9] The influence of group interrelationships and of the individual's participation in the group were cited by Mayo as major factors in the worker's performance.[10]

The Hierarchy of Needs

A later development in the approach to motivation, which contrasts considerably with the early theories, is that people will exert effort in order to satisfy a set of needs. Certain needs are considered more fundamental and must be satisfied, at least in part, before the less basic needs come into force. Thus, they are referred to as a hierarchy of needs. This concept was originally

---

[8]cf. M. S. Viteles, *Motivation and Morale in Industry* (New York: W. W. Norton & Co., Inc., 1954); and Opinion Research Corporation, *Public Opinion Index for Industry*, 1947.

[9]F. J. Roethlisberger and William J. Dickson, *Management and the Worker* (Cambridge, Massachusetts: Harvard University Press, 1939).

[10]Elton Mayo, *The Human Problems of an Industrial Civilization* (New York: The Viking Press, Inc., 1960).

suggested by A. H. Maslow.[11] He theorized that when a fundamental need is satisfied to a certain point, a person can then only be motivated to greater effort by appealing to the next higher need in the hierarchy. This means that the lower needs do not have to be fully satisfied before the next need in the hierarchy becomes a factor. Probably, none of the needs will ever be fully satisfied. Maslow felt that the higher the need, the smaller the percentage of the satisfaction of that need would be found in the average individual.[12] The needs which Maslow suggested, starting with the lowest need, can be summarized as follows:

1. Physiological needs, including food, shelter, and other similar fundamental needs.
2. Safety needs, concerning the protection against danger, threat, and deprivation.
3. Social needs, sometimes referred to as the love needs. These are concerned with man's needs for belonging to a group, to be accepted, and for friendship and love.
4. The needs for self-esteem, self-respect, status, recognition, and the respect of others, which are frequently referred to as the ego needs.
5. Self-fulfillment needs, which involve the realization by the individual of his potential.

The concept of the hierarchy of human needs has added to the understanding of human motivation. The idea that different needs exist and take on varying degrees of importance is a valuable tool. However, to state that this hierarchy applies to all individuals is misleading. There are those people who will strive to fulfill a higher need at the expense of a lower need. There are people to whom the ego needs are so strong that they will deprive themselves of food or disregard personal safety to achieve recognition. Others feel a strong drive for self-fulfillment which transcends the need for group acceptance or self-esteem.

This does not mean the concept of needs satisfaction, as a motivating device, should be discarded. It merely means that the needs priorities of individuals will differ. Each individual will place varying importance on his own need fulfillment. Management's recognition of a needs hierarchy and of the importance of a program for needs satisfaction is essential to the manpower plan of any enterprise.

X or Y?

An approach which has received considerable support concerning the best way to direct the energies of the workers to a higher level of achievement is concerned with the attitudes the managers themselves hold. This approach was presented by Douglas McGregor as Theory X and Theory Y.[13]

---

[11]A. H. Maslow, *Motivation and Personality* (New York: Harper & Row, Publishers, Inc., 1954).

[12]*Ibid.*

[13]Douglas McGregor, *The Human Side of Enterprise* (New York: McGraw-Hill Book Co., 1960).

Essentially, Theory X was viewed as the set of conventional attitudes management has held. It can be generalized by stating that people are normally passive, and opposed to working. It holds that management must use different devices to force or persuade people to perform their activities. The people must be directed, controlled, and punished to make their behavior conform to the organizational objectives.

Theory Y was presented as a contrast to Theory X. It contends that people are not opposed to work and that management can motivate the people by making them aware of their potential. Management should establish an organization climate which will most readily permit the workers to achieve their own goals by working toward enterprise goals.

McGregor's ideas were readily accepted by many people, particularly by those psychologically oriented, who saw this approach as the explanation of the problems of the implementation of the human relations approach; i.e., too many managers followed Theory X. Some advocates of this approach saw in it a suggestion for the abrogation of management's leadership role, in favor of a laissez-faire attitude toward the workers. This is not what was intended any more than the implication that these two theories were the extremes on a continuum of management strategies. Later McGregor was to write that these were only two classifications from among many possible ones, and that they were not at opposite extremes.[14]

The real value of these two theories is that they give an awareness of the different managerial attitudes found in practice, and create an appreciation of the impact and implications they have on the motivation of people. It may also be desirable to include in the manpower plan some approach for evaluating and changing prevalent managerial attitudes.

The Motivation-Hygiene Theory

This theory of motivation grew out of a study of 200 engineers and accountants made to test the needs-satisfaction concept. The subjects were asked to identify experiences which had improved their job satisfaction and those which had decreased it. In addition, attempts were made to determine why the subjects felt the way they did. The results brought forth a set of satisfiers and a set of dissatisfiers. Five factors were identified as satisfiers. Two — achievement and recognition — were identified as being of short duration; while three — work, responsibility, and advancement — were of long duration.

The satisfiers were identified as motivators, while the dissatisfiers were called hygiene factors, since they were external to the job and were primarily preventative or environmental. The contention is: The hygiene factors do not motivate when they are present, and they create dissatisfaction when they

---

[14]Douglas McGregor, *The Professional Manager* (New York: McGraw-Hill Book Co., 1967), pp. 79–80.

decline in significance. Working conditions, wages, supervision, and company policies are considered to be in this category.[15]

This dual-factor theory sparked considerable controversy, and additional studies have been undertaken, resulting in claims of verification or of disproof of the dual nature of an individual's attitudes toward his job. There have also been criticisms of the research methodology.[16]

Again, the value of this theory is that it gives further potential insight into the nature of human behavior, and of the ways management may plan to motivate its manpower.

Patterns of Performance

Likert reported an extensive study of the methods used by management and the effect of their methods on the performance of the people and the organization as a whole.[17] He states the most effective units in an organization tend to follow a pattern of management approaches. The units identified as high producing are usually characterized by a particular set of favorable attitudes and high job satisfaction for their members.[18] All units which possess these qualities, however, are not also high producing ones. In addition, it is necessary to have high performance goals, if this result is to be achieved.[19]

The results of the investigations lead to two generalizations:

1. There is a significant difference in the patterns of management used by those managers who achieve the best results, compared with those managers whose performance is less impressive.
2. Although a difference exists, this has not been formally recognized in any statement of a theory at this point.[20]

This research shows the importance of the particular pattern of management, which creates an attitude among the workers that leads to the desired results. The significance of the people-oriented attitudes found in the supervision of these high productivity units cannot be ignored.

Achievement and Motivation

Motivation is also viewed as closely related to achievement. The drive or desire to achieve a certain standard of success, or to achieve acceptance and

---

[15]F. Herzberg, B. Mausner, and B. Snyderman, *The Motivation to Work* (2d ed.; New York: John Wiley & Sons, Inc., 1959).

[16]cf. F. Herzberg, *Work and the Nature of Man* (Cleveland: The World Publishing Co., 1966); and Orlando Behling, George Labovitz, and Richard Kosmo, "The Herzberg Controversy: A Critical Reappraisal," *Academy of Management Journal*, Vol. XI, No. 1 (March, 1968), pp. 99–108.

[17]Rensis Likert, *New Patterns of Management* (New York: McGraw-Hill Book Co., Inc. 1961).

[18]*Ibid*, p. 58.

[19]*Ibid.*, p. 59.

[20]*Ibid.*, p. 60.

recognition, is considered the primary force which makes people willing to work.   Typical examples are the achievement desire of the entrant into the country fair cake baking contest for a blue ribbon, or the drive of the college football player to achieve all-American recognition.   However, in these cases, the achievement desire may be related to the motivating influence of money. The all-American athlete can demand a higher bonus from the professionals.

There is no denying the force of the desire for achievement.   It closely parallels the earlier mentioned need for self-esteem and status.   Naturally, as pointed out in the discussion of the needs hierarchy, the motivating effect of the desire for achievement will differ from individual to individual.

Some writers have related expectations to achievement as a motivating force.   Their thesis is: While the individual may have a high degree of desire for achievement, if he feels that the possibilities of achievement are poor, he will not be motivated to act.   He must feel that action on his part contributes some way to achievement of his goal.   For example, an individual may desire to achieve the position of president of the enterprise where he is employed.   However, if this is a company controlled by the Smith family, it is unlikely any action on his part will overcome the virtual certainty that John Smith, Jr., will succeed his father in the position.

This approach to motivation is specific, because it cannot be applied in a general sense in all situations.   It requires knowledge of individual expectations and desires for achievement.   The value is found in the recognition that if a person can be endowed with high expectations and desire for achievement, the possibilities of motivation will be improved.

Attitudes and Environment

Reference has been made to the attitudes of the managers as being significant factors in the motivation of the workers.   This was brought out in the discussion of McGregor's Theory X and Theory Y.   Attitudes of the managers are really only part of the total work environment in which employees find themselves.   The primary job of management, in its attempt to motivate the people in the work force, is to create an environment conducive to good work, where the workers will feel secure and satisfied.   To achieve this, approaches to change the attitudes of managers or to create the desired environmental conditions have been suggested.   Examination of the environment will be limited to the psychological or social rather than the physical environment.   This latter aspect will be discussed in Chapters 12 and 13.

The Managerial Grid.[21]   An integrative technique achieving some degree of popularity is the managerial grid.   This device attempts to show the relationship between the concern for production (which corresponds to the organizational needs) and the concern for people (related to the needs of the individual).   It is a schematic representation of different types of managerial behavior patterns

---

[21]Robert R. Blake and Jane S. Mouton, *The Managerial Grid* (Houston: Gulf Publishing Co., 1964).

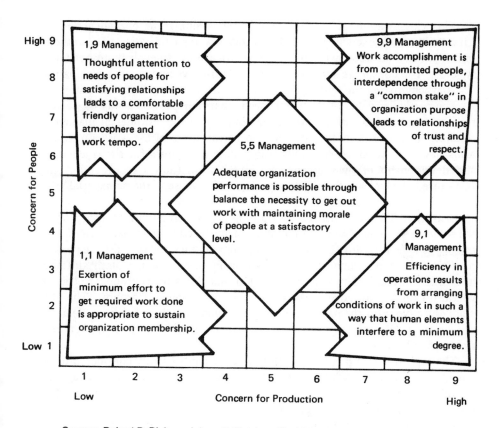

Source: Robert R. Blake and Jane S. Mouton, *The Managerial Grid* (Houston: Gulf Publishing Co., 1964), p. 10. Reproduced by permission of the publisher.

FIGURE 11-5

The Managerial Grid

represented on a two-dimensional nine by nine scale. The vertical grid is used to represent the concern for people, and the concern for production is found on the X-axis or horizontal grid. The 1 to 9 scale on each axis is used to indicate the degree of concern for the factor represented. A value of 1 indicates a low concern, and a score of 9, high concern.

The usual representation of the grid considers five patterns of management, as indicated in Figure 11-5. The 9,9 management is the desired pattern. In this pattern, the maximum concern for both elements is found. This is described as team management; the other patterns are described as impoverished management (1,1), country club management (1,9), task management (9,1), and middle of the road management (5,5).[22]

[22]Robert R. Blake, Jane S. Mouton, and Alvin C. Bidwell, "Managerial Grid," *Advanced Management-Office Executive*, Vol. I, No. 9 (September, 1962), p. 13.

This classification of management styles is similar to one suggested by Likert with two broad categories: authoritative and participative. The authoritative pattern includes exploitive authoritative and benevolent authoritative systems. The consultive system is partly authoritative and partly participative. The participative group system falls entirely under the participative pattern.[23]

The particular value of these schemes is that they provide a way of viewing the management job with an eye toward improving the attitudes of managers, resulting in increased motivation and job performance of the workers. Many firms have had satisfactory results using these techniques for the orientation and development of their managers. Humble Oil (now Exxon) and Aetna Insurance have had satisfactory experiences with the use of the managerial grid.

Sensitivity Training. Sensitivity training is a widely discussed approach to the solution of some of the attitudinal problems faced by managers. *Sensitivity training* is a device using the concepts of group interactions to assist the participant to understand human behavior by learning more about himself and how he relates to others. Through participation in a T (training) group, the trainee will also gain a knowledge of the nature and functioning of groups. The ultimate objective is for the participant to understand how these behavior elements can be used to improve motivation, management techniques, and organizational effectiveness.

The typical T group is small with ten participants usually considered to be the ideal. The approach is unstructured and nondirective, with no agenda provided. The members make up any rules for the operation of the group. The leader does not provide any control over what is done. At times he will comment to make them aware of what is happening; at other times, he will not participate, forcing the group to lead itself. This lack of structured activities is designed to make the members more sensitive to their roles as individuals, and as part of the group.[24]

Some organizations using sensitivity training are The American Management Association, Exxon Corporation, TRW Systems, and the Harwood Manufacturing Corporation. In spite of the acceptance of sensitivity training by some enterprises, it still remains a controversial device. The pros and cons of sensitivity training have been summarized in many places. No attempt will be made to list the arguments of both sides.[25] The use of sensitivity training appears to have value when used in the proper situation, in proper doses. There is currently no real evidence which conclusively answers the question of the value of sensitivity training. It is probably safest to consider it as a research device which requires additional evaluation before its true nature can be determined.

---

[23]Likert, *op. cit.*, pp. 223 ff.

[24]For a description of sensitivity training, including details of actual sessions, the reader is referred to: Alfred J. Marrow, *Behind the Executive Mask* (New York: American Management Association, Inc., 1964).

[25]See for example Yoder, *op. cit.*, pp. 381–383. This source also footnotes original source materials for this argument.

The Environment. Concern with the environment, at this stage, is with the psychological environment of work as opposed to the physical environment. Essentially, the discussion of motivation was primarily aimed at creating an atmosphere to encourage the workers to work toward accomplishment of the enterprise objectives. The problem arises when the environment negatively affects achieving the goals and objectives of the enterprise: goals of the owners, managers and workers. Thus, management has to create a setting which recognizes the needs of everyone. The needs of the organization must be balanced with individual needs in a way that they literally become one. This has been termed as fusion.[26] This condition would be similar to the 9,9 management suggested by the managerial grid, or to the participative group pattern of Likert. It would parallel the satisfiers of Herzberg, and approaches answering the self-fulfillment needs of Maslow's hierarchy. Fusion of organizational and individual needs appears to be a prerequisite to achievement of the psychological environment necessary to motivate the manpower of the enterprise to the degree desired.

Significance for Management

Several theories and concepts about motivation of the work force have been presented. There are differing viewpoints, and a single, clear-cut method cannot be set forth for management to follow. Should management ignore all these ideas since the experts fail to agree? Of course, that is not the correct action. Each concept has added something to knowledge about motivation.

Management must recognize that human behavior is largely determined by the individual's desire for achievement and realization in his relationships with individuals and groups. The essence of motivation can be seen in the attempts of people to achieve this feeling of self-actualization. The striving for acceptance and recognition, in terms of our own values and goals, is apparent in all our actions. This does not mean that people need to be pampered, but it indicates a need to instill in them a feeling of accomplishment from the tasks they are performing.

Some of the more basic factors held important by the early theories should not be ignored. Those elements identified by Herzberg as hygiene factors are still important. While money may not be a motivator, as some people have contended, if workers are not paid an adequate wage, management cannot expect a satisfactory performance level. On the other hand, paying a satisfactory wage will not in itself guarantee that they will achieve this level.

The problem of motivation is complex and important. Stimulating the people to meet organizational goals through satisfaction of their own needs is not all there is to motivation. It is also a matter of management's approach. Leavitt suggested that motivation is only one part of the problem, albeit an important part, and management must consider the other facets of getting the

---

[26]Chris Argyris, *Personality and Organization* (New York: Harper & Bros., 1957), and E. Wright Bakke, *The Fusion Process* (New Haven: Labor and Management Center, Yale University, 1953).

job done. He indicates that management must define the nature of the task involved, before deciding what steps to take. This will determine the need to emphasize either the people, the structure, or technology.[27]

All present-day approaches to motivation appear to be generalizations, although empirical evidence of applications of most of them in specific enterprises can be cited. What works in one case may not work in another. However, these approaches do present some of the important aspects of the problem of achieving the desired results from the enterprise's manpower. Until we discover the "elixir of motivation," management must examine and evaluate these existing ideas and make the best possible application in the environment where it must operate.

SUMMARY

Further consideration of planning the operations system leads to a determination of the manpower needs of the enterprise. The process whereby the quantity and quality of the work force are determined is manpower planning. While the process of manpower planning is conducted in different ways and in varying degrees in individual enterprises, certain general principles may be stated. The role of manpower must also be understood if manpower planning is to succeed.

The nature and importance of manpower policy is examined. Specific areas for which manpower policies must be established are considered. Among these is determination of the quantity of manpower required. This involves the establishment of a manpower forecast. Another area of manpower policy is recruitment and selection of the required manpower. A final manpower policy area concerns provisions for work force training and development.

The effect of the learning phenomena on the process of manpower planning is recognized. The application of a particular technique, the time-reduction curve, which has found some utilization in manufacturing is detailed. The basic concept of the time-reduction curve is: Each time the quantity of output is doubled, there is a constant percentage reduction in the average time required to produce the cumulative number of units. The computational aspects of this technique are explained, and its applications to manpower planning are discussed. The potential and underlying conditions of manpower planning are outlined.

Manpower loading is a specialized aspect of manpower planning, with specific relevance in manufacturing enterprises. This process is concerned with the actual assigning of the workers to the specific machines and tasks. It is an end process for the manufacturing manager. The relationship of manpower loading to the master schedule is considered, along with the means of controlling the loading process.

---

[27]Harold J. Leavitt, "It's a Valuable Management Tool, But . . . Motivation Is Not Enough," *Stanford Graduate School of Business Bulletin*, Vol. XXXV, No. 2 (Autumn, 1966), pp. 21–27.

The manpower plan involves achievement of a certain level of performance by workers. This is realized through the process of motivation. Numerous theories of motivation and the nature of human behavior have been advanced.

The earliest ideas tended to stress the economic factors as being the prime motivating devices. Money is still considered a motivating force, but there is recognition today that more than money is involved. The major impetus toward a realization of the importance of the human element came from the Hawthorne Experiments. From the results of these studies arose formulation of many human relations approaches which tend to emphasize the influence of the group and the individual's role in the group.

One theory of motivation developed is the concept of the hierarchy of needs. Another popular concept is Theory X and Theory Y advanced by McGregor. The Motivation-Hygiene Theory which classified into two categories the factors involved in the performance of a job is another theory. Another approach to the realization of the desired level of productivity suggests that patterns of performance can be designated. These patterns are related to the way the organizational unit is managed. A final view discussed is the relationship between motivation and the level of achievement an individual can expect.

The importance of the attitudes of managers and the psychological environment where the work is carried out were identified with the motivation process. The use of the managerial grid and of sensitivity training as ways to change management attitudes were evaluated. Theories regarding motivation are largely concerned with creating an environment which will contribute to the achievement of the objectives of the enterprise and of the individual. An evaluation was made of the significance to management of different theories and concepts regarding motivation.

INCIDENT I

MANPOWER FORECASTING

The Merta Manufacturing Corporation employs approximately 3,000 people. About 75% of the work force consists of semiskilled workers employed by the production department. Forecasts are developed for the total manpower requirements of the firm as well as for this principal segment, production. Total requirements are forecasted for five years into the future, and are prepared annually. In addition, forecasts for the total requirements and for the production requirements are prepared for the next year, for each quarter. Finally, the production work force is projected for the next six months on a monthly breakdown.

The forecasts in all categories are prepared by a member of the personnel department staff. Total manpower is forecasted on the basis of the predictions of the level of economic activity and in line with company policies for sales trends and product development.

The production worker requirements are predicated on the specific sales forecasts for the period involved, forecasts from the production department for the available internal manpower supply, and estimates of the required level of production from the production control department.

If the estimates of internal labor supply are lower than the forecasted production worker requirements, there are three alternatives for management to consider. The first is to increase the hiring to meet the demand. The second is to resort to overtime, and the third is to establish priorities on the scheduled work. If the differences are large, management favors the alternative of increasing the work force. On the other hand, where the excess requirements are expected to last for a short period of time, the second alternative is favored. The third alternative is only followed as a last resort.

If the reverse condition exists, where requirements are less than the workers available, the usual policy is to produce to inventory. If this is not feasible for any reason, separations are carried out.

Questions

1. Evaluate the manpower forecasting technique used by this company.

2. Do you agree with the priorities given to the alternatives considered?

3. Would you suggest any other alternatives which might be used when supply and demand estimates differ?

INCIDENT II

FEAR OR GOLD STARS?

William Hinds is the production manager of a medium-sized manufacturing company. He has often remarked that fear is the only way to make people work. Hinds operates on this theory, not only with those who report directly to him, but he also sees that this concept is applied to the production workers. Periodically, he has each worker in the shop report to his office for a discussion of performance. Invariably he uses this meeting to criticize the individual's performance, and to threaten him with loss of his job if he does not improve. To reinforce his point, he always gives some workers their notice of dismissal at this interview. Hinds feels that this will "straighten out those people," and that he can count on increased productivity in the shop for a period of time.

Henry Garrett holds a similar position in another company which is approximately the same size as the one where William Hinds works. Unlike Hinds, Garrett believes that you have to reward people in order to have them perform satisfactorily. He knows that money isn't enough and that people have to have some form of recognition. He has developed a system whereby any worker who performs at a level above the established standard, or in some other way distinguishes himself, will be recognized. He has posted a board at the workers' entrance with the names of all the production workers on it. Each week, if they qualify, a gold star is placed alongside their names. At the end of the year, the top gold star winner in each department is given a special recognition prize.

Question

Comment on these two contrasting styles of management. Evaluate them in terms of the motivating effect of each.

QUESTIONS FOR DISCUSSION AND ANALYSIS

1. Discuss the nature of manpower planning and its significance in operations management.

2. What is the objective of manpower policy? How is it related to the role of manpower?

3. Describe briefly the three areas mentioned in the chapter for which manpower policy must be developed.

4. How does the concept of learning and the learning curve relate to the problem of manpower planning?

5. What is the underlying concept of the time-reduction theory? In what way can it be useful in the area of manpower planning?

6. List and comment on some areas other than manpower planning where the concepts of the learning curve can be useful to the operations manager.

7. What is manpower loading? How does it differ from manpower planning? Why is it particularly significant to the operations manager?

8. Describe the relationship of motivation to the manpower-planning process. Include a definition of motivation in your discussion.

9. Comment on the concept of the worker as an economic man. How important do you feel money is as a motivating force?

10. Briefly describe the importance of the Hawthorne Experiments.

11. Do you agree with Maslow's hierarchy of needs? Compare it to your observations of people you know. Can you cite any examples of people you feel did not conform to this hierarchy?

12. Compare Theory X and Theory Y.

13. Evaluate Herzberg's Motivation-Hygiene Theory.

14. In what way is the pattern of management used by the manager of a particular unit of an organization, likely to influence the performance of that unit? How would you explain this relationship?

15. Comment on achievement and expectations as motivating forces.

16. Discuss the importance of managerial attitudes and the psychological environment as they refer to motivation.

17. Describe the managerial grid. Comment on its value. How does it relate to the theories of motivation described in the chapter?

18. What is sensitivity training? What is your evaluation of the use of T-groups as devices for changing management attitudes?

19. In your opinion, is it possible for management to motivate workers to the level of performance most desirable for the organization? If so, what are the most important things for management to do?

SELECTED ADDITIONAL READINGS

Andress, Frank J. "The Learning Curve as a Production Tool." *Harvard Business Review*, Vol. XXXII, No. 1 (January–February, 1954), pp. 87–97.

Greene, James H. (ed.). *Production and Inventory Control Handbook*. New York: McGraw-Hill Book Co., 1970. Chapter 10.

Herzberg, F., B. Mausner, and B. Snyderman. *The Motivation to Work*, 2d ed. New York: John Wiley & Sons, Inc., 1959.

Likert, Rensis. *New Patterns of Management*. New York: McGraw-Hill Book Co., 1961.

Maslow, A. H. *Motivating and Personality*. New York: Harper & Row, Publishers, Inc., 1954.

McGregor, Douglas. *The Human Side of Enterprise*. New York: McGraw-Hill Book Co., 1960.

Moore, Franklin G., and Ronald Jablonski. *Production Control*, 3d ed. New York: McGraw-Hill Book Co., 1969. Chapter 15.

Roethlisberger, F. J., and William J. Dickson. *Management and the Worker*. Cambridge, Massachusetts: Harvard University Press, 1939.

U.S. Department of Labor, Manpower Administration. *Employer Manpower Planning and Forecasting*, Manpower Research Monograph No. 19. Washington: U.S. Government Printing Office, 1970.

Yoder, Dale. *Personnel Management and Industrial Relations*, 6th ed. Englewood Cliffs: Prentice-Hall, Inc., 1970.

SELECTIONS FROM READINGS BOOK

Richards, Max D., and William A. Nielander. *Readings in Management*, 3d ed. Cincinnati: South-Western Publishing Co., 1969.
　McGregor, "The Human Side of Enterprise," p. 569.
　McClelland, "That Urge to Achieve," p. 579.
　Clark, "Motivation in Work Groups: A Tentative View," p. 591.
　Klaw, "Inside a T-Group," p. 962.

CHAPTER 12

Design of the Work System

Work is an important part of man's life, and he spends a considerable percentage of his life in work. Ever since man first appeared, he has looked for ways or devices to make work more acceptable. Development of the wheel, the stone tool, and other technological advances were certainly brought about as adjuncts to man's search to improve his abilities to carry out work and to extend his senses. Development of technology has continued and has moved man further from the actual work carried on in his environment. Many social, religious, economic, and political doctrines throughout history were indicative of man's attitude toward work. Examples are the various types of slavery, which are really only means of forcing the socially or economically inferior individuals to do the work; the Protestant Ethic and its concern for the moral virtues of work; the division of labor doctrine of Adam Smith; and the writings of Karl Marx.

NATURE OF WORK

Society's attitude toward work has varied from time to time. Some people have viewed it essentially as a four-letter word, others as a necessary evil, and still others do not even today accept it as a necessity. The philosopher's view of work has also changed from time to time. Aristotle looked upon the best possible performance of the work for which one was most fitted as a necessary element of the individual's happiness.[1] Other philosophers have looked upon work as the major purpose for man's being. The current status of work may best be described as being accepted as an important aspect of the achievement of the economic goals of a nation. Work leads to increased output, which results in improvements in the standard of living.

There are still people who have a pessimistic outlook about the future of work in our society. For example, Whyte sees society departing from the concept of the Protestant Ethic and moving toward adherence to the Social Ethic.[2] The Social Ethic is defined as a doctrine emphasizing society and the group, and sublimating the individual.

The changing nature of work has probably been influenced most significantly by the advancement of technology. At one time, the content of a job, to a large extent, was highly correlated with man's social status. He and his contemporaries tended to determine his worth and position in society by his work.

---

[1]Aristotle, *On Man In The Universe* (New York: Walter J. Black, 1943), p. 87 ff.

[2]William H. J. Whyte, *The Organization Man* (Garden City: Doubleday and Co., Inc. 1956).

The spread of technology has upgraded work in our society, and the majority of work now consists of some form of man-machine interface. This man-machine relationship has significantly changed the nature of man's task. Man's contribution has been lessened by increasing technology. As a result, the amount of physical energy used by man has declined.

While it is still true that a large part of the operations manager's concern with the design of a work system will center around man himself, the influence of the technical environment cannot be ignored. The concepts of the socio-technical system, as it is concerned with technology and its influence on job design, will be discussed in the next chapter.

WORK AND JOB DESIGN

The design of a work system involves the examination and evaluation of a presently existing or proposed method of performing a specific classification of work. The primary purpose of this investigation is to improve the operation of the existing system, or to develop the most efficient system possible. The determination of how well the desired goals are met is based on some measure of effectiveness such as productivity or cost. A variety of elements must be considered in the investigation and development of a work system. First, a description of the task or tasks involved must be developed. Next, the tasks must be analyzed taking into consideration the processes and methods used, the environment of the work system, and the required capabilities of the workers or machines involved in the work system. The work system must then be standardized. This standardization becomes a valuable aid in training the workers in the preferred method. Ultimately, the design of the work system will lead to establishment of work standards. From this, systems of job evaluation and a particular wage payment plan will evolve.

Once the design of the total work system has been set, the problem of how the individual tasks or jobs within that system can best be carried out has to be noted. This is the function of *job design*, which is concerned with compiling and combining the human elements of work. The designer of the work system, and consequently, the designer of a given job must be aware of the human components required by the system. Therefore, man is the most important element in the design of jobs.

MAN-MACHINE SYSTEMS

In the design of a work system, and consequently the design of jobs, the operations manager is primarily concerned with allocating functions between the primary resources available to him. In most cases, the primary resources are man and some form of machine.

A *machine* may be any device man uses to assist him to accomplish his particular work and job objective. He may use something as simple as a pen, a screwdriver, a shovel, or in the more usual sense of a machine, the lathe or drill press. A *man-machine system* exists whenever at least one human being interacts with one or more machines in a way that an input (data, material, or some other form) is processed so a desired output results. A man-machine system may consist of a number of men and one machine, or of several machines and a single man. The interface which takes place between the man and the machine elements of the system does not have to be constant. The interface between these two elements only needs to take place periodically for a man-machine system to exist. The major concern with this relationship in job design is determining those functions which may best be allocated to the two major elements of the man-machine system. The ultimate aim is to arrive at a proper balance which will enable the system to function at an optimal level.

A useful beginning for this determination is to examine some general characteristics, or functions, men and machines can best perform. Table 12-1 is a comparative listing of some characteristics.

TABLE 12-1

A Comparative Listing of Some Functions of Men and Machines

Men	Machines
Limited physical energy as well as psychological and sociological constraints.	No great physical limitations except those built in, and no comparable constraints in the psychological or sociological realm.
Reasonably sensitive, but some limitation in the range of the human senses.	Can be highly sensitive to very minute changes of various forms of energy, light, etc.
Identifying and perceptual ability very great.	Identifying and perceptual ability limited within a narrow range.
Limited channel capacity with regard to the amount of information which can be processed within a given period of time.	Virtually unlimited channel capacity.
Memory limits in terms of complexity and capacity are unknown, but believed to be very high.	Potential memory limits are quite high.
Quite flexible, and can be reprogrammed. Are able to adjust more readily to unexpected situations, and to select alternate means.	Relatively inflexible and difficult to reprogram. Cannot anticipate all possible deviations or contingencies.
Comparatively slow at computing.	Very rapid at computing.

This list of the functions is not intended to be a complete or comprehensive list of the characteristics of men and machines. It is offered as a partial example of some relationships found in a man-machine system important to the designer of a work system or job. Exceptions to the items in a list of this type, with many broad generalizations, are usual. The specifics of the given situation or system should be studied to determine the best man-machine relationship. What is true in one situation may not necessarily be true in another. In a given system, it may be unimportant to select the component which can perform most efficiently, because of other considerations. Chapanis offers three broad rules which can be applied to modify the list in Table 12-1 when considering the division of functions between men and machines.[3]

The first rule states that when an allocation of the functions to be performed in a man-machine system is made, the decision is almost always influenced to some extent by social, economic, and political values. In effect, job design is strongly influenced by the environment and culture found where it takes place.

The second rule involves the need for flexibility in man-machine allocations. Various conditions existing at the time the decision is made will influence the actual allocation. This means that a process of constant reevaluation of the man-machine system must take place.

The third rule states that a man-machine system often results from considerable trial and error. This occurs because of uncertainties of the system designers, and often a detailed review of the problems encountered in making man-machine allocations follows.

JOB DESIGN

The man-machine relationship is an important element of job design; however, it is only one part of the total problem. Traditionally, most managers have been largely concerned with establishing the design of the most efficient method to perform the job. The design of job methods has, for many years, depended largely on various tools of motion study; sometimes identified as motion analysis, methods study, or work simplification. Modern motion study techniques are generally conceded to have evolved from the pioneering work of the Gilbreths. The primary objectives of motion study are finding the easiest, most economical way to perform a job; requiring the least amount of effort; and making the best possible use of the manpower, the materials, and the equipment available. Through long and continued practice, those people who have used motion study techniques have found that a basic approach to all problems of this type is generally applicable. Before examining the tools of motion study, it may be well to review this approach.

---

[3]Alphonse Chapanis, "On the Allocation of Functions between Men and Machines," *Occupational Psychology*, Vol. XXXIX, No. 1 (January, 1965), pp. 5–6.

Pattern for Analyzing Job Methods[4]

It has been found convenient to utilize an analytical pattern for accomplishing the objectives of improving the design of job methods. While specifics may vary in different enterprises, the following five steps illustrate this pattern:

1. Choose the operation to be studied for possible improvement.

   If the operation is new and has not been performed, this step is quite easy. In fact, all new operations should be studied for this purpose. However, in the case of on-going operations, there are certain things one can look for in making this selection. Prime candidates are bottleneck operations requiring long periods of time or delaying other aspects of the process. Any operation which appears to have high cost, or an operation which requires considerable movement by either the individual or the object, should also be examined.

2. Analyze the job.

   List precisely all details of the job as it is currently being performed or planned. The details should cover all aspects of utilization of manpower, material, and equipment. For on-going jobs, details should be developed from actual observation; for new jobs, they can only be developed from a written outline of the planned method.

3. Examine and question all details.

   The questions, Why? What? Where? When? Who? and How? should be answered. Why is it done? What is done, and for what reason? Where is it, or where should it be, done? When is the job done? Who does the job, or should do it? How can the job be done? These questions can be applied to all details of the job. It is also important to question the materials, machinery and equipment, layout of the workplace, and other elements of the job.

4. Propose a new method.

   Eliminate all unnecessary details. Combine details of the job where practical. Rearrange the details of the job for better sequence. Simplify all necessary job details in an attempt to make the job easier and safer. The proposed new method should be developed in conjunction with others concerned with the job, and ultimately put into written form.

5. Institute the proposed new method.

   The new method must be sold to superiors and to those people who will perform the job under the new method. Therefore, approval must be received from all individuals concerned with the job performance. Once the new method has been instituted, it should continue in operation, but under constant surveillance, until a better method is developed.

---

[4]The reader is referred to any standard textbook in the area of motion and time study for more details on motion study. See for example Ralph M. Barnes, *Motion and Time Study: Design and Measurement of Work* (6th ed.; New York: John Wiley & Sons, Inc., 1968).

Motion Study Tools

A variety of motion study tools can be used in the application of this pattern. These motion study tools are usually tables or graphic devices, found to be useful for visualizing the total job design. Since these tools assume a variety of forms, not all of them will be useful for analyzing any single job design. The selection of the tools to use will depend largely on the nature of the process, activity, or operation under study. The traditional tools of motion study can be divided into three broad categories: process analysis, activity analysis, and operation analysis.

Process Analysis. Process analysis is the most gross or macroanalytic motion study tool because it takes the broadest view of job design. It primarily evaluates the sequence or flow of the work being performed. In making a process analysis, the analyst will usually use a flow process chart. A *flow process chart* is merely a graphic or schematic device which is convenient for recording the activities of a process in a condensed way. An example of a form of a process chart was given in Chapter 5. Examination of the flow process chart simplifies the analysis of the entire operation. The chart represents all steps, from the beginning to final output, in the total performance of a particular job. When the above five-step pattern for analyzing job methods is applied to the present process, as depicted on a flow process chart, possible improvements will become readily visible. Upon completion of the analysis of the present process, the proposed new process is recorded on another flow process chart.

A flow process chart may be one of two types: It may follow the activities of an individual, referred to as a man-type process chart; or it may be a material process chart concerned with the processes involving the material. A process chart may be only one of these types. Once the analysis is started with respect to the man or the material, it must continue to follow the same element.

SYMBOLS. A flow process chart uses a series of symbols to represent the types of activities in the process. Many sets of symbols have been, or can be used, to construct a flow process chart. The Gilbreths originally developed a set of four symbols which were used extensively for many years. Today, however, the most commonly used symbols are the ones recommended by the American Society of Mechanical Engineers.[5] These five symbols are really a slight modification and extension of the original Gilbreth symbols. These symbols, with their descriptions, are as follows:

◯ *Operation.* An operation occurs whenever some change in the item occurs at a particular workplace. This may be a change in the size or shape, an assembly or disassembly, or some other similar modification. The change may result from the expenditure of labor, a machining activity, or a combination of both. Computation, exchange of information, or a decision-making process may also be considered operations.

---

[5]*Operation and Flow Process Charts, ASME Standard 101* (New York: American Society of Mechanical Engineers, 1947).

⟁ *Transportation.* A transportation or move takes place whenever the item or person under study changes, or is changed, from one workplace to another.

D *Delay.* A delay takes place when the item or person must wait, or the item is placed in temporary storage prior to performance of the next scheduled activity. Onset of the next scheduled activity does not require any special requisition, order, etc., to initiate it when the item or person is in the delay state.

△ *Storage.* This is a controlled storage condition, and some form of order or requisition is required to remove the item from this state to the next scheduled activity.

☐ *Inspection.* An inspection takes place when a comparison or verification of an item, with either a quantity or quality standard, occurs at a workplace.

Under certain circumstances, two of the above symbols are combined when two activities occur at the same time at the particular workplace. An example of this would be the inclusion of a triangle within a square ◩ to show that an inspection was made at a particular point in the process while the item under study is in a controlled storage state.

FLOW DIAGRAM. Often it is useful to supplement the flow process chart with a flow diagram, to achieve a complete analysis of the process under consideration. The flow diagram contains the same information found on the flow process chart. This information is merely superimposed upon a scaled floor plan of the area in which the activity has occurred. The same symbols employed on the flow process chart are used in the flow diagram, and are placed on the drawing at the appropriate locations. Lines connecting these symbols show the movement of the item in the area diagramed. This technique may be used to solve problems of relative location of facilities discussed in Chapter 10.

Figure 12-1 shows a flow process chart for an office procedure under an existing method. This procedure is concerned with the steps involved in preparing and processing an expense account form from its origination by the employee through approval. The flow diagram for this process is shown in Figure 12-2.

Examination of this flow process chart and the accompanying diagram quickly reveals opportunities for improvement. In line with the suggestions in the pattern for analyzing methods, certain questions may be asked. Why does the manager have to approve the form? Where does the final authority for approval rest? Why does the form have to be typed from the handwritten copy? If certain answers to these questions are assumed, it is possible the form may go directly to the accounting officer for approval. This will eliminate several steps and effect a saving in time for this process. The resultant flow process chart for the proposed method is in Figure 12-3, page 306.

FLOW PROCESS CHART

No. __765A__

Page __1__ of __1__

Job __Complete Expense Acct.__

Man ☐ Mat'l ☒ __Form__

	Present		Proposed		Difference	
	No	Time	No	Time	No	Time
Operations	4					
Transportations	4					
Inspections	2					
Delays	6					
Storages	0					
Distance Travelled	1560'					

Chart begins _____

Chart ends _____

Charted by __B. Davis__

Date __7/27__

	OPER TRANS STORE INSP DELAY	Dist.	Time	(PRESENT) Details of (PROPOSED) Method
1				Expense account form written by employee
2				In basket awaiting interoffice mail pickup
3		20'		To department manager's secretary
4				Waiting on secretary's desk
5				Typed by secretary from written copy
6		15'		To department manager's desk
7				In basket awaiting approval signature
8				Examined by department manager
9				Signed by department manager
10				In basket awaiting interoffice mail pickup
11		1500'		To accounting department
12				Waiting on accounting officer's desk
13				Examined by accounting officer
14				Approved by accounting officer
15		25'		To accounting clerk's desk
16				On desk waiting for preparation of check
17				
18				

COMMENTS:

FIGURE 12-1

Flow Process Chart for Completing an Expense Account Form
Present Method

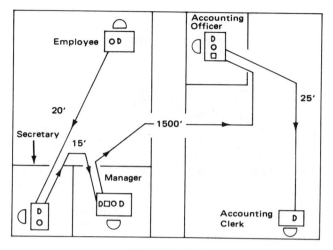

FIGURE 12-2

Flow Diagram for Completing an Expense Account Form
Present Method

Examination of this chart and the flow diagram for the proposed method in Figure 12-4 clearly indicates the potential savings. The summary table in Figure 12-3 shows the actual differences between the present and proposed methods.

Flow process chart techniques may also be used for assembly situations. They may be very useful to illustrate the case where component parts are produced singly, then come together to be processed or assembled.

The thermostat in Figure 12-5 is an example. This thermostat consists of three major parts: the shank, housing, and body. Each part is produced separately, then they are brought together to be assembled into final form.

The assembly flow process chart for this thermostat is found in Figure 12-6. The basic concepts of process analysis apply to the same extent here as for our prior example.

The flow process chart is a very flexible tool which can be applied to many kinds of activities in addition to office procedures or assembly processes in manufacturing. It may also be utilized in almost any other type of activity where a person, a form, or material is in some stage of process, no matter how simple or complex it may be. It could be used to show a simple personal activity, such as preparing a sandwich or purchasing a beverage from a vending machine. A process analysis of a laboratory test could be made, as well as one for a large-scale program, e.g., construction of a building.

Activity Analysis. In many cases greater detail must be developed than provided by process analysis. Activity analysis is a means of accomplishing this type of investigation. A schematic device, the activity chart, can be used

FLOW PROCESS CHART

No. 765B

Page 1 of 1

	Present		Proposed		Difference	
	No	Time	No	Time	No	Time
Operations	4		2		2	
Transportations	4		2		2	
Inspections	2		1		1	
Delays	6		3		3	
Storages	0		0		0	
Distance Travelled	1560'		1525'		35'	

Job Complete Expense Acct.

Man ☐   Mat'l ☒   Form

Chart begins _____

Chart ends _____

Charted by ____ B. Davis

Date ____ 7/27

	OPER TRANS STORE INSP DELAY	Dist.	Time	(PRESENT) Details of (PROPOSED) Method
1	○⇨△☐D			Expense account form written (4 copies) by employee
2	○⇨△☐D			In basket awaiting interoffice mail pickup
3	○⇨△☐D	1500'		To accounting office
4	○⇨△☐D			Waiting on accounting officer's desk
5	○⇨△☐D			Examined by accounting officer
6	○⇨△☐D			Approved by accounting officer
7	○⇨△☐D	25'		To accounting clerk's desk
8	○⇨△☐D			On desk waiting for preparation of check
9	○⇨△☐D			
10	○⇨△☐D			
11	○⇨△☐D			
12	○⇨△☐D			
13	○⇨△☐D			
14	○⇨△☐D			
15	○⇨△☐D			
16	○⇨△☐D			
17	○⇨△☐D			
18	○⇨△☐D			

COMMENTS:

FIGURE 12-3

Flow Process Chart for Completing an Expense Account Form
Proposed Method

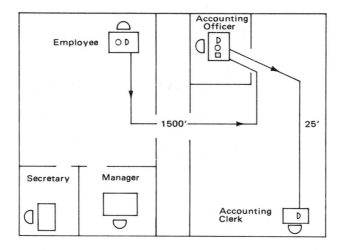

FIGURE 12-4

Flow Diagram for Completing an Expense Account Form
Proposed Method

FIGURE 12-5

Thermostat

ASSEMBLY FLOW PROCESS CHART

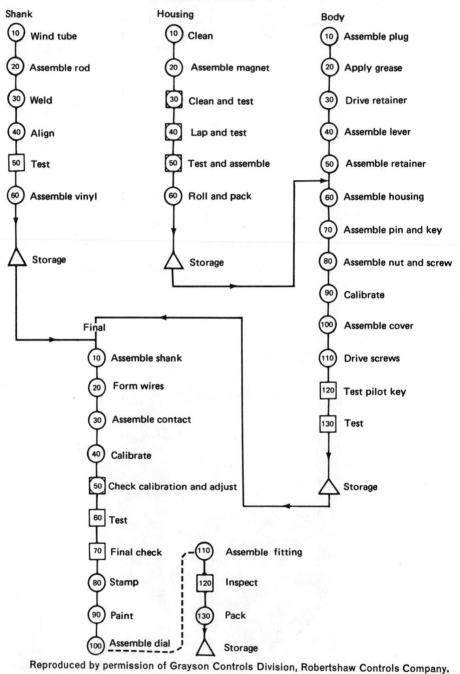

Reproduced by permission of Grayson Controls Division, Robertshaw Controls Company.

FIGURE 12-6

Assembly Flow Process Chart for Thermostat

to analyze the operation or operations in a process or activity by plotting it against a time scale.

A simple example to illustrate activity analysis is a library clerk in the current periodical room issuing a periodical requested by a user. The time used for walking to pick up the ordered periodical and returning to the desk is an average, based on the average distance involved. The activity chart in Figure 12-7 shows this operation.

More valuable, perhaps, are multiactivity charts to show details of work performed by an operator when done in conjunction with one or more machines or other operators having a time controlling effect upon the cycle.

The most common multiactivity chart is the man-machine chart, used to evaluate the method. Its ultimate objective is to improve the method by reducing any idle time experienced by the man or machine. Idle time cannot always be eliminated in the man-machine relationship, but its reduction is frequently possible. Man's idle time is most susceptible to improvement. For

	Activity	Time in min.
	Receive order slip from user and examine	.03
	Walk to stack	.08
	Pick up periodical issue	.02
	Carry back to desk	.08
	Stamp order slip and issue periodical	.02
	Place order slip in file box	.01

FIGURE 12-7

Activity Chart for Issuing Periodical in Library

example, it may be possible to add the operation of an additional machine, or performance of some supplemental operation during this idle time. Figure 12-8 is a man-machine chart showing the activities of an operator and two milling machines. The total cycle time for this case is 10 minutes. The cycle was determined by finding the elapsed time, from any point in the activity, until all steps have been completed and the same point is reached again. Each machine has 3 minutes of necessary idle time, during which it is being loaded and unloaded. Therefore, no improvement is possible in this category. The man is idle for a total of 2 minutes. The man could be given some supplemental task to perform during his idle period if it is desirable.

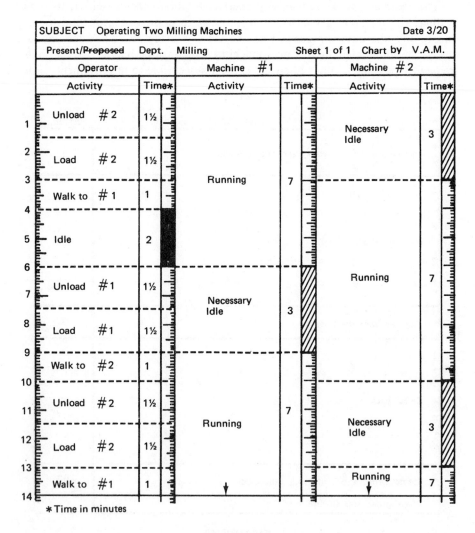

FIGURE 12-8

Man-Machine Chart for Operator and Two Milling Machines

Operation Analysis. The third and most microanalytic tool of motion study is operation analysis. It is used to make the most minute study of the method involved. It consists of a detailed analysis of the motions of each hand. The operation chart, another schematic device, is one tool of this type analysis. A detailed analysis of the movements of the two hands in performing a specific operation is possible using two symbols, a large circle and a small circle. The operation thus analyzed may be one which was represented by a single large circle on the flow process chart. The large circle on the operation chart indicates some sort of operation or specific action by the hand, and the small circle indicates a transportation or a movement of the hand.

It is also possible to carry out this kind of analysis with the same symbols used for the flow process chart. This may give a somewhat more specific picture than the two-symbol chart. However, the two symbols serve most purposes sufficiently, and will be used in the following examples. Figure 12-9 shows a right hand-left hand analysis of the motions involved in signing the expense account form in the process analysis example (refer to page 304). This is really a detailed breakdown of the inspection on line 5 and the operation on line 6 of the flow process chart for the proposed method in Figure 12-3. The object of this detailed analysis of the motions of the two hands is to help find a way to improve the specific task under study.

EXAMPLE OF IMPROVING AN OPERATION. To further illustrate use of operation analysis, the improvement of an operation which is a part of the assembly of the thermostat in Figure 12-5 is examined. This example involves the retainer assembly, part of the body of the unit. The operation is the assembly of a plastic button into a retainer plate. The set button retainer assembly #50092 is identified on an exploded diagram of the thermostat in Figure 12-10.

Originally the assembly of the button to the retainer plate was accomplished by using a hand arbor press. The details of the operation, including a sketch of the workplace, are in the operation chart (Figure 12-11, page 314).

After making an analysis of the original method, the Grayson Controls Division was able to improve the method, and achieve 68 percent increased production.

The two-handed method, use of two air presses, and use of gravity to feed the parts and dispose of the assemblies conform to the ideas of good work design. Note that these concepts are included in the principles of motion economy discussed below. The operation chart for the improved method is shown in Figure 12-12, page 315. A drawing of the new workplace layout is also included.

MICROMOTION ANALYSIS. Micromotion analysis, a form of operation analysis, is the most detailed and sophisticated technique available to study an existing method. It utilizes motion pictures of the operation under study. The pictures are taken, either by a regular camera with a clock shown in the picture, or by a special camera operating at a constant speed. Thus, a permanent record of the method used is provided as well as a means of timing the operation.

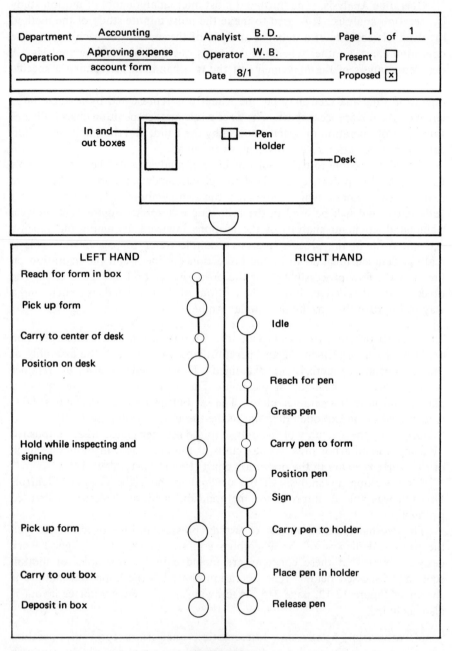

FIGURE 12-9

Operation Chart for Signing of Expense Form

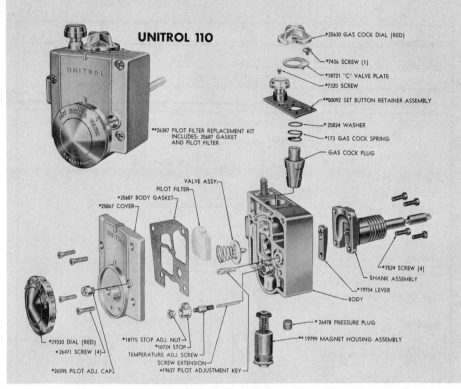

Reproduced by permission of Grayson Controls Division, Robertshaw Controls Company.

FIGURE 12-10

Exploded Diagram of Thermostat Showing
Set Button Retainer Assembly

In this technique, analysis of the work performed by each hand is broken down into fundamental hand motions called "therbligs". This is a coined word, derived from the name Gilbreth spelled backwards, with the "th" reversed. The seventeen fundamental hand motions classify the work performed by the two hands. These classifications are considered to be basic enough to describe any motions which may be observed. A list of the therbligs and the common symbols used to identify them are found in Table 12-2, page 317. Also included is a brief description of the nature of each motion the therbligs identify.

The analysis of a micromotion film requires a special projector which can be run both forward and backward, at varying speeds, to permit very close observation. Analysis of the motions of each hand is made separately by viewing the film. The information is ultimately transferred to a simo chart. A sample simo chart is shown in Figure 12-13, page 316. This chart illustrates the signing of the expense account form. A comparison of the additional detail found in micromotion analysis can be made by referring to the operation chart in Figure 12-9.

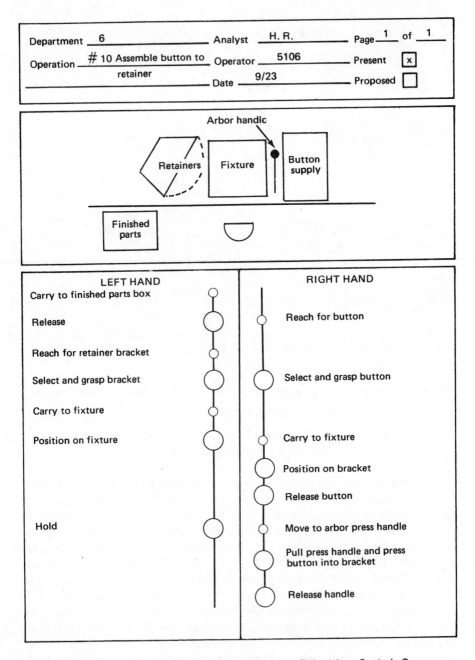

Reproduced by permission of Grayson Controls Division, Robertshaw Controls Company.

FIGURE 12-11

Operation Chart for Retainer Assembly
Original Method

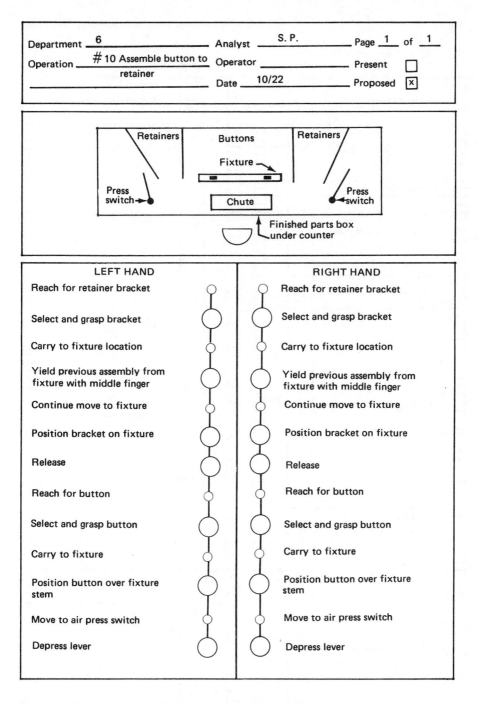

Reproduced by permission of Grayson Controls Division, Robertshaw Controls Company.

FIGURE 12-12

Operation Chart for Retainer Assembly
Improved Method

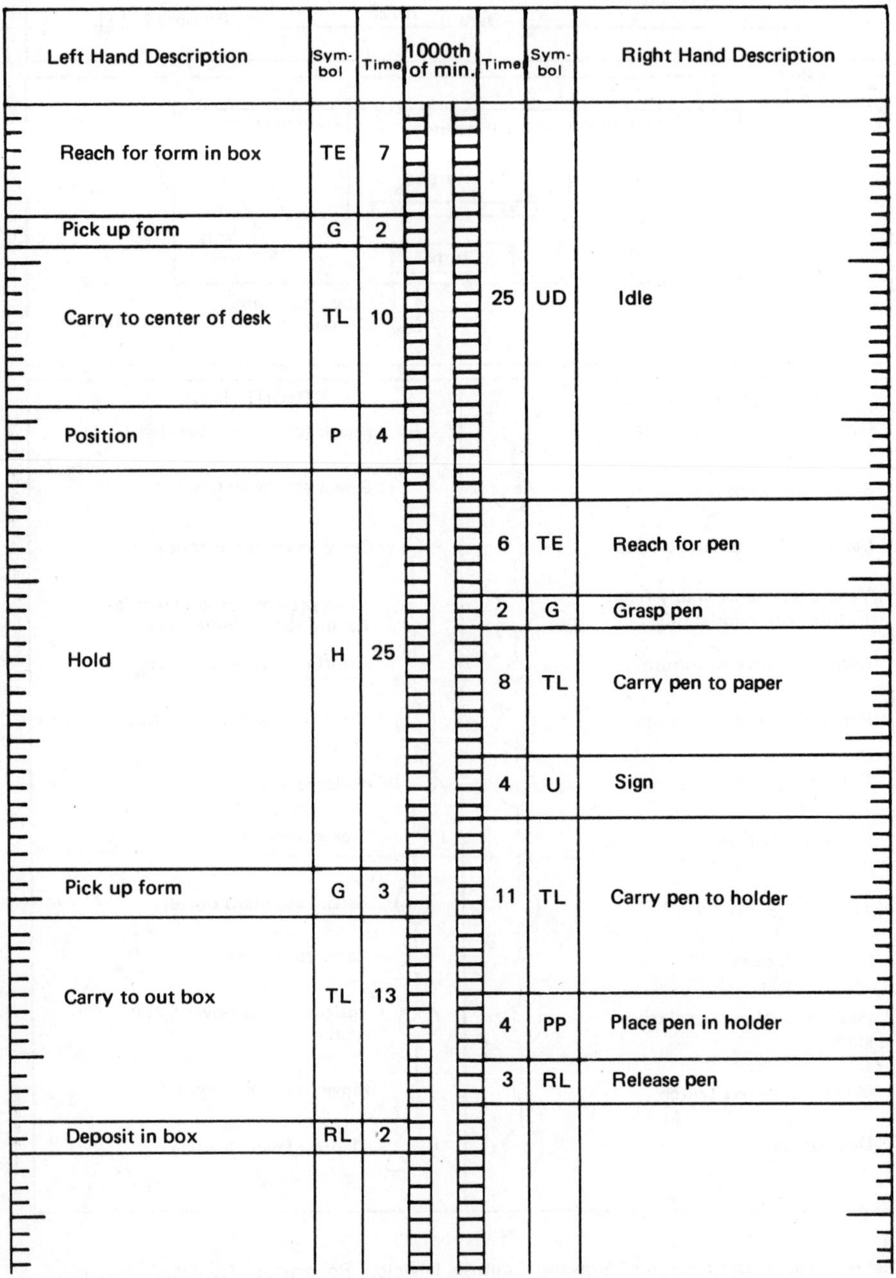

Left Hand Description	Sym-bol	Time	1000th of min.	Time	Sym-bol	Right Hand Description
Reach for form in box	TE	7				
Pick up form	G	2				
Carry to center of desk	TL	10		25	UD	Idle
Position	P	4				
Hold	H	25		6	TE	Reach for pen
				2	G	Grasp pen
				8	TL	Carry pen to paper
				4	U	Sign
Pick up form	G	3		11	TL	Carry pen to holder
Carry to out box	TL	13		4	PP	Place pen in holder
				3	RL	Release pen
Deposit in box	RL	2				

FIGURE 12-13

Simo Chart for Signing of Expense Account Form

TABLE 12-2

Symbols and Descriptions for Therbligs

Therblig Name	Therblig Symbol	Description
Search	SH	Trying to find item by using hands or eyes.
Select	ST	Finding and choosing the particular item.
Grasp	G	Contacting item and establishing control of it.
Release load	RL	Letting go of item; loss of control.
Position	P	Lining-up, locating, or orienting item.
Pre-position	PP	Lining-up, locating, or orienting item in preparation for later use.
Assemble	A	Putting items together.
Disassemble	DA	Taking items apart; separating one item from other.
Use	U	Manipulation of item, tool, or some device or control.
Transport empty	TE	Hand moves from one position to another empty.
Transport loaded	TL	Hand moves an item from one position to another.
Hold	H	Maintaining an item in a fixed position.
Unavoidable delay	UD	Waiting, which is a part of the method and beyond the control of the operator.
Avoidable delay	AD	Anything not part of the method. Idleness caused by the operator.
Inspect	I	Examination of an item to ascertain quality.
Plan	PN	Thinking of next step or activity.
Rest for overcoming fatigue	R	Delay, as a part of the method, to recover from fatigue caused by activity.

Micromotion analysis is a very specialized type analysis; consequently, very expensive. It requires specialized equipment and a highly trained observer. As a result, it is usually limited in its application to a very short cycle, highly repetitive operation.

Principles of Motion Economy. In the process of designing the best work method, the principal objective has been to achieve a certain economy and efficiency of the motion pattern. Work should be performed in the shortest time possible, with minimum effort and resulting fatigue to the operator.

Throughout the years, certain "principles" have successfully aided in achieving the above objectives. These principles are essentially a classification or codification of available information useful for developing the best possible method. They have been presented in various forms by different authors. For example, Barnes lists 22 which he subdivides into three categories: Use of the Human Body, Arrangement of the Work Place, and Design of Tools and Equipment.[6] Below is a summary of the usually stated ideas regarding the principles of motion economy. They are classified into three categories similar to those used by Barnes.

---

[6]Barnes, *op. cit.*, p. 220.

Human Body

1. Work should be evenly apportioned between the hands, which perform in a symmetrical pattern.
2. Reduce work to the smallest muscle grouping capable of performing the work.
3. Utilize momentum; rhythm; and smooth, continuous, curved motions, as opposed to straight-line motions which require sharp changes of direction.
4. Perform work so that the area utilized requires short movements of hands and arms as well as of the eyes.

Workplace

1. Location of tools and other items used to perform the work should be specific, close to the operator, and arranged to facilitate the best sequence.
2. Use gravity to deliver material and to dispose of parts whenever possible.
3. Have the proper amount and type of illumination necessary to perform the work efficiently and safely.
4. Arrange height of the workplace and the seat for comfort, to allow good posture, and to permit alternate sitting and standing to reduce fatigue.

Equipment Design

1. Use jigs, fixtures, etc., to replace the hands as holding devices.
2. Design equipment for ease of proper operation. This includes controls, displays, and the related response of the two.

This grouping is followed because it fits well into the concepts of the applications of ergonomics to job design.

In the next chapter the use of ergonomics will be examined, along with its relationship to the human body, the workplace, and the importance of the consideration of the design of tools and equipment in the design of jobs.

These "principles" are not truly principles in the sense that they are immutable truths. As Barnes points out, they are really "some rules for motion economy and fatigue reduction."[7] If these "principles," or rules, are applied correctly, they will materially help achieve the objectives of motion study.

SUMMARY

Different views about the nature of work are reviewed. The influence changing attitudes about work have had on the design of work systems and jobs is considered. Work design is primarily concerned with examination and

---

[7]*Ibid.*, p. 221.

evaluation of existing or proposed methods of performing work. Job design consists of developing the best way the individual tasks or jobs within the work system can be performed.

In the design of the work system, it must be recognized that a great deal of work today is accomplished by a man-machine system. Thus, it is necessary to understand the role of each component, man and machine, in the work system. A comparison of some functions of men and machines is presented.

In the area of job design, in the past, management has been primarily interested in the method used to perform the job. A five-step pattern for the analysis of job methods which has found wide utilization is presented. Traditional motion study tools which apply this pattern are then examined. These tools are process analysis, activity analysis, and operation analysis. The techniques of each tool are explained by examples.

Process analysis takes the broadest view of the method used. It is essentially concerned with the sequence of the work. The flow process chart and the flow diagram are schematic devices which serve as primary analytical devices for this type analysis.

Activity analysis is used to view the job in greater detail, primarily by plotting the work on an activity chart against a time scale. A more widely found form of the activity chart is a man-machine chart, which relates man's work to that of a machine, or to the work of other men and/or one or more machines. This appears to be a natural result of the fact that so many work systems are man-machine systems.

Operation analysis is resorted to for the most detailed study of the method used. It consists of analysis of the motions of the two hands by the use of an operation chart. Micromotion analysis is a specialized form of operation analysis. It results in an extremely detailed study of a method. This technique uses motion pictures of the operation to study the actions. The motions are identified by using the fundamental hand motions, known as therbligs.

Through broad utilization of the tools of motion study, practitioners have developed a set of rules, or principles, of motion economy. These principles classify concepts which are useful for developing a better method. These principles are summarized under three subdivisions: Human Body, Workplace, and Equipment Design.

Job design is concerned with more than the method used to perform the job. Design of the work system and of the specific job is extremely important to operations managers. The functioning of the operations system may be seriously impaired, without proper work and job design.

On the other hand, the problem of job design has not been fully investigated. Further study needs to be done in this area. A great deal of data are available for use. However, they have not been applied fully to the design of jobs. One reason is that much of these data come from a wide variety of sources normally not associated with the design of jobs. These data must be integrated into a single concentrated approach to the job design problem. Ergonomics is one attempt which will be discussed in the next chapter.

QUESTIONS FOR DISCUSSION AND ANALYSIS

1. What is the nature and major objective of job design? How would you differentiate between work design and job design?

2. Discuss the nature of man-machine systems. Give examples of these kinds of systems.

3. What types of activities have you observed where man's ability exceeds the ability of machines? Where does the machine exceed man's abilities?

4. What is the job-method analysis pattern? How is it useful in applying the traditional tools of motion study?

5. What is the primary purpose of process analysis? Describe the use of the flow process chart and the flow diagram.

6. Discuss the nature of activity analysis. In what types of situations is it of greater value than process analysis?

7. Describe operation analysis. In what circumstances is it used?

8. What conditions would you view as necessary to make a micromotion analysis useful and economical?

9. What are therbligs?

10. Are the Principles of Motion Economy really "principles"? Explain.

PROBLEMS

1. Observe an actual man-machine system and compare man's performance with the performance of the machine based on the functions in Table 12-1.

2. Make flow process charts of an activity as presently done, and for a proposed improved method. Suggested activities are:
   (a) A car wash operation.
   (b) Preparation of food for an order in a take-out food establishment (pizza, fried chicken, beef sandwich, etc.).
   (c) Changing a tire on an automobile in a service station.

3. Observe a man-machine system, and make a man-machine chart of the system. Try to make an improvement in the system, and draw an improved man-machine chart. Calculate idle time and cycle time of both methods.

4. Make an operation chart of one of the following:
   (a) Buying a cup of coffee from a vending machine.
   (b) Picking up, opening, and disposing of the top of an aluminum beverage can.
   (c) Putting a new filler into a ball-point pen.

SELECTED ADDITIONAL READINGS

Barnes, Ralph M. *Motion and Time Study: Design and Measurement of Work*, 6th ed. New York: John Wiley & Sons, Inc., 1968.

Krick, Edward V. *Methods Engineering*. New York: John Wiley & Sons, Inc., 1962.

Mundel, Marvin E. *Motion and Time Study*, 4th ed. Englewood Cliffs: Prentice-Hall, Inc., 1970.

Nadler, Gerald. *Work Design*, rev. ed. Homewood, Illinois: Richard D. Irwin, Inc., 1970.

Niebel, Benjamin W. *Motion and Time Study*, 5th ed. Homewood, Illinois: Richard D. Irwin, Inc., 1972.

CHAPTER 13 | Ergonomics

A major objective in designing the work system has always been development of the best method for performing the job. Operations managers have also been concerned with the amount of time needed to do the job. Thus, the techniques of motion study and work measurement (to be considered in Chapter 14) have been of primary interest to date. However, management and other people involved in job design must be concerned with considerably broader elements of the work system. Although this view of the work system has not reached the stage of universal application, most serious students of work and job design are convinced that another approach is necessary. This does not imply that the tools which have been useful in the past should be discarded. It simply means that additional factors must be brought into the design of jobs. The principal addition is an understanding and evaluation of *all* aspects of the performance of the task. Consideration of the method used is only one aspect. These approaches to job design have been grouped together under the general heading of ergonomics.

NATURE OF ERGONOMICS *BIOTECHNOLOGY*

Ergonomics is derived from the word ergon which means work. Consequently, the term *ergonomics* may be broadly defined as the study of work. More specifically, ergonomics is concerned with the study of the relationship of man to his work environment. The ergonomics approach to work design utilizes the fields of anatomy, physiology, and psychology to evaluate this environment. The important objective of ergonomics, then, is to design the work system to best consider the various abilities and limitations of man in the work system. It is concerned with the following: the man-machine relationship, in the broadest sense; the effects of the surrounding environment where the work takes place; the problem of energy expenditure involved in the specific task and the possibility of resultant muscular fatigue; the potential psychological effects of the work environment; and the role of job design as related to the exceptional worker; i.e., aging and handicapped workers.

+ MISTAKES

The field of ergonomics covers a rather broad area. Murrell summarizes the role of ergonomics as follows:

> Its object is to increase the efficiency of human activity by providing data which will enable informed decisions to be made. It should enable the cost to the individual to be minimized, in particular by removing those features of design which are likely, in the long term, to cause inefficiency or physical disability. By its activities it should create an aware-

ness in industry of the importance of considering human factors when planning work, thereby making a contribution not only to human welfare but to the national economy as a whole.[1]

Ergonomics may be viewed as the systems approach to work design. The work system is a subsystem of the total enterprise system. Since the concept of "system" implies that the concern is with the integrated whole, approaching work and job design in this fashion would necessarily take into account everything affecting job performance. The man-machine relationship is inherent in ergonomics, since there is a large degree of interface of these elements in any work system. Therefore, when considering the role of ergonomics in the area of job design, reference to the man-machine relationship is inevitable.

From an ergonomics viewpoint, various aspects of the human relations approach must play a part in job design. The theories of motivation (discussed in Chapter 11) are pertinent. Many interrelated factors are essential to achievement of the goals of ergonomics.

FACTORS IN ERGONOMICS

An examination of the function of ergonomics in the design of the work system requires a consideration of various elements or factors essential to a thorough work study. To achieve a systematic approach to an evaluation of these factors, they have been gathered into four groups. The first group deals with the characteristics of the human body: neuromuscular aspects, physiological response factors, and fatigue. Next, the importance of the environment where the work is performed is evaluated. Third, elements of the design and layout of the workplace and machines are considered. Finally, a variety of factors broadly classified as specialized human factors are viewed. Included here are job enlargement, shift work, and the exceptional worker problem in job design.

Characteristics of the Human Body

An understanding of man is essential since he is the principal element in the work system and in the design of jobs. Some aspects of man's psychological makeup were examined in Chapter 11, while his interface with machines was discussed in Chapter 12. In addition, some understanding of man's physical characteristics is necessary if a good job design is to be achieved. Thus, an understanding of the nature and functioning of the human body are essential.

Anthropometry. *Anthropometry* is the evaluation of relative body measurements, and there is a great amount of data available for application to job design.[2] Much of the data which have been developed, however, were not

---

[1] K. F. H. Murrell, *Ergonomics* (London: Chapman and Hall, 1965), p. xiv.
[2] See for example Henry Dreyfuss, *The Measure of Man* (New York: Whitney Library of Design, 1960); and Harold P. Van Cott and Robert G. Kinkade (eds.), *Human Engineering Guide to Equipment Design* (rev. ed.; Washington: Supt. of Documents, 1972), Ch. 11.

originally designed for industrial use but more frequently for specialized purposes, as studies of pilot performance for the Air Force. Considerable application has been made of data for positioning of arms and legs, working position, range of movement, and evaluations of the work potential of differing work postures (primarily related to special problems). Anthropometric variations, particularly in stature, seated trunk height, and lower leg length affect job performance and consequently job design.

Therefore, understanding of the anatomical makeup of the human body, including the skeletal framework, joints and muscles, as well as the functional relationships of these bodily elements, is important in the work system design. A basic understanding of these relationships, coupled with the consideration of body size, the movements of the muscles, particularly in the limbs which serve as levers and those which limit body movement, are important in designing the workplace and the equipment used. Muscular strength has little significance in the design or performance of work for the normally healthy individual.

Neuromuscular Factors. While these above discussed elements of the human body are important in work design, possibly more important are those aspects involving the central mechanisms of the body. An illustration of the elements used in the performance of a skilled activity involving these central mechanisms, and of the flow of the information which occurs, is shown in Figure 13-1. This familiar activity appears to be simple. However, it really involves a complex series of occurrences which require the integration of many job conditions and of responses of the operator.

Many tasks performed by workers do not require a large amount of physical effort, but are largely a combination of a series of small motions made in conjunction with one or more of the senses. These tasks involve the various neuromuscular response factors, and may be called *sensory-motor tasks*. Most assembly operations, clerical activities, and many white-collar jobs fall into this category. Of particular importance in these tasks is the perceptual capacity of the worker. In the area of work design, most of the attention to perceptual capacity has been concentrated on the worker's ability to perform two tasks at the same time; thus, to determine if there is a limit to the perceptual load imposed. In the man-machine relationship, the ability or inability to perform concurrent tasks is highly significant.

A considerable amount of interest has been directed to speed of reaction and speed of movement in designing man-machine systems. Inasmuch as the machine is usually a cycle-time determinant, it may have a direct effect upon the speed of work performance. Considerable emphasis in this area has been placed on the influence of age upon reaction and speed of movement times. It is widely accepted that these times increase with aging, but that the two are independent of one another.

Sensory functions are also important in the application of the neuromuscular factors to the design of jobs. Measures relating to visual efficiency like the critical flicker frequency test, hearing tests, light and dark sensitivity, adaptation measures, etc., have been used. To date, these measures seem to have little direct relationship to worker efficiency.   Perhaps the most direct relationship between sensory functions and work performance is in the area of the accuracy and speed of judgment in relationship to surface roughness.

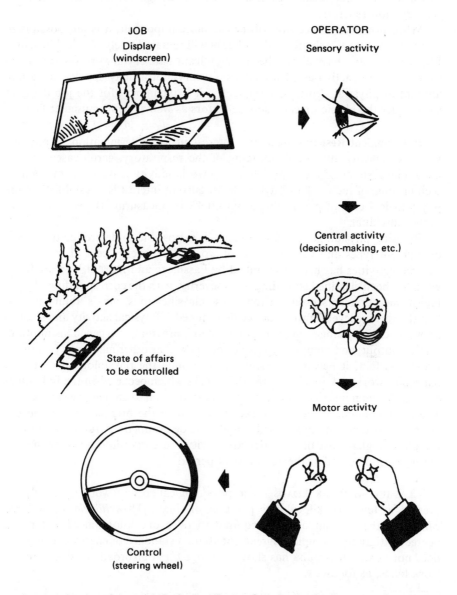

Source: Stephen Griew, *Job Re-Design* (Paris: Organization for Economic Co-operation and Development, 1964), p. 51. Reproduced by permission of the publisher.

FIGURE 13-1

The Flow of Information Between Operator
and Job During Skilled Performance

Current trends indicate that a very substantial share of work being performed now will become less physical as a result of increasing automation. This will lead to a larger proportion of jobs involving sensory-motor performance. Consequently, individuals responsible for job design must understand these sensory-motor factors.

While nonphysical activity will be the more important, it is not possible to ignore those jobs which are, and probably will remain largely physical in scope. Physical activities have always been a significant part of the work system. Even some of those activities identified as sensory-motor may involve a certain amount of physical effort. Consequently, it is incumbent for the job designer to consider the physiological response factors as well as neuromuscular factors.

Physiological Response Factors. Interest in the determination of physical working capacity and the functioning of the respiratory, cardiovascular, and metabolic systems of the body relative to work activity is not new, but can be seen in some of the work of Taylor. Most current interest is in establishing the physiological cost of performing a work task by measuring the energy output of the individual.

By using physiological measurements, it is possible to determine the effects of different types and varying levels of work. The energy cost of various industrial activities has been determined by Passmore and Durnin.[3] In addition, work has been classified according to its severity, with the corresponding physiological measurements given. From these classifications, man's ability to sustain the various levels of work can be determined.[4] Physical activity and stresses of work cause changes in heart rate, blood pressure, oxygen consumption, cardiac output, and pulmonary ventilation, as well as other metabolic functions. From this fact, it becomes possible to determine the physiological cost of a particular work task by finding the differences which occur when the individual changes from an inactive state to a working state, then to an inactive state again. The length of time it takes a worker to return to the original "resting level" after the work activity has ceased can also be determined. A full evaluation of the physiological cost of a particular activity must take into account this recovery period as well as the actual work period.

CLASSIFYING WORK LOADS. The physiological cost of work is usually expressed in terms of kilocalories per unit of time. The *kilocalorie*, or large calorie, is the amount of heat required to raise one kilogram of water one degree centigrade. Complete agreement about a standard of energy expenditure does not exist, but Brouha has shown a range for four broad classifications of work loads, as follows:[5]

---

[3]R. Passmore and J. V. G. A. Durnin, "Human Energy Expenditure," *Physiology Reviews*, Vol. XXXV, No. 4 (October, 1955), pp. 801–840.

[4]C. Frank Consolazio, Robert E. Johnson, and Louis J. Pecora, *Physiological Measurements of Metabolic Functions in Man* (New York: McGraw-Hill Book Co., The Blakiston Div., 1963).

[5]Lucien Brouha, *Physiology in Industry* (2d ed.; New York: Pergamon Press, 1967), p. 96.

Work Load	Energy Expenditure kcal/min
Light	2.5- 5.0
Moderate	5.0- 7.5
Heavy	7.5-10.0
Very heavy	10.0-12.5

These levels of energy expenditure are not intended to be applied for any long-term period, as the normal work day, but are valid only for short periods of a few minutes at a time.

Attempts have been made to utilize data of this nature in connection with the establishment of work standards. A fuller and more detailed examination of this approach will be made in Chapter 14.

MEASURING EFFORT OF MOTIONS.   Many concepts and techniques have been used to evaluate the physiological response of workers in industrial jobs. For example, Lauru applied the techniques of physiology to a study of the effort involved in different types of motions, by using a force platform.[6] This device is purported to measure the relative physiological load placed on specific muscle groups by the movements of the operator.   Thus, muscle loads which result from varying motion patterns on a particular work activity can be measured by this means.   The muscle loads attributable to different motion patterns can be compared, to achieve a more efficient method.

RECONCILING LABORATORY RESULTS WITH JOB PERFORMANCE.   Most investigations in the area of physiological responses have, of necessity, been conducted under laboratory conditions.   This is true because the instrumentation which is usually employed to make the required measurements hinders proper performance of a job when carried on in the actual situation.   However, new instruments and considerably less bothersome instrumentation are constantly being developed; e.g., telemetering equipment similar to that used in the space program for measuring heart rate and blood pressure.

There have been numerous attempts to achieve equivalents between laboratory measurements and direct measurements of work in the actual work situation.   Work equivalence studies have shown a high degree of reliability exists between the laboratory measurements and the work situation measurements. Müller, for example, has tried to determine occupational work capacity in the laboratory.[7]   Occupational work activities are conducted in a so-called *steady state*, where the metabolic measurements quickly level off and remain the same for the duration of the work period.   Even heavy industrial work is considerably below what is referred to as the maximal work level.   At the maximal work level the worker would evidence continuously increasing oxygen consumption and

---

6Lucien Lauru, "Physiological Study of Motions," *Advanced Management*, Vol. XXII, No. 3 (March, 1957), pp. 17–24.

7E. A. Müller, "Occupational Work Capacity," *Ergonomics*, Vol. V, No. 4 (July, 1962), pp. 445–452.

heart rate. He would only be capable of this performance level for a limited time until he reached exhaustion. In terms of the work load classifications indicated, anything in excess of moderate work would be a maximal load.

Müller's approach to measuring the occupational work capacity is a test identified as the work pulse index (L.P.I.). This index measures the rate of the rise in the pulse rate during progressively increasing work loads on a bicycle ergometer. The measurements are made over the normal range of energy expenditure found in industrial work. The L.P.I. is identified as the average increase in the pulse rate for each 0.12 liters per minute increase in oxygen intake. This can then be converted to the permissible occupational work level by a derived formula.

Many metabolic measurements used to evaluate physiological responses, especially heart rate and oxygen consumption measurements, are valuable; however, various psychological and fatigue factors tend to interrelate and modify both physiological and neuromuscular responses.

Fatigue. Everyone is well aware of what fatigue is. Everybody has experienced it as the result of heavy physical activity, and has also experienced fatigue following heavy or intensive mental activities. Many metabolic and neurophysiological measurements have been used to identify the results of fatigue in muscles. Electromyographic (E.M.G.) studies, visual tests, perceptual capacity tests, and measurements of heart rate, oxygen consumption, and lactic acid levels in the muscles have been used to identify fatigue.

The concepts of fatigue presently used as the basis for fatigue allowances and rest periods in actual work situations apply only to heavy physical labor. The present trend is away from this type of work, and these concepts do not apply to the fatigue which accompanies the less physical, more mental work activity which is becoming prevalent. The inability to measure, or even to define fatigue in most industrial work situations, has raised a question about the validity of making fatigue allowances when setting job standards. This does not mean to imply that the nonphysical work activities, which now constitute the majority of industrial jobs, do not show a decrease in performance, but rather is a statement of doubt that this poorer performance is actually the result of fatigue as normally defined. In fact, the reduction in performance efficiency is more likely related to psychological rather than physiological factors in these types of jobs.

Environmental Factors

The conditions under which workers may have to perform their assigned tasks can affect their ability and efficiency. The conditions can also affect their health and the safety of the job. Thus, the physical environment where man carries out a particular task is an important consideration in the design of the job. Among the environmental conditions which may vary, and consequently have the above mentioned effects, are temperature and humidity, lighting, noise, and vibration.

Temperature and Humidity. Brouha shows the effects of changes in temperature and humidity on the physiological cost of work.[8] He points out that extremes of temperature and humidity cause the metabolic functions of the body to concentrate on maintaining the homeostatic limits which are normal for the individual. Thus, extremes in these areas may significantly increase the physiological cost of performing any specific job. The heart rate, in particular, increases rather significantly under conditions of high temperature and high humidity, indicating an increased load on the individual performing the work. Brouha has also shown that there is a progressive strain on the cardiac system as intermittently cycled work is repeated under stressful environmental conditions. Some details of these studies will be cited in Chapter 14.

Lighting. Most jobs contain a visual element which is extremely important to their proper performance. Consequently, the amount of lighting or illumination that is available may be an important factor. The quantity of light is only one measurement of significance. The quality of the light, such as the amount of glare, the contrast, and even color may also be significant. Standards for artificial lighting have been established by the American Illuminating Engineering Society. However, artificial lighting is not always as satisfactory as natural daylight under all conditions. A great deal of study has gone into the proper quantity and quality of lighting needed for good working conditions, but determination of the exact lighting for a specific task is still not easily established accurately. The important thing is that a consideration of the proper lighting must be an essential part of the overall design of any job.

Noise. Sound is an almost constant element in any work environment. However, unwanted sound may have an undesirable effect upon the work situation. The level of noise, with respect to its intensity, is one important consideration, as is the intermittency or continuousness of the noise. The frequency of the sound waves is also significant in the effect noise may have on the individual. Certain frequencies may cause serious impairment of an individual's hearing.

The intensity of sound is measured in terms of decibels, which is a logarithmic ratio of the sounds audible to the human ear. An increase of ten decibels equals an increase of ten times in the sound intensity. Thus, an increase from 30 dB to 60 dB would mean an increase of 1,000 times and from 30 dB to 70 dB, an increase of 10,000 times. To give some indication of the level of common noises, the average vacuum cleaner operates at about 70 dB, and an exhaust fan at 90 dB. Above this level, certain physiological changes are noticeable. Pupils of the eye dilate and adrenalin flow increases, among other changes. Above 120 decibels, there is an onset of ear discomfort for most individuals, and pain is experienced at approximately 150 dB.

A limited amount of noise, usually unavoidable, in some cases, may even be desirable. Workers can be conditioned to some types of noise so that it will not have an unsatisfactory effect upon their efficiency. In other circumstances,

---

[8]Brouha, *op. cit.*, Ch. 2–2.

noise may be meaningful and, consequently, helpful in an efficient performance of the job. There are many examples of the introduction of music into the work environment as attempts to improve the efficiency of the workers.

It may be summarized here by saying that in the design of a particular job, consideration of the nature of noise in the environment is an important element. Some indication of the concern for the noise level in the work situation is indicated by the fact that the Occupational Safety and Health Act of 1970 established 90 decibels as the maximum continuous level of noise to which a worker may be exposed.

Vibration. The effect of vibration upon job performance is not entirely clear. Vibration may be annoying to a worker, and thus affect his performance. Individuals will react differently to given levels of vibration. Some individuals will find it distracting, others will find it intolerable, others will accept it, and still other workers will not notice it at all. While excessive vibration is bound to cause concern and inefficiency, it is presently impossible to establish a specific level as undesirable for all jobs. From a job design standpoint, the only rule which can be suggested is to minimize the vibration present in the environment or attendant to the specific job to avoid affecting performance efficiency.

Design and Layout of Workplace and Machines

The design and layout of the workplace embodies all things the worker has around him, including the machinery with which he interfaces. All these things should be designed and positioned to best fit the needs of the human operator. Cognizance must be taken of all workplace equipment: the chair or stool on which the operator sits; the table or desk where he works; instrument displays, and controls used to convey instructions to the machine.

Seating. The importance of anthropometric data was mentioned earlier. It can be applied to the design of the workplace. It is an important factor in aspects like the height of the seat relative to the work surface. It may also be used in the overall design of seating. Among the factors to be considered are the height of the seat from the floor, the contour of the seat, the position of the backrest, and the contour of the backrest. Seating used in industrial situations must be adjustable, with respect to the above factors, to assure comfort and minimal fatigue for all workers. Another important relationship is the ratio of the workplace height to the height of the seat. In some cases, the task may be performed either in a sitting or standing position.

Table 13-1 shows certain anthropometric data which are applicable when the workplace must be designed to satisfy both standing and sitting positions. These data are gathered from a variety of sources, and represent a consensus developed for this presentation. The populations used for the various dimensions are not necessarily the same. Some populations include both men and women, while others include only men. Subjective adjustments have been made to correct for these differences.

TABLE 13-1

Anthropometric Data for Design of Workplace to Accommodate
both Seated and Standing Operators

DIMENSIONS	HEIGHT IN INCHES BY PERCENTILE		
	5th	50th	95th
Standing			
Eye height	60.8	64.7	68.6
Shoulder height	51.0	54.8	58.8
Elbow height	40.6	43.5	46.4
Sitting*			
Eye height	28.4	30.3	32.1
Shoulder height	21.6	23.4	25.0
Elbow height	8.0	9.4	11.0

*Measured from sitting surface.

Some ergonomists feel that these data should be corrected for average shoe height, normal slump while standing, and normal slump while sitting. Ely uses + 1.1 inches for shoes, − 1.2 inches for standing slump, and − 2.0 inches for sitting slump.[9]

Where alternate sitting and standing is possible, or necessary in some cases, the operator's ability to change positions easily and the availability of a convenient work surface for both positions are significant. Usually, the seat will be somewhat higher than normal, and the worker's feet cannot rest on the floor. In these circumstances an adjustable footrest is required. A great deal of study has been conducted regarding seating and workplace relationships. It is not difficult to find data which can be applied to the particular situation.[10]

Instrument Displays. The primary way a machine communicates with its human operator is by means of visual displays. Other senses may also be involved in this communication process. Examples of audio communication from a machine to man are buzzers, horns, and bells. Other sensory forms such as vibration may also carry messages from the machine to its operator. However, an examination of the visual means of communication is sufficient.

The location of the instrument display is of prime importance. Its placement in relation to the operator's line of vision is the first consideration. It is also important that the plane of the display face, relative to the line of vision, and the viewing angle are correct for proper reading. Failure to consider these points may result in incorrect readings which can cause serious errors in the operation of the machine. The shape and contour of the mounting surface is also

[9]Jerome H. Ely, Robert M. Thomson, and Jesse Orlansky, *Layout of Workplaces*, WADC-TR-56-171 (Wright-Patterson Air Force Base, Ohio: Wright Air Development Center, 1956), p. 50.

[10]A collection of some research in this area can be found in the papers presented at the International Symposium on Sitting Posture, Zurich, September 25–27, 1968, sponsored by the International Ergonomic Association, in *Ergonomics*, Vol. XII, No. 2 (March, 1969).

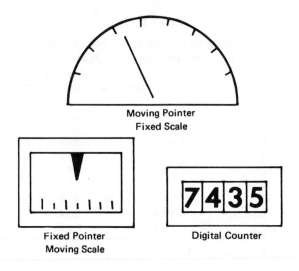

Moving Pointer
Fixed Scale

Fixed Pointer
Moving Scale

Digital Counter

FIGURE 13-2

Common Types of Dial Indicators

a factor. The placement must take into consideration the importance of the displays when there is more than one. The most critical display should be given priority in location relative to others. Grouping of displays is another point to take into account. Proper grouping facilitates reading, and the direction of alignment of the displays is also pertinent.

The relationship of the location of information displays to associated controls must also be evaluated. Some of the rules relating to this will be discussed in conjunction with controls.

Information displays may serve several functions. Chapanis indicates four: quantitative reading, check reading, setting, and tracking.[11] Quantitative reading involves the reading of a specific value. Check reading is merely observing whether the operation is within a certain range or level and noting any deviations therefrom. Setting is done in connection with some form of a control. The control is used to achieve some specific setting on the display. Tracking is also conducted in conjunction with some form of a control. However, in the setting function, the desired reading is merely set and need not be changed until a different result is desired; in tracking, there is a continuous monitoring and movement of the control. Information displays are found in many different forms, depending on the job to be performed.

Three of the most common types of dial indicators, moving pointer, fixed scale; fixed pointer, moving scale; and digital counter, are shown in Figure 13-2. The digital counter is the most accurate to achieve exact readings of specific values. Consequently, it is best utilized for quantitative reading. It is probable

[11]Alphonse Chapanis, *Man-Machine Engineering* (Belmont, California: Wadsworth Publishing Company, Inc., 1965), pp. 38–41.

the other two types are more common, however, because approximate readings are required frequently. They may also be used where an exact reading is desired. However, the possibility of error is greater than for digital counters.

A moving pointer, fixed scale is the most versatile of the types shown, and it is almost always preferred to the fixed pointer, moving scale indicator. In check reading and tracking, it is the preferred of the three types shown. As stated above, the moving pointer can give an accurate reading or an approximate reading. The approximate position of the indicator is often sufficient, as in the case of the hands on the clock. This type of indicator can also be used to determine the rate of change taking place. For performing the setting function, the moving pointer or the digital counter are equally acceptable.

In designing information displays, consideration must always be given to the scale, scale marks, and numbers used. These elements are necessary to insure accuracy in reading. The base used for the scale, the number of divisions used, the spacing and size of the scale divisions, the number of scale marks, and the value of the major scale divisions are all factors important in scale design.

As far as the numbers used are concerned, their size (height, width, stroke width, etc.), shape, and even color or density of color may play an important role in the accuracy with which they are read. Numbers are easily confused when read quickly, when partially obscured, or poorly lighted. The difficulty in differentiating between numbers is illustrated by the fact that optical scanners used in computerized systems were unable to read the numbers as they are normally reproduced. Consequently, special numbers had to be designed to be compatible with the scanners. The specially formed numbers, now imprinted on the bottom of bank checks, and read magnetically, were developed to overcome this difficulty.

Controls. Proper design of controls helps to avoid many of the problems and resultant mistakes experienced by operators. Controls are the way the operator communicates with the machine and achieves the desired results. Again, it is necessary to refer to available anthropometric data to determine the location of manual or foot controls. Placement should be within the normal operating areas as far as is possible. The exact location will depend on the particular requirement of the job in question, but certain general rules may be referred to. If controls are used in conjunction with displays, the relationship between the control and the display should be clear. If the controls are to be used in sequence, their arrangement should be systematic, horizontally if possible. When concentric knobs are used, the smallest should be used first; and where they are associated with displays, the small knob should relate to the display on the left. Spacing between controls is another factor in the proper location of controls. Figure 13-3 shows a series of recommended separations for different kinds of controls.

CONTROL IN RELATION TO SYSTEM. In order to avoid many errors resulting from the improper use of controls, the relationship between movement of the control and system response plays an important role. Have you ever taken a

Control	Type of Use	Measure of Separation	Recommended Separation (In.)	
			Minimum	Desirable
Push Button	One finger (randomly) [1]		1/2	2
	One finger (sequentially)		1/4	1
	Different fingers (randomly or sequentially		1/2	1/2
Toggle Switch	One finger (randomly)		3/4	2
	One finger (sequentially)		1/2	1
	Different fingers (randomly or sequentially		5/8	3/4
Crank and Lever [2]	One hand (randomly)		2	4
	Two hands (simutaneously)		3	5
Knob	One hand (randomly)		1	2
	Two hands (simultaneously)		3	5
Pedal [3]	One foot (randomly)		d=4	6
	One foot (sequentially)		D=8	10
			d=2	4
			D=6	8

[1] When finger- or hand-operated controls are used randomly or are "positioned blind," they should be separated by at least 5in. when mounted in the optimum manual area. This separation should be progressively increased to 12in. as the location of the control approaches the periphery of the limiting manual dimensions.

[2] When a group of levers are used simultaneously by the same hand, their maximum separation should be 6in. or less

[3] Either dimension d or dimension D should be met, preferably d.

From: *Human Engineering Guide to Equipment Design* by Morgan, Chapanis, Cook & Lund. Copyright © 1963 by McGraw-Hill, Inc., p. 313. Used by permission of McGraw-Hill Book Company.

FIGURE 13-3

Recommended Separations for Various Types of Controls

shower in a strange place and found that the hot water faucet turns counterclockwise to increase the flow of hot water? It is quite a surprise, when you think you are turning the hot water down, to get a gush of scalding hot water — not to mention the discomfort. Table 13-2 contains some recommended relationships between control movement and corresponding system responses.

Similar types of relationships may be found to be desirable with regard to control movement and a particular display response. In other words, control movement should have a normal correlation with a display response, as well as with that of the system. For example, when the display and the control are in front of the operator, an upward movement of the control should result in an upward movement on the display; a right movement of the control, movement to the right by the display; and a clockwise movement should result in a clockwise display response.[12]

TABLE 13-2

Control Movement and Corresponding System
Response Recommendations

CONTROL MOVEMENT	EXAMPLE OF CONTROL TYPE	SYSTEM RESPONSE Directional				
		Up	Right	For-ward	Clock-wise	Increase or On
Up	Toggle switch on vertical plane	+	−	0	−	+
Right	Toggle switch or lever on vertical or horizontal plane	−	+	−	0	+
Forward	Lever, toggle switch or slide switch on horizontal plane	+	−	+	−	+
Clockwise	a. Knob on vertical plane	0	0	0	+	+
	b. Knob on horizontal plane	0	−	0	+	+
Push	a. Push-button	0	−	0	−	+
	b. Push-pull knob or T-handle	−	−	−	−	*

*Pull is usually for increase or on with this type of control.

+ Acceptable
− Not acceptable
0 Provisionally acceptable

SELECTION OF CONTROL TYPE. Another function of the job designer is the selection of the proper control to perform the required task. The control selected must serve the needs of the system, as regards the function it is to perform and the job requirements. It must also meet the needs of the operator insofar as helping properly locate and position the control to achieve the desired response.

---

[12]Ely, *op. cit.*, p. 90.

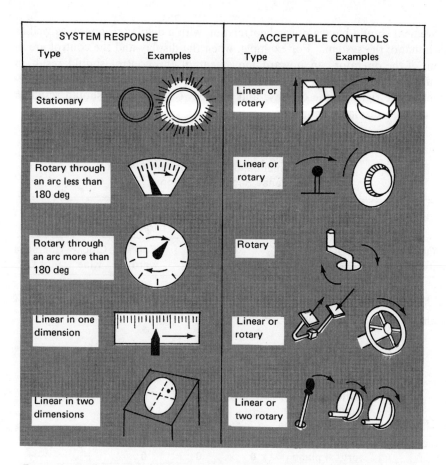

SYSTEM RESPONSE		ACCEPTABLE CONTROLS	
Type	Examples	Type	Examples
Stationary		Linear or rotary	
Rotary through an arc less than 180 deg		Linear or rotary	
Rotary through an arc more than 180 deg		Rotary	
Linear in one dimension		Linear or rotary	
Linear in two dimensions		Linear or two rotary	

From: *Human Engineering Guide to Equipment Design* by Morgan, Chapanis, Cook & Lund. Copyright © 1963 by McGraw-Hill, Inc., p. 248.   Used by permission of McGraw-Hill Book Company.

FIGURE 13-4

Acceptable Controls for Various Types of System Responses

It has also been found that certain general forms of controls are best to achieve a specific display or system response. Figure 13-4 shows recommendations for these types of relationships.

CONTROL SHAPES.   In many circumstances it is desirable that the control have a specific shape. The shape of the control will often assure that the right control is used; consequently, the correct response is achieved. If an operator is performing under a paced situation or in an emergency, the coded control will help him avoid using the improper control. This is particularly true when the situation requires that the operator not divert his visual attention to search for the proper control. A prime example is the airline pilot during landing.

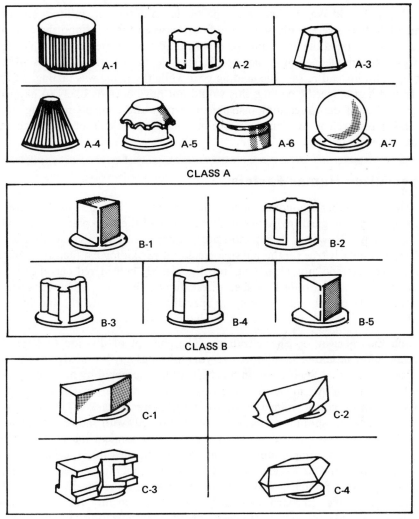

CLASS A

CLASS B

CLASS C

From: *Human Engineering Guide to Equipment Design* by Morgan, Chapanis, Cook & Lund. Copyright ©1963 by McGraw-Hill, Inc., p. 273. Used by permission of McGraw-Hill Book Company.

FIGURE 13-5

Shaped Control Knobs

Knobs in particular lend themselves very well to this type coding. Figure 13-5 shows a form of knob coding. Class A knobs are for twirling or spinning; position is unimportant. Class B knobs are for less than one turn, and the position is still unimportant. Class C consists of knobs requiring less than one full turn, but the position is significant.

During World War II there was a particular multi-engine, military airplane which had two levers depressed in the floor between the pilot and the copilot. One lever regulated the flaps, and the other raised and lowered the landing gear. It was not infrequent to have the copilot reach down to retract the flaps after a landing and instead retract the landing gear while the plane was taxiing. If the lever had had a specific coding, this would not have been as likely to happen. A great deal of data regarding instrument display and controls resulting from extensive research is available for use in solving problems of man-machine systems design.[13]

Specialized Human Factors

There are many ergonomic factors that cannot be included in the physiological or psychological environment, or the design of the workplace or machines classifications. However, these factors are still peripheral to these classifications. This is particularly true for the physiological and psychological factors. Therefore, since they do not clearly fit into the already considered classifications, they are arbitrarily grouped as specialized human factors. To be considered are the effects of job enlargement vs. specialization, shift work, and the exceptional worker; i.e., the aging and the handicapped worker.

Job Enlargement vs. Specialization. The concept of division of labor or specialization should be familiar to everyone who has any knowledge of current business practices. Specialization has been widely accepted by most managers since the time of Adam Smith. Advocates of specialization contend that a worker is more easily trained to perform the assigned task. Therefore, the resultant output should increase when compared with nonspecialization. Specialization is assumed to result in the most economical job performance.

In recent years, some doubt has been cast on the idea that specialization is always the best and most economical way to do a job. It has been suggested that a different approach would be more desirable in some cases.

The alternative approach suggested is job enlargement. Job enlargement has essentially taken the opposite viewpoint from specialization. In job enlargement, a worker performs a much larger segment of the total job than would be true under specialization. In some cases, under job enlargement, individual workers have been made responsible for producing an entire part or product, instead of performing a single operation required for that part or product. The basic contention is that this results in greater motivation and job satisfaction for the worker than he would experience under specialization. Generally, theories of human behavior have shown that a worker who is properly motivated will be more satisfied with his job. Walker and Guest found this to be the case in their study of performance on the assembly line, and suggested its use in the automobile industry.[14] To date, this recommendation has found little

---

[13]See for example Van Cott, *op. cit.*

[14]Charles R. Walker and Robert H. Guest, *The Man on the Assembly Line* (Cambridge: Harvard University Press, 1952), p. 151.

acceptance in the industry. As a result, reports of dissatisfaction with the working conditions on the automobile assembly line are prevalent.

While job enlargement has experienced notable success in certain companies, as Lehrer points out:

> . . . the simple enlargement of jobs is not sufficient by itself. Jobs must be *designed* so that they are both mechanically efficient, and efficient from the standpoint of the dignity of the individuals performing the work. There is ample experimental evidence to indicate rather conclusively that jobs can be *designed* to achieve both of these objectives.[15]

Concrete evidence in the form of actual experience with job enlargement is also available. I.B.M., Maytag, and The Harwood Manufacturing Corporation are organizations that have had remarkable success with job enlargement programs. Generally, it is agreed that the use of job enlargement should be selective, since all jobs do not lend themselves to this technique. It behooves management to have a careful study made of the potential results before designing any job for job enlargement.

Shift Work. In recent times, a great deal of comment has been made about the "biological clock" of man. Most of this comment has grown out of the problems of adjusting to rapidly changing time zones because of jet air travel. This has caused great discomfort to passengers. However, the major concern has been with the effects this phenomenon has on the efficiency of airline crews. A similar problem has been experienced by operations management for many years, insofar as they have had to face the problems their workers have adjusting to working different shifts. Everyone at one time or another has heard certain individuals referred to as "day people" and "night people"; that is, some people seem to function better during the day, whereas others seem to be able to function as well or better at night. Most people who are forced to change shifts from day to night have difficulty adjusting biologically, and usually efficiency decreases for these people. Some adjust more rapidly, and their efficiency may improve after being on the night shift for some period of time.

Few studies have been made comparing the overall efficiency of the day shift and the night shift. Those studies reported indicated a slight deterioration of productivity and accuracy in the night shift.[16] A possible conclusion is that these differences may result from a number of factors, in addition to difficulties of adjustment by the workers. One cause may be the lack of availability of higher-level supervision at night. As a result, certain problems may be ignored and left for solution by day shift supervision. Management must try to identify those individuals capable of adjusting to night work and to assign them to such

---

[15]R. N. Lehrer, "Job Design," *The Journal of Industrial Engineering* Vol. IX, No. 5 (September-October, 1958), p. 439.

[16]For comparisons of overall efficiency between shifts see: *Night Work in Industry* (New York: National Industrial Conference Board, Inc., 1927); and S. Wyatt and R. Marriott, "Night Work and Shift Changes," *British Journal of Industrial Medicine*, Vol. X (1953), pp. 164–172. On the increase in errors on the night shift see: B. Bjerner and A. Swenssen, "Shift-work and Rhythm," *Acta Medica Scandinavica*, Supp. 278 (1953), pp. 102–107.

work on a permanent basis. Conversely, those who are not able to adjust should not be assigned to night work.

The Exceptional Worker. The exceptional worker belongs to that group of workers who, for some reason, are physiologically or psychologically incapable of performing all types of work. Two characteristic groups of the exceptional worker are the aging worker and the handicapped worker. The effects of age on job design are more widely known than are those of handicaps. A great deal more research has been done regarding the abilities of the aging worker than has been done on the handicapped worker.

THE AGING WORKER. The average life expectancy in the United States today is over 70 years. Somewhat more than 18 million people, about nine percent of the total population, are over the age of 65. The aging population is becoming an increasing percentage of the total population, and the number of people over the age of 65 may exceed 26 million by 1990. Consequently, the problem for management increases in the area of job design. Equipment must be designed to facilitate its use by the aging population, and to develop and maintain suitable working conditions for this potentially more accident-prone segment of the work force. Chronological age is not a good measure of an individual's ability to adhere to an established standard of work performance. A more reliable indicator might be functional age, which includes biological, psychological, and social age.[17]

If an aging worker finds it difficult to maintain the performance level that has been established, several alternatives exist. His supervisor may make concessions about hours, required output, or rest periods. The worker is often transferred to a less demanding job within the same department, or to a more appropriate assignment in some other department. If possible, the job may be redesigned to make it more compatible with the reduced capacity of the worker. If these alternatives are not possible, the employee may be dismissed, or he may retire.

With the aging process in man there are certain changes in the neuromuscular responses of most individuals. Among these are changes in the speed of movement and reaction. Generally there is a slowing in the speed of movement and in speed of reaction with age. This apparently results from an increase in the period between the stimulus and the action. This leads to the assumption that the speed of movement and reaction are related to the central nervous system.

Age also seems to affect the speed of work performance. This is evidenced by the fact that jobs with a high speed requirement tend to be filled by younger workers. The percentage of workers over the age of 50 employed in jobs requiring speed or pace is significantly lower than for other tasks, including those having a heavy physical demand.

---

[17]S. R. Mohler, "Aging and Pilot Performance," *Geriatrics*, Vol. XVI, No. 2 (February, 1961), pp. 82–88.

Most of the sensory functions deteriorate with age. Attempts have been made to predict the job performance of aging individuals by the use of simple sensory tests.[18]

The effect of age on neuromuscular responses may be summarized as follows:

1. There is a slowing with age of the process involved when a sensing organ is stimulated through the central mechanisms back to the effector devices.
2. The exact location of the slowing is not known, but it is generally concluded that it is not in the peripheral organs.
3. Slowing is much more noticeable when the complexity of the reaction required is greater.

Attempts have also been made to determine the physiological responses of aging workers by measurements of ventilatory responses, cardiovascular responses, oxygen uptake, and work rate. It has been noted that the differences that occur with increased age in these measures primarily depend on whether the amount of work is maximal or submaximal. Actually, with minor exceptions, the differences are slight between workers of different ages when the measurements are made at submaximal work levels.

A recognition of the effects age has on the worker's performance ability and on the design of jobs is required. However, certain misconceptions exist regarding the abilities and capabilities of the aging worker. The potential of aging workers is higher than is generally believed. Much additional research is needed in this area. It is probable that determination of how older workers could benefit from the redesign of machines and jobs would lead to benefits for workers, regardless of age. Very slight changes might reduce the complexity or confusion in current job design and thus make the operation less difficult for all workers.[19]

THE HANDICAPPED WORKER. A large group of potential and actual workers are handicapped because of some disease or disability. Little is known about the work potential of these people. Most research regarding evaluation of the disability effect is primarily clinical in nature, and has been concerned mainly with functional impairment. This kind of approach to the problem does not evaluate actual work capacity, and it gives no indication of the performance possible in an actual work situation. One fact is clear, however: handicapped workers seldom have to use their maximum physiological work capacity. This is true despite the fact that a handicapped individual requires a higher metabolic level than does a "normal" person, irrespective of the type of handicap. The handicapped worker is similar to the aging worker because the neuromuscular

---

[18]Arthur C. Laufer and Bert Schweitz, "Neuromuscular Response Tests as Predictors of Sensory-Motor Performance in Aging Individuals," *American Journal of Physical Medicine*, Vol. XLVII, No. 5 (1968), pp. 250–263.

[19]For a more complete survey of the attempts to determine the abilities of aging workers see: Arthur C. Laufer and William M. Fowler, Jr., "Work Potential of the Aging," *Personnel Administration*, Vol. XXXIV, No. 2 (March–April, 1971), pp. 20–25.

responses are more critical than physiological measures. Even the handicapped worker, who generally has higher physiological requirements than the "normal" person, seldom finds it necessary to utilize more than 50 percent of his maximal working capacity. Therefore, physiological measures are not valid indicators of the potential job performance of the handicapped.

Perceptual capacity, dexterity, and speed of reaction and movement apparently are greater limiting factors in industrial situations. The most objective, valid, and reliable measures used to evaluate work potential of handicapped workers seem to be job and work samples used in conjunction with selected neuromuscular factors.

A detailed study suggests a new approach to the use of these types of measures. Attempts were made to identify factors which might be used to predict success of handicapped people in light industrial tasks.[20] The handicapped worker can perform industrial tasks efficiently in selected situations. Management must recognize this fact, and use this knowledge in its job design program.

Many disciplines can contribute to the evaluation of the handicapped and to the development of means whereby realistic selection, placement, and job design for all classes of individuals will be possible. This concept can conceivably be extended to all types of disadvantaged people, not just the handicapped.

Possibly the same sorts of considerations may be applied to workers identified as culturally deprived. Cultural and social environment may affect the ability of a person to perform a task. These workers may have physiological or neuromuscular limitations resulting directly from this environment which are not found in other workers. Those individuals concerned with job design would do well to consider these facts when they develop work systems where workers from the ghettos or high-impact poverty areas are part of the work force. These circumstances must be considered in the development of work systems in foreign countries. The multinational firms have found that the environment has a major influence on the way a firm must be managed. Since the workers will have unique social and cultural backgrounds, this will have a bearing on the way jobs are performed. It is necessary to recognize these environmental elements when jobs are designed in different countries.

SOCIOTECHNICAL SYSTEMS

The traditional approaches to job design have been directed very largely toward the physical aspects of job performance. The machine, the tools, the materials, and the process have tended to receive the lion's share of the attention. While no claim is made that the human has been ignored, it has often been assumed that this element of the work system must adapt to the others. Assuredly, the behaviorists have devoted a great deal of attention to this element. However, they have often been guilty in the opposite direction. The

---

[20]William M. Fowler, Jr., *et. al., Neuromuscular Responses and Work Samples as Predictors of Job Performance*, Final Report, SRS Research Project RD-1990-M (Los Angeles: Division of Rehabilitation, University of California, 1968).

assumption by some behaviorists, that the goals of the organization and those of man were irreconcilable, often led to the conclusion that technology, as represented by the machine, was dominating man. Only recently has an attempt been made to integrate these opposing viewpoints. This approach gives full and equal attention to all elements in the work system which is then identified as a sociotechnical system.

The Sociotechnical Approach

The sociotechnical system approach is essentially concerned with the man-machine system. The main point of emphasis in the sociotechnical system approach is that one element is not more important than any other, and in job design, no line is drawn between the two. The job designer must give equal attention to the potential and limitations of both. This process would eliminate the usual method of designing the technical parts of the work system, and then forcing the human element to conform. It would be an interesting experiment to design the system to achieve the maximum human satisfaction. The machine would then have to be developed to meet this criterion. The sociotechnical approach would be the midpoint between these two extremes (technical dominance and human satisfation). It emphasizes the need to consider the total environment where the work is performed. There has been general acceptance of the fact that each person is different. Thus, we would not question the fact that each segment of the enterprise, the individual, the group, etc., should be considered unique. The sociotechnical approach considers this difference, the social environment, and holds that there are differences in the technical environment as well. This would mean that a specific type of machine cannot be considered as being identical in all situations. It becomes necessary in work and job design to realize that both man and machine operate in their own individual environments which must be integrated.

Relationship of Technology to the Work System

In the discussion of technological forecasting in Chapter 9, reference was made to some social implications of technology. At this stage we are concerned with the impact of this force on the work system of the enterprise. There is no doubting the effect which technology has had on the way in which work is performed. From the development of the first stone tool, through the initial power-driven machine, to the numerically controlled machine tool of today, technology has been the most potent determinant of the design of jobs. These developments have each had tremendous social implications also. Often the social changes brought about are longer lasting and of greater total import. Can there be any denial of the enormous social change brought about by the application of mass production techniques on the world's society?

One area which has constantly received attention dealing with the influence of technology on the performance of work has been the assembly line. Some

early studies of behavior on assembly lines revealed that technological requirements virtually dictated the way work was performed.[21] The epitome of the
modern-day assembly line is in the automobile industry. This industry's social
system is probably more strongly influenced by the technological constraints
placed on the work system than any other.

A primary reason for many difficulties arising in the social-technical relationship is that technical advances have a tendency to occur at a more rapid rate
than society can comprehend their potential. It is doubtful that many people
were able to foresee the social influence of television when it was first developed.
How many could have foreseen the problems in the area of air and noise pollution when the Wright brothers made their historic flight at Kitty Hawk? Only
recently has society attempted to predict the implications of proposed technological developments. Examples of this are opposition to location of atomic
generating plants; to locations of airports; to the SST development; and to
destruction of natural resources, such as the California redwoods by freeway
construction. The problem of balancing the social and technical sides of the
work system has been investigated by numerous studies. Examination of some
studies will reveal that various approaches are available to reconcile the conflict between the technical and the social environments.

Examples of Sociotechnical Applications

Numerous attempts have been made to implement the integrative approach
of sociotechnical systems. It is believed that the terminology originated in the
studies conducted at the Tavistock Institute in England, starting in the 1950s.
One early study dealt with changing patterns of work in coal mines.[22] A
composite method of mining was used to replace the traditional one. The
essential element of the composite system was placement of the worker into a
situation involving a high degree of group relationships. The change in work
design resulted in improved output costs and other indices of the system's
efficiency.[23] While this and subsequent studies illustrated that both technology
and the social system are closely related, and that the technology may place
certain limits on the social system, there are combinations possible which are
better than others. Another study which gave similar results was conducted in
the textile mills in Ahmedabad, India.[24]

It is probable that no area of activity has received more attention in recent
times in regard to the sociotechnical relationships than those areas related to
aerospace. The problems of space flight, involving man's adaptation to highly

---

[21]Walker and Guest, *op. cit.*

[22]E. L. Trist and K. W. Bamforth, "Some Social and Psychological Consequences of the
Longwall Method of Coal-getting," *Human Relations*, Vol. IV (February, 1951), pp. 3–38.

[23]F. E. Emery and E. L. Trist, "Socio-Technical Systems," in C. West Churchman and
Michel Verhulst (eds.), *Management Sciences: Models and Techniques* (New York: Pergamon
Press, 1960), II, pp. 88–90.

[24]A. K. Rice, *Productivity and Social Organization: The Ahmedabad Experiment* (London:
Tavistock Publications, 1958).

technological requirements, and to social environmental pressures, are examples.[25] This is especially evident in the efforts applied to the design of the space capsule. Not only was this true in the manned space flights, but numerous instances are to be found in the unmanned ones as well. Many failures in the unmanned flights can be attributed to lack of consideration in this area of the sociotechnical aspects of the man-machine relationship.

Commercial aviation is replete with cases of near misses and catastrophic incidents which can be traced, at least in part, to a failure in the sociotechnical system. The mid-air collision of two airplanes over the Grand Canyon in 1956, which resulted in the death of 128 people, is one instance. The apparent cause was the failure of each pilot to see the other plane, because of poor visibility.[26] It is not necessary to cite the many instances, but investigations following such occurrences invariably indicate some conflict in the man-machine interface.

Not only aviation, but transportation generally, has been an area in which extensive investigation of these types of problems has occurred. A great deal of interest exists regarding the design of all types of transportation facilities: automobiles, airplanes, and highways. Most of the concern with regard to these elements, and with transportation systems as a whole, deals with the interactions of the human being with the system vehicle.[27]

While the emphasis in sociotechnical relationships is on man-machine relationships, other types of interfaces between man and his environment must be considered as falling into this area. One such problem area was the subject of an interesting investigation. A study of administration of drugs to patients in a hospital revealed there were 178 cases of error in a seven-month period.[28] The causes of the errors were largely determined as being the result of human error in relationship to the design of the system. This again illustrates the necessity of recognizing all elements of the work environment.

Ergonomics and the Sociotechnical System

The application of the techniques of ergonomics to the design of the work system is complementary to the sociotechnical system approach. Both can be used to evaluate the total environment where the work is to take place. Most of the interest in job design today centers around an integration of all elements of the system. This is particularly true with regard to the extremely complex man-machine systems which are so commonplace. It is important to recognize that we are dealing with an integrated system. In addition, the role of man in

[25]B. E. Flaherty (ed.), *Psychophysiological Aspects of Space Flight* (New York: Columbia University Press, 1961).

[26]Mary H. Cadwalader, "Air Mystery is Solved," *Life*, Vol. XLII, No. 17 (1957), pp. 151–152 *et passim*.

[27]Slade F. Hulbert and Albert Burg, "Human Factors in Transportation Systems," in Kenyon B. DeGreene (ed.), *Systems Psychology* (New York: McGraw-Hill Book Co., 1970), pp. 471–509.

[28]M. A. Safren and A. Chapanis, "A Critical Incident Study of Hospital Medication Errors," *Hospitals*, Vol. XXXIV, No. 9 (May 1, 1960), pp. 32–34 *et passim*, and Vol. XXXIV, No. 10 (May 16, 1960), pp. 53 *et passim*.

this system, as one of the elements, is a necessary consideration. The physical or technological aspects of the system are usually so evident in a work system that they often tend to dominate the designer's thinking. The place of all elements, the machines, tools, workplace, along with the abilities and limitations of the human operator, are important. Both ergonomics and the socio-technical approach recognize that the man's role in the work system is as an active element and not as a passive participant. The psychological needs of man, along with the social implications of any new technology, are necessary considerations in the development of the systems approach to job design.

Each system is unique unto itself as regards the way various elements will interrelate. A single prescription cannot be written about how these interfaces will occur. We recognize the limiting factor of technology, but it cannot be accepted as dictating the form the system will assume.

> Thus rather than being an absolute, fixed constraint, technology allows for various adaptations in the other systems. Increasingly, we are coming to recognize that one of the primary managerial functions is to facilitate the integration of the technical system with the organization structure and the psycho-social system — not only to improve efficiency but also to satisfy the various participants.[29]

SUMMARY

The use of ergonomics in job design is a relatively new approach which considers all aspects of the performance of the task. It is specifically concerned with the relationship of man to the working environment. Ergonomics is the systems approach to work design. It is also necessary to take into account the man-machine relationship of the work system in ergonomics.

Various elements are significant in the ergonomics approach to work design. First, the characteristics of the human body are examined. Included here are the anatomical aspects of the human body. Anthropometry, the consideration of body measurements, has a bearing on job design. Of possibly greater significance are those aspects related to the central mechanisms of the body. Here many neuromuscular factors are involved. Of particular relevance are those tasks which involve not only a series of small motions, but one or more of the senses as well. These are identified as sensory-motor tasks. Physiological response factors are of interest as possible determinants of the energy cost of various types of industrial activities. Work loads can be broadly categorized on this basis. Discussion of the problems of reconciling laboratory results with actual performance reveals some reasons for variations. The problem of fatigue is a final element of those characteristics of the human body reviewed.

A second set of factors in the ergonomics approach to job design is the physical environment where the task is performed. These include temperature and humidity, lighting, noise, and vibration. The nature of the problems related

---

[29]Fremont E. Kast and James E. Rosenzweig, *Organization and Management* (New York: McGraw-Hill Book Co., 1970), p. 167.

to each of these areas and some of the necessary considerations for good job design are outlined.

The design and layout of workplace and machines is the third group of ergonomic factors. Evaluations of such things as seating utilize earlier-mentioned anthropometric data. The primary way the machine communicates with the operator is through instrument displays. The locations and design of these displays are, in part, related to the function to be performed in conjunction with the display. Controls, which are the way the operator communicates with the machine and the way he achieves a desired response, are another element in machine design. The design, location, and shape of the control are also important elements. Recommendations regarding control movement and type relative to the system response are set forth also.

A final set of factors are designated as specialized human factors. A comparison of job enlargement with specialization and how they relate to job design is made. The effect of shift work on individual job performance as a factor in the design of a work system is also discussed. A final consideration in this category of factors is the nature of the problems of the exceptional worker. The aging worker and the handicapped worker are given primary emphasis, but other classes of workers, such as the culturally deprived, face similar conditions. The important fact is that the designer of a work system must consider these types of workers. If jobs are properly designed, these workers can make a significant contribution.

Another approach to job design which attempts to consider all elements of the work system is the sociotechnical system. It is primarily concerned with the man-machine relationship. It is an integrative concept which tries to balance the technical aspects and the social elements of the system. A few studies which have made use of the sociotechnical concept are outlined.

Finally, a reconciliation of ergonomics and the sociotechnical system is made. Essentially, both have the same objective. The role of all elements of the work system and the need to integrate them into a whole are recognized by these two approaches. The important thing is to increase the efficiency of the system with full regard for the needs of the elements of the system.

QUESTIONS FOR DISCUSSION AND ANALYSIS

1. Define ergonomics. What do you see as its role in job design?

2. Examine in detail your activities throughout a typical day and list those situations where ergonomics might be applied. Suggest possible improvements. For example, consider seating, table or desk height, lighting, temperature, noise, driving, etc.

3. What is meant by sensory-motor tasks? Give examples of these tasks. What is the relationship of the increasing level of automation to such tasks?

4. How would you describe fatigue? What factors contribute to the development of fatigue? How can job design be used to reduce fatigue?

5. What effect do the environmental factors of lighting, noise, and vibration have on performance of a job?

6. Which of the three basic types of dial indicators shown in Figure 13-2 would you recommend for the following:
   (a) An oscilloscope selector dial.
   (b) A steam gauge on a boiler.
   (c) A home electric meter indicating consumption.
   (d) An altimeter.

7. Table 13-2 contains certain recommended relationships between control movement and system response. For each type of control movement and for each system response listed as acceptable, give a specific example. For instance, in the case of the "up" control movement, a light switch would exemplify an "on" response.

8. Compare how job enlargement and specialization relate to the design of jobs.

9. Describe the possible effects of shift work on worker performance.

10. Discuss the importance of applying the concepts of job design to the problems of the exceptional worker.

11. What is the nature of the sociotechnical system concept? Describe its significance as regards the design of jobs.

12. Explain the relative roles of ergonomics and of the sociotechnical system approach in the design of jobs.

PROBLEMS

1. Measure the pulse rate of someone who has been sitting for at least two to three minutes. Have him jump in place for one minute. Take his pulse immediately after he has jumped. Measure his pulse again after he has been sitting for one minute, three minutes, and five minutes. Comment on the results and the implications for job design.

2. Measure the dimensions in Table 13-1 for ten or more individuals. Estimate the percentile into which each measurement fits. From your data, establish a workplace height you feel would be most desirable for your sample for both sitting and standing.

3. Try to design a set of digits from 1-9 which would be so distinctive they could not be confused in cases of poor lighting or even when partially obscured.

SELECTED ADDITIONAL READINGS

Barnes, Ralph M. *Motion and Time Study: Design and Measurement of Work*, 6th ed. New York: John Wiley & Sons, Inc., 1968.

Brouha, Lucien. *Physiology in Industry*, 2d ed. New York: Pergamon Press, 1967.

Chapanis, Alphonse. *Man-Machine Engineering.* Belmont, California: Wadsworth Publishing Company, Inc., 1965.

DeGreene, Kenyon B. (ed.). *Systems Psychology.* New York: McGraw-Hill Book Co., 1970.

Ely, Jerome H., Robert M. Thomson, and Jesse Orlansky. *Design of Controls,* WADC-TR-56-172. Wright-Patterson Air Force Base, Ohio: Wright Air Development Center, 1956.

_____. *Layout of Workplaces,* WADC-TR-56-171. Wright-Patterson Air Force Base, Ohio: Wright Air Development Center, 1956.

Fogel, L. J. *Biotechnology: Concepts and Applications.* Englewood Cliffs: Prentice-Hall, Inc., 1963.

International Labour Office, *Ergonomics and Physical Environmental Factors,* Occupational Safety and Health Series No. 21. Geneva: International Labour Office, 1970.

International Labour Office, *Ergonomics in Machine Design,* Occupational Safety and Health Series No. 14, 2 vols. Geneva: International Labour Office, 1969.

Jaques, Elliott. *The Changing Culture of a Factory.* London: Tavistock Publications, Ltd., 1951.

McCormick, E. J. *Human Factors Engineering,* 2d ed. New York: McGraw-Hill Book Co., 1964.

Mott, Paul E., *et al. Shift Work.* Ann Arbor: The University of Michigan Press, 1965.

Murrell, K. F. H. *Ergonomics.* London: Chapman and Hall, 1965.

Singleton, W. T. *Introduction to Ergonomics.* Geneva: World Health Organization, 1972.

Van Cott, Harold P., and Robert G. Kinkade (eds.). *Human Engineering Guide to Equipment Design,* rev. ed. Washington: Supt. of Documents, 1972.

Walker, Charles R. *Technology, Industry, and Man.* New York: McGraw-Hill Book Co., 1968.

_____, and Robert H. Guest. *The Man on the Assembly Line.* Cambridge: Harvard University Press, 1952.

Woodson, Wesley E., and Donald W. Conover. *Human Engineering Guide for Equipment Designers,* 2d ed. Berkeley: University of California Press, 1964.

14 | **Work Measurement**

Managers have long been interested in the amount of work that a worker can be expected to perform in a given period of time. If a true measure of work is to be achieved, a standardized way of performing the task involved must be used. This is the function of work and job design techniques. In the past, the main purpose of measuring the amount of work has been to develop wage incentives. Incentive systems were designed to motivate the workers to higher levels of performance. The methodology of work measurement is much more complex than first imagined. There are a variety of techniques available, and time standards are increasingly being employed for purposes other than incentive systems. Management has found the data useful in a variety of problem areas.

NATURE AND PURPOSE OF WORK MEASUREMENT

Work measurement is the technique used to determine the time a well-trained worker requires to perform a task using the prescribed, standard method; working at a pace specified as necessary and sustainable; and supplied with all the tools, materials, and other necessities. This time is referred to as the *standard time*. Standard time can be used as a base of measurement of the performance of all workers to determine any wage incentive which may be earned.

The determination of the time required to perform a task is a necessary prerequisite to efficient performance of the operations system. This is especially true where labor is an important part of the total inputs of the system. The use of work measurement techniques has largely been in relation to direct labor in manufacturing. However, with the increase of indirect labor and of service tasks, such as facilitating and clerical processes, greater need for measuring worker performance in these areas has become apparent.

Time standards can be of value in determining schedules and in the planning of the total work system. The establishment of a schedule for the system output will be easier if the amount of time the individual task requires is known. Time standards will be particularly useful in coordinating the activities of different departments or other units of the enterprise, if the same performance standards are used.

The time standards developed for labor will be an important element in the establishment of standard or planned costs. When anticipated costs are determined, the formulation of budgets becomes easier. Thus, time standards are valuable aids in the measurement and control of the performance of the operations system. Standards permit a comparison of actual and planned manpower performance.

Because time standards are useful in the determination of schedules and of costs, it is clear that they are useful in the area of manpower planning. Any manpower forecast must assume some manpower time requirements for the performance of the necessary activities. These time requirements can then be translated into the actual number of people needed.

While work measurement is designed to measure the output of labor, the establishment of time standards will materially assist in determining other resource requirements used as inputs of the system. Among these resources is the equipment needed. There is a close relationship between the man and the machine. If there is to be effective utilization of machinery and other equipment, the determination of time standards for the portion of the cycle performed by the worker is essential. Along with this is the determination of how many machines a single operator can run. On the man-machine form of the activity chart, a time scale is found which corresponds to the time standard for that activity. This time measurement is basic to the evaluation of a man-machine study. The same sort of situation may be found in making the decision of the number of workers needed to perform a task where gang or crew work is involved. Assembly lines exemplify this condition. The balancing of an assembly line requires consistent time standards for each operation performed on the line.

The estimating process is another area where the establishment of standard times makes a contribution. Whether the operations system is of an intermittent or continuous type, at times it is necessary to make a determination of the cost of the product or service prior to its being produced or performed. This determination may have to be made to establish the costs which can be used as a basis for making a bid to a potential customer. Even if a bid is not required, management will still want to establish a selling price for output.

Obviously, some form of time standards is needed by management of any enterprise. The way in which these standards are developed may vary considerably. Even where management does not acknowledge the need for work measurement, it will be found that some approach to setting time requirements is used. The method may be informal, or nonsystematic and highly arbitrary, but method there is. It may be simply looking at what was the case in the past and using that as the standard, or it may be a guess on the part of the supervisor. Of course, the accuracy of standards established in these ways is questionable. There are techniques available which can be defended as being more accurate and more consistent. In this chapter, the major work measurement techniques will be described and evaluated.

TIME STUDY[1]

In the minds of many people, time study and work measurement are synonymous. This is only natural since time study is essentially the basis of all work

---

[1]For a complete explanation of time study and other work measurement techniques the reader is referred to standard textbooks in the field. A number are listed at the end of this chapter.

measurement. In addition, time study is probably the oldest and still the most widely used technique of work measurement for determining the standard time. Because all work measurement techniques are really ways to study the time required to perform a job, the term stopwatch time study will be used to distinguish the time study form of work measurement from those of elemental data methods, predetermined time standard systems, and work sampling.

Equipment Used

The primary tool in stopwatch time study is a decimal stopwatch. The most frequently used type is the decimal-minute stopwatch. Another type which is sometimes used is the decimal-hour stopwatch.

The dial of the decimal-minute stopwatch, as pictured in Figure 14-1, has 100 divisions each one representing 0.01 minutes. The large sweep hand makes one revolution per minute. The totalizer, which is the smaller dial, has 30 divisions. The small hand moves one space for each revolution of the large hand. Thus, each division on this dial is equal to one minute. Starting and stopping the watch is accomplished by moving the serrated slide on the side of the watch. After being stopped, it is possible to resume from the point where the watch was stopped. The hands may be reset to zero by depressing the crown. The watch will not run as long as the crown is held down. When it is released, the watch will immediately start to run again.

Reproduced by courtesy of Meylan Stopwatch Corp.

FIGURE 14-1

Standard Decimal-Minute "Snap-Back" Stopwatch

The decimal-hour stopwatch is identical, in principle, to the decimal-minute stopwatch. The large hand makes one revolution in 1/100 hour and reads in decimal hours. Each division on the dial is equal to .0001 hour.

Although the decimal stopwatch is the primary tool used in stopwatch time study, other devices can be used to obtain and record decimal times. Foremost among these are motion picture cameras with synchronous drive motors. Time-recording machines that use a constant speed paper tape upon which markings can be made by finger operated buttons may also be used. The spaces between the markings represent the elapsed time between observed events. Electronic recording devices which use punched tape or punched cards to record the data are a final means of timing. The advantage of these is that the data can be processed directly by computers.

The Stopwatch Time Study Procedure

Although no two people use exactly the same approach in making a time study, certain steps need to be accomplished. The six steps which must always be completed are:

1. Planning the study.
2. Dividing operations into elements.
3. Reading and recording.
4. Determining the number of cycles to be timed.
5. Rating the operator's performance.
6. Computing and analyzing study data.

Planning the Study. The most important aspect of planning a stopwatch time study is to make sure that the operation is ready to be studied. The observer (or analyst) who is to make the study should discuss all facets of the operation with the foreman of the department involved. The observer must have a full understanding of the operation if he is to know whether it is ready to be time studied. Any pertinent information regarding the operation should be noted on an observation sheet. The analyst will especially need to ascertain that the operation is being performed according to the prescribed method. When he moves to the work area he will want to verify that the proper method is being utilized.

The observer will want to determine that the worker to be studied is a trained operator, capable of performing the operation properly. The operator should be informed, beforehand, that the study is to be made. This is important in securing the full cooperation of the operator. If necessary, a full explanation of the reason for the study and of the procedure should be given. Time spent in this phase will make the accomplishment of the study much easier.

When the analyst feels that these preliminaries are completed, he is ready to begin the next planning activity. He will want to observe the operation in order to verify the method. While observing the actual performance, he will proceed to the next step; dividing the operation into elements.

Dividing Operations into Elements. It is the usual practice to divide an operation being time studied into basic elements rather than to consider the operation in its totality. These elements must be written in detail on the observation sheet so that they will be fully recognized by anyone observing the operation. It is particularly important to list clearly the beginning and ending points of each element.

REASONS FOR ELEMENTAL BREAKDOWN. There are a variety of reasons for breaking down an operation into elements rather than timing it as an entity. Elemental division makes the process of timing easier, and the operation is more fully described by this type of breakdown. It is also possible to evaluate various parts of the operation with greater ease when it is subdivided into elements. If one part of the operation is poorly designed, improperly performed, or requires too much time in relation to other parts, it is more easily discovered when broken down into elements. Elemental times are useful in the development of standard data systems. Another value of elemental breakdown of operations is that it permits the application of performance ratings to each element. This adds accuracy to the standard time since many operators work at varying paces at different stages of their performance.

GUIDELINES FOR DETERMINING ELEMENTS. In making an elemental breakdown of an operation, there are certain guidelines which can be used. It is desirable that the starting and ending points of an element be distinctive and easily recognizable. One example of this is when a sound is associated with one of these points. This facilitates reading the watch and recording the time. The length of the element should be as short as is practical so the analyst can time it conveniently. When man and machine are both involved in the operation, the man's time should be separated from that of the machine. In certain operations, some elemental times vary because of some differences in the item being worked on. A part may differ in size, shape, or weight; or a paper form may require more information in some cases. Such variable elements should be listed separately from constant elements. Finally, not all elements necessarily appear in every cycle. These irregular elements are differentiated from those elements which occur regularly in each cycle.

Reading and Recording. Three methods of reading the time from the stopwatch are most frequently used. These three methods are (1) continuous timing, (2) repetitive or snap-back timing, and (3) accumulative timing.

In *continuous timing* the watch is started at the beginning of the study, and runs continuously throughout the entire study. At the end of each element the analyst reads the watch and records the time on the observation sheet. The times for each individual element are determined after completion of the study by subtracting the previous reading from the elemental reading. For example, if at the end of element one the time was recorded as 0.07, the time for that observation would naturally be 0.07 (0.07 − 0.0 = 0.07). In the same fashion, if the reading at the end of element two was 0.18, the time for that element observation would be 0.11 (0.18 − 0.07 = 0.11).

When *repetitive or snap-back timing* is used, the analyst reads the time at the end of the element and depresses the crown of the watch to return the hand to zero. The watch starts to run again immediately so that at the end of the next element the elapsed time can be read directly from the watch and the hand snapped back again. The repetitive method gives the observed time for each reading immediately, and does not require the subtractions as in continuous reading. The analyst can see the elemental times as the study is in progress and can note any variations which take place.

The snap-back procedure is somewhat more difficult to become accustomed to, and as a result it has been criticized as being less accurate than the continuous method. The empirical evidence does not bear out this contention. The differences in the times read by the two methods are not great enough to affect the final results significantly.[2]

In *accumulative timing,* use is made of two or more watches. Various types of mechanical linking devices are available to successively start and stop the watches. The time for an element can be read directly while the one watch is stopped and the next watch is running. When that watch is stopped at the end of the element being performed, the time for the second element can be read.

The observation sheet is designed to include all of the information pertinent to a time study. The observation sheet contains identification of the operation, the part, the operator, any machine and equipment, material, the analyst, and the date. In addition, there must be space to describe each of the elements. The space for recording the elemental times for each cycle is divided into two sections for use in continuous timing. One section is for the reading and the other is for the computed elapsed time. There is space for totals, for the select time, for the performance rating, and the calculated normal time for each element. Most forms provide for some sort of a summary and for the recording of the standard time. Some forms include areas for sketches of the workplace and of the part. An example of an observation sheet is found in Figure 14-2.

Determining the Number of Cycles to be Timed. Since time study is a sampling process, a sufficient size sample must be used. Obviously, the larger the size of the sample, the closer the study will be to the true situation. However, since it is impossible to do more than sample, it is important to determine the number of cycles to be timed which will yield the desired level of accuracy and confidence. The sample used in time study is not a random sample, but is an intensive sample, as all of the observations are made continuously at a given time.

The elemental times observed will vary somewhat between cycles. If all observed times were the same, a sample of one would be adequate. The greater the variation, the larger the sample needed. Thus, in determining the number of cycles to be timed, the element showing the greatest variability of times is used. There are a number of ways by which the analyst can estimate the sample size. A variety of equations, tables, charts, and nomographs are available. One can find examples of these mechanical devices and equations in any standard textbook

[2]Irwin P. Lazarus, "Nature of Stop-Watch Time Study Errors," *Advanced Management,* Vol. XV, No. 5 (May, 1950), p. 15.

TIME STUDY OBSERVATION SHEET

Study No. _____

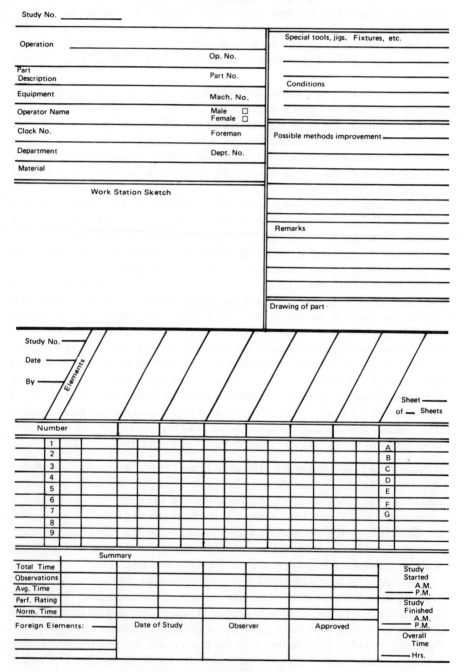

FIGURE 14-2

Sample Time Study Observation Sheet

on the subject. An examination of one of the more widely used equations will suffice as an illustration. This one is based on the standard error of the sample mean time for an element.

$$N' = \left(\frac{k/s \ \sqrt{N\Sigma\, X^2 - (\Sigma\, X)^2}}{\Sigma\, X} \right)^2 \tag{1}$$

Where:

N' = required number of cycles
k/s = confidence-precision ratio
X = observed individual elemental times
N = number of observed individual elemental times

The k/s ratio is based on the confidence level desired and the accuracy of the sample mean time for the element as compared with the true time. It is usual to use a 95% confidence level and a $\pm 5\%$ precision. In this case $k/s = 2/0.05 = 40$. The value for k is derived from the fact that a 95% confidence requires the observed times to be within ± 2 standard errors of the mean. The 0.05 value for s is based on the 5% precision requirement. To illustrate the use of this equation, assume that ten readings for an element have been made, and that they are as shown in Table 14-1. The computations for X^2, ΣX, and ΣX^2 are also shown.

TABLE 14-1

Values for Ten Elemental Times (X), X^2, ΣX, and ΣX^2

Element Times in 0.01 min.	X	14	17	17	19	17	18	16	13	13	14	$\Sigma X =$	158
	X^2	196	289	289	361	289	324	256	169	169	196	$\Sigma X^2 =$	2,538

Substituting in Equation (1) using a 95% confidence level and a precision of $\pm 5\%$ we have the following:

$$N' = \left(\frac{40 \ \sqrt{10 \times 2,538 - (158)^2}}{158} \right)^2 = \left(\frac{40 \ \sqrt{25,380 - 24,964}}{158} \right)^2$$

$$= \left(\frac{40 \times 20.4}{158} \right)^2 = \left(\frac{816}{158} \right)^2 = 27 \text{ cycles}$$

From this computation, the analyst would proceed to time a minimum of 27 cycles for this study. However, this is only a preliminary calculation based on 10 observations. After completing the total number of cycles indicated, it is necessary to recheck. That is, the analyst should check to determine that this number of cycles is sufficient to provide the desired confidence and accuracy. After a larger sample, he may find that the situation has changed, possibly because of increased variability, and additional cycles will be required.

Rating the Operator's Performance. During the course of the study the observer will rate the performance of the operator. *Performance rating* is the process whereby the performance of the operator is compared, on the basis of such things as speed, effort, and tempo, with what is considered to be normal pace. This implies that there is a definition of what is normal. Usually the normal pace is one which an average, well-trained worker can sustain throughout the regular workday without experiencing excessive fatigue. Of course, it would be difficult to determine an average worker. There would also be a problem agreeing on what is meant by well trained, and, as pointed out in Chapter 13, no clear definition of fatigue exists.

The usual method used to determine the performance rating of an operator is the analyst's own concept of normal pace. That is to say, it is a subjective judgment on the part of the time-study observer. Standards of normal performance exist, and are used as guidelines for developing the skill necessary to carry out performance rating. Examples of these standards are walking at the rate of 3 miles an hour and dealing a standard deck of 52 playing cards into four equal piles in 0.50 minutes. Time-study observers are trained to recognize normal pace and to compare an observed performance with this to arrive at a rating. The most frequent training technique is by means of motion pictures showing operations being performed at different paces for which consensus ratings have been developed. Often, a clip is shown of an operator performing one of the standard tasks such as walking at the rate of 3 miles an hour. The same task is shown at an undisclosed pace, and the observer must rate it. He can later compare his ratings for the tasks shown with the predetermined consensus rating and then analyze the results.

This aspect of time study is the one most subject to criticism because it is so highly subjective. Different methods of rating are used to attempt to improve the objectivity of the ratings. Performance rating is not only an element in time study, but also an essential aspect of all methods of work measurement. Some way of "normalizing" the raw times is necessary, otherwise it would be impossible to obtain a consistent standard since individuals differ in the speed and tempo with which they perform a task. The most common practice is to assign a rating to each element as opposed to rating the operation as a whole.

The most frequently used method for expressing the rating is a percentage system where the normal performance is expressed as 100%. Any pace faster than normal would be expressed by a figure greater than 100%, and conversely, performance which was slower would be below the normal figure. Thus, for example, if walking at 3 miles an hour is equal to 100%, a pace of 3.3 miles an hour would be expressed as 110%, and 2.7 miles an hour as 90%.

Another rating system is the Westinghouse System.[3] This approach applies a numerical scale to four factors: skill, effort, conditions, and consistency. The rating is arrived at by determining the levels for these four factors and summing the values. For example, assume that the following ratings are set:

---

[3] S. M. Lowry, H. B. Maynard, and G. J. Stegemerten, *Time and Motion Study* (3d ed.; New York: McGraw-Hill Book Co., 1940), p. 233.

Average skill, D	0.00
Excellent effort, B1	0.10
Fair conditions, E	−0.03
Good consistency, C	0.01
Total	+0.08

Thus, the rating for this element would be 1.08 or the equivalent of 108% as compared to normal performance.

Mundel developed a rating system called objective rating.[4] This method requires that first a pace rating, as in the percentage rating method, be made. This rating is made without any consideration of job difficulty. In addition, a difficulty adjustment is added. This adjustment is made by taking into account seven factors:

1. Total amount of body involved in the element.
2. Foot pedals used during the element.
3. Bimanualness of the element.
4. Eye-hand coordination required to perform the element.
5. Handling or sensory requirement of the element.
6. Resistance that must be overcome on the element — that is, thrust on levers or weight lifted.
7. Other special constraints on work speed.[5]

Tables have been developed for the first six factors from which the applicable adjustment factors can be taken. The observed time is first multiplied by the pace rating, then by the total difficulty adjustment. If the pace rating and difficulty adjustment were added, the difficulty adjustment would be affected by changes in the pace rating. Therefore, if the observed time for an element is 0.16 minutes, the pace rating 95%, and the difficulty adjustment 15%, the application of the rating to this element would be $0.16 \times 0.95 \times 1.15 = 0.175$ minutes.

A unique and somewhat new method of assessing the level of performance is by the use of physiological evaluations. In Chapter 13 comment was made regarding the use of measures of the levels of energy expenditure in connection with the evaluation of work loads. Certain broad classifications of work loads were presented (p. 327). Numerous studies have been conducted to evaluate work performance in terms of such physiological measures as oxygen consumption and heart rate. To date the applications of these measures to actual work situations have been limited, but some results are promising. The ability to relate work performance to a more objective norm like a physiological assessment would certainly be of great value and would remove one of the strongest criticisms of time studies. The potential significance of the application of physiological evaluations to the area of work measurement is considered so great that a detailed discussion of this topic will be undertaken further on in this chapter. It is sufficient at this point to simply state that this approach to the determination

[4]Marvin E. Mundel, *Motion and Time Study* (4th ed.; Englewood Cliffs: Prentice-Hall, Inc., 1970), pp. 558–595.

[5]*Ibid.*, p. 572, 574.

of the level of a worker's performance is arousing considerable interest on the part of those concerned with work measurement methods.

Computing and Analyzing Study Data. After completing the observations, it is necessary to carry out certain computations with the data collected. There are really three computational steps necessary after completing the actual study: determination of the select time, calculation of the normal time, and arrival at a standard time.

SELECT TIME. When the observer completes his study he has a number of readings for each element depending on the number of cycles timed. The question then arises as to which of these numerous values is representative of the time taken as observed.

Several methods may be used to select a representative time, but the most widely utilized method for determining the select time is to find the arithmetic mean of the observed times. In finding the mean, no time values should be eliminated without a specific reason. On occasion there are time values recorded which are extremely high or extremely low. If these are the result of improper reading or recording, they should be eliminated from the calculations. If, on the other hand, these values represent situations which are typical to the operation, they must be included. Extreme times may result from a variation in the metal. Some elements that are a regular, although infrequent, part of the operation may cause high readings. An example of an irregular element is found when the container for finished parts has to be moved and replaced with an empty one. This situation will occur only once in many cycles.

NORMAL TIME. Once the select time value is determined, it is necessary to apply the rating factor to it to find the normal time. The *normal time* is the time it would take an experienced operator to perform an element while working at normal pace. If the operator is rated as performing the task at below normal pace (less than 100%), then obviously the time observed will be greater than it should be. Conversely, if the rating is higher than normal (greater than 100%), the observed time will be low and must be adjusted accordingly. The application of the rating, frequently referred to as leveling, is similar to applying an index number to some value. If the select time for an element in a study is 0.09, and the performance rating is 105%, the normal time is calculated as follows:

$$\text{Normal time} = \text{select time} \times \frac{\text{rating in } \%}{100} \qquad (2)$$

$$= 0.09 \times \frac{105}{100} = .0945 \text{ minutes}$$

This, to repeat, is the time that it would take a well-trained worker to complete this element of the operation if he worked at the normal pace. It is necessary to compute this time for each element of the operation. If, for some reason, it was desired to know the normal time for the entire operation, it is a simple matter of addition of the elemental normal times.

STANDARD TIME. Once the normal time is established, it is then possible to determine the standard time. The assumption of the normal time is that the operator will work without any stop. Naturally, this cannot be expected. There will be numerous causes of intervals where the worker is not performing the operation. Therefore, certain allowances must be made for these interruptions or delays. There are typically three types of allowances which are identified. These are (1) personal, (2) fatigue, and (3) unavoidable delays.

Personal allowances are quite easily recognizable. These allowances include any time required for personal needs. Personal needs are not closely related to the nature of the task, although it is probably true that when the work is heavier and performed under poor environmental conditions there is a greater need for personal time. Often these factors are more closely related to the fatigue allowances. Under usual circumstances, the personal allowance seldom exceeds 5%. The amount of personal allowance needed can be determined by various techniques such as work sampling.

Because the definition of fatigue is not clear, the determination of an allowance for fatigue is difficult. Some people believe it is taken care of in the rating procedure and in the personal allowance. However, most time-study applications make some provision for fatigue, particularly where the work is heavy and the working conditions are poor. There is no question that under these conditions the worker will need more time for rest. These rest periods will vary in number and length with the severity of the work and the environmental conditions. Therefore, these allowances are needed in the establishment of the standard time. At present, there is no truly objective way to determine what this allowance should be. Some of the physiological techniques to be examined below may be helpful for this purpose as they are further refined.

The third type of allowance, unavoidable delays, encompasses any occurrences which cannot be considered as a part of the operation. Delays do occur, and must, therefore, be considered in establishing the standard time. Ideally, they would be timed and rated, then included in the standard. Practically speaking, this is not feasible. Delays caused by maintenance or repair of a machine, material difficulties, or discussions with the supervisor are typical examples. It is possible to determine the amount of these delays by work sampling; production time studies which cover a long period of time, such as a day or two; or by mechanical or electrical devices attached to machines to record details of the operation or delays of machines.

The usual practice is to express all allowances as a percentage and to apply them equally to all elements. Occasionally, allowances (particularly fatigue) are applied only to those elements where the operator is working and not to machine elements. Assuming total allowances of 15% for an operation, and normal time of 0.95 minutes for the total operation, standard time can be computed as follows:

$$\text{Standard time} = \text{normal time} + (\text{normal time}) \times \frac{\text{allowances in }\%}{100} \quad \text{(3)}$$

$$= 0.95 + (0.95) \times (0.15)$$

$$= 0.95 + .1425$$

$$= 1.0925 \text{ minutes, or } 1.09$$

This equation is the most frequently used for applying the allowances to the normal time. From a strict mathematical standpoint, however, this equation is not correct. An allowance of 15% amounts to 72 minutes for a normal workday (480×0.15). Thus, with a normal time of 0.95 minutes, the operator should produce 429.5 pieces. This is computed by dividing the 408 minutes available for work ($480 - 72 = 408$) by the normal time of 0.95 minutes ($408 \div 0.95 = 429.5$). Thus, the standard time should be 1.12 minutes ($480 \div 429.5 = 1.12$). The equation for determining the standard time which expresses this concept is as follows:

$$\text{Standard time} = (\text{normal time}) \times \frac{100}{(100 - \text{allowances in } \%)} \qquad \textbf{(4)}$$

$$= 0.95 \times \frac{100}{100 - 15}$$

$$= 0.95 \times \frac{100}{85}$$

$$= 1.12 \text{ minutes}$$

ELEMENTAL STANDARD DATA SYSTEMS

Another technique of work measurement, which is really an extension of time study, is the development of elemental standard data systems for establishing work standards. These systems are entirely dependent on stopwatch time studies as the original source of the data. Where the type of work performed is similar, and the operations are essentially the same, it is probable that the elements which make up most of the operations can be standardized. When the initial development of the work measurement system is undertaken, the elements should be selected so they can be applied to a wide variety of operations. In this way, standard times for these elements can be developed by time study, and, eventually, tables of standard-time data which are applicable to the constantly appearing elements can be developed. An example of a table of elemental time standards which were developed for use in one electronics firm, for one class of hand-wiring operations, is shown in Table 14-2.

Elemental standard data systems make it possible to reduce the number of time studies which must be made. When a new operation is to be used, it is possible, by reference to the standard data tables, to develop a standard time for it before it is ever performed. This is done simply by identifying the elements in the operation and then totaling the previously developed elemental standards. Such a system may be useful in estimating and bidding. It also tends to increase the consistency of the standards used by the organization.

TABLE 14-2

Example of Elemental Standard Data for Hand-Wiring Operation

Operation: Insert wire into terminal lug hole and crimp with pliers.
Lug Hole — Class No. 3

Previous	Attached First End		
Attachments	Wire Gauge		
	#18-#22	#16	#14
None	.069	.059	.061
1. #18–#22 Gauge	.072	.062	.063
2. #18–#22 Gauge	.074	.064	.066
3. #18–#22 Gauge	.077	.067	.069
4. #18–#22 Gauge	.080	.071	.073
5. #18–#22 Gauge	– –	.076	– –
1. #16 Gauge	.060	.062	.065
2. #16 Gauge	.063	.065	.068
3. #16 Gauge	.067	– –	.073
1. #14 Gauge	.061	.063	.066
2. #14 Gauge	.065	.070	.075

All times in minutes.

Example: The first end of a #18 to #22 gauge wire is to be attached to a Class 3
lug hole. Two #16 gauge wires are already in place. The standard time
is 0.063 minutes.

MOTION-TIME DATA SYSTEMS

An approach which is another form of a predetermined standard time system,
and consequently somewhat related to the elemental standard data approach, is
that group of systems which use normalized time values for therblig-like motions.
A number of these systems have been developed, but Methods-Time Measurement (MTM) is the most popular, and will be described briefly as illustrative of
all motion-time data systems.[6]

MTM was a result of an intensive research program over about eight years.
A full evaluation of hand motions was made in an attempt to determine what
elements influenced the time required to perform the various motions. The
results of this study culminated in the publication, in 1948, of a set of predetermined normal times for various types of motions.[7] The basic motions
used in this system are reach; move; turn and apply pressure; grasp; position;
release; disengage; eye travel and eye focus; and body, leg, and foot motions.

[6]A summary of the various systems of motion-time data is found in: Ralph M. Barnes,
Motion and Time Study: Design and Measurement of Work (6th ed.; New York: John Wiley &
Sons, Inc., 1968), p. 472–473 ff.

[7]Harold B. Maynard, G. J. Stegemerten, and John L. Schwab, *Methods-Time Measurement* (New York: McGraw-Hill Book Co., 1948).

The time values were derived from analysis of a large number of motion pictures of workers performing the basic motions in industrial operations. Applicable time values are shown on a series of ten tables found in Table 14-3.

The time values shown on these tables are designated as TMU's, or time-measurement units. A TMU is equal to 0.00001 hours, which converts to 0.0006 minutes. These time values are already leveled, which means that they are not subject to performance rating. The applicable allowances, however, must be added to arrive at a standard time.

The tables in Table 14-3 show that each motion has a variety of possible time values. This is true because the MTM system attempts to take into account all factors which might influence the time of a particular motion. For instance, in the case of reach and move, distance is a factor, as is whether the hand is in motion or not. There are also certain cases which affect the time required. For reach, the cases relate to the location of the object sought. For move, the location conditions at the point to which the object is moved determine the applicable case. Weight also has an influence on the time for moving an item.

In making an MTM study, a form similar to a simo chart (Figure 12-13) is used. There are columns for the two hands in which a description of the motions for each is written. In addition, there are columns for noting the appropriate MTM class for the individual motions for each hand. A final column is for noting the applicable TMU value. Naturally, the appropriate descriptive information about the operation and any other pertinent information are also included.

To illustrate the use of MTM, we will use a simple everyday activity. Assume that a man carries his wallet in the right inside breast pocket of his suit jacket. Table 14-4, page 368, is an MTM analysis of the removal of the wallet from this pocket, taking a bill out of the wallet, and returning the wallet to the pocket.

In Table 14-4, the MTM class for each hand is noted in a shorthand form. For example, the first motion of the left hand, reach to pocket, is designated as R12B. This represents a reach of 12 inches which is a Case B. Similar designations are used for all other motions. When motions are performed simultaneously, as with the first motions of the two hands, the motion having the highest TMU value prevails. Thus, motions where the TMU's are not included are circled. The total TMU's for this activity are indicated as 106.3. This comes out as 0.0638 minutes (106.3 × 0.0006).

In an MTM study, operations can be divided into elements in much the same way as is done in stopwatch time study. The same reasons cited for elemental breakdown in time study apply here also. The analyst can utilize previously completed elemental analyses to compute a standard time for a new or improved operation which contains the same elements. Two elements could be designated for the operation illustrated (Table 14-4). The first — get wallet from jacket pocket — would start with reach to pocket and contain all motions through tilt wallet to flip open. The second element — get one bill and return wallet to pocket — would start with reach for bill and end with release wallet.

The MTM system is particularly valuable because the MTM Association carries on a very strict training program. Only people who have been through a

TABLE 14-3

Methods-Time Measurement Time Values

TABLE I — REACH — R

Distance Moved Inches	Time TMU				Hand In Motion		CASE AND DESCRIPTION
	A	B	C or D	E	A	B	
¾ or less	2.0	2.0	2.0	2.0	1.6	1.6	**A** Reach to object in fixed location, or to object in other hand or on which other hand rests.
1	2.5	2.5	3.6	2.4	2.3	2.3	
2	4.0	4.0	5.9	3.8	3.5	2.7	**B** Reach to single object in location which may vary slightly from cycle to cycle.
3	5.3	5.3	7.3	5.3	4.5	3.6	
4	6.1	6.4	8.4	6.8	4.9	4.3	
5	6.5	7.8	9.4	7.4	5.3	5.0	
6	7.0	8.6	10.1	8.0	5.7	5.7	**C** Reach to object jumbled with other objects in a group so that search and select occur.
7	7.4	9.3	10.8	8.7	6.1	6.5	
8	7.9	10.1	11.5	9.3	6.5	7.2	
9	8.3	10.8	12.2	9.9	6.9	7.9	
10	8.7	11.5	12.9	10.5	7.3	8.6	
12	9.6	12.9	14.2	11.8	8.1	10.1	**D** Reach to a very small object or where accurate grasp is required.
14	10.5	14.4	15.6	13.0	8.9	11.5	
16	11.4	15.8	17.0	14.2	9.7	12.9	
18	12.3	17.2	18.4	15.5	10.5	14.4	
20	13.1	18.6	19.8	16.7	11.3	15.8	**E** Reach to indefinite location to get hand in position for body balance or next motion or out of way.
22	14.0	20.1	21.2	18.0	12.1	17.3	
24	14.9	21.5	22.5	19.2	12.9	18.8	
26	15.8	22.9	23.9	20.4	13.7	20.2	
28	16.7	24.4	25.3	21.7	14.5	21.7	
30	17.5	25.8	26.7	22.9	15.3	23.2	

TABLE II — MOVE — M

Distance Moved Inches	Time TMU				Wt. Allowance			CASE AND DESCRIPTION
	A	B	C	Hand In Motion B	Wt. (lb.) Up to	Fac-tor	Con-stant TMU	
¾ or less	2.0	2.0	2.0	1.7				
1	2.5	2.9	3.4	2.3	2.5	0	0	**A** Move object to other hand or against stop.
2	3.6	4.6	5.2	2.9				
3	4.9	5.7	6.7	3.6	7.5	1.06	2.2	
4	6.1	6.9	8.0	4.3				
5	7.3	8.0	9.2	5.0	12.5	1.11	3.9	
6	8.1	8.9	10.3	5.7				
7	8.9	9.7	11.1	6.5	17.5	1.17	5.6	
8	9.7	10.6	11.8	7.2				
9	10.5	11.5	12.7	7.9	22.5	1.22	7.4	**B** Move object to approximate or indefinite location.
10	11.3	12.2	13.5	8.6				
12	12.9	13.4	15.2	10.0	27.5	1.28	9.1	
14	14.4	14.6	16.9	11.4				
16	16.0	15.8	18.7	12.8	32.5	1.33	10.8	
18	17.6	17.0	20.4	14.2				
20	19.2	18.2	22.1	15.6	37.5	1.39	12.5	
22	20.8	19.4	23.8	17.0				
24	22.4	20.6	25.5	18.4	42.5	1.44	14.3	**C** Move object to exact location.
26	24.0	21.8	27.3	19.8				
28	25.5	23.1	29.0	21.2	47.5	1.50	16.0	
30	27.1	24.3	30.7	22.7				

TABLE III — TURN AND APPLY PRESSURE — T AND AP

Weight	Time TMU for Degrees Turned										
	30°	45°	60°	75°	90°	105°	120°	135°	150°	165°	180°
Small — 0 to 2 Pounds	2.8	3.5	4.1	4.8	5.4	6.1	6.8	7.4	8.1	8.7	9.4
Medium — 2.1 to 10 Pounds	4.4	5.5	6.5	7.5	8.5	9.6	10.6	11.6	12.7	13.7	14.8
Large — 10.1 to 35 Pounds	8.4	10.5	12.3	14.4	16.2	18.3	20.4	22.2	24.3	26.1	28.2
APPLY PRESSURE CASE 1 — 16.2 TMU						APPLY PRESSURE CASE 2 — 10.6 TMU					

TABLE 14-3 (Cont.)

TABLE IV — GRASP — G

Case	Time TMU	DESCRIPTION
1A	2.0	**Pick Up Grasp** — Small, medium or large object by.itself, easily grasped.
1B	3.5	Very small object or object lying close against a flat surface.
1C1	7.3	Interference with grasp on bottom and one side of nearly cylindrical object. Diameter larger than ½".
1C2	8.7	Interference with grasp on bottom and one side of nearly cylindrical object. Diameter ¼" to ½".
1C3	10.8	Interference with grasp on bottom and one. side of nearly cylindrical object. Diameter less than ¼".
2	5.6	**Regrasp.**
3	5.6	**Transfer Grasp.**
4A	7.3	Object jumbled with other objects so search and select occur. Larger than 1" × 1" × 1".
4B	9.1	Object jumbled with other objects so search and select occur. ¼" × ¼" × ⅛" to 1" × 1" × 1".
4C	12.9	Object jumbled with other objects so search and select occur. Smaller than ¼" × ¼" × ⅛".
5	0	Contact, sliding or hook grasp.

TABLE V — POSITION* — P

CLASS OF FIT		Symmetry	Easy To Handle	Difficult To Handle
1 — Loose	No pressure required	S	5.6	11.2
		SS	9.1	14.7
		NS	10.4	16.0
2 — Close	Light pressure required	S	16.2	21.8
		SS	19.7	25.3
		NS	21.0	26.6
3 — Exact	Heavy pressure required.	S	43.0	48.6
		SS	46.5	52.1
		NS	47.8	53.4

*Distance moved to engage — 1" or less.

TABLE VI — RELEASE — RL

Case	Time TMU	DESCRIPTION
1	2.0	Normal release performed by opening fingers as independent motion.
2	0	Contact Release.

TABLE VII — DISENGAGE — D

CLASS OF FIT	Easy to Handle	Difficult to Handle
1 — Loose — Very slight effort, blends with subsequent move.	4.0	5.7
2 — Close — Normal effort, slight recoil.	7.5	11.8
3 — Tight — Considerable effort, hand recoils markedly.	22.9	34.7

TABLE VIII — EYE TRAVEL TIME AND EYE FOCUS — ET AND EF

Eye Travel Time = $15.2 \times \dfrac{T}{D}$ **TMU, with a maximum value of 20 TMU.**

where T = the distance between points from and to which the eye travels.
D = the perpendicular distance from the eye to the line of travel T.

Eye Focus Time = 7.3 TMU.

TABLE IX — BODY, LEG AND FOOT MOTIONS

DESCRIPTION	SYMBOL	DISTANCE	TIME TMU
Foot Motion — Hinged at Ankle.	FM	Up to 4"	8.5
With heavy pressure.	FMP		19.1
Leg or Foreleg Motion.	LM —	Up to 6"	7.1
		Each add'l. inch	1.2
Sidestep — Case 1 —Complete when leading leg contacts floor.	SS-C1	Less than 12"	Use REACH or MOVE Time
		12"	17.0
		Each add'l. inch	.6
Case 2 — Lagging leg must contact floor before next motion can be made.	SS-C2	12"	34.1
		Each add'l. inch	1.1
Bend, Stoop, or Kneel on One Knee.	B,S,KOK		29.0
Arise.	AB,AS,AKOK		31.9
Kneel on Floor — Both Knees.	KBK		69.4
Arise.	AKBK		76.7
Sit.	SIT		34.7
Stand from Sitting Position.	STD		43.4
Turn Body 45 to 90 degrees —			
Case 1 — Complete when leading leg contacts floor.	TBC1		18.6
Case 2 — Lagging leg must contact floor before next motion can be made.	TBC2		37.2
Walk.	W-FT	Per Foot	5.3
Walk.	W-P	Per Pace	15.0

TABLE X — SIMULTANEOUS MOTIONS

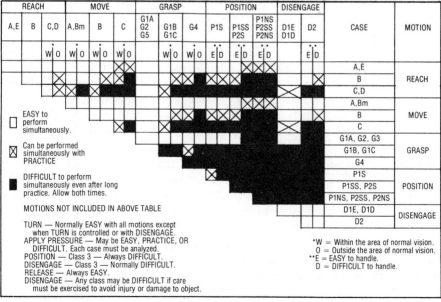

☐ EASY to perform simultaneously.

☒ Can be performed simultaneously with PRACTICE

■ DIFFICULT to perform simultaneously even after long practice. Allow both times.

MOTIONS NOT INCLUDED IN ABOVE TABLE

TURN — Normally EASY with all motions except when TURN is controlled or with DISENGAGE.
APPLY PRESSURE — May be EASY, PRACTICE, OR DIFFICULT. Each case must be analyzed.
POSITION — Class 3 — Always DIFFICULT.
DISENGAGE — Class 3 — Normally DIFFICULT.
RELEASE — Always EASY.
DISENGAGE — Any class may be DIFFICULT if care must be exercised to avoid injury or damage to object.

*W = Within the area of normal vision.
 O = Outside the area of normal vision.
**E = EASY to handle.
 D = DIFFICULT to handle.

TABLE 14-4

MTM Analysis of Taking a Bill From a Wallet

Description — Left Hand	LH	TMU	RH	Description — Right Hand
Reach to pocket	R12B	12.9	R6B	Reach to jacket lapel
Position fingers at pocket	P1SE	5.6	G1A	Grasp lapel
Move fingers into pocket	M2B	4.6	M2B	Move jacket away from body
Grasp wallet	G1A	2.0		
Move wallet out of pocket	M5B	8.0		
Regrasp wallet	G2	5.6	RL1	Release jacket
Move wallet toward R.H.	M8B ⎫			
Regrasp wallet	G2 ⎬	10.6	R5E	Move hand to front of body
Tilt wallet to flip open	M1B	2.9		
		2.5	R1B	Reach for bill
		2.0	G1A	Grasp bill
		5.7	M3B	Remove bill from wallet
Tilt wallet to flip closed	M1B	2.9		
Regrasp wallet	G2	5.6		
Move wallet towards pocket	M10A	11.3		
Move fingers to pocket edge	M1C	3.4		
Place fingers in pocket	P1SE	5.6		
Move wallet down into pocket	M2B	4.6		
Regrasp wallet	G2	5.6		
Push wallet to bottom of pocket	M3A	4.9		
Release wallet	RL2	0.0		
Total		106.3		

program conducted by a licensed instructor are issued certificates which qualify them as MTM analysts. The use of MTM requires a well-trained person to determine the nature of each motion in an operation. The issuance of certificates to such qualified people insures the consistency of the application of MTM data.

Some of the relative advantages of MTM as related to stopwatch time study should be obvious. The fact that the time values are already leveled eliminates the need for a subjective performance rating. Because it requires such a detailed analysis of the motions in an operation, MTM is valuable in developing better methods. Of course, the fact that it is not necessary to observe an operator with a stopwatch in hand overcomes a great deal of the psychological impact so often connected with the establishment of standards. Finally, MTM makes it possible to establish a standard for an operation which is in the "proposed" stage. The motion pattern can be determined by visualization as well as by observation. Once the motion pattern is established, time values for an operation can be set, even though the operation is not yet being performed.

WORK SAMPLING

Work sampling was initially utilized for purposes other than work measurement. It was originally known as Ratio-Delay Study or Random-Check Delay

Study. The purpose of these studies was to determine the percentage of time a machine ran and the percentage of time it was idle. A determination of the reason for the idleness was included. Work sampling was later used to make the same sort of determinations with respect to a worker performing a manual task. Such data can be useful for establishing personal and unavoidable delay allowances. Work sampling is now utilized to set standard times for some types of tasks.

Work sampling is a statistical technique founded on random sampling. A number of observations of a worker performing a task are made on a random basis. The state of worker activity is recorded, indicating whether the operator is working or is idle. If an adequate number of observations are made, the percentage of working time and of idle time in the sample can be considered as representative of what actually occurs within predictable limits of accuracy.

Tallying the Observations

To illustrate work sampling in its simplest form, assume that a study is made of an operation to determine the percentage of time a worker or group of workers are working. The observations are made at random, and a simple tally is made to indicate whether the operator was working or idle when each observation was made. A sample of the resultant tally of 60 observations made in a given day is found in Figure 14-3. From these observations, note that the operator was working during 49 observations, or 81.7% of the time, and idle during 11, or 18.3%. This is only a single day's observation, and not representative of the total picture. A larger sample would be required before any final conclusions could be made.

Determining Sample Size

It has been indicated that the size of the sample is critical to the accuracy of the study. As in determination of the sample size in stopwatch time study, it is necessary to establish the level of confidence desired in the results. Also, as in the case of time study, a 95% confidence interval is most frequently used. This is related to the fact that ± 2 standard deviations includes approximately 95% of all cases under a normal distribution.

State	Tally	Total	Percent
Working	THL THL THL THL THL THL THL THL THL IIII	49	81.7
Idle	THL THL I	11	18.3
	Total	60	100.0

FIGURE 14-3

Example of Work Sampling Tally

Tables and charts are available for finding the proper size sample for the desired level of accuracy, with a given level of percentage of occurrence of the activity being studied, at the 95% confidence level.[8]   Such tables have been derived from the use of the following equation:

$$S\bar{p} = 2\sqrt{\frac{\bar{p}(1 - \bar{p})}{N}} \qquad \qquad (5)$$

Where:

S = accuracy level desired

$\bar{p} = \dfrac{\text{No. of occurrences observed}}{\text{Total observations}}$ = the percentage of occurrence
of any class of observation being studied; i.e., working, delay

N = the total number of observations

To illustrate the use of Equation (5), use the data in the tally sheet in Figure 14-3. To determine the percentage of idle time of this operation with an accuracy of $\pm$ 2%, and a confidence level of 95%, substitute into Equation (5), with $\bar{p}$ rounded off to 18%, as follows:

Solve Equation (5) for N:

$$S\bar{p} = 2\sqrt{\frac{\bar{p}(1 - \bar{p})}{N}}$$

$$(S\bar{p})^2 = 4\left[\frac{\bar{p}(1 - \bar{p})}{N}\right] = \frac{4\bar{p}(1 - \bar{p})}{N}$$

$$N = \frac{4\bar{p}(1 - \bar{p})}{(S\bar{p})^2}$$

$$= \frac{0.72(1 - 0.18)}{[(0.02)(0.18)]^2} = 45,556 \text{ observations}$$

As can be seen from these computations, the statement that the original sample of 60 observations was inadequate was an understatement, to say the least. After the study has been completed, it is necessary to recheck the data to determine whether the sample size taken was adequate.

Charts are also available from which the degree of accuracy can be determined based on the number of observations and value of $\bar{p}$ at the desired confidence limit. The above analysis was based on a very small sample, and it is possible that later observations would change the situation. To illustrate, if the idle time turned out to be only 10% instead of the initial 18%, the sample size

[8]See Barnes, *op. cit.*, pp. 520–521; or Ralph M. Barnes, *Work Sampling* (2d ed.; New York: John Wiley & Sons, Inc., 1957).

needed to achieve the 2% accuracy would increase to 90,000. This is a large number of observations, but the extreme accuracy demanded in this case is a significant factor. If the accuracy was reduced to 5%, with an idle time percentage of 10%, the number of observations would be reduced to 14,400. The observations in this case require only a determination as to whether the person is working or idle.

Using Work Sampling to Determine Allowances

When making a work sampling study, the idle time may be classified. Each time the operator is idle, the observer will determine the cause and place it into the appropriate class. If, for example, it was ascertained that the idle time of the operator or group of operators observed was 10%, the idle time may have been classified as personal time, 5%; unavoidable delay, 3%; avoidable delay, 2%.

Thus, in establishing the allowances to be added to the normal time, 8% could be used as a figure for this class of work for personal and unavoidable delays. Any allowance for fatigue would be an addition to this figure.

Setting Standards by Work Sampling

Work sampling may also be used to establish time standards. In fact, for certain tasks, work sampling will probably be better than any other method. This is particularly true of long-cycle operations, some group activities, and work like indirect labor. In all these instances, stopwatch time study or other work measurement techniques may not be feasible.

The procedure for making this kind of study is essentially similar to that which has already been described. Only one additional step must be undertaken by the analyst during the course of the study. The analyst must rate the performance each time the operator is observed working. At the end of the work sampling study, the total number of pieces produced during the total time period required for the study must be determined. With this information, it is possible to determine a normal time, and from this, a standard. Suppose that in the course of a work sampling study conducted over a period of two 40-hour weeks, the data shown in Table 14-5 was obtained.

TABLE 14-5

Summary of Work Sampling Study Data

Total time covered by study (minutes)	4,800
Number of pieces produced	5,200
Percent working	84%
Percent idle	16%
Average performance rating	105%
Allowances	10%

From this data it is possible to first calculate the normal time by the following equation:

$$\text{Normal time} = \frac{\begin{pmatrix}\text{Total time}\\\text{of study in}\\\text{minutes}\end{pmatrix} \times \begin{pmatrix}\text{Working time}\\\text{as a decimal}\end{pmatrix} \times \begin{pmatrix}\text{Average}\\\text{performance}\\\text{rating in}\\\text{decimals}\end{pmatrix}}{\text{Total number of pieces produced}} \quad \textbf{(6)}$$

The standard time is computed by adding the allowances, using Equation (3) or (4), cited earlier. Substituting the data from Table 14-5 into Equation (6), we have:

$$\text{Normal time} = \frac{4,800 \times .84 \times 1.05}{5,200}$$

$$= 0.814 \text{ minutes}$$

Applying the allowances by means of Equation (4), the standard time is computed as follows:

$$\text{Standard time} = 0.814 \times \frac{100}{100 - 10}$$

$$= 0.904 \text{ minutes}$$

Work Sampling vs. Time Study

Work sampling has the advantage of being applicable to certain work which is not amenable to time study. In addition, work sampling is less complicated, and does not require the trained observer needed in time study and other work measurement techniques. The cost of a work sample is typically lower than stopwatch time study. This lower cost may result from the smaller amount of time involved, because a single observer can study a number of workers, and because no equipment is required. The fact that the analyst is not present for a long period of time, as he must be for a stopwatch time study, eliminates much of the psychological barrier in work measurement. In fact, in work sampling, since the observations are made randomly, and are brief, the worker frequently is not aware that he is being observed.

There are, of course, certain negative aspects of work sampling as compared with other methods. The operation is not subdivided in the same details as in stopwatch time study or MTM. There is no elemental breakdown or description of the method used. Therefore, a separate analysis is needed to acquire this information. If the proper methods for selecting the sample are not followed, the results of the study will not be a true picture of the actual conditions. It is also possible that too small a sample is used which can cause errors in the accuracy of the results. If the operators spot the observer before he observes them, it is possible they can induce errors in the results. They may change their normal pattern so the observation shows they are working more frequently than is normal, and they may signal other workers of the approach of the observer. These possible sources of error must be considered in planning a work sample.

PHYSIOLOGICAL WORK MEASUREMENT

Because of the subjective nature of some aspects of the more widely used work measurement techniques, a number of individuals have sought ways to make the results more objective. A promising approach to attain this objectivity is utilization of physiological measures. There are a variety of such measures which can be used to evaluate the work performance of an individual. The two which seem to be the most promising from a work measurement standpoint are oxygen consumption and heart rate.

Oxygen Consumption

The measurement of oxygen consumption is a way to determine the energy expenditure of an individual. Oxygen consumption is the amount of oxygen a person uses out of the air he breathes. The amount of oxygen in the inspired air is known. By collecting samples of the expired air and analyzing it, the difference between the amount of oxygen present in the sample and in the inspired air can be determined. This difference is the amount consumed by an individual. It is usually stated as a volume of oxygen in terms of liters per minute.

Measurement of oxygen consumption requires the use of equipment which can measure the total volume of air inspired and the volume expired and can collect the expired air. The equipment is usually cumbersome, and the individual must be connected with it in some way to permit collection of expired air. Most of this equipment is heavy and some permits virtually no movement at all. Newer equipment which weighs only 5 1/2 pounds is available from the Max Planck Institute of Germany. This can be carried on the back and permits freedom of movement, but the added weight does change the working conditions.

Oxygen consumption can be converted to energy expenditure measured by the caloric output. Energy expediture is usually expressed by the kilocalorie. The conversion is done on a factor of 5.0 as an average value which represents the caloric equivalent of 1 liter of oxygen consumed per minute. Thus, for moderate exercise, 1 liter O_2/min. = 5 kcal/min.

There is no precise standard for normal performance that is equivalent to the standard of walking at the rate of 3 miles an hour as used for time study ratings. The most widely accepted standard of energy expenditure is in the range of 5.0 to 7.5 kcal/min., previously identified (p. 327) as moderate work. In fact, the lower end of that range is considered by consensus as the level which should represent the average level for an eight-hour workday. It has been found that the rate of energy expenditure at the 3 mile an hour walking speed is close to this level (5.2 kcal/min. to be precise).[9] The relationship between performance

[9]B. Moores, "A Comparison of Work-Load using Physiological and Time Study Assessments," *Ergonomics*, Vol. XIII, No. 6 (November, 1970), p. 769, citing a comment by K. F. H. Murrell.

rating and walking speeds is asserted to be closely correlated at the lower limits,[10] and others have concluded that there is a close relationship between performance ratings and oxygen consumption.[11] Moores found that time study analysts have a tendency to underestimate the actual expenditure in their performance ratings. In addition, he noted that at higher levels of energy expenditure the ratings were increasingly below what they should have been to be a true representation of the work rate.[12] While this is a matter for concern and indicates a need for improvement in the accuracy of subjective performance ratings, it is perhaps not as serious as it appears on the surface. In the first place, most work performed today is at the lower end of the energy consumption spectrum. In other words, most work falls into the light or moderate category, and the corresponding levels of energy expenditure do not exceed the 5 kcal/min. level very often. This, the errors are not so great at lower levels as at the infrequently found higher ones. Secondly, the 5 kcal level is an average, and allowances for fatigue will be added on to the normal times raising the time allotted. Finally, the actual performance of the task is seldom consistent; there are interspersed periods of idleness and less demanding activities.

The time study analyst is aware of the failings of the normal performance rating process. It is for this reason that the interest in physiological evaluations of work has increased so markedly in recent years. To date, the major developments have been in other countries, primarily Great Britain, Germany, and Scandinavia, however, there is an acceleration of interest in a variety of universities and industrial organizations in the United States.

Heart Rate

Heart rate is a second measure used to determine the physiological cost of performing a task. When a person changes from an inactive to an active state, his heart rate immediately begins to rise, and there is a close relationship between the level it reaches and the length and severity of the activity. Obviously this indicates an increase in the physiological responses of the body, and thus may be an indication of the physiological cost of the particular activity. The advantage of using heart rate as a measure of the cost of performing a particular task as compared to energy expenditure is its relative ease of measurement. Heart rate can be measured directly or by means of electronic devices which convert the electrical impulses of each beat and indicate a rate or record it on a moving scaled tape. There are both advantages and disadvantages of heart rate as an indicator of physiological stress when compared to oxygen consumption. In addition to the advantage of ease of measurement, heart rate is more indicative of the total physiological effect of an activity than is oxygen consumption. For example, Brouha found that in certain types of activity, oxygen

---

[10]Barnes, *Motion and Time Study: Design and Measurement of Work, op. cit.*, p. 555.

[11]N. J. Aquilano, "Work Physiology: A Physiological Evaluation of Time Standards and Work-Rest Design for Moderate to Strenuous Work" (Doctoral dissertation, U.C.L.A., 1968), p. 37.

[12]Moores, *op. cit.*

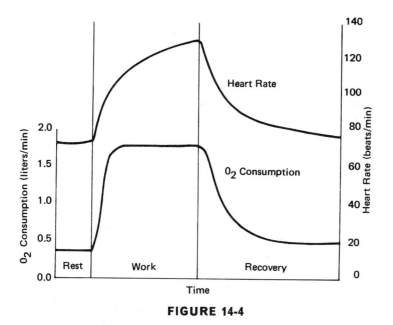

FIGURE 14-4

Comparisons of Changes in Oxygen Consumption and Heart Rate
Before, During, and After Submaximal Work

consumption reached a steady state during exercise, while heart rate continued
to climb throughout the four-minute period. He also found that following the
work period, the oxygen consumption returned to pre-exercise levels quickly,
while heart rate did not recover even after an hour.[13] It has been found by a
number of studies that the relationship between oxygen consumption and heart
rate is virtually linear for individuals up to maximal work levels. A typical
relationship between these two measures is found in Figure 14-4. This is for a
task falling into what has previously been classified as a heavy work load.

The relationship of heart rate and oxygen consumption is for a single individual. Although a specific relationship can be determined for any individual,
many factors have a bearing on the responses of each person. For example, the
physical fitness of the person studied will have an effect. Persons in good condition will start with lower heart rates, and will not reach as high a level during the
physical activity as will those less fit. In addition, a well-trained worker will
usually require less energy expenditure than an inexperienced worker, as measured by oxygen consumption. Sex, age, body weight, and body surface also
have a bearing on the energy expenditure of an individual. Thus, it is necessary
to determine the relationship between oxygen consumption and heart rate for
each individual. Once this is done, however, it then becomes possible to measure
the physiological cost of different types of work or different job designs for that
individual simply by measuring the heart rate.

---

[13]Lucien Brouha, *Physiology in Industry* (2d ed.; New York: Pergamon Press, 1967), p. 6.

It is important to note that total physiological cost is the most reliable measure of the stress imposed by any activity. However, in situations where it is impractical to measure heart rate during the actual work period, the recovery heart rate may serve as an acceptable substitute.[14]

The suggestion has been made that heart rate is a more accurate indicator of the amount of work an individual can perform without undue fatigue.[15] Generally, a person can sustain a heart rate of no more than 120 beats per minute throughout an eight-hour period. Approximate ranges of heart rate as compared to energy expenditure are as follows:[16]

Energy Expenditure kcal/min	Heart Rate Beats/min
2.5– 5.0	75–100
5.0– 7.5	100–125
7.5–10.0	125–150
10.0–12.5	150–175

Heart rate is also considered to be a potentially more valid indicator of fatigue than oxygen consumption. This is particularly noticeable in the recovery cost. As work increases, the recovery cost measured by heart rate becomes a progressively larger proportion of the total cost of work plus recovery.[17]

Not all researchers accept heart rate as an accurate determinant of total work cost. As suggested, it has some advantages over other measures. Perhaps the most important of these is its ease of measurement. At present, it is still considered best to use both heart rate and oxygen consumption for physiological work evaluation purposes. However, in certain situations heart rate may be adequate for determining physiological cost for an individual.

Effects of Environmental Stress

Not all work is performed under ideal environmental conditions. Many original studies of the physiological cost of a particular task were performed under laboratory conditions where factors of temperature and humidity were controlled at an ideal level. When the environmental conditions are not maintained at an ideal level, the physiological load is increased.

When the temperature and the humidity are increased, certain physiological responses indicate an increase in the physiological cost. Heart rate increases

---

[14]M. E. Maxfield and L. Brouha, "Validity of Heart Rate as an Indicator of Cardiac Strain," *Journal of Applied Physiology*, Vol. XVIII, No. 1 (November, 1963), pp. 1099–1104.

[15]E. D. Michael, Jr., K. E. Hutton, and Steven M. Horvath, "Cardiorespiratory Responses During Prolonged Exercise," *Journal of Applied Physiology*, Vol. XVI, No. 6 (October, 1961), pp. 997–1000.

[16]E. H. Christensen, "Physiological Evaluation of Work in Nykroppa Iron Works," in: W. Floyd and A. T. Welford (eds.), *Symposium on Fatigue* (London: H. K. Lewis & Co., 1953), pp. 93–108.

[17]Maxfield and Brouha, *op. cit.*

significantly with such changes in the physical environment.[18] The change in oxygen consumption is not significant, however. The effect is particularly noticeable in the recovery period where the heart rate decreases very slowly. In one experiment, subjects performed known work loads of a moderate level for 30 minutes. Then the work load was increased to a heavy level for four additional minutes. These studies were carried out at two levels of temperature and humidity; first at 72°F and 50 percent relative humidity and then at 90°F and 82 percent relative humidity.[19] The pattern of oxygen consumption and heart rate was similar to that illustrated in Figure 14-4 throughout the 30 minutes of moderate exercise. During the four minutes of heavy activity, both increased sharply. The recovery period found the oxygen consumption returning to resting level in about 25 minutes. On the other hand, the heart rate had not returned to its original level even after a 65 minute recovery period. This conforms with the normal pattern noted above. The different environmental conditions made no significant difference in the oxygen consumption values at work or during recovery. On the other hand, there was a noticeable increase in heart rate at the higher temperature and humidity.

Two other studies further illustrate the effects of such environmental conditions. In the first study, the subjects were asked to perform a standard amount of work for ten cycles of five minutes' duration each, at two different temperatures. In both cases they were allowed to rest after each exercise period until their heart rates returned to 110 beats/min. The results of this study are illustrated schematically in Figure 14-5. This shows the progressive physiological cost of performing a task under stressful environmental conditions.

The second study cited also showed the effect on heart rate for a standard work load for varying environmental conditions. The work was performed under three different environments. These are listed below:

1. Dry bulb temperature: 80°F
   Relative humidity: 60%
2. Dry bulb temperature: 90°F
   Relative humidity: 65%
3. Dry bulb temperature: 95°F
   Relative humidity: 90%

The results of this study, shown in Figure 14-6, indicate the stress of the environmental conditions caused a significant increase in the physiological cost. The particular effect of increased humidity can be seen in condition three. This again shows the heavy physiological load which is placed on an individual who must work in an environment of this type. The usual techniques of work measurement do not serve as an adequate measure of these stresses. In determining the amount of fatigue allowance which is applicable and the length of rest periods

---

[18]Lucien Brouha, "Physiological Approach to Problems of Work Measurement," *Proceedings Ninth Annual Industrial Engineering Institute* (Los Angeles-Berkeley: University of California, February, 1957), p. 13.

[19]*Ibid.*

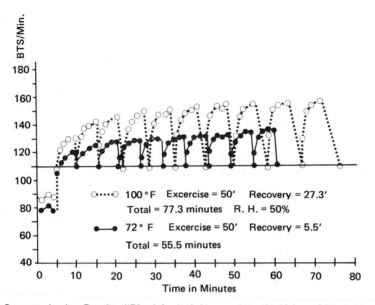

Source: Lucien Brouha, "Physiological Approach to Problems of Work Measurement," *Proceedings Ninth Industrial Engineering Institute* (Los Angeles-Berkeley: University of California, February, 1957), p. 14.

FIGURE 14-5

Average Heart Rates for Ten Work Cycles at Two Temperatures

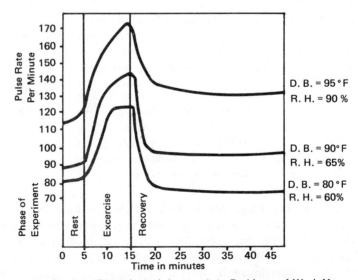

Source: Lucien Brouha, "Physiological Approach to Problems of Work Measurement," *Proceedings Ninth Industrial Engineering Institute* (Los Angeles-Berkeley: University of California, February, 1957), p. 14.

FIGURE 14-6

Heart Rate Before, During, and After a Standard
Exercise for Various Environmental Conditions

required, it is necessary to measure the physiological cost, with particular emphasis on the recovery time.

While the emphasis has been on the effects of temperature and humidity on the worker, it should not be ignored that other aspects of the physical environment may also increase the physiological cost to the individual. Recent evidence of the debilitating effects of air pollution confirm this fact. It is certainly necessary to attempt to make some evaluation of the other aspects of the physical environment in determining the safe work load.[20]

Physiological Measures as a Basis for Fatigue Allowances and Rest Periods

In determining a work standard, certain allowances must be added to the normal time. One of the categories of allowances used is for fatigue. There is not a clear definition of what constitutes fatigue. Karpovich points out that industrial fatigue may result from a variety of conditions. He classifies them into three groups:

1. Physical and Social Conditions at Work; Nature of Work.
2. The Worker Himself.
3. Home and Community Conditions.[21]

This substantiates the implication made in the earlier discussion of fatigue that there is more than physical work load involved. However, in heavy physical activity, fatigue is an important element. Physiological evaluations may be valuable aids in determining the amount of fatigue which results from a given task. The added stress from undesirable environmental conditions is one instance. Tasks requiring high concentrations of mental effort or close attention; being performed under hazardous circumstances; or having limited, but concentrated motions may also require a fatigue allowance. These latter types of situations are more difficult to assess by physiological means.

In most work situations, the problem of fatigue is combated by means of rest periods. Where the physiological load is severe, these rest periods are usually more frequent and of longer duration. In some instances, when environmental conditions are poor, the rest periods are taken in controlled areas, such as air conditioned rooms. Determination of rest periods is seldom based on a physiological evaluation. It is well known that when a person performs at a high level of physical activity for an extended period of time, he reaches a point where his body operates on a physiological debt basis. It is important under these circumstances that the individual be given an opportunity to rest and repay this debt. Indications of the physiological debt would be found when an individual's oxygen consumption or heart rate do not return to normal after a short rest. Because the individual has a certain reserve limit, the severity of the work and

[20]Lucien Brouha, *Physiology in Industry, op. cit.*, Chapter 2–3.
[21]Peter V. Karpovich, *Physiology of Muscular Activity* (5th ed.; Philadelphia: W. B. Saunders Co., 1959), p. 243.

the length of time which he is exposed to this load will determine when it is used up and he goes on a debt basis.[22]

There is some information with respect to continuous vs. discontinuous work which is related to the rest period question. The results are not conclusive, because each study has been made with different assumptions. Some studies have found that the best method, from a physiological cost viewpoint, was to perform the assigned task at a constant speed rather than on a work-rest cycle basis. It is believed that these findings resulted because workers usually set their own pace at a lower level than is required.[23] Other studies have found the work-rest cycle to be physiologically less costly.[24] Part of the disagreement may result from the fact that different types of work were used.

The use of physiological data in work measurement is in an early stage of development. Companies, such as DuPont and Eastman Kodak, have been using it in a limited way. Barnes illustrates an experimental technique for setting time standards by physiological methods.[25] As more work is done in this direction, techniques will probably improve. Many developments in both the equipment available and in the analysis of the data have taken place in the last few years. It is to be expected that this trend will accelerate.

Ultimately it is to be hoped that a stage will be reached where the use of physiological methods will supplement present work measurement techniques in achieving a true measure of what may constitute a "fair day's work." Only in this way will the subjective factors of work measurement be overcome and the establishment of the correct time for a work task be achieved. Then management and the workers can be assured that the task is being performed at its utmost efficiency, and at a minimum of physiological cost to the individual worker.

SUMMARY

Work measurement consists of the techniques used to establish a standard time for performing a task. It is necessary for any type of enterprise to develop some form of time standards, whether by a formal program or some informal method based on custom or past usage.

The most widely utilized method of work measurement is stopwatch time study. The primary tool is the decimal minute stopwatch, although other methods for determining times are used occasionally. Stopwatch time study procedure is divided into six steps: planning the study, dividing operations into elements, reading and recording, determining the number of cycles to be timed, rating the operator's performance, and computing and analyzing study data.

Each of these stages involves a number of individual steps. In planning the study, the analyst must make sure the operation is ready to be studied, secure the

---

[22]E. A. Müller, "The Physiological Basis of Rest Pauses in Heavy Work," *Quarterly Journal of Experimental Physiology*, Vol. XXXVIII, No. 4 (1953), p. 205.

[23]Müller, *Ibid.*; and E. H. Christensen, "Speed of Work," *Ergonomics*, Vol. V, No. 1 (January, 1962), pp. 7–13.

[24]Aquilano, *op. cit.*

[25]Barnes, *Motion and Time Study: Design and Measurement of Work, op. cit.*, pp. 560–562.

cooperation of the foreman in the department involved, and learn as much as possible about the operation to be studied. He must then observe the operation to verify the method and other preliminary information acquired.

The process for dividing the operations into elements is discussed. Reasons for elemental breakdown and guidelines for determining elements are presented.

The next step in stopwatch time study is reading the watch and recording the time. Three methods of timing are discussed: continuous, repetitive or snap-back, and accumulative.

It is also necessary to determine the number of cycles to be timed in order to achieve the desired level of accuracy and confidence. One commonly used equation for this purpose is illustrated. A significant aspect of stopwatch time study is the establishment of a performance rating by the observer. The rating procedure is primarily a subjective judgment on the part of the observer. A number of different approaches which attempt to improve the accuracy of ratings are examined.

Upon completion of the observations, it is necessary for the analyst to perform certain computations to arrive at the standard time. First a time must be selected from the numerous times recorded for each element. The most frequently used method for determining this representative time is the arithmetic mean. When the select time is calculated, this time must be normalized by applying the performance rating to it. To the normal time must be added the allowances for personal time, unavoidable delays, and fatigue. This results in the standard time.

A second work measurement method is elemental standard data systems. Such data are developed from large numbers of time studies. The elements are standardized to the highest degree possible. Thus, as time studies are made of these standard elements, the data can be collected, and eventually the average standards for the various elements determined. It is then only necessary to use such times to determine the standard for any job by summing the elemental standards previously developed.

A third technique of work measurement, motion-time data systems, is also examined. To illustrate these systems, a detailed study is made of the most widely used one, MTM. MTM uses a series of therblig-like motions for which normal time values have been developed from a large number of filmed operations. The normal time for an operation is determined by analyzing the motions used and the conditions under which they are made, and applying the time values previously developed. The relative value of MTM as compared to stopwatch time study is presented.

Work sampling is a technique based on random sampling. The procedure for tallying the observations, determining the sample size, using work sampling to determine allowances, and setting standards by work sampling are described. The relative merits of work sampling as compared to time study are examined.

A final technique of work measurement discussed is the use of physiological response factors to determine the level of worker performance. The aim of this relatively new approach is to make work measurement more objective. Numerous measures are available, but two are viewed as most useful: oxygen consumption and heart rate. A variety of examples of the use of these two measures as means of determining the physiological cost of a task are cited. The relationship of these measures is also examined. Particular attention is given to the effects of environmental stress on the physiological cost and on work performance. An evaluation of the use of physiological measurements as a basis for fatigue allowances and rest periods is also included.

While it is recognized that physiological work measurement is at an early stage of development, it has practical applications at this time. It offers promise of supplementing present work measurement techniques to the extent that an objective determination of the most efficient and physiologically economical way of performing a task can be made.

QUESTIONS FOR DISCUSSION AND ANALYSIS

1. What is work measurement? In what ways are time standards valuable to management?

2. What are the steps in the stopwatch time study procedure?

3. Discuss the practice of dividing operations into elements, including the reasons for elemental breakdown and guidelines for determining elements.

4. Compare continuous timing with repetitive timing.

5. What is the significance of the number of cycles timed in a stopwatch time study? How is the proper number of cycles determined?

6. Describe performance rating. Why is it necessary? What difficulties are encountered in performance rating?

7. Define select time, normal time, and standard time.

8. Evaluate MTM as a means of establishing work standards in comparison to stopwatch time study. Give particular attention to the potential areas of application, accuracy, cost, and worker acceptance.

9. Describe the work sampling process. What assumptions must be inherent in making a work sampling study?

10. Under what circumstances is work sampling preferred to stopwatch time study as a means of establishing work standards?

11. Discuss the potential of using physiological measurements in work measurement. Compare the use of oxygen consumption with heart rate as indicators of the physiological cost of performing a task.

12. Why are the effects of environmental conditions significant to the process of work measurement? Illustrate.

PROBLEMS

1. Below are listed the times recorded on a continuous reading basis for ten cycles of a two-element operation. The performance ratings for each element are also

indicated. If the total allowances are 20%, calculate the normal time and the standard time for each element, as well as the standard time for the total operation.

	1	2	3	4	5	6	7	8	9	10	Rating
Element 1	.11	.33	.51	.69	.89	1.11	1.27	1.47	1.67	1.86	90%
Element 2	.23	.42	.61	.78	.99	1.20	1.38	1.56	1.76	1.95	110%

2. You have obtained the following data from a work sampling study during a 40 hour week:

Idle time	20%
Performance rating	108%
Total parts produced	1,200
Allowances	15%

Determine the standard time per part.

3. Determine the required number of observations in a work sampling study at 95% confidence and a ±5% degree of accuracy. Use Equation (5) with $\bar{p} = 15\%$.

SELECTED ADDITIONAL READINGS

Aquilano, N. J. "Work Physiology: A Physiological Evaluation of Time Standards and Work-Rest Design for Moderate to Strenuous Work." Doctoral dissertation, U.C.L.A., 1968.

Barnes, Ralph M. *Motion and Time Study: Design and Measurement of Work*, 6th ed. New York: John Wiley & Sons, Inc., 1968.

——————. *Work Sampling*, 2d ed. New York: John Wiley & Sons, Inc., 1957.

Brouha, Lucien. *Physiology in Industry*, 2d ed. New York: Pergamon Press, 1967.

Floyd, W. F., and A. T. Welford (eds.). *Symposium on Fatigue.* London: H. K. Lewis & Co., Ltd., 1953.

Gomberg, W. *A Trade Union Analysis of Time Study*, 2d ed. Englewood Cliffs: Prentice-Hall, Inc., 1954.

Karpovich, Peter V. *Physiology of Muscular Activity*, 5th ed. Philadelphia: W. B. Saunders Co., 1959.

Lowry, S. M., H. B. Maynard, and G. J. Stegemerten. *Time and Motion Study*, 3d ed. New York: McGraw-Hill Book Co., 1940.

Maynard, Harold B., G. J. Stegemerten, and John L. Schwab. *Methods-Time Measurement.* New York: McGraw-Hill Book Co., 1948.

Müller, E. A. "The Physiological Basis of Rest Pauses in Heavy Work." *Quarterly Journal of Experimental Physiology*, Vol. XXXVIII, No. 4 (1953), pp. 205-215.

Mundel, Marvin E. *Motion and Time Study*, 4th ed. Englewood Cliffs: Prentice-Hall, Inc., 1970.

Nadler, Gerald. *Work Design*, rev. ed. Homewood, Illinois: Richard D. Irwin, Inc., 1970.

Niebel, Benjamin W. *Motion and Time Study*, 5th ed. Homewood, Illinois: Richard D. Irwin, Inc., 1972.

PART

Functioning and Control of the Operations System

Methods available for synthesizing the approaches to the individual problem areas are viewed in this section. Major segments of the operations system must be brought together to achieve coordinated performance. In addition to control of the individual subsystems, there are integrated control techniques. It is the purpose of the control systems to assure that the entire system functions as desired. Achievement of this goal requires an output when it is needed, where it is needed, at the required level of quality, and at an acceptable cost. A final perspective views the present and future status of operations management.

15 | # Logistics Systems

In the control of the operations function of any enterprise, the operations manager must be certain that the output of the system, whether it be a product or a service, is available at the point where it is needed, when it is needed, and at the most economical cost. While industrial logistics is of relatively recent origin, it has long been of considerable importance in the military. The primary meaning of logistics from the military point of view is the supplying, transporting, and quartering or storage of personnel or of equipment. Industrial logistics is concerned with the coordination of production or operations, marketing, and transportation. In attempting to supply users or customers, industrial enterprises view logistics as coordination of transportation, production and inventory planning and control, and storage. In other types of enterprises, logistics may be viewed as encompassing all of the activities related to the physical distribution or delivery of the product or service to the user. Logistics is viewed here as an enterprise subsystem concerned with the interrelated activities of the operations, marketing, and transportation subsystems. Involved are those activities necessary for the flow of all inputs, product or service, from their initial source through to the user of the output.

COMPONENTS OF THE LOGISTICS SYSTEM

Since the logistics system can be viewed as an open system from the definition in Chapter 2, it will have interchanges with the environment in which it exists. The components of the logistics system can be a part of either the internal or external environment of the enterprise. The internal components are those which are under some degree of control by the enterprise management. Those which are largely beyond any managerial control may be viewed as a part of the external environment. For convenience, the components of the logistics system will be grouped into these two categories for examination.

Internal Environment

Those components of the logistics system categorized as a part of the internal environment are largely in the areas of production or operations, and marketing. Other organization subsystems, considered as service or information systems, are also included. All activities from the receipt of the inputs to departure of the transformed outputs are involved. Acquiring inputs and certain activities designed to place outputs into the hands of the customers or users also belong in this category of components.

Production or Operations Components. Among the activities which may be included in this category is the overall production or operations planning and control function. This function can involve many complex activities and many elements of this function will be examined in the following two chapters.

INVENTORIES. The primary logistics activities in the production and operations area are related to inventory. Involved are the establishing of the needed amounts of inputs, and the requesting that they be ordered. Included also is the in-plant handling of all inventories. A final aspect of inventory involved in the logistics system is the finished parts inventory. The inventory control problem is an extremely complex one and it requires a separate treatment. This detailed examination will be deferred until the next chapter. However, it is impossible to discuss the logistics system without a recognition of the importance of inventories.

WAREHOUSING AND STORAGE. Logistics is concerned with those activities involved in the movement of the final output to the users. In the manufacturing enterprise especially, accumulations of basic inputs, partially processed inputs, and transformed inputs in the form of the final output will inevitably occur. The warehousing and storage of these inventories are critical activities. Warehousing can be viewed as a discrete function distinct from production or operations, or as a part of the procurement and marketing functions.

SCHEDULING. The scheduling of the total operations of the enterprise is naturally an element in the logistics system. Assuring that the goal of getting the output to the users at the time desired is achieved is a function of the scheduling activity. Scheduling will involve not only the setting of a timetable for the processing of the inputs, but also the determination of the time when inputs must be procured, as well as the timing of the completion of the output for placement in the finished goods inventory.

PROCESSING FACILITIES. The processing facilities must be of adequate size so that the capacity of the system can satisfy the demands for the system output. The capacity requirements and the techniques for making the related decisions have already been discussed in Chapter 8. Another significant aspect of this relationship is the location of the processing. The location of the processing facilities has a strong influence on the logistics system. The cost of the physical distribution of the output will obviously be related to the location. The effectiveness with which the distribution is carried out is also related to location of the processing facilities. In addition, the location of warehousing and storage facilities must also be a consideration in the logistics system.

Marketing Components. These components are concerned with all of the activities related to the creation of the demand for the output of the enterprise such as selling, promotional activities including advertising, and servicing of the customer to insure his satisfaction with the product or service. Physical distribution of the output is largely governed by the channels of distribution which the enterprise uses.

CHANNELS OF DISTRIBUTION. A wide variety of distribution channels can be employed for moving the output from the processing point to the point of use. The most frequently found channel is from processor to wholesaler to retailer to user. The number of wholesalers can be more than one in some instances, but essentially the channel is as listed. At each of these points there will be a warehouse or storage unit. The establishment of the particular channel to be utilized is an internal management decision, but the operations of the elements of the movement beyond the enterprise itself may not be entirely under management's control.

Other channels of distribution which are common are processor to consumer, and processor to retailer to consumer. Whatever the channel or channels used by an enterprise, the primary purpose from a logistics standpoint is to assure that the customer is being served. The management must determine the service level it wishes to achieve. That is, while it is the ultimate desire of any enterprise to be able to provide a level of service which will insure that the customer will always be able to acquire the product or service, practically speaking, this level of service is not possible. To achieve this ultimate in customer service would necessitate the carrying of unduly large inventories at all points in the distribution chain. This large inventory would be the only way to assure that there were never any out-of-stock situations. Obviously, the result would be excessively high inventory carrying costs. Thus, a level which balances the service and the costs that is attainable within the physical and economic constraints which exist must be determined. In the selection of the distribution channels to be used, this is the principal goal. While each level in a distribution channel wants to have the item demanded immediately available, no level wishes to accept the responsibility for maintaining the necessary inventory. The usual picture is that the processor must accept this responsibility by maintaining a sufficient stock of output at a point near to the other elements in the channel to provide the desired level of service.

Therefore, it is the function of the logistics system to select the channel or channels of distribution which will provide the desired level of service at the lowest cost possible. The determination of the inventory level required at the various warehousing or storage points is necessary. Consideration of the transport activities to assure that the needed quantities are moved to the appropriate locations at the time when they are needed is also required.

CUSTOMER SERVICE. The need for the determination of a level of service has already been mentioned in connection with the channels of distribution. The determination of a service level is the most important measure of effectiveness of a logistics system. This is the end result of all of the logistical activities. The service level determined must be achieved at a cost acceptable to the enterprise as well.

CREATION OF DEMAND. An important element in logistics from the marketing side is the creation and maintenance of a demand for the output of the enterprise. The purpose of the logistics system is to satisfy this demand. Thus, without the demand there would be no need for a logistics system. The major activities which create demand are sales, advertising, and other promotional activities. These elements can be considered as only peripheral to the logistics system, since they are not directly involved in the physical distribution of the output to the user. However, as just stated, it is only as a result of demand creation that the necessity of moving the output arises. Therefore, the importance of demand creation is undeniable.

OTHER MARKETING ELEMENTS. The relationship of the other marketing elements to the logistics system are more indirect. However, some may play a role and should be mentioned. Among these are price and product line mix. It is almost impossible to determine the relationship of elements like price and product line mix to the logistics function because they are so complex. These factors are frequently beyond the control of the management of the enterprise. External environmental forces such as competition may play a decisive role in shaping the influence of these elements.

A final comment regarding the marketing components is in order. While most enterprises have a marketing function, there are some where no such function is needed. This is primarily true of nonprofit enterprises and other service oriented firms. For example, it would be difficult to identify a function in the military which parallels that of marketing. To a lesser degree, the same statement may apply to a hospital or a state university. On the other hand, there is no questioning the fact that these enterprises have logistical problems, and hence must develop a logistics system.

Procurement Components. The procurement function is probably the most important activity in the physical supply side, or the material management phase, of logistics. Procurement is concerned with acquiring the inputs of the operations system and the actions involved in moving them to the processing phase of that system. The acquisition or purchasing of the system inputs is a highly specialized activity in most enterprises. It includes the selection of the sources, the actual purchasing, and the overseeing of the necessary transportation arrangements to get the inputs into the operation facility. This latter activity is carried on in conjunction with the traffic function of the enterprise.

Purchasing activities are determined entirely by the needs of the operations segment. The function of this component is to establish the needed inputs, and to set the schedule for their need. All of this will probably result from the forecasts developed as a result of the demand creation activities. Purchasing is notified of the needs, and takes action to supply what is requested. Purchasing is closely interrelated with other components of the logistics system. Purchasing is a service component to these other parts of the system. Because of this service relationship, the procurement function is frequently omitted from a discussion of logistics. The importance of this activity, however, dictates that it be included. The proper performance of this function can bear heavily on the total effectiveness of the logistics system. Since the procurement of the inputs is really the beginning of the delivery of the outputs to the users, efficient performance is vital.

Information System Components. The primary function of a management information system is to transmit data quickly to the managers, so that the information can be used for control and decision-making purposes. The principal areas of concern for the logistics information system are in relation to the processing of the orders to the suppliers of the inputs and the orders from the users of the outputs. The information system provides the necessary communication between the logistics system and the functional areas of the enterprises with which it relates.

The logistics information system should be designed to facilitate the receipt and transmission of all pertinent information and to permit the coordinated action of the various segments of the logistics system. The result will be various actions such as the customer order forms, replenishment orders, inventory records, status reports, processing orders, and other related communications. The characteristics of a good logistics information system are essentially the same as for any management information system. Information about the current status of orders being processed, purchase orders, and market information needs to be available immediately. Thus, the internal logistics system must be an "on-line" system. The ready availability of information to evaluate and measure the performance of the logistics system is vital. Only in this way can the control of this system be achieved.

Traffic Components. The traffic or transportation segment of the logistics system is obviously highly significant. Of course, much of the transportation activities will be external to the enterprise. Therefore, management has little or no control over the operation of the means of transportation. However, internally there are many aspects of the traffic function that have a bearing on the performance of the logistics system.

SELECTION OF METHOD OF TRANSPORT. The traffic section of the enterprise can play a large role in the effectiveness and in the cost of the movement of both the inputs and of the outputs. Management can choose the particular mode of transport to be used in the movement; including movement from vendor to processor, from processor to warehouse, and from warehouse to user. It is immaterial who is paying for the move. What is most important is to guarantee that the most efficient and economical method is utilized. From an internal viewpoint, in addition to cost, the traffic manager is interested in speed; the service availability, dependability, and frequency; as well as the capability of the carrier to handle the particular commodity class. This latter point not only refers to the physical ability of the carrier, but any legal restriction on a particular type of carrier in regard to the commodity involved.

MATERIAL HANDLING. Where physical goods are involved, it is usual to find a great deal of in-process movement required. Recall that in the discussion of the different types of production systems, the intermittent system was identified as one where the product requires a number of moves during the processing. Thus, in such a system the problems of material handling will bear heavily on the efficient functioning of the logistics system.

The logistics system will have interrelationships with systems of the enterprise other than those already mentioned. For instance, because cost is such an important criterion of the effective functioning of the logistics system, there will be an interrelationship with the cost control system. There will be interfaces with other subsystems of the enterprise as well. However, these interfaces will be indirect when compared with the interfaces between the components of production, marketing, procurement, and traffic. The important thing in relation to the internal environmental components of the logistics system is to recognize their interdependence. If the logistics function is viewed as a system, this recognition is assured. The coordination of the activities and components of this system will guarantee that it is efficiently operated.

External Environment

Certain components of a logistics system are largely or possibly completely beyond the control of the management of the enterprise. These are, therefore, considered as a part of the external environment. The general areas of these components are the source of inputs; the market conditions which prevail, such as the degree of competition, market locations, and demand conditions; distribution components in relation to the external links in the channels of distribution; and certain elements of the transportation system.

Input Source Components. In the procurement function it is assumed that the inputs will be acquired from the best source possible with regard to cost and delivery. In many cases, the choice of sources is limited and occasionally no choice is possible. Frequently, because the inputs are only available in one place (this is particularly applicable to certain raw materials), the problems of procurement of the inputs are governed by the enterprise's location. In such circumstances, the logistical decisions are beyond the control of the enterprise. These decisions are dictated by the location; and such things as delivery times, cost, and means of transport are usually dependent on where the inputs are available.

Market Conditions Components. In the process of the physical distribution of the output of an enterprise, it is certain that there will be a variety of market conditions which will prevail that will be beyond the control of the enterprise management. Even though they may be beyond the direct control of management, it is important to recognize these components in making the logistics decisions.

DEGREE OF COMPETITION. Attempts to regulate the competitive environment to the advantage of the enterprise are not peculiar to the logistics system. Any enterprise will constantly consider this environment in many of its management decisions. Among the logistically related responses which are made to adjust to the competitive environment are those which production and operations management must make in regard to the cost of producing the output and to the quality of the output. The most important responses will be in the marketing segment, however. Decisions related to price, promotion, and the like will bear on the competitive situation. Of course, these decisions are made internally, and have been briefly discussed. However, they are made in view of the circumstances found in the competitive environment which is the result of the actions of other enterprises. This aspect is not under internal control.

MARKET LOCATIONS. To a large extent, at least in the United States, a certain degree of regional specialization of industrial activity has developed. There are a variety of reasons for this. Some are historical, some culturally related, and some are the result of nearness to a source of supply or vital transportation facilities. As a result, the market for certain types of goods and services tends to be concentrated. Another reason for a concentration of markets is the relatively high level of population in certain geographic regions; e.g., northeast, north central, Gulf coast, and Southern California. As a result, the largest market for a good or service tends to be concentrated in a few areas. Beyond these areas the market will probably be widely distributed geographically. The locations of the primary markets for the output of an enterprise will influence the functioning of the logistics system materially. As one example, the mode of transportation utilized may be limited as a result of the location of the market. The problems in serving a concentrated market will probably be less than those attached to serving a widely dispersed market. Most of the internal problems involved have already been alluded to in the earlier discussion. Certain external factors which are not under direct control of the enterprise must be considered as well.

DEMAND CONDITIONS. Certain aspects of demand have been reviewed in connection with the activities involved in the creation of demand. As was mentioned at that time, demand considerations can be viewed as peripheral to the logistics function. Nevertheless, demand is a concern in the accomplishment of the physical distribution activities. Many aspects of the demand conditions are not within management control. Economic conditions will play a large part in the final demand. Such influences on the final demand will be external to the enterprise, but will be significant in many internal actions. The anticipated demand for the output will be reflected in the sales forecast. In the discussion of forecasting in Chapter 9, the effect that the forecast may have on various units of the enterprise was pointed out. The forecast will be a major determinant in many of the internal logistics decisions. The size of inventories, the quantity to be procured and produced, the requirements for warehousing and storage space, and other similar decisions will be affected.

Distribution Components. The choice of a channel or channels of distribution is obviously an internal decision subject to the control of management. The links in the channels of distribution should be considered as integral parts of the logistics system. The distribution channel used is the direct road to placing the output of the enterprise into the hands of the users. Thus, it is easy to see the importance of these channels to the accomplishment of the goal of

CONTROL OVER, — GM DEALERS —

the logistics system. However, since the institutions with whom the logistics system must deal (retailers, wholesalers, etc.) are external to the enterprise itself, the control which can be exerted over them is limited.

Transportation Components. Again, it must be stated that certain aspects of the transport of the outputs as a part of the logistics system have been discussed from an internal environment standpoint. *OWN TRUCK* However, as in the case of distribution channels, the agencies which carry out the transportation function are largely external. The carriers and shippers are separate entities and as such are not subject to internal control.

REGULATION. Many aspects of the transportation function are subject to a high degree of governmental regulation. In the first place, the types of carriers are defined by law. Each type of carrier is restricted as to method of operation with regard to rate, or safety, or both. Not only are the rates of certain of the types of carriers subject to governmental control, but in some cases the routes permitted and the types of commodities which can be handled are specified. Consequently, these matters are not in the jurisdiction of the user of the transportation.

RATE STRUCTURE. The majority of carriers, classified as common carriers, quote their rates on two major bases. The first of these results from dividing commodities into a small number of classes. Rates are quoted on the basis of the class rather than on the specific item to be transported. The second type, commodity rates, essentially ignores the classifications, and rates are quoted directly. The entire transportation rate structure is extremely complex and beyond the scope of this discussion. This brief mention of rate structure is simply to indicate that it is of great importance to the logistics system.

Typically, most enterprises have tended to view logistic activities as individual functions to be controlled separately. Since all of the elements which have been described are interrelated, it is difficult to achieve efficiency by this sort of subdivision. Each of the major entities of the enterprise will tend to perform the function to optimize its own objectives rather than those of the logistics function. The ideal production rate may not result in an output which is the most desirable from the standpoint of the needs of marketing. Conversely, marketing's demands may lead to an inefficient and costly production performance. There are numerous ways in which the logistics function can be organized, but no single form can be designated as best. The important thing is to view logistics in the systems concept, and consider all of the components of logistics as an integrated whole. Only then can any assurance be given that the logistics function will be carried out effectively. All of the components can then be coordinated in such a way as to achieve the objective of getting the output to the user when, where, and how he wants it, and at the lowest cost. With this idea in mind, we will examine a number of techniques which are useful for operating, evaluating, and controlling the logistics system, with the goal of arriving at decisions which will improve performance.

OPERATION AND CONTROL OF
THE LOGISTICS SYSTEM

The operation and control of the logistics system of any enterprise is primarily determined by the design and analysis of the logistics function. A complete comprehension of the activities of operations, marketing, transportation, and all other activities related to the supply and physical distribution needs of the enterprise is required. The supply needs are related to the inputs of the system and to those things which must be accomplished to satisfy these needs. Also included are demands made of the suppliers and vendors of the system. The distribution side is related to the satisfaction of the demands of the users of the output of the enterprise. Most emphasis with regard to development of techniques for the design and analysis of the logistics system, and hence its operation and control, has related to the physical distribution side. However, close examination will reveal that these techniques do not conflict with the supply side of logistics. Therefore, to a large extent, the fundamental concepts of these techniques are such that they can be applied to the total logistics system, supply and distribution activities alike. Some of the approaches that are useful with regard to the logistics system have already been introduced and only a brief reference to them will be necessary at this point. Others require detailed examination. The inventory system is one such example. Inventory will be the subject of the next chapter. Chapter 17 will include such problems as aggregate scheduling.

Among the more interesting and promising techniques for developing efficient operation and control of the logistics system are economic cost analysis techniques, quantitative analysis techniques, and industrial dynamics. Each of these will be examined within the context of logistics as a system.

Economic Cost Analysis

In operating and controlling the logistics system of any enterprise, one of the major criteria to be considered will assuredly be the total cost of the operation of the system. It is generally accepted that the cost of distribution is increasing regularly. Part of this is a result of pure growth and part of inflation-generated growth. A substantial portion comes as a result of greater competition to increase the value provided by the enterprise to the users of its output. Another factor is undoubtedly the increasing complexities of the distribution activities. Such things as more sophisticated products, improved packaging methods, and better methods of handling and transportation have contributed to the increasing cost of physical distribution. There is little doubt that this trend will continue in the future because of additional changes and increasing demands for service emanating from the users.

Traditionally, historical costs have been used in cost analysis. Such costs can be viewed as accurate and highly objective with regard to needs of the accounting reporting function of the enterprise. However, they are not adequate for the purposes of making the necessary decisions to improve the efficiency of the logistics system. What is needed is a cost analysis using projected costs that can be utilized for comparison purposes with regard to actual costs. Any cost analysis of the logistics system must keep in mind two somewhat conflicting goals. The first of these goals is to reduce the operating costs of the system to improve the profit position of the enterprise. The other goal is to improve the performance of the system to provide an improved level of service to the users of the output of the enterprise. What usually can be done to accomplish one of these objectives will tend to be in opposition to the other. The usual result of improved service will be an increase in cost. This is one of the reasons to view the logistics function as an integrated system. Only in this way can all of the elements affecting the cost of the system be placed in their proper perspective.

One of the problems frequently encountered in developing a cost analysis of the logistics system is that past practice has resulted in a limited view of its scope. As a result, the costs included will only cover the transportation and storage aspects of the system. This practice, of course, eliminates many other applicable costs from the analysis. Because of this practice, many accounting systems have not been designed for an accurate accumulation of all the costs of the logistics function. The systems concept makes possible a realistic analysis of available alternatives for the efficient operation of the logistics function.

The most important consideration in making a cost analysis of the logistics system is the incremental cost effect of a decision. For example, it is possible to conceive of a distribution system which could be designed to utilize a number of different warehouses centrally located. The number could be small with a large floor space capacity for each in order to handle the total requirements. Another possible design is to have a large number of warehouses, each located reasonably close to the markets served. The unit capacity of each warehouse would be considerably smaller, with the total square footage about equal to the other system. We can identify these two systems as system A and system B, each being an extreme on a scale of systems designed to include a varying number of warehouses. As the number of warehouses utilized moved from A to B, the total cost of transportation would take on a function which declined as the number of warehouses increased. It would take a variety of forms such as a linear function with the cost of transportation reducing in direct relation to the number of warehouses, or it could take some sort of a curvilinear form. An example of one such cost function is illustrated in Figure 15-1.

Also important in the decision about the number of warehouses to utilize are operation costs applicable to the warehouses. Among the components of the total warehouse operation costs are those of handling the items, and information processing such as billing and other clerical costs. These costs would tend to increase as the number of warehouses increased from A to B, but at a decreasing rate. Other costs that have to be considered are those related to carrying inventory and those related to the investment in the warehouses. With all of these individual costs determined, it is then a matter of comparing the total costs as a result of adding warehouses. The ideal system is found by

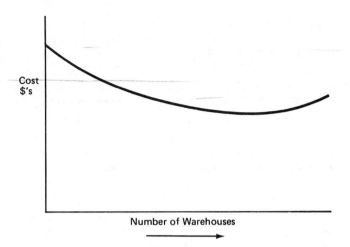

FIGURE 15-1

Typical Curvilinear Transportation Cost Function
with Additional Warehouses

determining the point where the addition of one more warehouse does not decrease the cost further, but results in an increase in the total cost. This warehouse is not added to the system.

Quantitative Analysis Techniques

Because the logistics system is interrelated with a number of problem areas
in the enterprise, a variety of general as well as specific quantitative techniques
are useful for the analysis of this system. Some of the generally applicable
techniques have been described. The role of quantitative analysis in the operation and control of the physical distribution activities of an enterprise tends to
be limited to use for analyzing individual components of the system. The
basic reason is the complexity of the total logistics system. Logistics involves
so many diverse functions, that optimizing the total system by a quantitative
model such as an algorithm would literally be impossible. However, these techniques can be valuable in the design and analysis of many component parts of
the logistics system.

Linear Programming. The transportation model of linear programming can
be utilized to determine the optimum shipping schedule in a multi-plant distribution system. It is also a useful technique for determining the location of new
processing facilities or for additional warehouses that optimize the logistics
system. The simplex model of linear programming is also useful in making
logistical decisions. Since these models have been demonstrated earlier, it is
not necessary to comment further on the mechanics of the models. Several
specific illustrations of their use are appropriate, however.

One of the most frequently cited applications of mathematical programming techniques to the logistics system is the variety of uses made by the H. J. Heinz Company.[1] Heinz utilized programming techniques to determine the minimum cost shipping schedule for their tomato ketchup which was shipped to about 70 nationally distributed warehouses from six plants spread from the east coast to the west coast. In addition, programming was used for such decisions as what and how much should be made at individual plants when capacity exceeded demands. Heinz also used programming to determine how to produce the output because the quality grade of raw materials available (tomatoes) as inputs will vary. Essentially, this was a type of mixture problem.

Oil refineries face a similar problem with regard to the quality of the crude oil available as input into the processing system. The use of mathematical programming enables such enterprises to determine the most profitable product mix of output. This is also an example of a mixture or a blending problem which varies on a daily basis according to the composition of the crude oil received for processing. Such applications are very commonplace today, and frequently institute significant results. One such application for a major oil refinery led to a $15,000 a day saving from an investment of approximately $2,000.[2]

There are available a large number of other similar examples of the use of mathematical programming as a means of improving the operational efficiency of the logistics system. One further interesting attempt is in regard to the selection of media to accomplish the most efficient use of an advertising budget. While this activity is somewhat peripheral to the logistics system, it is a related force in the final results.

Value Analysis. Value analysis, also referred to as value engineering, is a procedure that has as its objective the reduction in the cost of a product or service by examining the specifications and design of the item. It proceeds on the assumption that any aspect of the product or service which does not provide value, that is, does not serve a specific purpose, should be eliminated to achieve a minimum cost. As such, many of the considerations discussed in reference to the design of the product and the selection of the process are important factors in the use of this technique. However, most of these are internally oriented and reduce the operating costs of the company. Value analysis as a tool of the logistics system is largely externally oriented and is concerned with improving the value that the enterprise provides to the customers or users of the output. The value analysis technique tries to find ways of producing the output more efficiently and more economically. This process involves an evaluation of the function of the product or service to determine such facts as what it does, and what alternatives can be developed so that the same function can be

[1]Alexander Henderson and Robert Schlaifer, "Mathematical Programming: Better Information for Better Decision Making," *Harvard Business Review*, Vol. XXXII, No. 3 (May–June, 1954), pp. 73–100.

[2]William M. Young and Kurt Eisemann, "Study of a Textile Mill with the Aid of Linear Programming," *Management Technology* (January, 1960), p. 58.

accomplished. Accompanying these considerations is an evaluation of current costs and of the possible alternatives.

Some of the typical general alternatives are to simplify the design, or to use standard parts or methods in place of nonstandard ones. The substitution of cheaper materials is also a possible alternative. This latter alternative is particularly the case where the part under consideration is decorative rather than functional. In some cases, a change in the process can effectuate a substantial savings, or may result in better utilization of materials.

Specific examples are numerous. The use of aluminum in place of chromium plated steel for decorative trim on automobiles is one such example. Using plastic containers in place of glass or metal ones for certain liquids or powders reduces not only the original cost but the transportation costs as well because of the reduced weight. In many cases, it is possible to use smaller sized raw materials to reduce the swarf or wasted material removed in a machining process. A typical case of this would be to specify a smaller diameter bar stock in a turning operation. In the case of punch press operations, the manner in which the parts are laid out or nested on the metal plate or strip can reduce the waste. An illustration of such a case is found in Figure 15-2.

In this illustration, the improved rearrangement of the parts on the material resulted in a 56 percent decrease in the material scrap. A final illustration involves the production of a valve seat. Initially this part was machined from bar stock at a cost of 17.8¢ a piece. Figure 15-3 illustrates the savings which resulted when this part was made as a casting for a cost of 5.8¢ a piece.

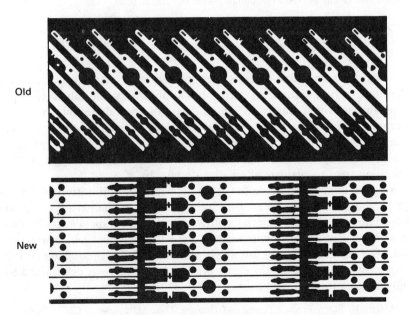

Old

New

FIGURE 15-2

Illustration of Improved Parts Layout for Punch Press Operation

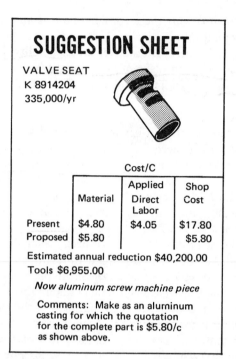

SUGGESTION SHEET

VALVE SEAT
K 8914204
335,000/yr

Cost/C

	Material	Applied Direct Labor	Shop Cost
Present	$4.80	$4.05	$17.80
Proposed	$5.80		$5.80

Estimated annual reduction $40,200.00
Tools $6,955.00

Now aluminum screw machine piece

Comments: Make as an aluminum
casting for which the quotation
for the complete part is $5.80/c
as shown above.

Source: L. D. Miles, "Value Analysis — A Plant Wide Creative Cost Reduction Program Under Purchasing Leadership," *Proceedings Fifth Industrial Engineering Institute* (Los Angeles-Berkeley: University of California, January–February, 1953), p. 96.

FIGURE 15-3

Cost Comparison for Alternate Valve Seat Production

As can be seen, value analysis is concerned with savings which are related to product or part design. As such it has applicability not only to the internal processing activities, but is an integral part of the relationship between the enterprise and its suppliers. The methodology used to evaluate alternative designs can be varied. Various types of economic cost analyses may be used. Break-even analysis is also useful in many cases. Starr has suggested the use of decision trees to evaluate alternative designs.[3]

Another unique technique for evaluating material utilization of a product or assembly is to develop a ratio of weights based on the partial utilization of each component.[4] The material utilization of each component is the ratio of the amount used for each component to the total amount which was initially used. The utilization figures are weighted by the relative production cost of the component. The total for the entire product or assembly is determined by the following equation:

[3]Martin K. Starr, *Product Design and Decision Theory* (Englewood Cliffs: Prentice-Hall, Inc., 1963), p. 9.

[4]Samuel Eilon, *Elements of Production Planning and Control* (New York: the Macmillan Co., 1962), pp. 180–181.

$$W = \sum_{i=1}^{n} w_i c_i$$

Where:

W = the total equivalent material utilization

$w_i c_i$ = the partial utilization figure

w_i = material utilization of component i

c_i = relative production cost of component i = $C_{i/C}$ = production cost for component i/total cost for entire product or assembly

A comparison of the partial utilization (representing the contribution of each component to the total) with the relative production cost (showing the maximum contribution possible if the material utilization is 100%) indicates the components to be analyzed.

An example will serve to illustrate the use of this concept. Assume an assembly which is composed of four components having material utilizations of 60%, 90%, 75%, and 25%. Table 15-1 shows the corresponding production costs for each component, and the other pertinent data used to achieve the partial utilization figures for the individual components.

An examination of this table reveals that the greatest potential for improvement of the material utilization lies in the last two components. These components contribute 52.5% out of a potential of 90%. Component d is especially susceptible to improvement since its present contribution is 7.5% as compared with a 30% potential.

Other Quantitative Techniques. There are a variety of specialized quantitative techniques available for use in the control of the logistics system. Some of these techniques are of a specialized nature and deal with problem areas not purely logistical in nature. Techniques utilized for inventory control problems are one example. A number of these will be discussed in the next chapter. Another class of techniques are those related to the discussion of large-scale systems. These systems will be examined in detail in Chapter 17.

TABLE 15-1

Partial Utilization of Four Component Assembly

Component	Material Utilization (Percent)	Production Costs	Relative Production Costs	Partial Utilization
a	60	$0.05	0.02 %	0.012
b	90	0.20	0.08	0.072
c	75	1.50	0.60	0.450
d	25	0.75	0.30	0.075
Total		$2.50	1.00	0.609

This discussion of quantitative techniques for analysis and control of the logistics system points up some of the newer decision tools available for use. All these techniques are complementary to each other. It is unlikely that any single technique would suffice to optimize the performance of the logistics system. Each method serves to assist in the improvement of one segment of the total system.

Industrial Dynamics

As earlier stated, one of the components of any logistics system is the information system. Information is an integral part of the feedback-control characteristic of any enterprise system or subsystem thereof. Industrial dynamics is a method for analysis of this segment of a system. As such, it is a useful means of evaluating the way various elements of the physical distribution activities are integrated. The interactions, over time, of these elements can be examined to determine how and why a particular result is achieved.

The term industrial dynamics is the outgrowth of research carried on at the Massachusetts Institute of Technology under the direction of Jay W. Forrester. Industrial dynamics is defined as "the study of the information-feedback characteristics of industrial activity to show how organizational structure, amplification (in policies), and time delays (in decisions and actions) interact to influence the success of the enterprise."[5]

The implications of this for the logistics system can be best illustrated by means of referring to a typical channel of distribution: processor, wholesaler, retailer. A retailer currently has a demand of 10 units per week for a particular item. Present policy is to order at the end of each week to replace actual sales and to maintain a beginning-of-week inventory of one and one half weeks' sales, or 15 units. Under these conditions, with instantaneous purchasing and resupply, the order for these units will be 10 per week. If the demand for this item now increases by 20% to 12 units per week, the inventory requirements will also increase by this percentage to 18 units. To meet this requirement, it will be necessary to increase the quantity purchased by more than the 20% amount. Increasing purchases to 12 will only replace the units sold, but will not replace in inventory the increased units removed as the result of the increase in demand. To achieve the policy of one and one half weeks' supply, it will be necessary to increase the purchases the first week by five units a week to 15, or a 50% increase. This sort of amplification will be passed on to the other levels in the distribution channel, with an increase in the amplification as the decision moves further away from the initial demand level. If such things as time delays are introduced into the system, the result will be even greater amplification. Such delays will be the case rather than the exception because of delays in the flow of the information feedback, in the decisions being made, in the processing of orders, and in the movement of replenishment shipments.

Industrial dynamics makes it possible to evaluate the effects of such changes in a distribution system by experimenting with the system by a form of simulation. The results of such a simulation for a system which experienced a sudden 10% increase in retail sales is shown in Figure 15-4. The system represented includes known delays in decisions and actions at all levels. Note that the disturbances which result from this change in retail sales affect all levels. The greatest fluctuations take place at the manufacturing level, and it is about 18 months before the system returns to a state of equilibrium.

It is possible to use industrial dynamics to evaluate the effects of varying conditions and the result of different policies on the distribution system. Forrester illustrates such uses by applying it to both rising and declining sales over a period of time, and to random sales fluctuations as examples of shifts in the system variables. In addition, it is used to measure the potential effects of reducing clerical delays; of eliminating the wholesale level; of changes in inventory policies, such as altering the timing of inventory ordering corrections; and of the effects of advertising policies.[6]   Obviously, since the tool of industrial dynamics is simulation, these effects are not precise predictions, but rather indications of the degree of dynamics or stability in a system when given changes are introduced.

In a highly dynamic system in which variations are violent, these variations in the elements of the logistics system bear on still other aspects of the enterprise. In the system illustrated in Figure 15-4, where factory production fluctuates from a high of plus 45% to a low of minus 3%, as compared with the original level, there will be ramifications with regard to the level of employment. Methods for dealing with this type problem are discussed in Chapter 17.

Industrial dynamics may be viewed as a means whereby management of the logistics system may approach the problem of control. Attempts at control may result in amplifications affecting areas not normally considered variables of the problem at hand. It should not be viewed as a total system control technique. It will not result in a homeostatic control system. What it does do is to indicate the results that changing variables will have upon the operation of the system. It indicates where some of the problems will originate in the overall control. Again, these can be from a source outside the normal confines of the system with which management is concerned. The use of industrial dynamics often results in the recognition of certain seemingly unconnected factors. For instance, the position and significance of the manager as a decision maker in this system may be brought more fully to the fore. Finally, industrial dynamics will point up the importance of management policy in the total control of the logistics system. This is really another way of saying that industrial dynamics will make it more apparent that the logistics function is itself a subsystem of the total enterprise system. Thus, the total systems concept is clearly indicated. The integration of the various elements of the logistics system will be facilitated, and the achievement of the goal of the total enterprise will be more easily reached as opposed to the satisfaction of the goals of sub-units of the enterprise.

---

[6]*Ibid.*, Chap. 2.

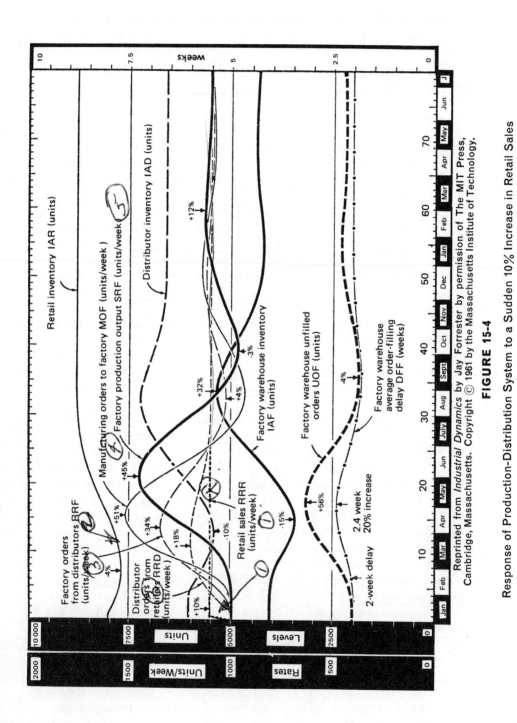

Retail inventory IAR (units)

Manufacturing orders to factory MOF (units/week)
Factory production output SRF (units/week)

Distributor inventory IAD (units)

+12%

Factory orders
from distributors BRF
(units/week)

+51%

+45%

+34%

Distributor
orders from
retailers RRD
(units/week)

+18%

+10%

+4%

-4%

+32%

+4%

-3%

Factory warehouse inventory
IAF (units)

Retail sales RRR
(units/week)

-15%

-10%

Factory warehouse unfilled
orders UOF (units)

+56%

Factory warehouse
average order-filling
delay DFF (weeks)

4%

2.4 week
20% increase

2-week delay

weeks

Units

Levels

Units/Week

Rates

Reprinted from *Industrial Dynamics* by Jay Forrester by permission of The MIT Press,
Cambridge, Massachusetts. Copyright © 1961 by the Massachusetts Institute of Technology.

FIGURE 15-4

Response of Production-Distribution System to a Sudden 10% Increase in Retail Sales

Logistics in Nonmanufacturing Enterprises

The emphasis upon the physical distribution aspects of the logistics function may lead to the conclusion that logistics activities are only found in the manufacturing enterprise where the output is a physical product. Logistical problems are found in all types of enterprises, whether they deal in products or services. The nature of the logistics system will differ with the type of enterprise. A differentiation can also be made among different kinds of enterprises that deal in products. One such instance would be between marketing enterprises and manufacturing enterprises.

Service Enterprises. The main difference between the logistics systems of service and manufacturing enterprises is the kinds of inputs found. In the manufacturing enterprise these inputs are some form of material and are almost entirely "physical" in nature. In the service enterprise the inputs are in a variety of forms and tend to be quite diverse. The inputs may not always be of a tangible nature or physical in form. Certainly, there are supplies which are indirect inputs, but often the inputs are in the form of a service as well as are the outputs. A part of the logistics system of a hospital concerned with providing medical services to its patients involves the availability of the necessary specialized medical skill at the time when it is needed. Thus, this input is really in the form of a service. It is necessary to have the facilities available, such as the operating room, respirator, and the like; to have the surgical supplies and drugs in the necessary amounts; but these things would be of little value if a doctor was not available when an emergency arose. ✕

Distribution activities usually do not have the same significance for a service enterprise as they do in manufacturing. A service is frequently performed for the user of the output directly and thus, the importance of place utility is decreased. There are, of course, problems of the flow of information and communication activities that take on a distribution form.

To further illustrate the nature of logistics systems in service enterprises, it is useful to identify some of the specific types of activities found in a variety of such enterprises. Another logistics system found in a hospital is the serving of meals to the patients. Not only is there the problem of acquiring the food and preparing it, but the problem of serving it is particularly acute. It is necessary to distribute the meals to the patients in their rooms. It is essential that this be done quickly so that the meals are served hot. Since the food is usually distributed from a central kitchen, the problem is complicated. A further factor found in this situation to make the problem more difficult is the necessity of preparing meals for patients on different types of diets; e.g., ulcer diet, salt free, low fat, etc. The design and control of this logistics system is a critical problem in a large hospital.

Scheduling classes at a university is a logistics problem. The timing of the offerings to meet the needs of the students, the availability of a qualified instructor, and the availability of the proper-sized room and other facilities are factors. Where equipment such as laboratory supplies are required, these elements also enter into the logistics system design. In public school systems it is necessary to establish a schedule for the utilization of certain supplies or facilities by a number of different classes. For instance, it may be that a particular textbook is not used by any one class for the entire school year. Thus, it is necessary to schedule the use of this book by all classes in the district. The planning of the sequence of the curricular topics so that this book can be distributed to all those who need it, and providing the system for accomplishing this are logistics problems.

The recently well publicized problems facing the brokerage firms in their so-called "back room" operations are logistical in nature. These activities involve the transfer of ownership of securities as they are bought and sold. Thus, the activities of acquiring the sold security certificate, recording the ownership transfer, and then forwarding the certificate to the new owner are really in essence a logistics system.

A final instance of a service type enterprise can be found in the airlines. The scheduling of flights, the selling of tickets and providing reservations, the providing of meals for the passengers, the providing of the necessary aircraft at the proper time and place, and the operation of numerous terminals and of maintenance facilities all go into the creation of a highly complex logistics sytem.

Marketing Enterprises. The logistics system in a marketing enterprise is not related to the type of marketing activity. It is primarily the same, irrespective of the type of marketing activity or the level in the distribution channel; i.e., retail, wholesale, etc. The essential differences from the manufacturing enterprise are that the inputs probably come from a greater number of sources, they are more diverse in nature, and their value varies widely. The output also possibly goes to a wider variety of customers (this is more likely the farther removed from the manufacturer the marketing enterprise is). A wider variety of output is probably found as well, and the unit size of the output is smaller. A unique feature of the logistics system of a marketing enterprise as compared with a manufacturing one is that, within the system, little or no change takes place from the time the products are inputs until they are outputs. In effect, the same items which arrive as inputs to the system depart in an identical state. All processing or operations within the system are of a logistical nature. It may be that in a marketing enterprise the operations system and the logistics system are identical.[7]

Other Nonmanufacturing Enterprises. Any enterprise must develop a logistics system in some degree or another. In some it may be merely the handling of supplies. In still other types it may be concerned with people. This is an essential element in the military logistics system as was brought out earlier. The army considers as an integral part of its logistics activities the "movement, evacuation, and hospitalization of personnel."[8] The logistics

---

[7]John F. Magee, *Industrial Logistics* (New York: McGraw-Hill Book Co., 1968), p. 334.
[8]U.S. Department of the Army, *Logistics Management*, FM 38-1 (Washington: U.S. Government Printing Office, March, 1969), p. 2-1.

system involved in research and development activities would also include the supplying of personnel as an integral function.

LOGISTICS AND OPERATIONS MANAGEMENT

At this point it should be clear that the development of a good logistics system is an essential activity in the overall management of the operations function. In the manufacturing firm, logistics includes a large part of operations, and in the marketing enterprise logistics and operations may be virtually identical. Thus, if the manager is to achieve a desired level of control over his operations system, an efficient logistics system is not something which can be left to chance. The relative importance will naturally vary between enterprises, but there is no denying the pervasiveness of logistics in all types of enterprises. The design of a logistics control system is not an easy matter. Consider, if you will, a company such as the H. J. Heinz Co., cited in regard to its use of mathematical programming to establish a minimum cost shipping schedule for tomato ketchup. This is only one of many products that this company produces. Even if we assume the "57 varieties" which they have advertised (and there are actually more), along with the numerous plants needed (recall that there were six for the ketchup), and the 70 nationally distributed warehouses, the designing of such a complex system for controlling the physical distribution problems would be a massive task.

Any examination of the components of a logistics system as discussed earlier in this chapter will reveal that the design of a system for controlling this function will be most difficult. Because of the activities involved, it is difficult to use any objective or quantitative means for evaluating such a system. Therefore, it can only be concluded that the primary measures of effectiveness of the logistics system must be of a subjective nature. It has been indicated that certain quantitative tools are useful in relation to certain segments of this system. However, the great diversity of activities involved is a deterrent to the application of such tools to the total system. For instance, cost data are difficult to obtain because the activities are so widely spread out. The desired characteristics of the logistics system are impossible to set forth specifically because of the complex nature of these activities. What must be striven for is a type of system that permits continuous control and that has feedback control as an essential element. A homeostatic control system would be the ideal.

SUMMARY

Logistics is a subsystem of the enterprise concerned with the interrelated activities of the operations, marketing, and transportation subsystems. Logistics is involved in the flow of all inputs, product or service, from their initial source through to the user of the output. The components of any logistics system are examined as being a part either of the internal or external environment of the enterprise.

The elements included as a part of the internal environment are those that are under some degree of control by the enterprise management. They fall primarily into the areas of production or operations and marketing, but also include certain service activities. Production or operations components are those that are related to the overall planning and control function of the operations system. Marketing components are those related to the demand-creation activities such as selling, promotional activities, customer service, and choice of channels of distribution. The service components are procurement, the information system, and traffic.

The external environment is composed of various components of the logistics system which are largely or completely beyond the control of the management of the enterprise. The areas of these components are viewed as input sources, existing market conditions, external distribution links, and certain transportation components.

Examination of a number of techniques available for the operation and control of the logistics system are undertaken. The first of these is economic cost analysis. Many elements are involved in the total cost of the logistics system. Probably the most important cost consideration is the incremental cost effect. The relative cost effect of differing alternatives is the basis for the final decision about the design of the logistics system.

Second, a variety of quantitative techniques useful for analysis of the operation of the logistics system are examined. Most of these are useful only for the analysis of small and specific segments of the logistics activity. This is largely a result of the extremely complex nature of the logistics system. Linear programming, particularly the distribution model, can be used for establishing the optimum shipping schedule to be used in a logistics system. Value analysis, which is used to attempt to reduce the cost of a product or service by means of a change in its specifications or design, is still another quantitative approach.

Finally, industrial dynamics, a method used to analyze the information subsystem of the logistics system, is reviewed. It is useful to evaluate the way the various elements of the physical distribution activities of an enterprise are integrated. It depends largely on a form of simulation that can indicate the results of changing variables on the operation of the logistics system. Through the use of such a technique, the integration of the various elements of a logistics system will be more easily achieved.

The nature of the logistics function in nonmanufacturing enterprises is described. Particular emphasis is placed on the differences which exist in service enterprises and in marketing enterprises when compared with the manufacturing enterprise.

The relationship of the logistics function to operations management is set forth. The development of a good logistics system is an essential activity in the overall management of the operations function. The complexity of the logistics function and the diversity of the activities involved make the proper functioning of this system difficult. Ideally a system can be achieved that will allow for the integration of the many activities and permit continuous feedback control.

INCIDENT

RX DRUG COMPANY

The RX Drug Company, a large manufacturer of pharmaceuticals, has a number of unique problems with regard to its distribution system.

In the first place, it produces about 1,500 different drug items, and they are packaged in 5,000 different sizes, depending on the nature of the item and the type of demand. Another factor which contributes to the complexities of the distribution system is the limited shelf life of most of the drugs. This may vary anywhere from a few months to two or three years. In addition, some of the items must be stored under specific temperature and humidity conditions. Some require refrigeration, and others require storage at very low humidity to avoid deterioration and spoilage. A final factor that affects the distribution system is the fact that certain diseases have higher or lower incidences than expected. Also, the incidence of a disease may be geographically dispersed or it may be concentrated in a local area.

Questions

1. What logistical components are the most important to the successful operation of this distribution system?

2. How would you proceed to design and control a logistics system for RX?

3. Discuss the relationship of the logistics activities in this situation to other activities or systems of the enterprise.

QUESTIONS FOR DISCUSSION AND ANALYSIS

1. Describe the nature of the logistics function. Briefly compare the usual concept of logistics with that described in this chapter.

2. What is the purpose of viewing the components of the logistics system as being a part of either the internal or the external environment?

3. What is the general nature of the components of the logistics system which are a part of the internal environment? Briefly discuss these components.

4. What components of a logistics system can be classified as part of the external environment? Identify and describe these components.

5. What is required to achieve efficient operation and control of the logistics system of any enterprise?

6. How may economic cost analysis be utilized to measure the effectiveness of the logistics system? What is the most important consideration in the use of this technique?

7. What are the types of quantitative techniques which are applicable to the logistics system? Illustrate the way in which each of the quantitative methods listed can be used.

8. What is industrial dynamics? How is it of value in controlling the logistics activities of an enterprise? Evaluate its potential contribution.

9. Compare the logistics function in the manufacturing enterprise with such nonmanufacturing enterprises as service enterprises and marketing enterprises.

10. Comment on the relationship and the importance of the logistics system in the total enterprise system. Give particular emphasis to the role of logistics in the performance of the operations system.

SELECTED ADDITIONAL READINGS

Constantin, James A. *Principles of Logistics Management*. New York: Appleton-Century-Croft, 1966.

Eilon, Samuel. *Elements of Production Planning and Control*. New York: The Macmillan Co., 1962.

Forrester, Jay W. *Industrial Dynamics*. Cambridge, Massachusetts: The M.I.T. Press, 1961.

Geisler, Murray A., and Wilbur A. Steger. "The Combination of Alternative Research Techniques in Logistics Systems Analysis." *Management Technology*, Vol. III, No. 1 (May, 1963), pp. 68-77.

Heskett, J. L., Nicholas A. Glaskowsky, Jr., Robert M. Ivie. *Business Logistics*. 2d ed. New York: Ronald Press Co., 1973.

Magee, John F. *Industrial Logistics*. New York: McGraw-Hill Book Co., 1968.

Marks, Norton E., and Robert M. Taylor. *Marketing Logistics: Perspectives and Viewpoints*. New York: John Wiley & Sons, Inc., 1967.

McElhiney, Paul T., and Robert I. Cook. *The Logistics of Materials Management*. Boston: Houghton Mifflin, Co., 1969.

McGarrah, Robert E. *Production and Logistics Management*. New York: John Wiley & Sons, Inc., 1965.

Mossman, Frank H., and Newton Morton. *Logistics of Distribution Systems*. Boston: Allyn and Bacon, 1965.

U.S. Department of the Army. *Logistics Management*, FM 38-1. Washington: U.S. Government Printing Office, March, 1969.

CHAPTER 16 | Inventory Systems

One of the elements or components of the logistics system and of the operations system is inventories. The inventory subsystem furnishes inputs into the operations system, into the logistics system, and into various other subsystems of the enterprise. For a variety of reasons, no other aspect of the operations function has received more attention than that of controlling inventories. One reason is that inventories are a significant element of cost; thus, the control of inventories has a major effect on the efficient performance of the enterprise. Where inventories consist essentially of physical inputs or the materials which are used to produce the output, they may be the largest cost item in the total of operation costs. Another facet of this attention to inventories stems from the growing emphasis on the use of quantitative techniques to the analysis and control of the operations function. No other area has been more subjected to the application of quantitative models than that of inventory systems. The reason for this is that most inventory problems lend themselves to the use of quantitative models better than any other single area of management. In the examination of the inventory problem and of the inventory system, this amenability to quantitative analysis should become clearer.

NATURE OF THE INVENTORY PROBLEM

Essentially, any inventory problem is concerned with the same set of considerations. One element of all inventory problems is the establishment of the level of service to supply to the user of the inventory. In addition, there is also the cost factor involved in the establishment and maintenance of the inventory. Presumably, some determination of the expected demand for the items in the inventory will be made.

The objective in any inventory system is to be able to make that set of decisions which will balance these factors. Ideally, these decisions would minimize cost, provide the level of service which was satisfactory to all users, and meet the demand which materialized. While these factors are inherent in any inventory system, the problems surrounding each inventory system and each item are unique. Thus, the methodology for controlling each inventory system will be different. There are, however, certain general methods or approaches item are useful for developing a systematic technique for analyzing and controlling inventory systems. The specific model has to fit the individual circumstances.

The Functions of Inventories

To understand the techniques used to control the inventory system, it is necessary to recognize the functions which inventories perform. Perhaps the major function of inventories, possibly even their *raison d'être*, is the separation or decoupling of the sequential stages in the total processing and distribution of a product or service. The *decoupling process* allows successive stages or departments to be independent of each other. Thus, the production of an item does not have to coincide precisely with the usage of the item. By maintaining inventories, the processor is free from concern about the delivery of inputs (e.g., raw materials) needed in the processing. If the materials are late, the processing can continue by drawing from the inventory on hand. At the same time, in a sequence of processing steps, the individual operation does not have to depend on the completion of a previous operation from which it may be separated. At the retail level, the maintaining of inventories allows the management to operate efficiently without being forced into the position of conforming to the needs of the processor. Attempts are made at all levels to establish forecasts for the usage of an item or service. However, forecasts are not 100% accurate. There will be variations in usage caused by a variety of forces. To offset the effects of these variations and to permit each level to operate most efficiently and economically, management maintains buffers in the form of inventories that it can draw upon when needed.

From these comments it can be seen that inventories exist for two reasons. One reason is that time is a factor in processing and in the logistics function of any enterprise. The operations to be completed require time; the transportation of the inputs to the processing unit, the movement of the inputs through the various operations, and the movement of the outputs all require time. In most cases, variations in these times will be present and cannot be accurately foreseen. The second reason for the existence of inventories has been described as organizational.[1] These types of inventories are necessary to create the decoupling effect. This decoupling permits the various organizational units to operate independently. Magee sees these situations as the cause of the most difficult problems for management in connection with inventory systems, because they:

> ... "buy" organization in the sense that the more of them that management carries between stages in the manufacturing-distribution process, the less coordination is required to keep the process running smoothly. Contrariwise, if inventories are already being used efficiently, they can be cut only at the expense of greater organization effort — e.g., greater scheduling effort to keep successive stages in balance, and greater expediting effort to work out the difficulties which unforeseen disruptions at one point or another may cause in the whole process.[2]

---

[1] It is believed that this precise description of such inventories was first used in: John F. Magee, "Guides to Inventory Policy: I. Functions and Lot Sizes," *Harvard Business Review*, Vol. XXXIV, No. 1 (January–February, 1956), pp. 51–53.

[2] *Ibid.*, p. 52.

Types of Inventories

It is convenient to consider inventories as a variety of types as opposed to grouping them all together. One group is based on the stage in the total process at which it is found. In this group are raw materials, work-in-process, finished goods, and supplies. The first type, raw materials inventories, is held so that processing may take place as needed. This type of inventory eliminates dependence on the performance of the vendor.

The second type of inventory found in the manufacturing enterprise is work-in-process. This type of inventory includes any of the inputs into the processing system which have undergone some transformation, but have not reached the final form. Of course, these inventories will be in various stages of completion.

When the processing is completed, the inventories are classified as finished-goods inventories. Circumstances will determine the necessity for these inventories. When processing is to customer order, finished-goods inventories may not be necessary. This situation is found in many intermittent operations systems. In the case of a restaurant, the final item to be served to the customer is not usually immediately available, but must be prepared for him. In this case, however, the customer is willing to accept this waiting period. Therefore, finished-goods inventories are not necessary.

Another type of inventory that is typical of almost any enterprise is supplies. In all manufacturing enterprises an inventory of many items not directly a part of the finished product must be maintained. Clerical supplies, tools, jigs, fixtures, and the like are examples. In the service enterprise, this may be the only type of inventory which needs to be maintained. Services in the form of "finished goods" are hard to visualize. In the restaurant example, the food to be prepared may conceivably be viewed as a supply, or as an in-process item, or even as a raw material.

Inventories can also be classified according to their function. It is usual to consider three types of inventories from this standpoint: lot size or economic order quantity inventories, anticipation stocks, and safety or buffer stocks.

Lot Size Inventories. These inventories result from the attempts of the manager to minimize the costs of maintenance of stocks. Items are stocked in quantities that are greater than are currently needed. These types of inventories will occur whether the items to be stocked are internally produced or are procured from an external source. Long production runs are necessary to internally produce these kinds of inventories. Frequent high setup costs resulting from short runs made to conform more closely to needs are avoided. For purchased items, the costs of placing numerous orders and of transportation will be reduced. In addition, discounts may be obtained. Naturally, additional costs are incurred as a result of maintaining higher levels of stock.

Anticipation Inventories. As the name implies, these inventories exist because of some planned future need. When the forecast of sales indicates a fluctuating or seasonal pattern of usage of an item, it may be more economical to build up inventories to handle this fluctuating demand than to attempt to change output levels to meet these variations. Other examples where anticipation stocks may be used are when an intensive sales promotion campaign is expected to increase demand significantly, or where a shutdown is expected as in the case of a vacation period, a model change over, or even an anticipated strike. When these events can be foreseen and planned for, this inventory situation is not a serious problem to management.

Buffer Inventories. Buffer inventories are held as a safety measure (hence, they are sometimes referred to as safety stocks) against unforeseen events. It has been pointed out at numerous times that demand often exceeds the forecast. When this occurs, buffer inventories serve to cushion the effect. Buffer inventories may also be useful when output deviates from the anticipated level. Buffer inventories are unavoidable, since these kinds of variations are inevitable, and management will want to avoid experiencing lost sales as a result of being out of stock.

Inventory System Costs

The most frequently used measure of the effectiveness of an inventory system is cost. It, therefore, becomes necessary to know the types of costs which appertain, and to understand their effect on the system. A basic problem in any inventory system is to achieve a balance between the cost factors which are in opposition to one another. Typically in these systems, if one cost is minimized, an increase results in one or more of the other applicable costs.

The cost figures which apply to the efficient operation of an inventory system are typically difficult to obtain. They are costs not usually contained in the chart of accounts of an enterprise. Note that the pertinent costs are variable or are "out-of-pocket" costs which are directly and immediately affected when a change in the operation of the system takes place. Thus, those costs which are incurred by ordering more frequently than in the past are considered, while salaries or depreciation are not.

There are three types of costs which are significant in any inventory system. At least two of these costs must be controllable if the system is to be considered as subject to control by means of the analytical techniques available. These costs are identified as replenishment costs, carrying costs, and shortage costs.

Replenishment Costs. These are all the costs which are related to the amount ordered. Included are the clerical costs incurred as a result of the procurement cycle for purchased items, or machine setup costs in the case of internally produced items. This class of replenishment costs is often referred to as preparation costs. These costs are usually constant, irrespective of the size of the order. Thus, the procurement costs may be $25 per order in a particular enterprise whether the quantity ordered is 10, 100, or 1,000.

Some replenishment costs are dependent on the quantity ordered. One such type of cost is the result of quantity discounts which are offered by vendors.

Usually the unit price of an item will be lower if larger quantities are ordered at one time. Transportation costs also fall into this category in some cases.

Processing costs can also be affected by the quantity ordered. Because fixed costs can be allocated over a larger number of units, the unit costs for long production runs will be less than for short ones. Another factor which has a bearing on costs for such runs will be learning time. As learning curve analysis revealed, full production is not obtained immediately.

Carrying Costs. All of those costs which are associated with the handling and the storage of the inventory are identified as *carrying costs*. Included here are the interest on the investment in the inventory, possible obsolescence of the item (perishables, high-fashion items, and items which are subject to rapid technological change), inventory taxes, insurance, and possible decline in the value of the items in the inventory over time.

Shortage Costs. *Shortage costs* are incurred when a sale is lost. Lost sales are a result of being out of stock at the time an item is demanded. This cost may include the actual value of the lost sale as one element of the total shortage costs. In addition, there may also be intangible cost elements which are somewhat difficult to ascertain. For instance, what cost can be attached to the loss of goodwill as a result of being out of stock? Not only is there the immediate loss of a sale and of goodwill, but there may also be a loss of future business because of the customer's dissatisfaction. As already indicated, one of the objectives of an inventory system is to provide a satisfactory level of service. The cost of lost sales must be weighed against the other costs which can only be decreased by increasing the total inventory system costs.

TYPES OF INVENTORY SYSTEMS

All inventory systems consist of some aspect of demand or usage, certain cost elements, replenishment characteristics, and a variety of constraints which affect these. The variations in the inventory systems found in actual operations are great. However, close examination will reveal that all systems are concerned with two basic factors. One of these has to do with time, and the other with quantity. Any inventory system must be designed to determine the time at which a replenishment should be made, and the amount which should be ordered. Any inventory system will attempt to control time and quantity in a way that the minimum cost position can be achieved. Two basic types of inventory systems, each of which approaches this problem from a slightly different viewpoint, will be examined. It is possible to classify literally any inventory system as some form of one of these two. These two types of inventory systems are identified as the fixed-reorder-quantity system, and the fixed-time-interval system.

Fixed-Reorder-Quantity System

The fixed-reorder-quantity system exists where a specific fixed quantity of the inventory item is ordered whenever the stock on hand reaches a predetermined

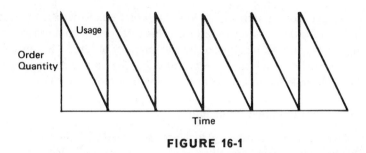

FIGURE 16-1

Inventory System with Immediate Resupply and Constant Demand

level. This level is specified as the point at which the items on hand will be just sufficient to cover the usage during the replenishment cycle time. If replenishment occurred without delay, the reorder point would be zero. In this type of system the quantity ordered is fixed and constant. The determination of this quantity is based on the minimization of the total costs. If the system were such that immediate replenishment could be achieved, and the demand or usage rate was constant for period after period, this system could be depicted by the diagram in Figure 16-1.

Obviously, the conditions assumed for this system are ideal, and highly unlikely to be encountered in a realistic situation. The most likely variation from this ideal is that the replenishment is not immediate. Therefore, some lead time is required to permit the necessary processing of the order from placement until receipt. Thus, some quantity to cover the replenishment period and assure receipt of the order before running out of stock must be established. This quantity is referred to as the reorder point. In addition to this variation, it is possible that the replenishment cycle will vary at times or that the usage rate will not be constant. For this reason it is usual in this type of system to find that management has decided to maintain a safety stock for coping with such contingencies. This situation is illustrated for a fixed-reorder-quantity system in Figure 16-2.

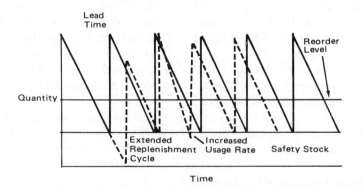

FIGURE 16-2

Fixed-Reorder-Quantity System with Reorder Level and Safety Stock

The dotted lines indicate how a longer replenishment cycle and an increase in anticipated usage will affect the operation of this system.

A particular form of this type of system is called the "two-bin" system; the regular supply is held in one location or storage bin, while the other stock is held in another location. When the regular supply is used up, the order is placed for the replenishment quantity. The supply in the second bin contains a quantity sufficient to cover the replenishment cycle and any safety margin which management may determine as necessary. In actual practice, it is not necessary to physically separate the two sets of stock, but merely to label the non-regular stock.

Fixed-Time-Interval System

This system is based on a periodic review of the quantity on hand. The period of time is fixed, and an order is placed at this time to replenish the inventory up to a predetermined maximum level. The primary distinction between this system and the one previously discussed is that the quantity ordered varies, and the orders are placed at fixed time intervals in this system, while in the fixed-reorder-quantity system, the quantity is fixed and the ordering intervals vary. The fixed-time-interval system is illustrated in Figure 16-3. Again the dotted lines are used to indicate the effect of variations in replenishment cycle and in anticipated usage.

Because the review period is fixed, and the order quantity is based on the maximum level desired less the inventory in stock at the time of review plus the anticipated demand during the replenishment period, a larger safety stock is typically required than in the fixed-reorder-quantity system. This increased stock is necessary because demand may be considerably larger than is expected, but this larger demand will not be noted until the review period arrives.

If we had the ideal system illustrated in Figure 16-1, with immediate replenishment, the two types of systems would be the same. The quantity ordered in

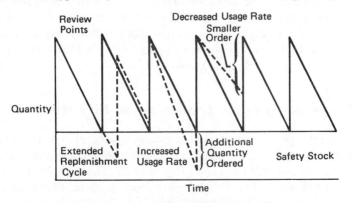

FIGURE 16-3

Fixed-Time-Interval System with Safety Stock

this circumstance, under both systems, is based on the economic lot size. Even when we move away from the ideal situation where we do have the already indicated differences because of lead time for the replenishment cycle, the economic lot size is still used to determine the order quantity or the review period in the two systems.

ECONOMIC LOT SIZE

Inasmuch as the determination of the economic lot size is fundamental to the operation of the two basic types of inventory systems, it is necessary to understand it fully. The *economic lot size* is that quantity of an item which can be ordered to replenish the inventory at the minimum total cost. There are certain assumptions which apply to the development of the model to be presented for the economic lot size. The demand and the lead time can be assumed as constant, or at the very least, assumed to have only minor variations. In addition, no price breaks as a result of the size of the order are applicable. Finally, ordering cost is constant for each order placed, irrespective of the number of orders, and the carrying costs per unit are also constant for any number of units stocked. This condition can be identified as certainty.

It is obvious even at this stage that all of these assumptions will apply only in rare instances. The question may then be raised as to the value of examining the techniques for determining the economic lot size. A parallel to a well-known economic concept can be drawn. The usual starting point for the study of the operation of economic systems is to consider the case of perfect competition. It does not take long to realize that such a thing as perfect competition is infrequently found, if at all. However, an understanding of this form of economic system is basic to the understanding of oligopoly, monopoly, and other systems which are found in actual operation. It is only with an understanding of perfect competition that it is possible to understand and evaluate the other systems. A similar statement can be made with regard to the ideal model for the determination of the economic lot size. All other models are essentially modifications of this basic model, wherein one or more of the conditions assumed above are changed. The actual situation can be compared with the ideal and an analytical model developed by modification of the basic one.

Cost Components of the Economic Lot Size Model

Earlier three types of costs were identified as significant in inventory systems. Of these types, only two are applicable to the development of the economic lot size model: replenishment costs and carrying costs. The third set of costs, shortage costs, are not involved in this model as a result of the assumption of constant demand and constant lead time. With these conditions, stockouts are impossible, and thus, there will be no shortage costs. As far as replenishment costs are concerned there are two applicable costs, and a single carrying cost element. The objective is to determine these costs at varying ordering levels to ascertain the minimum cost point. The total annual cost may be stated by the following:

$$TC = CR + \frac{PR}{Q} + \frac{iQ}{2} \tag{1}$$

Where:

TC = total annual cost
C = unit price
R = annual demand
P = order preparation cost (per order)
i = inventory carrying and storage costs per unit
Q = lot size

Determination of Replenishment Cost Elements. As was stated above, there are two cost elements in the total cost Equation (1) above that can be classified as replenishment costs. The first of these is the purchased cost of the annual inventory. This cost is represented by the term CR in Equation (1) that is the product of the annual demand and of the unit price.

The second cost element that falls into the category of a replenishment cost is order preparation. This is determined by first dividing the annual demand by the order quantity. The result is the number of orders placed annually. This quantity is then multiplied by the order preparation cost to yield the total preparation cost. This cost is represented in Equation (1) by the symbol $\frac{PR}{Q}$.

Determination of Carrying Costs. The total annual carrying cost is the product of the average inventory per year and the carrying and storage costs per unit. In Equation (1), this is represented as $\frac{iQ}{2}$. In this representation, i is assumed to be a dollar figure. Occasionally, a firm may estimate its carrying costs as a percentage of the value of average inventory. Under these circumstances, the total carrying costs would be represented by the statement $iC\frac{Q}{2}$. The actual value of these two alternate statements of the inventory carrying costs would be equal. It is merely a matter of whether the unit carrying costs are represented as a dollar amount or as a percentage of the unit cost.

Graphical Solution Method

The graphical representation of the total costs and the cost components as just discussed is shown in Figure 16-4. This figure is a schematic equivalent of Equation (1).

It is, therefore, possible to solve for the economic lot size by plotting the appropriate cost data on such a graph. The solution is at the point where the total cost curve is at its lowest. In this particular problem, this is also at the intersection of the preparation cost curve and the carrying cost curve. Note that the purchased cost of the annual inventory curve remains constant through all

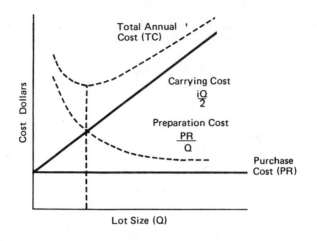

FIGURE 16-4

Inventory Costs vs. Order Quantity

ordering levels. Thus, purchased cost does not enter into the solution, but merely raises the base. The cost is included to illustrate all of the cost factors involved in the determination of the total inventory costs. It is possible to ignore this cost element and consider only the variable costs. The resultant equation is:

$$TVC = \frac{PR}{Q} + \frac{iQ}{2} \qquad (2)$$

Where:

$$TVC = \text{total variable costs}$$

The graphical solution would be lengthy and difficult to achieve accurately. This solution method does have one redeeming feature that makes it useful. It illustrates the effect of small changes in order quantity on total costs. This effect is easily seen by viewing the steepness of the slope of the curve on either side of the low point.

Tabular Solution Method

It is also possible to achieve a solution by substituting the appropriate figures into Equations (1) or (2) for different values of Q. However, this method could not guarantee an optimum solution unless one were to substitute all possible quantities of Q. This process could entail a very large number of computations. If the annual demand was 50,000, this would require substituting for all possible values from 1 to 50,000. However, certain lot sizes can be selected, and the lowest cost among these can be determined. Lot sizes of 1,000, 5,000, 10,000, 25,000, and 50,000 can be selected. The results of such computations could be presented in a form such as shown in Table 16-1. The appropriate data are:

$$R = 50,000$$
$$P = \$40 \text{ per order}$$
$$i = \$.20 \text{ per unit}$$
$$C = \$1.00 \text{ per unit}$$

TABLE 16-1

Computation of Total Inventory Costs for Selected Lot Sizes

Lot Size (Q)	1,000	5,000	10,000	25,000	50,000
Number of Orders (R/Q)	50	10	5	2	1
Average Inventory (Q/2)	500	2,500	5,000	12,500	25,000
Purchase Cost (CR)	$50,000	$50,000	$50,000	$50,000	$50,000
Preparation Costs (R/Q)P	2,000	400	200	80	40
Carrying Costs (Q/2)i	100	500	1,000	2,500	5,000
Total Costs (TC)	$52,100	$50,900	$51,200	$52,580	$55,040

From this analysis it can be stated that, of those lot sizes considered, an order size of 5,000 is the most economical. To achieve an exact economic lot size would require the same process for numerous quantities above and below 5,000 to find the lowest possible cost. Note that in this method, as in the graphical one, the purchase cost made no difference in the solution. Since it is constant, it could have been ignored and only the variable costs considered.

Mathematical Model Solution Method

A much more efficient method for determining the economic lot size is to resort to mathematical techniques. In the graphical illustration above, the economic lot size was at the lowest point on the total cost curve. The slope of the total cost curve is negative, or decreasing, prior to this point and positive, or increasing, beyond the low point. This illustrated in Figure 16-5. The slope of any curve is computed by determining the ratio between the change along a segment of the curve along the y-axis and the change along the x-axis for the same segment. This is identified in Figure 16-5 as Δx and Δy. The ratio can then be stated as $\Delta y / \Delta x$. In the illustration it is clear that $\Delta y / \Delta x$ is negative and $\Delta y' / \Delta x'$ is positive.

A little thought will quickly reveal that the slope of the curve at the lowest point is zero. This point is illustrated in Figure 16-5 by the straight-line curve represented by the dotted lines with the same low point. At the low point, the curve is neither decreasing nor increasing. It is then necessary to determine by mathematical means the point on the total cost curve at which the slope of the curve is zero. This point can be stated as:

$$\frac{\Delta TC}{\Delta Q} = 0$$

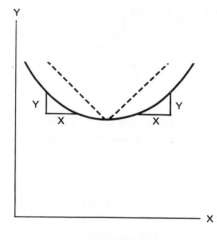

FIGURE 16-5

Illustration of the Changes in the Slope of a Curve

This point is computed by differential calculus. The process of differentiation is simply the determination of the ratio of change between two variables. The ratio is expressed as the derivative of one variable with respect to the other. The step-by-step process is as follows:

$$TC = CR + \frac{PR}{Q} + \frac{iQ}{2} \qquad (1)$$

taking the first derivative of TC with respect to Q we get:

$$\frac{d(TC)}{dQ} = 0 + \frac{i}{2} - \frac{PR}{Q^2} \qquad (3)$$

setting the derivative equal to zero we have:

$$\frac{i}{2} - \frac{PR}{Q^2} = 0 \qquad (4)$$

solving for Q:

$$Q = \sqrt{\frac{2PR}{i}} \qquad (5)$$

Note that the purchase cost disappears in this process. This result is in line with the observations made for the previous methods where it was found that purchase cost had no bearing on the solution. The use of Equation (5) enables the calculation, with relative ease, of the economic lot size for any situation which meets the original assumptions. Substituting the values used to compute total costs in the illustration represented in Table 16-1 yields the following:

$$Q = \sqrt{\frac{2 \times 40 \times 50{,}000}{.20}}$$

$$= 4{,}472 \text{ units}$$

Thus, in this situation the economic lot size would be 4,472 units (rounded to the nearest whole number). A brief analysis of the equation for economic lot size indicates some significant points for management. If the carrying costs were doubled to $.40, the lot size would be reduced by a little less than 30%. If the annual demand increased by some amount, the economic lot size would only increase by the square root of the multiple of the original demand which the new demand represented. That is, if demand increases fourfold, the economic lot size would increase by two.

Noninstantaneous Resupply Model

The above model assumes an instantaneous resupply, meaning that the entire quantity ordered is received at one time. This circumstance is likely for purchased lots, but unlikely for internally produced lots where the ordered items are placed in inventory as they are completed. As a result, the pattern of such a system will appear as in Figure 16-6.

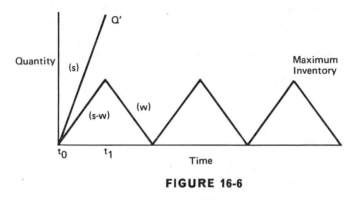

FIGURE 16-6

Inventory System with Noninstantaneous Resupply

Under these circumstances it is necessary to modify the original Equation (1) to take into account the supply or replenishment rate (s) and the withdrawal rate (w), both stated in the same units and same period of time. The supply rate is the rate at which the units ordered are placed into inventory. If the units are produced in the factory at the rate of 100 per day, and each day's output is sent to inventory, then s is equal to 100. If at the same time, the units are withdrawn from inventory at a rate of 50 units per day, this is the value of w. Notice that in this illustration s is larger than w. In such a system this difference is necessary to avoid running out of stock. The rate at which the inventory increases is equal to ($s - w$) and determines the slope of the line showing the increase in the inventory. This increase in inventory will occur over time period t_0 to t_1 and will be expressed as follows:

$$\text{Production period} = \frac{Q'}{s} \qquad (6)$$

Where:

$$Q' = \text{production economic lot size}$$

The maximum inventory which will occur at the end of this period is:

$$\text{Maximum inventory} = \frac{Q'}{s} (s - w) \tag{7}$$

Thus, it can be determined that the average inventory is one half this value, which is stated as follows:

$$\text{Average inventory} = \frac{Q'}{2s} (s - w) \tag{8}$$

Thus, the cost of carrying the average inventory can be expressed as:

$$\text{Carrying costs} = \frac{iQ' (s - w)}{2s} = \frac{iQ'}{2} \left(1 - \frac{w}{s}\right) \tag{9}$$

The total cost equation for the production economic lot size will then be as is shown below. The preparation costs (P) in this case involve such things as machine setup costs as well as any clerical costs attributable to the order. The value of (C) represents the manufactured cost of the item when placed in inventory.

$$TC = CR + \frac{PR}{Q'} + \frac{iQ'}{2} \left(1 - \frac{w}{s}\right) \tag{10}$$

The economic lot size equation in this case can be determined by the differentiation process as with Equation (1). The results of this process after solving for Q' are:

$$Q' = \sqrt{\frac{2PR}{i\left(1 - \frac{w}{s}\right)}} = \sqrt{\left(\frac{2PR}{i}\right)\left(\frac{s}{s - w}\right)} \tag{11}$$

Assume now that the following rates of replenishment and withdrawal apply. Compute the economic lot size for this model using the same values for the other variables as in the previous example.

$$s = 2{,}000 \text{ units per week}$$
$$w = 1{,}000 \text{ units per week}$$

Substituting into Equation (11):

$$Q' = \sqrt{\left(\frac{2 \times 40 \times 50{,}000}{.20}\right)\left(\frac{2{,}000}{2{,}000 - 1{,}000}\right)}$$
$$= 6{,}325 \text{ units}$$

A comparison of the value of Q (the purchased economic lot size) and of Q' (the production economic lot size) indicates an increase for Q'. This increase results because of the noninstantaneous resupply condition. The result will be fewer orders having to be placed, with a resultant reduction in preparation costs. Since preparation costs and carrying costs were equal at the economic lot size in the graphical solution, the conclusion is reached that the total costs will be lower as well. This conclusion can be verified by substituting the appropriate values into Equation (1) and into Equation (10).

Price Breaks

To this point the purchased or manufactured cost of the item has been considered constant, irrespective of the quantity ordered. However, in most situations, larger quantities will yield lower unit costs. Most vendors will offer quantity discounts at various order levels. In the manufacturing case, the costs can be reduced by using different types of machines, tools, or fixtures. Lower transportation costs are also possible when shipping larger quantities of an item which lowers the unit price. The problem of determining the economic lot size when price breaks apply can vary with the nature of the inventory system. Essentially, they will be merely a modification of the model used when there are no price breaks. We will illustrate one model for the purchasing case where one price break applies.[3]

Let:

$$Q_1 = \text{lot size with price 1}$$
$$Q_2 = \text{lot size with price 2}$$
$$b = \text{quantity where price break occurs}$$
$$P_1 = \text{price 1}$$
$$P_2 = \text{price 2}$$

The following general decision rules are established for this model:

1. Compute the value of Q_2 by means of Equation (5). It should be noted that Q_1 and Q_2 will differ as a result of a different value for i for each. This is true because the average inventory value will vary in each case with the different value of the units.
2. If $Q_2 > b$, then the optimum lot size is Q_2.
3. If $Q_2 < b$, the discount will no longer apply. This means that the lowest cost with P_2 will be at b.
4. Compute the value of Q_1 by means of Equation (5).
5. Compare the total cost of Q_1 with the total cost at b.
6. If $TC(Q_1) > TC(b)$, the optimum lot is b. If $TC(Q_1) < TC(b)$, the optimum lot size is Q_1.

A similar set of decision rules can be established to handle cases with two or more price breaks. The process starts with Q_n, until:

---

[3]The model suggested here follows the one presented in: C. W. Churchman, R. L. Ackoff, and E. L. Arnoff, *Introduction to Operations Research* (New York: John Wiley & Sons, Inc., 1957), pp. 235–254.

$$Q_{n-j} \geq b_{n-(j+1)}, \quad j = 0, 1, \dots\dots, (n-1)$$

Then, a comparison is made of:

$$TC_{(Q_{n-j})} \text{ with } TC_{(b_{n-j})}, \ TC_{(b_{n-j+1})}, \ \dots\dots\dots, \ TC_{(b_{n-1})}$$

The process involves at most n steps. The graphical representation of the problem when two price breaks apply is shown in Figure 16-7. The total cost curves for the three possible prices are indicated. The solid portions are those parts of the curves which are applicable. The dotted segments are not, because they pertain only above or below the price breaks $b1$ and $b2$. The economic lot size will be at the lowest point on the solid part of the curves. This point is indicated by Q^*.

A variety of conditions are possible, so the economic lot may be found on any one of the curves or at one of the price breaks in individual cases.

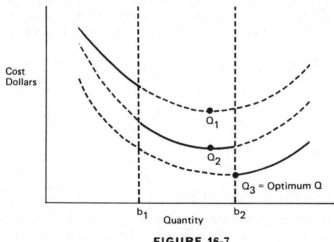

FIGURE 16-7

Economic Lot Size with Two Price Breaks

INVENTORY SYSTEM VARIATIONS

To this point, the consideration of inventory systems has emphasized the model for determining the economic lot size under very limited conditions. Essentially, these could be identified as conditions of certainty. The main circumstance that makes for certainty is the fact that the demand for the time period is constant and known. Because of this, the possibility of stockouts occurring is practically nonexistent. However, these conditions of certainty are found infrequently. What is more likely to occur is a situation where the demand is variable. If the distribution of the demand is known with certain probabilities, an inventory system under conditions of risk exists. When the distribution of demand is unknown, the inventory system can be said to be operating under conditions of uncertainty. The analytical approaches to the uncertainty problem become extremely complex and are beyond the scope of this discussion.[4] It is highly likely that the available information in a great number of cases will be so sparse as to put many inventory systems into the uncertainty category. The very complexity of the models and of the required computations necessitates the assumption of some knowledge to try to reduce the problem to a risk condition. Therefore, in many service enterprises, the inventory problem will approach uncertainty more frequently than in manufacturing enterprises. The results, with any decision-making problem under conditions of uncertainty, cannot be guaranteed to be optimum.

Risk Conditions

A large number of inventory systems fall into the category of conditions of risk. The principal reason for this is the variations in the demand which take place. However, it is possible to determine some pattern of the probability distribution for demand for many systems. In such cases, this pattern is drawn from the past distribution of demand. To use this demand, the same (or essentially so) distribution must be assumed for the future. Of course, a variable demand is not the only factor which can lead to conditions of risk. Conditions of risk can arise as a result of a variation in the replenishment cycle time. Whatever the case, there are a number of models which can be applied. Typically, they are for specific situations rather than for general ones.

Inventory under risk conditions will be illustrated by some fairly typical systems. They will be viewed as falling into two broad categories. The first of these categories will be the dynamic inventory system which is a continuous system wherein the number of orders to be placed is more than one. Most likely the number will be considerably more than two, but anything more than a one-order possibility makes for a dynamic system. Obviously, for most manufacturing firms and for most retail enterprises this is the type of inventory system found. The second class of systems is identified as static systems. These are single-order inventory systems. This means that only one order is possible. The usual circumstances where these types of systems are found are for enterprises which deal in perishable supplies, high style seasonal items, or one-of-a-kind type of orders. Such systems are not as rare as one might imagine at first consideration. Many of the nonmanufacturing enterprises would fall into this category. The baker; the newsstand; the high-fashion women's clothing store; the building of a new facility to provide sufficient capacity, such as sufficient seating capacity in a restaurant, sufficient beds for a hospital, or adequate classroom capacity in an educational institution (the problem would also be concerned with avoiding excess capacity as well); and what has come to be the classic example of such systems, the Christmas tree dealer, are all illustrations of the static inventory system where only a single order is possible.

---

[4]Some specific approaches to inventory problems under uncertainty are detailed in: Martin K. Starr and David W. Miller, *Inventory Control: Theory and Practice* (Englewood Cliffs: Prentice-Hall, Inc., 1962), Chapters 3 and 6.

Dynamic Inventory Systems

In a system in which there is a continuous demand for the items in the inventory, the possibilities of stockouts are brought on with variable demand or variable replenishment cycle time. An almost automatic reaction to offset this possibility is the use of safety or buffer stocks. In the determination of the economic lot size under conditions of certainty, the addition of a safety stock will increase the total cost because of the additional carrying costs incurred. However, since it is expected that the inventory will be replenished when the stock reaches the safety level, the economic lot size will not be affected. In the dynamic inventory system, demand can fluctuate or the replenishment cycle can vary, possibly causing inventory to go below the safety stock level. Therefore, the level of safety stock that can balance the cost of carrying additional stock and the appropriate level of service must be established. Unfortunately, there is no really accurate way of computing what the level of safety stock should be. About the only meaningful way is to find the reorder level based on some measure such as the minimum cost of lost sales and of carrying the inventory during the replenishment period.

Determination of the Lowest Cost Reorder Point. To illustrate one approach to this problem, assume the following data with regard to the sales during the replenishment period:

Sales	Probability
0	.03
1	.07
2	.22
3	.53
4	.14
5	.01

Under these circumstances, it can be seen that if the reorder point is five there is no need to carry any safety stock, as the replenishment order will always come in before more than five units are sold.

If the reorder point is set at four units, the demand will be greater than the stock on hand by one unit one percent of the time. The expected value of lost sales can be calculated if the cost of losing a sale is available. Realistically, this cost of a lost sale is difficult to ascertain. Will the customer take what is available and go elsewhere for the remainder of his order? Will he go elsewhere for the entire order? Will he return again once he has received satisfactory service elsewhere? Thus, much of this cost of losing a sale is intangible. However, for purposes of the example, assume that this cost is ascertainable, and that it amounts to $100 for each sale lost. The procedure for calculating the cost of lost sales for 100 replenishment periods with a reorder point of four is as follows:

$$(5 - 4) \times .01 \times 100 = \$1.00$$

In the same way the cost for a reorder level of three units is computed:

$$(4 - 3) \times .14 \times 100 = \$14.00$$
$$(5 - 3) \times .01 \times 100 = \underline{2.00}$$
$$\text{Total} \quad \$16.00$$

and for a reorder point of two:

$$(3 - 2) \times .53 \times 100 = \$53.00$$
$$(4 - 2) \times .14 \times 100 = 28.00$$
$$(5 - 2) \times .01 \times 100 = \underline{3.00}$$
$$\text{Total} \quad \$84.00$$

Assume that the cost of carrying an item in inventory is equal to $25 for the period of 100 replenishment cycles. The total costs can be compared for these alternative reorder points in Table 16-2. The carrying costs are computed for the units in inventory during the replenishment cycle.

TABLE 16-2

Costs of Lost Sales and Carrying Costs for Different Reorder Points
100 Replenishment Cycles

	Reorder Point			
	2	3	4	5
Lost Sales Costs	$ 84	$16	$ 1	$ 0
Carrying Costs	50	75	100	125
Total Costs	$134	$91	$101	$125

From this analysis, the lowest cost can be achieved by placing the order for replenishment when the level of stock is at three. This decision does not insure that there will be no stockouts. In fact, an examination of the sales distribution during replenishment indicates that there will be an out-of-stock condition 15% of the time, when demand is either four or five units. However, this is a chance that the enterprise will have to take if it wishes to achieve minimum costs. If the enterprise is satisfied to accept this service level, the reorder point of three will allow for no safety stock.

Level of Service and Reorder Point. Another approach to the problem of variable demand and variable replenishment cycle time is to attempt to determine a level of service which the enterprise wishes to achieve. This situation can be illustrated by means of a diagram such as found in Figure 16-8. This figure indicates the cumulative distribution of the demand for an item. The horizontal axis indicates the demand during the replenishment time, while the vertical axis is the percentage of the time that the indicated demand is exceeded.

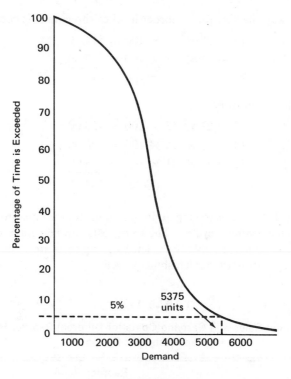

FIGURE 16-8

Distribution of Demand Exceeding Indicated Level

As can be seen from this curve, the average demand is approximately 3,025. If the management of this enterprise establishes a policy that stockouts are acceptable only 5% of the time, they will have to place a replenishment order when the inventory reaches 5,375 units. Under these circumstances the difference between the amount in inventory at the time of reorder and the average demand during the replenishment cycle is identified as the safety stock. In this illustration the safety stock would be determined as $5,375 - 3,025 = 2,350$. Management may be willing to accept a lower level of service, or putting it another way, be willing to accept a higher risk of running out of stock. The reorder point for any such level can be determined from this curve in the same fashion. A decision to accept a higher risk should only be made with the understanding of the effect that it will have on the relationships with the users of the inventory items. Again, it is important to emphasize that the determination of the cost of reduced service and of lost sales is not only difficult, but is frequently impossible. In moving from a greater to a smaller risk, management must take cognizance of the increase in carrying costs that accompanies any such decision.

The situations that exist under conditions of risk in a dynamic inventory system vary in a variety of ways from the illustrations used here. In some cases they become extremely complex, and require complicated mathematical models to represent the system. It is usually necessary to develop a model to fit the individual system. Thus, it is not within the scope of this discussion to attempt to go beyond setting up the generalized framework of inventory systems.

Use of Simulation. A final illustration of a way in which fluctuating demand and replenishment cycles may be treated is by the use of simulation techniques. As in all inventory systems, it is desired that a sufficient quantity be in stock to cover the demand during the replenishment cycle.

Assume that demand can be forecasted over time with reasonable accuracy, and that an average of 10 units per week has been found to be substantially correct. However, the pattern for this demand is such that any given week of a small group of weeks may show a considerable deviation from the average. On the basis of past experience, it has been found that demand may vary anywhere from 1 to 17 units per week. The probability distribution of demand for these items is indicated in Table 16-3.

TABLE 16-3

Probability Distribution of Demand

Weekly Demand	Probability
1	.01
2	.02
3	.03
4	.04
5	.06
6	.09
7	.10
8	.10
9	.09
10	.12
11	.10
12	.09
13	.05
14	.04
15	.03
16	.02
17	.01
	1.00

The distribution of the replenishment cycle, which was found to average about three weeks, with a range from one to five weeks, is illustrated in the same way in Table 16-4.

With this information it would be possible to simulate the performance of this inventory system. Starting with a given inventory level, and assuming a fixed-time-interval system, where orders are placed at the end of each week to

TABLE 16-4

Probability Distribution of Replenishment Cycle

Replenishment Cycle (Weeks)	Probability
1	.11
2	.14
3	.42
4	.21
5	.12
	1.00

replace the items sold during that week, simulation techniques could be used to establish a history of the operation of this system.

In analyzing this system, it is necessary to determine what measure of effectiveness will be utilized. One measure is that of lost sales. When demand for an item is made, and it is not in stock, a sale is lost. The obvious objective is to develop a system in which the performance is improved by reducing the number of lost sales. A normal step in the attempt to achieve this goal is to increase the amount of inventory carried. The best solution, however, is to find the point which gives the lowest cost combination of carrying cost and lost sales as in the previous example. It is possible to simulate the effects of various inventory levels and to calculate the balance of the added revenues versus the additional costs from carrying the different levels of inventories.[5]

Static Inventory Systems

While most inventory systems would clearly be dynamic systems, it is important to recognize the existence of static systems. A static system exists when only a single order can be placed to satisfy the demand. There is no replacement possible in these systems either because of the nature of the item involved, such as a highly perishable one; because of the nature of the demand, as in the case of a demand that will prevail only for a limited period of time, i.e., a few hours or one day; or because the cost of a replenishment order is excessively high, as in the case of a custom-made item that is uneconomical to replace or duplicate. While these systems may be relatively infrequent, they are a typical problem faced by many managers of inventories. The seller of the daily newspaper cannot sell today's news tomorrow, and he wants to have enough papers on hand to meet the demand for that day. The baker of pies which are sold as freshly baked

---

[5]A simulation using this approach has been described in: Kenneth C. Lucas and Leland A. Moody, "Electronic Computer Simulation of Inventory Control," *Electronics in Action: The Current Practicality of EDP*, Special Report No. 22 (New York: American Management Association, 1957), pp. 107–121.

today is in the same position, as is the fruit and vegetable section manager of the supermarket. This problem will be illustrated with a simple example which will be representative of a large number of cases. From this analysis a generalized model for these types of systems can be stated.

Assume a bakery that wants to prepare specially decorated cakes for St. Valentine's Day to sell on February 14. These cakes cost $.75 to make and they are sold in the store for $1.50. If they are not sold on that day, they are sold to the senior citizen home for $.50. An examination of the past experience for the sale of these cakes reveals the following probability distribution.

Sale of N cakes	20	21	22	23	24	25	26
Probability of sale of N cakes	.05	.10	.15	.40	.15	.10	.05

The problem facing the bakery is to determine the number of cakes to bake to achieve the maximum expected profit. No cost is attached to the loss of a sale because of an out-of-stock situation except the failure to achieve the revenue from that demand. There is also no goodwill attached to the sale of leftover cakes at the lower price.

It is possible to attach a probability of sale, then, to each cake that is baked. This probability can be stated as P_n, n being the number of cakes baked. Since the information gathered indicates that the baker will always sell at least 20 cakes, the value for P_n, $n \le 20 = 1$. Accumulating the individual probabilities, the following values for P_n apply:

$$P_1 = P_2 = P_3 = \ldots = P_{20} = 1$$
$$P_{21} = .95$$
$$P_{22} = .85$$
$$P_{23} = .70$$
$$P_{24} = .30$$
$$P_{25} = .15$$
$$P_{26} = .05$$

For each cake that is made and sold, a contribution of $.75 is achieved ($1.50 − .75), and for those cakes baked and not sold, a loss of $.25 each is incurred ($.75 − .50). A determination of the expected value of the incremental contribution of any cake, as represented by the possible values of n, can be made. The expected contribution of any cake made and sold, then, is the product of the contribution and the probability that that cake will be sold, or $.75P_n$. The expected loss for those cakes made but not sold is the product of the loss incurred and the probability that the cake will not be sold, which is $.25 (1 - P_n)$. Thus, the expected value of the contribution of any cake is the difference between these two values, and is stated as:

$$EC_n = .75P_n - .25 (1 - P_n) = 1.00P_n - .25 \qquad \textbf{(12)}$$

The problem now is to find the value of n which will result in the maximizing of the total expected contribution. The total expected contribution can be stated as:

$$TEC_n = \sum_{i=1}^{n} EC_n$$

Clearly, the contribution of the first 20 cakes is equal, in that each cake made has a probability of being sold equal to 1.00. Thus:

$$EC_1 = EC_2 = EC_3 = \ldots = EC_{20} = \$.75$$

and the total contribution for $TEC_n = 20 = \$15.00$.

Following this process, and substituting into Equation (12) for the values of n, the expected contribution for each cake is as follows:

$$EC_{21} = \$.70, \, EC_{22} = \$.60, \, EC_{23} = \$.45, \, EC_{24} = \$.05, \, EC_{25} = -\$.10,$$
$$EC_{26} = -\$.20$$

and for all $n > 26$, $EC_n = -\$.25$.

From this computation it can be seen that the maximum value for TEC_n will be achieved when $n = 24$. Up to that point, each additional cake made will have an expected contribution which is positive. The incremental contribution of cake 24 will average \$.05, while cake 25 will result in an expected loss of \$.10. The resultant total expected contribution from making 24 cakes is \$16.80.

Another approach to solving problems of this type which may be simpler from a computational standpoint is to first establish the probability distribution for a demand of less than n units. In the problem illustrated above, this distribution is as follows:

Demand n units	Probability Demand less than n units
20	0.00
21	0.05
22	0.15
23	0.30
24	0.70
25	0.85
26	0.95

Using the following statement of inequality, the quantity to make or to order can be determined:

$$\sum^{d'} P(n) \leq \frac{S - C}{S - U}$$

Where:

$\quad\quad P(n)$ = probability of demand less than n units

$\quad\quad\quad d'$ = demand level just below optimum order or production quantity

$\quad\quad\quad\, S$ = unit selling price

$\quad\quad\quad C$ = unit cost

$\quad\quad\quad U$ = salvage value of unused units

Using the information available for the Valentine cake example, we have the following:

$$P(y) \leq \frac{1.50 - .75}{1.50 - .50} \leq .75$$

$P(y)$ = cumulative probability of demand less than n units, at level just below optimum

The demand with a probability less than or equal to this result is the same as determined above, 24, with a corresponding probability of demand less than 24 units of .70.

PRACTICAL INVENTORY MANAGEMENT

The analytical approaches to the control of inventory systems as presented have wide and general application. They can be used for the determination of such things as order points and order quantities for anything which can be stocked. However, it is important to emphasize again the necessity for looking at each item separately, as well as taking account of the total inventory system. Some of the most common variations that affect the control of inventory have been examined. It has been assumed that management wants to control inventory because of the large proportion of the total cost inventories represent in many enterprises. This may not necessarily be true. The implication is that a varying degree of control of this problem area is possible. It is possible, at one extreme, to ignore inventory control by simply not carrying any inventory. Such a policy of control, while highly unlikely in most cases, can be followed. In fact, where the output of the operations system is only to customer order, this situation is often found. Many small businesses which perform a service to the customer's demand may fall into this category. A case in point may be the small automobile repair business. This type of enterprise may depend on the parts jobber completely for any parts which the mechanic needs. Parts jobbers usually carry a wide variety of parts, and the mechanic may acquire them virtually on an immediate order and resupply basis.

The other extreme would encompass a control system which used a very rigid reorder quantity or review period for each individual item in the inventory.

This type of system would be constantly under review to update the ordering information.

Analysis of Inventory by Value

In the establishment of the degree of control to be applied to an inventory system, it is useful to differentiate the items in the inventory on the basis of their relative importance. Not all items will have the same value or the same level of usage. Some items are more important because of their value, and consequently merit greater control and attention than others. Most often a small number of items in an inventory represent a very large percentage of the total inventory value, while a very large percentage of items have a low total value. Thus, it may be that about 15% or 20% of the inventory items may represent 80% of the total value while only 10% of the value is in 60% or more of the items.

The development of analysis by value is attributed to H. Ford Dickie of the General Electric Company. The analysis is usually referred to as the ABC method since it identifies all items in inventory as falling into one of three classes, A, B, or C. The A items account for the largest percentage of the total value of the inventory, but represent only a small proportion of the total items. At the other extreme, the C items are a large percentage of the total number, but account for a small part of the inventory value. The ABC analysis is represented in Figure 16-9.

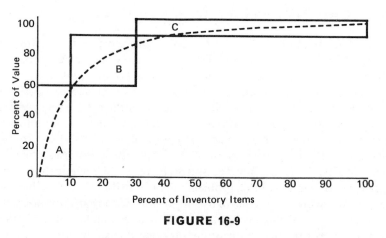

FIGURE 16-9

The ABC Method of Inventory Analysis

This analysis allows management to develop a selective type of control for all items in inventory, dependent on their relative value. Thus, for items in the A class, very extensive controls would be desired. It is for these types of items that the use of the high-level quantitative models would be most applicable. It would be possible to justify the building of a complex mathematical model for the items in this class because of their relative importance.

Items which fall into class B would be subject to moderate control techniques. The use of standard economic lot size analysis would probably be justified, but the development of sophisticated analytical models would not.

It follows, that Class C items would be of such relatively little value and importance that very simplified control techniques would be the most that management would want to utilize. In fact, it is not difficult to imagine that for some items in this class no controls would be utilized. For example, the cost of control of certain minor clerical supplies would make the institution of an inventory control system uneconomical. It matters little that the office runs out of staples — paper clips can be used as a substitute.

A system of analysis such as the ABC method can also be used for the usage rate of the items in inventory. That is, items may be classified according to their usage rate, with the high usage rate items identified as A items. It is also feasible to combine value and usage by using the product of unit value and usage to achieve a usage-value figure which can be used to establish the classes. It may be desirable from management's viewpoint to establish more than three classes of inventory items. There is certainly no reason why this cannot be done, if it serves the purposes of improving the control of the inventory system of the enterprise. The greatest value of this form of analysis is that it enables management to develop a system of controls which permits placing the proper amount of emphasis where the need is greatest and where the most efficient and economical results can be achieved.

Policy Adjustments to Meet Actual Needs

In the management of any inventory system it will always be necessary to adjust to meet the actual needs of the enterprise. In developing the optimum order quantity, it is often the case that certain restrictions may exist which are not reflected in the model. Frequently, the total of the optimum orders indicated will face a limitation. For instance, if the total indicated by the quantitative calculations were ordered, this total would exceed the available storage space. Another similar circumstance would be found when the enterprise is short of cash or working capital. In this case it would not be possible for the enterprise to pay for the total indicated. A final example in this broad category would be found in the instance of economic production orders whose total exceeded the manufacturing capacity of the plant. In general, these are situations where management policy will have to be modified. Frequently, the policy indicated by quantitative analysis is not attainable under the conditions in effect.

There are times when an enterprise, because of the competitive conditions, will have to deviate from the policy which is indicated as optimal from a cost standpoint. Such a case would be found when a small enterprise cannot always meet the price or the technology of large competitors. To offset this competitive disadvantage, the small firm may resort to a policy of maintaining an inordinately large inventory. In this way it may be able to "sell service" by always being in a position of having the items on hand.

Policy Review

The policies used in developing the control for any inventory system must be subject to periodic review. The data used to establish such things as the optimal ordering rules are based on some combination of past history and forecasted conditions. As the actual picture unfolds, there will be deviations from these premises. Thus, to be sure that the policies which are being followed are the best, management must examine the conditions that exist with regard to each item in its inventory. In the past, in large enterprises having many thousands of inventory items, this examination has been a tremendous task. Today, however, with the availability of computers, the frequent review of inventory items is a practical and economic possibility. Programs can be written to review all inventory items on a regular basis, yielding data on demand, costs, replenishment time, stockouts, and service levels. These data can be used to revise the order quantity or reorder period. Computer programs may be designed to utilize the ABC analysis idea in updating the inventory item. For example, A items may be reviewed by the computer weekly, B items monthly, and C items semiannually. The results of these programs will be to have the computer make routine inventory decisions; e.g., changes in order quantity or reorder points.

The approaches to controlling inventory systems discussed are of general applicability. The determination of the proper policy can only be made by an examination of each item in the inventory. Even with what appear to be perfect policies, there will be excessive costs and some shortages in all instances. However, by the proper use of the techniques suggested, difficulties will be reduced to a minimum.

SUMMARY

All inventory problems are concerned with a level of service, with cost, and with a usage factor. The control system aims at a balance among these factors. However, inventory problems are sufficiently distinct that each case requires a unique control model.

Probably the most important function of inventories is the decoupling effect that they have in regard to other stages of the operations system. They are necessary buffers against unforeseen variations in the actual performance. Inventories offset the timing variations which occur. They also are organizational in that they offset extra effort on the part of organization units.

Inventories can be classified in a number of different ways. The most useful way is by the function which they perform. This classification includes lot size inventories, anticipation inventories, and buffer inventories.

Costs are an important element of inventory systems and are the usual measure of the effectiveness. Replenishment costs, one of the significant inventory costs, are concerned with the amount ordered. Carrying costs are incurred in the handling and storage of the inventory. The final category of inventory system costs results from lost sales. These costs are referred to as shortage costs.

Two basic factors underlie any inventory system decision: time of replenishment and quantity of order. Two types of inventory systems are examined, each of which approaches these problems in a slightly different way. The fixed-reorder-quantity system is one of these. Where it is utilized, a specified quantity is ordered when the amount on hand is just sufficient to cover the needs during the replenishment cycle time. The idealized situation is where there is immediate replenishment and the demand is constant. However, this is not usual and variations occur. These variations are typically the result of changes in the rate of usage or in the varying of the replenishment cycle time.

The second type is the fixed-time-interval system. This approach uses a periodic review period as the basis for ordering to replenish the inventory. Therefore, the quantity ordered in this case will differ from period to period, based on the maximum level desired. This system typically requires a larger safety stock to offset variations which will not be noted until the review period. When the ideal conditions exist, these two types of systems are identical.

Fundamental to the calculation of the order quantity or the review period is the determination of the economic lot size. This is the quantity which can be ordered to replenish inventory at a minimum cost. The basic model assumes certain conditions which are found in rare instances. This model is helpful in understanding the models used in realistic cases. All of these models are modifications of the basic one. The cost elements of the economic lot size determination are identified as replenishment costs and carrying costs. Graphical, tabular, and mathematical solution methods can be used. In addition to the purchased lot case, there is also a model for the internally produced lot. This is referred to as the noninstantaneous resupply model.

The basic model assumes the cost of the item is constant at all levels of the quantity ordered. This is not the usual case, as larger quantities will usually result in economies which yield lower costs. A generalized model for determining the economic order quantity for these cases is presented.

The basic models are all developed for circumstances which could be identified as conditions of certainty. Since certainty is not usually the case, it is necessary to examine inventory system variations. One of these variants is identified as the category of risk. This results primarily from variations in demand. The use of probabilities applied to the demand distribution is the basic tool used here.

Dynamic inventory systems are found where the demand for an inventory item is continuous. To offset the possibilities of stockouts, a common reaction is to resort to the use of safety stock. A precise determination of a safety stock level is virtually impossible. However, some systematic process must be followed to achieve a reasonable decision. One useful technique is to attempt to determine such things as the lowest cost reorder point, or the desired level of service and the reorder point. Simulation is a useful tool for evaluating the effects of fluctuations in demand and replenishment cycles. The use of different order points, service levels, and inventory levels can be simulated to predict costs.

A less frequent situation is the static inventory system. This exists when only a single order can be placed to satisfy demand. No replacement is possible. The usual circumstance is where the item is a perishable one. A model for handling a particular case is presented.

Certain practical considerations beyond the analytical approaches to inventory management need to be included. On occasion, inventory control is ignored. One result is to eliminate inventories entirely. Another consideration is the analysis of inventory by value. A method identified as the ABC method is used for this purpose.

Management must continuously make necessary adjustments in its inventory related policies to meet actual needs. Numerous examples are possible. Policies should be subjected to continuous review. The computer is a useful device for assisting in such a review. Programs have been developed where the computer reviews all inventory items on a regular basis. The computer then makes the necessary routine revisions in inventory policies to update the system.

INCIDENT

HOKE'S HAMBURGER HUT

John Hoke is opening a short order restaurant. He is trying to develop an inventory policy for all items which he must order. He has tentatively established three categories of inventories: food perishables (meat, butter, etc.), food non-perishables (canned goods), supplies (napkins, dishes, silverware, cooking supplies).

Questions

1. Are these three categories sufficient to cover his inventories?

2. What information does he need to make a decision about the ordering and inventory policies?

3. What types of policies would you recommend for the different categories of inventories which you feel are necessary?

QUESTIONS FOR DISCUSSION AND ANALYSIS

1. In what way are all inventory problems the same? How do they differ?

2. Discuss the decoupling function of inventories. Explain what it is and why it is necessary to the operations system.

3. Identify the types of costs associated with an inventory system which may be controllable. Describe the nature of each cost and cite examples.

4. Compare the characteristics of the fixed-reorder-quantity system and the fixed-time-interval system. Under what circumstances are they the same?

5. What is the economic lot size? Why is it fundamental to the two types of inventory systems discussed in Question 4?

6. What are the assumptions which underlie the basic economic lot size model? Are these assumptions realistic?

7. Discuss the analogy presented in the chapter with regard to perfect competition and the ideal inventory model. Do you agree with the conclusion reached? Discuss your reasons.

8. Describe the composition of the various cost elements used in the determination of the economic lot size. Comment on the relative ease or difficulty of accurately identifying these costs.

9. Compare the practicality of the different solution methods presented. Under what circumstances would each be likely to be utilized? Give specific examples.

10. Explain the differences between the purchased lot and the production lot economic size models. Which of the assumptions of the basic model does the production lot situation violate?

11. What is the underlying concept of the model for determining the economic lot size when there are price breaks? Why is a modified model necessary?

12. Define the dynamic inventory situation. What are the major variables which complicate the control problem for such systems?

13. Discuss the necessity for safety stock in the dynamic inventory system. What criteria or measures of effectiveness can be used to determine the level of safety stock?

14. Describe static inventory systems. Give examples which you have observed other than those given in the chapter.

15. What is the ABC method? What is its purpose? Of what use is it to management in the control of inventories?

16. Why are policy adjustments and policy review necessary in maintaining control of inventories? Give some examples of unusual inventory policies which you may have encountered.

PROBLEMS

1. The usage of a purchased item is 1,200 units a year. The cost of placing a purchase order is $25 for each order. It costs $.15 per unit to carry the item in inventory. What is the economic purchase order size?

2. Assume that the inventory manager in Problem 1 was unaware of the true costs, and that he had estimated the cost of preparing a purchase order as $30 and the carrying costs as $.10 per unit. How much more is it costing him to operate his inventory under the incorrect estimates?

3. At the present time a firm is using 1,200 units as the economical production run. The annual requirements are 72,000 units. The cost per setup is $100 for each production run. The inventory carrying costs are $.50 per unit. When they are producing the part, the rate of production is 6,500 units a week, while the parts are used at a rate of 1,500 units per week. What would be the savings if the correct lot size was being used?

4. A magazine stand buys a weekly periodical for $.20 and sells it for $.75. A refund of $.05 is given for those copies not sold. Past records provide an estimated distribution of sales as follows:

No. of copies	Percent of time sold
15	5
16	15
17	20
18	30
19	15
20	10
21	5

How many copies should be ordered to achieve an average maximum weekly profit? What will this profit figure be?

SELECTED ADDITIONAL READINGS

Buchan, Joseph, and Ernest Koenigsberg. *Scientific Inventory Management.* Englewood Cliffs: Prentice-Hall, Inc., 1963.

Buffa, Elwood S., and William H. Taubert. *Production-Inventory Systems*, rev. ed. Homewood, Illinois: Richard D. Irwin, Inc., 1972.

Fetter, Robert B., and Winston C. Dalleck, *Decision Models for Inventory Management.* Homewood, Illinois: Richard D. Irwin, Inc., 1961.

Greene, James H. *Production Control: Systems and Decisions.* Homewood, Illinois: Richard D. Irwin, Inc., 1965.

Killeen, Louis M. *Techniques of Inventory Management.* New York: American Management Association, 1969.

Magee, John F. "Guides to Inventory Policy: I. Functions and Lot Sizes." *Harvard Business Review,* Vol. XXXIV, No. 1 (January-February, 1956), pp. 49-60.

_____. "Guides to Inventory Policy: II. Problems of Uncertainty." *Harvard Business Review,* Vol. XXXIV, No. 2 (March-April, 1956), pp. 103-116.

_____. "Guides to Inventory Policy: III. Anticipating Future Needs." *Harvard Business Review,* Vol. XXXIV, No. 3 (May-June, 1956), pp. 57-70.

Magee, John F., and David M. Boodman. *Production Planning and Inventory Control*, 2d ed. New York: McGraw-Hill Book Co., 1967.

Naddor, Eliezer. *Inventory Systems.* New York: John Wiley & Sons, Inc., 1966.

Plossl, G. W., and O. W. Wight. *Production and Inventory Control.* Englewood Cliffs: Prentice-Hall, Inc., 1967.

Prichard, James W., and Robert H. Eagle. *Modern Inventory Management.* New York: John Wiley & Sons, Inc., 1965.

Starr, Martin K., and David W. Miller. *Inventory Control: Theory and Practice.* Englewood Cliffs: Prentice-Hall, Inc., 1962.

| **Integrated Control Systems**

A major portion of the study of the operations system to this point has focused on individual problem areas while emphasizing the importance of the systems concept. It has been pointed out that the enterprise must be viewed as an integrated whole. The operations system is a subsystem of this enterprise system, and there are, in addition, subsystems of the operations system. It has been these sub-subsystems toward which we have directed much of our attention. Analysis of these individual areas in this way might be described as a "divide and conquer" approach. That is, by using this method it is easier to see the problems, and to recognize the methods which might be useful for solving them. Historically, managements have (and some still do) approached the problems of the enterprise and of the functional areas, such as operations, by analyzing individual areas. If the goal of full control of the operations system is to be achieved, however, some synthesizing of these diverse areas must be accomplished. There are available a variety of management techniques which can be identified as integrated control systems. This title is utilized here because the methods to be discussed are essentially designed to join together a number of the separate decision areas. The purpose of these techniques is to provide sets of decision rules which will solve a number of interrelated problems simultaneously and optimize the total functioning of the system. These control systems are also referred to as aggregate systems.

It is not claimed that the systems of control to be discussed are total systems control techniques. These systems unite a variety of individual decision areas of the operations system to achieve integrated decisions. It will be necessary at times to distinguish between the two types of operations systems already identified: intermittent and continuous. In addition, some differentiation of approach will be related to the scale of the operation. In particular, large-scale projects may be somewhat unique. As has been true throughout the book, a major emphasis will be placed on production activities. However, the application of these control systems to nonmanufacturing enterprises will be delineated where appropriate.

TYPES OF CONTROL SYSTEMS

In discussing the integrated control of the operations system, it is usual to associate the control system with the type of operation. Thus, the type of control associated with the intermittent system is known as order control, while flow control is related to the continuous type of operations. There are also certain types of hybrid control systems used for special forms of operations that are not strictly intermittent or continuous.

Order Control

Since in most intermittent systems the output is processed in small lots, frequently referred to as orders, the control system used for this type of operation is given the title of order control. This identification is perhaps a misnomer since not all such output is the result of a demand from a user in the form of an order. In some cases, the output is for stock, either in the form of a component of the final output or in its final form. Irrespective of the situation, order control is used. Where the output is in the form of a service, it is typically to customer order, since services are not capable of being stocked for later use.

Order control is a very difficult form of control because of the nature of the intermittent operations system. In these systems, the size of the order is variable, usually relatively small; and the inputs, the processing required, and the final output differ from order to order. Thus, it is necessary to perform the required planning and control activities many times. It is not possible to reuse the old plans in most cases. Because each order or lot is unique, the planning and control actions must be carried out for each one.

When the operations system receives an order for a specific output, it is necessary to determine what inputs are required for this order, what processes must be performed, the sequence of the processing, the timing of the various steps in the total process, and it is necessary to make any other decisions required to insure the completion of the order by the desired or scheduled date. These activities and decisions will have to occur for each order in an intermittent system, which is why order control is the most difficult type of operations control system. The identification of lots as orders is useful for purposes of comparing actual performance with that of planned performance. Progress can be more easily followed because each order is kept separate and distinct from all others. Cost collection and control are also facilitated by the use of order designation.

Generally speaking, order control is more prevalent in manufacturing situations than in nonmanufacturing ones. There are a number of reasons for this. The producing of a manufactured item is usually more complex than the performance of a service. The procurement of inputs in the form of raw materials and parts is more difficult. The processing involves various types of equipment which can be utilized in different combinations. The maintaining of the status of the order progress can become quite complex. In addition, the need for control of such elements as time and cost is usually greater in the case of manufactured items.

Everything said to this point about control, and specifically order control, is applicable to nonmanufacturing situations. In a restaurant, orders are taken and sent to the kitchen for processing. While the variety of orders is limited by the menu of the day, each order will be to customer demand. Thus, there are many parallels in this system to the intermittent production system. The problems, and even the necessity, of control are less than in production, but that control found is primarily order control.

At first thought the consideration of people as "orders" may seem to be dehumanizing, but strictly speaking, this is what patients in a hospital are from

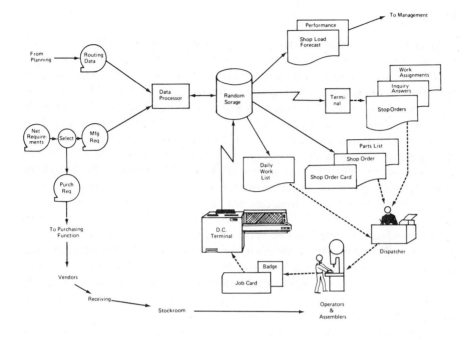

Source: *General Information Manual, Manufacturing Summary*, No. E20-8118 (White Plains, New York: IBM Corporation, Data Processing Division, undated), p. 5. Courtesy of International Business Machines Corporation.

FIGURE 17-1

Computerized Job Shop Control System

the viewpoint of operations control. The laboratory tests, the surgical operations, the X-rays, the patients' medication programs, and the prescribed diets are processes. From a systems viewpoint, the patient is the order to be processed, and any control of the system is directly related to the patient or order.

The introduction of computers into the decision-making process has had a strong influence in the control of operations systems. In order control, computerized systems have served as a means of coordinating the vast amount of information which affects the operations system, especially in the production situation. Computerized systems speed up the decisions so that real-time control is approached, if not fully attained. Figure 17-1 depicts a system which provides control for a job shop where a form of order control is found.

It will be noted by reference to Figure 17-1 that information such as shop orders, routing data, dispatching information, shop load forecast, and performance information is made available by this system. Consequently, the control of the system will bring improved decisions about scheduling and dispatching. Management's ability to react to deviations or changes in plans will also be improved. Clearly, such a system provides an integration of the various parts or subsystems of this operation.

Flow Control

In continuous operations systems, the processing is repetitive in that the same output results time period after time period. Ideally, the level of processing is established, and this level is maintained indefinitely. Under such conditions, the operations manager has relatively few problems of control. He plans and establishes the system. The processing and output then continue virtually without interruption or need to make further decisions. All of the decisions made in an intermittent system under order control are made here too, but only once, at the beginning. This situation does not mean that nothing has to be done in such a control system. There are times when the rate of output has to be changed or some other change in the requirements occurs. The control problem here is to see that all of the related subsystems are integrated so that the flow of inputs through the system is not impeded. This needed integration can best be exemplified by reference to a television manufacturing plant. It would be inadvisable to make cabinets at a rate in excess of chassis or vice versa. Under either of these conditions, the system would be out of balance, and problems would develop quickly. In flow control, management must constantly be aware of the actual as compared with the planned. Any deviations such as in the above illustration would be the signal of impending trouble.

In the "pure" continuous system, all items produced are completely standardized. In such circumstances, management needs to issue instructions regarding the specifications of the product only when processing is begun. However, in many continuous systems there are slight variations in the product. A variation may be as simple as a difference in color. Such variations increase the complexity of the flow control system. Each specific automobile on the assembly line is designated to be a particular color. All of the components to be color coordinated must be fed to the line properly. The upholstery must arrive when that car is being assembled. The proper colored body, fenders, and wheels also must be supplied from the appropriate feeder lines at the precise time. Any error will disrupt the flow of the system.

Therefore, while flow control may not be of the same degree of complexity as order control, there are many difficult problems facing management of such control systems as well.

Hybrid Control Systems

Since few if any operations systems are entirely intermittent or continuous, it follows that the control system utilized will at times have to be modified. Many of the operations are hybrids, in the sense that they contain elements of both intermittent and continuous operations. Logically there will be control systems which contain elements of order and of flow control. The two major types of hybrid control systems to be discussed here are block control and load control. One other control system, that of special or large-scale project control, will also need to be identified.

Block Control. It is possible to view block control as a modified form of flow control. The reason is that block control usually applies where the outputs are essentially the same and require the same processing. The difference is in some aspect such as size or style. In this type of control system, groupings of orders referred to as a block are released for processing. The key to the size of the block is the amount of time required to complete the group of orders. The block requires a specified period of processing time in the first department and in each succeeding department. A block of orders could require a week, four hours, two hours, or 15 minutes of processing in each department. Thus, each department will have equal capacity in terms of a given processing time. The size of the individual departments will have to be established on the basis of the time required to complete a block.

Block control serves to push the orders in the block through the processing departments. A block cannot be cleared from a given department until all orders in the block are completed. This fact tends to create a situation where it is desirable to keep all work moving. This type of control system can be used wherever variations in output do not significantly affect the required processing time. Clothing and shoe manufacturing are two places where this type of control is used extensively. Aerospace firms use a type of block control to release parts orders. The assembly activities would be subject to flow control. It is also possible to find some mail-order houses using block control. An order picker is given a block of orders, which represents a certain period of time, to fill from the stock area. Scheduling of classes in 50-minute periods is also a form of block control.

Load Control. This type of control system is found where the operations are closely related to the continuous form, but the type of control needed is similar to order control. The main feature which characterizes load control is the necessity to schedule all of the processing on some special operation or piece of equipment which becomes limiting with regard to the total processing. This limiting factor may be a key, one-of-a-kind, usually very expensive machine that cannot be duplicated because of cost.

The essence of this type of control is to schedule this critical process for its maximum utilization. All other processes are usually not a problem as each possesses sufficient capacity to process all other orders. A critical operation should never be delayed by lack of capacity in some other operation. Load control differs from flow control in that there are individual orders in load control. This difference results in a situation that requires the key operation to be stopped and to be rearranged to fit the need of the next order. In most cases the outputs require the same operations, so the controls must differ from order control where the operations are different.

The book printing industry is probably the best illustration of the application of load control. All books go through the same basic operations. The press is the key operation, and it determines the pace of the total process. As new books are released to the shop for printing, the presses must be stopped and set up for the new run. Certain clerical operations fall into this type of situation, as when the key operation is a computer. The computer sets the rate for the entire process. As in all such systems, the key operation determines what the total output can be. This operation is a bottleneck, and the control system is designed to alleviate the possible limiting effect of it.

Project Control. This type of control is associated with large-scale, one-of-a-kind output. Typically it is found in construction type projects such as a ship, a building, a dam, or something of this nature. It can also be exemplified by a major research and development program or a large banquet for thousands of people. Because of the uniqueness of the project, it is not usually possible to utilize past plans or experiences in planning and controlling the processing. There will undoubtedly be some similar aspects between projects, so there can be some sort of loose plan.

The keynote of project control is its informal nature. Because there are usually so many phases to these large-scale projects, and because one phase depends on the completion of preceding phases, control consists of attempting to integrate and coordinate the related activities. The planning and control of the total project is general in nature, but the individual component activities require detailed attention. In the case of a building, the controlling of the total construction is difficult because minor details cannot be determined except from a broad view. However, the activities relating to the plumbing or the electrical work can be scheduled and controlled in much more detail. Even in these component phases, detailed scheduling is difficult since these activities may be spaced out over a number of months. Some relatively new techniques for use in project control have been developed.

OUTPUT SCHEDULING

Scheduling the output of an operations system involves many activities which must be integrated. The scheduling activity has been closely identified with the logistics system. Therefore, one element of the total scheduling is the acquiring of the inputs at the time when they are needed. The main purpose of scheduling, however, remains that of establishing a timetable for the processing of the inputs that are to be transformed into the final output form.

Output scheduling is difficult because the level of demand fluctuates in most cases. (If this were not the case, scheduling would be much simplified.) To meet this demand fluctuation, it is necessary to forecast the output requirements for future periods in order to make a schedule. It is possible to schedule the processing aspect of an operations system in alternative ways. In general, a given level of output for a specified period, say a year, can be achieved by:

1. Varying the level of output in response to demand.
2. Varying the level of the work force, either in conjunction with a change in output or not.
3. Varying inventory levels to meet changes in demand.

Output Scheduling Alternatives

It is possible to view the scheduling alternatives as a continuum, with virtually an infinite number of variations possible. The three major controllable variables which may be utilized in various combinations are output level, work force size, and inventories. The objective in establishing the best combination of these variables to be used is some measure of cost. The two extremes of this continuum might be viewed as perfectly stable output, and as output which fluctuates in precise response to changes in demand.

Level Output. If a decision is made to establish a fixed output, it must be assumed that the output is capable of being stocked, and then withdrawn at the time when it is demanded. Thus, such a scheduling decision is essentially limited to manufacturing. As a result, the remaining discussion of this alternative will be from the viewpoint of a production system.

Level output means that the total demand is met by means of fluctuations in the level of the inventory or in order backlogs. This alternative also assumes that a constant work force is maintained. If the forecast of demand for a product is 60,000 units for the year, under this alternative the production level would be 5,000 per month, with the necessary work force to meet this output remaining constant as well. During periods of low demand, the inventory would be increased, and as demand moved to a higher rate than output, the items would be withdrawn from inventory. As long as cumulative demand was less than cumulative output, the company would be able to satisfy demand. If, however, cumulative demand exceeded cumulative production at some point, the items would have to be back ordered or a lost sale would result. This alternative can be illustrated graphically, assuming no inventory or back orders at the beginning of the year as in Figure 17-2.

Of course, actual demand will usually differ from that which has been forecasted. As a result, scheduling at a level output is not a particularly viable decision. This decision can result in large accumulations of inventory or an unsatisfactory level of service because of back orders, which implies the incurring of the costs associated with such conditions.

There is one advantage to the maintenance of an absolutely level production. Under this alternative there are no peak periods or slack periods, and this means that the plant is effectively operating at 100% capacity at all times. There is no idle capacity, so the system is at its optimum size, which eliminates investment in unutilized capital equipment and the attendant opportunity costs.

The maintenance of a constant work force is not contingent on the establishment of level output, but can be attained by changing the rate of output to meet demand through adjusting the hours of work. This is an alternative available in service enterprises. The adjustment can be accomplished by working overtime or undertime as the circumstances dictate. There are obviously costs attached to the use of overtime, and there are also limits to the number of hours which a worker can be expected to work before losing efficiency. In some cases of

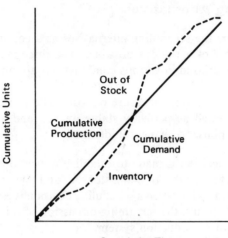

FIGURE 17-2

Cumulative Production Versus Cumulative Demand
Level Production

excessively high peak demands, subcontracting may have to be used in addition to overtime, resulting in still greater costs.

The cost of undertime or idle time when demand falls is not readily visible, but such costs do exist, and management must recognize that they will be incurred when this situation develops.

Output Fluctuating in Response to Changes in Demand. The opposite extreme to maintaining constant output is varying output in exact response to demand. If this variation is carried out precisely, there will be no need to maintain inventory. Thus, inventory costs, which are the major cost factors in the case of level output, are eliminated. On the other hand, in order to meet the fluctuations in 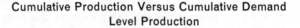 demand, it is necessary to increase or decrease the size of the work force. An upward movement in orders is met by hiring, while a decline results in layoffs. These work force fluctuations result in a variety of employment costs. The process of hiring or layoff involves costs of selection, testing, and terminal pay. In adding to the work force, provisions must be made for training and learning, which are costly. In addition, if the capacity of the plant is to be established by the level of peak demand, this can mean a considerable investment in plant and equipment that will be idle a large part of the time. Part of this investment can be offset by utilizing overtime or subcontracting at additional cost. It is also possible to effectively increase capacity by adding shifts, which involve premium costs as well.

The fluctuating output alternative is more likely to be utilized in intermittent operations systems than is level production. As a result, it is the type of scheduling

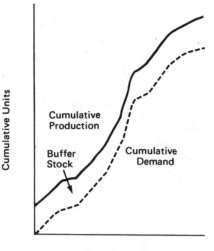

FIGURE 17-3

Cumulative Output Versus Cumulative Demand
Output Varied in Response to Demand

decision which a nonmanufacturing enterprise will most likely make. For example, a retail establishment would meet changes in demand by adjustment in its work force. In addition to hiring or layoffs (usually of part-time workers), the stores may adjust their hours of operation. The period between Thanksgiving and Christmas when the stores remain open longer hours and many part-time workers are used is typical.

A comparison of cumulative output and cumulative demand using this alternative is illustrated graphically in Figure 17-3. This situation assumes that the output can be stocked, and that a buffer inventory is maintained as a matter of management policy.

Combination Alternatives. Neither of the two extreme alternatives for scheduling output is going to be optimum in most situations. What is needed can be described as an eclectic alternative where the best combination of the relevant variables is used. This approach means that the output will have to be scheduled to meet the demand variations by resorting to some accumulation of inventory (when physical output is involved), some fluctuations in the output level, and by some changes in the size of the work force. The particular solution will depend on the applicable costs for the enterprise at the given time.

A hypothetical alternative, which could be described as a combination of the extremes somewhere near the midpoint in the continuum, can be set forth. The enterprise establishes a schedule in which the output and the work force remain constant for a period of months, and then output is raised or lowered dependent on the anticipated future demand. This new level remains in effect for a period

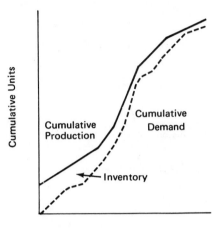

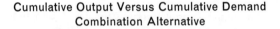

Cumulative Time

FIGURE 17-4

Cumulative Output Versus Cumulative Demand
Combination Alternative

of time and then is adjusted again according to forecasted needs. This type of schedule makes some use of inventory accumulation to meet periods of high demand, and adjusts output level and the work force size to absorb some of the fluctuation. Conceivably, the inventory costs under this alternative would be lower than experienced under level production where inventories were varied to offset the demand fluctuations. This combination alternative results in lower employment costs than when output is changed in response to demand. Probably, this alternative will have less excess capacity than the changing output response. Without precise cost data it is impossible to determine that this combination alternative would be better than the other two. Of course, this is only one of many combinations that could be adopted, but it is illustrative of the types of alternatives available between the two extremes. Figure 17-4 illustrates the relationship between cumulative production and cumulative demand for this alternative.

The situation illustrated in Figure 17-4 assumes output can be placed in inventory. Therefore, this alternative is not available to service enterprises which do not deal in physical outputs. It appears, however, that this scheduling alternative can be utilized in either a continuous or an intermittent operations system.

Output Scheduling Decisions Techniques

A number of methods for making the relevant decisions with respect to the scheduling of output have been developed. Generally speaking, all of these methods are designed to achieve a decision that will result in the optimization of some predetermined measure of effectiveness. The most frequently sought result is lowest total cost. The cost criteria usually include some aspect of the cost of the level of service furnished as well as a consideration of the cost of operating the decision system. Management not only wants decisions that give a specific outcome, but also wants to be able to achieve these decisions quickly and economically. We will examine some of the individual techniques developed for use in making output scheduling decisions under the conditions described.

Linear Decision Rules. One of the most interesting techniques available for making scheduling decisions to meet fluctuating demand is one developed by Holt, *et al.*, known as linear decision rules.[1] The *linear decision rules* (LDR) are equations derived from a consideration of the total cost function for output and work force size scheduling. This cost function considers all pertinent costs: regular payroll, hiring and layoff, overtime, and inventory related costs. The decision rules enable the enterprise to make decisions that minimize the sum of these costs. The mathematical process yields two decision rules, one for production, and the other for work force. They require a minimum of computation to achieve the necessary decisions at the beginning of a period. These decisions will be the optimum ones.

This technique recognizes certain relevant facts. In the first place, it is based on the understanding that there will be fluctuations in orders that have to be compensated for in some way. It is also accepted that there will be forecasting errors, and some way of dealing with these must be established. Finally, the method takes into account the fact that the production and work force decisions for any one period are interrelated with the same decisions for other periods. It is, therefore, necessary to consider the entire chain of decisions.

NATURE OF THE RELEVANT COMPONENT COSTS. For the purposes of achieving ease of mathematical solution, the assumption is made that most of the component costs of the total cost function can be approximated by a U-shaped curve. Reference to the total cost curve developed for the economic lot quantity model (Figure 16-4) will illustrate this type of curve. At lower inventory levels, the total cost was high, as it was at high inventory levels. The low point represented the minimum cost. The only exception to this assumption in applying the LDR was for regular payroll, which was linear. This follows the idea of making the necessary decisions only at the beginning of a time period. The decision is fixed for that period. Thus, if the size of the work force for the following month is set, the regular payroll costs are committed for the month. All of the other costs involve change (overtime, hiring and layoff, and inventory level) and can be approximated by the quadratic curve.

TOTAL COST FUNCTION. The total cost function is the sum of the component costs. It takes a quadratic form of the following type:[2]

---

[1]Charles C. Holt *et al.*, *Planning Production, Inventories, and Work Force* (Englewood Cliffs: Prentice-Hall, Inc., 1960). Earlier versions of these rules were published in two articles in *Management Science* in 1955. These articles are cited at the end of the chapter.

[2]*Ibid.*, p. 58.

$$C_T = \sum_{t=1}^{T} C_t$$

and

$$C_t = [(C_1 W_t) \qquad \text{(Regular payroll costs)}$$

$$+ C_2(W_t - W_{t-1})^2 \qquad \text{(Hiring and layoff costs)}$$

$$+ C_3(P_t - C_4 W_t)^2 + C_5 P_t - C_6 W_t \quad \text{(Overtime costs)}$$

$$+ C_7(I_t - C_8 - C_9 S_t)^2] \qquad \text{(Inventory-connected costs)} \textbf{(1)}$$

subject to constraints

$$I_{t-1} + P_t - S_t = I_t, \qquad t = 1, 2, \ldots, T$$

Where:

$W_t =$ the number of workers required for the period t
$P_t =$ the number of units to be produced in period t
$I_t =$ the inventory minus backlogs at the end of period t
$S_t =$ forecast of the number of units to be ordered for shipment during the period t
$C_k =$ cost coefficients to be determined for a given plant or situation

THE DECISION RULES. By means of a mathematical process of differentiation, the two decision rules are developed. The production rule, which is designed to set the aggregate rate of production, incorporates a weighted average of the forecasts for future periods. This weighting contributes to a smoothing of production. The assigned weights decrease quickly to reflect the high cost of producing for future orders and stocking the output.

The employment rule also utilizes a weighted average of forecasted orders. The weights for this rule do not decrease quickly, but extend some distance into the future. This procedure has the effect of making the forecasts more significant in arriving at the work force decision. The general form of these decision rules is as follows:

$$P_t = \sum_{t=1}^{T} \alpha_t S_t + k_1 W_{t-1} + k_2 - k_3 I_{t-1} \qquad \textbf{(2)}$$

$$W_t = k_4 W_{t-1} + k_5 - k_6 I_{t-1} + \sum_{t=1}^{T} \beta_t S_t \qquad \textbf{(3)}$$

Where:

$\alpha =$ weight given to individual forecasts to determine production level
$\beta =$ weight given to individual forecasts to determine work force level
$k_i =$ coefficients

EVALUATION OF THE DECISION RULES. An examination of these two decision rules indicates the dynamic relationship between the decisions with regard to output and work force levels. The level of output in a given period will be a determinant of the inventory at the end of that period. This inventory level, in turn, will be a factor in the employment decision in the next period, which will bear on the output decision in period three. The influence of the weights assigned to the forecasts is such that long-term variations will be absorbed by changes in the work force over the period, while output changes will be the system response to short-term variations.

These rules have been applied in a number of actual companies in an attempt to ascertain their value. In one case, a company's actual performance was compared for a five-year period with the performance that could have been attained using the decision rules. The decisions that would have been made during this period under the decision rules were simulated using two types of forecasts: a perfect forecast and a moving-average-of-past-orders forecast. The anticipated costs were compared with the actual costs to test the efficacy of the decision rules. If the perfect forecast is used as a base and is assumed to be 100%, the costs for the other forecast and for the actual costs can then be compared on a relative basis. Table 17-1 shows the percentage comparisons for the relevant costs.[3]

TABLE 17-1

Cost Comparison Percentages
Perfect Forecast = 100

| Component Costs | Actual Performance | Decision Rules | |
		Moving Average Forecast	Perfect Forecast
Regular payroll	102%	92%	100%
Overtime	143	177	100
Inventory	80	99	100
Back orders	390	154	100
Hirings & layoffs	91	125	100
Total costs	139%	110%	100%

Comparison of the data in Table 17-1 indicates that the use of the decision rules reduced the total costs substantially. The savings are attained essentially as a result of a reduction in back order costs. This is not the only area where savings can be achieved by use of the decision rules. In fact, studies of different periods of time in the same plant showed that the savings came about as a result of changes in a number of different costs.

Naturally, a perfect forecast is not a feasible alternative, but it is significant that substantial savings were made using the relatively simple moving average

---

[3]Computed from cost data found in Charles C. Holt, Franco Modigliani, and Herbert A. Simon, "A Linear Decision Rule for Production and Employment Scheduling," *Management Science*, Vol. II, No. 1 (October, 1955), pp. 1–30.

forecast. It is possible that larger savings could be made with a more sensitive forecasting technique.

The available evidence indicates that the use of linear decision rules as a supplement to management offers a great potential for improved decisions in scheduling. The rules integrate a number of problem areas into the decision process. Obviously, each enterprise must develop its own rules based on the applicable costs, but apparently the technique is useful in any enterprise where the costs can be approximated by a quadratic curve. It is not known how frequently this form of cost curve applies, but before using LDR, the U-shaped cost curve must be verified as an accurate representation of the costs of the enterprise.

Management Coefficients. The basic thesis of this approach to the problem[s] of aggregate scheduling decisions is that management's past decisions can be utilized to improve the current decisions.[4] In comparison with the linear decision rules, this technique does not resort to rigorous mathematical analysis to develop the coefficients in the decision rules. Instead the coefficients are derived from a statistical analysis of past decisions about output and work force. Decision rule coefficients developed in this manner are assumed to be better. Bowman contends that using the average of past coefficients will result in more consistent decisions. This conclusion was reached as a result of the observation that in the actual decision-making process managers have a tendency to respond in an inconsistent fashion to any change in the system variables. These reactions are typically such that the range of the actual costs is large. The wide variances resulting from management's erratic behavior will cause large departures from the optimum. If the average of past coefficients is used, the variations will be reduced. Thus, if the quadratic shape of the cost curve is assumed, such small biases will only result in small losses from the criteria, since the curve is relatively flat at its optimum point.

This concept of the coefficients was applied to several companies using simulation methods. The results were compared with actual performance and with performance resulting from the use of linear decision rules. In all cases, the coefficients resulted in better performance than actually experienced, but the outcome was mixed when compared with the use of linear decision rules. Probably, the use of the management coefficient has the most potential as a device for investigating the decision processes of managers in this complex area of output scheduling.

Simulation Applications. The powerful and highly flexible tool, simulation, is valuable in establishing an integrated control system, particularly when the complex scheduling in an operations system with fluctuating demand is considered. Systems of this type can become extremely complex to the point where the use of algorithms becomes an impossibility. As a result, the simulation applications to be presented will deal primarily with complex intermittent operations systems, which are identified as job shops in production systems.

---

[4]E. H. Bowman, "Consistency and Optimality in Managerial Decision Making," *Management Science* (January, 1963), pp. 310–321.

Job Shop Scheduling. The term job shop actually defines a broad variety of operations systems. The picture of a job shop most frequently conjured up in the mind is of a small machine shop engaged in producing a number of different metal parts in very small quantities for many different customers. This shop is the "custom" production shop, which produces only to order. While this is certainly a job shop, and most of the characteristics described are elements of any job shop operation, there are many variations to be found. The size of the operation is not necessarily a determinant of a job shop situation. Many job shops are large in terms of the number of employees and in the number of orders processed. In some cases, output, while "to order," may be placed into inventory for later use by some other part of the operations system such as an assembly department. Certain characteristics are assumed here as determining a job shop operation.

1. There is a wide variation in the output and a wide variation in the production time required.
2. Prediction of the future needs of the system is difficult because of the wide variation in demand.
3. A large number of orders are in process at the same time.
4. Alternate processing methods are possible as are alternate sequences for each order.
5. The level of activity of the processing segment of the system will vary, resulting in slack capacity or need for resorting to such devices as overtime or subcontracting in peak periods.
6. A large number of orders will be waiting to be processed at any given time, which contributes to the necessity for many decisions regarding which order to process next.

From these characteristics it can be deduced that the job shop operation system faces the same output scheduling alternatives as have been discussed. The problem is to coordinate the various activities to arrive at a balance among the relevant costs. Essentially, this balance is accomplished by regulating the sequence in which the processing is performed, and by controlling the flow of the work. Note, that while the job shop is typically viewed in the context of a production or manufacturing situation, the same basic conditions can be found in a system with a service output.

A number of simulation models of the scheduling decision in job shop situations have been developed.[5] The object of all of these models is to find some relatively simple decision rules for the control of the job shop. Most of these models are computerized systems, a condition that enables them to be dynamic. In this way the decisions can be made on the basis of constantly updated information. Thus, these simulation models are essentially data processing and data transmission systems that make computations from the feedback of actual performance.

Such a model could be used as an adjunct to a computerized job shop control system similar to the one illustrated in Figure 17-1. The performance data

[5]See references at the end of the chapter, especially, P. Mellor, "A Review of Job Shop Scheduling," *Operational Research Quarterly*, Vol. XVII, No. 2 (June, 1966), pp. 161–171.

sent to management could be utilized as a basis for analyzing all orders in process. The shop-load forecast, schedule, and work assignments could be revised from the simulated data. The simulation model could also be applied to the routing of new orders to generate the same sort of information output.

Some of the advantages of a job shop simulation model have been suggested by LeGrande as a result of the operation of the model used by the El Segundo Division of Hughes Aircraft Company. They can be summarized as follows:[6]

1. The determination of more reliable order waiting times.
2. The development of more representative output schedules by anticipation of trouble areas.
3. The evaluation of the effects of different priority dispatching rules.
4. The formulation of a shop-load forecast.
5. The more efficient planning of the relative location of processing facilities.
6. The creation of a means for evaluating the potential effect of different decisions.

INDUSTRIAL DYNAMICS. The application of the simulation technique of industrial dynamics lends itself well to the development of an integrated control system. Because the total operations system is so complex, and the interrelationships are so numerous, it is unlikely that optimization can be achieved. There are really no optimizing models available that can handle the magnitude of variables involved in a typical large operations system. Simulation which is related to the actions of the information-feedback system is seen by some as the ideal approach to the development of a system of control.[7]

The integrated decisions required to control the production-inventory-employment system are clearly made in a dynamic environment. An examination of the relationships of the individual subsystems would reveal the existence of information-feedback loops. The inventory levels for items stocked are adjusted in accordance with information about the level of demand. For instance, as inventories are depleted by shipments, and these adjustments are made, manufacturing orders are released. Any backlog of orders is transmitted into the decision about the employment level. This level, in turn, determines the rate of output possible. The output will affect the size of the order backlog and the level of inventory of the items stocked. This is a brief description of the closed-loop nature of the information-feedback system involved.

An industrial dynamics model can be utilized to evaluate the operations of an integrated operations control system. From this evaluation, revisions of existing policies and procedures can be implemented. These revisions are designed to improve performance. This improvement would be reflected in increased stability in the fluctuations of at least some of the variables. Fey reports a significant improvement in employment stability in one application.[8] Not all variables will

---

[6]Earl LeGrande, "The Development of a Factory Simulation System Using Actual Operating Data," *Management Technology*, Vol. III, No. 1 (May, 1963), pp. 1–19.

[7]Willard R. Fey, "An Industrial Dynamics Case Study," *Industrial Management Review* (Fall, 1962), pp. 79–99.

[8]*Ibid.*

experience the same kind of change. The fluctuations in employment may be decreased as a result of the use of one of the other parameters such as inventories to absorb the changes in the demands on the system. The degree of stability to be achieved will vary with the system. However, the use of industrial dynamics offers potential as a means of achieving a high degree of control of a dynamic and integrated operations system.

PRIORITY DISPATCHING RULES. The development of priority rules for the release of orders to be processed is largely a problem found in the intermittent type of operations system. In manufacturing, it is essentially related to the job shop situation. However, this type of decision rule can be found to have application in any intermittent system where orders are to be processed to produce an output. In a clerical operation where claim forms are to be processed, some alternate priority schemes might prove more efficient than others in the overall performance of the system. Basically, this is a form of a waiting-line problem, and many situations of a nonmanufacturing nature can be described in these terms. The waiting-line disciplines of first-come, first-serve, and by appointment have been illustrated. These are priority dispatching rules that determine the sequence in which the inputs waiting to be served are put into the system. Of course, other priority rules can be used. The number of rules, while not really infinite, is quite large. The technique of simulation to be described is designed to allow management to evaluate a variety of these possible dispatching rules to determine whether one of them would lead to a more efficient performance of the operations system.

The method will be described in a simplified form, using "hand" simulation techniques for purposes of illustration. Keep in mind that the simulation would normally be carried out through a computer program. The method used in the example has been called the card-pigeonhole method.[9] Cards with the sequence

Order No. 01			Start: Day 1	
Oper.	Mach.	Oper. Time Days	Due: Day 22	
			Priority	
1	M1	3.0		
2	M2	3.5		
3	M3	4.0		
4	M4	3.0		
5	M5	3.0		

FIGURE 17-5

Sample Job Order Card

[9]James R. Jackson, "Research in Production Scheduling," *Proceedings, Eighth Industrial Engineering Institute* (Berkeley-Los Angeles: University of California, 1956).

of operations and the time required for each operation were prepared for each order. A sample of such a card is shown in Figure 17-5.

Each operation or machine is represented by two pigeonholes or pockets: an "in-process" pocket and a "waiting" pocket. Each operation card is placed in the "waiting" pocket for the first operation at a time equivalent to its starting date. If only one order is waiting, the operation card is moved into the "in-process" pocket. For each operation having more than one job waiting, the job with the highest priority is moved to the "in-process" pocket. Using a Gantt chart, a record is made of the time for each job opposite the appropriate operation. A portion of such a chart for one operation is shown in Figure 17-6.

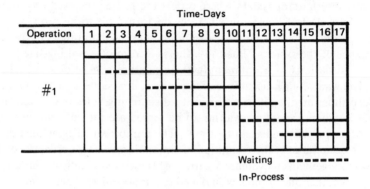

Time-Days

Operation	1	2	3	4	5	6	7	8	9	10	11	12	13	14	15	16	17

#1

Waiting ━ ━ ━ ━ ━ ━ ━

In-Process ─────────

FIGURE 17-6

Portion of a Gantt Chart for One Operation

When an operation is completed for the order in process, the card is moved to the "waiting" pocket of the next operation, and a similar procedure as just described is followed whenever the processing is available for a new order. In this way all jobs can be charted until their completion.

In conducting this simulation, certain assumptions, perhaps some unrealistic ones, were made to simplify the procedure. They are as follows:

1. No set-up (included in the operation time).
2. No splitting of orders. An order must be completed once the operation is begun.
3. The processing is begun on any available order immediately.
4. No breakdown time is incorporated.
5. No lap-phasing. The operation must be completed on the entire order before it can be moved to the next operation in the sequence.

Using this simulation procedure, a small number of orders were processed through a machine shop with five machines. Eight orders were introduced into this system, and an average of four machines was used per job. Each order was given a starting date and a due date. Six different priority dispatching rules were used in the simulation. These rules are as follows:

1. First-come, first-serve.
2. Minimum imminent processing time, i.e., smallest of the times required on the operation for which the orders are waiting to be assigned.
3. Maximum imminent processing time.
4. Smallest time for the remaining operations, excluding the present operation.
5. Smallest time for the remaining operations, including the present operation.
6. Smallest of (time until due) less (the expected time for the remaining operations, excluding the present operation).

The results of this simulation for three possible measures of effectiveness using these six decision rules are shown in Table 17-2. The measures of effectiveness used are percentage of utlized capacity, waiting time per order per machine (average), and the mean completion time for the orders. Mean completion time is the average of the difference between the actual completion time and the due date. Thus, a minus figure indicates late order completion.

TABLE 17-2

Summary of Results of Priority Dispatching Simulation

Measure of Effectiveness	Priority Rule					
	1	2	3	4	5	6
Utilized capacity, %	95	89	95	88	88	99
Waiting time, days per order per machine (average)	1.9	1.3	1.2	1.2	1.4	1.4
Mean completion time, days	−4.2	−1.4	−.125	−1.0	−.94	−1.6

These results are based on a limited sample and a particular case, and should not be taken as an indication of the total effectiveness of the rules tested. The effectiveness of the rules can only be determined by a complete study of any given system. The six priority rules tested were chosen arbitrarily. Any rule that seems feasible can be used in a full-scale computer simulation. Tests of significance can be applied to determine the relative value of the rules tested. Examples of different rules and the results of simulation studies under varying conditions are found in numerous sources.[10]

By utilizing the simulation results, a set of decision rules can be developed to improve the performance of the operations system as a whole. The improvement of the delivery date may be achieved as a result of a specified level of output. This in turn may also yield lower inventory costs as well. This simulation technique can be implemented into a highly integrated control system. As a result of

---

[10]cf. Alan J. Rowe, *Toward a Theory of Scheduling*, Report SP-61 (Santa Monica: Systems Development Corporation, 1959); Richard W. Conway, "Priority Dispatching and Work-In-Process Inventory In a Job Shop," *Journal of Industrial Engineering*, Vol. XVI, No. 2 (March–April, 1965), pp. 123–130.

a continuous information-feedback system, the latest data can be brought to bear so the effect of any changes can be evaluated. It is then possible to develop the most suitable decision rules.

LARGE-SCALE PROJECT CONTROL

Reference was made earlier to the general problem of controlling operations systems concerned with large-scale projects. Such projects have as characteristics the concentrated application of the available resources; the requirement of an extended time period to effect their completion, possibly measured in years in some cases; and usually, single unit one-of-a-kind output. The construction of a ship, a dam, a bridge, or a building are examples. Research and development programs may also be included in this category. A large-scale introductory sales promotion program or a system established to provide financing for a new enterprise could conceivably be included as well. Inherent in all of these types of operations are a large number of individual activities that have to be performed and coordinated if the final output is to be achieved. Because of their scale and the fact that they are unique, control is difficult. The relationship of these individual activities will vary. Some activities can be undertaken independently, while others must be dovetailed because they are sequentially dependent. Any control system must not only take account of these relationships, but it must integrate the performance of the individual tasks with the total project. It is necessary to determine the timing of all activities, and the effect that their scheduled completion or failure thereof will have on the total performance of the project. Therefore, some way of measuring changed conditions must be an integral part of such a control system.

The large-scale system is similar to the intermittent system. In manufacturing it is almost identical to a job shop, since much of the production is custom. However, the vast number of activities required, many of which are being performed simultaneously; the variety of the operations and processes; and other such multiplicities necessitate a different control system. As a result, certain specialized techniques for integrated control of large-scale projects have been developed. Among the most interesting are network models such as PERT and CPM, and heuristic models where resources are limited.

Network Models

Network models are essentially schematic models. They are detailed flow diagrams showing the activities which are required, along with their interrelationships, to complete a project. Network models differ from typical schematic models in that they are dynamic. A computer analysis system that serves to pinpoint potential problem areas makes solutions possible at a time early enough to prevent the difficulties from occurring. The two most popular forms of network models are PERT and CPM. A brief examination of these methods will be sufficient for purposes of a basic knowledge of network models.

PERT. PERT is an acronym derived from Program Evaluation and Review Technique. PERT was developed as the result of efforts designed to assist Special Projects Office of the Navy in the planning and control of the research and development of the Polaris Ballistic Missile. PERT utilizes statistical and mathematical methods to achieve the desired control. PERT evolved from earlier ideas and concepts developed for managerial control. Such things as Gantt charts, critical path analysis, and dynamic progress reporting were merged with newer ideas to develop this technique.

NETWORK EVOLUTION. The evolution of the PERT network from the basic Gantt chart concepts can be illustrated by a series of steps. A form of a Gantt chart which could be used in project planning is illustrated in Figure 17-7. This chart is representative of all of the tasks to be performed in the completing of a project. It shows only the overall plan for the completion of the individual tasks, and tells nothing about the needed accomplishments within each task.

From this chart a milestone chart is developed showing the accomplishment of significant events or milestones. The achievement of the milestones within each task, and their dependency on each other is illustrated in the milestone chart in Figure 17-8. However, there is no indication of the interrelationships or dependencies that usually exist between tasks. Thus, it can be clearly seen that milestone event 7 depends on the completion of event 1, and that event 9 follows the completion of event 4. This chart does not tell whether event 4 can be started before the completion of event 1, nor whether the completion of event 4 is necessary to the start of event 7. Without the knowledge of the existing interdependencies of tasks and events, management is not in a position to exert full control of the project.

The milestone chart can be transformed into a PERT network by showing the interrelationships between tasks and events in a fashion shown in Figure 17-9. The events are indicated by the numbered rectangles. An *event* is the completion of a milestone at a specified time. The events are joined by arrows which represent activities. An *activity* is the performance of the work necessary to achieve the completion of an event.

The times shown on each activity represent the estimated time required, in weeks, to accomplish that activity. From this it is possible to determine the critical path for the completion of this project. The *critical path* is the one that requires the longest time to complete, and is found by summing the times for all activities leading to the accomplishment of the final event 12. In this network the critical path is events 2, 5, 8, 12 which total 19 weeks. This path is indicated in the network by a heavy line.

TIME ESTIMATES. The PERT model does not use single time estimate, because this is too restrictive, and because it is impossible to predict the time needed to accomplish an activity with complete accuracy. Instead, the time estimates are stated as three points over the range of a distribution of time. These three time estimates are identified as the optimistic time, the most likely time, and the pessimistic time. These time estimates are points on the probability

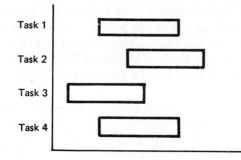

FIGURE 17-7

Gantt Type Project Planning Chart

FIGURE 17-8

Gantt Type Project Milestone Chart

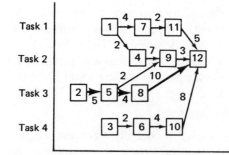

FIGURE 17-9

PERT Network

distribution curve of the time required to complete an activity. This curve is assumed to have one peak representing the most likely time, and the extremes are the optimistic and pessimistic time estimates. There is, therefore, a low probability of about one in a hundred that the work will be completed outside the extremes. In PERT it is assumed that the times follow the beta distribution which has the form $f(t) = K(t - a)^\alpha (b - t)^\beta$. Figure 17-10 shows a typical activity time distribution curve.

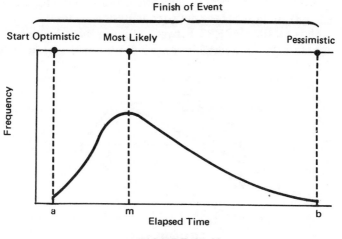

FIGURE 17-10

Activity Time Distribution Curve

A statistical expected time is then computed for each activity by solving:

$$t_e = \frac{a + 4(m) + b}{6}$$

Where:

t_e = the expected time
a = the optimistic time
m = the most likely time
b = the pessimistic time

From these same time estimates for each activity, a variance can be determined as an indication of the uncertainty associated with the time estimates for the activity. The equation for the variance is:

$$\sigma t_e^2 = \left(\frac{b - a}{6}\right)^2$$

PERT NETWORK ANALYSIS. Once a PERT network has been developed for a project, it is possible to analyze it for the purposes of obtaining certain information which is useful for management decisions. The analysis will enable a determination to be made about the earliest time at which the project can be expected to be completed. This determination permits management to establish the probability of meeting any scheduled or promised completion dates. This analysis will also reveal the critical activities. Certain events will be found to have slack as to their expected completion time, and are, therefore, of less concern. Those events with little or no slack, on the other hand, will have to be watched closely. Management can keep a close watch on progress by getting a current status report at any time. It is also possible to use the computations to evaluate the effect of any changes or alternate actions on the total project.

The easiest way to illustrate the network analysis is by means of an example. Figure 17-11 shows a simple PERT network of seven events and nine activities. The three time estimates for each activity are indicated on the arrowed lines in the fashion of 8-10-12.

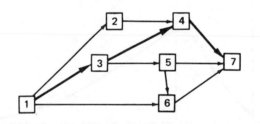

FIGURE 17-11

PERT Network

The calculations for the analysis of this network are shown in Table 17-3. A brief description of the individual columns follows:

Column A is simply a listing of each event starting with the end or objective event and working backward to the beginning event.

Column B contains a list of the preceding events. For each event, the event or events which come before it are listed.

Column C is the expected time for each activity using the equation discussed above.

Column D is the value of the variance for each activity. The equation for this computation has already been discussed.

Column E is the earliest expected time for each event. This is the total of all the expected time values for the activities which lead to the event. Where there is more than one path leading to the event, the longest time is used.

Column F is the latest time for each event. This is taken to mean that if the event in question is completed by this time, the completion of the project on schedule is still possible. It is computed by starting with the T_L for the objective event, which is equal to T_E, and subtracting the t_e values for all activities back to the event.

TABLE 17-3

PERT Analysis

A	B	C	D	E	F	G	H	J	K	L
Event	Pre-ceding Event	t_e	σt_e^2	T_E	T_L	$T_L - T_E$	T_S	P_R	$T_L - T_E$	Event
7	4	19.0	4.000	42.5	42.5	0.0	40.9	.26	0.00	3
	5	7.5	.694						0.00	4
	6	9.5	1.361						0.00	7
4	2	12.0	1.000	23.5	23.5	0.0			3.0	6
	3	16.0	4.000						3.5	2
6	1	30.0	7.111	30.0	33.0	3.0				
	5	4.0	.444							
5	3	5.5	1.361	13.0	35.5	22.5			22.5	5
3	1	7.5	1.361	7.5	7.5	0.0				
2	1	10.0	.444	10.0	13.5	3.5				
1	—	—	—	—	—	—				

$$\frac{T_S - T_E}{\sqrt{\Sigma \sigma t_e^2}} = \frac{40.9 - 42.5}{\sqrt{1.361 + 1.000 + 4.000}} = \frac{-1.6}{2.522} = -.63$$

Table Value of .63 = .23565

Column G is the slack time which is the difference between T_L and T_E. From this it is possible to determine the critical path. The critical path is made up of those events which have zero slack. They, of course, are potentially the major management problems.

Column H is the contractual completion date for the project. It is also possible that such schedule dates will exist for intermediate events in the project.

Column J is the probability of meeting the contractual date. It is determined by computing:[11]

$$\frac{T_S - T_E}{\sqrt{\Sigma \sigma t_e^2}}$$

This result is then referred to an area under the normal curve table. Since the computed value is negative, the table value must be subtracted from .50000 which is the mean of a normal curve.

Columns K and L are the listings of slack time in ascending order from low to high, with the corresponding event shown. Again, the critical path is identified by the zero slack events.

---

[11]The term $\sqrt{\Sigma \sigma t_e^2}$ in the following expression can be stated as the standard deviation of the sum of the variances of the events in the critical path.

CPM. Another network model is known as the critical path method. The critical path has already been identified as an element of PERT, and CPM is a technique similar to PERT. The main difference between PERT and CPM is the incorporation of cost into the network. A number of network models with the cost constraint included have been developed under the general title of PERT/COST. The primary goal of these models has been to enable management to have control of not only time but also of cost. In these models, this goal is accomplished by providing a technique whereby management can evaluate different mixes and find the anticipated cost differences.

A second point of difference between PERT and CPM is in the time estimating approach. CPM utilizes only two time estimates along with their related costs. These estimates are identified as the normal and the crash estimates. The normal estimate is essentially the same as the most likely estimate in PERT. The crash estimate is for the time it would take to complete an activity if no cost was spared.

CPM, as with all PERT/COST, uses a process of evaluating the trade-off effects of different allocations of time and money. The initial network is established for the normal time estimate with the attendant costs for each activity. The critical path can then be determined. If this results in a completion time for the project which is beyond the contract completion, the activities along the critical path are then reviewed to find the one that will result in the least cost increase if the crash time estimate is resorted to. If the new critical path is now such that the project can be completed by the scheduled date or sooner, it is considered as a possible solution. On the other hand, if it is still greater than the contracted completion, the next least costly activity on the critical path and its crash time estimate are put into the solution. Note that the first revision may have changed the network so that a new critical path is now found. This process can be utilized to find all possible ways of reducing the completion time and the cost increases incurred. In this way it is possible to determine all alternatives for meeting the scheduled completion and the cost of each of these. Thus, the time and cost of completing the project under normal conditions, and the amount of time that can be saved by spending more money on various activities are determined. Management will be able to make a decision about the project after a consideration of all of the time-cost options. They will have available the lowest cost option, the shortest time option, and interim alternatives with the appropriate cost and schedule data.

Evaluation of Network Models. Network models quickly achieved a high degree of popularity. To a great extent this popularity was a result of the fact that the Department of Defense made it a requirement in all major programs. As with many new techniques, network analysis was viewed by some as the answer to all planning and control problems to the extent that it was expected to replace management in these functions. Networks are only a tool designed to provide data to management so that sound decisions regarding the effective accomplishment of a program's objectives can be made.

Although it is possible to utilize networks for simple projects, they are of most value in complex system applications.   Networks are used in the research and development phases of special projects such as weapons systems, dams, bridges, and road construction.   For established operations programs as in continuous manufacturing, the traditional control techniques are more appropriate, particularly where the time and cost elements are reasonably well established as a result of experience.   Network analysis in these cases provides little or no valuable information to management that is not readily available from other control tools.   It is in the unique projects where the elements to be controlled are not known with any degree of certainty that network models can best be used. Another reason for the lack of applicability of networks to all types of systems is cost.

Even in the case of projects where the usefulness of network analysis is apparent, there are certain limitations which are inherent.   One study which analyzed the assumptions of PERT arrived at conclusions which are representative of some of these limitations.[12]   Three major sources of error were found in the PERT calculations with respect to the activities.   One source of error, the human estimates of the three probabilistic times for each activity, can be in the magnitude of 30% of the calculated mean and 15% of the range.   Another error source was related to the assumptions about the distribution of the time required for an activity when the true distribution is usually not known.   The final source of error in relation to activities stems from the assumptions behind the equation used to calculate the expected time of each activity (t_e).

Also, the calculations of the project mean completion and the standard deviation were found to be subject to error.   The mean always tended to be biased in an optimistic direction, while the standard deviation could be biased in either direction.   The greater the number of parallel paths through a network, the larger these errors were.   This was particularly true if the paths did not have many common activities and required approximately equal amounts of time. The researchers suggest that a critical activity analysis as opposed to a critical path analysis may be more useful and more valid.   They pointed out that the critical path may not actually contain the most critical activities.

Heuristic Methods

Another specific application of the heuristic technique is in the scheduling and control of large-scale projects.   It is natural that heuristic methods would be useful here because of the complexity of such projects.   Algorithms would be impossible to develop.

The discussion regarding project scheduling has made clear that the major problem is to achieve the contractual completion date.   If management had available all of the necessary resources this would be relatively easy.   However, it is a fact of life that a manager seldom, if ever, is in the enviable position of

---

[12]Kenneth R. MacCrimmon and Charles A. Ryavec, "An Analytical Study of the PERT Assumptions," *Operations Research*, Vol. XII, No. 1 (January–February, 1964), pp. 16–37.

having unlimited resources. Computer programs using heuristics have been developed for arriving at a hoped for satisfactory solution, although not usually an optimum one.

To some extent these programs are more concerned with the concept of critical events as opposed to the critical path. The program looks at those activities that have zero slack with a view toward shifting such activities within the resource restrictions to improve the scheduled completion date. Some programs will assume that the available resources are fixed at a certain level, and will schedule the activities within the project on the basis of the criticalness of the activity (slackless ones are considered most critical). As many of the activities as possible are fitted into the available resources for a given period of time. After that period is scheduled, the following period is scheduled using the same decision rule for selecting the specific activities.[13]

It is also possible to utilize a set of heuristic decision rules to allocate the available resources to activities in a way that the amount of resources utilized from period to period is the same. This situation is similar to the process of achieving level output. In this type of program, the activities with the most slack are moved to periods when the resource utilization is low.[14]

SUMMARY

The various problem areas of the operations system must be synthesized. Only in this way can the achievement of full control be realized. A number of approaches which can be identified as integrated control systems exist. Decisions encompassing a variety of areas are made possible. These decisions lead to aggregate results.

The types of control systems are conveniently related to the two types of operations systems identified as intermittent and continuous. Order control is the type of control system closely associated with intermittent operations. It achieves control through small lots of output often processed to customer order. It is a very difficult type of control because of the variations which occur from order to order. Order control is applicable to both manufacturing and non-manufacturing situations. Computerized systems have recently been developed which are of great assistance in making real-time decisions in order control systems.

The type of control most frequently associated with continuous operations systems is flow control. This type of control is concerned with integrating the related subsystems so that the flow of the inputs through the system is smooth. Flow control is not considered as complex as order control because of the level of repetition and standardization in the system. There are still difficult problems involved in these types of control systems, however.

---

[13]J. D. Wiest, "A Heuristic Model for Scheduling Large Projects with Limited Resources," *Management Science*, Vol. III, No. 6 (February, 1967), pp. 359–377.

[14]A. R. Burgess and J. B. Killebrew, "Variations in Activity Level on a Cyclical Arrow Diagram," *Journal of Industrial Engineering*, Vol. XIII, No. 2 (March–April, 1962), pp. 76–83.

There are hybrid control systems, as well, for those situations which are not clearly intermittent or continuous. One such system is identified as block control. It is closely related to flow control. However, the output is not as standardized as in the continuous system. Orders are collected and released as a block for processing. A block represents a specified period of processing time.

Load control, another hybrid, is more closely akin to order control. This is true even though the operations are quite similar to a continuous system. The major feature of these systems is a critical process or key machine. By controlling this process or this machine so as to achieve maximum utilization, control of the entire process is usually attained.

Project control is classified as a hybrid system also. The operation to be controlled in this case is a large-scale one. The output is typically one of a kind. Because of the size of the processing system and the uniqueness of the output, control is less formal.

Another aspect of integrated control is output scheduling. This involves the establishment of a timetable for the performance of the system. Probably the factor which complicates scheduling the most is the fluctuations which occur in demand. There are three variables which affect the scheduling. They are output rate, work force size, and inventory level. The possible variations in scheduling are large and the three variables may be changed in a number of ways. At one extreme is level output, and at the other is output which fluctuates in direct response to demand changes. There are many combination alternatives which can fit between these two extremes.

A variety of techniques for making the output scheduling decision have been developed. Among these are linear decision rules which use specially derived equations based on the total costs for output, size of work force, and inventory costs. Another approach is to utilize management coefficients which are developed from management's past decisions. A third technique in scheduling output is simulation.

One of the most difficult situations for developing an output schedule is in the job shop operation. Certain specified characteristics are assumed as determinants of a job shop. Thus, it can be found in manufacturing and nonmanufacturing operations. A number of models for scheduling in job shops have been developed. Because of the complexity of the relationships in a job shop, simulation is virtually dictated as an analytical tool. Industrial dynamics is one application of simulation in such a situation. A means of deriving priority dispatching rules for releasing orders is another area in which simulation is used.

A number of specialized techniques have been developed for use in controlling large-scale projects. The mere size of these projects is a major contributor to their complexity. The large size virtually dictates the need to use specialized techniques for the difficult control job. Network models are one of the broad categories of control tools for these types of projects. These are schematic models. However, because they are dynamic, they differ from the typical schematic model. The data are kept current through the use of a computer. The best known network model is PERT. The analysis of a PERT network will reveal information which will be valuable for making certain decisions regarding scheduling. Management can determine the probability of meeting the proposed schedule from this analysis. It can also determine which parts of the project are critical and need to be observed closely. Another network model is CPM. The primary variation from PERT is that CPM introduces cost considerations into the network. Through analysis, it is possible for management to determine the various time-cost alternatives available for completing the project. Management can make a decision after full consideration. While network models have found some popularity, they have limitations. A recognition of these limitations will help to insure their proper application.

Heuristics have also been used for scheduling large-scale projects. This results from the complexities of these projects. Large-scale projects do not lend themselves well to optimizing algorithms. With the use of heuristic techniques, a satisfactory solution can often be achieved.

INCIDENT

AIRLINE HOLIDAY SCHEDULING

A major airline has scheduled flights to most parts of the country. As is typical, there is exceptionally heavy passenger traffic in December, particularly around the Christmas holidays. In addition, this year, severe winter weather has complicated the problem. Some flights have not been able to depart as scheduled because of the weather, resulting in late arrivals. Delays en route because of weather and overloaded traffic in the approaches to the airports have also caused late arrivals. A number of flights have had to land at alternate airports because of this. Late arrivals have necessitated rerouting of passengers to later flights. As a result some flights have experienced demand well in excess of capacity.

The long delays, longer flights because of landing queues, and additional length of flights as a result of weather and flight diversions have increased the working hours of flight crews. Regulations limit the maximum number of hours for aircraft crews. Many of the employees reached their permissible limits by December 25. Consequently, the airline was concerned about maintaining its schedule for the remaining period of the heavy demand.

Questions

1. What scheduling alternatives does the airline have?
2. Evaluate the problems connected with each of the alternatives.
3. How might the airline avoid this situation in future years?

QUESTIONS FOR DISCUSSION AND ANALYSIS

1. Describe order control and give examples of the types of operations systems to which it can be applied.
2. What are the major elements of a computerized order control system? What information is made available in such a system?

3. In what ways does flow control differ from order control? Are there any similarities between these two types of control?

4. Why is it necessary to have hybrid control systems such as those described in the chapter? What are the characteristics of operations systems where these types of control would be applicable?

5. What conditions would favor the use of block control, and what conditions would favor the use of load control? Cite examples to support the answer.

6. What are the three variables which can be adjusted to establish a schedule that will meet fluctuating demand?

7. Compare the cost effects on the operations system of the two extreme scheduling alternatives.

8. Why is it that the scheduling alternatives available to operations systems which provide a service as output are limited?

9. What are the potential advantages of a combination scheduling alternative that is between the two extremes which were discussed in the chapter?

10. Describe the underlying concept of linear decision rules. What is the practical value of this technique?

11. What are the characteristics of a job shop operation? Why is simulation a valuable tool for scheduling in job shops?

12. What are priority dispatching rules? Give examples of such rules. What is the value of a simulation utilizing various dispatching rules?

13. What is the objective of network models? What advantage do they have over other techniques in controlling large-scale projects?

14. Define event, activity, and critical path as applied to PERT.

15. Why are three time estimates needed in PERT? Could a supervisor make these three estimates more accurately than he could make a single estimate? Comment on your reasoning.

16. In what way does CPM differ from PERT?

17. Enumerate and comment on the significance of the three major sources of error in PERT calculations.

18. What is the principal advantage of heuristic methods in regard to the control of large-scale projects?

PROBLEMS

1. A company has the following forecast of demand, in units, for the next year:

January	1,500	July	9,400
February	3,200	August	7,000
March	12,700	September	5,200
April	15,100	October	3,500
May	12,800	November	3,000
June	11,400	December	2,300

As of January 1, there is on hand an inventory of 1,000 units. The present capacity of the facility is 12,000 units a month working on regular time. A minimum of 35 production workers are maintained irrespective of the output requirements. When a change in the level of output is required, it necessitates a change of one employee for every 100 units of output change. A cost analysis revealed that the following costs are applicable:

Inventory carrying costs	$3.00 per unit, per month
Hiring/layoff costs	$25.00 per employee
Output level change costs (setup, teardown, etc.)	$50.00 plus $.25 per unit of change
Overtime costs	$5.00 per unit additional
Back order costs (out of stock)	$2.00 per unit, per month

Compare the costs for the following scheduling alternatives:

(a) Level output of 9,000 units per month.
(b) Output equal to demand. Assume that production can be in the same month as the demand.
(c) Output of 8,000 units for the first three months; 12,000 for the next three months; changing to 9,000 for three months; and 7,000 for the last three months.

In all cases, assume January production is the same as in the previous month.

SELECTED ADDITIONAL READINGS

Bowman, E. H. "Consistency and Optimality in Managerial Decision Making." *Management Science* (January, 1963), pp. 310–321.

Buffa, Elwood S., and William H. Taubert. *Production-Inventory Systems*, rev. ed. Homewood, Illinois: Richard D. Irwin, Inc., 1972.

Fey, Willard R. "An Industrial Dynamics Case Study." *Industrial Management Review* (Fall, 1962), pp. 79–99.

General Information Manual: PERT . . . A Dynamic Project Planning and Control Method. White Plains, New York: International Business Machines Corp., undated.

Greene, James H. *Production Control: Systems and Decisions*. Homewood, Illinois: Richard D. Irwin, Inc., 1965.

Holt, Charles C., *et al. Planning Production, Inventories, and Work Force*. Englewood Cliffs: Prentice-Hall, Inc., 1960.

Holt, Charles C., Franco Modigliani, and Herbert A. Simon. "A Linear Decision Rule for Production and Employment Scheduling." *Management Science*, Vol. II, No. 1 (October, 1955), pp. 1–30.

Jackson, James R. "Research in Production Scheduling." *Proceedings, Eighth Industrial Engineering Institute*. Berkeley-Los Angeles: University of California, 1956.

LeGrande, Earl. "The Development of a Factory Simulation System Using Actual Operating Data." *Management Technology*, Vol. III, No. 1 (May, 1963), pp. 1–19.

Lockyer, K. G. *An Introduction to Critical Path Analysis*. New York: Pitman Publishing Corp., 1964.

MacCrimmon, Kenneth R., and Charles A. Ryavec. "An Analytical Study of the PERT Assumptions." *Operations Research*, Vol. XII, No. 1 (January–February, 1964), pp. 16–37.

Mellor, P. "A Review of Job Shop Scheduling." *Operational Research Quarterly*, Vol. XVII, No. 2 (June, 1966), pp. 161–171.

Moore, Franklin G., and Ronald Jablonski, *Production Control*, 3d ed. New York: McGraw-Hill Book Co., 1969.

Rowe, Alan J. *Toward a Theory of Scheduling*, Report SP-61. Santa Monica: Systems Development Corporation, 1959.

Wiest, J. D. "A Heuristic Model for Scheduling Large Projects with Limited Resources." *Management Science*, Vol. III, No. 6 (February, 1967), pp. 359–377.

| **Output Quality Control Systems**

Management must develop systems to insure that the quality of the output conforms to established quality standards. In the design phase, standards are set which determine the basic characteristics of the output. This includes such things as the appearance, dimensions, and performance specifications. For a service, the standards, though less tangible, also determine the nature of the output. The successful achievement of these standards plays a major role in the acceptance of the output in the market. In addition, there are considerations with regard to the processing system which have a bearing on the quality. If the quality standards are to be achieved, it is necessary for the processing system to be capable of meeting the design specifications. This capability, quite naturally, includes the ability to meet the specifications within a predetermined cost limit.

Quality is relative in nature. Quality carries little meaning unless the end use of the output is clearly defined. When it is stated that something is of good quality, this merely means that the product or service is of a level which makes it satisfactory for the intended end use. Thus, a power saw which one purchases for a home workshop may be of "good quality" for the purpose intended. However, if the same saw was used in heavy construction work, it might be found to be lacking. Quality standards must be stated in specific terms. Chemical or physical properties can be quantitatively stated.

The purpose of the quality control system is to regulate the mix of the inputs into the operations system so that the goodness of the output is high. Most quality control systems are concerned with a continuous type of control which deals with the in-process activities, or with an evaluation of the final result in comparison with the standards established for the system output. The majority of such systems can therefore be designated as either process control systems or as acceptance sampling systems.

BASIC QUALITY CONTROL CONCEPTS

Today the term quality control means statistical quality control. Conventional inspection is clearly concerned with quality, but it is not necessarily a control oriented activity. Naturally, all quality control involves the use of inspection. Inspection is after-the-fact, while quality control is an ongoing process designed to keep the output within certain specified limits. It is before-the-fact.

Output Variables

The mere application of the inputs into any processing system (men, machines, materials, etc.) will result in variations in the output. It is impossible to avoid variations from a predetermined standard. However, it is possible to limit these variations. The usual method is to state a standard as an acceptable range rather than as an absolute. This range is referred to as a *tolerance*, a zone of acceptability which is stated as a permissible deviation from a standard. A tolerance for a product can best be exemplified by reference to a physical measurement. A tolerance for a particular dimension could be stated as $1.000^{\pm .001}$ inches; the $\pm .001$ is the tolerance for this dimension. Any part which measures from .999 to 1.001 inches is acceptable. The variations which occur in any process and which make tolerances necessary are of two types: chance variations and assignable variations.

Chance Variations. These types of variations are inherent in the processing system. They result from such things as the variations which can be found in the materials used. If machinery is utilized in the process, there will be variations in the way in which the machine performs. The machines are made to tolerances themselves. Therefore, the resultant play between meshing parts of the machines will lead to differences in their performance. Another source of chance variations is the performance of the human being in the system. No one performs precisely the same way at all times, even though he is following a standard method. There will always be variations from item to item. A well-known example of this is the fact that we never sign our names exactly the same way twice. These small chance variations tend to cancel out each other because some will be in one direction while others will be in the opposite. It is impossible to reduce these variations without a significant change in the processing system. This may entail new equipment, different material, or a redesign of the job method if smaller variations are desirable.

Assignable Variations. Variations of this class are a result of factors which are external to the system itself. Such things as the improper operation of a piece of equipment or some other type of incorrect job performance may be the cause of these variations. Others may come about as the result of inspection instruments which require repair, extremes in room temperatures, vibrations in the building, or any other type of variable that can be specifically assigned. These variations can be identified and controlled without altering the process itself. These are the types of variables about which management is concerned in regard to the control of quality. When such variables occur, they must be identified and corrected as soon as possible to bring the quality of the system output back into control.

Pattern of Variations

From the fact that there are item-to-item variations resulting from chance causes comes the ability to determine a pattern for the output of a processing system. This pattern takes a definite and predictable form for any given system. This fact in turn makes it possible to evaluate the quality of the output by sampling techniques and to predict the normal limits of the process in the future.

When these limits are exceeded, it is an indication that an assignable cause may be present in the processing system.

Frequency distribution. When the individual outputs of the processing system are compared with the established standard, the variables can be grouped conveniently for further analysis. The counting or measuring of a characteristic, when grouped into classes to show the number of observations in each class, is known as a *frequency distribution*.

Frequency distributions have been widely utilized in population statistics. The height of men can be tallied when a group of men are measured and their heights, to the nearest inch, are determined. The result would be a table showing the number of men found at each of the individual heights. We might find that, of the men studied, the smallest was 61 inches and the tallest was 78 inches. We would find that the number of men at the two extremes would be relatively small. As we moved from 61 inches upward, the numbers found at each of the heights would increase until we reached 70 inches. From this point, the numbers would decrease. A chart in the form of what is called a historgram would appear as found in Figure 18-1.

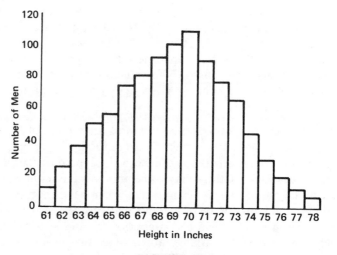

FIGURE 18-1

Frequency Distribution Histogram
Height of 1,000 Men

The same sort of analysis can be developed for any measurement or characteristic of the output of an operations system, if the variable can be clearly compared with a previously stated standard. Thus, for a part which has a standard of 1.000 inch in length, any part produced can be measured and sorted according to its deviation from the 1.000 inch standard. If we established class intervals of .001 inches, we would find that the largest number of parts would fall into the 1.000 inch category. The numbers in the categories on either side of

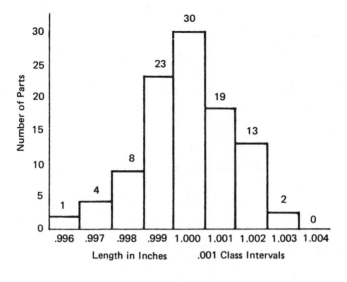

FIGURE 18-2

Frequency Distribution
100 Parts

the standard would decline. For a small number of parts, say 100, a pattern of variation such as that shown in Figure 18-2 would emerge.

As the number of parts measured increases, the distribution tends to become symmetrical if the controllable factors or the assignable variations have been eliminated. Only the chance variations would remain.

Normal Curve. When there is a perfectly symmetrical distribution after measuring an infinitely large number of parts, it is identified as a *normal curve*. In the normal curve, there is always a single peak which is the average, or the established standard, e.g., 1.000 inch. The normal curve decreases in either direction from the peak to zero and to infinity. An example of a normal curve is found in Figure 18-3.

The pattern of variation for individual items of output of an operations system almost always approximates the normal curve. This is particularly true of manufactured products. On occasion, however, the pattern is nonsymmetrical, or skewed. Skewing results for a definite and ascertainable reason. No matter what the exact shape of the curve, normal or skewed, the patterns of variation develop for the same basic reasons. This pattern results from a concept known as the law of large numbers.[1] This law states that, as a larger sample of a population is taken, the sample mean will more closely approximate the mean of the population, and the distribution will approach a normal distribution.

---

[1]For a detailed presentation of this concept, the reader is referred to one of the basic statistics texts listed in the bibliography for this chapter.

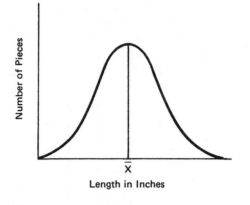

FIGURE 18-3

Normal Curve
Infinite Number of Parts

The characteristic of the variations to scatter about the mean is known as *dispersion*. The analysis of a normal frequency distribution requires the consideration of dispersion. The dispersion of the normal curve has a definite proportion that plays an important role in the effectiveness of the quality control system.

Measures of Dispersion. The methods of analyzing the scatter of the data about the mean are known as *measures of dispersion*. There are a variety of measures of dispersion which may be utilized for the purpose intended. In regard to the quality control system, we will concern ourselves only with two: the range and the standard deviation.

The range is the easiest of the measures of dispersion to calculate. For this reason, it has gained some degree of popularity in regard to control charts in quality control. The *range* is merely the difference between the highest and the lowest value in the distribution. Sometimes it is stated as the highest and the lowest values. For example, in the measurements of the height of men illustrated in Figure 18-1, the highest value was 78 inches, and the lowest, 61 inches. Therefore, the range could be stated as $78 - 61 = 17$ inches, or as 61 inches to 78 inches in height.

The range has drawbacks since it is based on only two measures. It, therefore, tells nothing about the values in between. It may be considered as a less accurate measure of dispersion than others that are available. However, it does have value as an indicator of the possible introduction of an assignable variable into a process.

Probably the most widely used measure of dispersion is the standard deviation. The standard deviation, defined in Chapter 9, serves as the basis for much of the underlying principles of statistical sampling in quality control. The standard deviation indicates the proportions into which the dispersion of a normal curve can be divided. Each standard deviation, or sigma, represents a zone of

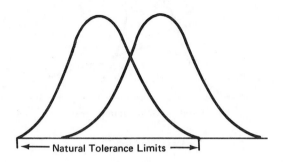

FIGURE 18-4

Distribution Shift

variation. When these zones are determined for the distribution of the output of a process, it is possible to predict the nature of the total population based on the results of a small sample. From this it can be inferred whether the process is in or out of control.

Prediction. Because the pattern of the variations of the output of an operations system is repetitive, it is possible to predict the limits of the process as long as no change takes place. The continuation of a pattern means that the process is being affected only by the chance variations and that no assignable variations are influencing it. Thus, as long as this circumstance exists and no new chance causes are introduced, the pattern will continue within limits of predictability indefinitely.

As long as the output of a process continues within the predictable limits, management has assurance that the entire output is in control. This means the output is acceptable, and it is not necessary to evaluate each individual item. The system is functioning within the limits of tolerance that have been established as acceptable.

A deviation from the pattern is an indication of a problem. This deviation signifies that the process is probably being affected by more than chance causes. An assignable cause that must be located and corrected is almost certainly changing the pattern of variation. When this is the case, the process is out of control.

There are many possible assignable causes of variation. In manufacturing, dull cutting tools, worn jigs or fixtures, and other problems relating to the equipment will cause the distribution pattern to shift. This shift signifies that the mean is now higher or lower than normal, and at least part of the distribution is beyond one of the tolerance limits. This situation is depicted schematically in Figure 18-4.

Other types of assignable causes can result in increased variation in the distribution. Examples of these are design imperfections, material instability, and improper sequencing of operations. An illustration of increased variation is shown in Figure 18-5.

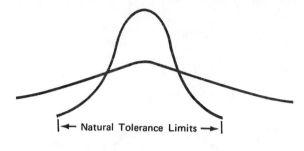

FIGURE 18-5

Increased Variation

Prediction is accomplished by the periodic measurement of only a few items of the output. It is not necessary to evaluate all items produced in order to determine quality of the total output. Therefore, it is possible to control the quality of output of a system by using sampling techniques.

Sampling. The selection of a small quantity of the output of the processing system is sufficient to attain the necessary control of quality. The sample selected, say five or ten items, must be chosen randomly. Each item must have an equal chance of being selected. Such a selection will mean that the sample is reflective of the nature of the total output or population within predictable limits of accuracy. In this way the risks of error can be held to whatever limit management determines as desirable from a cost and accuracy standpoint.

The sample is merely a means to an end. The end result is to assure that the quality of the total population is of a desired level. The sample is a way of predicting the quality. It provides a method for ascertaining, at an early point in the processing, when the quality is deviating from the standard. The sample is not important in itself. The sample is only of significance for what it indicates about the population.

Sampling inspection of system output can be utilized for two types of control. One type is process control, where the concern is about the nature and extent of the variations. Samples are taken periodically throughout the processing period. Sampling can also be carried out to determine if the items are acceptable or unacceptable. Attribute inspection, as this is identified, usually takes place after the processing of a group of the output items is completed. The interest at this time is the prediction of the percentage of defectives in the total.

PROCESS CONTROL BY INSPECTION FOR VARIABLES

When control is achieved by determining the degree of "goodness" or of "badness" of an output, it is referred to as inspection for variables. Exact comparisons are made between the output and the standard. Characteristics of an item's dimensions or other quantifiable standards are evaluated. Such inspection is limited to physical outputs. Each item inspected is compared with the standard, and the variation noted. Thus, if the length of a part is specified as

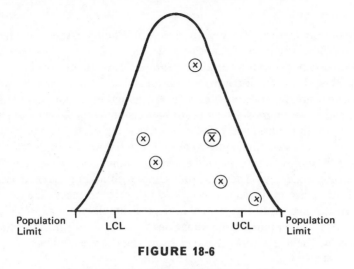

FIGURE 18-6

Control Limits, Sample and Sample Mean
in Relation to Population Distribution

$1.000^{\pm .001}$ inches, each inspected item will be measured and its length noted.
If the process is in control, essentially all of the parts in the population will fall
within the tolerance limits established. In this type of sampling a small number
of parts are taken from the process at random intervals of time. In a sample, the
mean of the parts will fall within narrower limits than the population limits.
This narrowing results from the highs canceling out the lows. These narrower
limits can be determined by a simple equation using data gathered from a series
of observations made at the start of the run. These limits are called the control
limits. The upper control limit is identified as UCL and the lower limit as LCL.
The relationship of the control limits to the population limits can be seen in
Figure 18-6. This figure also illustrates the way in which the average will fall in
these narrower limits. The parts in the sample are indicated by $\widehat{x}$, while the sample mean is designated by $\widehat{\overline{X}}$.

If a sample mean is beyond one of the control limits established, it is an indication that the process is almost surely out of control. A search is then begun to
identify the assignable cause.

A device which makes use of these concepts to achieve in-process control is
the control chart. The control chart can be utilized to keep a constant check on
the pattern of the process. A form of control charts was discussed in Chapter 9
as a means of controlling the accuracy of forecasts. In quality control, the control charts for variables consist of two parts. One part is used to plot the sample
means, and the other is for sample ranges.

Control Charts for Means

The sample mean can be an indicator of a shift in the pattern of variations.
As long as the sample means remain within the control limits, the process is

assumed to be in control. The distribution is continuing to show only the normal variations which result from chance causes.

It is necessary to select a variable to sample that will give the best indication of the effects of an out-of-control condition. The variable selected (usually a specific dimension from among many for a product) is the one that management believes will have the most direct cost relationship to the level of quality. The determination of the frequency and size of the sample is also an important consideration. In constructing control charts for variables, the initial samples used for setting the control limits should be selected at the outset of the run from items produced consecutively. The following samples should be taken at random intervals from items produced consecutively just prior to their selection.

The determination of the control limits is a simple process.[2] The UCL and the LCL can be computed from equations that require little calculation. The equations for the mean or $\bar{X}$ (X bar) control chart are as follows:

$$UCL_{\bar{X}} = \bar{\bar{X}} + A_2\bar{R} \tag{1}$$

$$LCL_{\bar{X}} = \bar{\bar{X}} - A_2\bar{R} \tag{2}$$

Where:

$\bar{\bar{X}}$ = the grand mean. This is the mean of the means of the preliminary samples

A_2 = a constant

$\bar{R}$ = the average range of the preliminary samples

The value of A_2 and other applicable constants used for $\bar{X}$ and R charts are found in Table 18-1.

TABLE 18-1

Table of Constants for $\bar{X}$ and R Charts

n	A_2	D_3	D_4
1	—	—	—
2	1.880	0	3.268
3	1.023	0	2.574
4	.729	0	2.282
5	.577	0	2.114
6	.483	0	2.004
7	.419	.076	1.924
8	.373	.136	1.864
9	.337	.184	1.816
10	.308	.223	1.777

---

[2]For the statistical basis for the determination of control limits, the reader is referred to: Charles T. Clark and Lawrence L. Schkade, *Statistical Methods for Business Decisions* (Cincinnati: South-Western Publishing Co., 1969), Chapter 9.

To illustrate, the data on Table 18-2 are from ten samples of three pieces each. The values are the deviations from a selected dimension of .990 inches.

TABLE 18-2

Results of Ten Samples of Three Each
Taken from Output

(Values in .001″ deviations from .990″)

Sample	Values			Mean	Range
1	4	6	5	5.00	2
2	9	13	5	9.00	8
3	6	11	15	10.67	9
4	18	10	7	11.67	11
5	19	15	21	18.33	6
6	9	6	19	11.33	13
7	18	12	2	10.67	16
8	9	8	10	9.00	2
9	6	17	7	10.00	11
10	6	3	13	7.33	10
Totals				103.00	88

From these data the control limits for this process can be computed and a control chart constructed. The computations follow:

$$\bar{\bar{X}} = \frac{103.00}{10}$$

$$= 10.30$$

and:

$$\bar{R} = \frac{88}{10}$$

$$= 8.80$$

The control limits are then:

$$UCL_{\bar{x}} = \bar{\bar{X}} + A_2\bar{R}$$

$$= 10.30 + (1.023)(8.80)$$

$$= 19.30$$

and:

$$LCL_{\bar{x}} = \bar{\bar{X}} - A_2\bar{R}$$

$$= 10.30 - (1.023)(8.80)$$

$$= 1.30$$

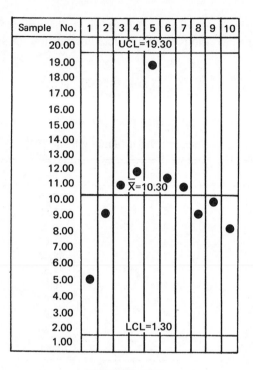

FIGURE 18-7

Control Chart for Sample Means

It is now possible to draw the control chart for the means of these samples. This control chart is shown in Figure 18-7. As can be seen, at this stage the process is under control. If one of the sample means was outside of the control limits this would not be true. Note that the control limits in the chart are not the limits permitted by the designer's specifications or tolerances. The control limits established for the mean are narrower than the tolerance limits.

Control Charts for Ranges

This form of control chart can be used to determine any shift in the amount of variation which may take place. The range chart or R chart is used to plot the difference between the highest value and the lowest value in each sample. The plot of the range is made at the same time as the sample mean is plotted on the $\overline{X}$ chart. If the sample ranges stay within the control limits, the process is considered to be in control as far as the variability is concerned. The control limits here are the upper range limit (URL) and the lower range limit (LRL). They are also identified as UCL_R and LCL_R. The LRL is often identified as 0 (zero) since for sample sizes of six or fewer it is always zero. This value results from the fact that the value of the constant used is zero for these sample sizes.

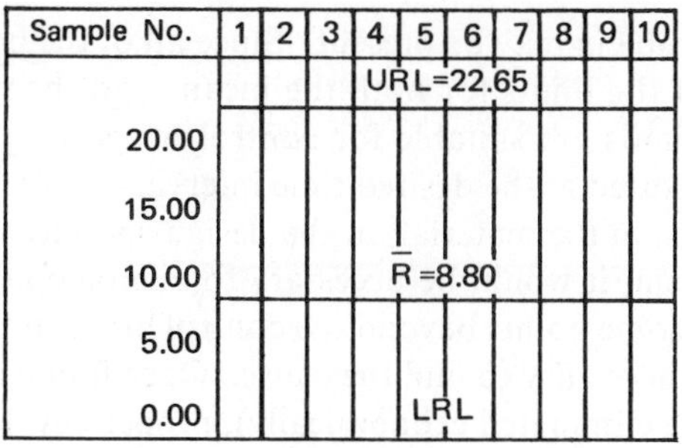

Sample No.	1	2	3	4	5	6	7	8	9	10
				URL=22.65						
20.00										
15.00										
10.00				$\bar{R}$=8.80						
5.00										
0.00				LRL						

FIGURE 18-8

Control Chart for Sample Ranges

The computation of the range chart control limits is accomplished in a similar fashion to that which was used for the mean chart. The equations are:

$$URL = D_4 \bar{R} \qquad \text{(3)}$$

$$LRL = D_3 \bar{R} \qquad \text{(4)}$$

The symbols D_3 and D_4 are constants whose values are found in Table 18-1. Note the values for D_3 are zero for sample sizes of six or fewer. This accounts for the zero value of the LRL in such instances.

The computation of the control limits for an R chart and the construction of such a chart can be illustrated with the data found in Table 18-2. The mean range was computed in the illustration for the $\bar{X}$ chart. It is:

$$\bar{R} = \frac{88}{10} = 8.80$$

The computations for the establishment of the control limits are as follows:

$$URL = D_4 \bar{R}$$
$$= (2.574)(8.80)$$
$$= 22.65$$
$$LRL = D_3 \bar{R}$$
$$= (0)(8.80)$$
$$= 0$$

The sample ranges can now be plotted on the control chart in Figure 18-8. The process is also found to be in control as regards the variability since none of the sample ranges is outside of the control limits.

These types of process control charts supply instantaneous information about the expected pattern of variation. When a point is beyond the control limits, it is a signal that a problem may be present. Since all of the points in the example used were inside of the limits for both the means and the ranges, it can be assumed that these limits are suitable for control purposes. Additional samples can be taken and plotted at the desired time intervals. If there is a change in the processing methods, in the material, in the design specifications, or some other variable in the system, it would be necessary to compute new limits.

Had there been some points beyond the control limits in these initial samples, it would have been necessary to find the cause. Once found and eliminated (this assumes they can be eliminated economically), proper new limits would have to be established. Only then can management presume that the process is in control.

ACCEPTANCE SAMPLING FOR ATTRIBUTES

Acceptance sampling for attributes deals with inspection for the purpose of determining whether a unit of output is defective or nondefective. The unit selected may be anywhere from a single item, some portion or component of the item of output, the entire order, the output of some period of time, or a total shipment.

Design of Acceptance Sampling Plans

The prime purpose of an acceptance sampling plan is to determine the extent of nonconformity which is acceptable for the unit of output of concern. This nonconformity is usually expressed as a proportion of defectives in the unit: most frequently, the percent defectives, using the equation:

$$\text{Percent defectives} = \frac{\text{Number of defectives}}{\text{Number of units}} \times 100$$

A distinction is sometimes made between defectives and defects. A unit is defective if it has one or more defects. When the sampling plan is designed to determine defects, the proportion of nonconformity is stated as the defects-per-hundred units, expressed as:

$$\text{Defects-per-hundred units} = \frac{\text{Number of defects}}{\text{Number of units}} \times 100$$

Any acceptance sampling plan should be designed to avoid two basic errors. The first error to be avoided is the acceptance of output as satisfactory when in fact it is unacceptable. The second error to avoid is the rejection of a lot as unacceptable which is of an acceptable quality.

Operating Characteristic Curve

To avoid rejection of acceptable output, an acceptable quality level is established for any given sampling plan. The *acceptable quality level* (AQL) is the

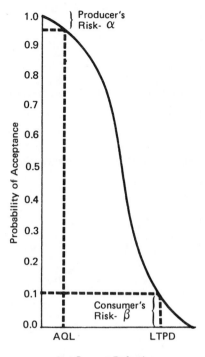

FIGURE 18-9

Operating Characteristic Curve for Sampling Plan

percent defective or defects per hundred determined as representative of "good" quality. It is desired to accept such lots most of the time. To avoid the acceptance of "bad" output, a level known as the *lot tolerance percent defective* (LTPD) is established. It is desired that lots of the output of this level be rejected a high percentage of the time. It follows that since sampling is being utilized, certain risks of the occurrence of the basic errors will exist. The *producer's risk* (β) is identified as the probability that output of the level of AQL will be rejected. The probability that a bad lot of the level of LTPD will be accepted is identified as the *consumer's risk* (α). The *operating characteristic curve* (OC curve) is a graphical representation of these relationships for any given sampling plan. Each sampling plan has distinct attributes. The terms defined above can be seen in the operating characteristic curve illustrated in Figure 18-9.

The operating characteristic curve for any sampling plan will show the relationship between the actual percent defective in a lot and the probability of acceptance. From the curve can be determined the probabilities of making the two kinds of errors found in any sampling plan. It is also possible to establish the economic effect of any sampling plan by establishing the indifference quality level or the break-even level.

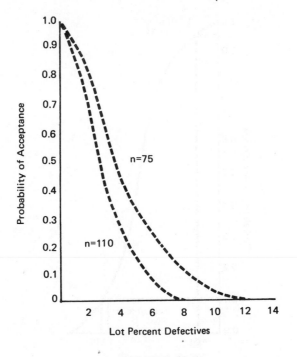

FIGURE 18-10

Change in OC Curve with Change in Sample Size

$$c = 2$$

The primary determinants of the shape of the OC curve for any sampling plan are the size of the sample (n) and the value of the acceptance number (c). As could be surmised, as the sample size is increased, given the same acceptance number, the probability of accepting a given lot percent defective declines. This probability decline means that the plan is more discriminating. The discrimination can be seen by comparison of two operating characteristic curves for plans with an acceptance number of two. Figure 18-10 shows one curve for a sample size of 75 and another of 110.

When the acceptance number increases while the sample size remains constant, the probability of acceptance of a given lot percent defective increases. Thus, the curve is less steep and the plan is less discriminating, as can be seen by comparing the family of OC curves in Figure 18-11. In this example the sample size is equal to 75. Increasing the acceptance number moves the curve to the right and makes it less steep.

Types of Sampling Plans

To this point the examples regarding acceptance sampling plans have dealt with the taking of only a single sample. This is the simplest type of sampling

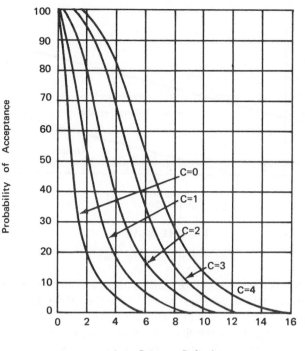

FIGURE 18-11

Change in OC Curve with Change in Acceptance Number

n = 75

plan since the decision as to whether to accept or reject is made on the basis of what the one sample indicates. When the number of defectives in the sample is less than or equal to the acceptance number, the lot is accepted. If, on the other hand, the number of defectives is greater than the rejection number, the lot must be rejected. It is possible, however, to design sampling plans which utilize more than one sample. The major objective of such plans is to get the same assurance of quality with a reduction in the amount of inspection. While such plans may result in a reduction in inspection time and consequent cost, this is not a certainty. A drawback of sampling plans that require more than one sample is the increased difficulty in designing them. The most frequent types of these sampling plans are double, multiple, and sequential sampling plans.

Double Sampling. These plans provide for the use of a second sample when the first sample is not conclusive enough to make a decision. If the number of defectives in the first sample is less than or equal to the acceptance number specified, the lot may be accepted. As in single sampling plans, if the number of defectives is larger than the rejection number, the lot is rejected. In double sampling

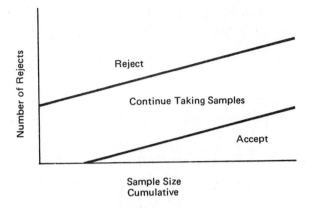

FIGURE 18-12

Sequential Sampling Plan

plans the range between the acceptance number and the rejection number for the first sample is greater than one. Thus, when the number of defectives in the first sample is between the acceptance and rejection numbers, a second sample must be taken because the results of the first sample in this case are not conclusive.

After the second sample is drawn, the cumulative number of defectives from both samples is compared with the second acceptance and rejection numbers. For the second sample the range between these numbers is one, as in single sampling plans. The decision to accept or reject is then made as in the case of a single sampling plan.

Multiple Sampling. Multiple sampling plans are essentially the same as double sampling plans with the exception that the number of samples required for a decision may be more than two.

Sequential Sampling. This type of sampling plan provides for the taking of an unspecified number of samples. If the lot quality is either very good or very bad, a small sample will suffice. It is only when the quality is between these two levels that a larger sample is required. The range between the acceptance and rejection numbers remains constant and greater than one. The sampling process is carried on until either the acceptance or the rejection level is reached. A sequential sampling plan is illustrated in Figure 18-12. The design of a sequential sampling plan can be accomplished by determining the appropriate acceptance and rejection limits. Tables are available to determine the proper limits for specified values of AQL, LTPD, α, and β.[3]

Double, multiple, and sequential sampling plans should typically result in less inspection than is required for single sampling plans for a given level of protection. However, the amount of inspection required will vary widely from lot to lot.

[3]Statistical Research Group, Columbia University, *Sequential Analysis of Statistical Data: Applications* (New York: Columbia University Press, 1945).

Control Charts for Attributes

Control charts can be utilized in attribute inspection as well as in variable control. The major difference in the control charts is that, in the case of attributes, the unit of measurement used is a distinct value while for variables it is a computed measure of central tendency; i.e., mean or range. The two types of attributes control charts are concerned with the percentage defective (*p*-chart) or with the defects per unit (*c*-chart).

Percentage Defective Charts. When control is concerned with attributes, a determination is made as to the acceptance or rejection of the output units. For each sample the percentage of defective units can be determined. The *p*-chart can be utilized to record the variations in the percentage defective in the lots sampled. Control limits are computed in the same way they are computed for variable control charts. As long as the points remain within the control limits, the quality is assumed to be in control. The control limits for a *p*-chart, based on three standard deviations, are computed as follows:

$$UCL_p = \bar{p} + 3\sqrt{\frac{\bar{p}(100 - \bar{p})}{n}} \tag{5}$$

$$LCL_p = \bar{p} - 3\sqrt{\frac{\bar{p}(100 - \bar{p})}{n}} \tag{6}$$

Where:
$\bar{p}$ = the mean of the percentage defective in a series of initial samples

Defects Per Unit Charts. If output is such that defects can occur at a variety of points within the unit of output, the control of the number of defects may be more useful. Examples of processes where this type of control might be valuable are:

a. Electronics equipment in which a variety of defects can occur.
b. Textiles which may contain numerous defects per yard.
c. The number of improper medications issued in a hospital for some unit of time.
d. The number of incorrect orders sent out by the audiovisual service of a school district.

The cases where this type of control is useful may be generalized as those where the possibility of defects is high, but is in fact small. This condition is found to approximate the Poisson distribution for fluctuations in the number of defects. Using $\bar{c}$ as the average number of defects per unit of output, again based on three standard deviations, the control limits are determined by:

$$UCL_c = \bar{c} + 3\sqrt{\bar{c}} \tag{7}$$

$$LCL_c = \bar{c} - 3\sqrt{\bar{c}} \tag{8}$$

The value of $\bar{c}$ is an estimate, as was $\bar{p}$, based on past accumulated data. The c-chart has many uses other than for quality purposes. Examples are found in the area of inventory control for controlling the number of stockouts, in equipment maintenance for the number of breakdowns, and for accident statistics.

STATISTICAL TESTS OF SIGNIFICANCE IN QUALITY CONTROL

The statistical techniques usually associated with acceptance sampling and quality control are really specialized applications of tests of significance. When the sample is taken and the necessary measurements made, it is for the purpose of testing the hypothesis that the lot is acceptable, or that the process is under control. This is usually referred to as the null hypothesis, H_O. When the null hypothesis is rejected, it is assumed that there is an assignable cause of the process being out of control. It is then necessary for management to isolate the cause of the variation. Statistical experiments can be designed which will indicate the source of the variation. The inputs into a process may be numerous: men, machines, material, sources of material, methods, to mention the more obvious ones. Tests can be made to test differences between sample means, sample proportions, and sample variances. A detailed exposition of these types of tests is not within the scope of this book, but a summary explanation of the more widely utilized tests of significance which have application to the control of quality will be useful.

Difference Between Two Sample Means

It is often useful in quality control to attempt to determine whether there is a significant difference between the mean of two samples. As an example, we may wish to determine whether the mean of a dimension for parts produced by two different machines was significantly different. If the population is normally distributed, while the standard deviation is unknown but can be determined from the two sample estimates, the t-test statistic can be utilized.

Assume that the mean of the five samples taken from Machine I is 0.946 inches, and the mean for Machine II is 0.943 inches. The null hypothesis is that the two machines are producing parts which are not significantly different for this dimension, that is, that the samples are from two populations which are the same. The results of the samples are listed below:

Machine I	Machine II
0.942	0.940
0.946	0.945
0.951	0.949
0.949	0.941
0.942	0.940
$\Sigma x_1 = 4.730$	$\Sigma x_2 = 4.715$
$\bar{x}_1 = 0.946$	$\bar{x}_2 = 0.943$

The test statistic for computing the value of the t distribution for two sample means is:

$$t = \frac{\bar{x}_1 - \bar{x}_2}{s\sqrt{\dfrac{1}{n_1} \quad \dfrac{1}{n_2}}} \qquad (9)$$

where s is the estimate of the population standard deviation, which can be computed from the sample data given above by:

$$s = \sqrt{\frac{\Sigma(x_1 - \bar{x}_1)^2 + \Sigma(x_2 - \bar{x}_2)^2}{n_1 + n_2 - 2}} \qquad (10)$$

Substituting into this equation, a value for s of 0.004 is achieved. The computations for finding the value of t from the data presented is as follows:

$$t = \frac{\bar{x}_1 - \bar{x}_2}{s\sqrt{\dfrac{1}{n_1} + \dfrac{1}{n_2}}} = \frac{0.946 - 0.943}{0.004\sqrt{\dfrac{1}{5} + \dfrac{1}{5}}} = 1.20$$

The value of t at the 0.01 level of significance for eight degrees of freedom $(n_1 + n_2 - 2)$ can be found on a t distribution table. This is found to be 3.355. The criterion for accepting or rejecting the null hypothesis is reject it at the level of significance if the computed value of t is greater than the table value of t; or reject it at the level of significance if the computed value of t is negative, and is less than the negative of the table value. In this case the null hypothesis would be rejected if $t > +3.355$ or $t < -3.355$.

Thus, the null hypothesis is not rejected in this example, and we assume that the difference in the two means is not significant at the 0.01 level. The difference is then a result of random variations only.

Other tests for differences between means are available. For instance, the z-test is widely used. This test is used for normal distributions where the mean and variance are known. The z-test can also be utilized in testing for the difference between sample proportions.

Difference Between Two Sample Proportions

The testing of difference between two population proportions is similar to the test for difference between means. The null hypothesis is that there is a zero difference between the proportions. The distribution is assumed to be normal, and the standard deviation is equal to the standard error of the difference between the two proportions. The sample sizes (n_1 and n_2) are large, but not necessarily equal.

The standard error of the difference between the two proportions is computed by the following:

$$S_{p_1} - p_2 = \sqrt{\frac{\bar{p}(1 - \bar{p})}{n_1} + \frac{\bar{p}(1 - \bar{p})}{n_2}} \qquad (11)$$

Where:

$\bar{p}$ = the weighted average of the two samples or

$$\frac{x_1 + x_2}{n_1 + n_2}$$

Where:

x_1 = sample 1, number of defects
x_2 = sample 2, number of defects

The z-test is used to test the hypothesis that the difference between the two proportions is zero. The test statistic is computed by:

$$z = \frac{p_1 - p_2}{Sp_1 - p_2} \qquad \textbf{(12)}$$

Assume that we wish to determine whether two different brands of purchased items are significantly different. In a sample of 500 of Brand X there are 130 defects, and in a sample of 300 of Brand Y there are 66 defects. Therefore, $p_1 = 0.26$ and $p_2 = 0.22$. If we wish to test the null hypothesis at the 0.01 level of confidence, it will be rejected if the computed value of z is greater than the table value of 2.58. The computations for finding the value of z are:

$$z = \frac{0.26 - 0.22}{0.0316} = 1.27$$

Therefore, since $1.27 < 2.58$, the null hypothesis is accepted, and the test does not indicate that Brand X is significantly better than Brand Y.

Differences Between Sample Variances

It is also possible to use similar methods for testing whether the different variances of sample data are significant or not. The variances of two sets of data can be compared by means of the ratio of the larger variance to that of the smaller one. The ratios of pairs of a series of samples will be distributed in a form known as the *F distribution*. This distribution uses the statistic:

$$F = \frac{s_1^2}{s_2^2} \qquad \textbf{(13)}$$

The null hypothesis is that the two variances are equal. The hypothesis is accepted only if the ratio of the larger variance to the smaller variance is greater than the appropriate point on the F distribution. The true value of F is determined from a table. The values of F are given for a specified level of confidence and for the degrees of freedom ($d.f.1$ and $d.f.2$) in each sample. The degrees of freedom are equal to the number of items in the sample minus one.

Assume that a particular task is being performed by three different people. The times that each of these people take will naturally vary. Management is concerned with determining whether the differences in times are significant. A sample of 25 times for each of the operators is taken and the variances of the samples computed. The computed variances are:

$$\text{Operator 1, } s_1 = 0.183$$
$$\text{Operator 2, } s_2 = 0.172$$
$$\text{Operator 3, } s_3 = 0.089$$

The null hypothesis is that the variances are the same, and that the differences are the result of purely random factors. A pairwise comparison can be made using the ratio of the largest variance to the smallest in a pair of samples. The F distribution value for 24 degrees of freedom for each variance is 1.98 at the 5% confidence level and 2.66 at the 1% level. The ratio of the variance for Operator 1 to Operator 2 is:

$$F_{12}[24,24] = \frac{0.183}{0.172} = 1.06$$

In the same fashion the ratios for the other pairs are:

$$F_{13}[24,24] = \frac{0.183}{0.089} = 2.06$$

$$F_{23}[24,24] = \frac{0.172}{0.089} = 1.93$$

Therefore, the difference between Operator 1 and Operator 3 is judged to be significant at the 5% level. The null hypothesis is rejected at this level for these variances. All others are accepted at the 5% level, and no rejection takes place for any hypothesis at the 1% level. It is possible to make a further test by pooling the variances of Operators 1 and 2, which did not show a significant difference. This new variance can then be tested against the variance for Operator 3. This pooled variance is equal to 0.177. The pooled variance is then tested against the variance for Operator 3 by:

$$F_{12.3}[49,24] = \frac{0.177}{0.089} = 1.99$$

The difference is again determined as significant at the 5% level because, from the table, it is determined that:

$$F[49,24]_{0.05} = 1.87$$

Again there is no significant difference at the 1% level where the value of $F = 2.45$. Operator 3 appears to be a significant source of variation in the times taken to complete the task. The same type of analysis could be used for any of the other inputs into the process which might be a source of variation. Possibly there will be factors in addition to the operator that cause a significant variation in the times.

A useful extension of the basic concepts just discussed can be achieved by means of the technique of analysis of variance. This statistical tool is valuable since it can be used to test differences within a single classification, or between a number of classifications, and any variation caused by interactions between the classifications. The details of this technique are beyond the scope of the present discussion, but full explanations can be found in the statistics references at the end of the chapter.

There are many tests of significance which have value in quality control beyond those outlined. Wherever sample data are utilized and differences exist, the significance of these differences is subject to test. The random nature of the sampling technique insures these differences. It is only after sufficient testing of the sample data that conclusions can be drawn with any level of confidence.

HUMAN PERFORMANCE AND QUALITY CONTROL

The great value of statistics in the quality control system has tended to overshadow other aspects of the problem of achieving a desired level of quality. One such aspect, which is now receiving increased attention, is that of human performance in the quality control system. Various facets of human performance in the operations system have been discussed, so it is necessary to mention only certain additional factors as they relate to the quality problem.

Despite the increasing amount of work performed by machines, the contribution of the human operator is still significant. The cause of the majority of defects in the output of a process frequently is a result of improper human performance. The application of the techniques of ergonomics in designing jobs will contribute much to improved human performance. Proper design of jobs, of the workplace, and of the total work environment will contribute to the reduction in defects caused by human error. Proper selection, training, and motivation will also be factors in improving human performance.

The quality control system is also influenced by human performance in the inspection process. The determination of the level of quality is the outcome of inspection activity. The decisions about quality control are made from the information flowing from inspection. While a great deal of inspection is carried out by utilizing precision instruments, the operation of the instruments is largely a human activity. In addition, much inspection is based on human judgment rather than on a specific quantitative measurement. Therefore, the possibility of human error in the inspection task is also high. There are indications that inspection accuracy can vary from 20 to 80 percent, and that individual inspectors rarely detect more than 50 to 60 percent of the defects.[4] The accuracy of inspection tasks would improve with the application of the principles of human performance found useful in processing tasks.

Some special consideration should be given to inspection performance because of the specialized nature of such tasks. They are typically complex and require higher levels of certain performance factors than do other tasks. Examples of such factors are scanning and vigilance. Special care in the selection of

---

[4]Douglas H. Harris and Frederick B. Chaney, *Human Factors in Quality Assurance* (New York: John Wiley & Sons, Inc., 1969), pp. 9–10.

inspection personnel is warranted because of these needs.   For instance, one study found that inspectors performing inspection tasks requiring a high level of visual discrimination had not been tested for eyesight.   Upon testing, some of the inspectors were found to have sight in only one eye.   Another similar example was found in electronics assembly inspection, which involved a considerable amount of color coding.   Here it was found that some of the inspectors were color-blind.

SUMMARY

Quality control utilizes statistical methods to assure that a process is conforming to preestablished standards. The need for the control of the quality of the output of a processing system stems from the variations which occur. These variations are identified as either chance variations or assignable variations. Chance variations are inherent in the processing system and they cannot be eliminated without a redesign of some significant aspect of the system. Assignable variations can be identified and controlled. They are the types of variations toward which management directs its attention. They must be eliminated to retain control of the output quality.

The existence of chance variations results in a pattern of variations. This pattern repeats itself. From this fact comes the ability to control a process. A change in the usual pattern indicates a probable deviation in the normal output quality. The variations in an output can be displayed in the frequency distribution. When large numbers of observations are made, the distribution of a particular attribute will appear as perfectly symmetrical. This is a normal curve. Items scatter around the mean of a distribution to create a dispersion. The analysis of the scatter can be accomplished by means of measures of dispersion. Two such measures of significance in quality control are the range and the standard deviation. The repetition of the pattern of variation makes prediction of the process limits possible. When a shift in a distribution or an increase in the variation occurs, a quality deviation is indicated. It is only necessary to use a random sample to predict the quality of output within set limits of accuracy. Sampling can be carried out to determine the degree of variations or simply to determine the acceptability or rejection of the output.

Control with respect to the degree of variation is identified as variable inspection. Comparison of each item in a sample is made with respect to some quantifiable standard. The mean of a sample falls within narrower limits than those of the population. These limits are the control limits: the upper control limit (UCL) and the lower control limit (LCL).

A graphical device for achieving in-process control is the control chart. The control chart for the mean is used to determine any shift in the distribution. An increase in the degree of variation can be noted on the control chart for range. When a plot falls outside of the control limits on one of these control charts, it is an indication of a probable out-of-control situation. It then becomes the job of management to discover the cause.

Acceptance sampling for attributes is a determination of whether a unit of output is acceptable or not. This type of sampling should be designed to avoid the acceptance of bad output, or the rejection of good. For any sampling plan, an operating characteristic curve can be developed. This shows the relationship between the actual percent defective and its probability of acceptance. The sample size and the acceptance number will determine this exact relationship.

In addition to the usual single sampling plan, there are plans which utilize more than one sample. The most frequent of these plans are double, multiple, and sequential sampling plans. The objective of these approaches is to reduce the cost of inspection by arriving at decisions with smaller samples. Such plans are more difficult to design than are single sampling plans.

Control charts also find use in attribute sampling techniques. Two types frequently used are the percentage defective chart and the defects per unit chart.

A number of the statistical tests of significance are useful in quality control. When a sample is tested, it is for the purpose of testing the null hypothesis that the process is in control. When this hypothesis is rejected, statistical tests can be applied to isolate the source of the variation. One of the tests used in quality control is for the purpose of determining if there is a significant difference between the mean of two samples. The t-test statistic is one such test. Tests for difference between two proportions are also useful. The z-test is one of these. Tests for differences between sample variances such as the F-distribution statistic also have value in quality control. These tests of significance are useful for making decisions, with a specified level of confidence, based on the results of sample data.

The close relationship of quality control and statistics has tended to over-shadow certain other elements of such a control system. A specific example of this is human performance. A large amount of work is still performed by human operators. Therefore, a substantial percentage of the defects which occur are a result of some form of improper human performance. In addition, the inspection task is largely a human activity, and human errors can affect the accuracy of inspection results. Special attention should be given to the selection, training, and performance of the human element in the processing and inspection tasks.

INCIDENT

FIELD MANUFACTURING COMPANY

The Field Manufacturing Company produces metal parts of various types in large quantities. Most of the parts are screw machine parts from a variety of metals (steel, aluminum, brass). Field also machines small gears and produces a few punch-press parts. All of these parts are later assembled into a precision piece of electro-mechanical equipment used in aircraft.

Statistical quality control techniques are utilized. The primary emphasis is on variable inspection. A study has been made of each part to determine its importance in the proper functioning of the final assembly. As a result, four categories have been developed into which it is believed any part, or dimension of a part, can be placed. The categories can be summarized as follows:

1. Critical dimensions or parts. Any errors will not be detected at a later point. Such a situation dictates 100% inspection.

2. Significant dimensions or parts where any deviations will not be detected in quality checks at Field, but which will be discovered by operational tests before actual use. A low level of parts that do not meet quality standards is desired in these cases. The maximum allowable defects are 1%.

3. Important dimensions for which any quality defects will be found either in subsequent tests at Field or at the time of assembly. Since the defective part will not become a part of the finished item, a 3% level for such parts is set as permissible.

4. Dimensions that have no functional significance. May fall into the category of appearance or skilled craftsmanship. Thus, a limit of 5% defects is determined as acceptable.

Questions

1. Evaluate this approach to quality control in such a situation. Give particular attention to the costs incurred or avoided.

2. Are these categories sufficiently discrete to include all possible parts or dimensions?

3. Do you foresee any difficulties in achieving the desired levels of defects in any of the categories?

QUESTIONS FOR DISCUSSION AND ANALYSIS

1. What is meant by the statement, "Quality is relative"? Give examples. Can the quality of similar items be judged by the relative prices?

2. Define tolerance. Why are tolerances necessary? Can there be tolerances set for services?

3. What are chance variations? Can they be eliminated or reduced? If so, in what way?

4. Give examples of assignable variables that may be found in a process. Why is it important for management to discover and eliminate these types of variables?

5. Why is it important to know that a pattern of variation repeats itself? What is the significance of (a) a distribution shift, of (b) increased variation? What are some of the possible causes of (a) and (b)?

6. How is it possible to make determinations about the quality of output from the results of a sample?

7. Why does the mean of a sample fall into narrower limits than the limits of the population from which the sample was taken?

8. In the control of quality through variables, why are the mean and the range chosen as measures for determining whether the process is in control? Does a sample plot beyond one of the control limits on a mean or range control chart indicate that the process is out of control? Explain.

9. Compare variables and attributes sampling.

10. What does an operating characteristic curve show? What determines the shape of an OC curve?

11. How can a sampling plan be made more discriminating? How is this greater discrimination represented on the OC curve?

12. Describe the types of sampling plans other than single sampling plans. What is the primary objective of these other types of sampling plans?

13. What is the difference between the p-chart and the c-chart? Under what conditions would each be useful in achieving quality control?

14. Discuss the application of statistical tests of significance in quality control. Give examples of situations where tests for differences between sample means, sample proportions, and sample variances can be used in quality control.

15. What is the significance of human performance in achieving quality control?

PROBLEMS

1. The data for the mean and the range shown below were derived from a series of samples of six each, taken at regular intervals as the parts were processed.

Sample

	1	2	3	4	5	6	7	8	9	10
$\overline{X}$	1.153	1.152	1.150	1.149	1.155	1.151	1.149	1.151	1.149	1.153
R	0.009	0.008	0.009	0.009	0.005	0.009	0.004	0.009	0.005	0.009

Draw $\overline{X}$ and R charts for use in controlling output in the future.

2. The output of a manufacturing process was sampled for 20 days. The items in each sample of 100 were classified as defective or nondefective. The following data show the results:

Sample Number	Number Defective	Sample Number	Number Defective
1	4	11	3
2	6	12	2
3	3	13	21
4	3	14	4
5	7	15	8
6	5	16	11
7	12	17	14
8	8	18	5
9	5	19	3
10	8	20	13

Is this process in control?

3. A manufacturer of molded rubber parts has each part inspected for any blemishes that are visible. If it is desired to hold the number of such blemishes to an average of no more than four per part, what would be the upper and lower limits of a control chart for defects with a 3 sigma limit?

4. In a sequential sampling plan, the following acceptance and rejection numbers apply:

Cumulative Sample Size	6	25
Acceptance Number	1	5
Rejection Number	3	7

(a) Construct a chart similar to Figure 18-12 to illustrate this sampling plan.

(b) What would be your decision under the following conditions using this sampling plan?

(1) Twenty parts with five defectives
(2) Three parts with none defective
(3) Fifteen parts with two defectives
(4) Eight parts with four defectives

SELECTED ADDITIONAL READINGS

Bowker, A. H., and G. L. Lieberman. *Engineering Statistics.* Englewood Cliffs: Prentice-Hall, Inc., 1959.

Clark, Charles T., and Lawrence L. Schkade. *Statistical Methods for Business Decisions.* Cincinnati: South-Western Publishing Co., 1969.

Cowden, D. J. *Statistical Methods in Quality Control.* Englewood Cliffs: Prentice-Hall, Inc., 1957.

Dodge, H. F., and H. G. Romig. *Sampling Inspection Tables — Single and Double Sampling*, 2d ed. New York: John Wiley & Sons, Inc., 1959.

Duncan, A. J. *Quality Control and Industrial Statistics*, 3d ed. Homewood, Illinois: Richard D. Irwin, Inc., 1965.

Fetter, Robert B. *The Quality Control System.* Homewood, Illinois: Richard D. Irwin, Inc., 1967.

Grant, E. L. *Statistical Quality Control*, 3d ed. New York: McGraw-Hill Book Co., 1964.

Harris, Douglas H., and Frederick B. Chaney. *Human Factors in Quality Assurance.* New York: John Wiley & Sons, Inc., 1969.

Juran, J. M. (ed.). *Quality Control Handbook*, 2d ed. New York: McGraw-Hill Book Co., 1962.

Stockton, John R., and Charles T. Clark. *Introduction to Business & Economic Statistics*, 4th ed. Cincinnati: South-Western Publishing Co., 1971.

A widely used measure of effectiveness of the operations system is minimum cost. In the profit-oriented enterprise, the reduction of costs in any of the operations subsystems will contribute to the improvement of profits. In some of these enterprises, it is possible to increase profits by ignoring costs and simply raising prices. This is not the usual circumstance, however. Even those firms that have some control over the market must usually control costs in order to improve the profitability of the enterprise. Profitability can be improved by identifying, through cost controls, that portion of the output that is most profitable, and by concentrating selling efforts in this area. In the nonprofit enterprise, the most efficient operation is the lowest cost position.

In the problem areas of operations management that have been examined, cost has been a major element in the final decision. It is not necessary to reiterate the various costs which have been involved in these decisions. The purpose here is to examine the specific methods which are available for evaluating the system's cost performance once the decision has been made. This does not imply that the decision is set in concrete and that costs are forever fixed. Just the opposite is the objective of a cost control system. A cost control system should be designed to compare the actual costs with those which are expected. Any variation can then be used as a basis for a new decision.

COST CONCEPTS

Cost in the operations system is taken to mean the value which is designedly relinquished for the purpose of achieving the desired output. While it is possible to state the sacrifices for achieving this objective in other than monetary terms, monetary measurement is most common. Measurement in other terms complicates the determination of costs.

Costs for Control

Costs that are used for controlling the operations system must serve the purposes of management. One use of costs is as a part of the management information system. The information system can be used to convey the objectives and plans of management to the entire organization. Since costs are part of the enterprise plan, they play an important role in conveying this planning information. A specialized form of this kind of cost information is the budget.

Another role of costs for management control is as feedback on the performance of the system. The actual costs incurred are reported and compared with planned or standard costs. In this way the efficiency of the performance of the system can be evaluated. Performance information can also be used as a basis for planning future operations and as a device for stimulating better performance. The timeliness of cost information for evaluation purposes is a significant factor. Cost systems that are current or in real time are the ideal.

Cost data can also be used as one form of incentive. The comparison of actual with planned performance is useful in achieving improved performance in the future. A device that has found some degree of popularity, largely in manufacturing, is wage incentive systems.

Cost Elements   *Show org chart*

The costs typically associated with the producing of the output of an operations system are direct materials, direct labor, and operations overhead.

Direct material cost is that cost associated with the materials included in the finished output. Naturally, such costs are found only where the output is physical in nature. There would be no direct material cost if the output is a service. Direct materials are the raw materials such as metal, wood, etc., which are transformed in the processing, but remain as a part of the finished product. They must be distinguished from such indirect materials as supplies. These supplies are used in the enterprise, but do not enter into the finished output. Costs of indirect materials are usually charged to overhead.— *List*

Direct labor cost is the cost of the labor used in creating the final output whether product or service. There are also indirect labor costs associated with all kinds of output. The wages and salaries of those who do not take part in the processing, such as operations supervisory personnel, are indirect labor costs, and would be classified as operations overhead.

The category of *operations overhead costs* includes all those costs associated with operations except direct material and direct labor. Costs such as utilities, maintenance, taxes, insurance, and other costs incurred in the functioning of the operations system are included in the overhead classification.

The sum of these three categories of costs is the total operations cost, which is also referred to as manufacturing cost in the case of a production system. Manufacturing cost is frequently used as the cost of goods sold as well. There are other costs incurred by the enterprise which would compose the total costs. Added to the costs of operations would be such costs as selling costs, and general and administrative costs.

The Costing Procedure   *42" × 48" STEEL PROBLEM 20% waste 26 ¢/POUND.*

The process of arriving at the total operations costs is usually designed to identify all such costs with a clearly distinguishable unit of output such as an order or a batch.

The costing procedure is concerned with allocating the cost elements to those units of the operation about which management wants information.

These units are referred to as cost centers. A cost center is any identifiable unit of action for which costs may be accumulated. It may be a department or some other organizational unit. On the other hand, it is not necessary that it be an organizational unit. As long as it is possible to allocate costs to it, it can be a cost center. For example, a single machine may be a cost center. A product or a product line may also be a cost center. The goal in operations costing is to collect costs to determine the cost of a unit of output. Consequently, this process is usually referred to as product costing. Product costing may be accomplished by one of two types of systems identified as job costing and process costing.

Job Costing and Process Costing.   Job costing is the more frequent type found in manufacturing. It can be used when the output is capable of being identified in specific jobs or lots. The costs are gathered together for each individual product or service. Job costing is widely used where a number of different kinds of output are found, in other words, intermittent systems.

Process costing is better applicable to the continuous type of system where there is a single type of output produced over a long period of time. The applicable costs are gathered for a specified period of time and then allocated to the number of units of output produced for the period. A costing system that is purely job or purely process in form is rare. The important thing is to develop a costing system that will provide the information which will assist in making the necessary decisions.

Difficulties in Costing.   There are numerous difficulties in costing. In regard to operations costs, two difficulties are of particular relevance. The first is the identification of direct material and direct labor cost incurred in the processing of the output. The second is the allocation of the overhead costs.

The problem of identifying direct materials is peculiar to the producing of a physical output as in manufacturing. While it may be presumed that the collection of such costs would be easy, this is not so. The problem stems from costing the material. The basic cost is the invoice price of the material. In most cases, the freight cost of bringing the material to the plant is included as well. The difficulties arise when the question of how to assign costs of storage, and other costs associated with the material once it has been received, are considered. The determination of the actual amount of material used is sometimes a problem. In some processes, the amount of material used may vary from item to item. Some material that is used in the product can be used for other purposes, thus creating a problem of identifying what portion is direct material and what is indirect.

The difficulties associated with identifying direct labor costs are parallel to those for material. It is not always easy to measure the amount of labor used in producing the output. This difficulty is particularly evident if some of the worker's time involves indirect work. On occasion, some of the time reported on the time cards cannot be identified with a particular order or product. The question of how to assign costs which are labor connected also arises. The various fringe benefits fall into this category. Certain wage-payment plans are designed to facilitate the measurement of direct labor costs.

Overhead costing is unquestionably the most difficult of the costing problems. What portion of such costs as indirect labor, plant depreciation, and the operations manager's salary should be allocated to each unit of output or to given operations cost centers? There is no completely correct rule for allocating such costs.

A factor which is a measure of the volume of activity with a direct cost relationship to output is selected. Typical factors are direct labor hours, machine hours, and direct labor dollars. The factor chosen and the operations overhead are budgeted. The budgeted overhead is then divided by the amount of the factor in the budget to achieve the overhead rate. This procedure results in a figure such as a certain number of dollars per direct labor hours, or in terms of the factor chosen. Each product or type of service is then assigned operating overhead costs by multiplying the actual quantities of the overhead factor used by the calculated overhead rate. If actual overhead differs from that budgeted, this difference is accounted for by an adjustment at the end of the year.

Costing of output has largely been associated with products, and thus with manufacturing enterprises. It should be emphasized that the same principles can be utilized in service enterprises. A brokerage firm can allocate costs on the basis of the types of securities in which it deals; hospitals can compute costs on the basis of patients, or on the basis of the types of services performed; e.g., laboratory, X-ray, emergency, maternity; and educational institutions can account for the costs per student.

STANDARD COST CONTROL SYSTEMS

Standards have been discussed in several areas. The establishment of time standards was the major function of the work measurement system. Standards of performance or measurement standards were the starting point for the determination of the quality of output. Standards are a yardstick by which results can be measured. Standards, in effect, are what should have been. In a cost system, expected costs, called *standard costs*, are assigned to the various elements of the operations system. These costs are those that management expects to incur as opposed to those actually incurred.

Types of Standard Costs

Standards for operations costs are established for direct labor, direct material, and for operations overhead. The direct labor costs are determined from the time standards for process performance. This cost is determined by multiplying the standard time per unit (e.g., pieces per hour) by the wage rate per period of time (e.g., dollars per hour) or by relating cost to output, if the wage rate is based on output as in the case of a piece rate (e.g., dollars per unit). Most standard costs are expressed in terms of a unit of output. Standard costs are also set for a unit of direct material and for the quantity of material used in a unit. A standard cost is set for operations overhead as well as in terms of the overhead factor chosen; i.e., standard direct labor hours or standard direct labor dollars. Once standard costs are set, they are not changed unless there is a change in the processing method or in the price of material or labor.

Advantages of a Standard Cost System

A standard cost system simplifies the cost control process. The standards serve as a basis for evaluating the actual performance. Since standards are established for the various elements of the processing, there are critical checkpoints which exist. These checkpoints can be utilized to compare the actual results with the standard while the process is in progress. This type of comparison avoids the after-the-fact determination of excessive costs. If costs are exceeding standards, the variations noted at the checkpoints will permit initiation of corrective action immediately. This also means that management can concentrate attention on the variances and not have to expend time on in-control situations.

Standards can be useful in establishing incentive systems. The workers can be motivated to improve their performance as compared with the standard. One of the most widely used of these systems is in the case of wage incentive systems. The operators are rewarded for performance which is better than standard. The standards used can be quantity, quality, or overall costs.

Variances

Cost variances will usually be the result of either a price change or a variation in the quantity used. If the price of a unit of raw material changes, this will cause the cost to vary from the standard. The same situation will exist if the price (wage rate) of labor changes. A variation in the amount of either labor or material from the established standard will also cause a variance.

The overhead rate is determined by dividing the total standard overhead by some measure of the volume of activity. This means that the standard overhead per unit is determined on the basis of an anticipated operating level. The measure of volume used will materially affect the determination of the overhead rate. If volume varies from this level, the actual overhead allocated will show a per-unit variance in the opposite direction from the anticipated. That is, if volume is lower than predicted, the overhead rate will be higher. Thus, the measure of volume used in computing standard overhead must be selected carefully.

Budgets

Budgets are similar to standards. In fact, in the determination of the standard operations overhead, it is usual to use a budgeted figure for the standard cost. The budget is not always regarded as a control device. This is because a budget is, in the first place, a planning tool. The budget is a statement of expected results in some quantitative measure, usually money. Whenever expected outcomes are set forth in specific terms, whether they be dollars, labor hours, unit sales volume, or some other, a formalized statement of the means of achieving the objective results. When action is taken to make actual results conform to the budget, the budget is a control tool. Budgets are made for various activities of the enterprise. Some of the common ones are cash budgets for financial planning, capital equipment budgets, personnel or labor budgets, selling budgets, and operations budgets.

Operations Budget

The operations budget can be classified in different ways. Of the three forms usually found, one is useful for control purposes, one has limited value in control, and the third is used for future planning. These are identified as the responsibility budget, the product budget, and the forecasting and program budget.

The responsibility budget identifies costs according to the individual responsible for them. Only the costs over which the supervisor of the unit has control are included. The actual costs are gathered by the same categories as budgeted and are not allocated. In this way, a comparison of actual with budgeted cost can be readily made, and the supervisor's performance measured.

The product budget (also referred to as the product costing budget) is similar to the responsibility budget. The major difference is the level within the organization at which the budget is found. The product-costing budget follows the general procedure of costing already outlined. Costs are allocated in such a way that they are related to individual items of output. Actual costs can be compared with budgeted costs for the different lines. This form of budget does not provide the same force of control as the responsibility budget because of the allocation of costs to products. This method of allocation blurs the lines of cost responsibility.

The third type of operations budget is the forecasting budget. A forecasting budget is designed as a means of future planning. However, its use as a means of motivation by making the future goals known is not precluded. A program budget is a specialized form of a forecast budget. The main distinction is that the program budget is concerned with the programs of the enterprise as opposed to the output. The program budget deals with allocation of resources to specific programs (e.g., research, sales promotion). It emphasizes the goals of the enterprise at the top management level. Program budgeting is used to evaluate the cost benefits of the various programs to determine which is best.

Variable Budgets

One of the problems associated with budgets is that they are established on the assumption of a certain output level or some other measure of activity.

Recall that, in a standard cost system, the overhead rate is determined by dividing the total estimated overhead by a standard measure of activity. However, this level of activity is also an estimate which may or may not be correct. If volume of output is used as the measure of activity, and this volume is greater than anticipated, what happens to the budgeted expenditures for overhead items? If the budget is fixed, these expenditures do not change, even though a greater amount may be required. Inflexibility can be a danger to the efficient performance necessary to achieve the goals of the enterprise. Variable budgets avoid these problems.

To develop a variable budget, it is necessary to analyze all costs to determine their relationship to activity. Some costs will vary in direct proportion to the volume of output. This variation pattern is usually the case for direct labor and direct material. Costs such as indirect labor and material, supervision, and utilities may not move in direct proportion to output. Other costs may not change at all with changes in activity. Examples of these latter costs are depreciation, taxes on property, and insurance. Some fixed costs are determined by management policy. The decision to maintain a minimum key management force is one such case.

The basic idea of a variable budget is that cost estimates are first developed for a number of different levels of activity. From these estimates, the budget for the appropriate cost categories can be established for the different output volumes. Departments or cost centers are given the projected relationship between the costs which they will incur and the potential levels of output. The cost centers are then assigned their fixed costs and the activity factors selected. By applying the activity factors such as direct labor cost per unit and direct unit material cost to the actual output, a cost center can determine the budgeted expenditure for any level of activity. If volume increases, the allowable expenditures will increase. The activity factors will tend to be different at different activity levels. For instance, the unit material cost will usually decline for higher quantities because of price discounts.

Variable budgets are a recognition of the need for flexibility in budgeting, and of the fact that the level of activity is subject to change. The ability to forecast activity accurately is an important prerequisite to an effective flexible budget. If the changes in activity are not reasonably well planned for, managers are unable to make anything like long-range plans. Perhaps the most important advantage of a variable budget is that it requires a thorough study of the relationship of costs to activity. This study permits management to have a better control of its operation costs when a change in the volume of output is required.

CONTROL OF LABOR COSTS

Direct labor may be the major cost element in many operations systems. In some, where a service is the output, it is the only direct cost. The increasing number and importance of service enterprises in the economy focuses emphasis on systems for controlling this cost. The control of labor cost is a difficult problem for management. Today, management has limited control over the setting of wages. One determinant is competition. It is difficult, if not impossible, to gather information which will permit direct comparison. Most companies do not like to make their wage structure public. Even when the wage schedule is readily available, the differences in duties of jobs with the same or similar titles may lead to incorrect comparisons. Union demands also dilute the control that management has over the cost of labor. There is also the minimum wage set by law which may apply to some jobs. Despite these difficulties, it is still possible to use certain techniques which will help to reduce costs, to make labor costing easier and more accurate, and to keep costs in control within the limits of available management action.

The type of wage payment plan which is utilized can be an important element in the control of labor costs. Essentially, there are two classes of wage payment plans. One of these is based on the time worked, referred to as daywork; and the other type is based on the output produced, broadly identified as incentive pay.

Daywork Wage Payment Plans

Wages which are paid on the basis of time worked are the most frequently used. *Daywork is payment of some specified amount per period of time*, irrespective of the level of output. The most common day rate is a certain dollar amount per hour. Computation of the payroll is easy, but the costing of output is complicated with daywork. If a worker is paid by the hour, the labor cost of his output is determined by the rate at which he works. There will tend to be wide variations in worker performance under these types of wage plans. If a worker produces a greater amount during a given period of time, the unit cost will decrease. This is advantageous to the enterprise since it does not have to pay more per unit for a greater output. When the level of performance declines, however, the reverse is true. Day wages provide little incentive since improved performance does not result in higher wages. What small motivation there might be is related to possible promotion or pay raises. These increases are not typically related in any proportion to a worker's performance, however.

Wage Incentive Plans

The purpose of a wage incentive plan is to motivate the employee to a higher level of productivity. This motivation is achieved by offering a financial reward to the individual or group for output of acceptable quality above a specified output standard. There are a large variety of wage incentive plans. While they may vary in detail, all well-designed incentive systems will have certain characteristics in common.

Characteristics of a Well-Designed Wage Incentive Plan. Any incentive plan must have a standard of performance as a starting point. The most accurate way of establishing such a standard is generally conceded to be through some means of work measurement such as stopwatch time study. However, there are many standards which are based on past performance or on estimates made by supervisors. Irrespective of the method of setting the standard, the presence of certain features will make the plan potentially more successful.

A good plan should reward the worker in direct proportion to the increased output. The majority of plans in operation today do this. Any other arrangement is not as acceptable to the workers. Plans which do not include this feature are sharing plans. In sharing plans, the worker does not receive full benefit from the extra effort, but is given only a percentage of the savings.

Today, most incentive plans guarantee a base rate or day wage for all workers. Thus, even if the standard is not met, the worker is guaranteed the base rate for his job. The base rate is one that is established by job evaluation and the collective bargaining process. This feature removes the uncertainties of wage incentive systems which made workers less willing to accept them in the past.

The plan should be simple, easy to understand, and fully explained. A wage incentive plan which is not fully understood by the employees will be suspect from the outset. Plans that require complicated formulas and calculations to determine the amount earned will appear to be attempts to limit earnings. Without the full acceptance and cooperation of the work force, no incentive plan can succeed. Management must see that the plan is fully understood. Workers are entitled to know why they are paid what they are.

It is important that precise work standards be developed and that they be strictly adhered to. The standard should be attainable, and it should be guaranteed against change because management believes the standard is too loose. This kind of change will threaten the security of the workers, and will result in a lack of confidence in the plan. Generally, most of the employees are expected to earn a bonus under a well-designed incentive system. The mean performance level would be between 120% and 130%. The typical distribution of performance is shown in Figure 19-1. Note that well over a majority of the workers would be expected to exceed standard and thus increase their wages.

Specific policies regarding all aspects of the incentive system must be developed. Management must make clear precisely what will and will not be done in all cases. For example, the method of handling circumstances where a machine breakdown occurs should be clearly covered. This condition is usually beyond the control of the operator, so he does not want to be penalized for being unable to earn a bonus while the machine is down. A similar circumstance is when raw material is out of stock. Justifiably, workers want to know what will be done, and want fair and equal treatment. Clear-cut policies are essential to insure the success of a wage incentive plan.

The period of time between the performance and the receipt of the payment for this performance should be as short as is practical. If the incentive is to have full impact, it is important that the workers be able to identify the extra earnings with the added effort. The most common practice is to pay the bonus weekly. This increases administrative costs, but any longer period creates

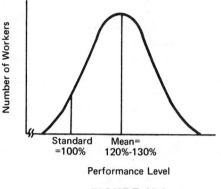

FIGURE 19-1

Expected Distribution of Performance Under a Wage Incentive Plan

dissatisfaction. The nearness of the reward to the effort is almost directly proportionate to the motivational effect.

Individual Incentive Plans. By far the most frequently found types of wage incentive plans can be identified as individual. That is, the performance of each worker covered is measured against the standard and his wage is determined from the amount of his output.

Today the most popular of the individual incentive systems is the straight piece rate or some variant of it. Under the straight piece rate the employee is paid a stipulated dollar value for each unit of output of acceptable quality. The standard is expressed in the monetary amount per unit rather than in time. The earnings can be expressed as:

$$E = R_p O$$

Where:

E = earnings
R_p = rate in dollars per piece
O = output

While this system meets the criterion of pay being directly proportionate to output, it lacks the security of a guaranteed day rate. As a result, most plans now incorporate a guaranteed day rate for all work below standard. The earnings under these conditions can be expressed as:

$$E = TR_h + (O_a - O_s)R_p$$

Where:

T = time worked
R_h = rate per hour in dollars
O_a = actual output in units
O_s = standard output in units
R_p = rate per piece in dollars

Earnings under these two plans can be shown graphically as in Figure 19-2. The dotted line represents the earnings below standard when there is no guaranteed base rate. Notice that since the premium is in direct proportion to output, the piece rate curve is at 45°.

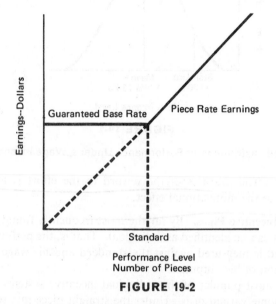

FIGURE 19-2

Earnings Curve for Straight Piece Rate

Because the standard is stated in dollars per unit under the straight piece rate, the workers relate setting of standards closely with their earnings. This attitude may reduce the motivational force of these plans. To overcome this objection, plans which are called *100 percent premium plans*, or standard-hour plans, have been developed. Such plans are essentially the same as piece rate plans. The difference is that for the 100 percent premium plan, the standard is expressed in units of output. The worker is still paid 100 percent of the earned bonus. The earnings under the 100 percent premium plan can be expressed as follows:

$$E = \left(\frac{0_a}{0_s}\right) R_h T$$

The majority of the individual plans which do not fit into the categories described are some type of *sharing plan*. Under these plans the worker's bonus is not in direct proportion to his output. Instead he receives some stipulated percentage of the value of the increased output. A guaranteed base rate is still a feature of most of these plans. The earnings are computed as follows:

$$E = TR_h + P(S - T)R_h$$

Where:

P = the premium percentage
S = the standard time for the task
T = the actual time used in performing the task

When $P = 100$, this plan is identical to the 100 percent premium plan. If the value of $P = O$, the plan is identical to daywork. In Figure 19-3, a graphical comparison of earnings under a 50-50 sharing plan and a 100 percent plan can be seen.

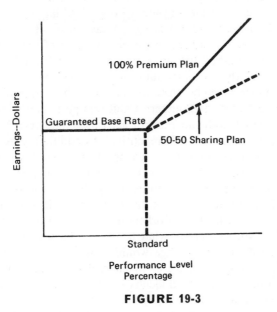

FIGURE 19-3

Comparison of Earnings Under 50 Percent Sharing Plan
and 100 Percent Premium Plan

Occasionally other forms of individual incentive plans are utilized, but the 100 percent premium plan and the sharing plans encompass practically all of the plans in use today.

Group Incentive Plans. Some wage incentive plans are designed to reward a group of workers rather than an individual. Generally speaking, these plans do not supply the same degree of motivation as individual plans. The individual is not able to identify his wages as closely with his performance when he is paid on the basis of the total group output. Probably the greatest advantage of group bonus plans is that more workers can be included. It is not easy to establish a standard for some jobs. The less repetitive a task is, the more difficult it is to measure the output. Consequently, indirect jobs, clerical work, and service tasks in general would fall into this category. A group incentive plan allows for a bonus system where many, if not all, workers can receive a bonus. The output of a work unit of some sort becomes the basis for calculating the bonus. The group size is not usually a factor and can be small or large. Each individual's share of the total bonus is computed on the basis of his base rate. Another advantage of a group plan is the lower administrative costs incurred.

Evaluation of Wage Incentives. The acceptance of wage incentive plans is variable. Some industries use them widely, while other industries are marked by the complete absence of such plans. There is also a difference in the acceptance of incentives between geographic areas. A great deal of this variation is historical. Some is a result of the attitudes of organized labor. The nature of the tasks performed has also had a bearing. A case in point is that incentive plans have been more widely utilized in the eastern part of the United States than on the West Coast. Part of this can be traced to the earlier industrialization in the East. Consequently, the early influence of the scientific management movement was felt more strongly. Another factor is the nature of the major industries on the West Coast. In Southern California particularly, most manufacturing has been related to the airframe or aerospace industry. Many of the tasks in these industries are not highly repetitive. In addition, these industries have depended largely on government contracts. Consequently, they have not been required to be as cost competitive as those enterprises in consumer goods.

Wage incentive plans are less numerous today than in the past. Surveys which have been taken have tended to get different results. It is safe to estimate that no more than 25 percent of the workers in production-type jobs are paid on incentive basis. If all workers in what have been identified as operations activities were included, this percentage would drop — perhaps to as low as 10 percent. The increasing incidence of machine-paced operations is a contributing factor in production. The difficulty of measuring productivity in the other types of operations areas has already been noted.

The most advantageous aspect of a wage incentive plan is the control it provides over labor costs. The unit labor cost is more easily and accurately determined. Under the straight piece rate and its variants, the unit labor cost remains constant starting with standard output and beyond. This constant cost leads to a reduction in total costs because the fixed costs are spread over a larger number of units per period of time. There is also the benefit of higher income to the workers. This higher income does not guarantee job satisfaction, but is certainly one factor in achieving it.

The use of wage incentives has some drawbacks which are generally recognized. Among the disadvantages is that when quantity is stressed by the payment of a bonus, quality and safety may be adversely affected. In addition, workers may build up resentments against management and the plan. This feeling can lead to restriction of output, resistance to changes in methods, and conflict. Naturally, these conditions will lead to increased costs.

Because of the great emphasis on increasing productivity, incentive plans are undergoing close scrutiny. Attempts to overcome some of the shortcomings can be seen. The major thrust seems to be in the direction of eliminating the

causes of resentment. One device utilized for this purpose is employee participation in the design of the plan. The greatest need for improved productivity
in the future will clearly be in the service areas. It is possible that there will be
a resurgence in wage incentive systems. They will, however, take on a new look
as compared with past and present-day plans.

Job Evaluation

All jobs, whether paid on a daywork basis or on incentive, have base rates
established for them. *Job evaluation* is a technique which is used to establish
the base rates for jobs on a systematic basis. It is a method for determining the
relative value or contribution of each job in an enterprise. Since there is no
measure of performance included in the job evaluation process, it is a difficult
undertaking. Job evaluation requires a great deal of subjective evaluation of the
elements of each job. Job evaluation does not assign a dollars-and-cents value
to each job. What it does is to make a comparison of such job elements or
factors as skill, education and experience, working conditions, responsibilities,
and effort required for the different jobs. The basic assumption is that those
jobs which have higher requirements with regard to these factors should have a
higher base rate. The method of establishing the specific rate is usually a separate and more difficult activity.

A variety of job evaluation systems exist, but the major ones are four in
number. In all of these systems, the evaluation process may be done by an individual or by a committee. The more acceptable method today is to use a
committee in making the evaluations. Usually, union members, or some employees if there is no union, will be on the committee.

Job Ranking Systems. This method involves the ranking of all jobs in the
order of their relative worth. Initially, a group of key jobs are selected. *Key
jobs* are jobs which represent a cross section of all jobs in the enterprise. Their
job characteristics should be well known. If possible, the list of key jobs should
contain jobs which represent the maximums and the minimums for each of the
factors to be evaluated. The current rates for these jobs should be competitive
with similar jobs in the industry, and the maximum and minimum rates paid
should be included. The key jobs are ranked first. Next, all other jobs are
ranked by relating them to the key jobs. The final result is a listing of all jobs
in a hierarchy of relative values. This method considers each job as a composite,
and does not consider each factor for each job.

Job Classification Systems. The *job classification system*, sometimes referred to as the predetermined grading method, involves the placing of all jobs
into established job levels or classifications. The classifications are first determined, and then each job is evaluated and placed into one of them. To make a
decision as to the proper classification, each job should have a detailed job
description prepared for it. These descriptions can then be compared with the
specific classification requirements.

The U. S. Civil Service uses two systems of job classification. One is for jobs such as technical, administrative, and clerical which are classified under the General Schedule. The "GS ratings" are set up into 18 categories identified as GS-1 to GS-18. The other system used is for crafts, protective, and custodial jobs which uses ten grades of "CPC ratings."

Other applications of job classification systems may be on a functional basis such as executive, administrative, operations, marketing, engineering, and any others applicable to the enterprise. There can be subgrades within each of these classes into which each job is then placed. The job classification system is also a composite one and does not give attention to the presence or absence of the job factors.

Factor Comparison Systems. These systems take into account the factors which make up a job in determining its relative value. The first step is to determine and define the factors to be used. Typically, from four to seven factors are selected, with five being the most frequent. The five generally used are mental effort, skill, physical effort, responsibility, and working conditions. The key jobs are then selected, and each of these jobs is ranked for each of the factors. The existing base rate for each of the key jobs is apportioned on a weighted basis to each of the factors. The weight assigned to each element is determined for each individual job so that the apportionment of the going rate differs between jobs. The remaining jobs are then evaluated by comparing them for each factor with the key jobs. In this process, a monetary value for each factor is determined. The sum of these values of the factors leads to the total wage for a job.

These systems are difficult to develop and administer as compared with other job evaluation systems. These difficulties may create some dissatisfaction on the part of the employees because of a resulting lack of understanding. When a wage change occurs, it is necessary to rework the job evaluations.

Point Systems. The most widely used systems of job evaluation are point systems. These systems arrive at an evaluation of jobs by comparing the degree of each of the characteristics or factors present in the job. As in the factor comparison system, the factors are assigned weights. Instead of using dollars, however, points are assigned. The jobs to be evaluated are studied to discover what characteristics or factors determine the worth of jobs in the enterprise. A scale or range of points for the presence of each factor is set and points for intermediate divisions or degrees for each factor are determined. Each factor and degree which is determined must be clearly defined. The factors are then assigned weights so as to include the maximum and the minimum degree of each factor that is present. The weights assigned to each degree of each factor become the points against which all jobs are evaluated. The key jobs are evaluated first and their total point value determined.

An enterprise may develop its own system by the above procedure, or it may resort to one of the already existing systems. Most of these have been developed for use in a particular industry. One of the most widely known programs of this sort is the one used by the National Metal Trades Association and the National Electrical Manufacturers Association. This plan, as do most standardized plans, has a manual containing detailed descriptions of the factors and degrees of each factor, and gives the point values for each factor and degree.

After the jobs are evaluated by the point rating system, it is necessary to price the jobs. This pricing is accomplished by a point-to-money conversion line. The current base rates and the total point values of the key jobs are used to determine this curve. The point values are plotted against the wage rates as is indicated in Figure 19-4. A trend line is then fitted to these points. A linear trend line such as illustrated in the figure can be fitted either by visual inspection or by a statistical method such as least squares.

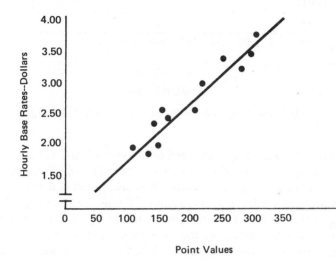

FIGURE 19-4

Key Jobs Point-to-Money Plot
with Least-Squares Trend

The line of best fit may not always be linear. A curvilinear fit may be a better representation of the trend. This latter type of curve is an indication that a point value is not worth the same amount of money for all jobs. The more skilled jobs are given more value. This difference in value may be difficult to explain to the workers, especially those in the low skill jobs.

The establishment of labor grades is the next step in the point rating plan. This step is necessary in order to avoid a situation where there would be a large number of base rates. Each job would have a base rate set for it according to its point value. By grouping jobs into labor grades, the base rates can be limited to the grades established. The groupings also permit the stating of a range of wages for each grade. A typical practice is to have each grade extend over the same number of points. Such a plan is shown in Figure 19-5.

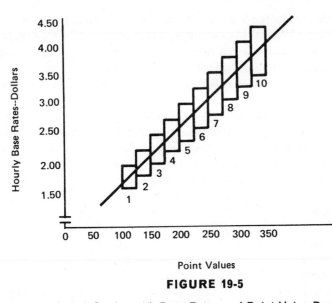

FIGURE 19-5

Labor Grades with Base Rates and Point Value Ranges

Overlapping labor grades as illustrated in the above figure are not the only form used. Among the other forms are those where the top of one grade becomes the bottom rate for the next grade. It is also found that the overlap is not equal between all grades in some systems. Within each labor grade there are usually a number of steps from the bottom to the top. Each step may have an equal increment. An employee's movement from bottom to top of a labor grade may be a result of seniority, may be based on merit increases, or some combination of both.

When the above steps have been completed, all jobs other than the key jobs are evaluated in the same way as the key jobs. After the total points for all jobs are determined, each job is placed in a labor grade. Theoretically, the jobs would fit into one of the wage ranges established for the point values. In fact, however, there will be some jobs that will fall outside the range. Those jobs which are below the lower limit should be moved to the base rate level established by the evaluation plan. The ones which are above the upper limit are more of a problem. The existing rates will have to be maintained for the incumbents. When new employees take over these jobs, the evaluated rate will be in effect. If possible, the present job holders will be advanced to a job which pays the rate they are currently getting. Additional training may be required to prepare them for the new job.

Appraisal of Job Evaluation. The greatest value of job evaluation is that it provides an impersonal method of determining the relative worth of jobs in an enterprise. The resulting structuring of jobs should reduce some of the concern which workers typically have about the fairness of their wages. In addition, an environment for developing a good wage payment plan should result. This improvement applies whether an incentive system is used or not. A well-designed job evaluation system will be valuable in achieving control of labor costs.

Job evaluation systems are not without their shortcomings. Since the process is so largely dependent on subjective judgments, it is not always readily accepted by workers. It is difficult to find job characteristics or factors that are discrete. The factors almost always encroach on each other. Also, jobs change with time. This changing means that periodic reevaluations should be made. The evaluations are also affected by the periodic wage adjustments which take place. These adjustments can create undesirable distortions in the wage system. A percentage increase will create a greater disparity between the top wages and the lowest. On the other hand, a flat rate increase lessens the percentage differences between classifications.

As would be expected, attempts to improve the application of job evaluation are being made constantly. One approach which has aroused considerable interest and consequent controversy is worthy of some comment. This idea proposes determining the value of a job by use of the time span of discretion. The *time span of discretion* is a measurement of work difficulty determined by the length of time a worker is permitted to use his own discretion in making decisions without some review by his supervisor.[1] Under this concept, the higher the level of the job, the less frequent the time span between reviews. These higher-level jobs would demand a higher wage. Such a system would require considerable research into the time spans of numerous jobs, and these time spans may not be easily determined.

One reason for the interest in the time span theory is that job evaluation is now being utilized in many enterprises for a greater variety of jobs. Many so-called white collar jobs are being evaluated, as are supervisory tasks. The time span theory offers a greater potential for classification and evaluation of these types of jobs. It is, therefore, of particular interest to operations managers in the emerging service types of enterprises.

COST REDUCTION

One of the objectives of controlling costs in the operations system is to find those areas where costs are exceeding expectations. It is then the role of management to take steps to bring these costs back into line. Not only should management take immediate steps to control a particular cost when it deviates from the expected level, but it should develop long-range programs aimed at cost reduction. The most easily identifiable costs in the operations system are direct labor and direct material. Since these costs are major ones, the emphasis on cost reduction is usually concentrated here. However, the overhead areas should not be overlooked. While any single item may not yield a large savings, the accumulation of many small savings can be significant.

[1]Elliott Jaques, *Measurement of Responsibility* (London: Tavistock Publications, Ltd., 1956).

Cost reduction does not mean merely reducing the amount of money spent. It means getting better results for the same amount of money or the same results for less outlay. Cost reduction programs should aim at improving the efficiency of labor, at improving material utilization, at improving the design of the output, and at any other improvement which increases the efficiency of the operations system. In essence this means the proper utilization of the tools and techniques which have been discussed throughout the book.

There are certain specific areas in which cost reduction programs are most successful. One area where cost reduction programs are frequently found is work and job design. Such programs are often labeled as work simplification programs. Not only are the efforts of those responsible for the design of jobs involved in these programs, but attempts are made to include all of the employees. The aim of these programs is to get everyone to be "work design conscious." One of the elements of such programs is frequently a formal training course in work simplification. The hoped-for outcome is that everyone in the enterprise will constantly look for ways of improving his own job and other jobs with which he is familiar. Frequently, there is a suggestion system included in the program. Workers make suggestions about work methods. If a suggestion is accepted by management, the worker submitting it is paid a financial reward. The reward is typically based on the savings expected from the improvement. Suggestion systems are not limited to work simplification programs, but can be utilized in any type of cost reduction program.

Related activities aimed at reducing labor costs are programs that attempt to improve the performance of the workers. Increased motivation, improved job satisfaction, and improved technical ability are all ways in which this may be achieved. Any step that will improve the performance of the workers and increase the productivity of labor will result in a cost reduction.

In discussing the techniques of inventory control, considerable attention was given to models which had lowest cost as their measure of effectiveness. Improving the control of inventories can lead to reduced costs by reducing the incidence of out-of-stock conditions. Proper inventory planning will also result in a better utilization of all other resources, and thus yield a cost improvement. Material costs may also be reduced by means of changes in specifications or design changes. Programs such as value engineering have cost reduction as their objective.

Cost reduction possibilities in overhead are many. Indirect labor is a prime target for cost reduction, especially in the service enterprises. The amount of indirect labor also increases with increased automation. Often a duplication of indirect activities in different departments of the enterprise exists. Clerical activities offer many possibilities for cost reduction. The improvement of performance, better paper systems and procedures, and control of the size of the staff are prime candidates. The use of time standards, standard costs, and budgets can contribute a great deal to the reduction of costs in the overhead area.

Improvement in facilities planning, location of facilities, scheduling, transportation, and output quality can also lead to cost savings. A potential for

Rotated handwritten notes:

Actual Col ① $(4800 \times 0 + 5400 \times 0 + 19200 \times 0) - 0 = 0$

Col ② $(0 \times 0 + 6 \times 0 + 150 \times 0) - 115 = -115$

B Col ③ $(3 \times 0 + 18 \times 0 + 0 \times 0) - 70 = -70$

Entry No Calculation

m_1 Row $= 4800/6 = 800$

m_2 Row $= 5400/0 = 5400$

m_3 Row $= 19,200/15 = 640$

Inventory II $0 = \dfrac{19,200 \times (-244)}{30} = \dfrac{+4,684,800}{30} = 156160$

$-115 - \dfrac{(150 \times (-244) - 115)}{30} = \dfrac{(-36.603)}{30}$

$= 122 - 115 = 7$

Mary Jo Vargas
351 Carnahan
San Antonio, Tx 78209

cost reduction exists in literally every area which falls under the concern of the operations manager. Management must continuously be alert for possibilities for cost reductions in all of its decisions.

COST-EFFECTIVENESS ANALYSIS

A recently developed technique which can be useful in the controlling of costs and also useful in evaluating the overall performance of the enterprise is cost-effectiveness analysis. *Cost-effectiveness analysis* (also referred to as cost-benefit analysis) is used to evaluate alternatives in circumstances where the objectives and the measures of effectiveness are not capable of being expressed in clearly measurable terms. Measuring performance in government, education, health services, and eleemosynary enterprises is difficult. The results are not clearly measurable in terms of sales dollars or profit margins. Business organizations are increasingly undertaking programs with social goals, and the effectiveness of these programs is difficult to measure. Pollution abatement and training of the disadvantaged are examples of these kinds of programs.

Cost effectiveness is utilized to evaluate the output of total systems. Consequently, the analysis is difficult. In the first place, the final output is not always predictable, particularly since it is the product of a large system in most cases. Additionally, costs are difficult to estimate, and the measure of effectiveness is not amenable to quantification. Each alternative is evaluated in terms of its effectiveness, and the cost of each is compared with this effectiveness. The effectiveness measure is a form of utility determination. The result is an ordering of the alternatives at a level of either cost or effectiveness. This level has been predetermined as the objective of the program. It may be desired to establish a total relationship for each alternative at all levels of cost and effectiveness. In this way, it can be determined how much the effectiveness will be affected by a change in cost and how much cost will change with an alternate effectiveness. An important element of cost-effectiveness analysis is the use of the program budget. Many governmental agencies, federal, state, and local, have adopted program budgets. The Federal Government uses the Planning-Programming-Budgeting (PPB) System. This system is designed to provide better analysis of programs in the civilian departments of the government. The analysis which accompanies each program should be useful in the development of final budgets.

Cost-benefit analysis is not a final answer to marginal comparisons between nonquantifiable goals. However, it does offer a means of getting better analysis than has been available in the past.

SUMMARY

Costs are frequently used as a measure of the effectiveness of an operations system. They are a means of conveying the plans of the enterprise throughout the system. As feedback information, costs serve as a means of comparing performance with plans. Costs are also used as a motivating device.

The major cost elements of an operations system are direct material costs, direct labor costs, and operations overhead costs. To arrive at the total operations costs, the cost elements must be allocated to the various cost centers. Costing can be either by job or by process. Costing problems arise from difficulties of identifying direct material and direct labor and from difficulties of determining the basis for allocating overhead costs.

Expected costs for the operations cost elements can be established as standard costs. These standard costs are the basis on which actual performance is evaluated. Attention is concentrated on variances in costs which may occur. These variances are usually the result of a change in price or the quantity used.

Budgets are similar to standard costs. Budgets as a control device are used to compare actual with that which was planned. The operations budget may be found in three different forms. The responsibility budget is the form which is used primarily for control purposes. The product budget allocates costs to product lines, but is not useful for control. The forecasting budget is primarily a planning tool. A specialized form of the forecasting budget is the program budget.

To introduce some degree of flexibility into the budgeting process, variable budgets can be used. This form of budget permits the budgeted costs to be changed with a change in the level of activity.

The control of labor costs is important in total cost control. One factor in achieving labor cost control is the type of wage payment plan in effect. Daywork is the most frequently found method of wage payment. Daywork payment is based on the period of time worked. Since it is not related to output, it provides little incentive for improved performance.

Wage incentive systems offer a financial reward to workers if they produce above a specified level. This higher productivity not only results in higher pay, but also leads to reduced cost per unit. All well-designed wage incentive systems have certain characteristics in common. A worker should be rewarded in direct proportion to any increased output. The plan should guarantee a base rate for all workers. The plan should be simple and understandable. The standard should be precise and adhered to strictly. Policies regarding the administration of the plan should be stated clearly. The reward should be paid soon after the performance. With these characteristics, a wage incentive system will likely be successful.

Most incentive systems are based on individual performance. Prominent among these systems are the straight piece rate and the 100 percent premium plan. Some plans are identified as sharing plans. These plans do not pay the worker in direct proportion to his output. Group incentive plans are also used, though they tend to lack the motivational effect of the individual plans. The utilization of wage incentive plans has declined in recent years. However, the great emphasis on improved productivity has caused their usefulness to be reevaluated.

A widely used technique for determining the base rate for all jobs is job evaluation. It is a systematic means of determining the relative value of each job. There are four major types of job evaluation systems. Job ranking simply ranks the jobs in order of their relative worth. Job classification systems place all jobs into specified levels or classifications. These two systems are composite methods that consider the job as a whole. The other two methods consider the individual factors that go to make up the job. The factor comparison system weights each factor of the job considered and apportions money values to each of the factors on the basis of the weightings. The point rating system is the most widely used technique. A job is evaluated by comparing the degree of each factor present in the job. This degree of presence is determined by a series of weighted point values assigned to each factor. Jobs are priced in the point rating system by determination of a trend line from the total points and the going base rates. The many base rates are consolidated into groups known as labor grades. These are established to encompass a range of point values and a wage range for each grade. Job evaluation can assist materially in achieving labor cost control.

Cost reduction programs are useful in achieving the control of costs. They attempt to improve the utilization of resources so that the cost per unit of output is lower. One type of cost reduction program which has been widely used is in the area of work simplification. Other labor-related cost reduction programs are also found. Attempts to reduce material-related costs are necessary as well.

A relatively new technique which is useful in controlling costs is cost-effectiveness analysis. Such an analysis can be used to evaluate various alternative programs in terms of cost vs. effectiveness at all of the possible levels.

INCIDENT I

BRITANNIA HOTELS, LTD.

Britannia Hotels operated a group of 75 hotels, motor inns, and small inns throughout the British Isles. These facilities varied greatly in size, types of accommodations, and location. Some of the hotels had several hundred rooms. Most of these establishments were located in cities, and could be classified as luxury or first-class hotels. Some of the motor inns were located near large and medium sized cities along the motorways. These inns averaged between 50 to 100 rooms in size, and were new. Another group of the motor inns of about the same size were located in medium sized towns, primarily those with strong tourist attractions. The inns in this group were older but well maintained. Some of them had recent additions built onto the older portions. The small inns were all quite old. Some dated back 400 to 500 years. They ranged in size from 10 to 25 rooms. All of the hotels and inns had eating facilities appropriate to the accommodations. Some of the larger establishments offered a variety such as one or more dining rooms and a coffee shop.

A job evaluation plan had been instituted by the central management. The system selected was a job classification plan. Eventually 15 classifications with appropriate salary ranges were developed. The plan included all positions below vice-president at the central office and all positions at the individual hotels and inns. This meant that each hotel manager and inn manager was included in the plan. A large number of these managers were opposed to the inclusion of their positions in the plan. Some felt that a plan which included chambermaids and porters could not be applied to the position of manager of a hotel or inn. It was also pointed out by those who opposed the plan that the duties of the managers of the different facilities were diversified and could not be accounted for in a general classification plan of this type. Additionally, they noted that the salaries paid to the different managers covered a wide range.

Questions

1. Present arguments in favor of this plan.
2. Are there any additional reasons for excluding the managers from this plan?
3. Present possible alternatives to the recommended plan.

INCIDENT II

STORE-TO-DOOR DELIVERY SERVICE

The STD Delivery Service has contracts with most of the major department stores in a large metropolitan area to handle all of the stores' package deliveries. These deliveries do not include "big ticket" items such as furniture and appliances. The packages vary in size from very small to a maximum size of about six cubic feet. The delivery radius from the STD distribution center is 25 miles, but the majority of the packages are delivered within a 12-mile radius.

All packages are picked up from the stores on a scheduled basis. They are taken to a distribution center where they are sorted according to destination. They are then loaded onto the trucks whose route includes the delivery address. Not only are the packages of varying size, but there are other differences in the packages. Some stores require a signed receipt for certain packages. This requirement usually is for packages over a stated value. If delivery of these packages is not possible, the driver must fill out and leave a notice. Some packages are C.O.D. for which the driver can accept only cash.

Performance standards have been established and have been in use for some time. These standards have been set for drivers after considering the number of stops on a route, the average mileage covered on the route, and the location of the route (central city vs. suburbs). Time standards also exist for all aspects of package handling at the distribution center. To date, these standards have been used only as a means of evaluating the efficiency of employee performance. No attempt has been made to use them in connection with a wage payment plan or to measure costs.

A proposal has been made that STD establish a standard cost system. The company wants to set a single standard cost per package. It is felt that the time standards now in existence can be used as a basis for establishing a standard labor cost.

Questions

1. Can a single standard cost per package be set?

2. What are some of the difficulties which you foresee in setting a standard cost in this situation?

3. What would you recommend as the means of allocating overhead costs?

QUESTIONS FOR DISCUSSION AND ANALYSIS

1. What is cost? Why is it an important factor in operations decisions in all types of enterprises?

2. Describe and exemplify the major types of costs associated with the operations system.

3. What is a cost center? Why is the identification of cost centers necessary to the costing procedure? How are cost centers and product costing related?

4. Distinguish between job costing and process costing. Describe the types of situations to which each is most applicable.

5. Identify the difficulties associated with costing, making specific reference to the three types of operations costs.

6. What are standard costs? Give examples. What are the advantages of a standard cost system?

7. Why do cost variances occur?

8. "The budget is essentially a planning tool." Do you agree? What is the relationship of the budget to cost control?

9. Which type of operations budget is most useful for control purposes? What other types of operations budgets are there, and what is the function of each?

10. What is the purpose of a variable budget? What difficulties do you see for the operations manager who must function under a variable budget?

11. What is daywork? Why is it the most frequently found method of wage payment?

12. What are the characteristics of a well-designed wage incentive plan?

13. Compare the effectiveness of individual and group incentive plans. What are the advantages and drawbacks of each?

14. How effective do you believe wage incentives to be as a motivator of greater productivity?

15. Describe the characteristics of the four major job evaluation systems.

16. What are some of the opportunities for cost reduction in the operations system?

17. What is the primary objective of cost-effectiveness analysis? What is its potential as a cost control technique in manufacturing and nonmanufacturing enterprises?

SELECTED ADDITIONAL READINGS

Anthony, Robert N., and James S. Hekimian. *Operations Cost Control.* Homewood, Illinois: Richard D. Irwin, Inc., 1967.

Belcher, D. W. *Compensation Administration.* Englewood Cliffs: Prentice-Hall, Inc., 1974.

Belcher, D. W. *Wage and Salary Administration*, 2d ed. Englewood Cliffs: Prentice-Hall, Inc., 1962.

Brennan, C. W. *Wage Administration.* Homewood, Illinois: Richard D. Irwin, Inc., 1963.

Carroll, P. *Better Wage Incentives.* New York: McGraw-Hill Book Co., 1957.

Jaques, Elliott. *Measurement of Responsibility.* London: Tavistock Publications, Ltd., 1956.

Langsner, A., and H. G. Zollitsch. *Wage and Salary Administration.* Cincinnati: South-Western Publishing Co., 1961.

Louden, J. K., and J. W. Deegan. *Wage Incentives.* New York: John Wiley & Sons, Inc., 1959.

Moore, Carl L., and Robert K. Jaedicke. *Managerial Accounting*, 2d ed. Cincinnati: South-Western Publishing Co., 1967.

Otis, J. L., and R. H. Leukart. *Job Evaluation: A Basis for Sound Wage Administration,* 2d ed. Englewood Cliffs: Prentice-Hall, Inc., 1962.

Prest, A. R., and R. Turvey. "Cost-Benefit Analysis: A Survey." *The Economics Journal* (December, 1965).

The evolution of operations management to its present state has followed a series of reasonably logical steps. Much of this evolution has been a response to the changes that have taken place in the types of problems and in the decision-making tools utilized. The importance of the efficiency of the operations system to the success of the total enterprise is unquestionable. Therefore, the management of this function must remain flexible to meet the changing demands. The details of the major failures in both large and small organizations reveal that these failures are largely attributable to inefficient management of the operations function. In addition, many problems currently facing all types of enterprises make strong demands on the performance of the operations system. In all probability, the same situation will exist in the future. Therefore, it will be useful to examine the present status of the field of operations management and of the associated problems. In addition, viewing the changes taking place will be helpful in considering the next phase of the logical development. Trends can be seen and prediction can be made from these trends about the future.

PRESENT STATUS OF OPERATIONS MANAGEMENT

Change is probably the one word which can be used to characterize the development of operations management to its current stage: change in the internal setting of the enterprise, and change in the external environment. The problems have changed, and the techniques for solving the problems have also changed. Perhaps the greatest responses have been the result of the changes in the socioeconomic area. While perhaps not as far-reaching, the effects of technology have been a strong and more visible influence for change.

Socioeconomic Factors

Economic and sociological forces are so closely intertwined that any attempt to identify trends as belonging exclusively to one of these categories is useless. For example, the increased education of the work force is both a social and an economic force. Certainly the fact that a majority of the college-age population is attending college is a factor of great social implication. At the same time, this occurrence is also having great economic impact.

A direct outgrowth of the greater educational level of the population is the increasing demand by the consumer for better performance by the producers of products and services. The consumer movement has led to calls for the establishment of, and adherence to, high standards of quality and performance. Coupled with this is the growing concern for the environment. These demands have obvious relationships to the performance of the operations system. The management of the operations system is perhaps affected by these demands more than is any other segment of the enterprise because this system produces the output. It is in the processing subsystem of the operations system that the changes must be made to reduce much of the industrial pollution.

Changing demands by consumers have led to a situation of shorter product life which places many burdens on the enterprise. A great deal of the shortening of the life of a product today is a result of rapid technological development.

Technological Factors

Clearly, technology is advancing rapidly, and little evidence exists that the increase will not continue at an even greater rate. The effect of technology on operations management comes from many different sources. In the first place, the new technologies bring on new products and services. The tremendous spin-off from the missile and space areas into consumer applications is just one example. A need for new processes, new methods, and new allocation of resources results. These requirements along with the new technology have brought innovations in equipment and associated problems of selection and introduction of such equipment. There are also questions of where to direct research efforts, and problems of organizational design related to technological change. These factors, among others, have brought on a need for improved operations management.

Problems of Operations Management

The trends currently taking place in the social, economic, and other environments have had effects as well. Problems have been created which are peculiar to the performance of the operations manager.

The systems approach has opened new vistas in the management of the operations system. Certainly the multiplicity of analytical techniques now available has more clearly defined the decision process. The tremendous impact of technology has forced an increase in the knowledge about how it can be managed. The problems of the relationship of policy and strategy of the enterprise to the operations function are apparently becoming clearer.

Despite these many advances, operations management is still faced with problems which must be overcome in order to achieve more efficient performance. Some of these problems are critical to the successful movement of the management of this function to the next stage of development. Among these problems are productivity and its improvement, the measurement of productivity, the evaluation of the performance of the system, and the consideration of the role of people in the system.

Productivity. Interest in improved productivity is not new. The attempt to get greater output from men, machines, and other resources is as old as work itself. The farmer has always been concerned with how much yield per acre he can get. In manufacturing, the attempt to increase output per man-hour is at least as old as the industrial revolution. The growth and efficiency of a nation's economy is measured in terms of total-factor productivity. The larger the unit for which the measurement is to be made, the more difficult it is. Even where physical units of output are involved, the task is complicated. Now with the shift to greater service activities it is more so.

Examples of the need for improving productivity in the service sector are almost infinite. Much concern has been expressed about the productivity of various governmental operations. Another area is education, while the efficiency of the health care delivery system has been the subject of much study. In addition, there are examples in banks; brokerage houses, and other financial institutions; the repair and maintenance services; communications; and marketing services.

The labor intensive nature of most service activities raises the question about the potential of improving productivity in this sector. There are those who argue that it can't be done. However, the application of many techniques, both old and new, is finding some success. The use of work design and work measurement; some forms of financial control, including budgets; standardizing of many aspects of the operations; and applying computers to the various decisions are found even in small-scale operations. These techniques are being applied in such diverse operations as real estate, barber shops, repair services of all types, restaurants, retailing, leisure-time related enterprises, and the health care services.

Measurement. The strict definition of productivity as the relationship between total input and total output appears deceptively simple. The problems of measurement are complex. Even where labor is utilized as the basic input, measurement is not easy. Acquiring an accurate measure of labor input in the sense of actual hours worked is hard to come by. When a consideration of the physical output is involved, this becomes even more of a problem. Getting accurate figures for the entire enterprise is problem enough. When an industry total is attempted, measurement is almost impossible. Then, when the services are considered, it appears insurmountable because the outputs are not physical. If dollar volume of output is used, it must be deflated by any price rise.

Much work is now being done to develop accurate measures of productivity for the service industries. Some interesting progress has been made. In 1972 a group of economists working in conjunction with the Bureau of Labor Statistics developed an index of productivity for federal civil service workers. Other agencies are working on indices for numerous governmental activities. New York City has established a program of productivity targets and progress measurement and reports.

The problem of measurement for the operations manager is not limited strictly to productivity, however. To date most measurements have been directed toward operational effectiveness. Now, there is added emphasis on measures of service effectiveness. How well the system is fulfilling the needs of the external environment is a pertinent question. This kind of measurement is less objective than measurement of the internal environment of the system. Management will have to develop better means for measuring service effectiveness.

One specialized form of this type of measurement is the social audit. This type of audit tries to measure the social contributions of the enterprise. This is a highly subjective concept, and is in an early stage of evolution. A recent study examines the development of such audits by some of the major corporations.[1] The implication is that as means of measurement are improved, the social audit will become a more common practice.

Evaluating Performance. Evaluation is the next step after measurement. Without good measurement, evaluation is of little value. On the other hand, measurement in itself is meaningless without evaluation. The evaluation process begins at an early stage, and is based initially on the planning process. An enterprise management must plan, measure results, evaluate the measurements, and then take some action. These are the steps by which management determines the effectiveness of the system's achievement of the objectives.

Since evaluation of performance presupposes a formal planning system, improvement of the evaluation process requires improved planning. The principal area where planning needs improvement is in respect to the period for which plans are made. Therefore, there is need for extending the time horizon of planning. Long-range planning has developed significantly in the last decade. Today's rapidly changing environment requires enterprises to plan further into the future. There will be a premium on spotting trends at an early date. New developments will have to be foreseen well in advance so the operations manager can be given the necessary lead times to accommodate.

A second aspect of the planning problem comes from the increasing influence of the external environment. Planning will have to take cognizance of the external factors which influence operations. Most planning in the past has been inwardly oriented. Today, the pressures of the socio-technical-economic system need to be accounted for in any plans.

A final area of planning needing improvement is budgeting. The increased number of innovations will necessitate better methods of capital budgeting. There will be more frequent expenditures for machinery and equipment required. The amounts of money needed will be larger, and the decisions made will be more complex. Management will need budgeting techniques designed to cope with such problems. Because of the expanded planning horizons, budgets must be developed for longer periods of time than has been the norm. Budgeting of large-scale programs will be required more frequently. Consequently, some form of program budgeting will be necessary. Program budgeting is a difficult process as it requires much more than changing the method

---

[1]Raymond A. Bauer and Dan H. Fenn, Jr., *The Corporate Social Audit* (New York: Russell Sage Foundation, 1972).

of developing the budgets and accounting for expenditures. This form of budgeting involves a change in the basic philosophies of budgeting. Therefore, the attitudes of those who must formulate, administer, and conform to budgets must be altered.

People. Since people are at the core of any operations system, a discussion of problems necessarily includes a consideration of people. One of the ongoing problems found in the operations system is the shortage of well-qualified managers. Part of the reason for this is simply absolute growth. As enterprises grow in size and number, the need for managers increases. Another reason is that not enough people are being trained in this area. This results partially from the increasing breadth and complexity of the field. There has been an expansion of the range of knowledge which is required for managers in this field. In addition, the operations area has not had the appeal to young managers that other areas of management have had. Consequently, there is a need to attract more and better qualified people to be trained in the operations area if the function is to be carried out efficiently.

Another problem related to people is need for motivation. This need is particularly significant in the labor intensive enterprises. Motivation plays an important role in the improvement of productivity. One of the significant elements in the drive for improved performance is the attitudes of the worker toward the job and toward management. Evidences of the problem are seen in the high level of absenteeism, high employee turnover, along with low productivity.

If the goals of the enterprise are to be achieved, the problems in the operations area must be overcome. The key to the solutions of these problems rests with operations management. How well they will be solved and how this will influence the nature of the operations system is a question for the future.

FUTURE STATUS OF OPERATIONS MANAGEMENT

The future is uncertain and unknown. However, it is possible to spot certain trends, and by extrapolation forecast future conditions with a reasonable degree of confidence. Certainly, many of the same problems currently present will still exist in the future. Most of the current techniques for solving the problems of operations management will still be used. This does not mean that the problems will be of the same level of difficulty or be of the same form. Nor does it mean that the solution techniques will not be refined and improved. Refinements and improvements will take place. Their exact nature we leave to an oracle.

Many predictions have been made about the nature of management and of the enterprise of the future. Some writers have predicted drastic changes, a few of which border on being classifiable as Orwellian. Usually these far-reaching predictions are based on a narrow conception of the probable changes, dwelling on one aspect of the enterprise management, and assuming only that aspect will be altered, while everything else will remain constant. Examination of past trends does not support this viewpoint of change. When significant change occurs in one area, other areas react and compensate to keep pace. It is true that short-run, disproportionate changes occur, which result in distortions and imbalances among the many phases of management. However, if the concept of the system is to be accepted, the integrated whole cannot continue to function in this way. It would be impossible to function with giant advances in planning techniques without equivalent improvements in methods of control also being developed. In essence, this means that the future operations system is not going to be too dissimilar from what we now have. Changes and improvements are inevitable. The changes, however, will continue to be evolutionary and the relationship of the offspring to its ancestor will be recognizable.

The most evident trends for the future are already well established. The application of quantitative techniques to the problems of operations management will not only continue, but will expand. The primary expansion will take place in the application of these techniques to new problem areas. For instance, there is considerable parallel between the socioeconomic system and the operations system. Both are adaptive, open systems. There is no reason to believe that many of the same analytical approaches could not be utilized for problem solving in the socioeconomic area. There are presently examples of successful applications of some of these methods to social programs. There have been reports of limited uses in the poverty program and in federal housing programs. The use of econometric models for predicting the level of the economy is another case in point. It is interesting to speculate how useful quantitative analysis will be in solving the problems of pollution and other ecologically related problems.

The continued growth of computer technology is another example of this kind of trend. The tremendous impact on information processing has already been discussed. A continuation of the trend of programming routine decisions is a virtual certainty. Better ways of utilizing computers will be developed. The use of computers in simulation and in heuristic decision making is really in its infancy. As these techniques are developed further, they will make possible decisions in problem areas not presently subject to systematic analysis. Along with these developments, brought on by the information revolution, will come, in reaction, some changes in the organization structure itself. This organization change will be accompanied by a consequent change in the way the manager performs his job.

Because of the continuing and growing impact of technology, management will learn to implement and make use of new advances and to predict the consequences. The problem of technology is far-reaching and is applicable to a wide range of areas. Management must consider the effect of different technologies on the operations system. Managers of the future will be more aware of the full impact of any technological change on the socioeconomic environment, on the total organization of the enterprise, as well as on the operations system. It will be important to avoid any further "future shock" caused by technology.

The future will see more emphasis on the human element in the operations system. There will be continued attempts to increase motivation in line with the desire for greater productivity. New techniques like the task-force approach used by General Electric, which calls for greater worker participation, will find favor. Methods such as flexi-time, which allows workers to set their own working time schedule within limits, will also be tried more. Approaches like behavior modification suggested by B. F. Skinner may be used for motivational purposes.[2] Attempts to widen or make better use of the individual's skills will be needed to meet new and greater technical knowledge on the job. This will bring about new and better training programs and techniques of development. At the same time, some better appraisal techniques than those presently available will be developed. All of this concern for motivation, development of skills, and appraisal of individual performance applies to both the workers and the managers.

L'ENVOI

The past, the present, and the future. The progress has been logical and systematic. There is no reason to believe that this evolution will not continue. The changes are coming faster than ever. New concepts, technologies, and tools appear at a rapid pace. To keep up, operations managers of the future will need to be better trained than ever. They will have to engage in a process of continuous education. Only in this way can they hope to meet the needs of the operations system of the future.

The need is there and the challenge is great. The management of the operations system will present an opportunity which will be equal to any in the enterprise. The successful accomplishment of the task will offer an unparalleled satisfaction to those who are capable of meeting this challenge.

[2]B. F. Skinner, *Contingencies of Reinforcement: A Theoretical Analysis* (New York: Appleton-Century-Croft, 1969).

Index

A

ABC analysis, 434–436
Absolute rate of return, 184
Abstract models, 39
Abstract system, 21
Acceptable quality level, 486, 487
Acceptance sampling, 486–492
Access time, 63
Accounting equation, 90
Accounting models, 87, 90–93
Accounting ratios, 93
Accumulative timing, 354, 355
Achievement, 287, 288
Activity, defined, 461
Activity analysis, 305, 309, 310
Activity charts, 99, 305, 309
Adaptive system, 21
Addition rule, 45–47
Adhesive joining, 244
After-tax return, 185
Aggregate systems, 441–468
Aging worker, 340, 341
ALGOL, 67
Algorithms, 38, 260
Allocation problems, 116
Alpha factor, 221–223
Alphanumeric terminals, 76
American Society of Mechanical Engineers, symbols of, 302, 303
Analog computers, 62
Analog models, 39
Analytical forecasting techniques, 210–222
Analytical premises, 201
Anthropometry, 323, 324
Anticipation inventories, 411, 412
Apollo program, 9
AQL, 486, 487

Arithmetic unit, in digital computer, 64
Artificial destination, 139
Artificial source, 140
Assembly, processes, 243, 244
Assembly chart, *see* assembly diagrams
Assembly diagrams, 103, 105
Assembly line, 4, 255, 259, 260
Assembly line balancing, 257
Assignable variations, 475
Attribute(s), acceptance sampling for, 486–492; defined, 20
Attribute inspection, 480
Authoritative management, 290
Automation, 9–11, 238, 245, 246
Auxiliary memory, in digital computer, 63
Auxiliary storage, in computers, 63, 66
Average net investment, 185

B

Babbage, Charles, 4, 5
Balance sheet, 90, 91
Barnes, Ralph, 317, 318
Barth, Carl, 8
Batch operations systems, 235, 236
Batch processing, 72
"Biological clock," 339
Bit, 63
Block control, 444, 445
Block diagrams, 103, 105, 106
Bonuses, *see* wage incentive plans
Boolean algebra, 89
Boring, 242
Brazing, 243, 244
Break-even analysis, 95–97

Break-even chart, 95, 96

Break-even formula, 96, 97

Break-even point, 95

Brouha, Lucien, 329

Budget(s), 502, 506, 507; budgeting, 530, 531

Buffer inventories, 412

Byte, 63

C

Cardinal utility, 50

Card-pigeonhole method, 457–459

Carrabino, Joseph D., 3

Carrying costs, 413, 416, 417

Cash flow statements, 92

Casting, continuous, 239; die, 239; permanent mold, 239; plaster mold, 238, 239; sand, 238

Cathode ray display terminal, 78

Cathode ray tube, 76, 77

c-chart, 491, 492

Certainty, 39, 40, 424

Chance variations, 475

Channels of distribution, 387

Chapanis, Alphonse, 332

Check reading, 332

Chemical milling, 243

Clerical processes, 237

Closed-loop system, 26, 27, 246

"Closed" models, 89

Closed system, 21

COBOL, 67

Coefficient of correlation, 219, 220, 225

Competition, 390, 391

Compilers, 67

Computer(s), 9–12, 61–83, 99, 102, 103, 124, 142, 156, 246, 260, 436, 443, 455, 456, 532; applications, 71–80; developments in technology, 72–77; digital, 62–64; input-output forms, 64–67; limitations, 82, 83; nature of, 61–67; programming, 67–69; role in decision making, 69–71; types of, 62

Computer assisted design systems, 76

Computer graphics, 76, 77

Computer program, flow chart for a, 99, 102, 103

Computer word, 63

Confidence intervals, 156

Console, in computers, 64

Consumer's risk, 487

Contiguous moves, 256, 257

Continuous casting, 239

Continuous operations systems, 236, 441, 444

Continuous path numerical control, 247

Continuous timing, 354

Contouring control, 247

Control, 27, 28; large-scale project, 460–468; process, 480–486; systems, 441–468, 502–521; see also controls

Control charts, for attributes, 491, 492; for means, 481–484; for ranges, 484–486

Control limits, 481–486

Controls, 333–338; relation to the system, 333–335; selection of type, 335, 336; shapes of, 336–338; see also control

Control unit, in digital computer, 64

Conventional decision models, 87–112

Cooke, Morris L., 6, 7

Correlation, 219–221, 225

Cost(s), 94, 95; concepts, 502–505; control systems, 502–521; defined, 502; direct labor, 503–505; direct material, 503–505; elements, 503; fixed, 94; indirect labor, 503–505; indirect material, 503, 504; incremental, 94, 95; manufacturing, 503; operations overhead, 503–505; overhead, see operations overhead costs; opportunity, 94; reduction of, 519–521; variable, 94; variances, 506; see also costing

Cost-benefit analysis, 521

Cost center, 504

Cost control systems, 502–521
Cost curve, 96, 97
Cost-effectiveness analysis, 521
Costing, 503–505; *see also* cost(s)
Country club management, 289
"CPC ratings," 516
CPM, 460, 466
CRAFT, 260
Crash estimate, 466
Criteria of pessimism, 41
Critical path, 461, 465; critical path method, 466, 467
Critical values, 225
Culturally deprived worker, 342
Cumulative average time, 276, 277
Customer service, 387
Custom operations, 234, 235
Cycle time, 258
Cyclical fluctuations, 218, 219
Cyert, Richard M., 21

D

DAC system, 76
Data, defined, 61
Data communication, 73–75
Data processing, 61
Data transmission, 73
Daywork, 509
Decibels, 329, 330
Decimal stopwatch, 352, 353
Decision(s), of the first kind, 35; making, 35–60; nonprogrammed, 36–38; programmed, 36–38; of the second kind, 35; of the third kind, 35; *see also* decision models
Decision models, 86–171; accounting, 87, 90–93; "closed," 89; conventional, 87–112; economic analysis, 87, 93–97; general, 87–90; logical, 88, 89; non-quantitative simulation, 87, 89, 90; "open," 87, 89; quantitative, 87, 115–142, 146–167; rule-of-thumb, 88; schematic, 87, 99–112
Decision trees, 54, 55
Decoupling process, 410

Deduction, 88
Deductive reasoning, 89
Defectives, 486
Defects, 486
Defects per unit charts, 491, 492
Delay, symbol, 303
Demand, creation of, 387, 388; conditions, 391
Dependent events, 48, 49
Design, of a product or service, 173–177
Dial indicators, 332, 333
Dickie, H. Ford, 434
Dickson, W. J., 7
Die casting, 239
"Difference Engine," 4
Digital computers, 62–64; arithmetic unit, 64; auxiliary memory, 63; control unit, 64; input devices, 63; output devices, 64; storage or memory unit, 63
Digital counter, 332, 333
Direct labor costs, 503–505
Direct material costs, 503–505
Dispersion, measures of, 478; 479
Distribution, components, 391, 392; *see also* distribution models
Distribution models, 128–142; of linear programming, 193; northwest corner rule, 129, 130, 135; stepping-stone method, 130–135, 140, 141; variations, 138–141; Vogel Approximation Method, 135–139
Division of labor (specialization), 4, 338
Dodge, H.F., 8
Double-declining tax depreciation, 187
Double sampling, 489, 490
Drawing, 239
Drilling processes, 241, 242; boring, 242, tapping, 242
Durnin, J.V.G.A., 326
Dynamic inventory systems, 425–430
Dynamic programming models, 141, 142

E

Eastern Rate Case, 6
Ecology, 203
Economic analysis models, 93–97
Economic considerations, 175, 176
Economic cost analysis, 393–395
Economic forecasting, 205
Economic lot size, 8, 416–424; cost components of the model, 416, 417; graphical solution method, 417, 418; mathematical model solution method, 419–421; noninstantaneous resupply model, 421–423; price breaks, 423, 424; tabular solution method, 418, 419
Economic order quantity inventories, 411
Electrical discharge machining, 243
Electroplating, 244
Elemental standard data systems, 362, 363
Ely, Jerome H., 331
Emerson, Harrington, 6
Emory, William, 41, 53
Empirical techniques, 209, 210
Enterprise strategy, 14, 15
Entities, 20
Environment, 20, 291, 328; forecasting premises, 202, 203; humidity, 329; lighting, 329; noise, 329, 330; temperature, 329; vibration, 330
Equal contribution lines, 120
Equal cost lines, 122, 123
Equipment investment analysis, 177–188; MAPI system, 184–187; models, 178–188; payback method, 179, 180; present value, 180–184; return on investment, 178, 179
Ergonomics, 322–347
Erlang, A.K., 8
Evans, Oliver, 4
Event, 461
Exceptional worker, 340–342; aging worker, 340, 341; culturally deprived, 342; handicapped, 341, 342

Excluded cells, 138, 139
Expected time, 463
Expense summaries, 93
Expensing, 187
Exponential smoothing, 221, 222
External premises, 201
Extrusion processes, 240

F

Facilitating processes, 237
Factor comparison systems, 516
Fatigue, 328, 379, 380
F distribution, 494, 495
Feedback, 26, 27, 502; feedback control, 28, 246; feedback control system, 30, 31
Financial management, 2
Finished goods, 411
Finishing processes, 244; electroplating, 244; galvanizing, 244; porcelain enameling, 244
Finite source, 158
First-come, first-serve, 158, 159, 162
Fisher, Ronald A., 8
Fixed costs, 94
Fixed pointed, moving scale indicator, 332, 333
Fixed-position layout, 254
Fixed-reorder-quantity system, 413–415
Fixed-time-interval system, 415, 416
Flow charts, 99, 100, 102, 103, 148, 255
Flow control, 441, 444
Flow diagrams, 99, 101, 255, 303–307
Flow process charts, 99, 302, 303, 305, 307, 308; man-type process chart, 302; material process chart, 302; symbols, 302, 303, 311
Flow reports, 92
Force platform, 327
Forecast(s), 157; revenue and expense, 92, 93; *see also* forecasting
Forecasting, 200–227, 271, 272; critical values, 225; economic, 205;

empirical techniques, 209, 210; moving-range chart, 226, 227; premises, 200–204; reliability of forecasts, 223–227; sales, 205, 206; standard deviation, 223, 224; standard error, 224, 225; techniques, 209–223; technological, 206–209; types of forecasts, 204–209; *see also* forecast(s)
Forecasting budget, 507
Foreign location problems, 194, 195
Forging processes, 239, 240
Forming processes, 238–240
Forms distribution charts, 103
FORTRAN, 67–69
Frequency distribution, 476, 477
Frequency tables, 44, 45
Fry, T.C., 8
Fusion, 291

G

Galvanizing, 244
Gantt, Henry L., 6, 106
Gantt charts, 6, 106–108, 461; limitations, 109; types, 107, 108
General decision models, 87–90
General Problem Solving program, 81
General purpose machines, 234, 235
Gilbreths, 300, 302; Frank, 6; Lillian, 6
GNP, 201, 202, 205
Governmental factors, 202
GPS, 81
Graphical solution method, 117–123, 417, 418
Graphic displays, 76
Grinding, 242
Gross National Product, 201, 202, 205
Group incentive plans, 513, 514
"GS ratings," 516

H

Habit, 37
Handicapped worker, 341, 342

"Hand" simulation techniques, 457–459
Harris, F.W., 8
Hawthorne experiments, 7, 284
Heuristics, 38, 260; heuristic methods, 460, 467; heuristic models, 88
Hierarchy of needs, 284
High impact premises, 201
Histogram, 476
Holidex system, 78, 79
Homeostasis, 27
Hoxie, Robert F., 7
Humidity, 329
Hunch, 37
Hybrid control systems, 441, 444–446
Hygiene factors, 286, 287

I

Iconic models, 38
Implied premises, 201
Impoverished management, 289
Improvement phenomena, 274
Income statement, 91, 92
Incremental costs, 94, 95
Independent events, 48
Index numbers, 125
Indirect labor costs, 503–504
Indirect materials, 503, 504
Individual incentive plans, 5115–513
Induction, 88
Industrial dynamics, 157, 400–402, 456, 457
Industrial Revolution, 2–4
Infinite source, 158
Infinity, 138, 139
Information, compared to data, 61; system components, 389
Information distribution charts, 103, 104
Information flow charts, 103
Input, 23–26; devices, 63; forms, 64–67; source components, 390
Inspection, 474; attribute, 480; symbol, 303; for variables, 480–486
Instrument displays, 331–333

Integrated control systems, 441–468; large-scale project control, 460–468; output scheduling, 446–460; types, of, 441–446
Integrated management, 22
Intensive sample, 355
Interactive devices, 76
Interchangeable parts manufacture, 4
Interface, 298, 299
Intermittent operations systems, 234, 235; types of control, 441–444
Internal premises, 201
Intuition, 37
Inventory, 157, 386; analysis by value, 434, 435; anticipation, 411, 412; • buffer, 412; dynamic systems, 425–430; economic lot size, 416–424; economic order quantity, 411; finished goods, 411; functions of, 410; lot size, 411; management of, 433–436; nature of inventory problem, 409–413; policy adjustments, 435; policy review, 436; raw materials, 411; safety stocks, 412; static systems, 425, 430–433; supplies, 411; system(s), 409–436; system costs, 412, 413; system variations, 424–433; use of computers with, 436; work-in-process, 411
Irregular variations, 219
Iscontribution lines, 120
Isocost lines, 122, 123
Iterative processes, 260

J

Job classification systems, 515, 516
Job costing, 504
Job design, 298, 300–318; motion study tools, 302–318; patterns for analyzing methods, 301
Job enlargement, 254, 338, 339
Job evaluation, 515–519
Job ranking systems, 515
Job shops, 454–456

Joining processes, 243, 244; adhesive joining, 244; brazing, 243, 244; soldering, 244; welding, 243, 244
Judgment, 37
Jury of executive opinion, 209, 210

K

Karpovich, Peter, 379
Keyboard terminals, 75
Key jobs, 515
Key number, 126
Kilocalories, 326, 327, 373
Kimball, George E., 35

L

Labor costs, control of, 508–519; direct, 503–505; indirect, 503
Labor grades, 517, 518
Large-scale project control, 444, 446, 460–468
Lasers, 243
Lathes, 240, 241
Lauru, Lucien, 327
Law of large numbers, 477
Layout, approaches, to, 254–256; fixed-position, 254; process, 252; product, 252–254
Layout chart, 107
LCL, 481, 491
LDR, 451, 454
Learning curve, 273–281; application of, 278–281; equation for, 273; time-reduction curve, 274–278
Least squares method, 212–217
Leavitt, Harold J., 291, 292
LeGrande, Earl, 456
Lehrer, R.N., 339
Level output, 447,448
Lighting, 329
Light pen, 76
Likert, Rensis, 7, 287, 290
Linear decision rules, 451, 454
Linear programming, 116, 117, 395, 396; distribution models, 128–141;

graphical solution method, 117–123; mathematical programming, 116–142; simplex method, 123–128
Line balancing, 257–260
Line of balance (LOB), 109–111
"Line of best fit," 212
Load chart, 107
Load control, 444–446
LOB, 109–112
Logic, 88; symbolic, 89
Logical decision models, 87–90
Logistics systems, 385–405; components of, 385–393; operation and control of, 393–405
Lot-feet-travel, 255, 256
Lot size inventories, 411
Lot tolerance percent defective, 487
Lower control limit, 481, 491
Lower range limit, 484
Low impact premises, 201
L.P.I., 328
LRL, 484
LTPD, 487

M

Machine assignment problems, 128
Machine(s), defined, 298; general purpose, 234, 235; special purpose, 236
Machining processes, 240–243
Magnetic tape, 64, 66, 67
Maintenance, 260–263
Major premises, 89
Management, authoritative, 290; country club, 289; defined, 1; evolution of, 2–11; fact-finding approach, 5; impoverished, 289; middle of the road, 289; participative, 290; philosophy of scientific, 4, 5; rule-of-thumb method, 5; task, 289; Taylor's four duties of, 5; team, 289; tool, 5, 6
Management coefficients, 454
Management information systems, 22, 69–71, 389

Management science, 7
Managerial accounting techniques, 90
Managerial grid, 288–290
Man-machine chart, 309, 310
Man-machine systems, 298–300
Man-made system, 21
Manpower, role of, 270, 271; policies, 271, 272
Manpower loading, 281–283
Manpower planning, 269–292; elements of, 269–272; learning curve, 273–281; manpower loading, 281–283; motivation, 283–292; quantity determination, 271, 272; recruitment and selection, 272; time-reduction curve, 274–278; training and development, 272
Man-type process chart, 302
Manufacturing cost, 503
MAPI system, 184–187
March, James G., 21
Marginal costs, 94
Market(s), 173, 174, 203, 390, 391
Marketing, components, 386–388; enterprises, 404; management, 2
Maslo, A. H., 285
Material handling, 389
Material process chart, 302
Mathematical model solution method, 419–421
Mathematical programming, 116, 117; models, 116–142
Maximin criterion, 41
Maximizing models, 140, 141
Maximizing problem, 117–121
Mayo, Elton, 7
McGregor, Douglas, 7, 285
Mean control chart, 482
Measurement of productivity, 529, 530
Measure of dispersion, 478
Mechanical processes, 237
Mechanization, 4, 9
Memory, 36
Memory unit, in digital computer, 63
Methods study, 300

Methods-Time Measurement, 363–368
Micromotion analysis, 311, 313, 317
Middle of the road management, 289
Milestone chart, 461
Milling, 242
Minimax criterion, 41, 42
Minimizing problem, 121–123
Minor premises, 89
Mixture problems, 116
Models, 22, 23, 38, 39; abstract, 39; analog, 39; conventional decision, 87–112; iconic, 38; management information system, 70, 71; quantitative, 87, 115–142, 146–167; simulation, 89, 90; symbolic, 39; *see also* specific models
Monte Carlo Simulation, 147, 148, 255
Morell, Robert W., 88, 89
Most likely time, 461, 463
Motion analysis, 300
Motion economy, 317, 318
Motion study, 300; contributions to, 6; tools, 302–318
Motion-time data systems, 363–368
Motivation, 283–292; attitudes, 288–290; defined, 283; early theories, 283, 284; environment, 291; Hawthorne experiments, 284; hierarchy of needs, 284, 285; motivation-hygiene theory, 286, 287; patterns of performance, 287; significance for management, 291, 292; Theory X, 285, 286; Theory Y, 285, 286
Motivation-Hygiene theory, 286, 287
Motivators, 286
Movement, symbol, 311
Moving averages, 211, 212
Moving pointer, fixed scale indicator, 332, 333
Moving-range chart, 226, 227
MTM, 363–368
Müller, E.A., 327, 328
Multiactivity charts, 309, 310
Multiple-channel waiting line, 159, 164–167

Multiple-phase case, 159
Multiple sampling, 490
Multiple spindle drill, 242
Multiple-station case, 159
Multiplication rule, 48
Mundel, Marvin E., 359
Murell, K.F.H., 322, 323
Mutually exclusive events, 45, 46

N

Nanoseconds, 63, 64
Natural system, 21
Negative exponential distribution, 161, 162
Negative feedback control, 27
Network models, 460–467; CPM, 460, 466; evaluation of, 466, 467; PERT, 460–465, 467
Network techniques, 108, 109
Neuromuscular factors, 324–326
Next-year capital consumption avoided, 185
Next-year capital consumption incurred, 185
Next-year deferment concept, 185
Next-year income tax adjustment, 185
Next-year operating advantage, 185
Next-year relative rate of return, 185
Niland, Powell, 41, 53
Noise, 329, 330
Nonadaptive system, 21
Noncontiguous moves, 256, 257
Noninstantaneous resupply model, 421
Nonlinear models, 141
Nonmanufacturing enterprises, 403–405
Nonprogrammed decisions, 36–38
Non-quantitative simulation, 87; models, 89, 90
Normal curve, 477, 478
Normal estimate, 466
Normal time, 360
Northwest corner rule, 129, 130, 135
Not mutually exclusive events, 46, 47

Null hypothesis, 492–494
Numerical control, 10, 245–249

O

Objective probability, 44
Objective rating, 359
Objects, defined, 20
Occupational Safety and Health Act of 1970, 330
OC curve, 486–488
100 percent premium plans, 512, 513
On-line, 72
On-line management information system, 70, 71
"Open" decision models, 87, 89
Open-loop system, 26
Open system, 21
Operating characteristic curve, 486–488
Operation(s), aspects of, 1; components, 386; custom, 234, 235; defined, 1; functional areas of, 1, 2; policies, 15, 16; problem solving, 17–19; symbol, 302, 311; types of systems, 234–237
Operation analysis, 311, 317; example of improving an operation, 311, 313; micromotion analysis, 311, 313, 317; symbols, 311
Operation chart, 99, 311, 312, 314
Operations budget, 507
Operations function, 1, 16–19
Operations management, 14, 405; future status of, 531–533; phases of development, 3–11; planning, 173; present status, 527–531; problems of, 528–531; system, 28–31
Operations manager, 16, 17, 87
Operations overhead costs, 503–505
Operations research, 7, 8
Opportunity costs, 94
Optimistic time, 461, 463
Optner, Stanford L., 23
Order control, 441–443
Ordinal utility, 50

Organization chart, 98, 99
Origin solution, 124
Output, 23; decisions techniques, 450–460; fluctuating, 448, 449; forms, 64–67; level, 447, 448; scheduling alternatives, 447–450
Output quality control systems, 474–497
Output scheduling, 446–460
Output variables, 474, 475
Overhead costing, 505
Overhead costs, 503–505

P

Partial ignorance, 42
Participative management, 290
Passmore, R., 326
Payback method, 179, 180
Payback period, 179, 180
Payoff table, 53, 54
p-chart, 491
Percentage defective charts, 491
Performance rating, 358–360
Permanent mold casting, 239
Personnel assignment problems, 128
Personnel management, 2
PERT, 460–465, 467
Pessimistic time, 461, 463
Physical system, 21
Physiological evaluations, 359, 360
Physiological response factors, 326–328
Physiological work measurement, 373–380
Planing, 242
Planning, 502; equipment investment analysis, 177–188; manpower, 269–292; operations management, 173; plant location, 189–195; product, 173–177
Planning-Programming-Budgeting System, 521
Plant, defined, 189; location, 189–195
Plaster mold casting, 238, 239
Plastic processes, 244

Point-rating system, for job evaluation, 516–518; for plant location, 192, 193
Point to point control, 247
Poisson distribution, 160–162
Pollution, 208
Polygon of technical feasibility, 120
Porcelain enameling, 244
Positioning, 247
Positive feedback control, 27
Powder metallurgy, 240
Precedence requirements, 258
Predetermined grading method, 515, 516
Prediction, 479, 480
Premises, analytical, 201; external, 201; for forecasting, 200–204; high impact, 201; implied, 201; low impact, 201; major, 89; minor, 89; procedural, 201
Present value, 180–184
Present Value for an Annuity table, 181, 183, 184
Present Value of $1 tables, 181, 182, 184
Preventive maintenance, policy, 262; programs, 261
Price, 388; price breaks, 423, 424
Principles of efficiency, 6
Priorty dispatching rules, 157, 457–460
Probability, 40–49, 157, 162–166; formulas, 43; objective, 44; rules, 45–49; subjective, 44; techniques, 35
Problem-oriented languages, 67–69
Procedural premises, 201
Process(es), 23; adhesive joining, 244; assembly, 243, 244; automation, 245, 246; casting, 238, 239; chemical milling, 243; clerical, 237; defiined, 333; drawing, 239; drilling, 241, 242; electrical discharge machining, 243; electroplating, 244; extrusion, 240; facilitating, 237; finishing, 244; forging, 239, 240; forming, 238–240;

galvanizing, 244; grinding, 242; joining, 243, 244; lasers, 243; machining, 240–243; mechanical, 237; milling, 242; nature of, 233–245; planing, 242; plastic, 244; porcelain enameling, 244; powder metallurgy, 240; production, 238–245; shaping, 242; .soldering, 244; stamping, 239; tapping, 242; technical, 237; turning, 240, 241; ultrasonic machining, 243; woodworking, 245
Process analysis, 255, 302–308; flow diagram, 303–307; flow process chart, 302, 303, 305, 307, 308; symbols, 302, 303
Process control, by inspection for variables, 480–486
Process costing, 504
Processing facilities, 386
Processing industries, 236, 245
Process layout, 252
Process planning, 157, 233–263; layout facilities, 249–260; maintenance, 260–263; numerical control of machine tools, 245–249
Procurement components, 388
Producer's risk, 487
Product(s), design of, 173–177
Product budget, 507
Product costing, 504; product costing budget, 507
Product development simulation, 148, 149
Product distribution inventory systems, 157
Production, 16, 17; classification of, 234–237; processes, 238–245
Production design, 175
Production progress curve, 278–281
Production-progress function, 274
Production-routing problems, 128
Productivity, 529
Product layout(s), 252–254, 257
Product planning, 173–189

Profit and loss statement, 91, 92
Program budget, 507
Program Evaluation and Review Technique, (PERT), 460–465, 467
Programmed decisions, 36–38
Programming, 67–69
Progress chart, 108
Project control, 444, 446; large-scale, 460–468
Punched cards, 63–66
Purchasing, 388

Q

Quality control, basic concepts, 474–480; human performance and, 496, 497; output systems, 474–497; statistical, 474; statistical tests of significance in, 492–496
Quantitative models, 87, 115–142, 146–167
Quantitative reading, 332
Quantitative techniques, 7–9, 255, 395–400
Quantity determination, 271, 272
Queue, 72
Queuing problem, 157
Queuing theory, 8

R

Random arrival and servicing simulation, 153–156
Random-Check Delay Study, 368, 369
Random number(s), 151, 152, 154
Random number generator subroutines, 152
Random number tables, 150–152
Random variations, 219
Range, 478; range chart, 484
Rates of return, 184
Ratio-Delay Study, 368, 369
Raw materials inventories, 411
Real-time systems, 72
Recruitment, 272
Regional specialization, 190

Regret criterion, 41, 42
Relationships, 20
Relative rates of return, 184
Repair policy, 261
Repetitive timing, 354, 355
Replenishment costs, 412, 413, 416, 417
Responsibility budget, 507
Return on investment, 178, 179
Revenue function, 95, 97
Risk, 39–41; inventory systems under conditions of, 424, 425
Roethlisberger, F.J., 7
Romig, H.G., 8
Routine sequence diagrams, 103
Rule of thumb, 88, 93; rule-of-thumb models, 88

S

SABRE, 79
Safety stocks, 412
SAGE system, 78
Sales force composite, 210
Sales forecast, 271; sales forecasting, 205, 206
Sample size, 156
Sampling, 480, 488–490; work sampling, 368–373
Sand casting, 238
Schedule simulation, 149–153
Scheduling, 386, 455, 456; output, 446–460; problems, 128
Schematic models, 23, 87, 90, 99–112; advantages, 111, 112; assembly diagrams, 103, 105; block diagrams, 103, 105, 106; drawbacks, 111; flow charts, 99, 100, 102, 103; flow diagrams, 99, 101; forms distribution charts, 103; Gantt charts, 106–108; information distribution charts, 103, 104; information flow charts, 103; line of balance, 109–111; network techniques, 108, 109; organization charts, 98, 99; routine

sequence diagrams, 103; summary of uses, 111, 112
Scientific management movement, 4–7
Scientific method, 17–19
Seasonal variation, 218
Seating, 330, 331
Second-degree parabola, 216, 217
Secular trend, 212–217
Select time, 360
Sensitivity training, 290
Sensory-motor tasks, 324, 326
Sequence diagrams, 103
Sequential sampling, 490
Service enterprises, 403, 404
Service rates, 162
Setting, 332
Shaping, 242
Sharing plans, 510, 512, 513
Shewhart, Walter, 8
Shift work, 339, 340
Shortage costs, 413
Simo chart, 313, 316
Simon, Herbert A. 36–38
Simple rate of return, 178
Simplex method, 123–128
Simulation, 89, 90, 146–157, 159, 160, 167, 255, 260, 454–460; application of, 157; in maintenance problems, 163; models, 89, 90; Monte Carlo, 147, 148, 255; product development, 148, 149; random arrival and servicing, 153–156; sampling, 156; schedule, 149–153
Single-channel waiting line, 159–164, 167
Single-phase case, 158–164, 167
Sintering, 240
Skewing, 477
Slack column, 139
Slack row, 140
Slack time, 121
Snap-back timing, 354, 355
Social Ethic, 297
Socioeconomic factors, 527
Sociotechnical systems, 342–346

Soldering, 244
Sound, 329, 330
Specialization (division of labor), 4, 338
Special purpose machinery, 236
Stamping processes, 239
Standard cost(s), 505, 506; control systems, 506–508
Standard deviation, 223, 224, 478, 479
Standard error of the estimate, 224, 225
Standard-hour plans, 512, 513
Standardization, 176, 177
Standard time, 350, 361, 362
Statement of manufactured costs of goods sold, 92
Static inventory systems, 425, 430–433
Statistical quality control, 474
Statistical sampling tables, 8
Stepping-stone method, 130–135, 140, 141
Stochastic model, 147
Stopwatch, decimal-hour, 352, 353; decimal-minute, 352
Stopwatch time study, 352–362
Storage, 386; symbol, 303
Straight-line tax depreciation, 187
Strategy, 14
Subassembly, 24
Subjective probability, 44
Subsystems, 23, 24, 31
Successful occurrences, 43
Successive maximum elemental time technique, 260
Sum-of-digits tax depreciation, 187
Supplies, 411
Syllogism, 89
Symbolic logic, 89
Symbolic models, 39
Synthesis approach, 22
System(s), analysis, 9, 19; approach, 8, 9, 19–31; classifications of, 20–22; continuous, 441, 444; cost control, 502–521; defined, 19, 20; elements of, 23–26; integrated control,

441–468; intermittent, 441, 442; inventory, 409–436; logistics, 385–405; man-machine, 298–300; output quality control, 474–497; sociotechnical, 342–346; standard cost control, 505–508; structure, 22–28; work, 297–318; *see also* specific systems

T

Tabular solution method, 418, 419
Tapping, 242
Task management, 289
Taylor, Frederick W., 4–6, 326
Team management, 289
Technical processes, 237
Technological forecasting, 206–209
Technology, 203, 206–209, 297, 298, 343, 344, 528, 532
Telephone terminals, 75, 76
Temperature, 329
Terminals, 75–77; computer graphics, 76, 77; keyboard, 75; telephone, 75, 76
Tests of significance, statistical in quality control, 492–496
T groups, 290
Theory X, 285, 286
Theory Y, 285, 286
Therbligs, 6, 313, 317
Thermostatic control, 26
Time-measurement units, 364
Time-reduction analysis, 274
Time-reduction curve, 274-278
Time-series analysis, 212–219
Time-sharing, 72, 73
Time span of discretion, 519
Time study, 5, 351–362
Timing, accumulative, 354, 355; continuous, 354; equipment, 352, 353, procedure, 353–355; repetitive, 354, 355; snap-back, 354, 355
TMU's, 364
Tolerances, 175; defined, 475
Total cost function, 451, 452

Total ignorance, 41, 42
Total operations cost, 503
Total systems approach, 22
Tracking, 332
Traditional management information system, 70
Traffic components, 389
Transaction-oriented information systems, 71
Transport, selection of method of, 389
Transportation, 389; components, 392; models, 128; symbol, 303, 311; of manpower, 272
Travel chart, 256; travel-chart technique, 260
t-test, 492, 493
Turning, 240, 241

U

UCL, 481, 491
Ultrasonic machining, 243
Uncertainty, 39, 41, 42, 424, 425
Unequal supply and demand, 139, 140
Unified management approach, 22
Upper control limit, 481, 491
Upper range limit, 484
URL, 484
U.S. Civil Service job classifications, 516
User's expectation, 210
Utility, 49–57
Utilization factor, 259

V

Value analysis, 396–399
Value engineering, 396–399
VAM technique, 141
Variable budgets, 507, 508
Variable costs, 94
Variables, inspection for, 480–486
Variances, 506
Variations, assignable, 475; chance, 475; pattern of, 475–480
Verbal models, 87, 88, 90

Vibration, 330
Vogel Approximation Method, 135–139

W

Wage incentive plans, 509–515
Waiting lines, 72, 157–167
Waiting-line theory, 8, 157–167, 255, 263; channels, 159–167; phases, 158, 159
Warehousing, 386
Watt governor, 26
Weber, Max, 7
Welding, 243, 244
Westinghouse, System, 358, 359
Whitney, Eli, 4
Wiener, Norbert, 10
Woodworking processes, 245
Workers, aging, 340, 341; handicapped, 341, 342; culturally deprived, 342
Work-in-process inventory, 411
Work loads, classifying, 326, 327

Work measurement, 5, 350–380; defined, 350; elemental standard data systems, 362, 363; motion-time data systems, 363–368; nature or, 350, 351, physiological, 373–380; purpose, 350, 351; time study, 351–362; work sampling, 368–373
Work pulse index (L.P.I.), 328
Work sampling, 368–373
Work simplification (motion study), 300; programs, 520
Work system, design of, 297–318; relationship of technology to, 343, 344

X

X̄ control chart, 482

Z

Zoning constraints, 258
z-test, 493, 494